BYZANTIUM INTO EUROPE

I. HEAD OF CHRIST

Mosaic in the narthex of St. Sophia, 886–912

JACK LINDSAY

Byzantium

into

Europe

*The Story of Byzantium as the First
Europe (326–1204 A.D.) and its further
Contribution till 1453 A.D.*

THE BODLEY HEAD

London

First published 1952

Made and printed in Great Britain by
WILLIAM CLOWES AND SONS, LIMITED, LONDON AND BECCLES
for JOHN LANE THE BODLEY HEAD LIMITED
28 Little Russell St., London W.C.1

CONTENTS

LIST OF ILLUSTRATIONS

HALF-TONE PLATES

LINE DRAWINGS

NOTE

THIS book attempts, not only to tell the story of Byzantium and its culture, but also to show the part played in the foundation of European culture by this Empire which, lasting over a thousand years, provided all the transitional forms between the Ancient and the Medieval State.

Although many books exist on particular aspects of this process, this is the first book in any language which asks, and keeps asking throughout its examination, what was the role of Byzantium in the creation of Europe. I hope to follow it in due time with books dealing with more specific aspects of Byzantine culture, particularly the literature.

At the end, I make various acknowledgments to historians; here I should like to make more personal expressions of gratitude. Robert Browning of London University requires a special word for his patient readiness to discuss large and small points alike, and to help me among Russian and other Slavonic sources. I must also thank R. H. Hilton, E. A. Thompson and John Mavrogordato for answering many queries and points of debate; Dr. Fiala and Mr. Pallis of Charles University, Prague, and the Czechoslovak Ministry of Information and Culture and D. Polishensky for getting me *Byzantinoslavica* and other materials; VOKS of Moscow for supplying me lavishly with Soviet works of historical research, and the Union of Soviet Writers for having enabled me to visit Kiev and Pskov in 1949; the Courtauld Institute for aid in obtaining illustrations.

I should also like to thank my publishers in the persons of C. J. Greenwood and Norman Denny, who suggested the book and who have discussed with me the many stages through which it has gone; Dr. Edith Sitwell for her heartening interest at each phase of the inquiry into Byzantine culture; and my wife for her work in transcription and correction, without which I could never have managed to complete the task.

JACK LINDSAY

FOREWORD

A SHORT while ago most people, even scholars concerned with the ancient world or the medieval West, would have described Byzantine History as remote and obscure, likely to interest only a handful of specialists and with little relevance to modern problems. This viewpoint, however, within the last few years, has begun to crumble away; and there has been an increasing awareness of the need to understand Byzantine culture, to examine the part it played in the transition from the Graeco-Roman world to medieval and modern Europe.

Indeed, Byzantium has become the most topical of themes; for any argument about the nature of Western or Eastern Europe, of Europe itself, holds at its root an assumption about the Byzantine world and the varying relations of the West and of Russia to that world. Unless we are aware what assumption governs our attitudes, we can hardly claim to be taking a rational attitude to the questions under debate.

This book is a study of Byzantine society which seeks always to keep in mind the relevance to the issues of our world today; but it is an historical study, and only at the end shall I attempt to relate to contemporary controversy the points which have emerged from the investigation. Those points are conclusions to which I have been impelled by the logic of the material itself, not theories with which I began the analysis.

The Roman Empire, at its limit of expansion in the second century A.D., held all the Mediterranean shores. On the Atlantic it reached north to take in Britain up to the Clyde, and the Belgic area up to the south banks of the Rhine. Across Europe it held the line made by the Rhine and Danube; but it had also moved over the Danube to set up the large province of Dacia, which extended to the Carpathians. Eastward it included Syria, Egypt, Mesopotamia and Armenia, touching the Caucasus and the Persian Gulf.

But the long internal peace which had held the Empire after the civil wars that founded it was broken in the third century by a violent resurgence of civil war in the form of military revolt and peasant uprising. The State was deeply shaken; and in the reconstruction by Diocletian towards the century's end many changes were introduced, intensifying the absolutist controls and their bureacratic machinery. This reconstruction heralded further clashes and disorders culminating in the triumph of Constantine, who as part of his civil-war policy extended toleration to the Christians and, in his efforts to consolidate the Diocletianic State, founded a new capital at Byzantium, Constantinople.

Here, then, is the point at which our narrative begins.

In concentrating on basic patterns and crucial moments I must omit much detail that clarifies side-issues, transitions, the complex criss-crossings characteristic of historical development in its fullness. But for the purposes of our inquiry the disentangling of basic patterns is the essential need; and the definitions, though compressed, will manage, I trust, to convey the general structure and an idea of the richness and vitality of the developments between 324 A.D., the year of the new capital's foundation, and 1453, when the Turks stormed the walls. During that period of more than a thousand years only one enemy, the treacherous Crusaders of 1204, had managed to break in.

In dealing controversially with material not generally known or accessible, one has a difficult problem of presentation—especially when the material is so vast in scope and involved in detail. Byzantine History does not even merely concern the later developments of the Roman Empire; it takes in the happenings in Syria, Egypt, Armenia, Georgia, Persia, as well as the relation of the Papacy and the Germanic West to the Empire; the rise and growth of the Moslem Empire and States as well as the rise and growth of the Slav Empires and States; and so on. It is necessary, therefore, to tell much of the story before analysing it, and to give some idea of other interpretations in setting out my own.

I

The Setting of the Scene

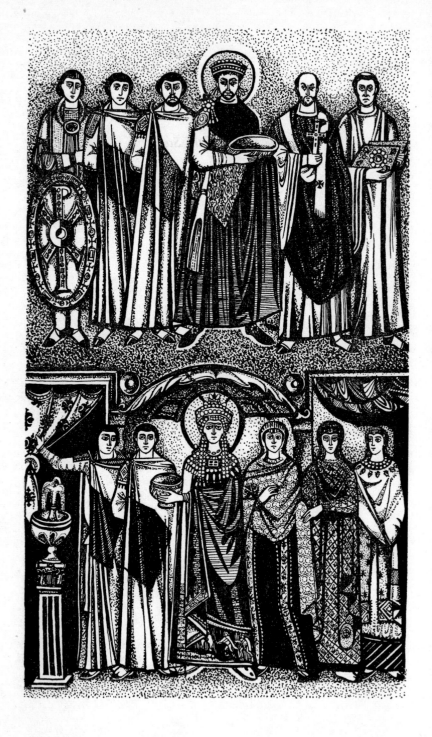

THE FOUNDATION OF BYZANTIUM AS CONSTANTINOPLE

THE SITE. Byzantium had more than a thousand years' history when it became the new imperial world-centre. Sailors from Megara (a town between Corinth and Athens) had landed there about 667 B.C., attracted by the fine harbour, some seven miles long, at the point of the European coast where the Propontis, the Sea of Marmora, was joined by the Bosphoros to the Black Sea. Between the harbour and the outer waters stood a hilly promontory, where the Megarians set up a trading-post.[1]

A disadvantage was the chilly north wind from the steppes in winter and spring, with sultry summers to follow; and this wind, aided by the strong southward current, gave ships a hard tussle to reach the port. But once round the point, they were sheltered in the harbour, which gained the name of the Golden Horn. The town itself was almost an island. 'The sea', wrote Prokopios, 'wreathes the city round, leaving the earth only a little space which serves as the garland-knot.'

Take a larger view, and we see the town set between two wings of the great mountainous barrier of Devonian massif that binds Europe and Asia and separates the Mediterranean and Pontic worlds. It straddles the transverse way linking Central Europe and the Indian Ocean, Danube and Euphrates. Only a few miles away, on the Asian side, stood Troy, the bridgehead trade-town that had first connected the early civilisations of the Near East with Europe. When Byzantium became the imperial world-city, it was reviving on a higher level the function that Troy had carried out two millennia before.

Situated on the point where the Black Sea breaks through the massif, it looked alike to Central Europe and Syria, to the Mediterranean and the South Russian steppes, to the Transcaucasian area (Georgia) pressed between the Caucasus and the Armenian massif, and opening both on Central Asia and Mesopotamia.

In its early years Byzantium had few trade-contacts with the Near East. Traffic from the East preferred to go to Smyrna, and then across the Aegean into Europe. Wild Thracian tribes inhabited the hinterland of Byzantium, and the area suffered from earthquakes: there were thirteen felt

[1] Recent excavations have shown a Phrygian settlement before the Greeks.

between 395 and 565 A.D. What first brought the town importance was
its strategic position between the Aegean ports and the corn-growing
Crimea—a position that had its value brought out in the interstate wars
in Hellas of the fifth century B.C. Later the Macedonians Philip and Alexander, in their imperial ambitions, realised that the town held the gateway
to Asia.

Its strategic value came up again as the convulsions of the Roman
Empire began. Severus demolished its fortifications after it held out against
him for two years; then he tried to rename it Antonina and began rebuilding its Hippodrome, Caracalla restored its political rights. Rebels in the
reign of Gallienus sacked it; and Gallienus did some more dismantling.

With the renewed clashes of the early fourth century its significance as
a key stronghold stood out yet more clearly. Licinius made it the pivot of
his campaign against his rival Constantine, who had ample chances to note
its possibilities. After the war Constantine had the area surveyed, and
building began. In 324 the new foundation was officially announced; on
11th May, 330, it was inaugurated as the new imperial capital, *The New
Rome Which Is Constantinople*. That remained its formal title to the end.[1]

The old Hellenic town was incorporated. Imperial agents gathered art-
treasures from all over the Empire, especially from the rich East. Thus the
three bronze serpent-pillars with gold tripod, which the Greeks had dedicated to Apollo for their victory at Plataia against the Persians, were now
set up in the Hippodrome. No expense was spared to rear in a few years
a city worthy of its imperial role.

A NEW START. Many factors converged to make Byzantium desirable as a
new capital. The violent dislocations, with their bloodshed, had made men
feel that a new start was needed; and a new capital helped to build up the
emotion of renewal. Almost four centuries before, right on the threshold
of the Empire, Julius Caesar had felt the eastward pull and meditated
transferring the Roman government to Troy. No doubt he was considering the strategy of the war he planned against Parthia, and realised that
Roman power rested ultimately on the Asian provinces; but he may also
have felt something of the millenniary emotions that certainly stirred
among the people and hoped for a removal from the scenes of fratricidal
bloodshed. A contemporary epode by Horace records how the masses
felt about the project:

> *The encircling Ocean waits for us, let's seek afar
> where the blest fields, the isles of richness are.*

[1] Oddly, *Nea Romē* does not seem to appear in literary texts till the end of the fourth
century, or in legal texts till the time of Justinian: F. Dölger.

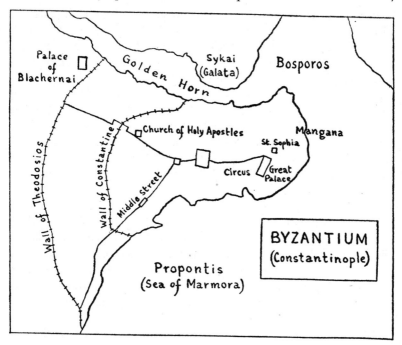

And his later *Carmen Saeculare* expresses the effort made by Augustus to give the people a conviction of renewal without a change of capital. Virgil's Messianic eclogue and the Sibylline verses of the East which proclaimed a new dispensation and the advent of a redeemer derived from the same complex of aspirations as Horace's epode; while the *Aeneid* strove to do the same work as the *Carmen Saeculare*, restoring men's faith by a return to what was believed to be origins.

For Troy, we must remember, was held by the Romans to be their place of origin; and tales went round that Constantine had first intended to build on Troy's site. It seems unlikely, however, that he ever really contemplated using the less strategic site: he was in fact celebrating his own naval victory at Byzantium, and it had been Licinius who held Troas. But the tales showed how important in men's minds was the idea that the Roman centre was coming back home. For the same reason Constantine was said to have taken from Rome the Palladium, the power-fetish believed to have come originally from Troy with Aeneas, and to have hidden it under the great porphyry column at Byzantium, on top of which stood his own image, constructed according to Apollo's statue at Troy.

A NEW DISPENSATION. The desire for a new start, for a world of peace and
plenty (which was evident in the travailing days of Caesar and Augustus),
in recoil from the imperial State's failure to achieve such a world, had
played a basic part in begetting Christianity. This desire could not but
come to a head afresh in Constantine's period. Once more there had been
a prolonged and bloody series of upheavals, based in the demand of the
masses for a different sort of life; and as a result of this tumultuous pressure
Constantine had been driven to take the dissident creed of Christianity
into the State-structure. Christianity in its deepest idiom of protest had
demanded a rebirth, a reversal of all things; and the whole complex of
historical forces which had compelled the fusion of imperial State and
anti-imperial creed lay behind the decision to leave Rome and build a
new capital.

Though in time Rome was to profit by its imperial memories which
gave weight to papal claims, at the moment the Church's triumph had
the effect of shaking the imperial tradition which had been cemented
by the cult of the emperor's genius. Rome was the headquarters of
the pagan opposition, the diehard section of the old aristocracy, rather
than the seat of the Bishop of Rome, whose importance was not yet
established.

Thus we meet once more a clash of opposites, which begets the new
form. The return to the region of Troy was based in the pagan concept of
renewal which had been given emotional expression by Horace and Virgil;
but the mass-forces which in their baffled but powerful way were shaping
certain aspects of the new State found their deepest utterance in Christianity. And so the Return to Troy became a forward movement to the
City of Christ.

This contradiction appeared openly in Constantine's own religious attitudes, which fused the imperial cults and Christianity in a strange way,
and which yet laid down the lines along which State and Church were
to develop.

A NEW CENTRE. Further, the trend into absolutism could culminate more
effectively in a new capital without the remnants of republican form that
persisted at Rome. At Byzantium the new centralised bureaucracy could
be built up more easily than at Rome.

But the last word must be given to the political and economic pressures
that made Byzantium a more adequate capital than Rome could now be.
Here the emperor was securely based on his rich and stable eastern provinces, and was much better able to deal with frontier troubles. He was
also closer to his best recruiting area, Illyria. Byzantium, with its sea-

defences, was a far stronger city than Rome, and later survived many terrible attacks and sieges.[1]

Before Constantine the emperors had realised the need to move eastward. Maximian ruled from Milan; Diocletian took Nicomedia as his chief residence; and Constantine, before settling on Byzantium, played with the idea of settling at his birthplace Naissos (Nish)—he also seems to have considered Sardika and Thessalonika.

The West and East of the Empire had never been equally civilised, and the language-division had remained as a sign of divergent developments. From Augustan days there had been a Greek as well as a Latin Secretary. Greek prevailed east of a line that included Illyricum; Latin extended in the more western area, driving out other tongues or dialects. But even at the height of the early Empire the thinkers, architects, artists, engineers, and great lawyers were men from the East, from Syria, Egypt, Greece. The world-religions were all eastern products, whether pagan like the Mithraic and Isaiac worships, or Christian. Later, Manicheism and Islam came from the East; and the great heresies were eastern, monasticism was eastern.

It is meaningless, then, to talk of the movement eastward as an orientalisation. The Orontes had already poured into the Tiber, as Juvenal complained. Even the thinker who gave Stoicism the form that became typically Roman was a Syrian. In this situation 'eastern' comes merely to mean 'civilised, rich in complex inherited techniques'. The breakdown of the Roman Republic and the setting-up of an empire which steadily developed towards centralised absolutism was not a sign of 'oriental influences', but was an expression of the inner contradictions of the Roman State, which was developing in the only effective way open to it. The crisis of the Empire was a crisis of slave-economy, not of oriental forms imposed on a deliquescent republican system.

We must therefore drop from our minds the term 'orientalisation', since it is invested with too many ready-made prejudices and emotional colourations. Its meaning in this situation is no more than that the Empire moved to its centre of stability which lay eastward of Rome, the previous centre, and that this new centre linked more directly with the ancient and still vital areas of urban civilisation. But scholars who use it mean much more than that. They convey a strong suggestion of moral collapse, as if

[1] The army on the Danube was largely responsible for increasing the prosperity of the East Balkans in the first three centuries of the Empire; and the East Balkans depended on Asia Minor trade. Thus Byzantium rose as an entrepôt. The Palmyrene attempt to break away in the third century and to detach Asia Minor showed the fissiparous forces at work; and thus Byzantium, set between the Balkans and Asia Minor, was equally a key-point from the economic and the strategic angle. (E. Gren.)

there was some virus of Orientalism that made men corrupt and servile; and they imply that the development under question can be defined as a losing battle between a republican independence of spirit, a rule of law, on the one hand, and an irresponsible rule, a sort of totalitarian submission, on the other. It would be just as correct to describe Charlemagne's effort to build a centralised State in Gaul as an orientalising of Gaul, or Louis XIV's Versailles as an orientalising of France.

If we throw this overcharged term away, we can go on to consider what was the actual contribution of areas like Syria or Mesopotamia to Byzantine culture without distorting our focus at the outset. In that culture we find in fact contributions from north, south, east and west; and we can define the result only as *Byzantine*—just as we define the culture of ancient Rome as Roman, even though Virgil was a Celt from North Italy and Apuleius was an African (probably with Punic blood), though Livy was another Celt and Galen was a Syrian, though Martial came from Spain and Claudian was an Egyptian.

STILL THE ROMAN EMPIRE. But though the term Byzantine is a convenient term to define the culture of the later Roman Empire, we must always remember that it is of the *later Roman Empire* we are treating. Byzantium was founded as the result of a period of revolutionary shocks, but it was still the Roman Empire within which the changes took place. England before and after Cromwell was still England, though a revolutionary movement had taken place, shattering the old State-structure and releasing new productive energies—those of the various inventors, enterprisers, small producers who built up industrialism and swung the world into new lines of development. It would still have been England if William III had decided to make Bristol his capital.

The early Roman Empire saw the ancient State, with a slave-economy, carried to its limit of growth. That State broke down in the third century, and the Constantinian State began the definite transition to feudal bases. With it began a new curve of development that embraces the various forms through which the later Roman Empire went, the Germanic attempts at imperial structures, the building-up of national States out of western medievalism, the building-up of the Russian State, the emergence of the Islamic Empire. The interrelation of all these phases will be indicated as our analysis proceeds. That in the long run the new feudalising process had very different effects in the West than in the East is no disproof of the generalisation. The differences were based in the situation already apparent by the fifth century: in the West the imperial State-structure disintegrated and in due time a new sort of town grew up; in the East the State-structure remained intact and the ancient type of town persisted despite many modifications. But in the total development from which Europe and the modern world arise, both East and West play essential parts—the centralised imperial State surviving in the East and the national State finally growing up in the medieval West.

THE NEW ROME. Many efforts were made to turn the New Rome into a replica of the Old. It was divided into seven hills and fourteen regions— though the sixth hill was outside Constantine's walls, on the Golden Horn. The thirteenth region, north across the waters, corresponded to the Trans-tibur region in Rome. A Capitol was built on the second hill; the Great Palace was set by the Hippodrome like the Palatine Palace by the Circus Maximus. Rome had a hieratic name, *Flora*; so Constantinople had one too, *Anthusa* (Flowering). The town-system was based on Rome's, with curator, beadle, five night-patrols, firemen with axes and buckets. Constantine is said to have copied several Roman mansions, to lure senators with an exact version of their old homes.

Latin remained for long the official language. Justinian's Code of Laws was issued in it; coin-inscriptions were Latin till the eighth century. The first wedge of Greek appeared in 439, in the orders of the prefect Cyros. The people's name for the new empire was *Romania*, which by the fifth century had become the current term, though unofficial, and held its own till the end, in the fifteenth century. Not only the Greeks used it, but also the foreign peoples who came up against the Empire. The Latin Crusaders knew Romania, and the Seljuk Turks fought against *Roum*.

The subjects of the emperor seated at Byzantium were Romans, and no one else had the right to use the name. When in 968 papal legates dared to submit letters in which Otto was called emperor of the Romans and Nikephoros emperor of the Greeks, they were thrown into jail; and in the 1488 treaty between the emperor John VIII and Venice the Greek text speaks of his subjects as *Romaioi*, but the Latin text translates as *Graeci*. At Byzantium *Graikoi* had an insulting colouration; and Hellenism was synonymous with paganism—a Hellene was an idolater. Late in the thirteenth century humanists tried to change this meaning and to use Hellenism as a patriot term reminding men of the glorious past of Athens; but their revaluation had a limited circle. Even under the Turks the Christians of the Empire called themselves Romans, and still today the Patriarch of Constantinople is the Patriarch of the Romans.

There, then, is Byzantium, a city which rapidly expanded and flourished, and which for a thousand years was the greatest city in the world (though in later years rivalled by Bagdad and Cordova). It carried on the traditions of antiquity, created a magnificently rich culture of its own, and in the process laid the foundations which made Europe possible. Its millennium of history is one of the basic phases of human development; and in this book we are going to explore it.

2

THE CRISIS OF THE ANCIENT STATE

THE ECONOMIC CONTRACTION. But before we look at the State of Constantine which inaugurated this new phase of history—a phase which lies along the main road of human advance and which therefore must be understood if we are to understand history at all—we must glance further at the crisis of ancient society. We must know more of the deep convulsion which brought about the new start, the new dispensation, the new centre. I have already spoken of the crisis of the Empire as the crisis of slave-economy. What does that entail?

Under the early Empire a considerable expansion of trade and industry had gone on, linked with a westward extension of town-life—in Gaul and Spain, and to a lesser extent in Britain and the Danubian area. But there were no radical changes in the techniques of production, in the modes whereby men were organised in the labour-process, in the social relationships growing out of those modes. That is, no deep changes in man's relation to nature, in the activities by which he strove to master and transform nature. Even the watermill, known for centuries, was little used. What happened was only a multiplication of the existing units of production. Sometimes these units were enlarged; more slaves were brought together in a single agricultural enterprise or workshop, especially for brickmaking or ceramics; but no movement towards improvement or integration of methods appeared.

For a while, local industries rose to a fairly high volume in parts of the West. In Africa Carthaginian lamps drove out Italian imports. The manufacturing centre of the widely used redware-pots moved from North Italy to the Cevennes, up into eastern Gaul, and settled finally near Speyer. Till the mid-third century Gallic wines and pots were exported as far east as Syria. Italy thus lost many markets and in the second century declined economically; by 395 Campania had more than 528,000 *iugera* (about 345,000 acres) of abandoned fields.

The expansion had no stability because no country-market was developed. The rise of the towns reposed on a worsening of the lot of the land-workers. This dilemma showed up sharply in the West, where the quick urbanisation was doomed to breakdown by its basis in an equally

23

quick depression of conditions on the land. The inability to nurture internal markets was not an accidental aspect of the situation, and was in
turn bound up with other limitations in a slave-economy: the inability
to devise new techniques and labour-saving methods—or to apply them
even when they were known.

FROM SLAVE TO SHARE-CROPPER. In Italy specialised crops, worked by slave-
labour, gave way to large-scale cultivation of cereals, in which slaves were
less used.[1] But this did not mean the rise of the free farmer. The wealthy
class, the landlords, needed to draw from the country-producer, not from
the town-worker, their main income; and so the wealth that made possible
the rise of the towns was primarily extracted from the man on the land.
The latter's buying-power was steadily lowered, here and elsewhere. The
farmer's status fell. He tended to become a *colonus*, often a sort of share-
cropper, who paid his landlord in kind and services for the use of the land,
even for tools and seed. The towns were hit; their capacity to draw on
the resources of the surrounding countryside was lessened. The town-life,
which Prokopios so aptly described in the following picture of Justinian's
effort to revive towns in North Africa, faded out:

> The Wall had been brought to completion, and with it a city, and the con-
> ditions of a farmland are suddenly changed. The rustics have thrown aside
> the plough and lead the existence of a community (*politikos*), no longer going
> the round of country tasks but living a city-life. They pass their days in the mar-
> ket place and hold assemblies to deliberate on questions that concern them;
> and they traffic with one another, and conduct all the affairs which pertain to
> the Dignity of a City.

'And they traffic with one another.' A poor life unless someone is producing the basis for the trade-profits. The rustics who remained rustics
had to do most of that; and their conditions and status sank slowly but
surely in the process. The trafficking business-men of the town sank with
them, consuming their own basis and in turn consumed by the tax-
machine and the magnates. For, while the farmer and the urban middle-
class went down, the large landlord rose.

> Not only large agricultural estates, but also mining camps, fisheries and hunting
> parks became to an increasing extent the nuclei around which handicrafts and
> industries agglomerated themselves. Sometimes these primary units were
> temple property, not only recalling the similar institutions of Babylon or
> Hellenistic Asia Minor, but also foreshadowing clearly the medieval monastery.
> (Walbank.)

[1] The *latifundia* or *massa* was a collection of farms, *fundi*: we must not think of it as
normally organised with a central control, though the degree of co-ordination would
vary. Land-slaves did gangwork under an overseer with whip and branding-iron.

Already in the first century the agriculturist Columella had pointed out that where land was poor or difficult it was more profitable to use tenant farmers, colons, instead of slaves; and soon the free tenant was crushed by debt into varying dependencies on the landlord. Also, slaves were often put in charge of farmwork on the same lines as the colon, becoming domiciled serfs, *servi casati*. Thus it grew hard to tell colons by contract from semi-colons by usage or customary tenure.

Frontius already in the first century A.D. saw the estates of the African magnates with dependent villages round them like bulwarks. Beside the *civitas* of the town-centre was the *saltus*, rough land under lord or imperial steward who in the most important cases was outside urban controls. The lord's dominion over the *saltus* provided a type towards which land-ownership in general tended to approximate, as smallholdings weakened before the large estates. *Patronus* had been a title given in compliment to a local man of wealth who built baths or founded a poorhouse; by the fourth century the term of ceremonial prestige had become an expression of political and economic power.

THE TOWNS WEAKEN. During the first two centuries A.D., prices had stayed fairly stable; by the end of the second century they were rising. With the turn into the third century they were 'at a level twice as high as in the first and second' (Segrè); by mid-third century they were out of control.

And this meant that the tax-system was thrown into confusion and basic new lines of approach had to be found.

There was rapid decay in the *municipia*, the towns with local self-government, on which the tax-systems had been based. Through the third century these trends hardened, and the administrative methods jammed. As the towns' capacity to pay taxes lessened, the government's demands went up; and the slackening central control meant a maximum of arbitrary and corrupt extortion by the local agents. Coinage deteriorated. In 260 at Oxyrrhynchos we meet a bank-strike: all the banks refused to take the imperial bad-money. Generally the civil service functioned, public works went on, communications were intact, but the *municipia*, the basic unit in the system of the early Empire, was going under.

The government's reaction was to attempt a total arrest of the situation. Not to grapple with what was wrong, but to hold things in a rigid structure of relationships. The emperors sought to impose a caste-system on what they considered the key-areas of society, land and army: to tie farmer's son to the land and soldier's son to the ranks. Caste-compulsions spread in turn to trade connected with the food-supply which interested the State, the sailors fetching corn from Egypt, the butchers and bakers, and so on.

The colon approximated to a serf tied to the land; and the big landlords, abandoning production for the town-market by slave-labour, divided their estates into farms worked by colons.[1] The propertied members of a *municipium*, who once aspired to the honours of the council, *curia*, now had curial rank imposed as a burden and were made collectively responsible for tax-collection. They in turn ruthlessly oppressed those below them: "So many curials, so many tyrants," said Salvian. The liberties of the township, gradually undermined from the Empire's early days, fell away, and Diocletian sought to lay on all curials a uniformity of obligations.

Throughout the third century the crisis had grown more acute. The curials fled, hid, turned brigands. A colon at Hermopolis in Egypt offered to give up his whole property if his son was released from the high municipal rank bestowed on himself; in reply the council ordered his arrest. An early third-century papyrus asks an oracle in an ascending series of calamity: 'Am I to be sold up? become a beggar? a fugitive? a municipal councillor?'

This pauperisation or at least depression of large sections of the urban

---

1 Slaves had become comparatively scarce and expensive after the wars of expansion ended: in the early third century a slave cost 200 *aurei* (500 denars) of full ancient coinage—a high rate.

middle-class was linked with the increasing wealth of a minority. The town-curials were seldom solely men of the town; they had their stakes in the land around. Their fall is bound up with the rise of the magnates to enlarged estates and enhanced political power.

The colons could not pay rents and taxes, and they wanted to escape from burdened farms. Tax-payments declined as land fell out of cultivation, and that made things worse for the remaining farmers or curials. The West, where the urban growth had been recent and insecure, saw its towns rapidly shrink. By 275 Autun had contracted from 500 acres to 25. After 300, scarcely any Gallic town had more than 60 acres covered. Sometimes crops were grown inside the walls. In the East too the crisis was felt; but the much higher level of economic development helped the towns to hang on, distressed, though with powers for recovery unimpaired.

LARGE-SCALE REVOLT. Here, then, lay the troubles that shook the Empire. The towns exhausted their own hinterland and in the process brought themselves down. Tax-burdens fell ever more keenly on the farmer in circumstances that weakened his powers to meet the demands of State and landlord. The bitter discontent and sufferings of the peasantry underlay the continual insurrections and revolts of the third century.

These armed protests took two forms: the direct uprising of the oppressed slaves, often joined by the colons, in Gaul and Spain, in Italy and Africa, in the Balkans—all the areas most hard hit by the agrarian crisis; and the revolts in the army, the soldiers of which were themselves mainly of peasant stock and kept continually deserting.

The civil wars of the third and early fourth centuries may thus be defined as a baffled revolutionary movement of colons, slaves, soldiers. Baffled because the infuriated farmers and labourers were blindly striking out at a hated State, but with no idea of what political form they wanted to substitute. Even the most rebellious sections of the peasant masses, such as the Bagaudae, were victims of this confusion; and the lack of a clear political goal prevented any effective link of the peasant uprisings with the army revolts in a common strategy.[1]

The insurrections in the countryside, though often ferocious and sustained, thus kept falling back in disorder or brigandage, intensifying the economic collapse against which they protested; and only the revolts canalised in a military *pronunciamiento* had a direct political effect—though

[1] We must not forget that as well as the big uprisings there was the ceaseless pressure of peasant 'brigandage' in these years, wherever the central control had slipped. The steadier urban life of the East, its more stable integration of town and country, meant that the revolts here were fewer and less violent.

not an effect which expressed the people's embittered hatred of the system itself. They merely changed one emperor for another and gave the rebels only the satisfaction of pulling down one oppressor before setting up another.

And yet the movement was revolutionary because in its total impact it brought about fundamental changes in the State and its economic system. It arose in a society still largely slave-owing—that is, using slaves, not only for domestic and personal services, but also in the main industries: a society in which the dominating factor was the town where this slave-labour was employed, and in which even agricultural production was in many areas carried on by slaves. And it died out in a society where slave-economy had been broken down or had received blows that were to prove mortal, and where the dominating factor was landwork carried on by a colon tied to the soil under a magnate claiming a coerced rent in money, kind, services.

MONEY THE LEVELLER. The dilemma we have found in the economic sphere can be traced throughout the social relations of the Empire.

Augustus, in seeking to find stable bases for his principate, had favoured in many ways the middle-class of the *municipia* and cemented them into his system. As the trading and industrial class, they provided the foundation on which the *municipia*, the urban forms synonymous with romanisation, depended, and without which the fiscal system supporting the State could not function. But Augustus rested his power ultimately on an alliance with the landed magnates. His imperial constitution essayed to find a balance between *princeps* and Senate, between the head of State and the big landlords in their political groupings. In this dual rule or dyarchy each side had certain provinces to administer. But the scales of power were tipped so heavily on the emperor's side that the Senate steadily lost even its semblance of an independent role and the republican formulas became a mere shell.

Kingly forms were adopted to some extent by Aurelian in the third century; and the third century saw the speeding-up of absolutist trends, which were linked with the breakdown of the *municipia*. Centralisation of State-power went on side by side with the failure of the middle-class, who were the main employers of industrial slave-labour. Money and land heaped up in fewer and fewer hands; and money sank overwhelmingly into land rather than trade. Hierarchical divisions intensified in society.

Yet these caste-rigidities emerged in an Empire which had begun with a considerable expansion of urban and monetary forms. And that expansion meant that previous forms of privilege or unequal status tended to be flattened out, reducible to the common denominator of the coin. The levelling effects of a money-economy appeared in the sphere of law as a tendency to equalise status. Under Caracalla all free men in the Empire gained full Roman citizenship, and in the eyes of the law there was substantially left only the basic division of free and servile.

Thus absolutist centralisation in the State and the equalising of legal status among the citizens appeared as opposed aspects of a single process. But the contradiction in turn begot new divisions in society, new class-stratifications, as money lost its mobility and came to rest in a few hands. The last remnants of tribal variations in status faded out under the levelling movements of money; yet in the further effect of these movements, concentration of wealth, sunk into land, was setting up a new structure of social differentiations which became decisive in the third century—a structure in which the great landlord and the colon paying a coerced rent grow increasingly the typical figures.

THE POSITION OF THE EMPEROR. But did the breakdown of the Augustan dyarchy mean that the emperor was fighting the great landlords and that the latter were losing power?

It meant the contrary. True, at moments the emperor had to fight certain sections of the landlords in order to maintain his position as the executive of the landlord class as a whole. But the need to prevent anarchy breaking up the system was in the interests of the system itself; and so the movement into centralisation worked out as the building-up of a State strengthened in its fight to save the system, to save intact the power of the landlords as a class.

This is a key-point, and to grasp it we must realise how the tangle of contradictions in the Principate worked out. The urban and monetary expansion made possible the complex bureaucratic structure on which alone the centralised State could function; but the absolutist centralisation obstructed and flattened the economic expansion because it leaned more and more on the big landlords as its source of power. And the reason why it did so, and had to do so, was the weakness of the industrial and trading middle-class, their inability to develop and apply new techniques and methods of productive organisation. Wealth accumulated in the form of land, not of industrial capital; and the State, seeking its power-base, had to repose squarely on the landlords.

Yet though the upheavals of the suffering masses in the third century had the ultimate effect of riveting instead of breaking landlord-power, they left profound marks on the State-structure, on the new system of absolutist centralisation. To stabilise his State, Constantine had to take over that creed of the masses which most powerfully expressed a protest of nonconformity, a rejection of the State. And though in making Christianity part of the State-structure he robbed the Church of its basic dissidence, yet only one aspect of the mass-protest could be thus taken over, disarmed, distorted. The forces of dissidence, seething with revolutionary potentialities, continually split off from the established Church and opposed the ruling State. However conforming as an institution, Christianity preserved an idiom necessarily full of anti-imperial ideas and attitudes.

The linking of Christian Church with Roman State must therefore be seen as a direct outcome of the third-century crisis, its main idealogical expression.

TRADE AND TRIBES. Reaching out beyond the frontiers, the mercantile and monetary expansion quickened the breakdown in the tribal systems of the near peoples. This outmovement of a money-economy increased inequality in the tribe; it facilitated the rise of the tribal noble, with the free clansmen falling into servitude under him, and the emergence of the war-king, as the lures of plunder called and intertribal dissensions increased. For Roman foreign trade here was largely a slave-trade.

The trade-nexus thus drew the tribes in towards the Empire and over its boundaries, as soldiers and settlers on military tenures—and then, as the imperial structure weakened, as raiders and large-scale invaders.[1] The changing relations of the tribes and the Empire were thus partly based on the internal changes in the tribes themselves (which trade speeded-up and to a considerable extent determined) and partly on the internal changes in the Empire (which the failing trade-nexus intensified). The invasions of the fourth and fifth centuries must therefore be interpreted as aspects of the crisis of the Empire, and not as external shocks which caused crisis. To ascribe the migrations to the impact on the tribes by nomads such as the Huns from the East is to mistake a contingent factor, which hastened things, for the basic cause.

With Byzantium then began a new phase of history, that of the later Roman Empire, in which the absolutist State was consolidated and Christianity accepted as part of the State-structure. But these steps which appear in the State of Constantine, do not settle the matter in any simple sense. At once new forms of struggle, operating on the new level of

1 We must remember also that large numbers of slaves, of barbarian origin, were ready to co-operate with raiders or invaders.

organisation, appear, with enormously vital and important cultural effects —effects that founded and shaped Europe. This book will explore the new forms of struggle and cultural expression during the millennium of Byzantium's rich life. And first, to get the bases clear, we shall look at Constantine's State.

3

CONSTANTINE'S STATE (I)

DIOCLETIAN AND THE TURNING-POINT. The preliminary work of reconstruction had been done by Diocletian (284–305), an Illyrian, perhaps a slave's son.

He brought the absolutist trends to a head. He reorganised the State-apparatus on bureaucratic lines to meet the emergency caused by the collapse of the self-governing township. He turned east for a new seat of government. And he tried, in vain, to stabilise money and control market-prices.

He recast the system of provincial government, making the provinces smaller and setting up between the reduced governor and the central officials two high authorities. Provinces were grouped in dioceses under vicars, and dioceses were grouped in four big prefectures under praetorian prefects—Gaul, Italy, Illyricum, East. By thus concentrating power in the hands of a few high officials Diocletian hoped to be able to watch and control them more effectively; to ensure that they should not be tempted to revolt, he separated civil and military functions.

He abolished senatorial provinces and replaced the Augustan Dyarchy by a system of dual emperors, one for West and one for East: each with a Caesar as heir. This delimitation of spheres of rule was not meant to divide the Empire; on the contrary it was an administrative device to hold the Empire together as well as the circumstances permitted.

He made the army more mobile, capable of meeting frontier-calls. He extended the bureaucracy and State-participation in production. From the early third century the emperor's personal economic acts had been indistinguishable from State-intervention in trade and industry. Long the largest landowner, he now became the main owner of quarries and mines and the largest industrialist. The State had first organised production in mints, iron-foundries, arms-workshops, textiles, brick-kilns, to supply its own needs; but in combating the third-century crisis it had to go further and recruit labour by forced enlistment. And new applications were tried: thus, with certain weavers, the State handed out materials, gained by a levy in kind, for working-up in home-cottages according to a fixed schedule. Methods drawn from Ptolemaic Egypt and the

Hellenistic kingdoms of Asia were revived, in terms of the changed situation.

TAXES. The levelling-out trend appeared in the introduction of uniform taxation, with increased State-control of local authorities. The basic source of income was the tax on land and agricultural labour, applied in two forms, *ground tax* and *annona*. The ground tax was derived from the old *tributum* exacted from a conquered area, and under the early Empire paid only by communities thus liable. The *annona* had once been an emergency tax in some provinces, levied against such needs as war supplies or food for Rome during famine. The total amount and its distribution were fixed by the emperor's Indiction. During the third century *annona* became general, paid even by imperial estates (and later by religious communities). The lack of metals, the weakening free market, the coinage debasement, led to army pay being made in kind, with money donations now and then. Diocletian stabilised this system and applied it throughout the Empire. The provisions per year per soldier were called an *annona*; and in the fourth century the system was applied to civil-service pay as well. The periodical declaration of the Indiction made revisions of assessment possible after new land-surveys. And tribute, which seems paid in coin save in the grain-lands of Africa and Egypt, was now fixed at the *annona*-surveys with their regular land-valuations.

The Diocletianic *annona*, with payment in kind for army and civil service, marks a heavy break in the old monetary free market. It is imposed on a whole community, to prevent losses to the State by individual default.

Here, then, we put our finger on a decisive moment of shifting bases; the Empire of expanding urbanisation, making an *urbs* of *orbs*, becomes an empire looking substantially to taxes in kind on peasants increasingly subjected to a new kind of servile status. Such a document as the edict of the praetor Aristius Optatus, in Egypt, confesses the breakdown of one fiscal system and the transition to another.

> Diocletian, whose words we may doubtless, with Wilcken, trace in the prefect's edict, established his new system of taxation, which was founded on the principles of the *annona*, because the old system had broken down and (the officials acting according to the needs of the moment) nobody knew any longer what was demanded of him. . . We do not know when this state of affairs began, but it may have done so long before Diocletian took action, and it may have manifested itself in some districts earlier than others. The Thebaid, always the region in which separatist and recalcitrant movements tended to appear whenever the central government grew weak, may well have set the example here. (H. I. Bell.)

It was in the Thebaid that by the sixth century we find a growth of powerful baronial manors.

We must not, however, get a picture of anything like a total failure of the monetary economy. Silver and gold were still needed for the barbarian soldier who after fulfilling his term of service wanted to go back home with something solid to show; and trade, though contracting (especially in the West), was still extensively carried on. Nevertheless the Diocletianic reforms show a large-scale shift of burdens on to the primary producer in the simplest of ways, the direct extraction of his produce by the State—which in turn was linked with similar extractions by the local magnates. Production by slave-labour of commodities for sale had received a severe setback. Caste-formations were also intensified.

RELIGION. But where Diocletian failed to realise the needs of the time was in his attempt at a religious solution of the conflicts seething under the State-structure. He sought to exalt yet further the sacral character of the emperor, to provide an ideological basis of cohesion for the fissured social edifice. He took over the haloed majesty of the Persian Sassanids. The emperor no longer moved freely among his subjects, he withdrew into a complicated seclusion of ceremony, chose eunuchs often as ministers, wore a sacral costume, and compelled those in audience to prostrate themselves. A divine descent was necessary. Diocletian claimed Jupiter as forefather; Maximian took Hercules; Constantius, Caesar of the West and father of Constantine, combined Mithraic and imperial cults by calling himself the scion of Apollo.

Thus Diocletian brought to a head the sacral character of the emperors which had been growing up ever since Julius Caesar, fusing elements from all the strong religious trends: Hero and Saviour, Genius of the Paterfamilias and the Universal Sun. The old high-gods had been more and more absorbed into the emperor's person. Thus, under Trajan we find unofficial titles such as Optimus Maximus, which blend the emperor with Jupiter:

> In the Greek East, temples of Rome and Augustus had at first been the unofficial order, but the goddess Roma was too abstract and shadowy for the clear-sighted Greeks, and the living emperor was so real and powerful that it was not surprising to find Dea Roma fading away, while the emperor remains in possession of the field, often equated with Zeus Eleutherios and Zeus Panhellenikos. In the West we can observe the emperor quietly absorbing the minor deities: thus we find dedications to Apollo Augustus or Minerva Augusta in Italy, Mercurius Augustus in Gaul, and even Vesta Augusta in Spain. They are tending to become 'the emperor's god's', as it were, the gods whom the emperor recommends: sometimes the epithet Augustus means

little more than 'imperial'. The attraction of the emperor was, in fact, too strong for all save the most revered gods and cults to withstand. (Charlesworth.)

But there was one god, one cult, that had no intention of being absorbed. So Diocletian had to strike at this enemy. He had no liking for persecution, but he saw that the Roman State with its basis in the cult of the emperor could not coexist with Christianity. His persecution was severe, the one really organised blow that the creed had to weather: it aimed specially at having all copies of the Gospels burned. But though it brought about many recantations, it failed to break the Church.

CONSTANTINE AND STABILISATION. Constantine was the son of a Dardanian from the hilly country north of Macedonia and his concubine Helena. His father became a Caesar under the new system, and Constantine succeeded him in Gaul and Britain. The Imperial College, which had excluded hereditary succession, thus fell to pieces in a few years. Civil wars began, ending with Constantine's triumph.

He carried on Diocletian's work, but he had the genius to see that something further was needed for the centralised bureaucracy. He made the decisive breaks expressed by the turning from Rome and the surrender of the imperial cult.

Though the triumph of Christianity was linked with the revolutionary upheavals of the third century, we cannot identify the dissident creed and the rebel movements of slave and colon. Those movements were strongest where Christianity was weakest, among the peasantry of the West and the Balkans; yet nonconformist creed and rebel outburst were only different facets of a mass-protest against the imperial State. Indeed we see in an area like Africa, where the old Graeco-Punic culture had deep roots, how Christian dissidence and peasant revolt could fuse. There, the persecution created a new belligerence. The *Circumcelliones* or Wanderers of Numidia, calling themselves the Soldiers of Christ, were homeless bands of Punic-speaking peasants, who roamed about the country, begging or taking from the farms. With Donatist leaders who preached against any tolerance of the brethren who had recanted under persecution, they made concerted attacks on towns like Cirta, and more than once in the fourth century broke in. Shouting their war-cry, *Praises to God!* they caused much destruction and refused in any way to accept the State.

The revolt of the colons tied them down more than ever to the soil and the lord's will; the triumph of Christianity meant a thorough distortion of the creed. Yet the situation was not so simple as those generalisations imply. The revolt had changed the State; elements of the original dissidence survived in the creed, capable of reviving their force at suitable moments. All mass-movements of rebellion or revolution henceforth used the dissident aspects of the Christian idiom for fourteen hundred years. The Cromwellian revolution was the parting of the ways: some of its most powerful formulations were Christian in their terms, but were mixed with political terms which then detached themselves, so that in the American and French Revolutions of the next century the secular idiom dominated.[1]

OUR LORD. The State-acceptance of Christianity did not destroy the sacral character of the ruler; it merely meant that this character had now to be fitted into the new terms of religious reference. The emperor ceased to be a god, but in return he became god's regent, with the whole weight of the Church backing his claim. To enter his presence, you adored, knelt and kissed the purple. *Dominus*, the slave's word for his master, had long appeared in addresses; but now the ruler applied it to himself. He became *Our Lord* on coins. He assumed regal insignia. Previously he had worn the purple cloak; now he takes the diadem (possibly worn at times by Aurelian and Diocletian) and red boots. The diadem came from Persia where the Magian high-priest set it on the king's head.

Power was centred in his person. He had entire control of finance and legislation, was commander-in-chief and head of the Church, appointed and dismissed ministers. Legislation sometimes took the form of an *oratio* to the Senate, but was mostly done by edict.

Republican Rome and the early Empire had detested the name of king, *rex*, but in the eastern provinces the Greek *basileus* had soon been used. There the term for the empire was *basileia*. Now *basileus* became the title of the Roman and Persian rulers; *rex* was allotted to barbarian kinglets. But so strong was the anti-monarchical tradition that not till the seventh century did the emperor use *basileus* in constitutions and rescripts. His official Greek title was *autokrator*, meant to be a translation of *imperator* but lacking the military connotation of the Latin. *Despotes*, a Greek slave-term like the Latin *dominus*, was used from Constantine's day.

THE NEW NOBILITY. Byzantium's Senate had been merely a municipal council; but Constantine's son raised it to imperial level. As in Old Rome it was an hereditary body, entered through the upper magistracies. But many offices had died out; others had changed in character. The praetorship, through which the republican Senate had normally been entered,

---

1 We must beware of thinking of the establishment of the Church as a simple surrender to the State. The conflict of compromise and no-compromise dates from the earliest days of Christianity; and various aspects of the pre-establishment conflict will come up when we treat the rise of the bishops, the early heresies and so on.

was no longer the department of a great law-officer; it was honorific and its holder had only to spend money on shows and works.

Most of the old nobility had refused to leave Italy where they had their estates. So the emperor found it easier to build up a new nobility largely based on the higher civil service and on allegiance to his person. There were now three orders, *Illustres, Spectabiles, Clarissimi,* each with cash-subsidies. The emperor could confer them on anyone, who then became eligible for the Senate. The City Prefect was the Senate's chief and kept in liaison with the emperor. The new character of the body is shown by the fact that all administrative posts were now open to senators, including those previously reserved under the Augustan scheme of balances for the *equites,* the middle-class. But this did not mean that the posts were limited to aristocrats; on the contrary, men of the lowest rank could and did rise to high positions which gave them entry to the Senate. A new nobility, based not on birth but on imperial service, was thus created.

But the fact that the Senate was now much more closely related to the emperor's person did not mean that it was divorced from the land. The body was still essentially a committee of the landlords and magnates— but a new relation between the landlords and the State-system had been brought about. They were indeed much more closely integrated in the State, since the Augustan balance-of-power, which tried to keep the middle-class as the agents of government and the magnates as the basis of power, had fallen away.[1]

An Imperial Council, *Consistorium,* advised the emperor. Derived from Hadrian's legal *Concilium* as enlarged and modified by Diocletian, it acted as high court for such cases as treason, and was consulted on policy and legislation. The Quaestor presided. The two Finance Ministers and the Master of Offices attended its meetings, which seem to have been both special and regular. It controlled a large department of secretaries and officials called tribunes and notaries, who had offices in the palace and drafted its proceedings and resolutions, as well as carrying out missions. A meeting of the *Consistorium* was called a Silence, *Silentium.*

The two highest officials were the Praetorian Prefects of Italy and the East, who had executive, legal, financial, even legislative functions. With treasuries, they dealt with army-pay and food; they were supreme judges

---

1 The history of *Patricius* is of interest. The Patricians were first the closed circle of noble families holding power in early Rome; Caesar and Augustus were empowered by law to raise rich plebian families to the status, to fill gaps in the peerage; and in time this power became an imperial prerogative. With Constantine *Patricius* is a title conferred for very special services on individuals. In the fifth century the supreme commander of the army became *The Patrician*—and at times was a barbarian like Ricimer the Suevian.

of appeal, cared for the food-supplies of Rome and Byzantium, issued their own edicts on matters of detail, appointed or dismissed provincial governors. They even wore purple robes, shorter than the emperor's; military officers had to bend knees at their entry; they rode in tall chariots and each had a big silver inkstand and heavy gold pen-case.

Rome and Byzantium were each under a City Prefect, a chief criminal judge, controlling the water-supply, the markets, the trading and manufacturing guilds, *collegia*.

The highest legal officer was the Quaestor of the Sacred Palace, who drafted laws and rescripts in reply to petitions.

CIVIL SERVICE. The head of the civil service was the Master of the Offices, who ran several ministries, especially the palace bureaux. Three *scrinia* or departments had been inherited from early days: *Memoriae*, records and issue office, helping other *scrinia* to find needed documents; *Epistularum*, in Latin and Greek sections; *Libellorum*, dealing with petitions. A fourth was added, *Dispositionum*, to arrange the emperor's programme. The Master controlled audiences and ceremonies, including the reception of ambassadors, and so had a corps of interpreters: he himself thus approximated to a Minister for Foreign Affairs. He also ran the State-post and the school of *agentes in rebus*, confidential messengers who acted as a secret service spying on governors, tax-collectors, and others. These agents were classed in five grades and could rise to the rank of first-class count and to provincial governorship. The Master had further a control of some frontier-commanders, and in 396 was set over State arms-factories, of which there were then thirteen in the East. He had legal jurisdiction over civil servants in the capital, and the Scholarian Guard was his care.

The whole civil-service was now fictionally military. Officials wore the military belt; and on completing their term of work they gained *honesta missio*, discharge without a stain—a military phrase. The imperial service had three main divisions, civil, military, palatine. Under the third heading came the staffs of the Finance Ministers, the Counts of the Sacred Largesses and the Private Estates. Every *scrinium* had a permanent official at its head, on whom its efficiency depended. Promotion was by seniority. The higher officials were all senators.

ARMY. The old legionary system of republican days, based on the levy of free farmers, had long faded out. Constantine carried further Diocletian's work of devising a mobile field-force. The cavalry was organised in separate units and the infantry formations were reduced in size.

The main army was composed of the *Comitatenses*, under the emperor—

the very name gives its origin in his personal troops, his *comitatus*—and the *Limitanei*, frontier-troops under dukes.

The field-army was divided into *Comitatenses* and the palatine troops that were now the imperial bodyguard proper. The small infantry legions were linked with *auxilia*, light troops recruited from Gauls, Franks and other Germans, under their own chiefs or Roman officers. The cavalry, *vexillationes*, was under separate command. All three arms were under Tribunes. The Master of Soldiers was Commander-in-chief.

All the new bodies of the third and fourth centuries show how the new army was built up out of imperial guards. Constantine abolished the old Praetorians, but probably before that a body of Protectors of the Divine Side had appeared, made up of Germans (often of princely origin) and Romans. Diocletian had added an élite corps, a new lot of Protectors, horse and foot; and Constantine created the Schools of the Palace. Till about the mid-fifth century the Germanic element grew ever more prominent. The two court-corps left the palace only to accompany the emperor; but there were also horse and foot guards under counts, who were generally at court but could be sent away on special missions. There were also Cuirassiers, and *armaturae* with lighter equipment.

In the early Empire all free citizens were still liable to legionary service, while subject peoples were enlisted in the auxiliaries. Now the distinction of citizen and subject had gone, and the legions were recruited from the wilder areas of the Empire, the highlands of Illyricum, Thrace, Galatia, Isauria. Urbanised areas were left alone. On the Danube the auxiliaries, mostly barbarians, ranked higher than the legions in the same command.

The recruits were sons of soldiers, men from barbarian settlements under Roman officers, homeless men who came to the recruiting office and took dust-money. Curials were exempt, tied to their councils; artisans were generally enclosed in the caste-system. Large landlords were supposed to provide one or more of their colon-tenants; but if they gave up anyone, he was likely to be a useless fellow, and so the State preferred to recruit barbarians and take a money-payment from the landlord in place of men.

The strong Germanic element is shown by the use of the barbarian war-cry, *barritus*, and a close formation of infantry, the Germanic *drungus*. The ancient and revered Eagle of the legions gives way, it seems, to the Dragon. A German chief elevated Constantine as *Imperator* in Britain; and Julian the pagan later attacked Constantine as a Germaniser.

There was no officer caste. A good soldier could become *centenar* or *ducenar* (the old centurion), and rise to the rank of tribune, over a unit, or might even be promoted count.

Private bands of retainers accompanied the growth of baronial estates. They were called Bucellarians, biscuit-men; and though long illegal, they steadily increased from the turn into the fifth century.

A complete change had taken place since the days of Augustus. Barbarians replaced the free citizen in arms; and this influx of Germanic tribesmen was linked with the growth of military tenures and the sinking status of the colon. There was a basic regrouping of forces around the emperor's person. Instead of a stress on civic aspects, as in the Principate, the whole government service, from soldier to law-clerk, was conceived in terms of army-organisation. Septimius Severus, at the outset of the third-century turmoils, had been the first emperor to wear in Rome the full insignia of military command; and now, through the concentration of the revolutionary forces in the army of colons and tribesmen, the whole State had been transformed as though it were a mere extension of the army.

Infantry lost in importance to the cavalry, as the free citizen and farmer faded out. The well-armoured horseman, the typical warrior of a society where the landed magnate dominates, became the main fighter. The decisive moment when the footman was finally shown as outdated was the battle of Adrianople in August 378, when the Germanic horse smashed up the enfeebled legions. Within a couple of generations Prokopios was writing of the legionary as a remnant of the distant past and the armoured horseman as the modern trooper. He eulogises the horse-archer with cuirasse and kneeboots, quiver and sword, sometimes lance and small shield. 'Some people, however, who choose to ignore the existence of these troops, persist in openmouthed adulation of Antiquity and refuse to admit the superiority of Modern Inventions.'[1]

[1] Iron-mailed cataphracts were tried by Maxentius against Constantine—their armour was made of square pieces of iron or brass overlapping, and covered both man and horse; the helmet fitted close to the neck and the face was protected by a visor with holes. Though too cumbrous, this heavy armour interestingly shows the tentative movement towards the later knightly equipment.

4

CONSTANTINE'S STATE (II)

THE MAGNATES. Let us see in more detail what was happening to town and country. Before Diocletian tax-incidence had been unequal, governed by a variety of conditions. Towns or districts once free or lightly taxed had become tributary and vice versa. Despite the trend to uniformity from Augustus on, many anomalies and diversities persisted, *e.g.* a gift of immunity to civic groups. Diocletian flattened these out, and imposed taxes on Italy, which had hitherto been tax-free.

The middle-man or *publicanus* was swept away. Using the curials or its own officials to collect taxes, the State supplanted the businessman. By the late fourth century most of the old impost-forms had gone; new taxes, new methods of assessment superseded them. And these new burdens had shifted on to land, taxed not by mere acreage but by productive value in corn, wine or oil. The unit was the area that an able-bodied peasant could cultivate and live on; and in fact such peasants carried the whole burden of the taxes.

The land was now substantially under large-scale ownership, held by the emperor or magnates, *possessores*, though when we look more closely at the East we must modify without denying this generalisation. Estates were made up of farms worked by tenants who paid rent and defrayed the land-tax; but the element of free contract was almost gone. The tied colons, *adscripti*, outnumbered small proprietors or free tenants; and through the fourth and fifth centuries the State kept on limiting the area of free action open to the colon. In both East and West the colonate is a transitional form between slavery and serfdom. But its continual extention does not mean that slave-labour was discarded.

Such free peasantry as survived, plebeians, tended to seek of their own accord the patronage of a magnate or high official. The times were too dangerous and the taxes too heavy if they tried to stand on their own feet. They often made themselves over by a fictive form of sale: they continued to work the land while handing over part of the products to their lord and, though they had no hold now on the land by law, they were sheltered to some extent by their lord's own privileged position. Whole communes in this way sought a patron. They lost their freedom, such as it was, but they gained an escape from the voracious tax-collector.

2*

The State attempted to hold up this form of tax-evasion. An edict of 368 put heavy penalties on the client and laid a fine of 25 pounds of gold on the patron. Then the fictive contracts were declared null, and notaries who drew them up were threatened with legal action. That the East was strongly affected by the breakdown of free farming is proved by the fact that of eight ordinances directed against the patronate between 366 and 534, six are addressed to the Praetorian Prefect of the East and particularly deal with Egypt. But in East and West alike the State's efforts to curb the patronate were futile.

The senatorial magnates had their own domain as well as their colonfarms; and they often still used slaves to work it. For this they themselves were taxable. The small-producers, the curials with lands near their towns, were being borne down and crushed on the lines already sketched. 'Like victims bound with fillets' for slaughter, the Law with surprising truth described them. They were collectively responsible for the taxes in the town-area and the upkeep of the State-post.[1]

TAXES AND MONEY. Special taxes were imposed when an emperor came to the throne and every five years thereafter (when he made donations to the army); the senatorials made an offertory, and the decurions had to get gold together. A tax on trade-profits, the five-yearly contribution or 'gold-and-silver', was set on every sort of turn-over, on beggars and prostitutes (even catamites, says Evagrios) as well as traders and shopkeepers; and this tax was much resented by the townsfolk. We hear of fathers selling their children or putting their girls in brothels to meet it. The richest class, the senatorials, had the easiest time. Immune from urban rates, they passed the land-tax, save for the domain, on to the tenants; they paid the offertory and at times had obligations as magistrates; they paid a property-tax, *follis*, in specie, assessed in three grades. But such payments as they did make were light in comparison with their means; and Constantine even set up *Defensores Senatus* in the provinces to protect the rich landlords against his own officials.

Customs-dues, after varying at fairly low rates in the early Empire, rose in the fourth century to $12\frac{1}{2}$ per cent and seem to have stayed there. In prosperous times the volume of trade and the yield in dues were high. The State also owned works and industries, such as mines and textile manufactories, as well as getting the return from the imperial estates.

---

[1] They could escape by begetting twelve children. The only way a soldier could leave the army was by volunteering to be a curial. A veteran's son who chopped off his fingers, or a disgraced priest became curials.

The Treasury was administered under three main controls. The Central Treasury, under the Count of the Sacred Largesses, took in most taxes and returns, and administered mines, customs, mints. The Chests of the Praetorian Prefect, still paymaster of the forces, looked after the *annona*. And the Chests of the Count of the Private Estates administered the imperial estates, which confiscations kept extending.

Interest in the fourth century was 4 to 6 per cent though it could rise to 12 per cent when no good security was offered. Senators, as before, were not allowed to lend at usury, but they evaded this regulation; and after the fall of the Patriarch John of the Golden Mouth, champion of the poor, they were granted the right to lend up to 6 per cent.[1]

The simplest proof of the success of Constantine's reorganisation lies in the coinage. He set up a gold standard, the *solidus*, bullion stamped with the imperial seal rather than a coin, to which the coinage was related. The *solidus* kept its value for eight centuries. In this fact alone we touch the vitally important economic role of Byzantium through that long and difficult tract of time. The *solidus* maintained a stable basis of international trade, extending its influence far past the Empire's borders and ceaselessly infiltrating into the broken West to stimulate and aid the revival of town-life and a monetary economy.

THE TOWNS AND TRADE. In taxation we see the contradictions of a levelling trend to uniformity and a deepening split between the rich, who became fewer, and the poor, who were flattened out by the levelling process. In law the same contradictions appeared. The third-century crisis had seen a levelling of legal status among all freemen, and a convergence of free and servile status; the result was the creation of a new and deeper social division —that between the *honestiores*, the rich, and the *humiliores*, the masses. A rich man and a poor man who committed the same crime suffered different penalties: a typical difference was that which linked exile for the rich with death for the poor.

As the crisis worsened, the gap between East and West increased, and the richer economic and cultural life of the East asserted itself ever more decisively. In Syria and Asia Minor trade carried on with considerable volume, as we can see from the *Expositio Totius Mundi*, composed in the East in the earlier fourth century. Alexandria, Antioch, Byzantium were cities with populations of hundreds of thousands, while the towns of the West had become mere villages; and after temporary setbacks the eastern

[1] John speaks of short-term loans by landlords to their tenants at 50 per cent. Though no doubt illegal, such loans were made, and naturally hastened the fall of the free peasant to the level of the adscript.

cities did not merely hold fast, they expanded again. Soon Themistios could tell with pride of the grandiose building in Byzantium, houses of seven to nine storeys, and the town itself 'a huge workshop of magnificence' where architects, decorators and workers of all crafts finely laboured.

Greece itself was hard hit; but throughout Egypt, Syria, Asia Minor, skilled craftsmen kept producing textiles of wool and linen, working at metals, glass, pottery, jewellery. Thus, Alexandria was an exporter of papyrus, glasswork, textiles. Mining and metallurgy were active in Pontus, in Asia Minor, in Macedonia. Egypt exported vast quantities of corn both to Byzantium and to Arabia. And trade with the farther East went on thriving. Syria and Mesopotamia traded with Central Asia, and Syrian embroideries and glasswork reached as far as China; Egypt was linked through the Red Sea with Ceylon; and the Black Sea ports had routes going north and east.

How far did the mercantile and industrial classes play an active political part in the East after they had broken down in the West? and how far did slave-production continue? These are important questions, which must be answered if we are to grasp the difference between the developments in the East and the West after the movement into a feudalised system was started off.

The merchants were mainly Syrians, Jews, Greeks, Egyptians, Armenians. In the fifth and sixth centuries eastern traders were busy in the West, picking up what threads of business remained and supplying luxury goods to the magnates and high clerics. They brought papyrus, textiles, wines, even herbs, and traded, not only in Sicily, Rome or Ravenna, but also in Paris, Orléans, Marseille, the Rhine area, Spanish ports.

These traders and moneylenders were officially plebeians; but their wealth enabled them to buy or worm their way into the higher ranks of the State-machine in the East. At least the upper sections of the mercantile class became closely identified with the State, to which they lent money and which they provided with financial experts. The job of collecting customs was sold, and in this way the traders and the treasury were in many ways drawn together. The merchants needed a strong State, and their economic role was never great enough to enable them to challenge the hold of the magnates on the Empire. At most they wanted to buy land and become magnates themselves. But this does not mean that there was no cleavage of interests between the merchants or financiers and the senatorial landlords. The former tended to want simply a strong State that kept traffic safe and profitable, whereas the magnates were continually rent by the intrigues of one group against another for control of the State-system.

And the former wanted the tax-incidence to fall less on trade and industry than on land, whereas the magnates wanted the reverse. But the upper sections of the merchants and financiers, by getting more drawn into the State-system and by aspiring towards the status of magnate, were liable to betray the interests of the small trader or shopkeeper or manufacturer, who wanted definitely to see the township's burdens lightened and the big estate's burdens increased.

The mercantile class thus provided an important cross-current in Byzantine politics, which could modify the situation from time to time, but which was not strong enough at any time to determine the main policy of the Empire or to control the State-structure. The bureaucracy, though often recruited from this class's members, always acted as a whole as the agents and upholders of the landed magnates, subserving in the last resort their interests.

SLAVES AND ARTISANS. The plebeians may be grouped as small-producers cultivating their own land, large and small traders, artisans of all sorts, workers of the colon type. The first and last group, we have seen, tended to fall to the level of the tied colon, though in the East this tendency was offset by the persisting urban life, which kept the traders going. The artisans had always been stronger in the East, organised communally as Imperial Workers under the Hellenistic Kingdoms, and carrying on to some extent through the early Roman Empire. They played here on the land a stronger role than did the *latifundia* worked by slaves, and free artisans, organised in guilds that descended from the Hellenistic State-corporations, were as active in the towns.

Under the early Empire trade-corporations were permitted; but the State was suspicious, and in cases of doubt inclined to suppression (so, Trajan in his letters to Pliny). But the economic contraction which drove the State to join widely in trade and industry made the State approve of such organisations, by which alone it could effectively control production and distribution; and members of a *collegium* were as tied down as the curials. If a man ran off, his property fell in to the *collegium;* if there were gaps, the State forced well-off persons in.

In State-industry, especially textiles, slaves were often employed; but the free artisans, organised in *collegia* and bound to their work, held their own. The *collegia* paid taxes and were liable to State-burdens.

The East then differed from the West in the survival of both *collegia* of artisans and slave-manufactories.

One of the distinctive peculiarities of Byzantium lay in the preservation of strong survivals of slavery concurrently with the development of servile forms of exploitation. The new modes of production are developed here without losing the external forms of the ancient State: imperial crown, bureaucratic and army organisation; also their working-out was slow and painful for the primary producer. But despite the similarity of the essential processes of development in the empires of the east and the west, we must not lose sight of the basic differences in the economy and social structure. Those differences it was that allowed the former to survive the latter. (Levchenko.)

VILLAGE-COMMUNITY. It follows that the large estate was not the same in the East as in the West. The extreme independence of the magnate in the West, his secure arrogation of political rights that had previously belonged to the State, were only partly to be seen in the East. Here the survival of the centralised State held back the full seignorial development of the estate, which did not become a self-sufficing economic organism. Here the town-life, the town-market and the wider trade-nexus still kept contacts with the estate, which found a profitable outlet in supplying the needs of the large town-populations.

Constantine in 324 had legally attached the tenant-farmer to the land of the large estate; and after that any tenant who left his farm could be brought back like a runaway slave in chains. 'He steals his own self', the Law ingeniously explained. The colon, however, remained otherwise a free legal personality, able to acquire and hold property. Against that was set the fact that the magnate had won the right to use force within his own estate: he called up army-recruits and produced persons accused or summoned to appear by the law-courts.

The colonate, which was introduced into different provinces at different times, saved agriculture, and thereby saved the State. If the farmer was tied down, at least he could not be evicted. There was a movement back to the village in some areas; and the villagers were not altogether helpless before attack. Thus, rescripts of Commodus in the late second century show the vindication of rights and customs by colons in large tracts of Africa against imperial stewards. In Asia Minor the peasants took similar actions; we find them threatening to leave work if oppressions do not stop. Private contract gives way before regional and traditional usages; individual claims are merged in communal claims.

There are many traces of group-management of local affairs. Peasants organised for sacral purposes, *e.g.* those on the Cyllanean estates in Phrygia formed *collegia* for the cult of Zeus Sabazios; and such *collegia* could provide the basis of discussion and common action on more than cult-matters. Often there was a communal control of woodland and pasture, and group-action to uphold some standard of customs. The colons acted and complained as a body; the emperor addressed them as such.

The *vici* (villages) of the Codex Theodosianus and the recent discoveries as to the organisation of the Asiatic *saltus* show that in this case, as in Western instances, communal institutions arose independently of ethnographic causes on the soil of the Roman provinces as well as on soil conquered or colonised by Germans or Slavs. These institutions were generated by several facts which occur in all the instances of which we have been speaking: tribal survivals, extensive semi-pastoral methods of husbandry, settlements which involved a good deal of intermixture of rights (on the wasteland), the necessity for territorial lords to organise their districts and possessions, not on the principle of the steward's absolute rule, but on that of hereditary self-government. (Vinogradoff.)

Communes of free farmers with a certain autonomy are to be traced in Egypt, Syria, Armenia, Isauria, inner Asia Minor, Illyricum, Thrace, Moesia, Dacia. Thus, in Thrace and elsewhere we meet free farmers who are descendants of the peasantry on the huge imperial domains of Hellenistic times.

5

CONSTANTINE'S STATE (III)

CHURCH-ORGANISATION AND THE EMPIRE. St. Paul's Epistles give no hint of a local clergy. The *Didache* shows that at the end of the first century at least many Christian groups depended on wandering apostles (permitted only to stay three days) or prophets who might settle down, and that deacons and bishops were held rather in contempt; it makes no reference to presbyters, priests. From Paul's account of the orders—apostles, prophets, teachers, those with the powers, those with healing gifts—it is clear that stress was on spontaneous expression and inspiration, and that the types which the later Church distrusted were those dominant in apostolic congregations. Only at the end of Paul's list do the presbyters and deacons tail in, the men concerned with organisational work.

By the second century, as the need to organise grew, bishop or overseer got a strong position as group-representative. But his close relation with the group fell away. By the third century new officers intruded, and by the fourth to fifth centuries the graded hierarchy had arrived. Originally, presbyters were the bishop's counsellors; the deacons carried out such work as poor relief. But now, with the growing split between officers and congregation, bishop and deacon were elevated by the additional offices beneath them of subdeacon, acolyte, exorcist, reader.

The bishop's election had once been free and open to all the group; but as the clergy steadily gained more control it lost its democratic basis, especially at centres like Rome. The parochial system was slow in developing, and was looked on suspiciously by the higher clergy; they feared that the common priest might find and express ideas of his own. Even by the end of the fifth century it was held down at Rome; but two or more centuries earlier it had appeared in the more democratic East. And it was a parish priest, Areios, who set off, at Alexandria, the first great heresy that shook the established Church.

A crucial step was taken when the bishops of near groups met for discussion. In the third century local or provincial councils were becoming regular and had supplanted the original system, that of an underground corresponding-society backed by personal intercourse—'a laired and light-fleeing nation', as Minucius Felix said.

2. GREEK-EGYPTIAN PAINTING FROM THE FAYUM

Second Century

3. ST. TRIPHONIOS

Macedonia, church of St. Panteleïmon of Nerezi, c. 1164

Early Christians met in groups or corporations to read the Scriptures, comment, exhort to correction or censure of one another; then came the *agape* or love-feast, a communal meal prefaced by prayer, in which the caste-divisions of Roman society were ignored. When the Church was established, it turned on these gatherings by which it had built itself up. Many groups, however, could not reconcile themselves to the State and world, and kept up their dinners in churchyards. The Church Councils condemn equally the *agape* and the pagan feasts of the Kalends.

The first stages of organisation had been based on the system of the *municipia*. The division of clergy and lay, *ordo* and *plebs*, appeared also in the *civitas* with its *curia* and *populus*. The Church's officers and overseers (*episkopoi*, bishops) were based on the officers and overseers of the *municipium*; both Church and civic officers dealt with the administration of the law (the Christians having their own system of arbitration) and *alimentaria*, doles. As late as Origen we find the Christians conscious of the likeness.

The later stages of organisation were based on the provincial and then on the whole imperial system. Rising in Syrian and Asian cities, the Church had had some difficulty in keeping contacts between its groups. Paul went from main city to main city; from provincial capitals the creed was carried out into the neighbouring areas. The capital was thus looked on as the mother-church of the region; and when the Church was established in the fourth century, it emerged with a structure built on the territorial forms of the Empire.

The role of the capital had been defined by councils of bishops in the second century, who came from all over the province to meet there. By mid-third century the synods were regular. The capital's bishop assumed a special importance and tended to be the synod's standing president; he gained much influence on the election of bishops anywhere in his province. When Constantine called the first General Council of the Church, it was decided that provincial synods be held twice a year under the metropolitan and that his approval be held necessary to the validity of a bishop's election.

Changes in provincial government-forms meant changes in church-organisation. Thus, the emperor Valens cut up the province of Cappadocia to weaken St. Basil's authority. And in the expanding Church the need for councils at which bishops from several provinces might come together was felt. Hence councils were held at the great cities, Antioch, Ephesos, Alexandria. The bishop of such a city won an overlordship above the ordinary run of metropolitan bishops, as they had one above mere bishops. These new dominant figures were called patriarchs. They represented the enlarged areas of control appearing in the Church as the prefects and vicars had represented an enlarged area of control in secular government. The election of metropolitan bishops needed patriarchial concurrence; and in Egypt the Patriarch had a special authority, so that all elections of bishops required his approval.[1]

Thus, in the elaborated system, the importance of a see was derived from its secular position, though the apostolic tradition linked with certain of the great towns underlined the sanctity of their patriarchs.

THE PROBLEM OF BYZANTIUM. Byzantium, New Rome, had an anomalous position, since it lacked anything like an apostolic tradition; it had not grown into ecclesiastical dignity by dominating in the course of centuries the parishes and sees around it. Before the new foundation, its bishop had been a minor one, under the see of Heraklea. Now its see outbid Old Rome's in secular significance. At once all the other patriarchs and metropolitans regarded it with fierce jealousy, coveted or opposed its power. Rome, Antioch, Alexandria were the main rivals.

In the fourth century, Antioch was, on the whole, won over by Byzantium to stand against the common foe, Alexandria, while Rome held aloof, ready to muster all her forces if Byzantium claimed supremacy. At the General Council of 381, Canon III tried to keep the peace by declaring that the Bishop of Constantinople, ruling the see of the New Rome, was second in honour to the Bishop of Old Rome. Rome was to some extent mollified; but Alexandria was directly challenged.

THE FIRST COUNCIL. Later I shall deal with the struggle in the Church. Here let us consider what Constantine had done in calling the first General Council of the Church at Nikaia, in 318, to which came bishops even from Armenia and Scythia.

He had made the decisive step that incorporated the Church in the State. The Imperial Church Council represented the Roman Senate in the sphere of *Res Divinae*. The old pagan Senate had dealt with both civil and religious matters; indeed the latter came first on its agenda; but after the Christian triumph, its control of religion ended, and what it lost the Church Council gained.

Just as the emperor nominated and summoned senators, so he determined the Council's composition. He paid the cost of the bishops' journeys and put the imperial post at their service. He or his delegate, not an ecclesiastic, presided. (And at this time the emperor was not yet personally

---

1 We must relate the gradual approximation of the Church to the imperial structure with the social changes going on inside the Church, of which the most important are the rise of the bishops (to the destruction of apostolic democracy) and the changes in the bishops' status as the rich and socially powerful invade the office.

a baptised Christian.) The Gospels displaced the Altar of Victory. The Council's conclusions, like the Senate's *consulta*, needed the emperor's assent to become valid.

The Council was in no sense a representation of dioceses or congregations. It was a charismatic assembly: its decisions were taken as revelations of the Holy Ghost. They must be unanimous. A persisting minority created a schism and destroyed the unity of the Church, denied its very nature. All that could then be done was to declare the lack of spiritual validity in the Council and start all over again, till unanimity was assumed to prove the divine presence.

In practice, this position meant that the emperor had to prepare unanimity by negotiations, threats, or persuasions. He must anticipate the workings of the Holy Ghost, or all was lost. However, he soon learned, to his regret and amazement, that he was not the only person who could pack or overawe a Council. In fact he discovered that the Church which he had taken over in order to build an ideological unity in the Empire was the vital source of a new and irreconcilable discord, however he might 'fulminate like a powerful herald of God against internal strife in the Church as more dangerous than any kind of war or conflict' (Eusebios). And in vain also he burned the books of Areios, 'not merely that his depraved teaching might be utterly destroyed, but that not a single record of it be left to posterity'. In establishing the Church, Constantine had unloosed forces which he could not foresee.

THE THIRTEENTH APOSTLE. He had possibly thought at first that pagans and Christians would live together. He attempted to bring about general toleration and end the clash of Christianity and State; but he soon found that Christians could tolerate neither pagans nor fellow-Christians with opposed views. Well might he write to the first contestants who rent the established Church, 'Restore to me then my quiet days and untroubled nights, that the joy of undimmed light, the delight of a tranquil life, may henceforth be my portion'.

The Church with its multiplied privileges and immunities, its new secular defences against paganism and heresy, was soon implicated with the State in all its workings, large and small. That was acceptable, as long as the Church, without schism, buttressed the State. Constantine was duly welcomed by the bishops to his seat in their midst 'as if he were one of them'. He became for the orthodox world *Isapostolos*, the Equal of the Apostles, the Thirteenth Apostle (while yet unbaptised). In return the Church demanded that he act as the guardian of dogma and enforcer of discipline. He proceeded to interfere in all church-matters, organise and direct, legislate for the Church, preside at Councils, and dictate formulas of faith: 'You others are Bishops within the Church, whereas I am divinely-appointed Bishop-General outside the Church.'

THE DEME. If in the Church, its orthodoxy and its heresies, the people had found a living relationship to the State, which enabled them to debate issues and take an active part in questions that affected high and low alike, there was also in Byzantium an organised way of direct political expression. This was through the circus-factions which captured the control of the Demes, the subdivisions of the citizen-body.

It is necessary to understand both the Deme and the Faction; for then we see both the way in which Byzantium carried on the structure and character of the ancient city, and the way in which she transformed them.

Demos has two meanings: the people in general and the population in an urban circumscription. The deme inside the city may be called a quarter or parish: a territorially based neigbourhood or group of neighbourhoods, *geitoniai*, inhabited by demesmen, *demotai*. The deme was the original cell of the Greek city of *polis*, and always kept some measure of local autonomy.[1]

It had its assemblies, its officials, its property; it kept the list of those liable to taxes or military service, took part in tax-collection, had charge of police-work in its area. After Alexander the Great, the deme-system spread with the new cities over the Near East; but the demes lost their military functions, their part in tax-collecting—displaced by the imperial army and mercenaries, the new bureaucracy. What remained was the control of cultural and religious matters; and with the collapse of self-government in the city, social life centred more and more in the theatre, circus, temple.

The Roman Empire ended the privileged position of the Greeks in the demes; and after 212 A.D. all citizens became demesmen. The demes in this form were carried over into the Byzantine world. At first they still elected their own officials; but under Justinian at least the main ones were State-nominated.

At Byzantium the demes were made up of rather small quarters or neighbourhoods; but not the whole population were *demotai*.[2] There was

---

1 In early Athenian society 'the vital unit of the new system was the *demos*' (cognate with *desmos*, the share or *moira* of land for a clan)—G. Thomson. Though the clan-system of tenure early broke down, a clan-sense based on association for civic tasks and rights persisted to the end of the *polis*, in the *demos*, in the deme.

2 It is tempting to hold that the *demotai* were those privileged to claim 'political bread', the free donations given (till Heraklios) from high-up buildings approached by stairs, dotted about Byzantium.

also the People, *ochlos*, in which we may distinguish the citizens proper and *xenoi*, strangers who for one reason or another were resident in the city, mainly visitors or emigrants from the eastern provinces. The *demotai* were the descendants of citizens of the old and new city, derive their rights from Constantine; but entry into their ranks could be given by assent of the city authorities, occasionally by grant of the emperor. The demes were under the city prefect, eparch. We may safely assume that they had many of the old functions such as control of street-order, docks, fire-services, cistern and aqueduct repairs. Rich demesmen built or maintained the temples—later the churches. But ever since Severus (at the outset of the third century disorders) the demes had lost the right to bear arms.

In Byzantium, and doubtless elsewhere, the demes regained this right when there was danger of attack on the city. In 400, when a Gothic sedition threatened, the *demotai* took arms to defend the city, but by their own initiative, not by government order. Only in the late sixth or early seventh century were the demes officially organised for city-defence. They had earlier played an important part in rebuilding and extending the walls under Theodosios II, in 447.

Their power grew in Byzantium, and was at its height through the fifth and sixth centuries. From Leo I (457–74), they played an important part in the election of emperors. The emperor constitutionally needed the people's approbation, though the election was formally made by Senate and army. The demes could legally express assent, *euphemia*, or dissent, *thorybos*, *tarache*, which they did, in the Hippodrome mainly, but also on the parade-grounds, churches, or other public places such as the Forum of Constantine, where the announcement was made.

Sometimes the emperors convoked the demes, not necessarily in the Hippodrome, to gain approval for political acts; some judicial matters also were taken up by the demes. But their basic and continuous function was that of controlling cultural and religious activities. Charges were met by the old method of liturgies, special obligations imposed on rich members.

THE CIRCUS-FACTION AS A POLITICAL PARTY. Now we reach the aspect of deme-life which developed so as to give more direct and organised political expression than the general assemblies of the demes, called sporadically, could give. Clubs or associations had to be formed to deal with the superintendence and running of the various shows that were part of the demes' work. These clubs were in turn linked with the rich and powerful demesmen who were given the various liturgies; and provided organisations which could be turned to political purposes.

Thus the clubs formed to look after the various teams, defined by colours, of charioteers in the circus became factions. These factions supported their colour in the circus, but they also became political organisations. The clarification of this point (carried out by Uspenskii, Manojlovic and Dyakonov) is of basic importance for the understanding of Byzantine society; for the viewpoint of Gibbon, restated by Rambaud, that the factions were simply sports-organisation, with no relation to the religious, social and political struggles of their world, has largely contributed to the false picture of Byzantine society as regressive, corrupt, dominated by the intrigues of eunuchism, the dementia of sport and the worst kind of religious ossification.

The race-course had been originally a Greek creation, which the Romans borrowed. Constantine in building up the Byzantine race-festivals looked both to Rome and to Antioch. The faction-clubs controlled the games and the personnel of the circus; they obtained funds from the State or from *choregoi*, patrons, among whom we find the emperor himself, high civil and ecclesiastical dignitaries, provincial magnates and rich men exalted by the demes. The common demesmen never had to pay anything. But though great men became patrons, the faction-chiefs proper were the primates of the demes, members of *ta proteia*. Platon, Green leader, under Anastasios, was City Prefect, and so on. The actual work of organising shows was, however, done by executant artists, whose positions were fixed by the government.

The whole system antedated Byzantium. In most of the large Greek and eastern cities we find the deme-system begetting circus-factions. Big hippodromes existed at Antioch, Alexandria, Apamea, Edessa. At Antioch under Caligula Blues and Greens had taken sides in anti-semitic troubles. The same sort of conflict appeared in Egypt, where the Greens were anti-semitic—a tradition that carried on into Byzantine days. Blues and Jews sat together; the Greens rose against the archon Thalassios, who was hit by a stone from a Greek bath-attendant, and the tumult turned into a pogrom, with the emperor merely commenting that Jews should be burned alive, not dead. Under Anastasios the Greens wrecked a synagogue and turned it into a church.

Throughout Egypt the towns imitated Alexandria. 'Among the expenses of the town of Oxyrrhynchos figure the salary of the hippodrome employees, and the price of an embrocation for the circus-horses. The big landowners, it seems, had equally their race-stables.' At Alexandria the circus-parties constituted the popular *collegia*, the *corporati civitatis Alexandriae*, of which the Theodosian Code speaks, and had their leaders. In large cities the faction organisation must have been considerable, dealing with large bodies of craftsmen and performers. More, by the fifth century at least, the factions of one city corresponded with their fellows else-where; and the capital's faction-leader could give the word for a common policy all over the main parts of the Empire.

GREENS AND BLUES. Byzantium added this co-ordinating centre, which raised the activity of the factions to a new level. The factions became sub-stantially political parties. The Blues and Greens, the main colours, stood for opposed economic interests. The traders, artisans, sailors, shopkeepers found in the Greens their mouthpiece, and the landed magnates, their retainers and hangers-on, supported the Blues. The Reds and Whites were subsidiary, the Reds being linked with the Greens and the Whites with the Blues. In origin the structure of the two factions was local: the Blues were based on the demes of the old city and the suburbs, the Greens on those of the new city. But we cannot distribute the factions around in poor and rich districts (as Manojlovic tried to do), as in fact the lower levels of the populace were to be found in almost all the areas. The key to the difference lay in the bosses of the factions. The bosses of the Blues were the landed nobility in old Byzantium, those of the Greens were the rich merchants and employers of the new city, who had close connec-tions with their fellows in the eastern cities.

The bosses of one party wanted to grab the power and property of the other; and one of the main fields of conflict was the distribution of taxes. The Blues wanted to shift as much as possible all tax-burdens from the big estates and put them on to the cities; the Greens wanted to do the oppo-site. At court the eunuchs, who often rose to high positions with much in-fluence, were on the whole easterners, with the outlook of the trade-towns and with a finger in the finance-bureaucracy. They were able to exert their influence on behalf of the Greens in a way that the Blues found it hard to counteract.

Many of the finance-experts that the State needed came from the ranks of the Greens. Even Justinian, a Blue, had to use as his finance-expert John of Cappadocia, who had risen as a Green. The Blues had their strongest base in the Senate; the Greens in the finance-bureaucracy. And thus we find even a split in the palace-guards: the Schools or the old guard were solid for the Senate, but the new guards of Excubitors, organised by Leo I and Zeno, from time to time supported the Greens.

At moments of political crisis, especially at the death of an emperor, the factions were liable to clash; and often the fear of violent outburst led to hurried accords between the bosses, with compromises extorted from the weaker side. We find battles between the factions, the rising of one faction while the other stays quiescent, and the union of the two factions

in revolt. When the union happened, it meant that the control of the
bosses had slipped, and that the ordinary demesmen had got together to
forget points of difference and to rise, not merely against the existing
government, but against the governing class altogether.

A potent factor that mixed in the disputes was the religious difference
between orthodox and heretic, especially Monophysite. The Monophysites, strongly concentrated in Syria, were largely made up of the mercantile and artisan classes that composed the rank and file of the Greens;
and so the Greens inclined to Monophysitism, while the Blues were orthodox. This linking of religious and political positions was, however, complicated at Byzantium itself by the fact that the capital-city had so many
workers, employers or traders who depended on the products required
by Court or Church. The Byzantine Greens were therefore not staunchly
Monophysite like the Greens of Antioch.

At a glance, then, we seem to have the scene set for a thorough political
contest between an urban middle-class and a landed nobility; and to some
extent that is what we find during the fifth and sixth centuries. The faction-
struggles then remind us with extreme vividness of the clashes in the
later communes of the West; and indeed they are orientated in that
direction rather than to the faction-fights which the ancient world had
known, *i.e.* the use of the *collegia* by political bosses in the period of
convulsions at Rome which founded the Empire. But we must always
remember what has been said already of the comparative weakness of the
mercantile and industrial classes in this world. Those classes were strong
enough to put up a good struggle at moments, but not strong enough to
consider at any time a resolute attempt to control the State. Such an
attempt would have meant a definite policy of breaking down the power
of the landed magnates.

The upper levels of the mercantile and employing class, of the finance-
bureaucracy, could not detach themselves from the situation in order
to attempt or even conceive such a policy; they lacked the stable basis.
They could only wage a struggle along more limited lines, in which they
sought to take over some of the power of the landed nobility—*i.e.* to gain
land as effectively as their adversaries. So, in so far as they won, they ended
by merging with their adversaries and strengthening the basis of the
nobility. They shared this limitation with the crown itself, which could
see the need at times to break down a group of nobles which had grown
too powerful, or even to attempt checks on the class as a whole in order
to strengthen State-power at difficult moments of attack from outside,
but which could not imagine a system in which the mainstay of power
was not the landed nobility. So, at moments, the Greens, with their roots

in the finance-bureaucracy, could become a sort of Court-party opposed to the Blues as Senate-party. But that did not mean that there was an essential, as distinct from a contingent, clash of interests. Nobody was challenging the basis of State-power in a class of landed nobility.

This again is an important point, without which the struggle inside Byzantine society cannot be got into a clear focus. Many historians have been deluded into thinking that the struggle which often goes on between State and a section of the nobility was a struggle of the State against the nobility as a class. That is incorrect; but we must not go to the other extreme and see only a round of futile struggles for power within a society made up of landed magnates. There is movement forward as well as a tussle to-and-fro; and this movement forward comes about precisely because there are a number of factors involved, factors of varying social basis and development. The farmers and artisans may seem always betrayed by their leaders; the Greens may seem in the end to shade off into the landed power that they oppose; the court is continually the plaything of magnates that it seeks to control in the interests of effective government. But out of the total struggle society is being driven forward, is severing its roots in the past, is developing productive forces which ultimately cannot be contained within the given system.

6

THE NATURE OF THE CHANGES

THE PROBLEM OF TERMS. Now we have looked a little more closely at what Constantine did, we must again consider the problems raised by his work. The conventional interpretation has seen it as only a stage in the coarsening and breaking-down of the ancient State. Constantine's world is compared with the world of Augustus, in the terms of Augustan values, and naturally is found wanting. If my analysis is correct, then there are certain losses, but far more important gains; and the Constantinean State is an advance on the Augustan, in that it widens the whole reach of social and economic potentiality.

Since our interpretation of historical development in general and of the nature of Europe in particular depends on the answer given to this question, we must look more fully at the implications. The conventional view, which I consider totally false, sees a black void between the ancient world and the feudalism that grows up in the West. That feudalism emerges (this view declares) from a welter of disintegrating tribal systems and various weak remnants of social organisation left over from the broken-down ancient State; there is no clear continuity and no line of coherent social development; the early middle-ages are a barbarised darkness after the élite civilisation of the Augustan Empire.

This view can be maintained only by cutting Europe in half, by ignoring what goes on in the East after the fifth or sixth centuries, by seeing the later Roman Empire as a 'decline and fall'. It is superficial and based on preconceived positions of propaganda which close our eyes to the fullness and the unity of historical process. Once we think in terms of the whole European scene, such a view shows up in all its meagre and distorting partiality. We realise then that the tribal welter in the West and the centralised State in the East are aspects of a wider process which embraces both and which cannot be understood if we abstract one aspect for isolated treatment.

How, then, are we to define this single process which includes both East and West with all their divergent and complex trends? It is the movement from the ancient State to the feudal State, from an economy in which slave-labour for commodity-production is the key fact to an economy in which serf-labour with its coerced rent is the key fact.

This change goes back, in its origins, into the second century A.D., but it is in the convulsions of the third century that a decisive shift occurs. Thereafter the world faces towards feudalism; and the work of Constantine consisted in salvaging as much of the ancient State as would fit in with the new bases, as would serve the new needs.

But though we are dealing with a single process, it is not a simple one. There are many survivals from the past, and the pace of change varies considerably in different regions. It is this irregular development of feudalism which makes analysis difficult, but which at the same time constitutes the living character of the new trend, its gathering of multiple forces and potentialities within a single line of advance. In the first stages in particular the new dominant structure is shadowy, insecure and torn with diverse possibilities; but is nevertheless the dominant structure because it holds the key to the future, and gradually its forms are consolidated.

The basic irregularity in this movement towards feudalism lies in the different levels of social and economic development in the East and the West. Thus, in the fifth century, when in the East we find a revival of town-life and an apparent movement back to ancient bases, in the Gaul of Aetius we are much closer to medieval France than to a province of the Antonine period of the Empire. Though far yet from medieval fiefs, we meet nobles like Ecdicius who raise their own cavalry detachments and support 4,000 poor folk in a famine; and the fortified home of Pontius Leontius, depicted by Sidonius, with its walls and towers, is already a baronial centre of power. The manor is surrounded by dependent villages; the bound colons pay rent partly in labour-services, though slaves, *casarii*, till part of the soil. The lord has his local court where he arrogates to himself many powers previously held by the State; and production is less and less concerned with the free market. The surplus is used by the lord for himself and his servitors.

Things, as I said, had not quite reached this stage in the East; in some respects they never quite reached it. But a general feudalising trend dominated both sectors. And if this is so, if there is a single arc of history in the period between the third century with its peasant uprisings and the seventeenth century with its Cromwellian shattering of the feudal State in its final absolutist stage, then we cannot treat the developments of western Europe as in a vacuum. We must see them as part of a larger whole, of which Byzantium and the Empire centred on it, the Roman Empire as it developed after the shocks of the third century, are an essential part. The foundations and growth of Europe then appear in a new focus.

THE UNITY OF HISTORICAL PROCESS. We are helped to grasp the unity of the processes under consideration if we look at the Germanic tribesmen, whose invasions were the result and continuation of the deep social and economic crisis that preceded them. By the third century the imperial army had huge numbers of Germans in its ranks; the western edge of their area had been incorporated in the Germanic provinces of Gaul; and Trier, Mainz, Cologne were Romano-German towns. After the Marcomannic wars of Marcus Aurelius, Germanic tribesmen had been settled in devastated areas as colons. Germans from beyond the Rhine were also settled in many places, particularly the Belgic provinces, as *laeti*, farmers holding land in return for military service. On the borders the special troops, *limitanei*, were given land for guarding the frontier-line; these were recruited more and more from Germanic colons. In the later fourth century tribesmen, Germanic and other, were settled in Italy and Gaul as *gentiles*, holding by military tenures.

Germanic colons had thus played their part in the upheavals; and their service-tenures helped in bringing about the general shift of small-holding from free contract to semi-servile status. When more and more tribesmen moved over the borders, what happened was not so much invasion as a speeding-up and extension of the methods by which the Empire had for long been gaining colons and soldiers. The large-scale movement of tribesmen into the Empire, as the Empire's powers of absorbing them in ordered ways lessened, was simply the completion of the processes of inner change that the third century precipitated. The inability to absorb the incomers in what I have called ordered ways meant only the inability to absorb them into a society remaining predominantly based on slave-labour; the disorder was the sign of the emergence of a new order, that based on feudal types of tenure.[1]

TRANSITIONAL FORMS. We may then call the third century the watershed between the ancient and the feudal worlds. But that does not mean that with the fourth century we can simply speak of a feudalised world. The

[1] Note how men like Synesios (*c.* 400) felt the presence of barbarians in high military posts (indeed in the army at all as dominant factor) as a *social* menace. Sidonius (West) and John Chrysostom (East) wanted the conversion of heathen or barbarian peasant, or the stable extension of episcopal controls, as the sole effective pledges against political unrest. The effect of the Bagaudae of Gaul in the fifth century to contact and gain Attila on their side against Aetius shows where the peasant in revolt felt that he could alone look for aid—to barbarians.

principle of irregular development must be borne in mind as the essence of the situation, of the conflicts and disequilibria which keep on driving society ahead to the full stabilisation and working-out of the new bases. That is why, and how, East and West play such complementary parts in the founding of modern Europe.

Slave-production of goods for the market did not cease at 324 A.D. In fact it importantly continued in the Byzantine world for many centuries. What happened in the third century was the violent emergence into the open of the crisis in slave-economy—an emergence that dealt a mortal blow to the ancient State and its basis in the locally autonomous city, the *polis*. But not for centuries can we say that the crisis has been overcome and slave-economy has been definitely transformed into feudal economy —that is, an economy where the basic factor is coerced rent, rent taken from the primary producer because of the lord's superior political position and not because of any genuine economic relationship between lord and farmer.

The crisis completed itself rapidly in the West, where the urban development and industrial forms of slave-production were very insecurely based, and where the uprisings of slave and colon and their middle-class allies had been most furious and sustained. But the reconstructed State centred on Byzantium reposed on an economic system which, though able to retain many more characteristics of the Graeco-Roman world, had ineluctably entered on the same path as the West, the feudalising path. As our inquiry goes on, we shall see how the long struggle between the inherited forms of the ancient State and the feudalising forces worked out in the East, and how this struggle was the key factor in world-development until the eleventh century.

The position here set out involves more than a mere change of terms; it strikes at the root of our whole conception of Europe. The events in the West during the so-called dark ages, it announces, cannot be considered in isolation. Though bringing many new factors into the situation— factors which later on become of extreme importance—they are peripheral events in an historical process centred on Byzantium until the eleventh century, when the western half of the European world reaches the Byzantine level and breaks beyond it in certain respects which hold the clue to the next stage of world-development.

For the moment, however, our problem is to define the nature of the Constantinean State, within the new focus which our inquiry has given us.

ACTION AND REACTION. The ancient world had witnessed many slave-risings, sometimes of prolonged fury; but only the upheavals of the third century were so sustained and broadly based as to have a powerful effect on the whole political and economic structure. This fact must be kept in the forefront of any definitions of the Constantinean State.

Yet that State was clearly a counter-revolutionary State in that it sought to end the disorders and unrest of the primary producers, to hold those producers down effectively once more within the State, to make them pay their taxes and maintain the State, to preserve the landlords in positions that enabled them to crush any rebellious moves of the farmers and labourers. So far from granting any demand of the colons and slaves, it sought to oppress them more thoroughly.

But that does not mean that it had not been deeply affected by the movement against which it was aimed. Thus, to take an example from much later history, the revolutionary overthrow of the feudal monarchy in Cromwell's day did not lead to any simple consolidation of power in the hands of the new classes with the clue to political and productive advance; it led to the Restoration of 1660, to a State which attempted to revive feudal power, to break down local liberties, to control Parliament in the interests of the Crown and its noble supporters. Yet all the while the basic changes which had gone on under Cromwell were operating, giving a new orientation even to the efforts to undo the work of the revolutionary period. Even so, a show of force in 1688–9 was needed from the magnates of the new system to undo the work of Charles II and James II, at least in some of its aspects.

How much more would we expect periods of reaction, periods which attempted to arrest forward movement and to turn back to previous systems of control in both political and economic spheres, in a world where the whole productive level was so much lower, where the immediate potentialities of advance were so much weaker, and where the revolting classes had never managed to grasp State-power at all.[1]

Further, the transition from the ancient State of the slave-owners to the feudal State of the rent-coercers was masked and blurred by two important factors. The ancient State, though driven forward by the development of slave-labour, was never able to rest stably on the industrial and mercantile classes; money always tended to move back into the land; and power (except for brief periods when strong mercantile cities like Athens were rising) always resided in the last resort in the landed

---

[1] We must remember too that Cromwell's revolutionary State became counter-revolutionary against Levellers and Diggers; and 1789 leads to 1793. The fact that the big landlords triumph in the fourth to sixth centuries does not disprove the revolutionary nature of the third century. The proof or disproof lies in the question whether or not a new social and economic system does develop from the rupture. And such a system does develop.

magnates. What characterises the changing forms of the ancient State is the varying relations of the landowners and the classes using slave-labour for commodity-production—relations which show the two sides at times merging or at least in some sort of accord, at times clashing and separating out. So the powerful role of landlord-power in the ancient State makes the transition to feudal landlord-power confused, full of obscure hybrids and forms of temporary balance.

Then, linked with this aspect, there is the fact that both the ancient and the feudal State involved forms of servile status in contradistinction to the bourgeois State in which the free money-market tended to flatten out all such divisions. Chattel slavery and feudal serfdom, though profoundly different in their social and economic implications, shared a servile status in the eyes of the law. Here again is a factor that produces hybrids of transition and masks as well as slows down the phases of basic change.

IRREGULARITY AND VARIATION. We are safe, then, from oversimplifying the process of change from the ancient to the feudal State if we bear in mind the broad contrast that in the West during the fourth and fifth centuries the imperial centralised State breaks down, while in the East it does not collapse at all. In the West the field is open to the great magnates, and from the fusion of Gallo-Roman landlord and tribal noble there arises in due time the fully matured type of military noble holding by fief.[1] And, as the economic level slowly moves upward, from the rivalries and conflicts of the nobles is born the feudally unifying kingship. But the economic progress which makes the new centralised kingdoms possible is based in large part on the rebirth of the towns, where appear the new social forces that later threaten and defeat the feudal system in Holland, Britain, France.

In the East, however, the pattern is very different, because of the persistence throughout of the centralised State. I shall not attempt here to summarise what happened; for the rest of the book will consist of the inquiry into the specific Byzantine contribution to Europe. But at the outset we must grasp clearly the points here briefly stated. The very strength and richness of Byzantine culture derive from the fact that the movement into feudalism in the East did not fall into the fairly simple pattern taken in the West. A long and complex struggle between the

---

[1] Before the Franks the major barbarian groups passing the borders were well-decayed tribal societies; the interest of the chief lay in agreement with the Roman govenment, though the tribesmen at large wanted at times to overthrow Rome— note Athaulf's statement of 414 A.D.

ancient inheritance and the feudalising pressures went on; and therefore it was at Byzantium that we find the key to the process whereby the ancient world was transformed into feudalism and its valuable elements made accessible to medieval and modern Europe. The simple pattern in the West is delusive; its simplicity appears only when we abstract it from the total process which in the last resort is what drives it on and develops it. In fact, the impacts and infiltrations from the East are going on at every phase of the western changes; and the changes are inexplicable unless we recognise this fact.[1]

THE KEY. The great interest of Byzantium, then, lies in the fact that it reveals the struggle to transform the ancient world into the feudal world at its maximal tension, conflict and resolution. For this reason we cannot even begin to grasp the relation of the ancient world to modern Europe unless we approach the problem through Byzantium; and so, if we omit Byzantium from our ken, we cannot understand the modern world at all, since all our preconceptions are false.

As this book brings out the concrete significance of the generalisations here laid down, the claim that Byzantium and its various achievements underlay the whole of medieval Europe will be seen in its full cogency. For the moment we need to bear clearly in mind the way in which the third century represented the open crisis of slave-economy and the ancient State, and the Constantinean State the first phase of a new world in which the feudalising forces fight to take over and control the ancient inheritance. The breadth and depth of the struggling forces will only be apparent when we come to discuss the political, religious and cultural conflicts and their social bases.

1 I use the term *feudalising* to express the new dominant forces that break through in the fourth to sixth centuries; *feudal* for the stabler phase that appears from the eighth century on; *medieval* for the period of feudalism when the new national State-forms began to achieve consolidation.

II

A Summary of Byzantine History

7

CONSTANTINE TO JUSTINIAN'S LINE

In the following summary I shall aim only at bringing before the reader the main events of Byzantine history. The summary is intended to give the reader the framework within which the discussions that follow are set. It is inevitably somewhat condensed: I suggest that the reader new to Byzantine history reads it through once for the general effect, and re-reads it later, or uses it for reference, to get his bearings when necessary in the detailed analysis.

THE NEW STATE, HERESIES AND INVASIONS. Constantine had begun by seeking a basis of accommodation; but the dynamic of Christianity was too great for it to accept a tolerated place among other creeds. Constantine began to treat it as the State-religion; and we have already had a glimpse of the problem of schism and heresy that he at once had to tackle. What he wanted above all was a unifying creed, and at the Council of Nikaia in 325 he had to crush Arianism, which refused the theologising trends that lifted Christ right off the earth as the Eternal Son. He sent his mother Helena to Palestine where with the aid of the usual dream she found on Calvary the True Cross, Lance, Sponge and Crown of Thorns. Part of these finds were transported ecstatically to Byzantium, and were of great use in sanctifying the new capital.

The frontiers still held. Constantine pacified the Danubian area, in part, by getting the enemy (Goths, Vandals, Sarmatians) to fight among themselves. Persia was threatening again; and he turned eastward, dying at Nikomedeia. But the Persian frontiers, quiet since the peace of 297, were not seriously disturbed.

Constantine, not a pleasant figure, was rent by the conflicts of his world. A massive man with large eye-sockets, comely mouth, and round, jutting chin, he burned alive a camel-driver who started a revolt in Cyprus; earlier he threw Frankish kings to the beasts; but in 325 he forbade the circus games. He killed a son as well as his wife, not to mention various friends, for obscure dynastic reasons. He was never officially a Christian till a few hours before his death; and then it was an Arian heretic who baptised him. He put off his purple and died in stainless white. And yet when all is said of his confused and syncretist tendencies, we have the conviction that he had come to feel, in his own way, that his empire and the new faith were inextricably bound up, and that he had a special destiny in bringing about this new start.

His greatness is undeniable. By completing the Diocletianic reorganisation, by finding the courage to make the decisive breaks with the past that the foundation of Byzantium and the acceptance of Christianity represented, he gave world-civilisation a new start. But in stressing his role, we must not forget that the ultimate pressures for the change had come from countless colons, slaves, peasant-soldiers, artisans, who took part in the long desperate revolts or clove through all dangers to the Christian creed.

His three sons quarrelled. By 350 two were violently dead. The third, *Constantius II*, ruled alone till 361 after defeating a usurper. An ardent Arian, he decreed, 'Let there be an end of all superstition and let the insanity of sacrifices be exterminated!' But though restricting paganism, he bore the title *Pontifex Maximus*. He exempted bishops from civil control, and ferociously persecuted Christians who refused the Arian communion.

The northern frontiers were in a bad way. When *Julian* defeated a German invasion, the army proclaimed him emperor. Constantius died soon after and Julian succeeded in 361 without conflict. A Neoplatonist, he tried to supplant Christianity with paganism organised as a Universal Church, but failed. Dying in an unexplained way while campaigning against the Persians, he was replaced by *Jovian*, a Christian, whom the army chose. When Jovian died after about a year, the army elected *Valentinian*, who chose to rule from the West, leaving Byzantium to his brother *Valens*, another intolerant Arian. Once more persecution raged. Ammianus Marcellinus, the Syrian historian, commented, 'I have never seen wild beasts so cruel to each other as these Christians.' There were several revolts, and Valens was killed at the battle of Adrianople by the Goths—the battle already mentioned as ending the foot-legions and finally establishing cavalry superiority.

During this period German domination in the army had been growing. And there was general unrest, both in the towns and on the land. Thus, a rising of Goths in 376 was joined by Thracian miners; a large Gothic revolt in Asia Minor in 399 was joined by the slaves (in Phrygia there were many slaves of Gothic origin); next year a revolt of slaves and colons broke out in Thrace. We understand why Constantine had enacted the penalty of burning-alive for anyone who helped barbarians to pillage.

Aid had been sent from Italy under a Spaniard, *Theodosios*, who was now appointed emperor, and who pacified the Balkans. Orthodox, he

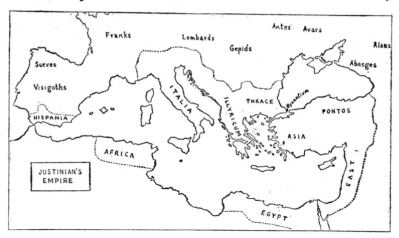

called a second General Council of the Church, in 318, to have Arianism crushed; made a treaty with Persia, partitioning Armenia; and in 394 took over from the West as well as the East, ruling from Britain to the Euphrates.

Pagans were persecuted. The distinction of orthodox and heretic was defined by law, so that the Church had a legal basis for attacking dissenters. The 380 decree permitted religious activity only to those who held the Nicene dogma of the Trinity; dissenters were proclaimed 'mad and insane', forbidden to meet, and put under severe penalties. In 392 pagan rites were prohibited.

Theodosios once clashed with Ambrose, bishop of Milan. He had billeted a large body of German mercenaries in Thessalonika, where they behaved badly. The citizens, stirred at the arrest of a popular charioteer, rose and killed the captain of the garrison. Theodosios turned the soldiers on the citizens assembled in the circus, and over 7,000 were massacred, men, women and children. Ambrose forced him to do penance. The episode gives us some idea of the emperor's fear and hatred of the common folk.

He left two sons, who divided the Empire. *Arkadios*, a short, dull, sleepy-eyed fellow, was given the East. The better choice, for the West was going to pieces. Visigoth, Ostrogoth, Hun were devastating the provinces; and though they broke into the Balkans, they all ended by turning west, to the easier prey. Italy was open to continual invasion; Gaul went down under successive Germanic waves; Spain fell even more easily. When North Africa with its capital Carthage fell in 439 to the Vandals, Byzantium felt the blow, for its control of the seas was menaced.

REVIVAL. *Theodosios II* has been abused by the aristocratic tradition because he listened to advisers whom the big landowners did not like. Under him Byzantium was refortified, a university was founded there (to offset the pagan element at Athens, and other seats of learning), and a comprehensive legal code was compiled, which was published simultaneously in East and West. In his later years, under the lead of the eunuch Chrysaphios, he inclined strongly to the Greens.

On his deathbed his pious sister Pulcheria persuaded him to name as successor, an old soldier, Count *Markian*, chief of the Bucellarians of the half-Goth, half-Alan general Aspar; then, though vowed to virginity, she married Markian to keep the dynastic link. Markian represented the full senatorial reaction. He was a dummy put in by his Scythian Arian master; and when he died in 457, Aspar was the most powerful man in the realm.

Aspar now put up a Dacian soldier, *Leo*, who was to warm the throne till Aspar's son was old enough to take over. But Leo, who had been a mere tribune of the commissariat troops, refused to give up. For four years there was a keen struggle. Leo set up a new guards corps, the Excubitors, mainly recruited from the red-cloaked Isaurian mountaineers, who defeated the Germanic soldiers when the latter tried to break into the palace. He continued with his policy of trying to enlist Isaurians in the imperial army (instead of letting them become retainers of nobles) to offset the Germanic sections, which were being used by Aspar and others. He married one of their chiefs, Taraisicodissa, to his daughter Ariadne, rechristening him *Zeno* and making him Master of the Soldiers in the East in place of Aspar's elder son. Finally Aspar was murdered in 471. Civil war broke out between the Isaurians and the federated Ostrogoths settled in Pannonia, which moved round, wasting region after region, for some twenty years.

Zeno had a troubled reign. He was first ousted by a stepbrother of Leo, who drove him for over a year back to Isauria. Then he had the Goths on his hands, but managed to divert their main leader, Theodoric (who was well Romanised), into taking on the job of reconquering Italy. And there were further revolts, with street-fighting in Byzantium itself. Ilus, an Isaurian noble, led a kind of pagan conspiracy, which was suppressed; and troubles kept on rising up in Egypt and Syria from the discontented populace. Zeno tried to placate the Monophysites in his declaration, the *Henotikon* of 481, which gained a thirty years' truce with the eastern dissidents.

In his reign the last emperor in the West fell, a usurper with the mocking name of Romulus Augustulus. The result was the founding of the

Ostrogothic kingdom of Italy under Theodoric, centred on Ravenna, with imperial assent.

Anastasios, the next emperor, was a civil-servant, who inclined strongly to Monophysitism. He carried on a defensive policy, settling Isaurians in Thrace, and building a Long Wall from the Propontis to the Black Sea— some forty-one miles in length, with round towers set in front of the line. He preferred peace and the payment of tribute to war against the nomad assailants of the Empire. His tax-policy was to lighten the burden on the traders and business-men of the towns; and under him we find the *annona* paid more in cash than produce. He did much to restore prosperity to the Empire, and heaped up some 320,000 pounds of gold in the Treasury. The Orthodox tradition described him as stingy: which meant that he was not interested in court-luxury and war. But he carried out many public works, built baths and aqueducts, and cut a canal in Bithynia from the Gulf of Nikomedia to Lake Sophin (which Pliny had wanted but failed to get four centuries before); he cleared out harbours and aided earth-quaked cities. In 499 he stopped the fighting of men with wild beasts in the circus.

His reign inevitably ended with a revolt, led by an Orthodox champion of the magnates. That groups of barbarians and of landless peasantry joined in, as they were ready to join in any movement of revolt, does not alter the nature of the movement. The next emperor, *Justin*, was a nominee of the senatorial reaction.

EAST AND WEST. Between the reigns of Constantine and Anastasios the East had seen a general revival of town-life, while the West had gone downhill with increasing speed. Gaul was divided between Franks, Burgundians, and Visigoths, in the first stages of semi-tribal kingdoms which absorbed enough of Roman law and procedure to make a quick start. The Germanic rulers were ready enough on the one hand to use such officials as remained from the broken-down imperial State, and to base their power as much on the big Gallo-Roman landlords as on their own nobles; and in the towns, such as they were, the bishops often became the dominant figures, carrying on elements of Roman organisation and allied to the big landlords.

In the East the revival of town-life was linked with mass-movements of protest, which took direct form in the conflicts of Greens and Blues, and which found a deep idiom of anti-imperial union in heretical creeds. Underneath the revival lies the hard work of the colons, the farmers reclaiming wasteland and in various ways reasserting communal forms of organisation as the State-controls weakened. In the reign of Anastasios the peak-point of development along these lines occurred, and we see plainly revealed the divergent trends of East and West within the common field, the crisis of slave-economy. Anastasios is the great emperor of this phase, belittled by historians because the aristocratic tradition disliked him.

Following him came the aristocratic reaction of Justin and Justinian; and because Justinian was able to squander the resources heaped up by Anastasios and the other Green emperors,[1] he has been acclaimed by the historians as a great ruler. But in fact what happened under Justinian was the maturing of the system's contradictions afresh. To build what he considered a strong State he speeded up once more the feudalising trends, the power-positions of the landed nobles—though historians have failed to see this key-point because in strengthening the trends to feudalism he had at certain points to fight anarchic elements among the nobles, and they interpret this fact as a fight against the nobles as a class. In the process the emperor clearly emerges more than ever as himself the supreme landlord, and a decisive turn into feudalism is taken. Thus the Justinianic effort to revive the glories of the ancient State ends in chaos, breakdown and the sharpened swing into feudal bases—and finally in the dismemberment of the Empire, the loss of Syria and Egypt.

REACTION. *Justin* had come to the capital as a lad, with a bag of bread on his back, a more or less illiterate Illyrian; now aged sixty-six, Commander of the Guard, he was well placed to bargain with the Senate, promising a reversal of the Anastasian policy in return for election. Six days after his accession the Patriarch announced from the ambo of St. Sophia that the Council of Chalkedon was once more recognised, and an edict required the adhesion of all bishops and imperial subjects. Persecutions of dissenters followed.

Justin had a nephew, Peter Sabbatios, better known as *Justinian*, a hard-working, sombre and capable man, who became boss of the Blues and secured the succession to the throne. He married an ex-actress, Theodora, who sympathised with the Monophysites. The imperial pair, however, agreed that their power must be supreme. Justinian favoured the senatorial nobility, and sought for an accord with the bishop of Rome. He meant to use the prosperity cultivated by Anastasios to restore the

---

1 In the fifth to sixth centuries there is a clear line of division in foreign policy—the 'progressive' emperors are for peace; the reactionary, for war. Peace meant paying tribute, which, at least partly drawn by taxes from the senatorial class, returned in trade to the benefit of the trading and industrial classes. Part of the pressure for war came from exiled nobles of Italy and Africa who wanted their lands back (for these see the letters of Theodoret).

Empire in the West. He recaptured North Africa from the Vandals and re-established control of the seas; then he regained Italy and South Spain. The whole Mediterranean was once more under imperial rule. He fought the Persians in the east and extended Byzantine influence in the Caucasian area.

He was a lavish builder and patron of the arts. Under him Byzantium reached a new magnificence. He had the imperial constitutions since Hadrian codified, a great work of inestimable importance for the future; and a digest made of the decisions of the famous jurisconsults of the second and third centuries. He constructed vast frontier-fortifications and a shrewd system of outlying vassal-States, which acted as buffers against nomad attacks or as counterweights to one another.

He carried on Justin's religious policy, modified by Theodora's intrigues, but in his later years he confused himself with a quest for a formula that would reconcile the warring sects, and himself fell into a heresy. He extended the bureaucracy and State-participation in industry.

Factional clashes went on during both Justin's and Justinian's reign, with their climax in the great revolt of the Nika, when the rank-and-file of both Blue and Green factions united and for a few days held the capital, at a time when their numbers were swollen by discontented farmers. But their lack of a political programme enabled the State to split their ranks, and then to defeat them with much slaughter.

BREAKDOWN. Justinian died in 565 and was succeeded by his nephew *Justin II*, who tried weakly to tackle the problems that he inherited—an Empire exhausted by Justinian's use of its resources for war and lavish building, and rent by the intensification of the mass-unrest and revolt that his pro-magnate policy had provoked. This policy it was that turned the expansion and the building programme into heavy burdens for the commoners of the Empire, and rapidly brought his system down in a wreck through its exacerbated contradictions—the effort to build once more the full imperial structure while sapping its bases by favouring the magnates at the expense of the village-community and the industrial town.

Justin continued his uncle's policy. Thus in 568 he enacted that a provincial governor be appointed at the request of bishop, magnates and inhabitants—which meant in fact the delivery of the appointment up to the magnates. When dying, he is said to have bidden *Tiberios*, who was being elevated to the rank of Caesar, to beware of the landed nobility as men who had led him into his sad plight. If he ever did make that comment, he had learned the lesson too late.

Relations with Persia were strained. The Persians were undoing
3*

Justinian's efforts to control the Ceylon trade through getting a hold on Yemen; but Justin could do nothing about it. He made a treaty with the Turks, who now appeared on the scene, holding down four subject kingdoms and controlling the silk-route to China; with a disorganised army the Empire was in no condition to wage wars. (Maurice had later to reintroduce even such elementary matters as the custom of a ditch around the camp.)

In 574 Justin went mad. To stop him from jumping out of windows, they put him behind bars. He bit the chamberlain, was drawn in a little wagon through the palace, and was calmed by music. If he grew too obstreperous, they said, 'The Son of Gabilo is coming', and that scared him into quiet. (The reference was to the king of an Arab tribe.)

Tiberios carried on Justin's social policy, but definitely gave up the Justinianic concept of empire. In Italy the Viceroy held the marshes round Ravenna, and the southern coast remained under imperial control, but otherwise the Lombards, who had entered Italy in 568, were left a free hand. Rome thus won semi-independence, though an imperial commissioner still lived in the palace of the Caesars. Spain had fallen back into Visigothic hands; and most of Gaul had been conquered by the Franks.

Maurice, son-in-law of Tiberios, a Roman of Cappadocia, had a scheme for local militia, and was the first emperor to realise the value of Armenia as a recruiting ground. He made the basic step towards what was later called the Theme System. Justinian had in some cases given a prefect the duties of a general; but now on the most menaced borderlands Maurice out of set policy combined civil and military functions, conferring on the Masters of Soldiers in Africa and Italy the new title of Exarch. The Exarchs were imperial vice-regents against the Berbers and the Lombards.

Avars and Slavs were now threatening the Balkans. At one moment the Slavs took Thessalonika. Monemvasia, important in medieval days, was founded on the Lakonian coast by Greek fugitives from the Slavs. John of Ephesos records under 583:

> Though very weakly armed with two or three javelins, the Slavs got hold of many strong places on their route; they had every chance to establish themselves and extend over the conquered areas, to carry off all the herds; they have become rich; they own gold and silver; they have learned how to make war better than the Romans.[1]

1 Michael the Syrian gives us a picture of the bands of Avars and Slavs in Thrace. Outside the towns they shouted to the people within, 'Come out, sow and harvest; we'll take only half the old tax from you!' When they took Anchialos, 'they found there the purple garments that Anastasia, Tiberios' wife, had left when she visited the Baths'. The khagan dressed up in them. 'Whether the Emperor of the Romans likes it or not, here's the Royalty he's given me.'

Factional conflicts in the cities broke out again. The rising popular tide showed itself in the new large-scale festivals that Maurice organised, which had considerable cultural significance and lasting effects on church-ritual and music.

Maurice's reign ended in a military revolt and violent civil war all over the Empire. *Phokas*, the choice of the army, captured Byzantium and murdered Maurice and all his family. Again a confused situation appeared as at the time of the Nika. Something of a popular reign of terror was instituted; but Phokas had no coherent policy, and in his furious effort to maintain power he veered from side to side. Bloody clashes were going on all over the East between Blues and Greens, be-tween the King's Men (Melkites in Egypt) and the masses expressing embryonic aspirations to separatist nationhood.

Finally the magnates of Africa took action. They sent *Heraklios*, the son of the exarch, with a fleet against Phokas, who was defeated and executed.

THE FRANKISH WEST. In the century between Anastasios and Phokas a great expansion of the Empire had taken place, based on the revived prosperity of the towns and breaking down because of the resurgence of landlord-power under Justin and Justinian. The expression of the breakdown was the fierce civil wars in which the sun of the Justinianic Empire set. But the tenacity and extent of those wars showed what forces of protest and what uncowed energies lived in the people.

In Italy from 568 the irruption of the Lombards from the middle Danube dominated the scene. These Germanic folk were soon absorbed. They took to Latin, gave up being Arians, found city-life to their taste, and intermarried with the local populations.

In Gaul, by 507, Frankish power had reached to the Pyrenees under Clovis, who had been converted to orthodoxy from paganism. Clovis made Paris his capital, and was buried there. In the following half-century there was a slight expansion at the expense of other peoples such as the Burgundians, and Provence was gained from the Ostrogoths at the price of supporting them against Justinian. Then for over a century (561–688) there was a prolonged tussle between the weak kingly power and the nobles: the Merovingian kings kept granting Crown land to the nobles, and the viceroys or mayors of the palace held the real power. Save for the enfeebled towns, all land was broken into large estates, *villae* or *fundi*. A *villa* was made up of land round the house of the pro-prietor or grantee, and lots of holdings, *mansi*, farmed by slaves, freedmen, or freemen—each keeping what he could of his products after meeting rent and services. A *villa* was self-sufficient, with its own mill, forge, wine-press, chapel.[1]

The Church, lacking enough slaves or freedmen to till its estates, let them out by life-grants called benefices. Lords used the same method. Beneficiaries easily turned into vassals. Soon a man's position was measured by the number of *vassi* that he could call out. Thus benefices in time developed into military fiefs. But before that development could come effectively about, many things had to happen. The economic level had to rise, and the first forms of an imperial State-system had to be laid by Charlemagne.

Slaves existed and still sometimes ran *mansi;* but the trend was towards freeing them. Then as freedmen, *liti,* they became dependent on their previous master, paying him a yearly fee and generally working his land as *lidiles.* On the large estates were *mansi ingenuiles,* descendants of Roman colons, theoretically free but in fact bound to the land. At first the freed-men were divided into Franks and Gallo-Romans, each under their own set of laws, but the two races were steadily mingling, or being con-founded. Free men more and more commended themselves to a patron.

The king's system of controls was still rudimentary; but the tribal assemblies had soon lost their force. Some of their powers were taken over by the king's *comitatus* or council (and later survive in the baronial *concilia*); in general the kingship gained what the tribal group lost. The tribal assembly became a military parade in the spring (first March, then May) without any basis for systematic political action. Production was carried on, in small-scale forms, by agricultural communities, not for the market. Peasant families worked small arable holdings of their own, but also did much of the productive work of the group in common. Handicraft was not separated out from agriculture.

The magnates extorted as much of the peasants' products as they could, in the form of rent in kind, money or labour; and this rent was achieved by some form of direct coercion. The total wealth thus gained was not enough to support a centralised State which could co-ordinate the system and obviate the need for direct coercions decentralised into the hands of the local landlords. In consequence the latter carried out on the spot the military, fiscal and judicial functions needed to maintain the system.

This system had, as we noted, grown up substantially before the

---

[1] The Franks were much less developed than Visigoths or Burgundians; the matri-lineal clan stands clearly out in the Salian law-code and the State apparatus is almost non-existent—while in the Visigothic and Burgundian codes the matrilineal system has left hardly a trace and the State is seen everywhere.

barbarian invasions, which merely completed the process of dislocating the imperial administration. In the East the magnates were never able to reach such an autonomous position; but the prevailing system—the forms of rent, and the social relationships resulting from them—had an essential kinship with what was happening crudely in Gaul. That is, the central dynamic of the eastern area was a feudalising movement as in the West, though it was complicated by the very much larger set of factors carried over from slave-economy.

8

THE HERAKLIANS

CRUSADE AGAINST PERSIA. Heraklios had to face the threat of Avars and Slavs at home and that of the Persians on the eastern frontiers. He bought off the Avars and prepared to fight the Persians, who had broken right into the Empire (612–17). Their success was in large part the measure of the discontent in Syria and Egypt; they took Antioch, Damaskos, and then seized Egypt, cutting Byzantium off from its main corn-supply. The Monophysites, and even more the Jews, welcomed the Persians, or at least did not fight them. Heraklios lost heart and wanted to go back to Carthage, but the Senate caught him in time, and he had to swear not to run off.

In these early years of his reign, Heraklios was a mere puppet of the Senate, which carried on diplomatic activities in its own name. He reacted to provincial disaffection by anti-semitism, and tried to start off a general persecution, drawing in the Visigothic king of Spain and the Frankish king. The imperial Church realised that if the rot went on, the Persians and Monophysites would bring the State and its Church down together. When the Persians took Jerusalem, fired the Holy Sepulchre Church and carried off the Patriarch and part of the True Cross, the Church saw its chance, its need, to work up a crusade. 'The evil enemies entered the City with a rage like that of infuriated beasts and annoyed dragons', wrote Antiochos Strategos (whose work has survived in Georgian). All the orthodox felt the challenge.

But the fear and anger would have failed if the Church had not taken the decision to lend from its vast wealth to the emperor, so that he could build up an effective army. In 622 the crusade started, with some bad moments for Byzantium, which was besieged in 626 by Avars on the land side, while the Persian army broke through to the Propontis. But Heraklios won in the end. Chosroes the Persian was said to have written: 'Do not deceive yourself with a vain belief in Christ who wasn't able to save himself from the Jews who killed him by nailing him on a cross.' The orthodox had their revenge when at Gansca they smashed up a statue of Chosroes in the Temple of the Sun, round which hovered winged images of sun, moon and stars;

and they burned the Persian Holy City, considered the birthplace of Zoroaster.

The True Cross was regained. Heraklios' manifesto to his capital declared, 'O be joyful in the Lord!' Chosroes was Judas gone to burn in Hell. But though the emperor entered Byzantium drawn by four elephants instead of white horses, welcomed with tapers and myrtle-boughs, he still had the disaffected provincials on his hands. He racked his brains to find a formula of reconciliation that wouldn't give too much away, and devised Monotheletism; but the Monophysites were unimpressed. And the Church wanted to be repaid, undoing with its greed the work it had done in its moment of fear. Also, it considered Heraklios' second marriage (with his niece Martina) as incest.

In this reign the Slavs and Croats settled down in the regions where they later come up into the full light of history. And the emperor, having decisively defeated the Persian king, at last officially took the title of *Basileus*.

ISLAM. But no sooner had the lull come than a worse danger than ever rose up out of the desert. Mohammed had provided a religion for drawing together the Arab tribes in the first unions from which emerged a tremendous war-dynamic and an embryonic State-basis. Weakened Persia could not withstand them; and in 634 they burst into Syria and defeated the imperial troops. Two years later they routed the great army that Heraklios had got together. Syria was lost and Jerusalem fell. Heraklios made another belated effort to draw the Monophysites into accord. Antioch fell. Two years later the Arabs were in Egypt. Everywhere the peasants and the Jews hailed them. In Egypt the Monophysite Greens rose and attacked the imperial troops. The nemesis of the inner split in Christianity had at last come home to the Empire with a vengeance.

The mingled effect of the Slav settlements and the flight of the magnates from their estates in Asia Minor was to bring about a resurgence of the free small-producer, the autonomous village-commune throughout the Empire—*i.e.* in the Balkans, Greece and Asia Minor. Thus, in the hour of disaster, when there seemed nothing that could save the Byzantine world, a vast social and economic change was affected, which provided powerful new thews of resistance for the Empire. Now, when in the West the independence of the peasant was being generally wiped out and a complex system of vassalages built up, the East saw the free village-commune reborn, released into fresh energy and breeding sturdy soldiers.

The Arabs moved on along Africa, where a revolt made things easier for them. An imperial effort to take Alexandria failed. Cyprus fell, then Rhodes. Byzantine control of the seas was lost. Yearly the Arabs made incursions into Asia Minor; but already their expansion was becoming tied up in its own inner contradictions—the free tribal spirit resenting the new inequalities as the structure of the State steadily emerged from their successful wars.

The Senate broke an effort by Heraklios' widow to seize power; and *Constans*, Heraklios' grandson, was made emperor. After being defeated in a hard-fought sea-battle off Lycia, with an army almost wholly Armenian he sailed west and tried to rebuild imperial power in South Italy, where his heavy war-taxes caused much discontent. In his edict, *The Type*, he tried to close down the dogmatic discussions that rent the Empire. The only result was a clash with the Pope, whom Constans arrested, tried for treason at Byzantium, jailed and exiled to Cherson in the Crimea. Finally in 668 Constans was murdered at Syracuse—knocked on the head in the bath with a silver ewer after being blinded with soap. The army in Sicily chose an Armenian as emperor, but was soon defeated.

The Arabs had founded in 660 something of a stable state under the Omayyad Caliphs, at Damaskos.

INCREASING PRESSURES. Under Constans' son, *Constantine IV*, things went militarily from bad to worse. The Bulgars were growing in strength south of the Danube, ruled by a khan with a council of six bolyars. The Arabs besieged Byzantium from 673 to 678; and were only defeated by the projectile Greekfire. But now the peasants of Asia were taking a hand, to save the land which they had shared out among themselves. They fought as guerrillas in the hills. Strong on Mount Taurus, they extended as far as the Lebanons, attacking and plundering the Moslems whenever they could catch them off their guard. 'A Wall of Steel' they were described. The Greeks called them Clubmen, *apelatai*; the Moslems called them rebels, *mardaites*.

And so by 678 the Arabs were ready to sue for peace.

The West recognised that Byzantium had saved the situation. Various nations sent embassies with gifts and asked for treaties. Even the khagan of the Avars joined in. The Papacy itself still looked on the Empire as the sole bulwark of salvation. Thus in 680 Pope Agatho wrote to say that a Roman Synod had expressed the wish that the Empire in which was located Peter's Seat, revered of barbarians, should have the primacy over nations.

The big blow had been the loss of Egyptian corn and Syrian industry, of the great harbours, and trade-towns, Alexandria, Gaza, Antioch,

Beirut. But though the blow had been heavy the Empire still held with its system substantially intact over the surviving area. Only, the domination of the magnates had been rudely shaken.

The result was the stormy reign of *Justinian II*, who was only sixteen when his father died. He is one of the rulers whom the orthodox histories blacken, because, coming in a period of violent change, he took rough-and-ready steps to strengthen the State, so that the Senate's control was shaken. That he had dreams of imperial renovation is shown by the fact that he took his name seriously and called his wife Theodora, to make his likeness to Justinian I more obvious. As Justinian had refounded his Illyrian home-town as Nova Justiniana and given it primatial rights in North Illyria, so Justinian II found a New Justinianopolis for the Cypriots whom he had moved in large numbers to the Hellespont, and the synod of 692 recognised the metropolitan of Cyprus, now the new city's bishop, as primate of the Hellespont, independent of the Patriarch.

He had to fight Bulgars and Slavs, resettling many Slavs in north-west Asia Minor, organising them as a military force under the name of Peculiar People; and managed to retake Armenia which he alienated by trying to impose orthodoxy. Then, defeated, he massacred the Slavs, who seem to have gone over to the Arabs, and lost Armenia again.

In the peace treaty he agreed to withdraw the Clubmen from the frontier areas; and succeeded in transporting at least large sections of them to Thrace, the Asian side near Byzantium, and elsewhere. 'From that moment', says Theophanes (an historian in whom we get glimpses of the popular viewpoint), 'the Roman Empire had to suffer from the Arabs evils of every sort, and they still suffer them till this day.'

Did Justinian act thus because he had no choice but to accept Arab terms? or because, in his general policy of regrouping forces capable of resistance around Byzantium, he liked the idea of having the fierce fighters nearer at hand? or because he recognised the threat to the land-lord-system which these guerrillas represented, and wanted to break it? Probably all three motives were present.

However that may be, his ruthless efforts to raise funds and strengthen the State made large sections of the magnates his enemies. He was de-throned by a general who escaped from the jail into which he had been flung; and the Senate exiled him to Cherson with a sliced-off nose. Anarchy broke out; and Justinian managed to get away from the Crimea. He plotted, fled to a group of near Goths, contacted the Khazars and married a Khazar princess, defeated (through his wife giving the secret away) a plot to kill him, strangled with his own hands the minister who had been instructed to do the killing, slipped off by boat, sent a servant to rally his

adherents in Cherson, and sailed west along the Black Sea into a terrific
storm, got up the Danube and gained the support of the Bulgars, who
helped him back to his throne.

In his ferocity he tried to take revenge on Cherson and attacked the
groups of magnates who had had him exiled. After an effort to reform
the Church, which produced the Synod of the Domed Hall with its canons
of discipline against corrupt and incompetent clergy, he clashed with the
Papacy and ordered the Pope's arrest; but the army in Italy took the
Pope's side against the imperial commissioner. Then another revolt, of
the fleet, ended his embittered reign.

DECISIVE TURN. The seventh century, then, saw the loss of the richest and
most industrialised of the provinces, those in which the great heresies
of Nestorianism and Monophysitism had opposed the State-Church and
the State. But replacing the old forms of struggle emerged the armed
groups of guerrilla-peasants, based on the village-commune as it revived
after the sharing out of the land among Slav clansmen or Asian villagers.
Nestorianism and Monophysitism, as well as expressing a general anti-
imperial attitude, embodied embryonic national aspirations in the Syrian,
Mesopotamian, Egyptian areas; but now various heretical attitudes converged on a new basis, later to appear as Paulicianism, in which the
anti-imperial aspirations of the free commune were given a powerful utterance. Thus, on the whole, struggle weakened in the remaining towns and
the faction-parties broke down, but an intensified struggle was born
among the peasantry, who fought hard to hold their gains.

What was the role of the State here? The State strove to maintain
its central controls, its bureaucracy, its military powers. The main need
was to repel the enemy in Asia, in the Balkans and on the seas. The considerable collapse of landlord-power meant corresponding modifications
in the social attitudes of the State, which, to survive, had to accept the
new commune and use it as the basis for an army capable of defending the
Empire. The Farmers' Code, probably compiled under Justinian II, shows
the effort to integrate the commune in the imperial system. But this does
not mean that the State became a State of free small-holders. The landlord controls remained in various parts, and the State, deprived of its
great mercantile towns, could not envisage a secure basis which did not
rest ultimately on the senatorial class.

All the same, in facing up to its military needs, the State swung as far
as it could, at moments, to support of the free peasant, without transforming itself into a new kind of State, a State based on a middle-class of
producers in town and country who worked for a free market without

servile labour. The climax was to come under Constantine V, as we shall see in the next chapter.

Administratively, the Theme System was extended over the remaining provinces. And, driven back on the areas where Greek was a predominant tongue, Byzantine society now achieved a cultural homogeneity that it could not previously attain. The Empire approximated more and more to a nation. And this happened while the West was still in the throes of passing from broken-down tribalism into the first stages of the feudal State proper. Here, as in all significant Byzantine developments, we see how the Empire blazed the way ahead, developing forms which it could not fully work out, and providing all the transitional forms between ancient society and medieval society.

9

THE ISAURIANS AND AMORIANS

ICONOCLASM. The eighth century opened with a sense of world-end on all sides, the result of the long interlocked wars:

> Under the influence of the outcome, among the Christians, as well as the Moslems, the idea of the triumphant State changed to the idea of repentance and both were expecting the end of the world. It seemed to both sides that only before the end of the world will the final aims of their States be attained. In the Latin as well as the Greek world a legend became current to the effect that before the end of the universe the Christian ruler (the Frankish king or the Byzantine emperor) will enter Jerusalem and hand over his earthly crown to the Saviour, while the Moslems expected the end of the world to be preceded by the fall of Byzantium. (Barthold.)

The new start was given to Byzantium by *Leo*, a commoner, who rose to the rank of Spathar of the Guard by furnishing Justinian II with fifty sheep in the Bulgarian campaign; after a mission to the Caucasus, he rose to command of the Anatolic Theme. He thus represents the new men, the new military nobility. His family was probably eastern, transported or migrating to Thrace.

He set himself to rebuild a strong State, based on what areas were left in the Balkans, Greece and Asia, and looking towards the Pontic or Black Sea area. He kept as firm a hold on imperial Italy as he could without being drawn in too much. He increased direct State-controls, *e.g.* replacing the last remnants of the curial system of tax-collecting by special State officials aided by assessors. He made judges wholly State-paid instead of letting part of their recompenses come from persons needing their services. He organised an up-to-date law handbook, the *Ekloga*, in which a Christian and humanitarian note invaded the Roman code. An Army Code, aimed at restoring army discipline and morale, probably belongs to this period; and the Farmers' Code, whether the work of Justinian II or the early Isaurians, certainly reflects the attitudes of Leo and his son.

Absolutism gained a new stress; and the resolute nature of the reconstructed State appeared in a tough attitude to Church and monastic property. What the Church had done in voluntary usury under Heraklios,

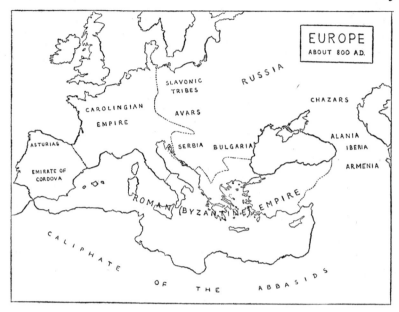

it was now forced to do under measures of expropriation. The sections aimed at were the monasteries, which were less directly linked with the State and its needs than the State-Church proper, and which were rich in lands. In the Isaurian policy of confiscation of monastic lands, the State was supported both by the magnates, who hoped to recoup their fortunes by sharing in the spoils, and by the bishops, who often were jealous of the monks and their influence. But though the basic cause of what became the Iconoclastic movement was the need of the State to confiscate the only single source of great landed wealth left to the impaired Empire, this movement chimed in with the nonconformist emotions of large sections of the peasantry and artisans. And so it worked on a powerful ideological basis, attacking the cult of the Virgin and of the Ikons, attacking the monastic creed of celibacy, and generally denouncing the more superstitious aspects of religious practice.

We must therefore define the Iconoclastic Movement as the first Reformation; what happened in the sixteenth century was the second Reformation. The latter had a wider scope and different effects, on account of the much more highly developed mercantile and industrial middle-class; but essentially the two movements were closely akin. No doubt Leo III had at first no more intention of furthering a mass-movement of dissent than had Henry VIII in England when he confiscated the abbeys' property; and no doubt many of his supporters, especially among the nobles, were no more concerned with religious motives than were many of the nobles who hastened to grab abbey-lands in Tudor England. But the whole set of historical circumstances which brought Henry VIII or Leo III to their actions, indissolubly included the mass-movement which willy-nilly they furthered. And so in the working-out royalty and nobility became themselves caught up in the ideological struggle and found themselves taking sides, often with intense passion.

The advent of the Iconoclastic creed in the Byzantine East, as part of the struggle against Islam, is of further interest in showing the unity of development embracing the whole Near East. Islam appeared for long to the Byzantines as a Christian heresy; John of Damaskos, born and bred among the Moslems, thought so. And to the orthodox Iconoclasm seemed a version of Judaism and Islam.

EFFECTS ON ITALY. The Iconoclast decrees had the effect of strengthening the imperial hold on South Italy, since large sections of Greek-speaking orthodox fled there. This Greek influx, which ensured that South Italy would remain Greek and Byzantine for another four centuries, had very important cultural effects, transmitting Byzantine influences with renewed force to the rest of Italy and other parts of the West.[1]

There was a revolt in Italy. Pope Gregory II withheld the tax that Leo was trying to raise for war against the Arabs. At Rome the Pope, and in Venice an elected Dux, took over the imperial prerogatives. The *dicio* (State-power) went from the emperor to the local authorities (magnates), even where there was formal adherence to the Empire. The Papacy had no wish to set up a counter-emperor; its own position was too weak. When the revolt was quelled, the *dicio* returned to the emperor. But the effects of independence could not be wiped out. Now it was impossible to appoint imperial officials in place of the local tribuniciate, which fell wholly into the hands of the landed lords, with an hereditary principle dominant. The imperial civil service was finally pushed out in Central and North Italy, dislodged or left high and dry, by the seignorial powers; and no more efforts were made there to reimpose the controls of the centralised State.

CLIMAX OF ICONOCLASM. Leo's son, *Constantine V*, carried on his work. The attack on the monasteries reached its climax: Constantine tried to

---

[1] J. Gay finds Hellenisation begins in the late sixth, early seventh centuries. Greek-speaking peasants still survive in Calabria. (On linguistic grounds these peasants are held to descend directly from the ancient world, though no doubt reinforced from time to time by Byzantine immigration: Rohefs.)

extirpate the monks altogether. A first-class organiser and general, he drove the Arabs back over the Euphrates and regained land-contact with Armenia; made strategic transportations of populations inside the Empire; kept the Balkans safe from Bulgarian attacks. But while he carried one aspect of the Iconoclastic programme to its limit, and was looked on as a prophet by many of the eastern nonconformists, he revealed the inner contradiction of the imperial position, its inability to break from landlord-power as its basis. His restoration of town-prosperity depressed the lot of the peasants; and he began the charistic system of land-tenure which corresponds to the western benefice. Still, he had to put down a vigorous revolt of the orthodox magnates.

The Gallic Church was closer to the Iconoclast position than to the papal, and Constantine made efforts to win its support; but the Papacy by its intrigues was able to control the Frankish king Pepin, who imposed his will on the Church Council held at Gentilly in 767. The power of the Frankish kings was increasing, and the last three years of Constantine's reign saw the destruction of the Lombard kingdom in Italy by Pepin's son Charles. The Papacy realised that there was a power close at hand which it would have to confront, and henceforward its policy was to use the Franks against the Empire and the Lombards, without allowing them to break from papal leading-strings.

In place of the religious art which they banned or destroyed, the Iconoclasts encouraged a secular art, drawing its motives from both the Hellenistic past and Sassanid secular imagery, and stressing the joy of life. They encouraged also a return to Hellenic humanism.

REACTION AND SECOND WAVE OF ICONOCLASM. Constantine's son, *Leo IV*, had a brief reign. He died leaving his wife *Irene*, an ambitious Athenian, as regent for his young son Constantine. She took up the cause of the orthodox magnates and Church-dignitaries; and despite violent demonstrations of the Guards against the ikon-worshippers, she managed finally to rig a Council and restore images. Military disasters followed and she was deposed.

A treasury-official, *Nikephoros*, was elected; he returned to a secularising policy on Iconoclast lines, and had to put down two revolts by the orthodox magnates. The eastern nonconformists, the Paulicians, supported him; and the pious Theophanes shudders to tell us that under him tolerance went so far that in Byzantium a group openly declared it wrong to kill heretics. He seems to have introduced the *Allelengyon*, which passed the burden of taxes from poor estates on to rich neighbours. Before his last campaign he had the poor enlisted in his army, rich neighbours had to supply their equipment. We hear also of peasants armed with gourds to replace mutinous soldiers.

His son *Staurikios* reigned only a few months: his wife intrigued with the orthodox magnates and his sister pushed forward the claims of her husband *Michael*. Michael got the throne, and he too took up the orthodox cause, pouring out money on monks, hermits and magnates. He sought an accord with the Papacy and was badly defeated by the Bulgarians. The army couldn't bear it any longer, deposed him, and set up *Leo the Armenian* to lead another Iconoclast movement.

Probably half-Syrian, Leo renewed the attack on image-worship and monasteries; but his friend *Michael* murdered him. The new emperor, an Amorian of humble birth, continued the Iconoclast tradition, but without persecuting the Iconodules. He wrote to Louis the Debonair in the West, trying to win him over; and the Frankish bishops agreed on the compromise-formula reached at the Council of Frankfurt (images as decorations or memorials), but the Papacy side-tracked the issue.

INNER SPLIT. Now when revolts broke out in Asia, the Paulicians sided against the government; and there was a great rising in Asia and the Balkans under Thomas the Slavonian—a movement of 'slaves against masters, of rank-and-file soldiers against officers', says the Continuator of Theophanes. 'Like the bursting Nile-cataracts, it flooded the earth, not with water, but with blood.' Here, then, is the moment when the mass-basis, which had long been weakening, finally deserted Iconoclasm. The peasants realised finally that they must stand on their own feet.

Michael's son *Theophilos* was an Iconoclast. Intellectually rationalist, he encouraged secular art, built splendidly, and fought the monks; but the revolt of Thomas had made Court and magnates alike equally afraid of the stirring masses, and Theophilos could not call on the people for aid as Constantine V repeatedly had.

When he died, his wife Theodora brought the orthodox worshippers of images back to power. Her son *Michael III*, when he came to power, was a mocking character, who with his boon-companions was said by his enemies to have played at some kind of black mass. In his reign, however, many important things happened, perhaps due largely to his uncle Bardas or the patriarch Photios. Some of the secularising trends of the Iconoclasts were preserved, in a revival of humanist education; the Arabs were decisively defeated; the Russian attack (860) on Byzantium by sea was repelled; and the break with the Papacy, growing ever since 800, reached its first full and systematic level in the controversy over the dogma of the Procession of the Holy Ghost (the Ghost coming, according to the Papacy, *from both* the Father and Son, not *from* the Father *to* the Son). This period also saw the evangelisation of the Slavs in Bulgaria and Moravia.

Then Michael was murdered by his favourite, *Basil the Macedonian*, of Armenian stock settled near Adrianople, who began work as a doctor's groom and rose through pleasing a rich widow of southern Greece. With Basil the full tide of reaction set in. The epoch based on the revival of the free village-commune was ended.

CHARLEMAGNE. During the ninth century the Bulgarian empire in the Balkans was rising; the Russian Kievan State was founded; and the Norman raids which had been going on ever since the late eighth century grew in intensity and became movements of conquest. Among the Arabs the Omayyad Caliphate had been overthrown by an Abbasid claiming descent from the Prophet's uncle; and al-Mansur retired from Damaskos to his newly built capital Bagdad in 766. Islam was continually rent by sects who resented the imposition of State-power on the tribes, and who looked for some Messianic advent or sought to set up a theocratic egalitarian republic. Early in the century had come the completion of Charlemagne's work of building a Frankish Empire; and in 1800, the Pope crowned Charlemagne, while the populace of Rome shouted in acclamation—an act precipitated partly by the intrigues of Irene's court in Byzantium, which wanted an alliance with Charlemagne and seems to have offered him marriage with Irene, indeed perhaps the imperial title and throne as consequences of the marriage; and partly by the intrigues of the Papacy, which sought to use the Franks against Byzantium without endangering its territorial claims in Italy. This act was not, and was not meant to be, the creation of a Western Empire; it was simply an act of usurpation, attributing to Charles the imperial title of the Roman Empire.

Charles had been on his way to Sicily when the Pope crowned him; but the first clash with the Empire came through Venice, which throughout this period acted as the main Italian port linking Byzantium with the West. Violent civic struggles had been going on there in the eighth century between the magnates and the popular party. Charles's intrusion into Italian politics led to fresh splits and fights, till in 810 he recognised Venetia, Istria, Liburnia and the towns that he held in Dalmatia as Byzantine—in return for a validation of his imperial title from the emperor Nikephoros—that is, he realised all along that the title was usurpation unless accepted by Byzantium; and when in fact thus accepted, it meant nothing except an honorific gift by the emperor.

In the earlier eighth century Gaul had been in such confusion that the

Church there lacked the organisation or moral energy to do anything about its own reform, let alone the conversion of the Germanic tribesmen east of the Rhine. Both works were carried out by Anglo-Saxons, led by the vigorous Boniface (Winfrid) of Wessex. Charles Martel had based himself on pledged vassals, to whom he gave Church-estates as fiefs, and made a considerable step towards building a coherent feudal State. Charles his grandson completed his work and built up a ramshackle kingdom, aided by the Church in establishing the idea of absolutism. (Pepin was the first Frankish king anointed.) In the State thus constructed, tribal forms modified by the fusion with disintegrated imperial forms in the Gaul of the fifth to sixth centuries (and such of the imperial tradition as the Church preserved) were mixed afresh with imperial forms and ideas borrowed directly from Byzantium in the eighth century.

A high-sounding title and Byzantine court-ritual were used. Chancery (for preparing documents) was staffed by the clergy, deacons and sub-deacons as clerks and notaries: the link of Chancery and the Court Chapel strengthened till its culmination in the later half of the ninth century. Administration was mainly by the *graf*, a definite organ of the kingship, replacing such forms as the dukeship through which the magnates had operated. The governor was usually a count, who represented Charles in the district, held assemblies, led levies, tried important cases, held the king's ban and helped the bishop in Church matters. The bishop too was a State-official. (Louis the Pious arranged for counts to report on bishops and bishops on counts.) Contact and control were largely kept through the king's envoys, *missi*, and king's law was steadily growing up beside customary usages. Efforts were made to encourage trade by making it safe, by restricting excessive privileges, etc. For State-works the people were called on, *e.g.* to repair or build a road. Revenue was based on the Crown-lands—with the addition of foreign gifts, tribute of subject peoples, war-loot. What was exacted from the people was services, not taxes.

War-service was a heavy burden. Each step in the building of the State involved a specialisation of military duties, linked with the development of the benefice into the fief. *Vassus* had once meant a dependent of any sort; now it means a freeman rendering service to king or lord, and subject to his jurisdiction. The manor-system was growing up, with the model provided by the Crown domains. There we find groups of home-farms under stewards, tenements held by free and semifree, allotments worked by serfs—at times concentrated into benefices granted to privileged tenants, *vassali*, for service; or managed by a king's steward, several *mansi* under a *villa* or set round a *palatium*, the great manors where the head-stewards lived and kept accounts and stored things. The king and his family moved from one *palatium* to another, consuming its products.[1]

Popular units or institutions, derived from tribal days, could carry on inside these looser formations, *e.g* the open-field system with compulsory crop-rotation, collective management of pasture and woodland. Customs of the village-commune were everywhere tangled up with issues of seignorial authority and perquisites.

Generally the freemen fell in status as the landed nobles rose. Thus *Bonde (Bauer)* means in Norway and Sweden a freeman standing on his rights; in Denmark and England, the *Bonde* becomes bondsman.

SLAVS AND GERMANS. With the eighth century conversion of the Germans lying east of the Rhine and the creation of Charles' unstable kingdom, there began an eastward expansion of the Germans, which characterises the whole medieval period. When vast masses of Germanic tribes moved westward in the fifth century, there had been a corresponding westward movement of the Slavs, who filled up much of the vacated space. Towns such as Berlin were Slav foundations. Now, as the Germans developed unsteadily the first stages of the feudal kingship, they pressed in on the Slavs and tried to push them eastward. The Anglo-Saxons who had converted the Saxons and other tribes had been zealously papist in their religious politics; and so, after Boniface, the Papacy gained a strong hold on the Germans.

CHURCHMEN AND MONKS IN THE WEST. We may also note the different function of the Church in the West and the East. Charles' Chancery was composed of churchmen on account of the almost total illiteracy of the lay; and this grip won by the Church on the machinery of secular administration was held for long, especially in the Germanic area. No less striking was the different function of monasticism in the West and the East. In the East it arose as a dissident movement, practically a heresy, which

[1] One of the differences between Western and Byzantine feudalism in their advanced medieval forms was that the concept of the fief had a strong military element, whereas *pronoia* or charistic tenures never became identical with fief-holdings in this way. The explanation must be sought in the fact that western medieval States developed out of the fusion of tribalism and the Roman bases of the fourth to fifth centuries, whereas in the East the State held and was able to attempt adaptations of the early Empire: soldiers' holdings under State-control.

The early forms behind the French word *fief* seem derived from a word for cattle, *vieh*, used by the Germans. In the tenth century the word took over the colouration of gifts of land or goods by lord to vassals (in seignorial households). *Feos* or *feus* was roughly used to express *beneficium*, and finally supplanted the latter word, in its Latin form *feudum*. (M. Bloch.)

the Church managed to subjugate but which never submitted to a central control; and though at times the bishops disliked and felt suspicious of it, on the whole it acted as a fighting wing of the Church, watchful for secular encroachments. In the countryside, however, it often still continued as a breeding-ground of heresy.

The monks of the West were soon controlled by the Papacy (after the defeat of the Celtic dissidents); and the monasteries acted to some extent as vanguard forces of artisan-craft and productive method, as well as preservers of certain traditions of literate culture. Further, in adventuring into the wilds, to escape the world, they acted as pioneer-groups, clearing the forests and providing nuclei for lay settlements—thus carrying the world into new regions. The eastward movement of forest-clearance was another important aspect of the whole medieval epoch.[1]

[1] The monastery in the West had a further economic function, in later medieval times. The pioneer group like the Cistercians, 'lord of undeveloped tracts of hill country restricted by the rule of his order from obtaining income from the usual manorial sources of profit, would perforce respond quickly to the opportunity of getting rich through the sale of wool'. Hence their concentration on big sheep farms supervised and worked by lay brethren. They thus helped the growth of industry and money-exchange. (M. Gibbs.)

THE MACEDONIANS

ABSOLUTIST STATE. *Basil I* (867–886) stabilised the State-power once again on the landed magnates, and the modifying vital elements that had carried on through the period of the Iconoclasts were crushed down. This reign opened with an unrelenting campaign against the Paulicians who had established their own towns towards the eastern frontier, and destroyed them despite their fierce resistance.

Absolutism now triumphed, without the limiting factors that had previously been exerted by the populace at election-time and at other political crises. The Iconoclast law-work was denounced and banned, and Basil and his successor, his son (perhaps really Michael III's son) *Leo VI*, compiled a new handbook and manual of law, which facilitated the magnate power and made serfdom (*enapographoi*) legal once more. The bureaucracy was extended again, but without the energy that the existence of a vigorous mercantile class had given it. The city-demes were reduced to the status of mere parade-groups; and the Senate itself lost its main political powers, of scrutinising legislation. The emperor now named all functionaries himself.

A vast court-etiquette grew up, rigidly enforced. And this Byzantium of the reaction, fast falling into feudal petrifactions, is the epoch of the Empire that has been taken as typical of 'Byzantine Culture' and lauded as the great epoch of magnificent achievement

> . . . returns to the empire an extension that it had not known for centuries and a magnificent prosperity (Diehl).
> . . . internal recovery from the troubled period of Iconoclasm continued. The reigns of Basil I and Leo VI are the last of the creative ages of Roman legislation (H. St. L. B. Moss).[1]

And the triumph of reactionary orthodoxy, the creed of the magnates, is continually described as a triumph of 'popular' religion.

Leo, intimate with monks, was defeated by the Bulgarians and saw

---

[1] It is significant that the Macedonian law-work abandons many of the Isaurian advances and returns for its basis to Justinian's Code: showing the agreement of the two periods in their narrow landlord-bases and pointing to the broader basis of the Isaurian system.

Thessalonika, now the Empire's second city, sacked by Arab corsairs. In his efforts to get an heir, he married four times—an atrocious sin in ecclesiastic eyes, which led to a complicated tension between Church and State. And when he died, his brother, who had disliked him, caused much trouble. After intrigues and clashes Leo's young son, *Constantine Born-in-the-Purple*, became sole emperor; but his ambitious mother Zoe kept control of things till her army was defeated by the Bulgarians and the shrewd Armenian admiral *Romanos Lekapenos*, a peasant's son, ousted her and became co-emperor with the lad.

Romanos was a capable general, who maintained imperial power in South Italy, turned the Serbs and Croats on the Bulgarians, signed a treaty with Peter of Bulgaria, and defeated an attack on Byzantium by the Russian kniaz Igor. He tried to stop the decay of the free village-commune by a law forbidding the magnates to buy their way into them, or to get in by any means whatever. This law of 922 was repeated in a law of 943, which attempted to nullify the inroads of the lords and compel them to return at cost-price all lands taken from the 'poor'. Clearly the first efforts had had little effect.

Romanos was at last dethroned by his own sons; but the populace of Byzantium demonstrated and thus saved *Constantine VII*, who became sole emperor. A mild, scholarly man, who compiled and encouraged others to compile encyclopedic works, and pottered about at architecture and shipbuilding, painting and sculpture, goldwork and canticles; he tried ineffectively to repeat the land-legislation of Lekapenos. His son, *Romanos II*, succeeded him, a weak man, who married a tavern-girl named Theophano.

Theophano, widowed, married the general *Nikephoros Phokas*, who took the crown despite the two sons of Romanos II. He won back Cilicia, Cyprus, Antioch; and clashed with the Church through forbidding donations to monasteries or new monastic foundations. He was probably aiming at ascetic reforms rather than expressing anything iconoclast, since he was a tough, hard-living, taciturn man who loved monks and soldiers. He gave the magnates back their rights of buying into large properties falling into decay.

Theophano, after a while, murdered him with the aid of another general, his cousin *John Tzimiskes*, a large landowner. John then chased her out and was crowned after making peace with the Church by abandoning the right to appoint bishops and giving half his personal property to the poor, half to hospices. He withdrew the reform-measures aimed at the Church; won half Bulgaria, defeated a Russian attack, and marched with his army close to Jerusalem and Bagdad. The great landed family of the Phokai revolted and tried to seize power, but was defeated. John, like his cousin, loved soldiers and monks, and was the first emperor to put Christ's image on gold and copper coins, with reverse legend, 'Jesus Christ King of Rulers'.

LAST SHOW OF STRENGTH. *Basil II*, son of Born-in-the-Purple, belatedly got his throne at John's death. As a lad given to drink and wenches, he now became a strict disciplinarian and devoted his life to war. His long reign opened with feudal anarchy, which he mastered. Then, though also enlarging the eastern frontiers, he spent most of his time fighting the Bulgarians. Tsar Samuel ruled from the Macedonian Mountains to the Black Sea and had built up a rival power threatening the Empire, but after some twenty years, using the strategy of dividing the enemy, enveloping them, and acting with extreme mobility, Basil emerged victor.

Psellos gives a clear picture of him, with his round face encircled with a beard, which 'he kept rolling between his fingers in thought'. He stood with arms akimbo, and spoke slowly, with little pauses, 'more like a peasant than an educated man; and his laugh was a great roar, an ebullition of his whole body'. When riding

> he seemed moulded like a statue by a master, firm and upright in the saddle . . . and then, checking his mount with a pull of the bridle, he jumped off as if he had wings, and kept the same position in the saddle as in the descent.

He was followed by a series of weak rulers and stupid empresses, brilliantly described in the pages of Psellos who knew them all and who tells of their petty doings, crimes and futilities with subtle psychological insight. Their general effect was to weaken the Empire and produce a cleavage between the State-machine, carrying on by its own momentum, and the magnates chafing in their country-seats. Hence the historians talk of a Civil Party arising at Byzantium—a phrase which merely masks the fact of the rapidly increasing contradiction between the overgrown apparatus of the centralised State and the strong centrifugal tendencies born of un-fettered magnate-power.

And grave new dangers were closing in. In the West the Normans had arrived in Italy under Robert Guiscard. On pretence of being allies of the Lombard prince of Salerno, they murdered, burned, raped and tortured prisoners. Only the Byzantine ports could hold out, with mutinous populations. The German emperors were also taking a hand in Italian politics and wars. And in the East the Bagdad caliphate had succumbed to the Seljuk Turks whom it had called in as mercenaries. In 1048 came the first inroad of Seljuks into Byzantine territory.

The magnates plotted with the patriarch and decided to put the great landowner *Isaac Comnenos* on the throne. The patriarch started tumults at Byzantium, and the magnates brought up the Asian armies. Isaac entered the port in a boat of flowers.

THE GERMANS AND THE PAPACY. Out of the welter of conflicting lordships and claimants to power the Carolingian Empire broke down and no stable centre emerged till the early tenth century. Then it was eastward, in the tribal duchies, that the State-form began to cohere again. In 919 the Saxon and Franconian nobles set Henry the Fowler, of Saxony, on the throne; and a new epoch began in the West. Henry and his successor, Otto I, carried on knitting their control, pushing frontiers further, colonising or conquering. In 962 Otto's kingdom was made up of the duchies of Saxony and Bavaria with the neighbouring marks of Franconia, Lorraine and Swabia (Burgundy was not gathered in till 1033). Bohemia was tributary from 950; Carinthia became a duchy in 976.

Swabia reached to the sources of the Rhine, and Bavaria opened into Italy through the passes, which included the St. Gotthard and the Brenner. Once again the Papacy in its entangled politics drew the Germans in, asking for protection; and in 962 Otto, outside Rome, swore to return any lands claimed by the Papacy which he recovered, and to bind anyone whom he set up as ruler of the Italian kingdom to act as the Pope's protector. The German emperor thus became the Pope's suzerain and held the right to control the papal elections till the middle of the eleventh century: no Pope's election was valid unless passed by the German ruler.

From now on Italian politics were a series of conflicts and alliances between the Papacy, the Germans, the Lombards, the Normans and the Byzantines—with moments of common action against the Moslems who invaded Sicily, threatened South Italy, and held strongholds on the coast as far north as Provence. The seaports of Naples, Amalfi, Bari, Genoa, as well as Venice, played an important part, growing steadily in power and often treacherously acting in conjunction with the Moslems against their fellow-Christians.

As German power grew, the lure of Italy and the desire to measure swords with the Empire increased; but the definite clash never emerged. The Germans were never strong enough. It was left for the Crusaders to swing the full tide of rising western energies against the Empire which had enabled Europe to grow up, by its long wars against Islam.

The tenth century saw a strong Byzantine trend at Rome. We meet officials with Greek titles and many Greek names, and a demand for highborn Byzantine ladies as brides. A certain link between the local nobles and the Empire appeared, *i.e.* in the clash of 1009 when Benedict VIII was elected with the support of the German Henry II against the candidate of the Crescentii, nobles of Rome. This Pope offered Henry a gold globe with a Cross above—a usurpation in Byzantine eyes.

The mid-eleventh century saw the struggle between the Papacy and the Germans over the right to appoint the holder of the See of Milan. The conflict soon broadened its issue. Royalist bishops backed the king; and grumbling Saxon and Thuringian nobles backed the Pope. The Pope encouraged subjects to rebel, claiming the right to release them from their oaths of obedience; and the wrangle between secular and ecclesiastical powers had begun, which carried right on, one way or another, till the Reformation, and beyond. At the same time the Cluniac movement of reform in the Western Church aimed at giving the Papacy close control everywhere of the churches and monasteries for purposes of political struggle against the new emerging States.

The mid-eleventh century saw also the breach between the Papacy and Byzantine Orthodoxy intensified through the actions of the headstrong patriarch Michael Keroularios and the rivalries of the two churches in the Balkans and Bohemia, and even in Russia.

THE WESTERN COMMUNE. But I do not wish to take up space here in dealing with matters of Western history that are easily accessible. One point, however, must be stressed—the emergence in the West of the free town, a new sort of town which had broken away from ancient forms and which provided the key-basis on which modern Europe has been built.

In the earlier medieval centuries of the West the economic level fell so low that the citizens lost all rights and were governed by a bailiff presiding over a seignorial court. For long urban and agricultural production were confused together: burgesses traded but also tilled acres in the common fields. Teutonic lawyers preferred to treat each town as an anomaly, a privileged abuse.

Towns grew up round abbey or castle, palace or cathedral; or on frontier-lands or newly won areas, with men-at-arms holding lands on military tenures—though in the Mediterranean region the nobles from the neighbourhood had town-houses and intrigued among themselves for control. An involved and unceasing struggle went on between the overlord, lay or ecclesiastic, and the townsmen. The lord wanted to appoint the chief magistrates: only then did he feel safe in granting privileges of trade and tenure. And the townsfolk wanted to elect their own council or magistrates; then only did they feel safe.

As areas like Flanders, North France and parts of Italy outside Papal

4

control began to thrive, the towns wanted full self-government; they strove to become communes. The commune was a sworn confederacy, a *conjuratio*, with elements akin to the merchant-guilds or the fraternities for the enforcement of the Truce of God, set up in the eleventh century—with the new feature that it was formed in defiance of authority and desired republican form. Traders and artisans largely composed it; and it was ready to fight, as we see with the Milanese or the men of Ghent. The basic form of commune-organisation was the committee with executive powers, and one or more councils which gave advice. In the first phases a mass-meeting was held for elections to magistracies or the councils, for voting of taxes, for the admitting of accounts of expenditure, for decisions on all important matters of policy. But popular control tended to weaken as wealth grew; offices were filled by co-options or by elections in the craft-guilds, or even became hereditary. As oligarchic control took the place of mass-participation, strong factions grew up, *e.g.* in fourteenth-century Florence.

The communes had a hard fight, and often they were bloodily smashed down by lords and bishops; but where industry was rooted, they held out and played a key-part in building the national State and all that that State implied.

Free institutions were late in German towns; they lacked any strong basis in struggle and never had the vital element that we find in Lombardy or Flanders or North France. Sometimes these towns became the capitals of petty principalities.

It is significant that in the areas where the commune grew stubbornly up, the settlements had strong cohesive survivals of the clan-kindred. Thus in north-east France kindreds were active till the fourteenth and even the fifteenth centuries—and kindreds cannot be deliberate groupings such as arise from guilds, secret societies or submissions to lordships.[1] It is clear then that the immigrants who formed the nucleus of the towns in Picardy and the Netherlands did not enter as individuals but as kin-

[1] Further west we have evidence only of the nobles, among whom the principle of kin-solidarity was still strong in the late thirteenth century; such scraps of evidence as there are suggest a certain degree of kin-solidarity in Champagne and Burgundy till about the same time. The chroniclers tell the same story as the documents, *e.g.* Jean d'Oucremese and Henricourt (fourteenth century) have the term *lignage* on almost every page, *e.g.* 'The Sire de Hermalle summoned all those of his kindred and demanded their aid in order to have vengeance and they all remained with him' (Henricourt, *Miroir des Nobles de la Hasbaye*, 341). It is the tension of kindred-forces and urban industrial production that underlies the commune. (I am aware of the rapid breakdown of kindreds into patriarchal family-forms of an extended kind and so on. Detailed analysis would have to go into this. For broad purposes my generalisations suffice.)

groups; the great merchant-families rose on a basis of kin-solidarity. The Lombards in Padua and elsewhere had associations, *consortia, comminia* or *vicinia*, which owned grasslands, woods, moors, farms and which provided the link between tribal forms and the trade-guilds that rose in the eleventh century. These *consortia* took part at Padua in the politics of the clash between German ruler and people; and it seems that the former 'granted ampler rights to these associations known as *vicinia* or *consortia*, and thus the last step was taken which fostered the birth of the Commune'.

Thus the struggle to reconstitute clan-democracy in the town developed new forms of political struggle in the western communes as in ancient Greek cities; but now there was the great difference that a slave-economy did not evolve underneath the struggle. The communes led the way into the free-market that played an integral part in breaking down feudalism and its serfdoms; they were the vanguard force breaking through into the modern world. That in the struggle the egalitarian element weakened, and oligarchic forms of control thickened, does not alter this fact.

Here then is the key achievement of the West, which the Byzantine area could not manage. But it is only with the rise of the commune and all that it entails, from the eleventh century onwards, that Byzantium begins to fall away from its role of world-centre; and we must see the rise of the commune as conditioned throughout by the general economic and social process in which Byzantium played the basic role, radiating influences and setting the pace, providing techniques and standards, and driving Europe forward.

THE LAST PHASES

THE THREAT OF THE WEST. *Isaac Comnenos*, acting for the magnates, cut down the salaries and privileges of the bureaucrats, the scholars, the clergy; but his party found that running the complicated State was not simply a matter of retrenchment, and after two years he abdicated. *Constantine Doukas* took over, and restored the policy of the 'civil party'. But there was no solution that way either. Pressures went on all round the Empire, Pechenegs raiding on the north, and Seljuks on the east, Croats independent, Serbs and Dalmatians in revolt, Bulgaria seething, and Normans looting town after town in Italy. The Turks took Armenia and went on devastating parts of Syria, Cilicia, Cappadocia.

The military party put *Romanos IV* on the throne. He was shatteringly defeated at Manzikert in 1071, and Asia Minor was overrun. The Turks set up a sultanate at Nikaia, only a few miles away from Byzantium.

Once more the desperate magnates put their man in, *Alexis Comnenos*. The Normans attacked Durazzo, the Adriatic fort holding the western end of the Roman road leading to Byzantium, but were defeated through the aid given to the Empire by the Venetian fleet. Venice, however, always exacted her price; and now she gained freedom from dues in all Byzantine ports. Nowadays most of the shipping trade was in the hands of the Italian merchants, so that to surrender the right to levy customs-dues on a group so active in carrying goods to the West was a heavy blow, a token of the end. The gold bezant, the imperial gold standard that had been maintained undebased since Constantine's day, now started going downhill.

In 1095 Alexis beat off a combined attack on his capital by Pechenegs and Turks; and next year the first Crusaders appeared. The Byzantines naturally felt dubious; they rightly interpreted the Crusades as aimed rather against themselves than against the Turks or Arabs, as the final phase of an ever more powerful challenge that since Charlemagne had been closing in from the West. They had long had bitter experiences of the Normans, and the Normans were keen Crusaders. From the Byzantine viewpoint the matter was simple. For many centuries the Empire had been the bulwark protecting Europe; now that they were in a tight corner, any Crusade should come as the work of allies sustaining the Empire in its rights. But the Greeks rightly suspected that the Crusaders had other ideas.[1]

The First Crusade was successful in taking Antioch and Jerusalem; and though the Empire recovered most of western Anatolia, small feudal States on the western system sprang up at Jerusalem, Tripoli, Antioch, Edessa. Alexis found himself in a complicated world where the Westerners with no loyalty of any kind to Christian principles were ready to unite with Turko-Arab emirs against Sultan, Caliph, or Byzantine Emperor alike. In particular he had a difficult time with the Normans, who kept on trying to strike Byzantium down, and against whom he had only an army of rough folk from Thrace, Macedonia, Thessaly, supplemented with mercenaries (now, since 1066, largely composed of Anglo-Saxons), with detachments of Franks, Turks, Serbs. To make matters worse, the Bulgarians began again growing restive.

The centre of mass-heresy was now Bulgaria and Macedonia. There heretics were directly carrying on the Paulician faiths, while others had embraced a more pacifist but equally uncompromising form, Bogomilism.

Alexis' son, *John II*, went on gaining back parts of Asia and strengthening the hold on Antioch, which the Empire had successfully claimed. But in the West the coronation of Roger II, Norman, at Palermo in 1130, meant the loss of South Italy; and both John and his successor, *Manuel I*, tried to build an alliance with the German emperor against the Norman threat. How implacable the West was growing was shown by a coalition of Roger II, France, Serbia, Hungary and the Papacy against Byzantium. The Germans did not join in; but when imperial troops landed in Italy in 1154, Venice and the Germans came out against Byzantium with the others. In 1158 imperial troops left Italy, never to return; and a disaster in the Phrygian mountains ended the hope of winning back Asia. To defend the coastal districts was now the highest hope of Byzantium.

THE CRUSADERS ATTACK. Under the strain a strong anti-Latin feeling grew up in Byzantium, which led to a massacre of Latins there in 1182, in return for which the Normans sacked Thessalonika. A popular wave set *Andronikos I* on the throne. (The 1182 massacre had been provoked by the intrigues of the Venetians and other Italians aimed at keeping Andronikos out; their intervention led to a revolt of the fleet, which went

[1] Individual Crusaders, high or low, had varying motives, religious and economic: they included high nobles, out for new lands and political power, knights of France and Germany hoping for eastern plunder, Italian merchants eager for new markets, peasants escaping from serfdom and wanting land, etc. The Reform movement played its part, and so on.

over to Andronikos, and the people attacked the westerners' quarter near the Golden Horn, joined by Andronikos' Paphlagonian soldiers.) He tried to inaugurate a strong anti-magnate policy and to defend the small-producers. So popularising was his policy that he ordered his portraits to be denuded of all splendours and himself to be depicted as a poor farmer in a smock of blue with a big sickle in his hand. He began to exterminate, the nobles; but the Normans came up from Thessalonika, and the scared population acquiesced in his overthrow by the bigoted and pusillanimous noble *Isaac Angelos,* who escaped from jail into St. Sophia.

Now the Empire was under the weak Angeloi. Bulgarians and Serbs broke away. When the Fourth Crusade arrived at Byzantium, ostensibly to proceed and attack Egypt, the Crusaders interfered in imperial politics by putting their nominee on the throne; when the populace rose, they stormed and sacked the city with the utmost violence and rapine on 13th April, 1204. The wealth of Byzantium was scattered all over the West; and the Empire was parcelled out among the Latin adventurers in small feudal kingdoms and principalities, with a Latin emperor and patriarch at Byzantium.

It is of some interest to English readers that the defence of Byzantium in 1204 was largely in the hands of English and Danes. When the Crusaders tried to land on the Imperial Pier they were driven back by the Greeks, Pisans and axe-bearing barbarians (Niketas says), Villehardouin describes the walls as manned by '*d'Englois et de Danois*', who resisted in hand-to-hand fighting with axe and sword. Also when the Latins sent envoys in, they passed at the Gates, and all along the way to Blachernai, English and Danes with battle-axes. Robert de Clari, telling of the attack on the walls from the ships, recounts how sergeants, English, Danish and Greek, in one of the tower-storeys, defended themselves vigorously with axes and swords.

NATIONAL REVIVAL AND BREAKDOWN. The national forces gathered at Nikaia under Theodore Laskaris and John Vatatzes; and in 1261 the Latin emperor Baldwin II was driven from Byzantium with the Venetian settlers.

There is no need here to examine in detail the tale of the enfeebled State between 1261 and 1453. Centralised controls have fallen away. Now Byzantium is only one minor State among many other feudal States in Europe, fighting against foes on all sides; and the confused and frustrated efforts of the Palaiologoi to pose Venetians against Genoese, to win over the Papacy by persecuting the orthodox, to gain help from one western power or another against the Turks went indefinitely on, till the Turks stormed the walls.

Not that Byzantium made no contribution to European development during those two centuries. Though broken-down, the Empire still held a number of key trade-routes; and though it could not even attempt to compete with the Italian ports, it provided the rich system which the others could exploit. Other Greek States had emerged, which played their part in cultural diffusions and in facilitating the Western invasion of the Eastern markets—Trebizond, the despotat of Epiros, Mistra in the despotat of Morea with its court that anticipated the intellectual and artistic life of the Italian courts of the fifteenth century, their humanist positions.

In these last years of doom there was a final efflorescence of Byzantine culture, of vast importance for Europe, an effloresence which we now recognise as the first phase of what became the Renascence later in the West and without which that Renascence cannot be conceived.

And in the mid-fourteenth century there was a last flare-up of the popular forces of revolt, a furious attempt to break through the heavy pressures of frustration closing in on town and country. The people rose and killed all the magnates, all the officials of the State, whom they could catch. They rose in Adrianople, Byzantium, Thessalonika; and this time they knew that there was no salvation in a mere change of masters, that they must work out themselves the forms of their freedom. From 1342 to 1349 the Zealots held out in Thessalonika, and then were bloodily crushed.

THE TRADE-EXPANSION OF THE WEST. During these last centuries the medieval West had been building the new national States, in France, England, Spain (from which the Moslems were finally driven in the late fifteenth century)—with the German Empire reaching its culmination under Frederick II in the twelfth century and then declining. That Empire lacked a strong civil service of the sort that developed in France and England, and could not achieve a point of central stability. Russia had been invaded and occupied by the Tartars in the thirteenth century—except for Novgorod and the extreme north—with the national forces regathering round Moscow, from which Ivan II liberated his country in the later fifteenth century.

The Germanic expansion eastward, with the clash of Papacy and Orthodoxy in Bohemia, Moravia, Dalmatia and Bulgaria, was part of a general trade-pull in that direction. This trade-pull operated partly through the Mediterranean sea-routes (to Syrian and Black Sea ports, and to India via the Red Sea) and partly through overland routes, running to Vienna or Regensburg, or across Germany southward to Bohemia or

eastward to Silesia and Poland. From Vienna the Moravian Gate gave easy
access to Cracow and through South Poland to Kiev. There was also the
river-route from the Baltic via Novgorod down to Kiev and the Black
Sea. In the eleventh century contacts between East and West were made
easier by the conversion of Hungary (freeing movement from Vienna
down the Danube to the Byzantine frontier-posts in Bulgaria) and the
breaking of Arab sea-power through the regaining of Corsica and
Sardinia by the Pisans and Venetians, and of Sicily by the Normans.

For a while Turkish domination closed routes into Asia. Then in the
thirteenth century the Mongols unified a large part of Asia under their
rule, and the routes to Central Asia and through the Persian Gulf were
open again. Only the Egyptian route was held by the Turks. In the eastward thrust of trade after 1204 the Venetians Matteo and Nicolo Polo,
who left Byzantium in 1250 to trade in the Volga region but found a
local war going on there, decided to 'go forward by way of the east'.
But instead of finding a circuitous way home, they arrived at Bokhara.
Their venture heartened Nicolo's son Marco to make the overland journey to China, returning by sea to Ormuz; and many traders followed
their route.

Everything seemed set for a great movement of trade eastward by land
and sea across Asia; but the conquests of the Turks and the fall of the
Tartar dynasty closed the routes once more. The Turkish middleman took
his heavy toll of the trade still reaching eastern Mediterranean ports, and
'a policy of strict seclusion stifling trade once again prevailed on China's
marches towards Central Asia' (Stein).

But the new mercantile energies of western Europe were not going to
be bottled up. Genoese and Venetians pressed into North Africa, and by
the fifteenth century traders were getting across the Sahara to the Niger
regions. In the late thirteenth century sailors were already venturing out
into the Atlantic, and had found the Canaries and Madeira; the Portu-
guese sought and achieved the sea-way round Africa to India in 1434. The
voyage of Columbus in 1492 completed the out-movement, and the
attention of Western Europe swung out over the ocean.

III

State Forms and Bases, and the Forms of Struggle

4*

12

STATE AND LAW

IDEAS AND PRACTICE OF ELECTION. The Byzantine world took over the fundamental ideas of the early Roman Empire, but gave them its own new orientation. It assumed the Rule of Law, and the elective basis of all rightful power, with the correlative that the ultimate source of power was the People. The Justinian Code declared 'To submit Our Authority to the Law is truly a greater thing than the Imperial Power.'

Augustus had built up his constitutional position by a manipulation and extension of republican forms and offices in complicity with the Senate, though the formula was *Senatus Populusque*. What happened as a result of the revolutionary third century was that the *Populus* part of the formula achieved more reality. The emperor was elected by the three main components of his society, Senate, Army and People (of Byzantium) —with the troops stationed in the capital speaking for the Army. Without acceptance by all three sections, an emperor had no valid title; and though normally the Senate's word was what controlled things, the Army could and did in moments of crisis carry the day with its nominee, whether he was a man put up by fellow-magnates or some popular figure genuinely swept into power by the rank-and-file. And in moments of crisis the People too could exert a strong and sometimes determining influence. After election, the emperor was crowned; and while he gave satisfaction, his power was absolute. But if he failed or outraged public opinion, it was open to the electors to proclaim a new ruler.

Though erratic in effect, with the Senate or Army-commanders in the normally preponderant position, this elective system was real enough; it carried on vigorously, if nothing else, the idea that the source of power lay in the People. Its contradictions appeared in the united notions that the Rule of Law was supreme over all personal considerations and that the emperor embodied law or was above all law, or that the law was an emanation of the emperor's deity. Justinian's *Lex de Imperio* expressly stated that the People had transferred their power to the emperor: theoretically they could take it back; but in fact no one contemplated such a constitutional possibility—though the Paulicians and Zealots put the idea into practice.[1]

CHURCH AND STATE. The contradiction appeared indeed further in the whole union of Christianity and State; for the origin of Christianity had involved a *total rejection* of the State in its very nature, so that the State's acceptance of the creed could not logically make the State Christian. It could only make the opposition of State and Christ worse; for it meant, and could only mean, that the State was trying to use Christ to gild and disguise its own essential evil. That was precisely what the various heretical sects felt in their deepest bones when they rebelled against orthodoxies that accepted the State or the world.

Yet in no other way could the two elements necessary for the future of men, for the forward movement of history, come together—the social organisation representing the attained level of productive activity and the dream of a unity without the existing contradictions of the world. Hence, however debasing and distorted were the ideas and methods of State and Church in bringing about and carrying on the union, there was something in it that went beyond those ideas and methods. That kept alive both the forward movement of history and the rebellious dream of a valid harmony. And in the process both State and Church were modified and facilitated the historical movement forwards to greater freedom and universality. From one angle the Church had sold out to evil and was distorting the dream of a true unity to sanctify the rule of division and greed; from another angle it was enabling the masses to throw off servile ideas, to feel the right and need to participate in social development, and was standing out over against the State with the criterion of a fuller and better life, criticising division.

The whole history of theological ideas, orthodox or heretical, could be analysed from this focus. We should then find that each important enunciation defined a point of arrest in the complex relationship, a point which enabled men to get at grips with their world and accept or repudiate in the degrees that they felt most fruitful, most satisfying, most truly integrative of dream and actuality. If the Augustinian thesis of Two Cities merged in the unifying experience of the faithful became in many ways the key-definition for the Latin West, in the East it was rather the thesis

---

1 There was no law against a female ruler, but a woman could not incorporate proconsular *imperium* with tribunician *potestas* (military power with the inviolability of the people's defender) on which Augustus formed his rule—though empresses took regent rights. Irene (late eighth century) was the first empress outright; but by that time the Greek term *autokrat* had practically eliminated *imperator* with its military colour. From Arkadios, the emperor's wife was an Augusta.

of an organic unity from which emerged hierarchical structures and relations (as in the pseudo-Dionysios' treatise) that may be regarded as typical. But against this position beat the Monophysite demand for a different sort of unity, or the Paulician reply that the world was indeed two, rent by a hopeless contradiction, but that he who resisted could fight his way through to the resolution, the unity.

Thus, Christianity had given the common man an idiom by which he could lay hold of historical process and define his own position, with a conviction that his position mattered. It had given the State a new re-conciliation formula, but it had also provided the people with a new idiom of struggle. And this religious development was linked with the dissident mass-movement which had begun in the first days of the Empire and which had reached a culmination in the broad conflicts of the third century.

REVOLUTIONARY RITUAL. The new active mass-element in the Empire can be seen in the ritual of election which had no basis in the Augustan period and which emerged during the army-revolts of the third century. The crucial moment of election occurred on the parade-ground of the Hebdomon, when the emperor stood in the midst of the soldiers, was given a golden torque, and was hoisted up on a shield. Both these usages were revolutionary in origin, and show an obvious derivation from the Germanic tribesmen who were numerous in the third- and fourth-century armies. To stress the democratic moment the torque, a military decoration, was handed to the emperor by a simple under-officer, the *compactidor*.

This ritual had become so deeply linked with the new monarchy that the elevation on the shield lasted till the end of the Empire, as art-works show (as well as the description in the treatise of the pseudo-Kodinos in the second half of the fourteenth century, which tells of the elevation taking place before the coronation, on the first storey of the patriarch's palace looking out on to the Forum Augusteum where the people were gathered—though in medieval days the shield was held by the patriarch and high officials).

CODES OF LAW—(A) JUSTINIAN'S. Since the Empire carried on the full Roman tradition while modifying it, the study and restatement of Roman Law continued. And at each of the decisive periods, that of Justinian, that of the Isaurians, and that of the Macedonians, a thorough effort to overhaul the legal tradition and fit it afresh for the tasks of the epoch was made. In the process, not only was Roman Law continually developed and related to the changing needs of the State; it was also carried into new areas—*e.g.* into those of the conquered or allied Slavs—and was handed on in forms which the West took in as its economic and social level rose to the point where a fully devised law of private property and the State was required.

Roman Law was made of statute law and jurisprudence. In the early Empire the sources of law were statutes (*leges*), which became rare after Tiberius; decrees of the Senate, which, proposed by the emperor, took the place of *leges*; edicts under his name; his final decisions as judge of appeal; mandates, instructions to governors; rescripts, answers on points of law to judges or private persons; the edict of the law-officer, the praetor, as revised and consolidated by the lawyer Salvius Julianus at Hadrian's command; treatises by authoritative jurists, embodying the common law and court-practices.

But from the mid-third century there was a juristic decline: with the emperor as sole source of law, expressing his will in constitutions. Publications became mere compilations, extracts of constitutions and the work of old jurists. Nothing was officially defined. The judge was supposed to look into all the imperial constitutions and all the old classical literature of the law—an impossible task, even if there had been a central organ for publishing the constitutions, which there wasn't. Yearly the constitutions piled up, scattered in various archives, complicated by changes and repeals.

The first effort to grapple with the problem was by Theodosios II. His Code met the existing needs far more than the only two previous compilations, much lesser works; it codified customary right, collecting the ordnances since Constantine's day; and it thus defined the extended power of the landlords. In the West it exerted an important influence on the legislation of the barbarian kingdoms in their attempts to develop tribal customs into State-law.

But there was still much confusion, and by Justinian's reign many more changes had occurred. The mass of existing law had to be reduced to manageable shape and dimensions; and the trend to simplicity and equity in civil law had to be brought out. A commission of ten was set up in 528; and, led by the lawyer Tribonianos and the professor of law at the University of Byzantium, in little more than a year they classified in a single Code the main constitutions since Hadrian. Then came the problem of covering the decisions of the great jurisconsults of the second to third centuries, who had completed the classical period of Roman Law (*i.e.* the period of the expanding free-market and the property-relations thereon based). First the lawyers drew up fifty decisions dealing with basic issues; then in 530 a commission of sixteen began the full job, to omit repetitions, reconcile contradictions, and make a coherent whole of the legal tradition which reached far back to early Rome. Three groups worked for three years; and the result was the Digest in fifty books. At the same time, with the aid of the professor at the leading law-university, that of Berytos in Syria, a handbook of civil law for students was prepared. All law-schools but those of Byzantium and Berytos were closed; and Justinian forbade any future changes in the finalised legal system. Further laws were issued as *Novellae*.

The preface to the Novellae shows that most of the men who carried out the great work were Easterners. It was a work of creation as well as digestion: the whole mass of Roman Law was oriented to suit the new world—and incidentally to serve as the basis of modern law.[1] When in the twelfth century the West had revived enough to need an elaborated law of property, Justinian's work became the real law of many countries, and had a profound effect even in a place like England which never directly embodied Roman Law.

Justinian's law showed both the levelling process of money-values at its climax and the new class-split, of *honestiores* and *humiliores*, that ran deep across the levelling. Thus, it continued to flatten out tribal forms with their exclusiveness and their close texture of kin-relations: Justinian broke up the system of land-tenures in Armenia where clan-bases were still strong and as a result Armenians henceforth drifted more thickly to Byzantium. He also tried to break up the old wedding-rites of the Mesopotamian folk. Procedure was simplified, in manumitting slaves or acquiring land. But class-distinction ruled in the penalties of criminal law: if a rich man forged, he was deported; if a poor man, he went to the ghastly toil of the mines. Now the poor could be tortured as once only slaves had been.

The criminal code, partly through Church influence, was harsher. Thus, a murderer was liable under Justinian as under Augustus to exile; but death was now imposed for marrying one's niece. Theodosios I enacted loss of property and burning-alive for the man who married his cousin, though Arkadios cancelled his law. A man who abducted was put to a painful death by Constantine; the girl, if consenting, died in the same

---

1 Old Roman Law had long been changing under the impacts of Praetorian and then Imperial Law: in both cases the law of Rome proper is modified and expanded to meet enlarged issues, to deal with contacts and incorporations resulting from the mercantile and political extensions. Praetorian Law brings in the solvent of the *Ius Gentium*—i.e. seeks to find general principles governing the intercourse of peoples and the impacts of diverse systems and prepares the way for the influence of the more philosophic idea of the Law of Nature. The Empire kept intensifying the need for comprehensive yet simplified systems.

way; if she resisted, she merely lost the right to inherit; if a nurse abetted, she had molten lead poured in her mouth. With slight mitigations, this law stayed in force, extended to the seduction of women under chastity-vows. Constantine had sodomites burned; Justinian concurred, observing that sodomy caused famines, plagues, earthquakes, but imposed a mere death-penalty. We hear of bishops and senators, convicted of sodomy, sexually mutilated and tortured, then paraded in the streets before execution.

Mutilation appeared as a penalty only after the triumph of the Church; the Church also created the new crimes of Seduction and Heresy. By Justinian's time mutilation was much used on the Biblical principle of punishing offending members. A tax-collector who falsified accounts, or a man who copied out Monophysite writings, was liable to have his hand chopped off; loss of nose or tongue was common. The late Republic had tried to abolish capital punishment; the early Empire reversed the humane trend, but only under Constantine did a full savagery burst out, with a sharp class-differentiation in application.[1]

Despite attempts to curb certain of the feudalising developments, and to fight sections of the magnates, Justinian's Code as a whole securely based the new absolutist State on its magnate basis. It was the first statement which tried to sap the elective idea by opposing to the people's will Divine Grace as source of supreme power. 'Nothing is superior or more holy than the Imperial Majesty.'

CODES OF LAW – (B) ICONOCLAST. With the Iconoclasts the need for a new Code appeared. For one thing, Justinian's Code, Digests and Institutions were in Latin; and the loss of the mercantile and industrial East had changed in many ways the basis of the State. In the provinces customs or arbitrary decisions tended to usurp Imperial Law. Hence the *Ekloga*, or Selection, 'proffering Justice to all earthly beings'. It was described as an 'abridged extract' of Justinian's law, arranged and 'corrected with a view to greater humanity' (though some historians take *philanthropotron* to mean 'with a view to improvement').

Absolutism was further stressed. 'All depends on the Prince's care.' The last remnants of the curials were swept away; and even the Senate lost its administrative role, till in the tenth century its purpose was mainly ceremonial. The consulate was a mere title. (A new aristocracy of

[1] The dual role of Christianity appears in both aiding the humanitarian trends against slavery and giving it new ideological defences. The Law's 'barbaric features were due either indirectly to the institution of slavery, or to the influence of the Church in those domains which specially engaged the interest of ecclesiastics' (*e.g.* divorce or sodomy), says Bury, somewhat simplifying.

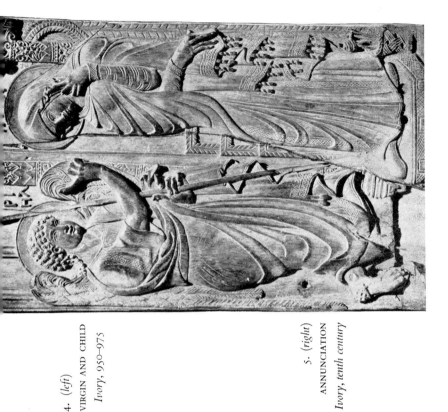

4. (left)
VIRGIN AND CHILD
Ivory, 950–975

5. (right)
ANNUNCIATION
Ivory, tenth century

military leaders has supplanted the old magnates, linked with the Theme System of government by generals.) And absolutism got an increased religious tinge. Law was the discovery of God as well as a social function; the emperor's duty was to maintain the Scriptures and the decisions of the Seven General Councils as well as Roman Law. When the *Ekloga* rebuked bribed judges, it appealed, not to the secular tradition, but to the Hebrew prophets such as Amos ii, 6. Thus we find for the first time a full medieval coloration in the State and its concepts; the integration of State and Church has considerably advanced. But this does not mean submission by the State to the Church; on the contrary, it means that the State feels it has successfully swallowed the Church. It was no accident that this State proceeded to overthrow Orthodoxy and confiscate ecclesiastical estates.

There is stress on Constantine the Great, 'who first in Christ's Name rendered the Imperial Crown more splendid and august'. Mutilations increase, and so do incest-taboos—cousins up to the sixth or seventh degrees are forbidden marriage, and a third marriage is treated as unthinkable (though formally forbidden in 800). Church-influence appears in the withdrawal of permission for peasants to work the land on Sunday, the forbidding of sabbath rites, the denunciation of blackpuddings as made of blood, the measures against gambling priests. But some penalties are mitigated, *e.g.* that for seduction; and there is tolerance except for Montanists and Manichees. The Church is told to look after heresies without secular aid. And a higher conception of marriage is seen than in Roman Law proper; man and wife are given theoretical equality of rights and dignities and community of goods. Thus, Justinian's law required a father's consent to a child's marriage; now the mother's also is required.

The weakening of the old bureaucracy and the medieval element are visible in the practical readiness to take account of 'accepted usages'. The principle is laid down that out of the business of common life comes the occasion of the law's application, and that for each new reality which cannot be related to some old law, a new law must be made. Further, laws should be simple, understandable by children.

The *Ekloga* had an enduring influence in the Slav areas. It was used by the Bulgar Judiciary Law for the People, *Zakon Sudnii Ljudem*; in the oldest monument of Serbian Law, the *Zakon* of Tsar Dushan; and in the *Nomokanon* put out in Moscow in 1653, known as the Directory or *Kormchaja Kniga*. Nikon (seventeenth sentury) refers to *Ekloga's* rulings as to the Tsar's authority. The profound importance of the organising forces and forms of Byzantium for the future is exemplified by the fact that provisions of the *Ekloga* were still in force in Bessarabia in the 1920's.

CODES OF LAW—(C) MACEDONIAN. The Macedonian reaction made a violent attack on all Isaurian works including its legal codes. (We have the *Ekloga* only because it was incorrectly ascribed in manuscripts to the Macedonians: otherwise all copies would have been destroyed.) First came a manual, the *Procheiron*, with a brief account of the laws of imperial rule—establishing righteousness 'by which alone, according to Solomon, a nation is exalted'. Forty chapters give the main norms of civil law and a list of penalties; for the first twenty-one the main source is Justinian's work (in its Greek revisions and abridgements). The *Ekloga* is denounced as a 'subversion of good law, useless to the Empire'. So 'it would be unwise to keep it in force'. All the same, the manual in its later section borrowed largely from the denounced work, thus proving how soundly based it had been in the Empire's changed conditions.

Then came the *Epanagoge*, Introduction to forty volumes of 'purged' laws (which are not extant, but which probably provided the basis of the *Basilica* issued under Leo). It too denounced the *Ekloga* as Isaurian nonsense intended to 'oppose the divine doctrine and destroy the saving laws'.

The Macedonian legislation and codification aimed at fully restoring the power of the nobles; the hatred of Isaurian law was partly based in dynastic rivalry, but also expressed the feeling that that law had to some extent hindered the magnates. Serfdom was legalised afresh; the parts of the Justinian Code which forbade governors to acquire landed property in their administrative areas were weakened. And the centralised bureaucracy was built up with enhanced power; the breakdown of the old senatorial class had made this development possible. The State—emperor and bureaucracy—was now both linked and opposed to the new military nobility. That is, the ultimate basis of the State in the landlords was not disturbed, but a simpler line of division ran between civil and military power, derived from the enfeebling of the urban elements and the expropriation of the village-commune. Here the development under the Isaurians, which deprived curials and senators of any powers of direct political organisation, was brought to its formal conclusion.

The ninth and tenth centuries saw a revival of juridical literature, in commentaries, scholia, manuals and abridgements.

There was now nothing to prevent the steady progress of feudalisation, breaking down the elements of the ancient State which Byzantium had carried on, and approximating Byzantium more and more with each century to the feudal West. This approximation comes about largely by contrary movements. The East saw the feudalisation of the centralised State inherited from the ancient world, with one big break in the process when the free village-commune rose and fell, the West saw the building-up of feudal States out of the merging of disintegrated tribalism with remnants from the trampled Empire and traditions carried on from the Empire (both its Roman past and its Byzantine present) by the Church. In the twelfth century the two systems were coming close together, despite many strong differences caused by the opposed processes that had made them what they were; and in the clash the West triumphed. Thus modern Europe was born.

13

FACTION AND CIRCUS

CHARIOTEER AND APOTHEOSIS. Probably the four-colour system of chariot-races went back to Republican Rome. Each colour stood for one of the associations with its stables, grooms, messengers, and so on. The government paid each group by a regular tariff. John Malalas, an historian with popular elements, links the factions with the origin of Rome; he thinks the four colours represent the four elements. There is this much truth in his thesis, that the symbolism underlying the four colours had ancient roots as well as many contemporary points of reference.[1] When Domitian had tried to bring in the imperial colours, gold and purple, the people objected and the attempt was given up. In any event, Malalas' ideas certainly represent a popular attitude, not a learned interpretation.

The hippodrome or circus, near the main palace-complex, was the scene of both great festivals and political assemblies. On race-days, from dawn men waited at the gates, even cripples; latecomers tried to hire an over-looking room. The main shows were in January's first week, when Consuls were inaugurated, on May 11th, the city's foundation-day, and other dates of national importance. The praetors, chosen yearly, superintended. Twenty-four races were run a day, with interval in the middle; between came fights of men with beasts, rope-walking, boxing, wrestling. Each race went seven times round the length of about a mile and a half. The victors, amid chants, with faction-delegates carrying crosses of flowers, waited on the emperor for their awards. The imperial box or *kathisma* stood along the side by the palace. At the emperor's entry the Protector Guards elevated their standards, and he greeted the People from the balustrade with the sign of the cross. Acclamations were chanted. The *kathisma* was directly connected with the palace behind it.

---

[1] It went back to Babylonia, related to the Elements, Planets, levels of Space (Heaven, Air, Earth, Underworld); and seems to have had this significance on the Ziqqurat. (Still in the early nineteenth century some Wallachian towns had quarters marked by colours; and the custom has persisted.) At Antioch the factions stood for the four city-quarters; and Dyakonov thinks the four Byzantine factions of Syrian origin. A Jewish midrash testifies to the political significance of the colours. Constantine VI noted the hair-colours in names of Pecheneg tribes, corresponding to the sky-region towards which the tribe in question was orientated.

Crack drivers became popular heroes. We have several poems about them which show a strong religious element: in them the people's chari-oteer takes over the attributes of the Sungod from the divine emperor. Thus, Porphyry was called the Wonder of the Blues, mounting to join the Sun in his heavenly courses. A statue of Faustinos of the Greens was described as held down only by the roof: 'Take off the roof: he'll reach the Sky'. And the dead driver-hero creates universal mourning like a saviour-god in his dying phase:

> Since Constantinos entered the House of Hades
> the race-course is dark with mourning faces.
> All Joy has left the People, not even the streets
> wake the old bandying of Friendly Strife.

Not that the Strife was always friendly: another poem calls Driving the Abusive Art.

The Chariot-god in Hellenistic and Roman times in the Near East de-rived mainly from Iranian sources: Mithras appeared in the *Vedas*, not on a horse, but in a chariot. And the chariot-image grew increasingly important to express resurrection, apotheosis, ascension. The pagan apotheosis of the dead emperor often took the form of a chariot-ascent: we find it used of Marcus Aurelius and Constantine's father. The people's chariot-victor was thus a sun-hero opposed to the imperial cult; and the poems which defined this attitude help us to understand why such power-ful popular emotions gathered round the circus-races.[1]

We can thus find a new significance in the fact that the first large-scale clash of people and emperor after the shift to Byzantium occurred in the Circus, about a charioteer. At Thessalonika this driver, 'seeing one of Botheric's cupbearers indecently exposed, made overtures to him'. Captain Botheric had him arrested; the people rose and killed Botheric because 'a great racing-show was to be held and they demanded the release of the prisoner, who was (they said) necessary for the festival's success. The request was refused, and they rose in sedition.' So Theo-dosio I massacred them while they were watching the races.[2]

[1] Thus it was a cognate development which gathered popular emotion round Elijah (2 Kings ii, 11), who went up in a fire-chariot to heaven (cf. the dying-reborn gods like Herakles-Melkart of Tyre). Throughout the Balkan and Slav world Elijah was a tremendous figure, taking over many of the attributes of the Slav Thundergod Perun; in Greece mountaintops were taken as his shrines. Like Apollo he drove away diseases. (They called him *Helias*, which suggested *Helios*.) And he was connected with Midsummer Fire-Festivals

[2] There is one odd example of the ascetic saints mixed with the racing passion: St. Hilarion (early fourth century) is said to have released the horses of a Christian's chariot from the spells cast by a pagan invoking the god Marnas, in the port of Maioumas, near Gaza.

THE RISE OF THE GREENS. The development of the faction-parties goes on as the curial middle-class go down. They emerge effectively in the first half of the fifth century under Theodosios II, who at least in his later years, under the domination of the eunuch Chrysaphios, favoured the Greens. The magnate and orthodox tradition in the historians described him as weak and cowardly because he bought off the Huns rather than fight them. That is, he inclined to the Green policy of taxing the landlords to pay tribute to the barbarians (who used the gold to buy goods from the Empire and thus stimulated trade and industry). The people remembered him gratefully. In 583 (some 133 years after his death) the Greens asked Maurice to name his son Theodosios: which he did, against the wishes of the Blues, who wanted the name Justinian.

He changed the seats of the Greens in the Circus to the left side, the side of greater honour. That act marks the rise of the Greens to the point of strength where they could challenge the Blues. The eastern cities had regained much of their old wealth and energy, and for some fifty years the Greens were generally in the ascendancy. Markian removed the tax from senatorial estates. The historian Priskos lauds him for creating a Golden Age (for the landlords). He was a Blue and set out an Edict depriving the Greens for three years of the right to occupy official posts, civil or military. But Zeno was a Green and reverted to Green policy. Anastasios called himself a Red: a Green to all intents and purposes. Under him Green policy reached its climax.

The struggles under Anastasios can be better dealt with when we come to religion: we must keep in mind throughout that the political battle of the Greens is always entangled with the religious protest of the Monophysites. Here, however, we can glance at the economic policy of Anastasios. His right-hand man was Marinos, a Syrian financier and Monophysite, who began as a clerk and rose to control of the tax-department. The Receipts Tax, which weighed heavily on trader, shopkeeper and small-producer, was abolished in May 498, and extreme care taken to stop its reimposition. All documents and registers were burned in the Circus; and then Anastasios gave out that he had changed his mind, got in any withheld files from officials, and burned them as well. We catch a glimpse of what these steps meant in a provincial town like Edessa, where 'both small and great in their rejoicing donned white clothes, and carried lighted tapers and burning incense'. Praising Anastasios, they went to church. 'All the artisans were reclining and enjoying themselves, bathing and feasting in the yard of the great church and in all the city-porticoes' for a week; and the citizens decided to hold the same festival every year.

One story says that Anastasios was moved to his act by the picture of hardships given in a tragedy by Timotheus of Gaza. Though he certainly did not need to be reminded by a poet to carry out such a decision, it is of interest to find the poetry of his day using such themes—and coming from the Syro-Palestinian area. He made up the revenue-loss by a land-tax, applied to the support of the army; the army itself lost requisition-rights.

He removed from the curials the task of tax-collecting and set up an official, the *vindex*, whose office was auctioned out—an effort to return to the practices of the Republic, which shows the extent to which a monetary system had revived, and with it the trading middle-class.[1] The orthodox historians say that the effect was to ruin the provinces, but Priscian in his panegyric, echoing official policy, proves that the aim was to ease things for the small-producer:

> *Pitying you lessened the farmer's bitter expenses,*
> *for all the Councils gave up their villainous ways*
> *nor could the unjust as before deride the laws.*

But the *vindex* could not resist the powers at the disposal of the magnates; and without repeal the office seems to have faded out.

The *annona* was increasingly paid in cash, not kind; and large copper coins and small change were minted, to make small trading easier and help the poor who were afflicted by the insufficient small-coins and their bad marking. On the land the *epibole* was still the main method used to stop lands from falling out of cultivation; it made the whole farming group responsible for individual taxes. Much struggle went on round the application of this system: the rich tried to use it for tax-evasion, making poor villagers pay for part of a large estate that fell into their territory or lay close by. The provincial governor decided how *epibole* fell; and the State tried to have land transferred to those made fiscally liable, with decisions based not on contiguity but on the history of a property. These positions, however, derived from the wish to keep the tax-system efficient rather than any policy of helping the small-producer. In fact in his land-policy Anastasios revealed the way in which even a strong Green government could not resist the basic feudalising process. He made the free farmer who had been settled for thirty years a tied colon.

BLUE REACTION AND THE NIKA REVOLT. The magnates mustered their powers, and Anastasios' reign went out in tumults of rebellion. With

---

[1] One matter that shows the basic difference between the Augustan and the Constantinean State. In the earlier period efforts to settle veterans on inalienable lands were defeated by *speculators*; now they are defeated by noble *landlords*.

Justin the Blues were in power again. In June 518, during the election-clashes, the Blues rose and fought the followers of the tribune John; they fought the opposed section of the palace guards. And Justinian was thick with the Blues long before his succession; indeed he may be called their party-boss. He filled posts with them, paid them well, and protected them from the consequences of their riots. Justin's reign was filled with such riots; and in 524 came a big scandal. The Blues murdered a Green in St. Sophia. Justinian was ill, and so the case came up before Justin. The Prefect was ordered to carry out exemplary justice, and there were many executions; but as soon as Justinian was well again, he had the Prefect exiled.

On his accession, however, he tried to curb factional fighting; and some five years later both Blues and Greens were arrested for a riot in which deaths had occurred. The Prefect condemned four men to be beheaded and three to be hanged. At the time there was much unrest in the capital: a dearth, added to Justinian's tax-methods, had bankrupted many farmers and thrown others into the hands of the magnates; Byzantium had many impoverished provincials inside its walls. Of the three rioters to be hanged, two fell twice to the ground, still alive, a Green and a Blue. Monks took them over the waters to a church-asylum; the Prefect sent soldiers to guard the church. Three days later, on the Ides of January, the people gathered in the Circus and demonstrated. At the twenty-second race there were cries, *Long live the humane Greens and Blues!* The two factions were fraternising. After the races they agreed on a common watch-word, *Nika*—Conquer! In the evening they broke into the jail and freed the prisoners, setting fire to the building. In the Augusteum they started more fires. The Bronze Gate of the palace was burned down, then the Senate House and St. Sophia. Next morning Justinian ordered the races to go on, but the united factions fired part of the Circus, and near buildings caught as well. The people demanded justice on the Prefect and on the ministers John the Cappadocian and Tribonianos the Questor. Justinian appointed a new Prefect and Questor.

But the riots were now an insurrection. The people, however, had no policy, no idea what to do with their own triumph. Someone started the plan of deposing Justinian and setting up one of Anastasios' nephews. But all three were missing, one had fled, and two were in the palace. Justinian was at a loss. He had two generals with him, Belisarios and Mundos; he sent the former out with his Gothic bodyguard, but the people beat the soldiers. The next two days were filled with street-fights and burnings. Soldiers set fire to a house in which were some Blue-Greens; the flames spread over church and palace, and raged along Middle Street, the great street of shops and works that curved through Byzantium.

Justinian, scared, sent out the two nephews of Anastasios, with every-one whom he suspected of treachery. On Saturday morning he tried to pacify the people by swearing an amnesty from the *kathisma*. They yelled that he was a liar, and got hold of one of the nephews, Hypatios. A council was held among the senators who were disaffected. In the palace Justinian debated whether or not to flee; but his wife Theodora scornfully advised to fight things out.

A court-eunuch sent out agents to split the ranks of the rebels by spreading rumours that Hypatios would favour the Greens, and by talking about Justinian's great goodnesses to the Blues. The generals prepared to attack. The palace guards refused to let them out, so Belisarios had to lead his men over the charred Bronze Gate; they got round to the west entry of the Circus, the Portico of the Blues, and charged in on the packed mass within, while Mundus attacked by another gateway with his Herul bodyguard. The massacre was easy. Justinian was saved by the Goths and Heruls, and some 30,000 people are said to have been butchered.

Hypatios was executed. Eighteen senators were exiled and lost their property; but later they were pardoned and got their estates back. Had these men played a key-part in the Nika? It seems unlikely. We can best interpret the rebellion as the result of the rank-and-file of the factions getting together despite the bosses, aided by the desperate farmers; then, as the tumults swept on, a group of senators, opposed to Justinian and the Illyrian magnates whom he favoured, tried belatedly to use the masses for their sectional policy. The people seem to have turned to Hypatios because of his kinship with Anastasios, in a vague hope that thus there would be a return to the Anastasian policy.[1]

The Blues held violent power through the rest of Justinian's reign, wore uniforms and bore weapons, killed, looted, raped. If the Greens re-torted, they were dealt with by the law. The Blue controls were to be met in all the cities: thus the governor of Cilicia was impaled for executing two Blue murderers. Not that the Greens did not often fight back fiercely: at Tarsos in a riot they killed the local Blue boss, and they continued to demonstrate at Byzantium.

Thus, in the capital, there were tumults in 539: the arrested men

[1] John the Cappadocian was ruined by Theodora. Exiled to Cyzikos, he hated the bishop there. The bishop was killed by a faction-group of young men in the market-place. There were no proofs against John, but later Theodora got hold of two young Greens, and by cajolery and torture gained confession from one: she then had the hands of both cut off. Prokopios says of the faked sex-prosecutions under Justinian that the men selected to be discredited and to lose their property were rich men dis-liked by Justinian or Greens—*i.e.* the senatorial section opposed to the emperor's own section, or the finance-bureaucracy with its eastern connections.

(Greens) were thrown into the sea or killed. In 541 and 542 heads were broken and houses burned. In 544, more burnings. In 547 there were riots suppressed bloodily by the (Blue) Excubitors. In 533 there was trouble over a new Prefect, the arrested had their fingers cut off. In 548 and 551, more riots. In May 556, demonstrations against the City-Prefect after a three months' dearth (this time leaders of the Blues seem to have been punished). In May 556 the factions fought for two days, and there were fires; the Praetorian Prefect's house was burned down, and the Excubitors were called out. In 562 and 563 there were more troubles; and we hear also of undated clashes.

EMPEROR AND PEOPLE IN DEBATE. We have a contemporary document, apparently from the Green archives, which brings before us the very words of a clash between the Greens and Justinian. A Chamberlain, Kalopodios (Prettyfoot), has offended the faction: they pun on his name in their second speech. To conjure up the scene we must imagine the packed intent Circus, the emperor in his *kathisma*, a herald (*mandator*) in front speaking for the emperor, a spokesman of the Greens confronting him. The speeches obey metric laws—based, not on classical quantity, but on the number of syllables and the accentuation of the last word in a clause: to speak thus in a rhythmic chant presupposes a special training in improvisation. The theological references play round the concept of Oneness (*i.e.* Monophysitism):

GREENS Long may you live, Justinian Augustus. May you win! I am oppressed, O best of masters, and my grievances, God knows, have gone past bearing. I fear to name the oppressor in case he prospers all the more and I endanger my own safety.

MANDATOR Who is he? I do not know him.

GREENS My oppressor, O thrice august, is found in the Shoemakers' Quarter.

MANDATOR No one is wronging you.

GREENS You know him well, O thrice august, I am oppressed this very day.

MANDATOR We do not know of any oppressing you.

GREENS It's Kalopodios the Spathar who wrongs me, O lord of all.

MANDATOR Kalopodios had nothing to do with you.

GREENS My oppressor will perish like Judas, God will requite him.

MANDATOR You've come here, not to see the Games, but to insult your rulers.

GREENS If anyone wrongs me, he shall perish like Judas.

MANDATOR Silence, you Jews, Manicheans, Samaritans.

GREENS Do you disparage us with the names of Jews and Samaritans? The Mother of God is with us all.

MANDATOR When will you cease cursing yourselves?

GREENS If anyone denies our Lord the emperor is orthodox, let him be anathema, like Judas.

MANDATOR I'd have you all baptised in the name of One God.

GREENS (*tumultuously*) I am baptised in the One God.

MANDATOR Truly if you refuse to be silent, I'll have your head off.

GREENS Every man seeks a post of authority, to secure his personal safety. Your majesty must not be indignant at what I say in my tribulation, for the deity listens to all complaints. We have good reason, emperor, to mention all things now. For we do not even know where the place is, nor where the government. If I come into the city once, it's sitting on a mule (like a prisoner drawn to execution), and I wish I hadn't come then, your majesty.

MANDATOR Everyone is free to move in public where he wishes, with no danger.

GREENS I'm told I'm free, but I'm not allowed to use my freedom. If a man is free but suspected of being a Green, he's sure to be publicly punished.

MANDATOR Have you no more care for your lives that you thus brave death?

GREENS Let this Green be once taken off, then Justice disappears. Put an end to the scenes of murder, and let us be lawfully punished. Behold, an abundant fountain: punish as many of them as you like. Truly, human nature cannot tolerate these two contradictory things. Would that Sabbatis [Justinian's father] had never been born, to have a son who's a murderer. It's the twenty-eighth murder committed in the Zeugma. The man was a spectator in the morning, in the afternoon, O lord of all, he was butchered.

BLUES (*joining in*) Yourselves are the only party in the Hippodrome with murderers among its ranks.

GREENS When you murder, you run from the city.

BLUES You shed blood and debate. You are the only party here with murderers among it.

GREENS Lord Justinian, they challenge me, and no man slaughters them. Wrath will compel assent. Who killed the woodseller in the Zeugma, emperor?

MANDATOR You killed him.

GREENS Who killed the son of Agapathos, emperor?

MANDATOR You killed him too, and you slander the Blues.

GREENS Now have pity, Lord God. The truth is suppressed. I'd like to argue with those who say that affairs are managed by God. Whence comes this misery?

MANDATOR God cannot be tempted with evil.

GREENS God, you say, cannot be tempted with evil? Who is it then who wrongs me? Let some philosopher or hermit explain the distinction.

MANDATOR Accursed blasphemers, when will you hold your peace?

GREENS It's the pleasure of your majesty, I hold my tongue though I don't want to. I know everything, everything, but I say nothing. Good-bye Justice, you are no longer in fashion. I'll turn and become a Jew. Better be a Greek [pagan] than a Blue, God knows.

BLUES You're detestable, I can't abide the sight of you. Your enmity dismays
me.

GREENS May the bones of the spectators be exhumed!

That is: Let the spectators all be killed! A customary curse in the Hippodrome. The Zeugma was an area past the Stairs of Sykai, kept for wood-
storage. (Huge quantities of wood were needed for fuel as well as building, and supplies were shipped from the Black Sea.)

The whole astonishing document, with the emperor's herald calling the
Greens Manichees and Jews (Monophysites) and the Greens jesting with
the charge and calling the emperor a murderer, gives us the very pulse of
struggle in Byzantium at this epoch.

THE LAST PHASES OF FACTION-FIGHTING. Justin II tried to break down the
spirit of the populace altogether. He reduced food distribution and games.
In 568 he told the Blues, 'Justinian is dead for you', and the Greens,
'Justinian stays alive for you'—that is, no favours for the Blues and continued repression for the Greens. But in practice he carried on Blue policy,
as did Tiberios (though he remitted the tax on political bread, the dole-
food).

With Maurice, however, a new situation emerged. His scheme for a
local militia, in which all freemen were to learn archery and own a bow
and javelin, showed less fear of the populace. At his accession the people
in the Circus cried: 'God grant you well, you have freed us from subjec-
tion to many!' And we hear also of a crowd (presumably of the Orthodox) crying that he was a Markionite, a believer in Two Gods: the kind
of charge that would be used against a Nestorian. Under him the demes
gained military functions, and enlarged church-festivities delighted the
people. The events that led to his downfall are confused. When Phokas,
leading the army-revolt, appeared before Byzantium, Maurice called on
the leaders of both the Blues and the Greens to man the walls but 'they
sent and asked his son Theodosios who was hunting with his father-in-
law Germanos to come and take over the Empire or leave it to Germanos'.
Maurice found out and had his son scourged, though Germanos got away
into a church. The people were turbulent and Maurice fled; then Germanos tried to get support from the Blues. But 'they went instead to
greet the tyrant Phokas'. (So the abbot Theophanes tells us.) Phokas, however, seems to have won Green support as well; for a few days after he
took power, he gave a decision in favour of the Greens in the Circus, and
the Blues shouted, 'Remember, Maurice still lives!'—so he sent soldiers
to murder Maurice. Soon after the two factions clashed violently; the
Greens burned down the houses of Blues and much of Middle Street

was once more destroyed. Phokas had the Green demarch, John Kroukis, burned alive. The Greens yelled at him in the Circus, 'So you're still drunk, eh? and off your head too?' He proscribed them from public functions and took up with the Blues. All the Greens of the Empire joined against him. Revolts broke out in Anatolia, Cilicia, Palestine, Asia, Thessalonika. A ruthless general, Bonosos, was sent to put down the Egyptians, but the Alexandrians resisted 'with the aid of barbarians, citizens of the Green faction, sailors, archers'. And the Greens in Byzantium supported Heraklios when he arrived.

Under Maurice and Phokas then the politics of the factions grows complicated, though in the provinces the Greens are solidly anti-imperial and anti-orthodox. At Byzantium itself a clear lead is lacking. Maurice, though a man of goodwill compared with the four preceding emperors, has no policy of reconstruction; and the people seem to turn on him in the end because of their feeling that he is only making confusion more confounded.[1] Phokas rises to power as a popular champion; but after he has struck down many of the nobles, his terrorism loses any social basis and becomes a mere personal effort to hold power. He turns to the Blues and the Pope; but isolates himself alike from the military and landed nobility and from the Greens.

THE END OF THE FACTIONS. Factional warfare fell into abeyance during the Persian war of Heraklios; and then the loss of Syria and Egypt cut away the main Green base. But already the situation which brought Heraklios to power betokened the end of the party-system based on the factions. The senatorial landlords were supreme in the early reign of Heraklios and the crown seemed in danger of becoming a mere cipher. Maurice, working on hints given by Justinian, had laid the first foundations of the Theme System; and the Arab attack only rudely and sharply speeded up changes which were already under way since his reign.

The factions do not seem, however, to have entirely lost their old functions till Justinian II. Enough of their forms and forces lay quiescent to allow a strong Blue support for the first overthrow of Justinian by the landlord-opposition. But the civic turmoil at the end of the seventh century was a last flicker of life. The factions were already turned into mere

---

1 See the next section for the popularity of Maurice with the Syrian Jacobites (Monophysites). His hold on the popular mind is shown by the tales that he wasn't dead (also that his son hadn't been killed). And the tale of the Nemesis on his killers. All soldiers of the rebellion against him were said soon after to die by disease, sword or fire from heaven. When Heraklios went fighting the Persians, he found only two of the partisans of Phokas left, and even they spoiled the army's luck till they were killed.

ceremonial appendages of the court. The Hippodrome itself was in decay, and the lapse of the sports-passions was one with the lapse of political vigour. (In the West the early city-decline had brought about the same result much more quickly: there the factions had declined fast after the fifth century; and at Rome and Carthage had long been the sports-organisation that they ostensibly were.) When in 667 Justinian II in a letter to the Pope spoke of delegates of the *Collegia Popularia* beside those of Senate and Army, he referred to a token-presence. The faction had become a sort of parade-troops used for acclamations and a unit in the demes concerned with municipal matters, with a geitonarch (a chief-of-the-quarter), a cartulary, a notary and other civil servants.

The phase of the Byzantine city when the ancient *collegia* developed into a new sort of political party, foreshadowing the social conflicts of the western medieval commune, was now at an end.

14

TOWN, COUNTRY AND ARMY

STATE AND LANDLORDS. To understand why the system in which the Greens and Blues fought came down in disaster long before the Arabs irrupted, we must consider in more detail what was going on in trade and industry, and how the peasants were faring; and the changes in the army which were linked with the changes in social organisation.

The contradiction rending the State appeared clearly in the early fifth century when, after struggling to arrest the growth of patronage, the State had simultaneously to remit forty years' arrears of taxes in the Prefecture of the East and to codify the relations of patron and client, making the patron responsible for tax-collection (415). The expansion of the large estate went rapidly on, with the landlords organising their retainer-troops; and Leo I in 468 tried to halt the process by forbidding the sale of land in a free village-commune except among its members.

This law shows that the State considered enough such villages still survived to make its clauses worth promulgation. And we know from papyri of the fourth to the sixth centuries that communal life persisted in Egypt: villages with common allotments and pasture, and with the right to collect their own taxes, control irrigation, distribute State-burdens. The State wanted this commune-element, which made it possible for the whole group to be held responsible for waste or neglected land. A similar village-life persisted in Asia and Syria, in Thrace and the Balkans. And the intrusion and settlement of barbarian groups, Goths or Slavs, increased the number and vigour of such communes.

The year 468 also saw a law which revealed a fear of free group-life by forbidding town or village to use mercenaries or armed slaves. And another attempt was made to threaten landlords with a fine if they acted as patrons, or peasants, if they asked for patronage.

Zeno sought to carry on Leo's work, forbidding the lords to collect taxes on their own lands or jail colons for arrears; and he tried to keep the village-commune intact by stopping the arrest of members for debts and arrears of their fellows. He tried also to encourage reclamation of waste; and though there was nothing new in this policy, he caused much discontent among the magnates.

With its weakening controls, the State was thus in a position where it had to rely on either the magnates or the free group for the estimated revenue of an area. It preferred the latter course in so far as the small peasants did not throw up rivals for the throne, but at the same time it feared their rebellious energies. It disliked seeing any noble or section of nobles growing strong enough to challenge the emperor; and yet it could not see how to keep the masses down and ensure taxes and recruits unless there was a landed nobility in action. It was thus kept in a ceaseless oscillation, trying to preserve a balance threatened by the very methods called on to preserve it.

JUSTINIAN'S POSITION. Under Justinian the same problems came up in extended and more pressing form, and the balance grew even less secure. Futilely he repeated the protests and demands for reform:

> We are almost ashamed to refer to the conduct of these. Men of great possessions, with what insolence they range the country, how they are served by guards, so that an intolerable crowd of men follow them; how daringly they pillage everybody, among whom are many priests, but mostly women . . . (to the Prefect of Illyricum).
>
> What can be more trying than the driving-off of oxen, horses, and cattle in general, or even (to speak of small matters) of domestic fowls . . . whence a multitude appeal to us here, hustled from their homes, in beggary sometimes to die here . . .
>
> News has come to us about such exceedingly great abuses in the provinces that their correction can hardly be accomplished by one person of high authority. And we are even ashamed to tell with how much impropriety the managers of landlords' estates promenade about, surrounded by bodyguards, how they are followed by large mobs, and how shamelessly they rob everything. . . . State property has almost entirely gone over into private ownership; for it is robbed and plundered, including all the horse-herds, and not one man spoke up against it: all the mouths were stopt with gold (to the Cappadocian Proconsul).

Magnates claimed land by simply putting up notices and taking the holders as colons. In Egypt the officials harried even the villages under imperial protection. In the sixth century the Apion family held large estates comprising whole villages; households with stewards and secretaries, masses of workers, assessors and tax-collectors of their own, treasurer, police, even their own postal service, troops, prisons—though private jails were forbidden.

The State's attitude was throughout dictated by its need to raise taxes. Justinian called on all officials to treat loyal citizens with fatherly consideration, protect them against oppression, refuse bribes, and so on—

'increasing the State treasury and exerting all possible effort for its benefit'. After the wastage of his western wars he declared:

> It is imperative the government taxes be paid in full and willingly at definite dates. Then, if you meet the rulers willingly and help them collect for us the taxes with ease and despatch, we shall laud the officials for their zeal and you for your wisdom, and beautiful and peaceful harmony will reign everywhere between the rulers and the ruled.

Whatever happened, it wasn't that harmony. The *epibole*, imposing collective tax-responsibility, was kept up—'a plague that fell suddenly on the farmer, definitively ruining all his hopes of being able to subsist', says Prokopios. A new tax, the *aerikon* (perhaps a kind of hearth-tax), was devised, 'as though fallen from the clouds'.

Efforts at reform were futile when the State would forgive anything for ready cash. Justinian forbade the traffic in provincial posts, the *suffragia* paid to emperor and praetorian prefect by an official (who borrowed the money and then extorted it with interest from the provincials). But within a year, says Prokopios, he was breaking his own law. He promised to bring in no new taxes, then did so. And the result was that Justin II had to lament in his first Novell 'a treasury overburdened with a plethora of debts and reduced to extreme poverty', and 'an army so desperately in need of all necessities that the Empire was frequently and easily attacked and raided by barbarians'.

Agathias the poet records that 'They squandered the money needed for the army on lewd women, circus-drivers, people of no account, capable only of getting worked up for social disorders and faction-strife.' Since we know that Justinian detested the Greens, this statement can only mean that money was lavished on the Blues and their bosses.

Local self-government was curbed. The peasants' lot was terrible. John Lydos says that in the towns and villages of Asia 'a foreign invasion was less dreaded than the visit of the tax-collectors'. Governors (in 553 and 556) were made responsible for taxes, and did their best, or worst, 'to make the earth yield up the obol that it hid'. The high officials like John of Cappodocia had an arsenal of tortures for extracting money. John Lydos records that along the highways by which grain was carted to the ports, 'there were strewn the corpses of women and children, dead of privations while carrying out these forced-services'. The colons, said Justinian, 'must each submit to his lot'.

And so the State fell back on the magnates after all. Justinian deferred to the Senate, increased its numbers in 537, made it the supreme court of appeal; and he later delivered provincial administration into the hands of the magnates, with whom the higher clerics were now assimilated. And

5

despite the complaints about seizures of State-land, the emperor was becoming an ever larger magnate himself. His estates were extending partly
through confiscations; some fifteen years after his death in almost all the
provinces we hear of private land taken over by imperial officials. The
Patrimony administration which Anastasios set up was ended; the emperor's domains came under Curators of the Divine House. Everywhere
the mercantile mobility visible under Anastasios, with its middle-class
reassertion, faded out; and things hardened, with emphasis on the emperor's personal ownership as supreme magnate rather than on his role
as supreme administrator.

THE TOWNS AND TRADE. For local public works, Anastasios had preferred
to send officials to superintend; in 530 Justinian put everything (works,
costs, accounts) under the bishops and magnates, merely reserving the
right to send a special accountant to look things over. Local authorities
were warned not to recognise anyone with the praetorian prefect's war-
rant. Later Justinian gave the governors the job of looking after basic
public works (roads, bridges) and food; but they had to act through sub-
ordinates, and their powers were limited. The bishop and curials were to
elect a City-Father, a Corn-Commissioner, etc.

Thus the State kept wavering, seeking to assert its central powers and
yet falling back on bishop and magnate.[1]

In the towns, the old amenities had largely gone, street lighting, games
and so on. The liberal professions lost their roots in towns that could not
afford to pay teachers and doctors; and lawyers were in a bad way.
Against this decay the State sought to tighten its hold on industry and
trade. It made a profit from its bakeries. All arms and armour were
fabricated in State-works, forged, inlaid with gold, etc., and sales to
private persons were forbidden. Under the Master of Offices, works existed

---

1 Novell cxxvii gives a slight autonomy to local budgets, but the trend is to restrict
any fiscal independence. The *Defensor Civitatis*, set up originally to defend local interests, is changed in character: he is now a local leading-citizen (by two-yearly
rotation) who cannot hold his own against the magnates. The State intrudes into
municipal affairs through direct finance-controls and through the intervention of the
Church into secular administration: at Alexandria the patriarch had officials regulating weights and measures. In country towns the officials are a sort of corps-of-
notables concerned with tax-collection rather than local affairs: of the old system only
a few obligations as to public services (sometimes hereditary) are kept. In some towns
the notables themselves collect taxes. In 543 the State distinguishes more sharply
imperial and municipal taxes, and local expenses are regulated on the spot by officials
with the function of pay-treasurers. Edict xii shows (for Alexandria) the dependence
of the curials on an official, an Augustal, who looks after both taxes and dues and
expenses for such things as Baths. This official has military authority over two Egyptian provinces and is specially concerned with the somewhat disordered corn-supply.

at Adrianople, Thessalonika, Antioch, Damaskos. At Tyre was the dye-works of the State, with a fleet of fishing-boats. State textile-works for wool and linen were at Cyzikos and Scythopolis, under the Count of the Sacred Largesses, who also controlled the manufacturers and traders in the guilds.

Industry was still considerable: well known were the carpets of Sardes, cottons of Kos, linen of Laodikea, Scythopolis, Byblos, purple cloths of Syria (less costly ones of Miletos), glass of Sidon, pots of Samos, chased iron of Cibyra, paper, glass, textiles of Alexandria, parchment of Pergamon, cabinet furniture of Thessaly. Flax was grown in Elis, spun and woven by the women of Patrai; vegetable dyes came from Phrygia; wines were exported from Lesbos or Askalon and Gaza; sylphium, much used for cooking, came from Cyrene, raisins and figs from Rhodes, cheese from Dardania and Dalmatia; dates from Phoenicia, preserved tunnies from Byzantium. The northern frontier saw a busy trade in slaves, furs, amber.

Routes by land-caravan ran from the Volga, or Cherson in the Crimea, to the Caspian and Turkestan; more south there was a trade-road from Trebizond across Armenia and then North Persia, or through Syria to the Persian Gulf and thence by sea to Ceylon. And Ceylon was reached also through Egypt and the Red Sea. The main worry was Persian obstruction and competition. For Persia lay across all the nine desert-routes. Its merchants chaffered with the Chinese who came through Sogdiana (Bokhara), and controlled the Ceylon trade. To Ceylon goods came from all over the East, silks, aloes, cloves, sandalwood, pepper, copper, musk, castor, jewels; they were loaded in Persian ships which carried them to the Persian Gulf and up the Euphrates to the Byzantine customs at the frontier. Justinian wanted to break through directly to Chinese and Ceylon trade, but failed.

He tried to use a port he held in the north-east corner of the Red Sea (with caravan route to Palestine) and another in the north-west communicating with the Mediterranean, with a customs house in an island near the south end of the Sinai peninsula; but lack of Byzantine ships in the Red Sea checked him. So he tried to use the Abyssinians of the Kingdom of Axum to break the Persian monopoly. But the Persian colony in Ceylon was too well dug-in; and the Empire couldn't use the Greek-speaking colonists in Malabar and Kalliana, as they were Nestorian heretics. The amount of indirect Byzantine trade with India is, however, testified by the coins found in Indian market-areas, brought by Persians and Axumites. Kosmas, a sea-captain turned theological geographer, declared:

All the nations carry on their trade in Roman money from one end of the earth to the other. This money is regarded with admiration by all men, to whatever kingdom they belong, since there is no other country in which the like of it exists.

And he tells a story about its supremacy in Ceylon.[1]

Byzantium itself was a great shipping clearance-centre: silk and other oriental goods from one side, furs from the north (through Huns at Cherson, in exchange for stuffs), slaves, skins, corn, salt, wine from Lazica. Imports dominated. There had long been a market for fine textiles, glass, enamels from Syria in China; but exports to India, China, Arabia were small next to the spices, gems, silks coming in from those areas.

Customs, a flat 10 per cent. rate, were collected at Byzantium, but there were observation-posts at Abydos and the Hellespont. No ship could pass into the Aegean without papers signed by the Master of the Offices; and many articles, wine, oil, lard, weapons, were forbidden as exports to South Russia or the Caucasus. The toll on exports was made at Byzantium. Goods carried from port to port for sale were liable to transit dues, with a limited amount of things for personal use going free. Licences for goldmining involved a yearly fee.

There was a great plague in 542: after which the price of labour rose. In 544 the State issued an Edict. Since the visitation of God, 'traders and artisans and husbandmen and sailors have yielded to a spirit of greed and demand prices and wages two or three times what they formerly got'. The Edict tried to restore the old levels, it forbade a building contractor or an employer of farm-labour to pay more than before 542. (Before the Plague there had been a slump; credit fell and measures were taken to protect the interests of the big Corporation of Bankers.)[2]

When war began with Persia in 540, the private silk-factories at Tyre and Berytos were hard hit. The *commerciarii* of the State-factories bought up all available raw silk, gave their own works what they needed, and sold the rest to the private firms. Buyers were told not to pay more than

---

1 Two embassies were sent to Abyssinia itself, which gained promises but little else. The men of Yemen had no wish to cross deserts to beat the Persians, and couldn't shake the Persian hold on the silk-entrepôts. The Abyssinians also traded with Central Africa, sailed south, then marched inland. Sometimes Byzantine merchants co-operated. Kosmas had seen an albatross on a southern voyage. Justinian (Orthodox) and Theodora (Monophysite) competed for two tribes of the Upper Nile; she got in first with one, and it then converted the other.

2 Interest tended to rise after 472. Under Justinian, the normal rate was eight per cent. (less on good securities); he reduced the minimum of twelve per cent. to eight per cent. but left twelve per cent. for sea-ventures (proof of the risks and profits of trade); four per cent. was maximum for loans to peasants; senators could only take four per cent. That trade stayed brisk is proved by two new mints (Thessalonika and Cyzikos) added to those under Anastasios (Byzantium, Antioch, Nikomedia). Also Alexandria and Cherson minted; and under Justinian, in the West, Rome, Ravenna, Carthage, Sicily. Gold was coined only at Byzantium; silver, there and at Carthage.

15 gold pieces for one pound of silk, but the Persian merchants refused to sell, or sold little; and so there was scant surplus for the private firms. The State fixed a maximum price for silk strips (8 gold pieces) and many firms went bankrupt. In 542 the Count of the Sacred Largesses made all silk-production a State-monopoly, and took over some of the bank-rupted houses. Then ten years later, two Nestorian monks from China or nearby arrived at Byzantium and told the secret of silk. Justinian offered a good reward for the eggs of silkworms, and the two monks returned in due time with eggs in hollow canes. Syria had lots of mulberry trees, and so a new industry was born. Silk was still imported (so much was needed for court-dresses) even when later the Turks occupied Persia; but much of the burden of imports was lifted as the industry grew.

At Byzantium the police-system was tightened up. The Quaestor dealt with non-citizens, inquired into all arrivals, helped those with legitimate business to speed things up, expelled others; and forced the workless into State-industries. A Prefect of the watch acted as chief of police and judge, and a Praetor of the Demes handled crime-waves and corrupt collusions among the *agentes*. The consulship (after a thousand years) was let lapse, to the benefit of the magnates who as consuls had had to spend heavily on a week's festivities.[1]

THE CHURCH AND PROPERTY. The inner contradiction of the established Church was to be seen most obviously in the monasteries which, origina-ting in the wish to reject the world, private property and money, became the main centres for heaping up land in the Church's hands. The estab-lished Church itself took over and increased the immunities of the pagan priesthoods; there was a rush of business-men into the clergy to grab the new advantageous positions of exploitation. Valentinian III withdrew the clergy's trade-concessions, but with little effect. By the sixth century, in Byzantium alone, the church of St. Sophia owned some 1,100 duty-free shops; and every other church, monastery, hospital, etc., claimed the same sort of privileges. But the Church's grip on land was far greater than its grip on trade, especially after it grew fashionable for a rich man to build a monastery for his retirement. Church-lands were exempt from the tax on land changing hands; and exempt, like the land of the rich senatorials, from the *descriptio*, a special tax for difficult times (assessed on the basis of the land-tax). In Egypt, and probably elsewhere, the Church

---

[1] Justinian's economies usually had a pro-magnate bias: he reduced the Shows, ended the corn-dole for the town of Alexandria, delayed army promotions, cut civil, service pensions, stopped the five-yearly donations, kept pay in arrears (when paid, the soldiers were tackled by tax-collectors).

imitated the violence of the magnates. It had its own fighting troops: we meet such a troop collecting arrears. The church of Hermopolis, with a large administrative machine for its estates, had its own soldiers. And the monastery of the Metanoia near Alexandria had its own fleet of corn-ships. Well might Zosimos complain of the monks:

> They renounce legal marriage and fill their populous institutions in cities and villages with celibates useless for war or any service to the State: gradually increasing from Arkadios' time to the present they have appropriated the larger part of the earth, and on the pretext of sharing all with the poor, they have reduced practically everyone to poverty.

THE ARMY AND THE PEOPLE. The army now quite changed from what it was in the early Empire; the Legion was gone, and, with the Guards, there were five groups—Regulars (*comitatenses, stratiotai*) recruited from areas where living was rough and tribal elements persisted, the highlands of Thrace, Illyricum, Isauria; Frontier-troops; Federates, now the most important part of the army, almost wholly cavalry, who, originally barbarians under Roman command, could now be joined by citizens; Allies (previously called Federates), bands of Huns, Heruls, etc., bound by treaty (guaranteeing land or subsidy) and led by their own chiefs; and Retainer Bands, organised by governors and praetorian prefects, but also by lower officials and magnates.

The Retainers were divided into Shieldmen, rank-and-file, and Spear-men, officers; both seem mounted, and were usually foreigners or hill-men. They took an oath to both their own lord and the emperor (which implied State-recognition). They stood by the lord at meals and fought close to him in battle. Belisarios was a Spearman of Justinian before the latter became emperor.

The main change was the complete eclipse of the citizen Legionaries; and the emergence of the Federates as a strong cavalry-force, the key-element of the army. The basic unit was the *numerus*, two to four hundred men under a tribune—a smaller unit than in the legions, suitable for times when many places needed garrisons: a town had its one or two *numeri*. Equipment had come close to the Persian, and was much more akin to the medieval knight than to the ancient legionary. Elaborate defensive armour dominated, cuirass, mailcoat, helmet, metal greaves. In the fourth century the cuirassiers were a *corps d'élite*: now they were an important section of the army, the Cataphracts, carrying the bow and arrow that the Roman citizen-army despised; also lance and sword.

From Maurice's time the demes appear organised in two military de-tachments made up of the factions for the defence of the capital. Now the term demarch applied to the commander of the detachments. Those demesmen who did service in the detachments were listed in special rolls; and through the seventh to eighth centuries they were linked with the palace-guards. They were under the Domestiks of the Schools and the Excubitors.[1]

This late and limited effort to use local and citizen forces for the defence of the Empire brings out even more clearly how scared the State had been to call on the people to fight. An extended picture is given by Synesios of Cyrene of the bedevilled position of the farmer and small-townsman round about 400 A.D., forbidden to take arms in their own defence and suffering the corrupt oppression of imperial officials as well as the ravages of invaders. In a speech which he declares that he delivered before Arkadios at Byzantium he made a stirring call for a citizen-army:

> We should recruit the learned professor from his lecture-hall, the craftsman from his lowlier calling, from the market whoever is there busied, and finally the mass of drones infesting the theatres in their boundless idleness. . . . Peace is assured only when soldiers have been trained to treat the unarmed population as their brothers and to take only such property as has been assigned to them.

And in his letters he speaks bitterly: 'Evidently the government is full of anger against those who try to save themselves', and he gives us vivid pictures of the infuriated people at last taking up arms and fighting back—sometimes when the imperial soldiers had been beaten and hid themselves. Here were the forces of regeneration that the emperors resolutely tried to beat down at all costs. Thus, the passes of Thermopylai had been guarded by the local peasants; Justinian put in a garrison of 2,000 soldiers instead. And a man from Viminakion, who had gone over to the Huns, sharply defended his behaviour to the historian Priskos, pointing to the terrible exactions of the taxes and of a corrupt law-system, and to the hopeless position of the common man in a war: 'The Romans are very liable to perish in war, as they have to rest their hopes of safety on others, and are not allowed, on account of their tyrants, to use arms.'

Sometimes the men of a small town in the danger-zone took things in their own hands. When in 595 the Slavs had been defeated, an officer, Peter—after yielding to the wish of the townsfolk of Novai to celebrate

---

[1] The demarchs became civil officials, probably charged with the police-work of the demes. Of the palace-troops, the Scholarians are now mere parade-soldiers. Young men with a bit of cash buy a place in them, the pay is good and the uniform handsome: Justin I took in 2,000 more for their entrance-money, and Justinian threw them out without compensation. We hear now of a new corps, *Scribones*, used for special missions. For the later part of Justinian's reign: Agathias tells us of the reduced army with soldiers often in beggarly condition forced to desert.

their saint's festival—came next day to Asemos, where he was received with such pomp as the place could command. The town-guard marched out with flags, and he was told they had been set up to fight the barbarians (they had in fact resisted the Huns in 447) and that Justin II had formally recognised them. Peter then tried to take them over in his imperial detachment. They replied that the citizens had borne the cost of their own militia, which was recognised by an imperial rescript; they were their own masters. Peter insisted. They refused and barricaded themselves in the Church. Peter sent an infantry-commander, taxiarch, to the town's bishop, but the bishop sided with his people. Peter degraded the taxiarch and charged one of the Scribonian Guardsmen to arrest the bishop. The whole people rose, chased the guardsmen out and closed the gates. Peter hesitated, then went on his way, while the citizens yelled from the walls praises of the emperor and insults of the emperor's troops who were going off to fight the barbarians.

15

FREE PEASANTS AND THE THEME SYSTEM

THE THEMES. Justinian's effort to extend the Empire while breaking down its prosperity by his decisive fostering of the magnates had had the effect of introducing the first modifications of the Diocletianic basis on which Constantine had built. Already indeed in the fifth century points of strain had shown up, provinces were further subdivided, and Anastasios created a new Vicariate (of the Long Wall). But Justinian made the first large breaches in the system, though unsystematically. He combined smaller provinces in a single large circumscription, did away with most diocesan governors (the link between the provincial governor and the praetorian prefect), and in some cases united civil and military functions under a governor with the rank of *spectabilis*. He was experimenting. Thus, some of the regions of the 536 reform had soon to declare a veritable state of siege: in the diocese of Pontus, the Vicar, suppressed, was set up again in 548 with the attributes of a special commission invested with the widest powers. And in the West the incursions of Moors and Lombards forced the following emperors to create exarchs, army-commanders who subordinated the civil administration to their defence needs.

Maurice first formalised the situation. For a while high civil officials hung on beside the military commander; but in the sixth century they weakened and were wholly replaced by military officials. The Ravenna Exarch took over imperial attributes; his place was the *sacrum palatium*; at Rome he was given an imperial reception. The African Exarch too soon assumed the same semi-independent attitudes. But so powerful was the imperial system that where it maintained control the new military governors were kept in control as its servants, and to some extent the bureaucratic network was able to function and control them. With all the omens of anarchy provided by this militarised system and the extension of retainer bands among the magnates, only at points of extreme stress did the central control slip, and then, after a burst of clashing interests, it was soon reimposed.

Justinian II seems the ruler who made the next important stabilisation. The Theme System proper emerged. A Theme was originally an army-corps, then the area of the corps, then an administrative circumscription.

5*

The two great Themes which first were formed in the seventh century were the Armeniac (the north-west area bordering Armenia) and the Anatolic: these two covered the whole middle of Asia Minor from Cilicia to the Aegean. The Opsikian was set up in Asia, as a bulwark of the capital on its eastern side; Thrace, against the Slavs and Bulgars. The Kibyraiot a maritime Theme (the name is perhaps eighth century), included the southern coast of Asia Minor and the near islands. Perhaps late in the seventh century came Hellas, against the Slavs, and Sicily, against the Arabs.

Normally a Theme was under a General—though the Kibyraiot was under a Drungary and the Opsikian under a Count. It was the governmental form which substantially persisted till the end of the Empire, with many reorganisations of districts and so on, according to the changing fortunes of war, but otherwise surviving as the best way of combining the civil State-apparatus with a dominating military defence-system.

What gave a stability to the Theme, counterpoising the power of the new military nobility, was the linking of the theme-army to the soil. The army was thus largely kept under imperial control, despite the extension of the General's prerogatives. The General, the most important figure in the new system, had risen to this position out of the wrecking of the old senatorial dominances during the convulsions at the end of the seventh century: 'The senatorial order lost its importance, in connection with the crises of the large estate. The decisive blow was given to it under Justinian II . . .' (Levchenko).

The General, with the title of Patrician, has his group of high officials, his Domestik, his Cartulary (who looked after supplies), his Protonotary (in charge of civil affairs and provincial lawsuits). The troops were divided into *turmoi* under turmarchs, subdivided into bands. The full organisation did not evolve till the tenth century, by which time the system of a military caste was stably based. Each soldier was given an allotment according to his time of service and the arm in which he served. Land worth five (or at least four) pounds of gold was the allocation of a cavalryman; a sailor got three pounds' worth. The land was hereditary. Waste was given to volunteers, or war-prisoners were put on it. Soldier-farmers had to pay land-tax like everyone else, but they were freed from all burdens of service, carryings, roadmaking, contributions in kind, etc. If through dire need they were called on for such matters, they were properly paid.

Beside the theme-troops there were cavalry-regiments, usually kept in Bithynia or Thrace, who went with the emperor on campaigns.

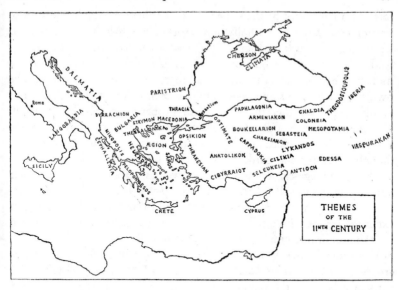

THEMES
OF THE
11ᴺᵀᴴ CENTURY

THE VILLAGE-COMMUNE REVIVED. Contemporary with this development, and in many ways conditioning it, was the rebirth of the free village-commune through the settlements of invading tribal groups, of which the Slavs were by far the most important, and through the sharing out of the land in areas where the magnates fled. We saw how in Asia there rose the Clubmen, fierce guerrillas who shook the Arab power in the rear: and this resurgence of the free peasant, which lasted a couple of centuries, left enduring effects on Byzantine society, its structure and its culture.

The document which enables us to see the way in which the State grappled with the situation is the Farmer's Code, long ascribed to the Isaurian emperors, but probably the work of Justinian II, though carried on by the Isaurians. It is divided into three sections: (1) cultivation of the ground and the relations of farmers to each other; (2) cattle, trees, sheep-dogs; (3) produce, implements, farm-buildings. Its concern is with the *chorion*, the area of the village community, and its internal relations and exchanges. It visualises a countryside divided into *choria*, where all the landowners are working farmers. If a farmer lacks the means of working his land, he may let it to a better-off neighbour; but only in two clauses (9–10) is there any trace of a big owner outside the *chorion* drawing rent.

Each *chorion* is a fiscal unity, where the whole group is jointly respons-ible for the tax-total. The land, which we may presume to have been originally common, has been cut into lots among the community's mem-bers. This division may be set aside on grounds of unfairness; and the lots may or may not be the same in size or value—we don't know. Also we don't know if a lot is wholly of one sort of land. All the area, however, has not been cut up; for successive allocations are contemplated. Grazing land is perhaps always held in common. The whole group is the commonalty, *koinotes*, and the members are the commoners, *koinonai*. The owners of a lot are sometimes plural; it seems the lot is thought of as family-property rather than individual property. It may be cornland, vineland, figland, woodland, vegetable-garden or waste. Corn and wine are the main products. There seem no divisions between cornlands, though vineyards and gardens are marked by trench or fence.

There are wage-earners and slaves as well as peasant-owners and their families: wages are cited for neatherd, crop-watcher, shepherd. The farmer seems to have no right whatever to sell to outsiders, though he can exchange his lot with a fellow-commoner for a season or for good, can let it to him or hire him to work it; but that is all.

The anomaly of the code is sections 9–10, which deal with share-cropper, *mortites*, and big landlord, *chorodotes*. Here the cropper takes nine parts of a harvest; the grantor, one part. And the punishment for not keeping to this apportionment is not so much legal as ecclesiastic—a curse. It sounds more like a council canon addressed to ecclesiastical landlords than an imperial enactment.

The Code is not a complete agricultural code meant to cover all land-working classes in the Empire; it is the law of a village-community of farmers working their own lands. Save for sections 9–10, there is no question of transfer or any other economic exchange or land alienation, except that of one farmer letting to another. Nor does the law give the right of free movement, as it has been taken to do. Some chapters refer to a farmer leaving his lot and going elsewhere; but the terms are doubtful. Two speak of flight, and others could be taken to mean illegal departure. And even if there were freedom to move in the group, it would not prove a similar freedom for farmers who did not belong to such a community.

The Code is partly civil, partly criminal. The civil section (discussed above) seems mostly new, concerned with the new settlements in the Empire and based at least in part on their customs. The criminal part is mainly based on early material, Roman in character, though in a few sections with similarities to Visigothic or other Germanic laws.

Scrutiny shows the Code is in the key of Byzantine legislation. Its basic consideration is fiscal. The commune it considers is an institution of fiscal law. Is it then a legal fiction? The crucial terms are *idios*, *allotrios* and *kyrios*. If *idios* means merely private owner, it may be claimed that the law, so far from dealing with a socially integrated commune, lays all emphasis on private ownership in land. Here is the point to be determined; for *allotrios* merely refers to someone else's land and its coloration will be settled by that of *idios. Kyrios*, master or owner, generally owner of a whole *chora* or village-territory, is hard to pin down, since its basic significance is simply the right to enjoy land.

An analysis of the administrative use of the term *idios* in Egypt proves that it defines a man purely as viewed by the fisc: the man in relation to the dues he is fiscally responsible for. *Idia* means the place for which each individual is registered on the roll of taxes and inscribed on the population-census. Each member of a *chora* has his own particular fiscal domicile, and this can be equally private property or crown land.

It is possible, then, that the Code's terms are drawn from Egyptian practice and applied to the Slav settlements and other free villages. If we set the law in the earlier years of Justinian II, we may suggest that the exodus of high officials from Egypt a generation before, with their manuals of procedure, had helped to bring this particular idiom into prominence at Byzantium itself. We know that bishops and other clergy fled from Asia and Syria with ikons and relics to escape the Arabs, and that they lent the strong Syrian trend to the reformatory Trullan Synod of 692. (And anyway if we had fuller evidence we might find *idios* with a similar reference in other provincial areas.)

In any event the fiscal meaning of *idios* may be taken as proved; and it therefore provides no argument against the position that under the fiscal commune of the Code lay the social and economic commune of the Slav settlers. The Code shows the adjustment of the imperial system to the new situation caused by the Arab shock and the Slav invasions.

Thus in the East as in the West—though later in time by a couple of centuries—the tribal irruptions created village-communes. But the effects are quite different. The continuance of the centralised State, weakened and modified but still imposing its tax-network, made the new village a source of strength in the East, whereas in the West the collapse of the State ensured that the village, controlled by the war-nobility, became a separatist cell.

TOWN AND COUNTRY. Now it was that the Isaurian State, strengthened for its war-task, turned to attack the huge monastic estates; and in doing so drew polemically on a dual set of influences, which mingled for a while and then separated out—a secular humanist trend which disliked monachism as harsh, rigid, dogmatic, anti-humanist, and a dissident religious trend which wanted an egalitarian group-unity. Both trends agreed on disliking image-worship and the cults of the Virgin and the Saints. I shall, however, consider the Iconoclastic movement fully in the next section, and here shall touch only on some economic aspects.

As Iconoclasm broke down through the State's fear of its mass-allies, there appeared an increasing surrender to the big landlord, with the inevitable result of deepening misery on the land and in the towns. The undaunted small-farmers formed their Paulician communes, or, where more distressed and downtrodden, they burst out in violent revolt, as under Thomas the Slavonian.

But in the earlier Iconoclastic period, when the free village was being stably incorporated in the imperial system and there was a certain alliance between the small-producers of the Empire (especially those who were linked with the system of theme-soldiery) and the emperor, there was a lull in such unrest. The towns prospered. Byzantium had never lost the techniques and mathematics of the ancient world; it managed to maintain and reapply them from time to time. The great richness of Byzantine art had behind it the accumulated techniques of the ancient world with further developments largely coming from the eastern provinces; and this applies equally to textiles as to ivory-work, to embroidered pictures as to enamels, to furniture as to mosaic. Mechanical skills, going back to Hellenistic days, were used for grandiose toys—a tree with golden birds that flitted and sang, golden lions that stood up and roared, a throne that rose into the ceiling and descended with the emperor in new clothes. Devices to impress ambasssadors and barbarians, and to express the ritual of death-and-rebirth that ceaselessly attended the emperor.

But the Isaurians were not exempt, more than any other emperors, from the contradictions inherent in Byzantine society. In helping the towns, they depressed the countryside; and however much they wanted to preserve a peasantry suitable for army-recruits, they fell back on the landlords in the last resort. Constantine V, after a bad drought, decided in 766 to restore the aqueduct of Valens, which the Avars had damaged but which had lasted more or less till Heraklios. He brought in 1,000 masons and 200 plasterers from Pontos and the West Asian coastlands, 5,000 labourers and 200 potters from Thrace, 200 pottery-makers (for the pipes?) from Greece and the Isles. The patrician in charge was aided by engineers and overseers. Such works meant increases in taxes. So the orthodox chroniclers accuse Leo III of greed and Constantine V of shutting up all the Empire's gold in his treasure-chests. Nikephoros, a ferocious orthodox opponent, gives us the following picture:

> This enemy of Christ was friend of Gold, and he gathered all the earth's gold in his palace. As the taxed populations were forced to pay the tax, it came about that the earth's fruits and the soil's produce were sold cheaply, so that for a

gold piece you got 60 measures of wheat and 80 of barley, and the same for all provisions. . . . This terrible and inexorable exacter raised as high as possible the tax assessments by extraordinary levies and oppressed the peasantry so heavily that for a piece of gold you could get the whole fruit of a man's labour (for a year?). Refractory peasants were hanged from the trees. Myself I have witnessed such executions.

Nikephoros is speaking shortly after Constantine's death, so we may accept his facts. The increase of cash-taxes meant that the peasants had to sell on a falling market for coin to meet the State's demands. The result was unfortunate for the peasants, but pleasant for the townsfolk who attributed the lowered prices to soil-fertility, good trade, general prosperity: 'This year Constantine made goods abundant in the towns'. Even Nikephoros cannot deny that.

The town-prosperity which showed up clearly in the ninth century meant a considerable demand for slaves. Slaves came mainly from the north—from the Khazars in the Russian steppes. A special tax-tariff was fixed for each sale of slaves in the Empire; the slaves were used mainly for domestic and personal service, but also to some extent for agriculture and industry. Thus, in the ninth century Danielis, the patroness of Basil I, owned large textile works in the Peloponnesos: at her death 3,000 slaves were freed.

Trade was thriving. Merchants arriving at Byzantium were received by the eparch's assistant, who inquired about their business, inspected stocks, laid down terms of sale, and named the date by which the capital must be vacated. When going, they were taken before the eparch to whom they gave a list of the goods they proposed to export. For some time the loss of the Syrian merchant-marine had given the Empire a heavy blow; but in the long run the capital itself profited, now incomparably the main port of Mediterranean trade. For a while all direct trade with Syria stopped, though exchanges went on in a roundabout way, via Egypt, Africa, Sicily, to Monemvasia and the Aegean (the plague route under Constantine V). But slowly direct contacts returned, through Trebizond or by highway across Asia Minor. Altogether a new stress appeared on the Black Sea areas—Trebizond, Colchis (Georgia), Crimea and the steppes. Byzantium was now silk-producer as well as consumer: its State-factories had a monopoly of silk-products all over Europe, though Arabs and Khazars wanted her brocades as much as the West. Hence the basis of ninth-century prosperity.

FEUDAL TENURES. The other side of Isaurian rule, the building-up anew of landlord-rule, appears in the fact that under Constantine V we find the

first definite traces of feudal tenures of the sort that were emerging in the
West. Constantine began the Charistic System, which became dominant
in the eleventh century and which corresponded to the western Benefices.
Land was made over without contract: if the unwritten compact was not
kept, the land was taken back. Constantine no doubt used this method
for the creation of military resources and reserves; but it reveals the breakdown of Roman forms of contract and a weakening of the monetary
forms which he was trying to build up through town-prosperity.

The Charistic System and *Pronoiai*, resumable imperial grants, which
were strong by the eleventh century, were similar to one form of *bene-
ficia*. The other form was to be seen early in the tenth century when poor
landowners gave up their land to lords for protection. This process was to
some extent resisted by the employers, and was linked with the charistic
development: it cannot be proved for the East before the ninth century.
Commendations, frequent in the West, whereby a poor or weak person
commended himself as a client to a rich and powerful person, do not appear
in the East. Neither do grants of immunity. The State remained too strong
for such forms, which emerged in the confused tangle of tribal forms
growing into feudalism in the West.

How are we, then, to define the Iconoclast State, when the Charistic
System begins and when a large-scale setback is given by the Slav settlers
to magnate estates? Though from one aspect the situation reveals a
reversal of feudalising trends, from another it reveals a sharp point of
break from previous systems, so that what comes out of it is something
much closer to the fief-feudalism of the West than anything in the
Justinianic State. We must therefore define the State as a feudal State,
but one with such a heavy ingredient of free village-communes that it is
quite unlike any phase of feudalism in the West. It is clearly not in any
sense a movement-back to ancient forms, a revival of slave-economy.[1]

THE STATE-MACHINE. The ninth century, when Iconoclasm weakened and
faded out, saw the increases of the big estate again and the failure of the
village commune. From the *Saints' Lives* we note how small farmers, even
sons of labourers, could rise to a magnate level. We find also an agitated
movement of population under the incessant attacks of Moslems or
Bulgarians, and drastic methods for resettlement: thus St. Athanasia

1 Angelov stresses the setback to feudalism. Picheta defines the state of tribal disintegration among the Slavs as a 'military democracy'—*i.e.* the war-chief has not
risen to the stage where inequalities of status have importantly begun. (We must
remember that one of the characteristics of the East throughout has been the considerable numbers of free farmers persisting from Hellenistic days, as pointed out by
Levchenko.)

wanted to be a nun, but was forced to comply with the edict ordering all widows or maids to marry barbarians settling in the area—an episode that gives us a glimpse of the way the barbarians were assimilated. State-police were well organised, chasing robbers and jailing suspected spies. There were still many free farmers, but they were declining; by the tenth century the magnates had things well in their hands; and the Byzantine and provincial nobility had intermingled.

Under the Isaurians the administrative machinery of the treasury was much changed. Instead of the two controllers and the praetorian prefect, we meet eight ministries: the General Logothete set over tax-collectors, surveyors, customs-officials and controlling mine-bullion; the Military Paymaster; the Wardrobe Cartulary concerned with military and naval supplies; the President of the Special Department dealing with mints and State-industry; the Cartulary of the Sakellion handling the revenue of the imperial estates, mostly in Asia; the Great Curator administering the estates; the Logothete of Herds; the Count of the Stables running the army-stables of Malagina.

The Sakellion, the central treasury, could inquire into what the other ministries did. The basic taxes were on Land and Hearth; and there were receipt-tolls, death-duties, judicial fines, customs-dues.[1]

This reorganisation shows a further movement to direct controls of economic life in the Empire, with a stress on war-needs.

Nikephoros (802–11) had been General Logothete; he tried to tighten up the State-machinery and extend the monastic confiscations but without any social reforms, except that he did his best to end the tax-evasions by the magnates which Irene had allowed or connived at. He laid down that all monastic or other religious bodies which had been evading taxes must pay all arrears that they had cheated the State out of since his accession; he ordered a new land-survey and added a charge for receipts; he extended the principle of the epibole (of making the whole village or the whole estate liable to the fisc, and not the individuals therein).

This policy must have helped to break up the free village. In fact Nikephoros tried to turn the disruptive effects to the benefit of the State in its war-needs: he conscripted the tax-defaulter into the army, making the local magnate responsible for equipment.

He took over the better land of the rich monasteries (probably by

---

[1] The Hearth-tax was a modification of the old Capitation-tax, levied on the household, at a uniform rate. City-dwellers did not pay it, at least in the capital and the East: they paid an assessed charge on sites, Urban Tribute. All landed property, including holdings on the imperial estates, was due for law-tax. Death-duties (five per cent. under Constantine) was abolished by Justinian, but reintroduced later, then let slip by Irene, revived by Nikephoros.

forced sales at prices fixed by the treasury); and sold farmland on the
Asian coast at fixed prices to unwilling buyers, men used to seafaring and
trade. He re-enforced death-duties, and announced taxes on increment of
unearned income, treating such increment as treasure-trove and bringing
it under a law of Justinian which gave treasure-trove to the crown. But
such a law could never have been applied save in unusual cases of gain.

Usury was forbidden; and the State offered to advance loans at high
interest ($16\frac{2}{3}$ per cent. to ship-owners and traders). The Abydos Customs,
abandoned by Irene, was restored; and a tax of two gold pieces put on all
slaves sold west of the Hellespont. (Previously only a tax on house-slaves
in the capital had been tried.) Nikephoros was strict about market-dues;
quartered soldiers in monasteries and bishop's mansions; sold gold and
silver plate dedicated to religious uses; raised taxes paid by church-bodies.
And he looked out for all of his own officials who were evading taxes,
and made them pay arrears.

Our account of his work comes mainly from a very hostile monk,
Theophanes, who wants to depict him as a malevolent miser; but we may
take it as substantially correct. Under him the State sought to recover
from Irene's policy with its extreme servility to magnate and ecclesiastical interests. It set out an Iconoclast policy stripped of its religious terms
and solely concerned with taxes and army. And though the reaction under
Michael I undid much of its work, certain stabilising elements persisted.

The attack on usury was not new. Far back in pagan days, *e.g.* the Lex
Genusia of 342 B.C., attempts to curb or destroy it had been made; but
the mass-elements in Christianity had an even sharper anti-usury feeling.
After Justinian this Christian attitude is always present, however diluted;
but the Church's tie-up with all possible exploiting forms and forces
made any direct attack difficult. The Iconoclasts, in so far as they expressed
the mass-attitude of the Asian heretics, opposed usury. The *Ekloga* did
not mention it, but the *Procheiron* forbade it. With the triumph of reaction under the Macedonians usury regained legality. What is new under
Nikephoros is the effort to make the Iconoclast position workable by
putting the State in the place of the private usurer.

THE THEME ARMIES. The early Isaurians generalised the Theme. There is no
need here to follow out the changing boundary-lines and the growth of
new Themes; for the system remained the same. What is new, however,
is the emergence of Kleisourarchies, smaller districts in the Anatolic and
Armeniac Themes, controlling the passes and free to take their own initiative against attack. Theophilos, interested in the Black Sea area, brought
the Crimea into the defence-system as the Klimata Theme, and set up

Chaldia, cut out of Armenia, with the Duchy of Koloneia south of it. Before 863 this duchy and Cappadocia also became Themes.

Local militia were organised under an imperial edict. Cadres were sent round (chiliarchs, centenars, chiefs of the squads of fifteen men) to train raw recruits. They called all inhabitants of an area to a meeting, each man to bring a pair of horses and chariots. To disobey involved a death-penalty. We hear of a poor soldier who had lost his last horse, begging one from Philaretes, a magnate of Little Armenia.

The early Isaurians issued an Army Code, which shows the moral tone of the new Iconoclast army. Adulterers cannot serve; a soldier conniving at his wife's unchastity is cashiered; desertion is punished by burning or crucifixion. A soldier must have no connection with trade.

The Theme soldiers were mainly horsemen, with scant pay but with military holdings. Soldiers not in the Themes were called *tagmata*: the old guards of the Schools and the Excubitors, the Watch—with a new lot of guards added by Nikephoros I. Domestiks still command the guards; and there were also infantry-troops, *numeri*, under a Domestik; garrison troops under the Count of the Long Walls; and the emperor's bodyguard, *hetaireia*, barbarians.

The troops were given much consideration: thus there were fine large baths at the station Dorylaion. There were *depoutatoi*, whose work was to rescue the wounded and carry them to the medical staff in the rear: they had water-flasks and two ladders on the left of their saddle for getting a wounded man on horseback. Generals still orated before battles, but there were now also professional speakers, *cantatores*, commissars for inspiriting the men before a fight. They used a religious idiom for building morale. Generally an army was kept in its own Theme. When a general campaign could not be evaded, an envoy consulted the generals to find out what they needed and what they held at their disposal; and to supply gaps, requisitions could be made from towns and monasteries.[1]

---

[1] The footmen of the Katalogs served for usufruct of land, like the Theme cavalry, but on a lower level. The *hetaireiai*, the foreign legion, had special provisions: thus renegade Moslems got land and even seed, and tax-exemption for some years. Punishments were flogging, or shaving of head, beard, moustache, eyebrows (*deirein kai kairein*). The Navy had a big revival in the ninth century (having fallen back after Heraklios reorganised it): the attack from Africa forced attention to the sea. Constantine V and then the Amorians gave much thought to naval matters. The main fleet was at Byzantium under a Drungary: five other fleets were stationed in the Themes. This was the period, however, of Arab supremacy (Magreb and Spain). From 960 to 1043 the Byzantines regained sea-power, with the West coming up and entering the gold-based mercantile worlds of Islam and Byzantium: A. R. Lewis, *Naval Power and Trade in the Mediterranean*, 1951.

16

FINAL TRIUMPH OF THE LANDLORDS

THE NEW LANDED NOBILITY. With the Macedonian Reaction both People and Senate lost their last remnants of political importance; and the basis of power was manifestly left in the hands of the State and the Military Nobility. The decisive shift to magnate supremacy occurred. The Senate was now only a State-council of tame functionaries, a docile witness of imperial acts; and the men of power were the provincial aristocracy, the metropolitans, bishops and abbots of the Church, the high military and civil officials—that is, the provincial aristocracy were the class who dominated the situation: from them came the high officials and bishops. They could buy both the offices that mattered, and dignities and titles. If anyone rose to a high rank without large landed property, he hastened to buy his way into the magnates' ranks. The old noble families and the new functionaries were welded in a single class.

> This class-grouping weighed with a double yoke on the population, grinding them down in the State's name, in the role of Generals, Protonotaries, etc., to draw from them taxes and other charges, and also acting on its own account, covering itself with acquired titles and seeking to reimburse itself as quickly as possible at the peasantry's expense. Harshness in greed, egotism, absence of all scruples in every cheat or carrying-out of irregular affairs, such was the common patrimony of all the powerful, as the very imperial Novells of the tenth century witness. (Vassilievsky.)

The *Lives* of Asian Saints show the big estates growing up. Even lesser magnates have 50 farms with good crops, 800 horses at pasture, 80 trainhorses and mules, 12,000 sheep, a horde of servitors, with a mansion in the domain's heart. In the house, reception rooms finely decorated, a triklinion with a big rounded table for 36 guests, and separate women's quarters. Basil's Danielis had 24 domains: when she visited Byzantium she moved with the splendour of a fellow-ruler; the officials taking off her stock at her death, blinked at the heaps of silver, money, jewels; and 3,000 slaves were sent to be colons in South Italy. The chamberlain Basil, an imperial bastard and a self-made man, had even in his worst days some 3,000 attendants.

Farmers on a noble's lands were called *paroikoi* from the ninth century on: some of them, *mortitai*, paid only a tithe over to the landlord, others were held on harder terms. These *paroikoi* and the surviving free farmers made up the whole peasantry and were classed as poormen, *penetes*.

As Asia in the ninth and Europe in the tenth centuries found some security from attack, investment sank rapidly into the land; and not only the ordinary peasantry, but also the men with military holdings fell, often by force, into the hands of the nobles. The *Peira*, a kind of jurisprudence set up in the eleventh century, shows how the nobles found varied means of grabbing land. They took it from one set of tenants to pass it on to others at more burdened terms, raided villages, made peasants buy back their own stolen farms in mock-markets. They once more controlled tax-collection, and got more and more of a hold on the army.

The new nobility built up powerful families, the Phokai, Doukai, Skleroi, Comnenoi, Palaiologoi in Asia—the Bryennoi, Tornikoi, Melissenoi, Kantakouzenoi in Europe after the conquest of Bulgaria.[1] A new feeling of class-solidarity, as well as feuds and rivalries, appears among these families. And a strong clannish emotion sometimes unites a whole family-group: thus the Comnenian brothers acted together under their mother Anna Daliassena for the good of their ablest but not eldest brother Alexis. These nobles had their country-houses for the summer: to be forced to live at Byzantium was a sort of exile and disgrace—though many had government appointments or court-dignities, on festival days they filed before the emperor, their wives before the empress. They tried to make their mansions small courts, patronising poets and ascetics. They plotted and intrigued. At a pinch the men rode off to the army to rebel; the women hurried to the altar. Under Nikephoros Phokas, Romanos Saronites, very wealthy, objected to surveillance so much that he meditated revolt, but on a saint's advice he went back to a monastery.

The monastics were not far behind the magnates as expropriators of the peasantry. The ninth and tenth centuries saw a vast increase once more of monasteries founded by rich men, by the emperors, sometimes as refuges in cases of political defeat. Poormen sought their protection from tax-collectors and nobles; and monks at times took part in trade. Psellos writes about a monk-merchant Elias:

> Happy to go climbing heavenwards, he is obstructed by earthly cares and the charge of a crowd of relations. . . . It isn't curiosity that sends him gadding, the wish to know the distance between us and the Thule of the Britons, or how the famous ocean washes the earth, what Ethiopians live in the East and which in the West: his will is entirely bent to a single end, to buy merchandise at one place and sell it at another.

[1] In the ninth century the great family seem to be Melissenoi (apparently rising on town property); the Doukai later get European estates as well as Asian.

Monasteries won immunities from the fisc, judicial and administrative autonomy. And the chrysobulls of exemption have the interest of conjuring up the heavy burdens under which the ordinary laymen groaned.[1]

THE STATE AND THE PRIMARY PRODUCER. The efforts of the emperors to arrest the failure of the small proprietor, and above all of the military holder, reveal the State's awareness of the dangerous trend and its inability to take effective measures against the class on which it based its own power. Romanos Lekapenos, tough old Armenian, made the strongest attempt. In 922 and 943 he stated in his laws his strong opposition to the expropriations. He called the *dynatoi*, the powerful, 'a plague of gangrene to the unhappy villages, bringing them closer to final peril'. He tried to give the villagers the right of first sale or lease of any local property falling in (first relatives, then co-proprietors, then near neighbours, then members of the same unit of taxation, could take up the right). *Dynatoi* must not get the poor's land by donation, will, patronage, purchase, rent, or exchange. Soldiers must not alienate their land; any military land alienated over the last thirty years could be reclaimed back without compensation.

> If we have attained such success in our struggle with the external enemy, how can we fail to crush our domestic and internal enemies of nature, men, and good order, through our rightful desire of freedom and the sharpness of the present law?

But he failed. The 928 winter was bad and was followed by several bad harvests; farmers, already hard-hit, had to pledge land to the magnates. Since 922 the *dynatoi* had been permitted legally to buy or otherwise gain land from small-holders only when relatives; and the property was still redeemable within ten years. But in the general distress these clauses were a mockery. So Romanos cancelled all transactions since September 927, allowing compensation for improvements and trying not to close up all loopholes of evasion. Infringement was menaced with heavy penalties; and if a landowner turned monk he could take only the land-price, not the land, into the monastery.

1 In the eleventh century a monastery is freed from the burdens 'of lodging officials, employees of the *tagmata* or themes, auxiliary troops and Roman mercenaries, payment of replacement-indemnities, the putting-up of judges, generals, tax-collectors, entertainment of dignitaries, gifts of any sort, food-supplies for fortresses, requisition of mules, asses, horses, bulls . . . chicken and game, eggs, supplies of products due under the land-tax, capitation taxes and dues, hearth-money, taxes on certain forms of built property, business taxes, taxes of post, roadmaking, taxes on *paroikoi*, furnishing of horseshoes and nails, hay, entertainment of judges, dukes, catapans, collectors, protocentarchs . . . all imperial officials for any cause whatever, equipment of sailors, soldiers, shipbuilding of any sort, sawing . . . any charges or burdens whatsoever.'

These regulations were copied in South Italy; but they failed. Constantine Born-in-the-Purple, reissuing, admitted that they hadn't been observed. And his own laws and the others that went on being promulgated during the tenth century had the same fate. Yet the emperors knew well enough what Romanos had clearly formulated:

> It is the masses, the large number of small men, who supply the State's needs, meet taxes, meet military charges. Everything breaks down as soon as they make default. (Novell, 934.)

Nikephoros Phokas made another attempt to stop the rot. In 964 he complained that the Empire was back at the abnormal condition that had prevailed before the Iconoclasts.

> If we abandon to the monastery the lands from which we gain our revenue, we shall inescapably arrive at the situation which formerly existed, it will no longer be possible to remedy the disorganisation and the insufficiencies of life, for we shall not dispose of any of the means to do so, and our imperial hands will be found paralysed.

In 967 he repeated Romanos' law of pre-emption, but made no effort to attack the magnate bases. His attempts to deal with the monks were more vigorous. In 964 he pointed out that they

> owned no evangelic virtues; they thought at every moment of their lives only how to get hold of new earthly possessions, to raise huge buildings, to buy vast numbers of horses, bulls, goats, every kind of beast of burden; they dedicate all their forces, all their energies to enriching themselves in this way.

He forbade new foundations, forbade the higher clergy and abbots to take over land from peasant or noble. Also, sharply cutting court-expenses, he submitted ecclesiastical property to heavy taxation.

He was murdered. John his murderer made large concessions to Church and court-officials, and when he noticed the magnate Basil ruining rich regions with his greed, 'he expressed his regrets, his vexation, and scolded Basil for his cupidity and cruelty'.[1]

---

[1] Documents of the monastery of St. Andrew at Peristerai near Thessalonika show how the pre-emption laws were evaded: 'Part of an alienated property need simply be "donated", and then the donated part and that offered for sale declared a single unit, for the entire property to pass—despite the law of preferential purchase—into the hands of the recipient of the "donation". It can be surmised that others apart from abbot Stephen and judge Samonas may also have hit upon the method. So the greed of Byzantine landowners, both secular and ecclesiastic, was breaking down all legal barriers, and the good intentions of the legislator were being wrecked by the resourcefulness and cunning of Byzantine judges who sided invariably with the "powerful".' (Ostrogorsky.) He points out also that the government itself gave orders that contradicted the law. So despite legislation against large estates we see the monastery 'receiving land in gift and buying it from private individuals, buying escheated land for next to nothing from the State', and rapidly gaining wide land-estates including property in Thessalonika itself.

Basil II tried to keep some of the checks on magnate encroachments, to revive Romanos Lekapenos' work and to make the magnates pay for taxes which poor farmers or soldiers could not pay. But though no serious effort was made to break down the power of the nobles, Basil had had enough trouble with feudal anarchs early in his reign to dislike an over-strong subject: an attitude set out by Psellos in the advice that he depicts the defeated noble Skleros gives to Basil. Once, in passing through Cappa-docia, he was so well entertained by a noble (who had played a part in the early revolts) that he took him off to Byzantium and kept him there; then on his death confiscated his vast estates. Also when hearing how a poor peasant in Asia had gained hold of a whole village and bought dig-nities, he razed the man's mansion, gave his land back to the villagers, and sent him back to his peasant-status. This act, however, has the stamp, not of any wish to help the villagers, but of an aristocratic hatred of the jumped-up peasant.

In 988, on the advice of monks, Basil definitively repealed the laws of Nikephoros Phokas which limited monastic property, on the grounds that 'they were an offence not only to these very pious monasteries, but to God himself'. After his death Romanos III repealed the laws forcing rich neighbours to pay for poor defaulters.

Historians have usually stressed the good intentions of the emperors in these restrictive laws; and especially in the case of Romanos Lekapenos there is at times a strong feeling for the small farmer, if only because the emperor is intelligent enough to see how much the State needs him for taxes and for defence. But the most striking thing is the almost total in-capacity of all the laws and declarations to divert in the least the feudalising process.[1] We have only to look back to the early Iconoclasts to see how a genuine assault on church-property worked out, though even there the emperors could not move from their main basis in the great estate.

The *pronoia*-system of land-holding grew ever more dominant. As the eleventh-century crisis deepened, the State granted the lands of the peas-ants in *pronoia* (literally, in protection): the possessors guaranteed tax-payments. They divided the land and gave it to farmers on terms. Once they got a footing in the village, the commune was doomed. The free cultivators became bound to tithes and services; and the *paroikoi* grew ever more burdened. As the *pronoia*-owner could not bequeath his land, he tended to wring all he could from the peasants and the earth, not caring

---

[1] We may compare Tudor legislation against the landowners (*e.g.* the good in-tentions of Somerset as Lord Protector) following on large-scale confiscation of monastic lands, and its inability to arrest the trends it deplored—because it sided with the landlord against the peasants.

for improvements. By the later eleventh century free peasants were almost crushed out in Asia.

WORLD-CENTRE. Byzantium remained the world-centre of trade. In the twelfth century, when the capital was about to lose its key-position, the Jewish merchant Benjamin of Tudela declared:

> Merchants of every sort come here from Babylonia, Persia, the Indies, Egypt, Canaan, Russia, Hungary, the lands of the Pechenegs and the Khazars, Lombardy and Spain. It's a great business-city where the merchants come from every country by land and sea; no other city in the world is comparable but Bagdad, Islam's capital. The countless riches which flow into this city from each State, each place and town, surpass all imagination and are superior to the riches of the whole world outside.

By the tenth century the growth of Kievan Russia had made the northern trade of increasing importance. Russian traders could stay in the capital up to six months, residing in the suburb of Saint Mamas. They had to show a safe-conduct from their prince; and could go into Byzantium only in small unarmed groups (less than fifty) controlled by an official. They engaged not 'to commit nuisances', could not buy goods above a certain price and quality, and had their purchases marked by an official. Lodging was free.

In cases of criminal law, the accuser could claim to have the trial carried on by his side's procedure. Varangian-Russians became an important section of the imperial bodyguard.

Trade with Italy was strongly on the increase, through the ports of Venice, Bari, Amalfi. Venice brought slaves, iron, rough cloth, Dalmatian wood for shipbuilding. Round the turn into the eleventh century the Venetians who now controlled the Adriatic, gained a reduction of customs-dues in return for carrying imperial troops when required. The Amalfians too had their warehouses in the capital, and provided recruits for the army; by 1060 their Patrician Pantalcon had a fine palace at Byzantium. Naples and Gaeta also played their lesser part; and then came Pisa and Genoa, greedy for trade.

Thessalonika, as well as being a great trade-centre, produced work in copper, iron, tin, glass—all 'the arts of fire'. As a transit-port between Italy and Byzantium, it gathered traders from France and Spain, from Egypt and Russia. The author of the *Timarion* satire has depicted it so vividly that his account is worth citing, both to show what a fair-day in this world looked like and how the Byzantines of his period wrote. Note how we already have here the kind of fair that later sprang up in the West.

The Demetria is a Festival, like the Athenian Panathenia and the Milesian Panionia, and at the same time the most thriving fair held in Macedonia. Not only do the folk of the country flock thickly to it, but crowds come from every land, every people. Greeks (from wherever you find Greeks), the various tribesmen of Mysia who live on our borders as far as the Ister and Scythis, Campanians and other Italians, Iberians, Lusitanians, Transalpine Kelts. To be brief, the shores of the ocean send pilgrims and suppliants to visit the martyr whose fame is spread throughout Europe.

Myself, a Cappadocian from beyond the Empire's frontier, I had never been at the Festival before, though I had heard it described. So I was anxious to get a bird's-eye-view of the whole scene, to pass over nothing unnoted. I went to a height near the fair, where I sat down and surveyed everything at leisure.

What I saw was a multitude of trading-booths facing one another in parallel rows for a great length and set wide enough apart to leave a broad space for the free passage of the streaming people. The booths were so close and so regularly placed that you took them for straight lines drawn lengthwise from point to point. And at right angles to these were set other booths, also in rows, though not so long—so that they suggested the tiny feet that grow along the bodies of certain reptiles. Odd indeed it was, though there were in fact two rows, they gave the appearance of a single animal through the closeness and straightness of the booths. The lines gave the effect of a long body, the cross-lines looked like the supporting legs. I tell you, when I looked down from high above on the fair's groundplan, I couldn't help thinking of a centipede, an attenuated creature with innumerable small feet under its belly.

And if you're keen to know what it contained, my inquisitive friend, as I saw it afterwards when I came down from the hills—well, there was every sort of textile woven or spun by men or women, all those from Boeotia and the Peloponnese, and all that are fetched in trading ships from Italy. Besides, Phoenicia sends many articles, and Egypt, and Spain, and the Pillars of Herakles, where the finest coverlets are made. These goods are brought direct from their place of manufacture to old Macedonia and Thessalonika. But the Black Sea also contributes to the splendour, sending its products to Byzantium, whence they are brought by horses and mules.

All these things I carefully looked over after I had come down; but even while still sitting on the heights above, I was astonished at the number and variety of the animals, and the extraordinary confusion of sounds that assailed my ears, horses neighing, oxen lowing, sheep bleating, pigs grunting, dogs barking. For dogs too accompany their masters as a defence against wolves and robbers.

In the tenth century a large Jewish community did silk-weaving at Mistra in Sparta, and Thebes too was an important silk-centre, producing webs 'finer than the spider's'. Theophanes declares that at the Fair of Ephesos, on the day of Saint John, up to a hundred pounds of gold was taken in various taxes. And Manuel Comnenos is said to have gained from shop-rents, market-dues and customs a yearly revenue of 7,300,000 pounds of gold. This figure may be exaggerated (Benjamin of Tudela gives it), but certainly such returns were still high. Liutprand tells how the courtiers of Nikephoros Phokas taunted him: 'With our wealth in gold we'll lead all the peoples of the world against the king (Otto of Germany), we'll break him like an earthenware pot which, once broken, can never be put together again'.[1]

MONEY AND INVESTMENT. But despite the trade-activity the basic area of investment was the land, and the middle-class remained unstable, limited, politically passive.[2] Even the town middle-class were half-farmers. In a drought the townsfolk of Thebes organised a procession round their walls to pray for rain.

> At Byzantium, as in the ancient world, economics assumed essentially a char-
> acter of consumption: that is, in its ensemble, production was intended, not
> for external markets, but for internal consumption. Mercantile elements, if
> they existed in the Byzantine economy, played only a secondary role. (Lev-
> chenko.)

Traders were in a small way liable to many ups-and-downs. Typical was Metrios, a peasant of Pamphylia, who lamented under Leo VI, 'As for me, brother, I was a wandering trader of good repute, with a thousand *nomismata*. To this thousand I added more belonging to some third parties, and procured a big stock of merchandise . . . and I put in my purse a sum of 1,500 *nomismata*.' Then all was lost, 'and I fell from great riches to extreme poverty.'

The only extensive production was by the State. Private industry tended to be small, carried on in workshops, by an owner with two or three companions or apprentices. By the tenth century the only alternatives for investment (apart from land) were hoarding or luxury-objects—or the buying of a government-job, which worked out as a sort of annuity. For a good sum a title such as Protospathar might be bought, with 10 per cent.

[1] Other trade-towns of importance were Dyrrachium, Corcyra, Demetrias, Adrianopolis, Selymbria; and in Asia, Antioch, Mistra, Trebizond, Tarsos, Attalia, Chios, Phocaia. In the eleventh century the Venetians demanded the right to instal trade-depots there. An Arab geographer says of Trebizond, 'All merchants frequent it. All Greek textiles, all the brocades that we receive, pass through it.' Benjamin of Tudela found a city on his route in almost every day's journey; the Comnenoi conceded the Venetians the right to trade-colonies in twenty-eight towns; other sources cite many other towns.

[2] The tenth century saw a slight change in interest to the lender's benefit. Under Diocletian the terms (12 per cent. for sea-ventures; 8 per cent. claimable by professional userers, 6 per cent. by ordinary persons, 4 per cent. by senators) were based on a 100 *nomismata* to one pound of gold. Constantine reduced the ratio to 72 *nomismata* per pound, and the fixed rate tended to adjust itself to the new ratio. By the tenth century interest was reckoned as 6 out of 72, etc., *i.e.* normally $8\frac{1}{2}$ per cent.—with magnates getting 5·55 per cent., usurers 11·11 per cent., and sea-speculators $16\frac{2}{3}$ per cent. Retail profits were fixed by law at $16\frac{3}{4}$ per cent.; there were no middlemen.

for life on the outlay; a minor court-post brought in about 2½ per cent. and could be left to heirs or sold. Hoarding often reached high levels. In the early eleventh century we find a patriarch with 2,500 pounds of gold, and a Bishop of Thessalonika with 3,300. John Kamniates says that at Thessalonika in his time many citizens had large hoards of gold, silver, jewels.

Wealth gained by financial adroitness (as by the Patriarch Niketas in the tenth century) was not respectable.[1]

But Byzantium remained financially intact, never even holding up payments. 'By her money she controlled both the civilised and barbarian worlds' (Gelzer). And while in every century after the breakdown in the West, she fed the outlying areas, northern and western, with as much economic energies, goods and techniques, as they could absorb, after the fourth Crusade her wealth was spilt all over the West, rapidly speeding up economic development. The term *bezant* (*i.e.* Byzantine money) was used in the West for all gold coins, even Arab ones. And the Arabs took over the Greek coin-term *aspron*. Also, from *charagme* (*charasso*, to engrave) came the Arabic *haradj*, used to express taxes in kind, as well as the Venetian *caradjii*—an excellent example of Byzantine economic penetration east and west.

THE ORGANISATION OF THE GUILDS. At Byzantium the State had its mint, its arsenals, dockyards, textile workshops (for the most costly silks and purples). Otherwise the shops were small, working for the luxury-market. Along Middle Street, between the square of the Augusteum and the Bull, were shops with gold embroideries, goldwork and jewellery, silverwork, bronzework, ivories, enamels, ikons in mosaic or paint. An Edict of Leo the Wise enables us to see in detail the kind of organisation that persisted through these later years.

This Edict is not concerned with the inner organisation of the trade-corporations or guilds; it is an administrative act dealing with their relation to the State and its monopolies, with the guarantee of essential supplies for the population; but twenty of its twenty-eight chapters deal with the guilds and we can learn much from them.

The preface shows how the concept of divine law giving limits and a fixed order to all social groups now pervades legislation and thought. The Law is set out by His Serenity the Emperor 'so that the human race may be governed as is fitting and no man may oppress another'. And so the man who makes soap out of animal fat in Lent or on a fastday and 'thus

---

[1] An anecdote tells how Theophilos considered a trading venture by his wife disreputable.

soils his workers' is to be whipped, shaven, and deprived of his right to carry on the trade. He has upset the universe's balance. For the same reason no man may exercise two trades at the same time. Things, however, are much less rigid than in Justinian's day: a master may change trade if he does it in an orderly way, and workers are engaged temporarily with wages.

The Count of Sacred Largesses controlled State-firms; the prefect looked after private firms. For obvious political reasons the State had intervened in or built up (i) the food-supply, which was looked after by its guilds and sold at low prices (apart from supplies needed for the palaces, for holiday distribution, for soldiery), (ii) army-equipment, to ensure efficiency and to keep certain things like Greekfire secret, (iii) goldmines and mints (a small part of bullion going to the smiths, the rest to the mint), (iv) most public works—a small church might be built by contractors for a private patron, but the larger ones were reared by State and Church together. Under the prefect's control the guilds had various civic jobs, such as drainage.

After the crisis in the silk-trade in Justinian's day, private manufacture was allowed, but under supervisions. The primary materials were imported and made-up by the State (and often corruptly traded-in by court-officials): the surplus was bought by the guild of silk manufacturers and allocated to members. A similar method was used in all industries where materials had to be imported. Over the years provinces of sale had been worked out between State and private maker; everyone knew pretty well the market he was producing for. The *gynaikia* or female sweatshops of the State were worked by slaves in the palace-area; though also a number of specialists, *e.g.* for dyeing, would be needed. The State-works, being larger than the private shops, brought together a number of processes, and thus were in advance of the shops; but on the other hand slave-labour dominated in them.

The guilds were liable to be called on to fill any gaps in State-production. Their services could be requisitioned, and they had the duty of meeting State-demands at whatever recompense the State decided. The best quality soap was reserved for court-use. The guilds also acted as official experts and valuers, and as police: silverworkers had to inform the prefect if a woman tried to sell silver or gold objects, pearls or precious stones (with the view of seeing that they were not exported). Bankers and moneychangers also acted as police agents.

The State thus controlled sales (especially of food), fixed prices, watched weights and measures. It prevented the building-up of stocks for price-rigging. And the fines for trade-infringements, much mentioned in the law, helped its income. A trader paid a fee on joining his guild, a part of which went to the State: he must keep up his industry's good name and have no foreign contacts.

There was no policy of trade-expansion: only of conservation and of attraction. Byzantine shippers had fallen away before foreign competition, but all the State was concerned about was to control the foreign traders their length of stay, their movements, their business. The prefect carried on the surveillance, and tried to get rid of the traders as quickly as possible. We hear, however, of a Syrian trader domiciled for over ten years at Byzantium, so there must have been ways of getting privileges. Indeed the Macedonian epoch was one of trade-treaties, *e.g.* three times with Russia in the tenth century.

The State entered into every business relation, inspected stores and accounts, owned a swarm of officials (though guild-members were also encouraged to denounce one another). If you refused an inspector entry, you were whipped and shaved. Everything was arranged so that the big man had the small one at his mercy, and could crush him if necessary.

Guarantors were needed for a candidate to a guild. In the Silversmiths, five members had to guarantee to take all risks resulting from the entry. Only substantial men could do that. There was no general consultation of members. The corporation-head and the prefect settled matters. The policy was to divide guild from guild, member from member. A master could not buy where he chose; he was told what merchant would suppply —with heavy penalties for disobedience. Also he might not infringe a State-monopoly: thus, there were three kinds of silk—one not for sale at all, one for which a special certificate was required, one that any master could make.

An advantage was the common capital from which buyings were made, with proportionate sharings-out. Middlemen were strictly suppressed. Each guild had its patron saint, its private and public festivals.

The prefect had under him all the guilds (indeed all the citizens); he kept the registers (the lists, the solvency-declarations, etc.); appointed his deputy, assessors, minor officials; named the guild-heads; controlled entries; was police-chief of the city, judged infractions of rules, carried out his own judgments; had direct access to the emperor on matters of trade and industry; had charge of the public peace, approved openings of shops, sites, methods of display, fixed prices; set his mark on goods and on weights and measures; controlled exporting; and saw that safety-precautions and Sunday-rest were obeyed. The assessors were specially attached to a guild; for some trades they kept the stocks of raw materials.

The guild-heads held the treasury and saw that all was in order, but took police-action only at the prefect's charge. They could arbitrate on matters that did not need to go to the prefect. Typical regulations ran as follows. Shops must be shut and fires out by 8 p.m. to stop boozing and brawls; moneychangers and bankers on market-days must attend their own counters; grocers (of spices) might set up in any quarter and make a 16 per cent. profit; linen must not be displayed in the shops or on benches, but on shoulders, during market-days; shops must shut Sundays and festivals, save for candle-sellers outside churches; also on such days food and wine could be sold after 10 a.m.; food could be set out in the streets in open sacks and barrels.

Exports were controlled with special rigour. Cult-objects were particularly important among exports: they spread the imperial influence. 'The blood that the martyrs shed served to open up new markets' and to extend the diplomatic network.

THE WORKSHOP. What sort of workshops do we find? The State kept up a slave-system of production, but the guilds show a combination of familial labour and wage-work. The State, using hired labour and slaves, brought both down towards a servile status; the workshops show the contrary trend. It was thus a misfortune for the workers to come into the State's orbit, *i.e.*, when, say, a weaver perfected some method and was attached with all his employees to the court: he got a good rank in the administrative hierarchy, but the employees' status fell. Or, say a man married a shell-fisher's daughter: he was attached to State-industry and his children after him. Condemned men were often sent to mines or quarries. And if a slave in a State-workshop was freed, he still did the same work, under practically the same burdens. Pay under the State was in the hands of the master of the *corpus*: he often gave his workers just enough to keep them alive. The only escape for the worker was to rise to mastership by ability or influence, or get into the Church.

Private workshops were small. At the most they had a dozen men under a master, *mastoros*, with sales-bench cutting workshop from buyers. A defaulting guildsman could be expelled, lose his goods or slaves, be fined, beaten, head-shaved (in which case he'd be howled-at in the streets). A worker was taken on by a contract specifying the nature of work, the time for completion, materials to be supplied; once he signed he must do the job or find some fault on the master's part. In a big job (palace or church) each section was worked by a group under a foreman, *e.g.* painters were quite distinct from marblers or carpenters at their side; and there were masters undertaking the walls, the dome and so on.

If a master thought he had underestimated costs, he could complain, and the Prefect decided the case on the advice of experts. The law admitted the possibility of a master's negligence; but greed, malice, cheating and the trouble of 'foolish words' were all attributed to the worker. If a master failed to complete a job, he paid damages; if a worker, he got bodily punishment and might be banished from Byzantium.

A workshop had its basic cadre, its wage-workers, its slaves. The cadre was made of the master's family, plus a worker or two chosen for ability or hard work; its members weren't paid by exact contract, but had security. The hired men had an exact contract, but were only there for the job. Apprentices were taken on by contract, paid by being fed and taught, and often lodged in the shop. Slaves suffered different and worse penalties than the free for defaulting, and could set up shop only when guaranteed by a master. They were used by the richer guildsmen, sometimes as workers with the cadre and hired men, sometimes on their own. They must have made up a good proportion of the small-workshop's men, doing the hard and dull jobs; but though still with no juridical personality, they must generally have had a better time in the small works than in the State-factories.

The guilds never became centres of political intrigue like the factions; they never even attempted to put out a trade-policy. Still from the eleventh century the workers were a force to be reckoned with: Leo Phokas in 970 tried to win over the Controller of the Silk Guild on account of his influence with the workers.[1] At Byzantium was a reserve of cheap labour, with wages kept down by law. A month's contract, with a month's pay in advance, was laid down as the mode of contract—a mode which clearly shows a desire to keep labour mobile and cheap. What is surprising is the mixture of strict controls and free labour. What prevented the situation from breeding a bourgeoisie like the western towns was the State-regulation and the State-factories with slave-labour; but we cannot separate these factors from the larger process which in the East maintains a town-form with strong elements of the ancient *polis* and a State-system able to enforce its basic demands.

The Byzantine guild-system had important influences both on the East and the West. The Turkish sultans copied the prefect's edict, and some of its provisions were still in force in the Istanbul of Mustafa Kemal Pasha. In western laws of the twelfth century many provisions resembling those of the edict have been found. There were 'remarkable similarities between the organisation of the silk industry at Constantinople and that of the

1 The populace remains turbulent (*e.g.* 1042, it breaks in the doors of the Sacred Palace, losing some thousands in the battle with the guards, pillages and destroys), but has no independent role; it can only effect a change of masters. In 963 a court official, Bazil, led thousands of his slaves in revolt, merely making Nikephoros Phokas' rise the easier.

cloth industry at Florence and Douai in the tenth and eleventh centuries, and that of England in the later centuries'. How could it be otherwise? The western textile industries matured in periods when Byzantium was still the world-centre of trade; and the merchants from the West must have gained all information they could when at Byzantium about its guilds.

OFFICIALS AND SOLDIERS. There is no need here to enter on the highly complicated officialdom which had emerged. Too much attention has been paid to the systems of etiquette and the court-flunkeys under the Macedonians, to the detriment of a serious understanding of the vital elements in Byzantine culture. The central government remained civilian, despite the themes, and was run by two kinds of officials, *kritai* and *sekretikoi*— the latter being mainly finance-ministers. A very important man was the Logothete of the Post, who, by controlling communications, became a sort of Foreign Minister as well as co-ordinating relations between the emperor and the other ministers. He looked after the diplomatic service.

In the ninth century, the *tagmata*, the four cavalry regiments of imperial guards, grew in significance, stationed near the capital. The Generals of the Eastern Themes had a fixed salary from the State, with the General of the Anatolics ranking highest. Each General had eleven classes of officials for both military and civil work. Despite his great powers, he could be deposed at the imperial will, and complaints could be lodged against him. The Chartulary in the bureau, who paid soldiers and officials, and the tax-collectors of the Theme, were directly under the central government; and legal cases of importance went to Byzantium. Special Generals could be sent anywhere in emergencies.

The Theme System was now at its height. With the successes of the Seljuks and the irruptions of the Crusaders, the imperial system rapidly declined and broke up.

The heavy cavalry, *kaballarioi*, with steel caps, mail shirts, steel frontlets (for officers and front ranks), with cloaks coloured according to regiments, were the basic force. Footmen were mostly light archers. The foreign legion had so many privileges that men paid to get in. Bardas Phokas, a noble, had a picked Georgian guard all equally tall and clad in white armour. Varangians became prominent in the earlier eleventh century; and soon the bodyguard was composed of all races, Russians, Turks, Franks, Germans, Bulgars. In the eleventh century foreigners, however, held no high commands: Peter, 'Nephew of the King of Germany', under Basil II, never rose above the rank of provincial Domestik, for all his merits. But

6

under the Comnenes things changed, as the theme-armies weakened and
mercenaries grew more important.

Wars were waged as follows. The Moslems crossed the border; the
local commander reported; the General warned the near themes; his
cavalry set out to harry the foe; his foot soldiers occupied the passes on
return, while the near themes sent troops converging on the point for
which the foe was thought to be making. That is, strategy was generalised
from the methods whereby Umar in 863 was trapped on the Halys.
Counter-raids might also be made, and the fleet sent out to ravage the
enemy coast.

For an offensive, the emperor led out the *tagmata*, joined at points along
the great military highway across Asia by theme-detachments (mainly
footmen, though each theme sent horsemen too). Caution was high: the
army cost a lot, men and materials must not be thrown away. Trickery
was advised, such as the spreading of stories of imaginary victories, to
raise morale, or the despatch of incriminating letters to an enemy general
to embroil him with his commanders. But a pledged word must be kept,
women unharmed, captives spared. A study was made of the weaknesses
of the enemy. Thus, the Franks, rash, were easy to ambush; their commissariat was bad, so they were liable to desert; they were generally insubordinate and corrupt, so delaying tactics were better than a pitched
battle. Slavs, lightly armed, were dangerous only in difficult country.
Saracens were strong fighters, but not well organised; their morale fell in
defeat: so attack them by night when they were laden with booty, or in
bad weather. Stress was laid on finding new methods of war.

The navy had revived in the ninth century. After the storming of Crete
in 961, Arab sea-power went down. Nikephoros said to Luitprand, '
alone command the sea.' Constantine VII claimed the rights to the Strait
of Gibraltar. But weakening showed again when Basil II gave the Venetians the duty of policing the Adriatic.

There were dromons or runners, bireme with a hundred to three hundred men, swifter biremes and galleys with a single oarbank. The ships
had rams, but the main weapon was Greekfire. Navigation was carefully
studied, and weather rather than battles was used to destroy the enemy.
If the fleet fought, it used the crescent-formation of the ancient Greeks.
The ships signalled by flags or lights.[1]

1 Merchant-ships could be commandeered; stores of Greekfire existed in the main
ports. When Krum captured Mesembria in 812, he got the supply there. In the army
Kabbalarioi also wore linen or woollen cloaks over armour; sword, dagger, bow and
quiver, lance, cap-tuft, lance-pennon. Of footmen, some provinces supplied javelin-
men; and to hold the passes there were heavy infantry with mail, axes, shields,
swords, lances.

17

LAST PHASES

THE WEAKENING STATE. The Macedonian State broke down in the mid-eleventh century through a cleavage between the top-heavy bureau-ratic machine and the feudal nobility of the provinces. The inevitable result was a period of anarchy, with a reorganisation of the State-form on a lower level of unity and complexity. The twelfth century saw the Empire in decay, shattered by the Seljuks, while in the West the cities and kingdoms which it had integrally helped into existence were rapidly advancing. Till 1204, however, Byzantium was the world-centre, radiating vital influences in all directions.

More and more the central government yielded its powers to the provincial nobility, while in Byzantium and the other ports the Venetians, Genoese, Pisans and others gained the economic upper-hand. The emperors were growing as impotent as western kings hedged in by insubordinate barons. The nobles became steadily more independent, and even took arms with the enemy against the Empire. Under the Angeloi Trebizond became an independent State under an Armenian family.

As the State failed, its exactions in the areas that it controlled grew more vexatious and violent. At Athens Akominatos denounced the pillaging officials: 'They behave like barbarians at Athens, this ancient once-happy town, the enemy of tyrants, the common fatherland of all instructed persons.' Especially in Greece there swarmed 'farmers or gatherers of taxes, praetors, collectors of taxes for naval construction more than the number of frogs with which Jehovah infested Egypt.' And the local magnates behaved as outrageously as the officials. The lord of Nauplia put double the burdens on impoverished Athens than had fallen on Nauplia and Corinth. Akominatos could not collect moneys due to the Patriarch from the isle of Aigina close by: most of its people had fled and the remnant were in collusion with the ravaging pirates.

In other parts the unhappy people fled to the Serbs, Hungarians, Turks. Recruitment for the army grew harder; and dukes replaced the generals in the straitened territory. The mercenary army increased. And the civil population feared the imperial troops as much as any invaders.

The troops, strong with imperial decrees, irrupted into the towns and village
and plundered townsmen and villagers of the fruit of their labour and eve
of all their goods, so that the wretches, to avoid becoming their slaves, sough
safety in flight, or indeed, as a last resort, joined the army-ranks. (Akominatos

Fallow or cultivated land had increasingly been granted to lords an
officials in *pronoia*. In the twelfth century the system expanded. The land
of a *pronoia*-holder formed an independent circumscription, in which th
lord enjoyed the judicial and administrative rights formerly held by th
State, imposed burdens and charges on the tillers, and paid a part of wha
he gained to the Treasury. These *pronoia*-enclaves tended to extend, en
gulfing the Empire like monastic lands. Originally they had been cede
for a term; but now they have been taken over in hereditary ways. Mor
and more they approximated to the western benefices.

The two sections of Europe had thus in the twelfth century grown to
gether by devious and often contrary ways. 'So when, after 1204, th
western feudalists had established themselves on the borders of the ancien
Roman power, they adapted themselves without difficulty to the usage
and customs of the Byzantine provinces' (Levchenko).

The Comnenes had to fall back even more thoroughly on mercenarie
in such a situation. The twelfth-century army was made up of Anglo
Saxons (who fled from England in numbers after 1066 to Byzantium)
Pechenegs, Turks, Georgians, Slavs, Franks, Germans; and besides oppres
sing people, these soldiers had to be well paid, which increased the ta:
pressures. Efforts were made to train the strange crew in large camps
and discipline was enforced by savage penalties, with donations and dis
tributions of equipment to encourage.

EAST AND WEST CONVERGE AND CLASH. I have stressed the way in whicl
eastern and western feudalisms were at last converging; but we must no
make the error of considering them identical. To the last the Byzantin
city held elements of the ancient *polis*, arrested by the centralised State
control which might weaken but which survived in so far as city-lif
survived. Therefore the Byzantine city and the State that reposed on i
was different in certain fundamental ways from the city born out of th
western commune and the national State which arose to co-ordinate th
new burst of economic and social activities. Because of the break in th
West, where the State had been broken down and only built up slowly an
confusedly, that new burst had become possible. But Byzantium, becaus
of the very virtues that had kept it strong during the troubled centuries
now went down, unable to grow in pace with the West.

In grasping this twelfth-century position, we must, however, alway

:eep in mind that the new life now appearing in the West had only been
nade possible because Byzantium had held back and civilised many
)owerful foes, had maintained the trade-routes, had continued with its
ich cultural life, transforming the ancient inheritance into forms most
·itally assimilable by the twelfth century.

Its great work was done. If at this moment it had been wiped out
inally, the future course of Europe would not have been so very different
·rom what it was. But all the same its continued existence till the mid-
ifteenth century had valuable effects. It meant that the impact of the
Turks on the Balkans and Central Europe was considerably delayed, and
hat Byzantium could continue with its work of cultural transformation,
naking possible the Renascence in the shape in which it appeared.

Though already in decline, Byzantium was still in 1204 the greatest
·ity in the world. 'The whole medieval world has dreamed of Constan-
inople as of a city of marvels seen in a mirror of gold' (Diehl). And
Villehardouin has recorded what the Crusaders felt in 1203, as they
inchored in the Golden Horn.

> They couldn't think that in all the world so mighty a city could exist, when
> they saw those lofty walls and those rich towers with which it was almost
> wholly surrounded, and those rich palaces and high churches, so many that
> no one could believe it unless he had seen it with his own eyes; and the length
> and largeness of the city which over all others was sovran.

Since the world was created,' he admits of the sacking, 'never was there
;o much booty in one town.' This booty, treacherously carried off, had
he effect of spreading Byzantine standards of art and luxury all over the
West in a single wave, and did much to speed up the economic developments already begun.

> The booty was so great that nobody would be able to give you an account of
> it. Gold and silver, and vessels, and precious stones, and satins, and silk clothes,
> and cloaks of vair, of grey, and ermine, and all the costly things that ever were
> found on the earth.[1]

Not that the common people lost much; they had little or nothing to
ose, as Niketas Choniates admits: 'The general disaster delighted them,
ind they said, God be praised, now we are better off!' They hoped for a
lightening of burdens, though they were mistaken in their hope. For the
moment, however (Niketas tells us), they were able to buy pillaged
valuables cheap; and the tillers and shepherds of Thrace scoffed malici-
)usly all along the route of his flight. He had to pretend to be a beggar,

---

[1] Much was destroyed. The brutal and uncultured Crusaders smashed and burned
a vast amount of art-treasures and of libraries, an irreparable loss to Europe and the
world

and his womenfolk had to go muffled up and bent to look like old women to escape the ravishing Crusaders in the streets.

A BAFFLED EFFORT. One effect of the Latin kingdoms set up in the East was the stimulus given to the theoretical basis of feudalism: for in devising constitutions, the feudal lawyers were able to work out logical constructions like the Assizes of Jerusalem. But the purpose of this book is to examine the part played by Byzantium in the creation of Europe; and since with the thirteenth century the political importance of Byzantium is slight, I do not wish to consider these later centuries in detail, till we come to their cultural and religious contributions. In the next section I shall deal with the fourteenth-century revolt of the Zealots, the last great flare-up of the throttled energies in the Byzantine towns. Here it is enough to point again to the value that the expiring Empire was to Venetians and Genoese who invaded its ports, used its protections and controls, and poured wealth into Italy, making possible the vital city-life of the thirteenth, fourteenth and fifteenth centuries.

But there is one episode of the twelfth century, noticed in chapter 10, that I should like to describe more fully, since in it we see the last attempt of the people to assert themselves before the doom of 1204.

In 1180 the Byzantine populace sacked the palace of the prefect and the procurator of the supreme court; they attacked and pillaged many houses of the wealthy. In particular the concessions to the Venetian merchants had exasperated them; and they felt that the regent, Mary of Antioch, a Latin, was betraying them. Andronikos, who belonged to a lateral branch of the Comnenes, came forward as a popular leader. A man who might be called 'the Byzantine Alcibiades-Nero, epicurean, ambitious, well endowed, a genially ferocious liver . . . brave, base, crafty perfidious, chivalric' (Marx). He had spent six years in prison on a treason charge; escaped and took refuge with Yaroslav, prince of Galich, then wandered in Palestine, Syria, Bagdad, Georgia. Pardoned, he lived in a Paphlagonian town. When in 1182 a revolt broke out at Byzantium, he was sixty-seven, but he marched with some soldiers to Chalkedon, opposite the capital, 'to unburden the emperor of evil counsellors'.

The Venetians took measures to keep him out, but the fleet then revolted, and the populace massacred the Italians, who numbered some 60,000. Their rich quarter was burned down, and 4,000 survivors were sold to the Turks as slaves. Andronikos was proclaimed emperor. Though he had been supported by a group of nobles, he now called himself emperor of the peasants, and gave his government the task of breaking the territorial aristocracy and driving out foreign exploiters.

To read these aims correctly, we must, however, see them as a radical effort to revive State-power by basing it on the only class that could reverse the process of decay. Niketas Choniates, a strong enemy, had to admit that in his few years Andronikos restored internal administration to a remarkable degree.

He sought to help the poor and the farmers; personally examined complaints and gave justice without concern of rank; and set out a series of measures to suppress the exactions of officials, the claiming of 'voluntary gifts'.

> If a man paid his taxes, nothing more was asked. He wasn't plundered of his last shift as before, he wasn't killed by violent treatment. The mere sound of Andronikos' name acted like a spell, the greedy tax-collectors were dispersed, he acted like a scarecrow for those who piled up taxes against orders. . . .
>
> It followed that people, sunk in slumber for so long and reduced to a death-level by social evils, as if they heard the Archangel's Trumpet, woke up from a long painful sleep, and revived. (Niketas.)

He suppressed wreckers. Fugitives returned to the land, and the Italians did not carry off the profits of trade. Food-prices went down.

The nobles were harassed, and swore to break Andronikos. He replied with a terror. The nobles fomented revolts in Asian towns, and a noble took charge of Cypros and declared it to have seceded from the Empire under his rule—an unprecedented act in Byzantine history. Andronikos went on hanging, burning, blinding the nobles who opposed him. As a result the noble Alexis Comnenos made a pact with the Latins; and the Normans in Italy attacked the Empire. In the summer of 1185 William of Sicily assaulted and took Dyrrachium, then turned to Thessalonika. In August he captured it by assault, and the citizens were butchered.

The Byzantine populace in fear accused Andronikos of failing to defend his country. Niketas, who hated both Andronikos and the people, thus described the latter:

> Stupid and impudent citizens of Constantinople, pork-butchers and curriers above all, as well as those who spend all day in shops and cookhouses and gain their living by mending shoes and hardly earn their bread with the needle . . . In any other city the populace is unreasonable and ungovernable; but that of Constantinople is distinguished specially by its frenzy and obstinacy, since it is made up of various races. It is justly blamed for its inconstancy, weakness, and fickleness. To manifest its lack of respect for authority seems natural to it. Those it chooses today will soon be chastised like criminals.

A noble, Isaac Angelos, escaped from the secret police and took refuge in St. Sophia. The agents of the nobles managed to raise the people against Andronikos, who was caught trying to flee to his Tauro-Scythians (at

Galich). The triumphant nobles put him to death with terrible tortures, while his army was fighting the Norman invaders.

FROM EMPIRE TO NATION. Thus the demoralised city-populace put an end to the 'attempt, unique in the history of Byzantium, to create a democratic monarchy' (Levchenko).[1] That the Church had played its part in aiding the reaction was shown by Isaac Angelos using St. Sophia as the centre from which to launch the counter-revolution.

This episode of Andronikos and that of the Zealots in the fourteenth century, are the two cases when the Byzantine city tried to break through into the new bases which were emerging in the West. And it is notable that the bold effort by Andronikos appeared as part of a frustrated effort to assert Byzantine nationhood.

For, just as we find in Byzantium the transitional forms between the ancient State and the western medieval State, so we also find the transition from imperial State to national State. The first decisive shift in this direction occurred in the seventh century, when Syria and Egypt were lost and something of homogeneity appeared in the area ruled from Byzantium. The development then initiated continued, with a long oscillation between imperial ideas and efforts of expansion, and ideas and forms more proper to the national State which in the West appeared finally in France, England, Spain.

In the tenth century, the new sense of nationhood was strengthened, partly through the work of the Humanists who since Iconoclast days had looked back to the great Greek past. Thus the dialogue *Philopatris* (*The Patriot*) was written in the days of Nikephoros Phokas; and Psellos in the next century calls himself *philoromaios* and *philopatris* (terms which show the conflict and fusion of the two ideas of empire and nation). The words *patris, philopatris, patrios*—fatherland or nation, patriot, national—take on more and more a modern coloration. By the fourteenth century a thinker like Thomas Magistros of Thessalonika, who defines a city as made up, not only of houses and monuments but by the accord of the citizens on all questions and their respect for traditions, is fumbling at a reconciliation of ancient ideas of the *polis* and modern ideas of the nation.

[1] Clearly there were demogagic elements in Andronikos; and we cannot attribute to him any clear-cut scheme for a bourgeois democratic monarchy. No doubt he looked finally to a system of landed nobility. But Levchenko's phrase can pass to express the fact that Andronikos made certainly the most ruthless attack before the Zealots on noble privilege, and that he does express the baffled social forces which in Byzantium as in the West were trying to beget the responsible monarchy (the rule of law as opposed to feudal privilege) and the liberation of the producing classes from feudal fetters.

IV

Struggles in the Religious Sphere

18

THE CHURCH BEFORE ESTABLISHMENT

PAGAN BASES. The problem of pagan elements in the Christian religion is sometimes treated as arising from the later influx of pagans into the Church, an influx often the result of compulsion or convenience. And though this aspect has its importance, we must begin by realising Christianity as a trend which differentiates itself out of a much wider stream of ideas and emotions. A stream which on the one hand went back to the first urban developments, and which on the other hand reached a crucial stage of conflicting elements brought together along a broad front by the convulsions of the last century B.C.

Among these elements we must notice the trend to unite the Greek cult of the Hero with the Saviour-cult of the dying-reborn god, to set the Hero within a ritual-structure born from the mystery-play of death-rebirth; the trend to set popular rites of immortality and apotheosis against the imperial rites; the gathering of popular emotions around the mystery-hero, with a deepening sense of the split in life.

The early Empire saw the advent of the emperor as the middle-class god or hero-saviour. Thus, Greek cities set up inscriptions in honour of Augustus:

(i) Through Him have come Good Tidings (the Evangel)
(ii) The Saviour sent to end Wars and spread Order (Harmony) through the World.

And Virgil, as the poet of new State, wrote in 41 B.C. of Augustus:

> *A god has wrought this Peace for us.*
> *He shall ever be my god, a gentle Lamb*
> *shall often wet with blood for me his altar.*

But for the masses, for the workers and peasants of the highly developed East, the Lamb sacrificed to the imperial cult was the god himself, was their own oppressed and crucified lives.

So, on one side, we meet the acceptance of power as god, the State as deity. A second-century papyrus has a sort of catechism: 'What is God?' 'Power.' 'And what is Power?' 'The Basileus.' With this crudely

expressed view Stoical acceptances of the universe more subtly accommo-
dated themselves. On the other side were the myths and rites of redemp-
tion, desperate demands for world-end and judgment, which the imperial
cult could not satisfy; and as the crisis grew inside the State, these dissident
elements increased in strength. By the third century it is obvious that no
manipulation of the imperial cult with additions from solar monotheisms
and mystery-sacraments could provide a satisfying social sanction. The
two claimants for the position which the emperor had failed to fill were
Mithras and Christ.

Mithraism had the advantage that its *Sol Invictus* could easily coalesce
with emperor-worship; but Christianity had far deeper social roots, a
more comprehensive element of revolt, a stronger organising force. Both
cults had forms of mystery-ritual: baptisms, initiations, communions,
redemptions, blood-baths. In Mithraism the blood-bath was literally
accomplished; in a ritual cave with a spring near the mouth, the Mediator
Mithras offered up a bull to aid rebirth and heaven-ascent. In the cave-
pictures the Bull, tracked by the deathbitch and stung in the testicles by a
scorpion, is stabbed in the neck by the gòd; from its tail sprout ears of
wheat, grapes grow from its blood; and the Redeemer, breaking bread
and drinking from a cup, bids farewell to his disciples. In another phase he
mixes the soul a cup of immortality, wine and bull's blood, and the soul
climbs a sevenfold ladder. In ritual the worshipper went down naked into
a hole over which were loosely set planks; a bull was sacrificed on the
planks; the blood ran down over the worshipper, who was thus reborn
(for five years).

But Mithraism was a male cult; it excluded women. The appeal to
manly virtues gave it a strong basis in the army, but weakened its social
scope. Christianity, with its original total rejection of the State (and a
belief that world-end was due any moment), provided an idiom of wider
resistance and cohesion. If the State took it over and thus inverted its
original basis, what greater strengthening could the State ask? So to the
State the establishment of the Church meant the winning-over of vast
dissident forces into allegiance, the building-up of quite new bases of
social participation. To the Church it meant the defeat of the State. The
result was a fusion of both aims. Christ was to some extent merged in the
divine emperor; but the Christian idiom preserved elements of the original absolute refusal to take part in a society based on discord, division,
greed.

CONSTANTINE. Constantine veered from one religious position to another.
He began by claiming Herakles as his god-ancestor, then returned to his

family-faith as the Son of Apollo, inclining to Mithraism. In the Civil War his opponent was anti-Christian; so he himself tried to win the support of the Christians. But he continued with a mixed attitude. He adored Tyche, his Luck, till his baptism (a few hours before death), the Temple of his *Gens Flavia* was never closed; he went on being *Pontifex Maximus*. Byzantium was consecrated by pagan ritual, an astrologer drew up its horoscope, and Tyche as the City-Luck was respected. We have already noticed his giant statue of Apollo, on which he stuck his own face: the Emperor Sungod—though the nimbus of seven rays could be taken to represent Christ's Nails. In the base were impartially closed the Luck of Rome, splinters of the True Cross, the Crosses of the Two Thieves, Noah's Adze, the Baskets that held the Crumbs after the 5,000 ate, the Alabaster Box of Spikenard, etc.[1]

Later it was said that Byzantium was dedicated to the Virgin Mary; but that was because of a statue of the Great Mother, praying, without Lions.

It has been estimated that Christians in the early fourth century made up about a fifth of the Empire's population. That is probably an overestimate, but in such matters majorities do not sway the world. Certainly, if the matter could have been put to the vote, the creed would have lost the day; but the Christians had their powerful organisation, their fierce dissidence. The Milan Edict of Toleration seems one of the many lies surrounding Constantine; but he was too shrewd to commit himself without experimenting with the force he wanted to harness. And as soon as he gave Christian clergy parity with the pagan priesthoods (exemption from taxes and State-duties), the rapid triumph of the Church was certain.

THE NATURE OF THE MARTYR. To grasp the mass-element in the new creed, an element which persists after establishment, we must grasp the role of the Martyr in the early Christian communities. He was the Hero of the group which had witnessed his confession of faith. His Death was felt

---

[1] He recommended in Rome the building of St. Peter and the Lateran; but on his coin-reverses he kept the image of Mithras and the legend: 'To my Comrade the Unconquerable Sun.' When he prohibited sacrifices in the temples, he was partly hoping to stop conspirators divining by entrails. While building Byzantium he left the old temples and built new ones for pagan workers. Only in the later years of his reign do we see *Sol Invictus* displaced by Christ.

Even the tale of his Conversion is dubious. In a dream he was told to adopt the Labaron before the decisive battle in the civil war. But the dream equivocated for the symbol was congenial to both sides. *Laboron* is cognate with *labyrinth* and *labrys*, the sacral sky-axe and thus combined Jupiter and Christ. 'Under this sign you will conquer.' (I do not accept the derivation from *lauratum* though that too would make it a pagan emblem.)

as giving a new life, a new basis, to the group—a decisive point from which there was no turning back. It was the pledge, the proof, of a new dispensation; and as witnesses of this pledge the community achieved stably its new life, its true life. 'Christ is in the Martyr,' said Tertullian.[1] The *Acta*, the account of the martyrdom, was carefully made and jealously preserved.

When Polycarp was martyred in 156, we are told that the Jews at Smyrna pleaded with the magistrate not to give the body back to the Christians lest they 'abandon the Crucified and begin to worship this man'. And still in the fourth century the local basis was strong. Eusebios felt that he had to explain why the relics of Romanos, martyred at Antioch were found in Palestine.

The Martyrdom was conceived as a Heavenly Birthday—opposed both to the pagan hero-cult in which the death-anniversary was treated as a birth into deity, and to the earthly birthday of the emperor which was a holy day. The martyr-cult thus concentrated the anti-imperial emotions of the masses as nothing else did. The whole community assembled at the Martyr's Tomb for a yearly celebration, a communal meal. Thus they took their oath of allegiance to a new life, a life which had opposed the existing State to the final pledge, death. The election of the bishop in early days often took place at the Tomb.

The martyr-ritual was substantially taken over from the pagan cult of the Hero. What it did was to oppose the people's Hero to the Hero of the State, to turn the pagan meal of communion into a last-supper of union absolutely opposed to the existing world, its self-divided society. And so Julian, in trying to revive paganism, sharply attacked the martyr-cult. 'To the original corpse a host of other new-dead corpses have been added.' 'Irreligion is the worst of all evils. This is the situation of those who have turned from the gods to worship corpses and relics.' His sophist friend Eunapios declared, 'Pickled heads and mouldy bones have become the new gods of the Roman people.'

The martyrs, as the persons in whom the force of the anti-imperial cult was concentrated, were felt to have 'a sort of claim on God' enabling them to 'call on him to bring things to an end'. In *The Assumption of Moses* eight martyrs bring about the climax; in *Enoch* the martyrs demand vengeance at once and will get it as soon as their number is complete. The same position appears in *Revelation*: 'They cried with a loud voice, How long O Lord holy and true, does thou not judge? . . . And each was told to rest for yet a little season till the number be completed of their com-

1 The word *Martyr* simply meant a Witness (to the Truth) in the *N.T.*, but by the time of the *Acts* the idea of death has been added. Tertullian distinguishes Martyrs and Confessors; so does Cyprian.

rades . . .' Then comes world-end and the day of judgment against 'the kings of the earth and the great men, the captains, the rich and the mighty'—the vision of the total overthrow of Rome in chapter xviii.

With establishment, the cult entered on a new phase. The comparative isolation of the local group was broken down in many ways; the local hero was more merged in Christ, in the Catholic Community. But the original nucleus of emotion and action was not lost; it lived on in the expanded sphere of reference and provided an incessantly renewed centre of aspiration and revolt, as important culturally as politically.

A community without its saint, its martyr's relics, was not a true community in the Christian world; it lacked its witness to the new life, its pledge of communal resistance and rebirth. Martyred bodies were therefore discovered by all sorts of divinations, usually by dreams. Trafficking in relics began, forbidden in 381 and 386. And the great cities, especially Rome and Byzantium, became magnetic centres, breaking down the localisations and amassing relics from all over the Empire. To Byzantium the alleged remains of Timothy, Luke, Andrew were brought, and Jerome tells us of the frenzy over the supposed bones of Samuel.

The sanctity of Rome in these years lay in its role, not as an imperial but as an anti-imperial centre. It was the City of the Blood of the Martyrs. Having been the State-centre of paganism, it was rich with martyrdoms; and only later did the bishop of Rome try to exploit the memories of imperial grandeur to glorify his seat. With the ravages that burst in on Italy, particularly in mid-sixth century, many local relics were sent to Rome for safe-keeping from all over central Italy, and Rome's sanctity was enhanced.

IN THE WEST. But Rome was a special case for the West, which was poor in early martyrs (except for Africa, which was soon lost to Vandals and Arabs). The economic wealth of the Empire and what Christians considered its 'spiritual wealth' or heavenly treasure, the relics, were both concentrated in the East. Indeed the West first showed a more rational attitude to relics: Vigilantius of Aquitaine attacked night-vigils and relic-worship: it was pagan to light tapers in the day and offer pinches of dust in small preciously-wrapt vessels to be kissed. Jerome replied with his usual ferocity that the martyrs went on praying for the Church after death. That was the distorted and abstracted version of their original unceasing demand for world-end and judgment on the mighty and the rich.[1]

---

[1] The idea of Intercession was pagan: tomb-inscriptions show pagans praying to their dead for aid or benevolence. Early Christians similarly invoked their dead— the family-dead, not any special saints. The Martyrs inevitably gathered this nexus of idea and emotion about them.

But the demand for relics in the West increased, quickened by Ambrose's discovery (through a dream) of bones believed to be those of SS. Gervasius and Protasius at Milan—during a siege when the people needed a lift in morale. Linen cloths that had touched these bones were kept in western churches, especially in Gaul, to make up for the lack of local witnesses. Victorinus, who as Bishop of Rouen got thirteen relics from Rome, wrote a treatise arguing that there was no reason why God shouldn't turn the martyr's flesh into light. The Blood had then the nature of heavenly fire, and the least fragment of a martyr the virtue of the whole, able to put a worshipper into direct contact with the Trinity.

But it was in the East that the potence of the martyr-cult vitally lived, with deep and far-reaching effect on culture. The specific Byzantine quality in architecture was a derivation from the *Martyrion*, as we shall see in the next section. For the moment it is enough to realise that the deep-rooted eastern cult of the martyr as the people's Hero was linked with the powerful rebellious forces that keep expressing themselves in religious terms, unable to accept the terms of settlement between Church and State.[1]

CHRIST AGAINST THE STATE. If we look at the *Lives* we see how the actual event of the martyrdom expressed perfectly the anti-imperial resistance, and how the story of it served to keep the original emotion alive. This is how it goes.

An imperial edict was set up in a public place with pomp and ceremony —for instance with trumpets. Criers cried it at the cross-roads, or the people were called into the Circus or the Temple of Fortune to hear it read. Sometimes the proconsul assembled all the city-notables and read out the order. Seventeen times they acclaimed 'May Augustus Live Forever Victorious', and the proconsul replied, 'Glory to the Propitious Gods.' This demonstration of State-power continued into the fourth century. John Chrysostom remembered: 'When the emperor's decree was read to us, a great silence fell on all sides. Each man listened keenly, afraid to miss a word, woe to him who made the least noise.' At Nikomedia an unknown man tore down the posters.

Next the police went round to arrest the dissenters. We find different officials making the clean-up, a *strator* at Ikonion, an eirenarch at Smyrna, with police on foot and horseback, soldiers of the garrison. At times the

---

[1] The use of the Relics as potent emotional emblems of new social unions has its pagan analogy in ancient Greece—*e.g.* the use of 'Theseus' bones' to sanctify the earlier formations of Athenian democracy.

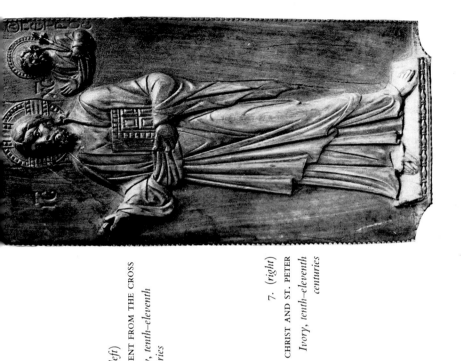

6. (left)

DESCENT FROM THE CROSS

Ivory, tenth–eleventh centuries

7. (right)

CHRIST AND ST. PETER

Ivory, tenth–eleventh centuries

town councillors or the curator ordered the arrests, and imperial soldiers rounded up the rebels.

Then came the confrontation, sometimes in the market-place, as with St. Nestor at Magydos in Pamphylia, before the local senators, with the people all round. For the trial of St. Mammarius the proconsul sent the criers to bring in all the townsmen and the people of the neighbourhood. Besides the Forum, the Baths or the Circus were used for the assembly.

The *Lives* bring out strongly the clash of opposed social and political views. Theodora, asked if free or slave, replied, 'I've already told you. I am Christian. Christ's coming has set me free'.

'Call the Curator Civitatis,' said the judge, and was brought her full dossier.

The fact that so many words of fundamental importance had a different meaning for judge and dissenter showed the irreconcilable oppositions. 'Hit him on the mouth so that he won't answer one thing for another.' And the way in which there had grown up conformities around the central decision of rejection can be read in the following dialogue from Scyllium in Africa, 180.

> PROCONSUL We also are religious, and our religion is simple. We swear by the felicity of Our Lord the Emperor, and we pray for His Salvation. You must do the same.
>
> SPERATUS If you are ready to listen quietly to me, I'll explain the mystery of true simplicity.
>
> PROCONSUL Just swear by the Emperor's Genius.
>
> SPERATUS I do not recognise the Kingdom of the existing world. But I praise and adore my god, whom no man has seen, whom no mortal eyes can behold, but whose true light is revealed to the believing heart. I have committed no theft. If I carry on my trade, I pay the tax because I know our lord king of kings and master of all the peoples. . . .

TWO-EDGED WORDS. As an example of the new meanings given to words, which seemed quibbling and obstinate equivocation to the examining magistrates, we may take *sacramentum*. First, it meant juridically the sum which two parties to a suit deposited and then were bound for. (Either the sum forfeited by the loser was used for religious purposes, such as the *sacra publica*, or it was put in a holy place, becoming *sacrum*, tabooed.) So the word came to mean a civil suit; and as an army-term, the preliminary engagement of the recruit, followed by an oath, at first voluntary, then after the Second Punic War, demanded by the military tribune. It was thus taken to express the military oath of allegiance itself, then any solemn oath. Later, from its nexus of meanings linked with loyalty to the emperor's person, it was developed into a Christian term suggesting a secret, the Gospel Revelation—the pledge of a dispensation opposed to the existing State—a sacrament, and finally the office of the ministry.[1]

Thus it grew from a monetary pledge to a military oath, then to an oath of allegiance to the emperor's person, then to the token of a new community life; and was finally recanalised into ritual and the glorification of the hierarchical clergy separated out from the people.

THE NATURE OF HERESY. The Church was rent by many schisms and heresies before establishment, but then lacked the means of putting them down by force. This ceaseless inner cleavage was inevitable after the failure of the Second Coming in the apostolic age or immediately afterwards. Conformities or compromises of one sort or another had to grow up; and what became orthodoxy was the line of compromise that enabled the Church to keep a maximum fusion of the original idiom and the conformist needs. The key-struggle continued against the imperial creed; but as the compromises necessary for working, marrying, etc., in a rejected world went on, this struggle tended to lose much of its social significance and to be theologically abstracted. The process of abstraction had had to go on for many generations before the possibility of union with the State by the act of substituting a Christian theology for the imperial theology could become feasible. And it necessarily involved an effort to state the Christian position in terms of pagan philosophy.

But each stage of compromise evoked fierce resistances from the revolutionary element still vital in the movement. And so a dual struggle appeared in the Church—on the one hand against the collapse represented by submission to the imperial cult, and on the other hand against the elements that wanted to maintain a total rejection of the existing world. Only thus could the Church maintain the central position that enabled it to survive, develop as a coherent body, and play its continuous part in history. (It is significant that Clement of Alexandria in the later second century expresses both the decisive effort to express Christian ideas in terms of Greek philosophy and the casuistic dissolution of plain gospel-meanings that makes the Church safe for the rich man.)

The dissident elements took the form of violent social nonconformity or of retreat into mystery-abstractions which severed contacts with the world. We may take Montanos of Phrygia as an example of the first form. A priest of the Great Mother, he was converted to Christianity; his fol-

---

[1] To the emperor the soldier owed *Pietas*, having taken the *sacramentum* to him. *Pia Fidelis* was an honorary title bestowed on a legion that had distinguished itself. *Pietas* came to mean loyalty, obedience, of all sorts, civilian as well as military. Then it was transferred to the Church.

lowers held him to be the Paraklete or Holy Spirit promised by Christ. With two priestesses he proclaimed a renewal of the original dispensation, classed sins as mortal and non-mortal, attacked second marriages, baptised in Memory of Christ's death for men, despised the old prophets as men possessed of demons. His ideas spread west and strongly influenced Tertullian.

Here we meet the demand for a sudden and total renewal, a demand for a fuller break with the world. Similar were the doctrines of men like Markion of Sinope, who believed that there were two Christs, one sent to save the whole world, the other whom the Creator would one day send to save the Jews. His followers denied bodily resurrection and held Christ's body to be like a man's only in appearance. Here we meet the signs of a dualism which was to tear the Church with increased force after establishment, opposing the dream of unity to the fact of division.

On the other hand thinkers like Origen, who sought to bring the valuable elements of Greek thought into the service of the Church, tended to lose themselves in symbolism, to dissolve history in an inner drama of death-rebirth, and to develop esoteric forms of belief inaccessible to the masses. They thus acclimatised in Christianity the form of creed developed by the Gnostic groups out of the breakdown of the old Greek mystery-cults, turning symbols of fertility and mass-life into spiritual abstractions of quest and discovery, and making ecstasy an all-sufficient end (whereas in mystery-ritual proper it was merely a turning-point in a movement of withdrawal-and-return, solitude-and-union, by which the initiate sealed his new relation to the group).

In the early days theological questions hardly arose. Such concepts as Son of God were concretely enclosed for the devotee in the mystery-experience of a union which denied the divided world. But the more that world-end and second-coming receded, and forms of adaptation to existing society had increasingly to be found, the exact meaning of such terms had to be worked out. For on one's understanding of them depended the nature of one's adaptation. Hence the enormous importance of formulations, which, viewed abstractly, seem hair-splitting and trivial.

Thus, late in the second century Praxeas, an Asiatic who had come to Rome, taught along lines that the Son and Spirit were not distinct from the Father, but merely functions of One God, the Father having come down into the Virgin and been born as Christ. At once he was accused of having made the Father 'suffer on the cross', and his sect were called Father-sufferers, Patripassians. Noetos of Smyrna taught something the same, and Sabellios of Libya set out the thesis with more philosophic fullness. Other groups, such as that led by Theodotes of Byzantium, a tanner at Rome, held that Jesus was only a perfected man. And in the third century a strong restatement of what we may call the unitarian thesis was made by Paul of Samosata, who defined the *Logos* or Word not as a person but as the Father's *Sophia* or Wisdom, which descended into Jesus but was not united with him.

Two Councils, meeting 264 and 269–70, condemned Paul's teaching; but Queen Zenobia of Palmyra protected him. It is of interest that when in 272 the emperor Aurelian took Antioch, which Zenobia was holding, the bishops appealed to him, and he supported them against Paul. Here we meet an anticipation of Constantine; for Aurelian decisively quickened the pace of absolutism, and led the way into the Diocletianic State. And the fact that the bishops were ready to use the pagan State against a heretic shows how far already they had come from the apostolic age.

How may we enter into the minds of these men to grasp what they felt to be at stake? Without claiming to make an exhaustive analysis, we can get the general social and political bearing of their terms of struggle along the following lines.

Originally we have the mass-hero whose life and death-resurrection are felt to embody the deepest possible pattern of the sufferings and hopes of the people, the mass-hero who dies the death of a slave and is reborn as the vindicated Son in a world where the present men of power have been damned for ever and a reign of harmony introduced. But as there is a loss of the faith that this pattern is going to be actualised *at once* in history, the devotee has to adapt himself to society in some way, whatever reservations he may make, however he may hope that the pattern will be actualised at some indefinite time in the future. At once the problem of the relation of the Son to the Father crops up. It is no longer possible to imagine the son of mercy fully and immediately united with the father of justice in a last-judgment. The agony goes on, the crucifixion never ends, the ritual pattern has coincided with existence only in its first half, the half of suffering and death. And so a complex set of tensions is born round the Father-Son relationship. Why does the pang go on? If the Father is supreme power and authority, and the Son suffers under his righteous will, what is the connection between the absolute pattern of mercy and justice and the existing pattern of suffering and power?

It is not that there is an identification of imperial power and God. It is precisely against that that Christianity is protesting; but already by compromise and adaptation its devotees are in part accepting the State, and to the extent that they do so, the identification operates. More, after establishment, the identification makes a tremendous leap forward, and the burden of contradictions borne by the Church and individual Christian is very much intensified. In such a situation what is needed is a dogmatic definition of the relation between suffering Son and omnipotent Father which simultaneously justifies the degree of compromise reached and yet maintains as much as possible of the original basis of revolt.

The type of statement that we find in Paul of Samosata is that which rested more fully and directly on apostolic positions. It shows the clearest basis in mystery-ideas. Jesus, it says, was a worthy man who by completing the forms of initiation in the greatest possible purity of heart became the perfect leader, the embodied symbol of the new-life. That is, all stress is laid on the *process of change*, of initiation (conceived as both ritual and as spiritual crisis-and-resolution), because by such a stress the way is opened to everyone else to follow in the leader's steps; and all efforts to abstract and hypostasise the relationships of Father-Son are resisted, since they remove attention from the concrete process of actualising the kingdom of heaven on earth—of overcoming the deadly contradictions and discords of the existing world.

THE SIGNIFICANCE OF BAPTISM. Hence the importance of the varying ideas and practices of Baptism. The basic notion is of initiation: rebirth, second-birth, or god-birth. And allied is that of illumination, since the crucial moment of initiation is that of the change from darkness to light, the revelation of that which constitutes the mystery (the thing-to-be-kept-silent), the thing that cannot be said but can only be realised in the experience of crisis and resolution, in the discovery of a new basis of harmonious union. Thus Justin, 'The bath is called illumination as enlightening the mind of those experiencing it.'[1] It was prepared for by fasting and vigils, and was originally a total immersion of the naked body. Methodios says, 'The Church is big with child and travails until the Christ in us is fully formed into birth, so that each of the saints by sharing in Christ may be born a Christ', and 'That is why in a certain scripture we read, Touch not my Christs . . . which means that those baptised by participation of the spirit into Christ have become Christs.' And even Augustine says, 'We give thanks for being made not only Christians but Christ.'

Thus the initiates became Christ as the Dionysiac became Dionysos, and Christ's birthday was not the day of his birth from Mary but the day of his baptism in the Jordan. Not till late in the fourth century, well after

[1] It is called a Seal or *Character Dominicus:* a metaphor drawn from Property (*Seal of Lordship*, Gregory Nazianzen) and from the Army, the brand put on recruits (Chrysostom). Some heretics Karpokratians and Heraklians branded the ears of initiates as a sealing of the Spirit. (Cf. the ivy-tattooings of Dionysiac devotees.)

establishment, did the Festival of the Virgin Birth appear to displace the Baptism Birth. In Egypt, Armenia and Mesopotamia, the new festival is merely added to the others, and both were held on January 6th, the Jordan date. Where the State-Church had a better control the Virgin Birth was set on December 25th, that is, it took over the pagan festival of the Birth of the Sun; an act aided by the fact that December 25th was also the day of King David. A pilgrim of Piacenza (sixth century) reports that on this day and the next Jews and Christians assembled in Hebron to celebrate David. As David and Christ were in some respects closely identified—as the Anointed, the Good Shepherd, the King of Israel—the merging of Jesus (and his brother James, also linked with this day), David and Mithras, expressed the handing-over of Messianic hope to the State-Religion, the compromise with paganism and abandonment of the old community-basis. Jesus became David-Mithras as the lord of the Roman State.

This change in the Nativity date is the crucial point of break with apostolic traditions and their social basis. The original reading of *Luke* iii, 22 (preserved in Justin Martyr, in Clement of Alexandria, in Codex D, and in the oldest Latin version), is, 'This day I have begotten you.' Thus speaks the heavenly voice to Christ as he is baptised in the Jordan; but now, with the decisive break, the Church corrected the text to, 'In thee I am well pleased.' The emphasis had swung from initiation to incarnation, from the unity of the group in equalitarian brotherhood to the unity of the group in a mystical conception that glorified the existing structure of society, from the idea of Christ as a Man leading into a new-life to that of Christ as the Word descended from aloft.

Originally only adults could be baptised; but the practice crept in of baptising babies. In Tertullian's day baby-baptism was already common, though he attacked it as a bad practice. It was a powerful factor, combined with the other forms and forces of compromise, in weakening the original bases. It stressed the magical aspect, to the exclusion of the mystery-experience of separation-out from the existing world of evil and of entry into a new union, a compact and a sealing of a new way of life.

In an effort to relate the initiation-experience directly to the hope of historical change, in early days baptisms were carried out at Easter and Pentecost. Tertullian explains why. Easter represented the crucial experience of change, death-to-the-old and rebirth-in-the-new, and Pentecost represented the collective expression of the individual experience, the moment of waiting among the disciples when 'the Spirit's Grace was bestowed and the Advent of the Lord suggested'. This attitude was still strong in the fifth century.

We have an account by Cyril of Jerusalem, delivered in Lent 347, of the baptismal procedure while it still held strong elements of initiation and of milleniary emotion. All Lent the catechumens gathered in the anastasis of the church for prayer and instruction. On Easter Eve in the dusk they assembled in the outer room of the baptistry, facing the west (the place of darkness and its powers). They stretched out their hands and 'with a gesture of repulsion' they renounced Satan. They cried 'I renounce you, Satan.' Then, 'And your works.' Then, 'And your pomp.' Then, 'And all your worship.' Then, 'when they had renounced Satan utterly, breaking all covenants with him', they turned to face the East, the home of light, made a profession of faith, and went into the inner room. There they put off the *chitones* that clad them, and were anointed naked from head to foot with oil. Led by the hand to the font, they again made a profession of faith, dipped themselves thrice right under—in token of the three days' burial of Christ and his resurrection. The water was both 'a tomb and a womb' for them.

Then, clad in white clothes, to express the new life, they were anointed on brow, ears, nostrils, breast (to represent the dove-descent of the Spirit on Christ), and they celebrated communion together, 'one body and one blood with Christ'. Now they were brothers in the new bond of freedom.

The link with Easter ceremonial was maintained, to fuse the individual with the collective hope. The baptism occurred during the night which moved to the dawn of resurrection; and Cyril pictures this moment when at the doors of the anastasis the white-robed band of initiates were seen approaching from the near baptistry, 'and the darkness was turned to day' in the innumerable gleams. And as the song burst out, it seemed that the angels were chanting of blessedness—as if the desired harmony were actualised on earth.

FROM SYNAGOGUE BACK TO TEMPLE. The Church was not only linked closely with Judaism in its origins; the relationship long persisted and the final severance was not made till the Council of Nikaia. Some areas such as Armenia were more strongly permeated with Judaic elements than others; but none was left untouched throughout the first three centuries.

Thus the Pauline creed of a universal Gentile Church did not win at Rome till a full century after Paul's death, and even in the third century (as the pseudo-Clementines show) Gentile and Judaic Christianity were still disputing there. At eastern centres like Antioch Judaising tendencies were still powerful in John the Golden Mouth's day; he denounces many of his Christian flock, especially for finding the synagogue courts more binding than the Church's.

From one angle we may define the Church's growth as a movement from the synagogue-basis of its origins back to the structures of hierarchy and the ritual pomps that ruled in the Temple. Not that the Temple could have any direct effect after its destruction; the effects were indirect —through the ideas that Christian theologians had of what it had been like, and through the Synagogue of the Dispersal, which took over certain institutions of the ruined Temple.

The Temple with its rich liturgy, its hierarchy and rigid organisation, its sacrificial cults, showed a sharp division between the ritual officials and the all-but-passive congregation. The Synagogue had been an informal lay institution which depended on the congregation's activity, with liturgy and administration both in lay hands. When the Temple fell, the Synagogue took over many of its functions, though changing them: prayer was substituted for sacrifice, scriptural readings for offerings. The Temple had had a professional priestly choir and orchestra; and though the Synagogue always resisted musical instruments, it gradually admitted a professional element—*hazan*, cantor, psalmist, reader—and sections of temple-liturgy were taken over.

The early Christian synagogues had often been in the rural areas of Palestine, where the poor peasants hated the learned rabbis and rich priests of Jerusalem, and were ridiculed by the latter in return. And so the slow progression of the Church to a hierarchical system with complex liturgy and professional practitioners or priests was in a sense a movement backward to the Temple-system—but a movement in terms of the full Graeco-Roman area into which Christianity, culturally and politically, broke and expanded.

19

PAGANS AND MONKS

GOD'S MOTHER. Theodosios II in 431 heaped disabilities on pagans, and seven years later claimed that he had wiped them out. He exaggerated, though he had made even private sacrifice treason, and the hanging of a ribbon on a tree a crime involving confiscation of property. But the compulsion of the pagan masses into the Church meant a vast influx of pagan ideas and practices.[1] Thus, the pagan practice of pilgrimage to shrines of saviour-gods was taken over; the healing-shrines of gods like Asklepios, Serapis, or the Twins were made into sanctuaries of SS. Kosmas and Damian, without much change in the magical and oracular methods of cure. (The pagan temple of Epidauros had pilgrim accommodation and dormitories, and the loving devotion of the worshippers is to be read in the inscriptions.) Many gods became saints, e.g. Saint Bacchus; gnostic and theurgic magics in general were often inextricably mixed with the new faith; and sometimes the Church, in its zeal to supplant the pagan hero with the martyr, merely made a hero (e.g. Hippolytos) into a saint.

The most important effect of the new influx, however, was to build up a Mother Goddess inside the Christian creed. Such cults as those of Isis had from the outset a strong effect on Christianity. Isis with her well-organised priesthood, who owned prayer-books, liturgies, tonsures and vestments, stately processionals with pictures and symbols, complex ceremonials, left a deep mark on the young Church: the great liturgical addresses to Isis near the close of *The Golden Ass* already hold the diction, rhythm, sonorities of medieval Church-Latin. Her inner devotees were called the Religious like medieval monks; her service was called a Holy War, with the worshippers graded as militia. Isis-Cybele provided much of the substance of the Virgin Mary. It was no accident that the Church-Council that settled Mary's place in Christian theology was held at Ephesos; the populace who cheered the decision were the descendants of the crowd who called in Paul's day, 'Great is Diana of the Ephesians',

[1] Sometimes a pagan had deliberately entered, e.g. the bishop of Ilion whom Julian met: he had become bishop to protect the shrines from Christian desecration, himself worshipping the Sungod. 'Make me bishop of Rome,' said a pagan prefect, 'and I'll be a Christian'.

and Mary's body was supposed to have been buried in their city. (Later the Church decided the body had been rapt to heaven.)

Mary's role was that of reconciliation: she became specially attractive where the direct political struggle had collapsed. The Great Mother then became the Mother Church, a fostering refuge from the world. Therefore, when struggle re-awoke and the problem of resolving conflict took the place of the fall into formulas of reconciliation, the attack on the Mary-cult became acute. The Iconoclast Reform and the later Reformation in western Europe both had the opposition to Mary at their root, because they opposed the helpless surrender to the consolations of ritual. But for the moment Mary appeared to the orthodox as the true mediating figure, displacing her Son and mediating between him and the Father, between earth and heaven, *Logos* and Man.

Pagan rites survived strongly in the countryside, and the fourth-century Fathers kept telling the landlords to build churches on their estates. But the real strength of paganism lay in the classics. The break in the West meant an almost total loss for centuries of the Graeco-Roman traditions of art and literature, but in the East ancient humanism never faded out. Its forces had their ebb and flow, yet never receded so far that a quick resurgence was not always possible. But though pagan discontents were mixed with other motives in fifth-century rebellions, the day of paganism had gone when the great Mysteries were stopped, the Olympic Games ended, the Athenian University closed. The last oracle was said to have declared, truly enough:

> *Tell the king that the glorious temple is fallen away,*
> *Phoibos has lost his shrine, the prophetic bay,*
> *the babble-spring, and the tongue of water has dried away.*[1]

THE MONASTIC REVOLT. Monasticism was a dissident movement inside the Church which would have wrecked it unless controlled. It emerged in the later part of the third century, expressing a conviction that the attempts to adapt the Christian way of life to a divided world were futile and had resulted only in corruption, complicity in evil.

It was therefore one of the offshoots of the revolutionary turmoils of the third century—though its origins go far back, as far back indeed as

---

[1] Tales of omens show the transition of disquiet. Athens was saved in 375 by an old man who obeyed a dream, made a statue of Achilles, and set it up in the Parthenon— earthquakes hit the other cities, but Athens was safe. And in 396, when Alaric was prowling round, he saw Athene Promachos march on the walls, with Achilles on guard; so he went off. But soon Mary took over the function of Athene as city-guardian in war as well as peace. (Justinian, in an important guardian-statue at Byzantium, was represented as Achilles.)

the periods of ritual withdrawal (fast, vigil, ordeal, bodily and spiritual tests) during tribal initiation. The shaman or witch-doctor is the person who under tribal conditions feels the impulse to continue indefinitely in this experience of crisis; and at times we find shamanistic groups in withdrawal, generally living a sort of communistic existence, *i.e.* among the Siberians. The groups of prophets among the ancient Hebrews were associations of the same sort, often inhabiting caves; thus the Haioth at Ramah, 'probably ought to be rendered dwellings, a sort of cenobium'. The correct term is a *hebel* of prophets, a rope or string of them, and probably refers to the round-dance.

Close to the *hebel* of prophets were the various withdrawn groups of the Graeco-Roman period, sometimes living in the world but with special ascetic observances, purifications and communal observances (and often with a semi-communistic attitude to property). The Pythagorean sect was the most famous; but the Orphic and other mystery-clubs or cult-fraternities were always liable to throw up similar groupings, open or secret; and Egypt developed its Serapion recluses. The Essenes and Therapeutai were the main example in the Hebrew sphere of influence in post-prophetic days. But we also find similar groupings on the borders of civilisation, *e.g.* in the Thracians who exercised an influence on Greek religion in the direction of fraternity-formations. Among the Dacians were the *Polistai*, whom Josephos equated with the Essenes; among the Moesians on the Danube, the *Ktistai*, vegetarian ascetics with community of goods, also known as the Godfearers.

The Christian Church before establishment was a semi-secret society, both in and out of the world, with communal meals; then in Egypt occurred the first considerable effort to use the fully dissident fraternity-form to express Christian opposition to the world—the form which involved a total rejection of sex as the force which more than anything else tempted a man to accept the existing system, adapt himself to it, and, to maintain his family, retreat from devotion to the new-life. The movement was ascribed to St. Antony of the later third century, though he may be an invented figure who personified a general trend. He was depicted as poor and ignorant, haunted by the Gospel command to sell all property and give the proceeds to the poor. He left the world for the desert, living for twenty years alone in the ruins of an abandoned fort by the Nile; then withdrew more and more into solitude, yet kept on defeating the demons of temptation. 'He was never gloomy, for his mind rejoiced.' He saw gold exposed in some rocks and ran from it as a terrible evil.

The cult of withdrawal spread in the fourth century through Lower Egypt along the Nile and up to the coast by the later fourth century. The

monks lived alone, in twos or threes, or in crowds: there were 600 at
Kellia. The Antonian type, a community of hermits, reached its height
in the deserts of Nitria, the valley round the nitre-lakes, and Skete. Palladios tells us that 5,000 had gathered at Nitria: after the first year each
man had to follow his trade. 'Physicians live in the mountains, and con-
fectioners. They use wine, and wine is sold. They all make linen by hand,
so that they have no needs. And about 3 p.m. you may stand and hear how
the psalmody rises from each dwelling, and fancy yourself rapt in to
paradise.'

In South Egypt, Pakhom, a pagan, born about 290, was converted
after army-service, and lived under a hermit near the Nile. An angel, says
Palladios, told him to found a monastery and gave him a Rule on a
brazen tablet. He founded his first house near Denderah; and his Rule
soon spread. With his more co-ordinated system he expressed the transition from the Antonian type to the monastic cenobium. Palladios saw
the Pachomian monastery at Panopolis, with 300 monks doing handi-
crafts and out of the surplus aiding nunneries and prisons. The work
varied from fieldwork to smithying, carpentering or tanning, calligraphy
or camel-keeping. The monks also learned the Scriptures by heart and
gathered in Church four times a day, with communion on weekends.
The Rule jostled moral exhortations with details about cleaning pots and
pans.

> All the machinery of centralised government, such as does not appear again in
> the monastic world until the Cistercian and the mendicant orders arise in the
> twelfth and thirteenth centuries. (Dom Butler.)

The abbots of such houses soon grew powerful—Pakhom himself had
already had clashes with bishops and clergy. And it was these men, such
as Schnouti and Bgoul in the fifth century, who laid the basis of the
national Church, that of anti-imperial Monophysitism.

THE CHURCH GETS CONTROL. The Antonian form of loose collections of
worker-ascetics was introduced into Palestine in the early fourth century.
In Syria and Mesopotamia about the same time came a burst of asceticism,
and we find Sons of the Covenant sworn to celibacy and a hard life; but
the origins of monasticism proper are obscure. In both the great heretical
groups of Nestorians and Monophysites the first stage of withdrawal was
normally cenobitic, communal—with the aim of attaining such personal
sanctity that one could retire into a hermit-cell, coming to the monastic
church only on Sundays and festivals.

Austerity was the goal: long abstinences, exposures, ordeals; Rabbula
forbade the carrying of huge lumps of stone or iron about on the back

except by hermits. And there was a type of ascetics called Grazers, who ate grass.

Monachism of an extreme type spread over the Asian area from Paphlagonia to Armenia: turbulent Massalians or followers of Eustathios of Sebaste who liked Church as little as State. It was St. Basil who provided a stable basis for bringing Greek monasticism into the Church's fold. He spent a year touring Egypt and Syria, and then, about 360, withdrew to a deserted place in Pontos. There he worked out a cenobitic system that became the basis of Orthodox Monasticism—and also (with elements from Cassian, a Greek, who lived in the Egyptian deserts and then went to Marseilles) the basis of St. Benedict's western monasticism.

Basil sought more coherence than the Pachomian rule allowed. He insisted on a common table and common prayer. Also he set himself against the assumption that a hermit life was superior to a cenobitic. He argued that work was more desirable than austerity for its own sake, and that a monk must do good to his fellow men. Thus he instituted orphanages nearby, for educating boys. There were yet no vows, but a sense of strict obligation. Prayer, work and Bible-reading were basic. The monks rose while it was still dark for common psalmody, chanted till dawn, assembled for prayer six times a day, worked at farming (from ploughing to making drains); their food, clothes, houses were rough and austere; their virtues were obedience to the superior, personal poverty, self-denial, cultivation of the spiritual life.

This form spread through Asia Minor and Armenia; and after the Council of Chalkedon it made its way over all the Greek area of the Empire. In the fifth-century Palestine, however, was the most thriving region of monasticism, owning both Basilian houses and lauras of semi-eremitical settlement (separate huts in an enclosure), a form organised by St. Sabas of Cappadocia.

Women's groups existed in Egypt in the mid-third century. Female hermits lived in tombs, and women dressed as men to get into the monasteries. Pakhom founded two nunneries; and Palladios tells tales of the houses of his day—of old Mother Talus at Antinoe who needed no locked doors to keep her nuns in, 'they were tied fast by love of her', and of a man Doretheus who sat at a window overlooking a convent to keep peace among the nuns. Syria had its Daughters of the Covenant, but we cannot trace its first nunneries—though it soon had them, like Palestine. Rich ladies left Rome to set up houses in the latter area. When Basil began as a monk his mother and sister were in a nun-community nearby, over the river.

Under Theodosios II a Syrian founded a monastery outside Byzantium;

and soon monasteries were to be seen all round. One important foundation was that of the Sleepless at Gomon near the north entry to the Bosphoros, later brought down the Asian side. Control by the bishops began effectively at the Council of Chalkedon, when monks were forbidden to leave a monastery without their abbot's permission. Not that a few canons could settle the problem of monkish restlessness and dissidence; but the first important step had been made to keep monasticism within the Church. The Council's resolutions, however, would have been useless without the Basilian rule, which substituted obedience for revolt and tamed the furious impulse that sent men crying doom and hastening from a damned society corrupt at the core. The desire to get right away and set up groups without the kind of private ownership that divided society was still there, but Basil found the way of using it to strengthen the Church, which was now part of the State; he drew it back into the very nexus from which the monks or hermits sought to escape, and thus turned the hatred of private property into a dynamic force accumulating such property for the Church.

IN THE WEST. Western monasticism was derived from the East. Athanasios gave it its first stimulus when he visited Rome in 339 with two monks. Soon a movement began in and round Rome. Eusebius, bishop of Vercelli, made the cathedral clerics live in community under a rule (which led later to the practice of monks becoming priests). Augustine took the Eusebian form to Carthage in 368. St. Martin of Tours, a Pannonian, had been a monk before becoming a bishop in 372; he had set up a house at Poitiers, now he set up another close to Tours, where some eighty monks lived in caves and huts, meeting for meals and services, with long fasts— a scheme Egyptian in type. Then with the fifth century monasticism began in South Gaul under John Cassian, who had come from Egypt.

But it was Benedict who did for the West what Basil had done for the East. He too deprecated ascetic rivalries and drew up a Rule of work and prayer. An Umbrian noble, born about 480, he was repelled by licentious Rome, went to the Sabine hills, to a cave over Nero's lake on the Anio, a rugged solitude, for three years. Disciples flocked round, and he set up a community on Monte Cassino, about 520. His rule drew on both Basil and Cassian, but mostly on Basil. Obedience becomes the primary monkish virtue, and monasticism in the West had been made safe for the Papacy.[1]

---

[1] Celtic monasticism stands apart. St. Patrick seems educated at Lerins in South France; but Celtic forms drew largely on tribal ideas and practices: the Abbot was often the clan-chief or a relation. In the sixth century Celtic monasticism had a great missionary force and many fine cultural qualities; but it was crushed by the Papacy.

CHRIST'S ATHLETE. The Greek term for asceticism is *askesis*, the normal term for exercise, training, practice of an athlete or a craftsman. An ascetic, originally, meant anyone who carries on an art or trade; but the word came to refer more and more to the athlete. *Askesis* is the way of life by which a man trains himself to become victor in the great festival-contests.

While the Greek *polis* survived, the athletic victor was one of the great men of the city, the popular hero. But when the free life of the *polis* had decayed, we find the term *askesis* applied to new purposes. In the Mithraic cult we can see the transition from the athletic training grounds, the *palaistra*, to the spiritual wrestling-arena that fitted the soul for a life-in-light:

> The Mithraic aspirant could ascend only after a life of strenuous endeavour demanded by his cult. Only blessed souls might be lifted by the rays of the Sun. In the instructive scenes of apotheosis in the underground basilica of the mystery-cult near the Porta Maggiore in Rome, there is an elaborate symbolism of the palaestra of life and of purifications before the reception of the crown of victory. The way to heaven was unambiguously the steep and rugged path of the Hesiodean parable and of the Pythagorean Y. (Angus.)

The symbolism entered Christianity through Paul and is common in the Fathers. Thus, Gregory Nazianzen, in welcoming a confessor of the faith, speaks of the crowns he has won, comparing him to a conqueror in the arena. And Tertullian's defence of Fasting explains that ascetic practices were meant to build up morale, to accustom a Christian to the tortures that the State kept in store for him:

> That is how one is hardened against prison, hunger, thirst, privations and agonies. The martyr's dried-up skin will serve as a cuirass, the iron claws will slide over them as over thick horn. Such a man will be he who by fasting has often come close to death and discharged himself of his blood, that heavy and importunate burden for a soul impatient to get free.

But after establishment the orthodox Christian did not need to train in order to be fit for the ordeals of torture and jail. In a wild burst of misery men broke away from society altogether, and now they trained themselves against what seemed an eternal and iniquitous enemy. They carried on the discipline as an end in itself, a proof that somehow they were still true to the dream of unity, the truth of uncorrupted love. They wrestled with history, with the State, in the abstract—incarnating the whole conflict in their own flesh and spirit. And the common folk admired and adored, for they darkly and powerfully felt in these fierce struggles a pledge of the day of freedom, when the historical conflict too would be resolved in a last-judgment.[1]

The ascetic saint now becomes the *Athlete of Christ*, a basic phrase in the *Lives* to express the nature of the striving for perfection. The Martyr set the seal of his blood on the mass-demand for a new life; the Saint in his *askesis* carried on the martyr's work in a perpetual rejection of compromise, which rent him to pieces but exalted his spirit. For his sufferings were felt, both by himself and by the people, as the pledge of a future triumph. He was the Victor in a dark arena of history.[2]

[1] There is also a relation to the pangs of labour, as Christ is identified with the broken body of the toiler, *e.g.* 'The body is not cherished in the mines with couch and cushions but with the refreshment and solace of Christ. The frame wearied out with labours lies prostrate on the ground, but it is no penalty to lie down with Christ. Your limbs unbathed are foul and filth-disfigured, but within spiritually cleansed though the flesh is defiled. There is lack of bread, but man lives not on bread alone but on the word of God. Shivering you lack clothes, but he who puts Christ on is abundantly clothed and adorned' (Cyprian). This attitude which identified Christ with the toiler is later used to justify the toiler's having only spiritual comfort. But the ascetic makes himself *one* with the sufferers.

[2] There is thus a link between the people's love of both the circus-charioteer and the ascetic saint—both are heroes of *askesis*, the mass-heroes opposed to the world of power.

20

THE ARIAN SCHISM

THE ARIAN PROTEST. The first great crisis, apart from monasticism, which the established Church had to face was Arianism. Constantius II and Valens were ardent Arians who violently persecuted the Trinitarians; and in this phase the most strenuous resistance to imperial positions came from Egypt. The Council of Nikaia had added to the creed the term *homoousios* (of one essence or substance) to define the Father-Son relation: a term with an unnoted ambiguity, for it could mean that Father and Son were 'the same thing' or 'of the same essence'. This definition we may take roughly to express Constantine's desire for 'Unity in the Church', a submission of everyone to his will as revealed through the Holy Ghost in the Council.

Egypt promptly reacted against the formulation. Areios, a parish-priest of Alexandria, replied that Christ was a created being who at one time did not exist; but tried to evade the plain rationalist position (the Adoptionism of Paul of Samosata, Christ as the Adopted Son) by denying the full humanity of Christ, asserting that he only took a body through which he acted. Athanasios, patriarch of Alexandria, refused to accept this position, and defied Constantine's effort to patch things up after Areios submitted to the emperor.

Areios was denying the imperial concept of unity; but Athanasios was denying the acceptance of division. That the Athanasian position did not mean an underwriting of the imperial concept was proved by the fact that Athanasios at once came into furious collision with the emperor and was exiled. The great significance of this event was its demonstration that in the Church there lived a force capable of defying the State and all its powers in defence of a formulation felt to embody the truth, to hold the clue to human life, to ensure the future of relentless judgment and true harmony.

We must realise that the theological distinctions which now caused such dissension were not matters discussed by an intellectual élite, like Greek philosophy after its early days. Gregory of Nyssa gives us a picture of the popular passion for exploring the logical distinctions:

> People swarm everywhere talking of incomprehensible matters, in hovels, streets, squares, market-places, crossroads. When I ask how many coppers I

7   *193*

must pay, they reply with minute distinctions on the Born and the Unborn.
If I ask the price of bread, I'm told the Father's greater than the Son. I call to
ask the servant if my bath's ready, he replies that the Son was created from
Nothing.

Thus the achievements of Greek thought were made common property
and transformed. But only in the East, in the Greek-speaking areas, in
Syria and yet further East. In the West, after the fall of Africa, there was
little intellectual activity even among the highest Church dignitaries, let
alone the masses. And in fact the problem of even translating the Greek
arguments into Latin (where the terms were lacking or were wooden,
rigid, lacking the subtle flow of suggestion and interrelation with life in
Greek terms), contributed to the increasing split between Western and
Eastern religious thinking.

Athanasios was driven five times into exile in his bitter conflict with
imperial authority. He had a strong mass-backing. At his election the
people cried, 'Give us Athanasios the Good, one of the Ascetics!' He
consorted with the desert-monks and probably wrote the important *Life
of St. Antony*. His struggle stiffened the national spirit of Egypt and prepared the way for the full anti-imperial schism of Monophysitism.

The emperors had become Arians, feeling that the Arian formulation
exalted the Father of Authority at the expense of the suffering son.[1]
Bloody persecutions tried to break the Egyptian spirit. Athanasios, himself a violent and unscrupulous man, tells us of the jailings, lootings,
floggings of naked virgins, lashings of men with thorn-boughs, depor-
tations. We touch the spirit of the man and his people in his account of
the effort to arrest him in 356. It was night, the people were at vigil, preparing for communion, General Syrianos with 5,000 soldiers surrounded
the cathedral. 'I sat on my throne and directed the deacon to read a psalm.'
When the General broke in, Athanasios evaded him and escaped abroad.

After an effort to discredit the aged bishop Euphrates by putting a
prostitute into bed with him, the people demonstrated against the new
imperial bishop, and the soldiers cut them down. Sokrates says that some
3,150 were killed or trampled to death. All who refused to communicate
were arrested.

Their throats were prised open and the sacraments forced in . . . women
refusing, had their breasts squeezed in a wooden frame and cut off. Other.

[1] The Germanic barbarians were largely converted to Arianism, and stuck to it
after the Empire had reverted to the Nikaian formula. We may suppose that the more
rational positions, which did not make the Son co-eternal with the Father, appealed
to their minds which had not been conditioned by the atmosphere of Greek philosophy or the long anguish of a self-divided class-society with its yearning for a unity
without inner contradictions.

had their breasts burned with red-hot irons, or had hard-boiled eggs pressed against them. This kind of torture, which the pagans had never used, was invented by men who called themselves Christians.

Virgins were scourged with thorns, made to sit on hot plates or charcoal fires, ravished. 'These atrocities were committed in all the cities of the East, but especially at Byzantium.'

The persecutions revived under Valens. Sokrates says, 'They were mocked and scourged. They were stript, bound, stoned, stabbed, driven wandering over the desert in skins of sheep and goat.' Soldiers were sent against the desert-monks. 'Some they beat and reviled, some they fined and jailed. They inflicted every kind of intolerable evil.'[1]

With Theodosios I the Nikaian brand of Trinitarianism was restored. The State had been defeated by the steady resistance of the people. But the State and the people always interpreted terms in opposite senses, and so the creed that now triumphed, however formally related to the Athanasian position, could not be acceptable to the masses who had fought under Athanasios. The struggle merely moved on to a new level.

JOHN OF THE GOLDEN MOUTH. Athanasios had established the prestige of the Alexandrian patriarchate; and the next step was an attempt by his successor Theophilos to control the Church. However, John of the Golden Mouth was appointed patriarch of Byzantium; this meant a triumph for Antioch, whence John came, against Alexandria, whose nominee was turned down. John, a Syrian of great preaching powers and moral earnestness, was appointed through the influence of the eunuch Eutropios, who controlled the Empire.

The empress Eudoxia, however, soon brought Eutropios down in rivalry for dominance over her weak husband Arkadios. And John clashed sharply with her in his desire for social reform. He detested the inequalities and greeds of the great cities; Antioch had been bad enough, but Byzantium was worse. 'A lamp burning before sore eyes', his biographer called it. When an earthquake came, he declared that 'the vices of the rich caused it, and the prayers of the poor averted the worse consequences'.

He attacked the pomp and pride of Eudoxia's court; and gave a weapon to his enemies by thinking rather of reform than correct procedure in deposing thirteen bishops for simony. Meanwhile in Egypt Theophilos

1 Valens when riding to disaster at Adrianople was, a tale said, warned by a hermit to repent or perish; and another tale said that he took shelter wounded after the battle in a peasant's hut. The enemy, Arian Goths, set fire to the place. So he was burned alive (a prelude to hell-fires) by his fellow-heretics, thus suffering the legal penalty for obdurate heresy. A typical propaganda-tale.

had quarrelled with the Nitrian monks, who were accused of anthropo-morphic views of God; and when an ecclesiastic whom he had ex-communicated fled to the Nitrians, he sent emissaries to use violence and arson and break the monastery up. The four Tall Brothers who presided fled in their sheepskins to Byzantium and appealed to John, who tried to reconcile Theophilos with them. Theophilos did not reply but sent counter-charges.

The Tall Brothers, however, won Eudoxia over, and Theophilos was summoned to Byzantium. He came with a horde of followers, monks and bishops from all over Egypt, Syria, Asia—after having sent a boatful of bishops ahead by sea. At the same time John embroiled himself with Eudoxia by talking about the priests of Baal who sat at Jezebel's table, and Eudoxia was touchy about references to Jezebel or Herodias.

Theophilos acted as if he were the accuser, not the accused. Various matters were trumped up against John (such as gluttony, because, having ruined his digestion with fasting, he ate alone); and he refused to appear before the Synod at Chalkedon. He was deposed amid a lavish dispensing of bribes by Egyptian agents. The emperor against his conscience acquiesced.

The people rose and flocked round John's palace and St. Sophia, guarding them for three days. John gave two discourses about Jezebel and Herodias, and the authorities could not arrest him; then he stole away by night over the water to Asia. The people, however, refused to be pacified. But an opportune earthquake scared Eudoxia into calling John back. He returned, but a few months later resumed his comments on Herodias; and Eudoxia took up his plea for a General Council. The Council was called in 401. Huge crowds filled the streets, dispersed from time to time by the soldiers. Forbidden to hold Easter services in the city, John held them in the fields.

Then on June 20th he once more slipped off to Asia, and that night a fire burst out in St. Sophia and spread to the Senate House. John's followers were persecuted; and four years later John, having kept in correspondence with his adherents all over the Empire, died while being taken to a distant Black Sea port. (Eudoxia died in October 404, apparently scared badly by a hailstorm which the people declared to be a pro-John demonstration from on high.) Theophilos had won the day.

This episode is the only occasion when a great churchman based his position on a demand for social justice; and its inconclusive nature shows how impossible it was to rally the forces of the Church behind any such position. John had a conviction of the need to do something about an unjust world, but no idea of how to act politically about righting things.

His inability to take a definite stand against Theophilos or Eudoxia derived not from cowardice but from this confusion. He wanted social reform but was terrified of social unrest; in his discourses he argued strongly against those who interpreted the Christian creed as implying the need for direct and uncompromising action against injustice, slavery and social inequality—which interestingly proves that there were many who still made the plain social application of the evangel.

21

NESTORIANS AND MONOPHYSITES

THE EGYPTIAN CHALLENGE. Theophilos was succeeded by his nephew Cyril on the Egyptian throne, and in 428 another challenge was made to his positions when Theodosios II appointed as Byzantine patriarch Nestorios, an Isaurian born on Mt. Tauros and educated at Antioch, who rejected the Alexandrian concept of unity. Both Cyril and Nestorios concurred in opposing Apollinaris, who virtually absorbed the man Christ in the *Logos*, but Nestorios opposed in turn Cyril's position that Christ's Two Natures (human and divine) were joined in indissoluble personal (hypostatic) union yet distinct, so that Mary was God's Mother, having borne Flesh that was one with the Word-spirit. He declared that he could not accept the idea of a God who was swaddled, and saw Christ as divided into Two Natures: Jesus was a Man become God. And so he refused to call Mary God's Mother or to use her cult-title *Theotokos*. He inclined to Theodore of Mopsuestia's notion of a union-of-opposites at every stage of growth, each union being fuller. Theodore, a Syrian of Antioch and a friend of John of the Golden Mouth, had fought for interpretations of Scripture that held to a direct historical meaning and did not blur that meaning away in christological symbolism. He saw history (*i.e.* the two testaments and the events of Roman history) moving along a definite progression in which the prophecy of ultimate human unity was steadily fulfilled.

Cyril, with clubmen who clattered bells and burned books in Alexandria, decided to fight Nestorios on the issue of Mary.[1] He attacked him (without mentioning names) in an Easter Pastoral, 429, and in a letter to his Egyptian priesthood. Nestorios, informed, decided to call a General Council. Cyril was keen to take the challenge up. 'Let not your Piety doubt for a moment,' he wrote, 'that we are ready to suffer anything, even prison or death.' His agents were busy in Byzantium, and he sent a report of the dispute to Rome, changing the chronology to make Nestorios out as aggressor. Not that the bishop of Rome needed any

[1] The *Parabolanoi* or Reckless, a sort of mercy-corps (for the sick), acted as leaders in mass-action against pagans or against bishops imposed by the State against the national positions.

stimulus in such a matter: he at once bade Nestorios denounce his (unstated) heresies, and Cyril launched anathemas. The emperor called a Council to inquire into Cyril's action.

Once more Egypt won. Nestorios had to be guarded by soldiers against Cyril's riotous followers. 'I was accused,' he said, 'by Cyril, who had got the Council together. Cyril was the head of it. Who was judge? Cyril. Who was accuser? Cyril. Who was bishop of Rome? Cyril. Cyril was everything.' He was deposed. The emperor confined Cyril, who was freed by Egyptian gold and from Alexandria sent round benedictions (gifts of carpets, ivory chairs, ostrich eggs, cash). Cyril had had to accept an Antiochene creed, but he saved his anathemas.

He died in 444. A letter attributed to Theodoret advised a heavy stone on his grave, as the dead would soon be trying to chase him back. Dioskouros tried to carry on, but now the political situation had sharpened. The Green faction was making headway under Theodosios II, and the dissident religious sects of Syria and Egypt were gaining a clearer political programme. The alliance of Rome and Alexandria against Byzantium broke down, for Rome normally inclined to support the most reactionary positions. At the second Council of Ephesos (called the Robber Council by those who disliked it) in 449, Dioskouros had everything his own way, refused to let the bishop of Rome's letters be read, and deposed Flavian, patriarch of Byzantium—in full pontificals he kicked Flavian in the belly 'like a wild ass', and three days later Flavian died. Back in Egypt, Dioskouros behaved as master, confiscating, murdering, exiling, as he pleased. 'The country is mine more than the emperor's!'

He was working with the eunuch Chrysaphios, the leader of the Greens; but in 450 Markian came to the throne, and the senatorial reaction triumphed. The eunuch fell, and in 451 the Council of Chalkedon broke the control of Egypt on the religious situation.

This was a decisive moment. It meant that the mass-demands uttered by Alexandria and Antioch had been defeated. When Markian's letter reinstating the men exiled by the Council of Ephesos reached Alexandria, the clergy saw what had happened. 'Death is in this letter, Man of God.' Dioskouros could have kept his see by submitting; but that was not possible. When he left Chalkedon, he had said, 'With me the faith of the Fathers is destroyed.' He refused to appear at the later sittings and went into exile at Gangra. But the faith which he championed was not destroyed; it fell back more deeply upon its mass-basis.

Chalkedon did not crush the dissident forces; it made them more recalcitrant. Now they do not seek to gain control of the imperial Church but to oppose it. In Egypt was born the Monophysite or Jacobite Church.

It was born out of the fierce resistance of the masses to Markian. When the imperial patriarch came, 'a terrible riot' burst out, says Evagrios. He adds:

> The rhetorician Priskos tells us in his *History* that he visited Alexandria at the time and saw the crowds attacking the civic authorities. When the soldiers tried to suppress them, they were stoned and chased off; they hid in the old Temple of Sarapis, but the people besieged it and burned them alive. The emperor in reply sent 2,000 solders, raw levies . . . making things worse than ever; for they raped the wives and daughters of the citizens.

Then in 457 came news of Markian's death: the people rose again.

> Taking advantage of the absence of the military commander, they chose a certain Timothy the Cat as bishop. . . . The commander returned on account of these atrocities; and some Alexandrians, instigated by Timothy, murdered the imperial bishop, stabbing his belly when he took refuge in the Baptistry. They then showed the body hung from a rope in the place called Tetrapylon, jeering and boasting they'd killed him. They dragged his body through the streets and burned it, and (according to a petition presented to Leo by the bishop and clergy of Alexandria) they even like beasts ate part of the intestines. (Evagrios.)

And so, often savagely, but always indomitably, the resistance went on. Greek was giving way to Coptic, the old Egyptian tongue in its vernacular development; and the patriarch of Alexandria had taken on the supremacy of the High-priest of Amen Ra: he was

> the most Divine and All Holy Lord, Pope and Patriarch of the great city of Alexandria, of Lybia, Pentapolis, Ethiopia, and all the lands of Egypt. Father of Fathers, Bishop of Bishops, Thirteenth Apostle and Judge of the World.

Leo and Zeno, who followed Markian, tried to find formulas of re-conciliation; but the Egyptians hardened in their emphasis on Unity—an absolute Unity which was opposed to the discordant world; Father and Son, Power and Love, absolutely one. This sharply monistic creed had great fighting powers, as had later Islam, which to a considerable extent issued from it. Zeno's accession was marked by rebellions in which the Monophysites played a part. His *Henotikon* of 481 threw a sop to the creed by supporting the formulations of Nikaia and denouncing all contrary doctrines whether set out 'at Chalkedon or elsewhere', and evaded all references to either One Nature or Two Natures. He thus won a thirty years' truce, though some extreme groups like the Headless in Egypt stood out.

The Monophysite cause, which was also that of the Green factions, steadily increased in strength during that period; the next emperor, Anastasios, was a staunch Monophysite.

GREENS AND MONOPHYSITES. The enemy's tales called him the son of an Arian mother with a Manichee uncle. A tall man with fine eyes of different hues, while still a palace-usher he set up a chair in St. Sophia and used to give not-very-orthodox instruction to a select audience till the patriarch expelled him. When he became emperor the Church tried to tie him down by demanding a written statement that he would maintain orthodoxy. But he soon showed that he had a will of his own, deposed two Byzantine partiarchs, threw out Flavian, the patriarch of Antioch and put in his place Severos, the great theologian of the Monophysites.

The kind of mass-unrest that underlay such acts can be read in Evagrios:

> The monks of the Kynegourika district and all who lived in the first province of Syria gathered and burst into Antioch with much tumult and disorder. They wanted to compel Flavian to anathematise the Synod of Chalkedon and the Epistle of Pope Leo. When he strongly refused and the monks still pressed, the people rose against the monks and killed a huge number, who found their graves in the Orontes.

'The people' in that last sentence must be the Blue faction; for Antioch was largely Green, at peace under Severos the Monophysite who followed.[1]

About the same time came riots in Byzantium over the Trisagion chant, the Monophysite slogan, invented by Peter the Fuller, a staunch bishop of Antioch a while back, who held his see though twice expelled by the orthodox. It consisted of the addition of 'who wast crucified for us' to the words 'Holy God Holy Mighty Immortal pity us'. Anastasios ordered it to be sung in the churches at Byzantium. The orthodox, the Blues, rose in horror at what they considered a blasphemy, and fired the houses of suspected Monophysites, such as the finance-minister Marinos the Syrian, and cut the head off a monk whom they found in Marinos' house. Then with the head on a pole they marched the streets, demanding a new emperor and saying the monk had been an enemy of the Trinity.

The orthodox account is that Anastasios came humbly and uncrowned into the Circus, to plead his case. But John Malalas, an historian with many popular elements, calls his speech 'divine' and does not mention it as humiliating. No doubt, however, the Trisagion was too strong for Byzantium. Evagrios links the whole episode with the general resurgence of Monophysitism in the eastern cities, and remarks, 'Archbishop Severos

---

[1] Two bishops could only get a writ of deposition to Severos by using an archdeacon dressed and veiled and 'pretending in all ways to be a woman' who slipped the writ to the patriarch 'with a lascivious air', then disappeared in the crowd—a proof of Severos' very strong position in the city.

7*

in a letter to Soterikos tells how the patriarch Makedonios and his clergy were responsible for this sedition.'

Anastasios must have agreed with Severos, for in 511 he had Makedonios deposed and a Monophysite·partisan made patriarch of Byzantium.

The horror that the orthodox felt at the words which added to the praise of the Trinity the claim that the Son was crucified for men, gives us an insight into the social bases of the dogmatic distinctions. The Monophysite masses want the conviction that the Son was *one* with them, *one* with their sufferings, and they find the clue to the meaning of unity in that conviction; the orthodox want the unity abstracted far from the earthly fact of suffering and division, so that it sanctifies that suffering and division from above.

We may, then, believe that the *Life of St. Daniel the Stylite* records something of what the common man felt about Anastasios: the saint prophesies that Ariadne would reign after Zeno with a man,

> a model of sobriety to all men, one who in gentleness and justice would surpass all who had reigned at any time. 'He will turn aside too,' he said, 'from that love of money which according to the apostle is the root of all evil. He will govern the State impartially and honestly, and in all his reign will grant peace and confidence to the most holy churches and the order of monks. In his time the rich will not be favoured, nor shall the poor be wronged; for this above all, in peace and war, will be the surest guarantee of prosperity to the world.'

JUSTINIAN'S DILEMMA. With Justin I and Justinian came the senatorial reaction again; and the suppression of the Greens was equally a suppression of the Monophysites. Justinian strengthened the imperial hold on the Church. Justin I had already set the pace. Under him heretics, Jews and Samaritans were put under severe disabilities. An accord was reached in 518–19 with the bishop of Rome—the usual sign of an attack on the people—and at once efforts were made to put down Antioch and Alexandria. More than fifty bishops were exiled; monasteries in Syria were shut; anyone who resisted was jailed or cut down. Justinian carried on with the same policy. A Samaritan revolt of 529 was bloodily crushed; in 551 the Samaritans rose again, with the Jews, at Kaisareia. One of the disabilities laid on Jews was to deny them the right to read the Old Testament in Hebrew. Montanists and Manichees were tortured, burned, deprived of all property. Justinian, we are told, liked to argue with them, but 'with satanic obstinacy they cried fearlessly that they were ready to face the stake for the religion of Mani'.

Justinian called on Leontios, a bishop skilled in the work of Aristotle, to draw up the imperial position; thus into the formulations came the

Aristotelean terminology of substance, species, genus, qualities, which dominated the later scholastics of the West. At the moment this Aristotelean intrusion into orthodox theology came from the need to stand up against the strong Aristotelean element in some of the last pagan philosophical works, an element taken over by the Monophysite thinkers like John Philoponos of Alexandria or Severos of Antioch.

In 529 Justinian reconsidered his policy; he let exiles return, and in 531 a conference without results was held at Byzantium. The obstinate resistance in the eastern provinces had shaken him; and he tried to weaken Monophysite opposition by dallying with the Theopaschite doctrine that one of the Trinity suffered in the flesh. In 533 he attempted an edict on the subject, and asked the bishop of Rome to confirm. With no results.

A 536 Council anathematised all dissenters and led to fresh persecutions. Theodora, however, worked for a reconciliation with the Monophysites. She got an undercover-Monophysite into the Byzantine patriarchate, and hid the deposed Severos in her palace-quarters. The orthodox patriarch at Antioch informed the bishop of Rome, who came to Byzantium and gave the show away. Severos went off in exile to the Egyptian desert, but various other heretics still hid in Theodora's rooms.

Justinian had attempted a reconciliation-formula in his *Three Chapters*, which cited, and condemned, extracts from three Nestorians (in chief Theodore of Mopsuestia) approved by Chalkedon. He hoped thus to win over the Monophysites, but what he did was to embroil himself with the Papacy. Pope Vigilius arrived in January 545 and tried to juggle statements condemning Theodore's work without repudiating Chalkedon. Then, scared that he was undermining the papal basis in the West, he suggested a General Council and withdrew his statement. Justinian, as a preparation for the right sort of Council, deposed the patriarchs of Alexandria and Jerusalem, and issued a new edict. Vigilius, resisting, was arrested at the altar; in his fear he pulled the altar over on top of himself and was let go injured home, guarded. Justinian weakened and agreed to let his patriarch make submission to Vigilius; he couldn't now stop the Council, but delayed it till May 553. Then it met and obeyed his instructions. The bishop of Rome and the three cited theologians were condemned. After six months in jail, Vigilius agreed with the Council, then died on his way back to Rome. (Oddly, under Pope Gregory I, the 553 Council was proclaimed valid.)[1]

1 Theodora had had her brush with Vigilius. She rigged the papal election and got him elected, but he failed to carry out his promises to her. He was carried off from a church in Rome by imperial soldiers to Sicily for ten months.

PANTHEISM AND SOCIAL PROTEST. In Palestine and Syria a new line of
heresy appeared, led by Stephen Bar Sudaili. Coming from Edessa,
Stephen spent some years in a convent near Jerusalem. His heresy was defined as Origenistic: it had affiliations with the semi-pantheist elements in
Origen. Thus, he was strong against eternal damnation: 'God will pass
away, and Christ will cease to be, and the spirit will no longer be called
spirit. Essence alone will remain.' He was probably the author of the
treatise ascribed to Dionysios the Areopagite, one of the basic works of
Byzantine culture. His teachings were condemned by edict in 543(2),
and among the ideas attributed to him was the belief that resurrected
bodies would be spherical, and that the stars were animated, and acted
directly on our world.

Something of this element, in the simple form of absorption in the
fullness and manifold beauty of the world, the sense of a luminous unity
of man and nature, appears in what became orthodox Syrian thought,
in the work of men like Ephraem of Edessa who disliked the analytic
divisive element in heresies tending to Manichee oppositions or to intellectual abstractions. 'The hateful sight of the image of four faces is from
the Hittites; accursed disputation, that hidden moth, is from the Greeks.'
The children of strife seek 'to taste fire, see the air, handle the air'. What
matters is the translucent pearl 'whose wall is its own beauty'.

> The daughter of the sea am I, the boundless sea. And from the sea out of which
> I came up is the mighty treasury of mysteries in my bosom. Search out the sea,
> yes, but do not search out the lord of the sea.

Such an attitude, though easily exploited to hide the discords and conflicts of society, was born from a deep sense of human unity abstracted
from struggle and projected on to nature as on to the pure dimension of
its own potentiality.

The Monophysite world was gaining new strength yearly. The great
organiser was Jacob Bardaios, bishop of Edessa. While hiding at Byzantium under Theodora's protection, he ordained Monophysite bishops;
and he roamed far and wide over the East, Asia, Syria, Mesopotamia,
clad in the stitched saddlecloths of asses. He escaped all snares, and went
on organising his rebel Church till his death in 578. In 550 he had gone so
far as to set up a patriarch of Antioch in open opposition to the emperor.

How strong was the local patriotism in Syria and Mesopotamia we
can judge from poets like James of Sarug. Edessa is for him 'the daughter
of the Parthians espoused to the Cross', who alone has been found faithful:

> Edessa sent to Christ by an epistle to come and enlighten her. On behalf of all
> the peoples she made intercession to him to leave Zion which hated him, and
> come to the peoples who loved him.

And this local patriotism is linked with an intense social feeling. In Christ is the saviour and lord of Edessa; he is also the fellow of the Syrian poor.

Shamuna, our riches, you're richer far than all the rich of the world.
For look the rich men stand at your door and ask that you relieve them.
Small was your village and poor your land, who then bestowed on you
that lords of villages and cities beg you for your favour?
Look, the judges in their robes and vestments stooping
for dust from your threshold as if it were the medicine of life.
The cross is rich and swells the richness of its worshippers
and its poverty depises all the riches in the world.
Shamuna and Guria, sons of the poor, look at your doors
the rich bow down that they may receive from you their wants.
The son of God in poverty and in privation
showed the world that all its riches are nothing.
His disciples were fishermen all, all of them poor and weak,
all men of no importance, whose name was famed through their faith.

Justinian died in 565, still desperately seeking for the formula that would unify his empire. He was caught up by what was termed the aphthartodocetic heresy (which had a tinct of the docetic idea that Christ was never incarnated in a human body, but merely 'appeared'). His own patriarch resisted, was arrested and exiled. Opposition flared up; and Justinian was preparing for strong repressions when he died.

22

THE CHURCH IN PERSIA

THE NESTORIANS. The heresies of Egypt and Syria had now taken the form of full-grown separatist movements, and especially in Syria and in Persia a strong dissident culture was being formed.[1] The extension of the Church into Persia deserves some notice; for there, free from the controls of the Roman state, heresy could flourish. In Persia, despite persecutions from the Magian priesthood, the Christians could win adherents among worshippers of the old cults of Assyria and Chaldea. Here too were Jewish communities of farmers and craftsmen under their own Prince of the Exile, who had carried on the study of the Law and founded schools—of which the most important was the Sidra of Sora, set up by doctors from the Galilean schools in the early third century.

About 250 a definite Christian Church had appeared, probably largely the work of men from Edessa; and in the fourth century attempts were made to co-ordinate the various groups under the see of Seluekia Ktesiphon. Monasticism was now common, and a local literature was evolving. Then, as war between Persia and the Empire appeared in the mid-century, persecution grew serious. Messianic hopes burned high, and the Christians looked to liberation by the Empire. Many died by the Nine Deaths, many recanted, but the Church survived.

Persecution slackened and the Church built itself up afresh. Yezdegerd I accepted the Christians, no doubt as a balance against the Magians in the feudal disorders that were afflicting Persia. A Council in 410 accepted Nikaia, and strengthened central organisation, with a primate and five metropolitans. When the Church started getting too strong, Yezdegerd changed his policy and began flaying Christians or putting them in pits of rats. But in 422, after war with the Empire, liberty of conscience was guaranteed. Then more persecutions came under Yezdegerd II.

In the later half of the fourth century a school had developed at Edessa, linked with Antioch. A strong Nestorian group arose, who, led by Barsauma, dominated the school. Barsauma put out the idea that if the Persian king wanted to keep the Christians loyal, let them have their own

[1] The Armenian Church rejected Chalkedon all along: here there was a fairly direct national-separatist issue from the outset.

dogma opposed to that of Byzantium. He attacked both Monophysites and Orthodox, and advocated a married clergy. As at this period Zeno's *Henotikon* had at least pacified the Monophysites within the Empire, Barsauma was able to argue that only the Nestorians were reliably anti-imperial.

Zeno purged the Edessa school of Nestorians, and Barsauma gathered them into a new school at Nisibis. A council held at Seleukia tried to control the monks by putting them under bishops and allowed the clergy to marry even a second time. Missionaries went out, even into the Kurdish mountains. In 492–5 Barsauma died.

THE NEW RATIONALISM. Syrian thought, whether Nestorian or Monophysite, had a far more rational element than is to be found in orthodox or papal formulations. The Nestorian schools, in fact, looked rather to Theodore of Mopsuestia than to Nestorios. Barses, a Nestorian writer, summed up plainly what the creed owed to Nestorios, who, he said, suffered for defending the true faith that was being wrecked by Egyptian guile and gold, for having distinguished the image of Servant from that of Master, and for refusing to call Mary God's Mother. Nestorios thus gave the creed its emotional stimulus, but its working-out was in terms of Theodore's cool and rational attempts to carry a scientific spirit into the examination of Christian ideas.

How may we differentiate the Monophysites and Nestorians? I have already indicated the reasons for the Monophysite clinging to the concept of unity as a defiance of the divided world and its false impositions of order. In such a view the Two Natures appear as a defence of the world's evil. But to the Nestorians Monophysitism seemed a slurring over of the fact of division. They held that one must begin from the fact of Two Natures, of a division in the life-process, and *then* strive to attain unity—not the unity of the imperial idea, which they detested as much as the Monophysites, but a unity developing out of the clash and fusion of the opposites, the two-natures.

There was thus an embryonic yet powerful scientific element in the Nestorian schools, a fumbling but vital effort to develop Aristotelian thought along more dialectical lines. On the other hand the Monophysite slogan of unity had a simpler fighting-force to rally the people against the imperial State. And Monophysite thinkers, because they opposed the State with a different concept of unity, also sought to develop Aristotelianism along new lines, to give a new concreteness to his logical oppositions and interrelations.[1]

1 'The struggle against the Two Natures symbolises in their eyes the struggle against the Devil, with whom they connected all that had a compact with the world, all that

We may generalise by saying that in these two heretical movements the abstractions of Greek philosophers were brought down to earth again. Involved in the Father-Son problem and the arguments over the Natures was the old question of unity and multiplicity, their relation, their opposition and identity. But whereas in the purely philosophic levels that question had become hopelessly abstract and etiolated, here in the masses fighting against the imperial State it was revitalised, given all sorts of new connections with life, with history, with struggle. The basis was being laid for an enormous new advance of thought.

THE PROPHET MANI. Meanwhile, linked with Christian and Gnostic elements in the Empire, a new prophetic religion had been born in Persia, which expressed dissidence even more sharply than the two heresies we have been considering. This was Manicheanism, a product of the second half of the third century.

Mani began preaching round 242, and came into collision with the Magians. He travelled widely in Central Asia, and seems to have reached China and India. His disciples went even further. He had been brought up in a sect called the Baptists in South Babylonia, related to the Mandaeans and the early elements in Christianity centred round John the Baptist. He declared himself the Leader, the Ambassador of Light, the Paraklete, the final Prophet who completed the work of Jesus (who did not suffer the Passion). His system was ruthlessly dualistic, an absolute opposition of good and evil, light and dark, spirit and body. Adam was begotten by Satan with the aid of Sin, Greed, Desire. Evil included an Earth of Darkness, part of the great kingdom from which Satan came, eternally opposed to Light and God's Primal Man. Irrupting into the Earth of Light, Satan defeated the Primal Man. God, with new Aions, then rescued the Primal Man: but the latter had lost some of his light and five dark elements had mingled with light's generations. Into Adam and Eve Satan put some of the stolen light, so they were not wholly of the dark, and the problem was to reject the world and liberate the seeds of light.

In the Manichean Church were two levels, the elect or perfect, and the catechumens or listeners. The perfect had to give up sex, meat, wine and all compromises with the world; the others had only to abstain from idolatry, lies, witchcraft, fornication, greed and the killing of any living creature.

Mani's ideas drew largely from Christian Gnostic sources. His dualistic

by which lived the rich Graeco-Roman exploiters and the native hellenist exploiters'
—Dyakonov, *John of Ephesos* (in Russian).

9. THE PRAYER OF ISAIAH

Paris Psalter, tenth century

8. MOSES RECEIVING THE TABLETS

cosmogony came from Bardaisan; from Markion he took his opposition of the Old and the New Testament, his eternal dualism, and his sect-organisation. Here, and in similar groups, lay his main sources rather than in the old Zoroastrianism of Persia, which, though opposing Light and Darkness, defined man as the product of light, goodness, truth (Ormazd), and as thus endowed with a will free to choose the right course.[1]

Mani's faith burst over the world in two big waves, the first in the third to seventh centuries, the second in the ninth to fourteenth. It went east to Turkestan, India, China; west all over the south and part of Central Europe. Wherever men felt gripped in a remorseless mechanism which could not be broken, and yet refused to surrender to it, Manicheanism had a deep appeal. In particular it underlay peasant revolts right through the medieval world.

Mani was said to have sent disciples to Syria and Egypt; certainly his creed had a strong hold in those areas by the fourth century and in some parts threatened the Church's grip. Aspects of it persisted powerfully through the great dissenting creeds, from Paulicianism to Puritanism. Among the monks who could not stomach the Basilian system, Manichean elements were often strong, *e.g* the Massalians, who refused to leave the world in order to be fitted back into it, or the Enkratites, a sect who condemned marriage, meat and wine. This sect was pre-Manichean, as it arose in the second century; and its attitudes show how linked was Mani's movement with the more dissident peasant movements of Asia. It was still thriving in Phrygia and Asia Minor (central and southern) till late fourth century. Montanism, though not thoroughly dualist, was another forerunner. It accused the Church of wordly compromise, and had two orders of worshippers, pneumatics and psychics, while Montanos like Mani called himself the Paraklete. It won over Tertullian and flourished till the eighth century. The Novatians, arising in mid-third century, demanded stricter disciplines and gradually fused with Montanists. Augustine, we must recall, was a Manichee in his youth.

---

[1] Gnostic creeds, amid much confusion, had often held that matter was wholly evil and so not of God—the work of someone between matter and God, a demiurge corrupted by his fall from the divine pleroma or fullness. Man they held a dual being with body as soul-tomb (an idea found in Plato). Only death released; meanwhile avoid all that strengthened the jailing, especially sex. Zorastrianism did not see man as dual; it looked to a final restitution, a bodily resurrection, a new heaven and earth, with all creation reconciled to God. It condemned self-mortification, being the ethic of cattle-raising farmers, who held marriage and the getting of sons a primary necessity. Its dominant form now under the Sassanids was Zarvanism: or at least that was a widely-diffused form, which held to a single primal principle that got two sons; the firstborn fell, but the younger will fight to the end, restoring unity and harmony.

Such creeds were diffused by wandering monks. Thus, Eustathios, once a disciple of Areios in Alexandria, founded cenobitic monasticism in Asia Minor and Armenia, and was condemned at the Council of Gangra, 330, for ascetic excess, teaching that the married cannot be saved, forbidding meat, encouraging women to cut off their hair and dress like men, and preferring his own gatherings to church-services. A significant section of this Council's attack on the uncontrolled ascetics was that 'as saints' they claimed the right to the first fruits that normally went to the Church. That is, if the ascetics prevailed, the Church's grip on the peasants would be broken down.

There was thus no lack of antecedents to Mani's creed in the heretical groups. To all such positions the Church opposed the ideas of the Incarnation and the Sacramental Use of Nature. These ideas vindicated the normal matters of living, on which human society depended, but in terms of the political and theological compromises laid down by the Church.

EVENTS IN PERSIA. In Persia things were quiet in the earlier sixth century. A Magian dissident, Mazdak, preached community of goods and women, and King Quwad took up the creed for use against the nobles with their wealth and pride-of-birth. A revolt led by the Grand Mobed and the high nobles deposed Quwad in 496; then came a further period of toleration. At length a strong Nestorian primate emerged, Maraba.

But renewed war with the Empire provoked fresh persecutions from the Mages. Maraba, arrested, was in a difficult position, as he had once been a Magian and the penalty of renegadism was death. However a revolt of the king's son, to whom Christians thronged, saved him, for he was freed to do what he could in quieting things. The next *Catholikos* was named by the king, not elected—Joseph, a doctor, who had studied in the Byzantine Empire and come back as a monk. He behaved in an arbitrary way till the bishops got at the king through another doctor and were allowed to depose him.

Though the Nestorians were the accepted Christian Church in Persia, the Monophysites had become strong too, and even won over a king's son at one time. Deportees from Syria and missionaries along the desert trade-routes under the protection of the Ghassanids, brought the creed in. A 585 Nestorian synod attacked the Monophysites as disturbers of the peace emerging like dungbeetles and crickets from the ravines and ditches of error, and called Henana of Nisibis a 'friend of elegant language opposed to truth, like whores who love a provocative dress'. (The Henanans believed in the Two Natures, but looked to John of the Golden

Mouth rather than Theodore of Mopsuestia, and so rejected the Pelagian rationalism of Theodore with its stress on free will; they held that human nature is sinful and errs involuntarily.)

There followed a troubled period of feudal revolts in Persia: when Chosrau II regained his throne with Byzantine aid, things looked bad for the Nestorians and the *Catholikos* fled. But the king was easy-going, and the problems that arose were of those conflicts among the Christians themselves—Nestorians, Monophysites, Massilians, Henanans. The last-named group caused a revolt, which led to their town Nisibis being sacked by Persian soldiers and many notables massacred.

The Monophysites had centres at Tagrit and the monastery of Mar Mattai, and were aided by a court-doctor. When the primacy fell vacant, they held debates with the Nestorians. What faith did the Apostles preach? Is Mary mother of god or man? Then persecutions began yet again, with the primacy still unfilled. But things bettered in time, with the king's treasurer working for the Nestorians. However, war with Byzantium came in 604. Difficult times were ahead. No sooner was the war between the Empire and Persia over than Persia fell to the Arabs. The Nestorian monks, who had managed to amass estates in the northern areas, resisted most strongly of the Christian groups.

THE FIRST THEOLOGICAL UNIVERSITY. The Nestorian Church had developed on lines as hierarchical as those of the imperial Church. The people were excluded from elective power, and juridical controls were in the hands of the upper hierarchy. Church-property was administered by *oikonomoi*, laymen of high social status, under the bishop; and the monasteries were drawn effectively under the bishops also, so that the hierarchy benefitted directly by the land-gains.[1]

Still, the rational and scientific bias of their thinking long remained, well into Islamic days. Dogmatic issues, except in a devoted reiteration of the bases on which the Church differentiated itself from the Orthodox and the Monophysites, were rather ignored. That is, its attitudes were political and national rather than dogmatic. The Nestorians needed, however, to resist and answer the strong missionary zeal of the Monophysites. The efforts of Barsauma and others from Edessa had founded schools, but this wave of intellectual activity declined in the first half of the sixth century. Under Maraba a second wave rose up. Each church or monastery was a centre where men learned hymns, canticles, responses, songs for

[1] Rather late in starting. They had a reform movement under Abraham of Kaskar (towards mid-sixth century): in his Mt. Izla monastery he tried to introduce rigorous methods of an Egyptian type. Here, later, Babai the Great was abbot, a doughty worker for Nestorian ideas. Abraham's disciples founded many houses.

popular use. At the same time a school for a higher level of work was needed, and this was built up at Nisibis.[1]

A Theological University, the first instituted anywhere.

The rule was cenobitic. Not that all the students were to be monks; some were to be priests or remain lay. Three obligations were imposed: regularity, residence, readiness to work. From clothes to hair-style, all was laid down, with fines or exclusion for infringement. Holidays ran from early August to late September, and only then might students leave Nisibis—unless sent by the Superior to take classes in near townships. They lodged in, unless all places were filled; must not eat in shops, inns or gardens; must not visit the nunnery inside the university-walls.

The building was composed of small rooms, each used by eight to ten students under a cell-chief. A cell-group ate together, and spent most of their time at study or in church. There was no manual labour save for poor students in holiday-time. Rich lads could lend if they did not take more than one per cent. yearly interest. The course lasted three years, and was based on the transcribing of Scriptures and liturgy, on which the professors later lectured. Theodore of Mopsuestia's commentary was the basic work; but almost all the great theologians were now translated into Syriac and were studied.

From these courses came many Nestorian tracts, *e.g. Instituta Regularia Divinae Legis* by Paul of Nisibis, translated into Greek at Byzantium in 551. The method is patently Aristotelian. Paul examines each book of the Scriptures, its aim, use, authenticity, order, title, significance, the divisions into chapters, the tendency. The text is studied in detail (with Porphyry's *Isagoge* as model). The Biblical canon is that of Theodore: after a critique into the historical materials Paul divides the books into those of complete authority, middling, and none, apocrypha. He touches on various difficult matters such as the Messianic sense of passages in the Ancient Law.

The Nestorians were thus well prepared for their great work of handing on the Hellenistic and Syriac traditions to the Arabs. In the brief narrative above, it will have been noted how doctors intrude. The Nestorians were keen students of medical science. They knew well the earlier parts of Aristotle's *Organon*. When the Edessan scholars moved into Persia, they worked not only at Nisibis but also at Gandisapora in East Persia; there arose an important school of Greek medicine, which spread its work all over the country, carrying with it Greek systems of thought.

[1] There was a school at Seleukia from the early fourth century, which expanded to take 800 students, but could not rival Nisibis won back to Nestorianism. Here Barsauma put Narses, of whose vast work we have only fragments. (Eighth-century schisms led to the setting-up of two monastery-schools.)

Not that the Monophysites were inactive in this kind of work. Their school at Resaina had by Justinian's day become famed through Sergios, one of the important translators of Greek works. Their monasteries at Kinnoesrin (Chalkis) sent out many versions of the introductory treatises of Aristotelian logic, concentrating on Porphyry's *Isagoge*, Aristotle's *Categories* and *Hermaneutike*: which they expounded, epitomised, made into compilations and so on.

23

THE LOSS OF SYRIA AND THE PAPACY

SEPARATIST MOVEMENTS AND NEW UNIONS. The century of Justinian went out in faction-fights, army-revolts, feudal anarchy, in which the rebel religious groups played a strenuous part. Justin II had weakly tried to put the Monophysites down with his *Programma*, but Maurice was described by the Syrian Monophysites as a righteous king, a martyr. They said that he prayed to God to be chastised on earth rather than after death, and an angel came to tell him that he was being taken at his word; he persisted, and even refused to let a nurse substitute her child for one of his own sons in the slaughter of his whole family. He was set in a blazing boat with hands tied; and as the boat drifted out, the cords burned through and he lifted up his hands in praise and thanks amid the leaping flames

In the invasions of the Persians and of the Arabs, the Monophysites, as we saw, took the side of the invaders or remained neutral. In Egypt their hatred of the King's Men, the Melchites who supported the imperial Church, was so great that they attacked the soldiers.

Thus the strong separatist movements, which had taken form in the idiom of the heresies, broke up the Empire before the invaders came, or at least weakened it so much that the invaders had no trouble in Syria, Palestine, Egypt. And just as the Nestorian and Monophysite expansion eastward, linked with trade-movements, played an important part in setting off the forces which cohered into Islam, so the cultural bases of these dissident creeds provided the main secular materials of Arabic culture. When we look at the full picture, we find that the forces breaking off Syria, Palestine and Egypt from the Empire, and those begetting Islam, are parts of a single movement.

IMPERIAL POSITIONS. Heraklios tried in vain the last imperial formula of reconciliation with the Monophysites. His Monothelitism declared that Christ has Two Natures but One Energy—the Two Natures were meant to please the adherents of Chalkedon, the One Energy to please the Monophysites. But nobody was pleased; Sophronios, a monk of Palestine, living in Alexandria, replied that the formula was mere political opportunism. Heraklios in his *Ekthesis* then forbade all mention of One or More

Energies, and asserted the doctrine of One Will. The pope dissented; the exarchs of Carthage and Ravenna revolted.

The increasing trend of the autocracy at Byzantium to elevate the status of its patriarchate had long worried the Papacy. Under Maurice the patriarch John the Faster took the title of Oecumenical, and Pope Gregory was horrified as at a sign of coming Antichrist:

> I am compelled to cry out and say O Times O Manners of Men. When all Europe has been given over to the power of barbarians, when cities are destroyed, camps overthrown, provinces depopulated, when the farmer no more tills the soil, when idol-worshippers rage and lord it for the slaughter of the faithful, yet priests who should lie weeping on the ground and in ashes seek for themselves names of vanity and glory in new and profane titles.

And when Maurice tried to stop soldiers, officials and curials deserting to become monks, Gregory again made a violent protest.

So far the Papacy had been able to maintain its political position largely by playing one patriarchate against another. But when Alexandria, Jerusalem and Antioch were lost to the Empire, Rome and Byzantium confronted one another without space for feints and complicated balances of power. Rome's position was much worsened. Now she had only one important asset, her comparative independence after the Justinianic edifice tottered and fell; but even that asset had its severe dangers. Who was to protect Rome from attacks by Lombards or Franks or some fresh barbarians? Rome now began to think in new political terms, feeling her way, but gradually moving towards the idea of becoming an independent power. This aim, long dim and tentative, was quickened after the shattering attacks of the Arabs on Byzantium. Who knew but that the Empire might fall? and then what was going to happen to the Papacy?

PETER OUT OF JANUS. It would be as well to pause here and look more closely at Rome. The Papacy up to the twelfth century was one of the main factors canalising Byzantine influences and transmitting them over the West; but after it managed to break away, partially in the ninth century and more fully in the eleventh, it took the lead in constructing the thesis of a unique and independent development of the West—the thesis which, prevailing one way or another, has distorted almost all inquiries into the nature of Europe and the changes between the ancient world and the medieval.

The see of Rome claimed a special position from the words 'You are Peter' (*Petra*, rock): You are the Rock of the Church. But in fact the name Peter seems to refer to the thunder-stone (in the earliest text of St. Mark's gospel) as the twin-apostles are called *Boanerges*, Sons of

Thunder. Also, it is more than doubtful that Peter ever visited Rome, though the see later claimed him as its first bishop. In any event there were no bishops in Peter's days! and it was with the see of Antioch that Peter was more convincingly connected. Latin churches still keep the Feast of the Chains of St. Peter at Antioch on February 22nd.

In apostolic days there may have been a committee of *episkopoi*, over-seers, but certainly no Bishop; and it is not till a hundred years after Irenaeus that the term Pope, *papa*, appears. There is in fact no higher title than bishop in the hierarchy. Pope Gregory the Great in 598, writing to the bishop of Alexandria, remarked that all bishops were equal, and Pope Zachery (in 751) referred to himself as *co-episkopus*, a fellow-bishop of St. Boniface. The term *papa* was used as late as the sixth century in the Latin Church for any specially virtuous bishop.[1]

However by the third century Rome had a special dignity, partly as the seat of Empire, but basically as the seat of the most extensive martyrdoms. *Revelation* had already expressed this, but with hatred, defining Rome as the spot most marked out for destruction.

It is not Peter but *Janus* that the Papacy based itself on. Janus was a sky-god, a god holding the sky-door:'Janitor of Heaven and Hell', said the pagan Macrobius, seeking to identify him with Apollo Thyraios, the Gate-keeper. In the Vatican Temple of Apollo, where Peter was buried according to the Papacy, in the basilica the Rod of Janus still stands beside the Canon Penitentiary: it was used to touch a penitent on the head, con-ferring an indulgence. Ovid says of Janus, 'In his right hand the Rod, in his left the Key', and calls him the guardian of the god's *limina* (threshold). *Ad limina* was used at least from the fifth century onwards, through medieval days, for a visit to St. Peter in the Vatican. The Vatican Hill itself was the Janiculan, the valley below being sacred to Janus. The first day of his month, January, was made the festival of St. Peter.

There is no doubt then that the see of Rome took over the powers of Janus, the god with the keys of heaven and hell, and simply identified Janus with Peter, to Christianise him.[2]

THE FORCE OF TRADITION. Of sites with apostolic traditions, Antioch and Alexandria had securer traditions than Rome; Jerusalem had an incom-

---

1 The Formularics of Marculf (*c.* 650) are dedicated to a *Papa* who is a bishop. Even after the ninth century the election of the Bishop of Rome is only a local matter for the clergy of the City of Rome, not concerning bishops in other sees. And today cardinals anywhere in the world hold their elective rights only as clergy of the *tituli* or parish-churches of the City of Rome and as bishops of the suburban sees.

2 In the earliest representations (*e.g.* mosaic of SS. Cosmas and Damian, at Rome) Peter has no key. About the eighth century he gets keys as his basic symbol—some-times one, generally two.

parably higher status as a martyr-centre, but lacked political importance. Rome, however, had no difficulty in preserving a high prestige while the seat of empire; when the seat shifted to Byzantium, Rome had a severe jolt, and for some time played for safety, backing one or another of the patriarchates to enhance its own value as the see controlling the balance of power. The Papacy thus tried to put itself forward as a sort of ultimate court of appeal on basic matters of faith, though the actual decisions came through General Councils.

The appeal to tradition had then a significance we find it hard to grasp: even among the Jews with their extreme respect for sacred books, the written word was made of no account by the traditions of the expositors.

> The votaries of the Greek mystic cults deliberately avoided writing down their more important formulae. Several considerations were in favour of this curious policy. There were no scientific canons for the interpretation of written texts; allegorising commentators read their own wild fancies into the plainest sentences. The only way of meeting them was to fall back on the traditional interpretations. We use the text to test the traditions; but criticism in its early stages pursues the opposite course, and as natural consequence rates tradition above Scripture.
>
> Other reasons which discouraged the use of writing were, first the fear that no literary skill might be equal to the difficulty of accurate statement; secondly, the natural reluctance of the religious mind to let the deepest truths be exposed to vulgar scoffs and criticism of the uninitiated; thirdly, some remnant of the primitive superstition that the formulae of a ritual are magic spells which would lose their potence if published to the world; and, finally, the natural instinct of a sacerdotal class to reserve the knowledge of deepest mysteries to a select inner circle.
>
> For all these reasons a jealously guarded tradition, commonly designated as the *arcana* or *secreta*, was to be found in all the early Christian Churches.

There is much of this attitude in Paul (the distinction of milk for babes and food for adults, and 'We speak wisdom among the perfect . . . we speak God's wisdom in mystery, the concealed wisdom . . . which none of the archons of this aion knew') and in *logia* like: Cast not your pearls before swine. Irenaeus, polemising against the Gnostics, does not base his position on the Scriptures, but says, 'The true *gnosis* is the teaching of the apostles and the primitive constitution of the Church throughout the world.' Celsus' first objection to Christianity was that it was a system of secret societies; Origen could not deny the charge, but justified a co-existence of exoteric and esoteric creeds from the examples of philosophy and the mysteries. Clement takes the same line, 'The Word loves concealment', he cites the *logion* of Jesus, 'My mystery is for me and the sons of my house.' The Apostles' Creed was oral till the fourth century and was recited to the initiate only at baptism. The Church was reluctant to set on paper the operative parts of the Mass; written texts are mentioned in the fourth century, but only much later was a standard text issued; the key-part was recited by the celebrant in a whisper and called *secretum*. Even the rules of penitential discipline were first written down by Theodore of Tarsos near the end of the seventh century, and some synods strongly criticised him.[1]

In such a situation Rome's claim to a traditional prestige could have much effect.

THE RISE OF THE PAPACY. Till the third century eastern influences dominated the Roman Church and the liturgy was in Greek. That is, only after the foundation of Byzantium did the see of Rome become decisively Latin. Hippolytus, a Roman Christian, wrote in Greek; with Novatian, in mid-third century, Latin is found.

The Papacy first gained something like a constitutional position at the Council of Sardica, in 343, a gathering of some western bishops not recognised by the African Church. So weak was this council's position that later popes lyingly attributed its decisions to the Council of Nikaia. But after it bishops of Gaul and Spain began asking decisions from Rome, who, however, used the prerogative for long with much caution, though losing no chance to talk about Petrine primacy. So barbarous had the West become that a pope like Innocent I could assert without contradiction that 'no man has founded any church in Italy, Sicily, Gaul, Spain or Africa, excepting those which Peter and his successors have ordained as priests'. Indeed how backward in theology and general knowledge was the West is illustrated by the fact that Saint Hilary admits he never even heard of the Nicene Creed till his exile in 356.

What enabled the Papacy to make such claims was the destruction of the

---

1 In mystery-ritual the power lay in the *drōmenon*, the completed rite, not in things said about it, which tended to become inflated allegories like Plutarch's work on the Osirian cult. Clement took up writing about the faith with much trepidation; the Elders, holding to apostolic tradition, wrote no books; he felt it would be dangerous to expose the ideas of the creed to general view. A perilous sword would be put in a child's hand, pearls of truth cast before unclean swine. Even in his oral teaching he distinguished among his pupils as to how much 'truth' be set out. Book V of his *Stromata* is a defence of concealment. The Scriptures like Mary are pregnant with hidden truth. The test of true doctrine is continuity of tradition. He himself saw a fourfold meaning in the *O.T.* (Origen's pagan teacher Ammonios refused to put his doctrines on paper and made his pupils swear not to tell his secret teachings.) Origen himself found threefold meanings (for flesh, spirit, soul). 'It is not without danger to commit to writing the elucidation of such things, inasmuch as the masses do not need more teaching than that about the punishment of sinners.' Stobaios says, 'The mystical secrecy of the rites renders the divine more awesome by imitating this nature which eludes our comprehension,' etc.

African Church by the Vandals. For the Africans had high intellectual achievements and held strongly to the apostolic idea of a confederation of self-governing churches which acknowledged only the rule of a General Council. Cyprian called Pope Stephen 'Bishop of Rome, who seeks by tyrannical threats to compel his colleagues to obey him'. The African position was close to that of the Orthodox Church, which allowed coequal churches bound in unity by communion with the Oecumenical Patriarch, the General Council being the executive of the whole. The Council of Chalkedon had declared that Rome and Byzantium had equal prerogatives, *ta isa presbeia*; but Rome could not accept that at any cost.

The African thinkers, Tertullian, Cyprian, Augustine gave the Latin Church its intellectual basis; but after the fall of Carthage, so weak was the culture of the Western Church that before 1000 it had only one theologian of importance, Gregory I, and he merely restated some of Augustine's views. The only important mission sent out by the Papacy was that of the later Augustine to England. The Anglo-Saxons had to take the initiative in converting the outer German tribes and in reforming the demoralised Frankish Church. Before Gregory VII the popes are merely politicians, occasionally of an impressive stature like Leo I, concerned to grasp the government of Rome, extend their Italian estates, and use their prestige to play a part in balance-of-power tactics.

In the disordered West the best security for a monastery was to come directly under the pope's aegis and thus escape as far as possible from the environing feudal politics. This was so particularly in the big missionary areas, where the monastery thus gained a sort of extra-territorial status linking it directly with Rome. And in Italy by the early seventh century the papal estates had spread over parts of South Italy and Sicily, as well as round Rome; and reaching out into Corsica, Gaul, Sardinia, Dalmatia. They were controlled by a central administration at Rome that based its system on that of the imperial estates. From these two sources of landed power, the monasteries and the *patrimonium* of Peter (ostensibly held for the poor), the Papacy was steadily building up its real political basis.[1]

In Italy its policy aimed at preventing at all costs any political unification under the Lombards. And its political rise was helped by the general chaos of seventh-century Gaul: when the Church was reformed, the Papacy was able to impose its forms and attitudes.[2]

[1] Its income included *solidi*, coins, from payments for land, sale of goods or 'contributions' for levies; income from corn or other food; cloth and made-up clothing.
[2] Boniface and the Anglo-Saxons in general were strongly pro-papal. When Charles visited Rome in 787, Pope Hadrian gave him a copy of the Dionysian collection of

Thus it was that by the eighth century, as the Empire was struggling
for life-or-death against the Arabs, the Papacy was able to emerge
tentatively as a political power, experimenting with the use of Franks
against Lombards, but not daring to detach itself openly from the Empire.

canons and later additions, which served as the basis for canon-development affecting
all the Latin Churches of the medieval world. At the same time he gave the Roman
Sacramentary, which served to reform and unify the mass-books of the western
Churches. Charles also chose to support the Roman mode of singing rather than the
Gallic and asked the pope to send Roman singers north with him.

24

THE ICONOCLASTS: FIRST PHASE

IKONS AND THE STATE. The political and economic aspects of the Iconoclast struggle against Orthodoxy have already been touched on; here we shall look at the struggle of ideas thus precipitated. The first phases brought together the State and the dissident sects of the eastern provinces; but as soon as the latter began to assert their own viewpoint too strongly, a split rapidly matured, which wrecked the Iconoclast State and returned the Empire once more to the full feudalising trend. For whereas, say, the Tudor State in England soon had to suppress the more dissident aspects of Protestants but produced a revolutionary situation through this split, which came to a head under the Stuarts, here the town-workers, merchants and free peasants were not strong enough to challenge the Byzantine State and transform it. But they did not give in, and the forms of struggle that they devised have a continuous history into Tudor days.

The dissident creeds were various, ranging from the Massilians with a vow of poverty, to the Paulicians who sought to build free republics on an apostolic basis; but what they all agreed about was that the State-Church was corrupt, sold to pomp and property. Though they often had their own cherished cosmic myths, they united in rejecting the forms of Christianised Neoplatonism which had become the central position of Orthodoxy and which drew men together in a sacramental mysticism that made class-division holy.

That Neoplatonism, merging with the new centres of idea and emotion expressed in the Martyr-cult, had provided much of the great dynamic which created the new culture of Byzantium. Its climax came when Maximus the Confessor used it to repudiate the compromise urged by the State, but thereafter it settled solidly into a mysticism of acceptance.

The intensification of hierarchical attitudes that set in with Justinian I had involved a concentration of emotion on the worshipped ikon. Architecturally this appeared in the building of the ikonostasis to cut the apse from the rest of the church and enclose it from further development. (In the West development went on in the apse, where the altar and its relics were still the magnetic point determining the lines of construction but in the East the relics were isolated, cut off from the people, and the ikonostasis rose up, a barrier glorified by the glittering images that demanded adoration.) The cult of the martyr-relic, originally based in the uncompromising demand for a new sort of life, was thus abstracted into the ikon-cult where the Orthodox State triumphed. A transition form between ikon and relic was found in the acheiropoietic picture of Christ and Mary, supposed to be miraculous productions, or in the *eulogiai* which pilgrims took home from cult-centres, such as the *ampullai* of St. Menas in which the flask itself, its holy water or oil, its painting of the saint, were all merged in a common aura of sanctity.

So, in the areas where the energies of social revolt were broken down the ikon-cult became a deeply needed source of consolation. The desire for a love that does not betray, an uncorrupted union, given concrete expression in the art-work as in the social struggles revolving round the martyr, was abstracted by the orthodox worshipper, cut off from life, made its own satisfaction. That was why the art-works were needed: they were concrete, and the abstraction of unity from the world of conflict which the worshipper felt in adoring them was thus given, as it were, a displaced concrete basis of reference. So the ikon was felt as the sole pledge of union, harmony, happiness, love. But for the groups who still held to social struggle and wanted to actualise unity without the contradictions inherent in the State, the ikons were temptations of the devil, giving a false consolation and breaking down the true struggle for righteousness.

That was the position of the artisan and peasant iconoclasts; but the rulers and their supporters among the magnates and bishops took their stand against the ikons because ikon-worship strengthened the monks whose estates they wanted to confiscate, and because the quietist element in ikon worship ran counter to the needs of a fighting ethic. If the State was to survive (and the nobles to become big landowners again), the monastic lands must be taken and the people must supply good soldiers. The State thus moved towards a secularised and humanist position while the mass-supporters of Iconoclasm moved towards new group-formations based on an apostolic idiom of fellowship.

We must also recall that the adoring of pictures of Christ, Mary and the Saints had directly come out of the divine honours paid to portraits of the emperor. The Theodosian Code made laboured efforts to distinguish worship of Christ and veneration of the emperor's images. And the sacred images, revered or hated, were also an insignia of aristocracy. Embroidered images of saints decorated the noble's State-dress; and we hear of one senator's robe that depicted the whole of Christ's life.

There is thus no need to drag in Islamic influences to explain Iconoclasm. Rather we should see Islam in its early formative phases and the mass-cults with an iconoclastic outlook as different aspects of a vast movement of revolt and change embracing all the Near East. The main group of dissenters who in Asia Minor looked for a return to apostolic days had become the Paulicians, and they were iconoclast before there were any Moslems; the Nestorians had a touch of the same attitude.[1]

> In the 5th century one of the Syrian bishops had advocated the denunciation of ikons before he was ordained to a high post. In the 6th century there was a serious upheaval in Antioch directed against the worship of pictures, and in Edessa the riotous soldiers flung stones at the miraculous image of Christ. We also know of instances of attack upon images and the destruction of some ikons in the 7th century. (Barthold.)

SECULARISING FORCES. The first decree abolishing the use of images came in 726. When the Christ over the Bronze Door of the palace was destroyed, the Orthodox rioted, and the officer in charge was killed by women. Leo closed the college (between St. Sophia and the palace) where religious instruction was given; and the Orthodox spread the lie that he had burned it down with all inside. The patriarch was deposed after being given four years to make up his mind; and an iconoclast was appointed. The Papacy refused to acknowledge him; revolts were stirred up in Greece and the Islands, but easily put down. A submarine earthquake threw up a new island in the Aegean in 726, and the Orthodox blamed it on Leo. The *Acta*, however, cite only one martyrdom, that of the spathar Gregory and his companions.

Leo was abused by the Orthodox as a Friend of the Arabs, Nestorian, Jew-favourer, Manichee, Phrygian, Amelekite, Chameleon, Sennacherib; but that was nothing to the things said of his son Constantine V, who carried on the iconoclast policy much more rigorously. He was called Ahab, Diocletian, Herod, the Many-headed Dragon, and accused of necromancy, magic, bloody sacrifices, poisoning, corpse-dissection at dead of night, adoration of Bacchos and Aphrodite, celebration of evil

---

[1] The Church before establishment was generally iconoclast, but the problem had not yet been strongly posed, *e.g.* canon xxxvi of the Council of Elvira, and Eusebios of Kaisareia refers to the worship of images of Christ, Peter, Paul as 'a habit of the Gentiles'. In the sixth century the Bishop of Marseilles (a place in close contact with the East) ordered all ikons to be taken from the churches and destroyed. Pope Gregory I praised his zeal but reprimanded him for the destruction, setting out the plea that pictures are the books of the illiterate.

Among the Moslems Yezid II had issued an iconoclast decree (and Quran V, 92 could be taken to support it). At the seventh Council, 787, a monk said Leo had corresponded with Yezid through the Bishop of Makolia; Theophanes called Leo Saracen-minded. But this is just abuse. Even wilder was it to call Iconoclasm Jewish: Leo tried to have Jews baptised by force (they were inevitably suspect of partisanship for Islam).

rites as the Pope of Joy at the palace Sophianon. He was denounced as a
debauchee, but the only precise charge was a taste for harp-music; a
pederast; a villain, who, against the Bible, bade his people shave their
faces to as to seem young and 'to swell up everywhere like mare-mad
horses', so that 'nowadays we see old men of seventy still keeping this
fashion and shaving their faces as he wanted'. And of course he was said
to have died in burning (hell-fire) agony, calling in vain for hymns to
the Virgin and the Saints.

These stories are of interest in showing the terrific hatred that he caused
in the Orthodox Church; and one is worth looking at, as it illustrates
the way in which propaganda gets into history. At his baptism he was
said to have fouled the font and the patriarch prophesied he would 'dirty
the Church'. This is a typical bit of symbolic invention; 'proving' that
he was destined to foul the faith at its source, but many historians have
taken it at its face-value, as well as its derivations; that he grew up mad
on horse-dung, and loved to live in stables, amid obscenities and ordures.
Thus, Theophanes says he turned the shrine of Euphemia into a dung-
store; George the Monk cites a saying that such behaviour was natural
for a man whose Name was Dung; Nikephoros suggests that the iconoclast synod of Blachernai be called the Dung-synod as the Dung-lover
summoned it. The one point of fact behind all this is probably the use of
confiscated monasteries as cavalry-barracks.

He took his first steps against the monks in 765 (some forty years
after Leo's first iconoclast decrees). He had been brought up by iconoclast scholars from Asia and was surrounded through his reign by scholars
working at iconoclast formulations. His support was wide, ranging
from land-hungry nobles to artisans who disliked the monks for competing in the manufacture of church-objects. Theophanes stresses the
Paulicians' support: 'They hold Constantine the Jew-minded in memory
as Conqueror and Prophet, and venerate his impious dogma that destroys
the Incarnation of our Saviour.' The core of the movement was certainly
in the army. When St. Ioannikos the Great was named in 773 an excubitor
of the 18th Company (*bandon*) he had to accept the iconoclast creed of his
comrades, and as a result of distinguishing himself in the Bulgarian
campaign was in 797 attached to the emperor's person.

At the 753 Council Constantine tried to build a stable iconoclast
Church. He himself took part in the arguments, and composed thirteen
sermons without any invocations to the Saints, which he ordered to be
read in the churches. All the accounts make him specially hostile to the
cult of Mary, and he seems to have gone further than his bishops, who in
two canons of the Council allowed intercessions of Mary and the Saints

—presumably against his arguments. The Orthodox said that he punished people who merely used the common phrase, 'Help me, Theotokos!' and tried to stop them referring to Saints even in the names of churches, *e.g.* 'I'm off to the Holy Apostles.' One tale said that he tried to get his patriarch to agree to calling Mary the Mother of Jesus and not God's Mother, but was deterred by the latter's horror. Once he filled a purse with gold, then emptied it. The filled purse was worth a lot, the emptied purse nothing; so Mary was 'just another woman' after bearing Jesus. And during a rebellion the patriarch sent the story round, 'The emperor has told us that the son whom Mary bore, Christ, wasn't God's son but only an ordinary man: Mary bore him as Mary bore me.' (Mary was his own mother's name.)[1]

What is clear is that Constantine went further in his religious ideas than did the higher clergy who were ready to support monastic confiscation and ikon-attacks. In the theological debates, the abstractions born from Monophysitism and Nestorianism gained a new life. The iconoclast bishops accused their opponents of Nestorianism (the heresy of the Two Natures) in isolating the image of the Human Nature. And so when Constantine went close to Nestorianism in denying Mary her cult-title, he weakened their argument that the ikon-painters and the ikon-worshippers were in a cleft stick—they put in a single form the divine nature, and so were Monophysite, or declared they were dealing only with the Flesh and so were Nestorian, separating the indivisible; worse, they made the Image a fourth in the Trinity.

The Orthodox based their reply on the dogma of the Incarnation. The image was guarantee that Christ truly had a human nature, that the Word was made Flesh. To deny that he had all a man's characteristics, including that of representability, was to be Monophysite. Also, who could deny that the Saints might be shown as men?

The 753 Council, by failing to go all the way with Constantine, left open to the iconodules to base themselves on the Incarnation and argue that it was the original they adored, the archetype not the image. What the iconodules feared was the charge of idolatry, set out in the opening statement, 'God has taught us to worship him in spirit and in truth, but the Demon has reintroduced idolatry into the Church.' (The patriarch was denounced as a wood-worshipper, and Constantine hailed: 'Glory to you, Salvation of the World, who have delivered us from Idols!')

---

[1] Photios says the Paulicians held Christ passed through Mary's body as through a conduit-pipe. They defined the Virgin as the Type of the Heavenly Jerusalem 'into which Christ came as a reconnoiterer'. (Tertullian had held Mary as the Type of the Unbelieving Synagogue and the Paulicians said Christ denied her to be blest.)

But this position could not be fully set forth without an adoption of Constantine's position on the Incarnation.

He called the people together to swear they would treat the images as idols; and all the texts show him rebuking monks and iconodules as idolaters. He cited Gregory Nazianzen, 'It's a blasphemy to fix by material colours that which ought to be believed by the heart and confessed by the mouth.' And the later Orthodox Council of 787 attacked him thus: anathematising 'whoever calls holy images Idols, whoever says the Christians accost images like gods, whoever asserts that anyone else but Christ has saved us from Idols'. (The anyone else is clearly Constantine himself.)

THE STRUGGLE AGAINST THE MONKS. The 753 Council's remarks make clear that though there had been no thorough-going iconoclast fight since Leo launched his campaign, yet there had been such work done by individual zealots—and also by bishops who used the campaign as a pretext for grabbing church-wealth. That the support for iconoclasm was very wide indeed was not denied by its Orthodox opponents. Theokterikos says, 'The venom of heresy had penetrated everywhere', and Nikephoros, comparing Constantine to Jeroboam 'who divided the people', admits that he took with him 'the greater part'. The iconoclast solidarity of the army too was admitted. Theophanes says, 'The persecution was carried out by the Emperor, his accomplices Antonios Domestik of the Schools and Peter Magister, and the soldiers of the *tagmata* whom they had reared up and instructed.' Not one bishop refused to subscribe to the 753 Council, and it was a representative council, with bishops from all over the Empire. (Strong reform-movements had been going on among the clergy of Armenia and Phrygia.) Nor can we say the bishops were all cowardly and time-serving. In 786, when the Orthodox regained power, many stayed true to iconoclasm; and when the soldiers burst in to smash the Council up, these bishops welcomed them, 'We've won!' When next year Irene set up a rigged council to restore Orthodoxy, she had to get in a mob of monks and abbots to fill the gaps; and even so there were outspoken iconoclast bishops, though this time they were overborne.[1]

The year 753 was one in which the fighting spirit was uppermost. The Moslems had been driven back, and peasants from the further east of

[1] Yet historians keep on saying things like this: 'The triumph of the icon-defenders was a victory for popular religion and popular ways of thought' (Moss, 1949). The iconoclasts did not close churches as their enemies said, except when the shrine existed solely for an ikon (*e.g.* that of Euphemia's relics was made an arsenal). Churches were built, as later the iconodules worried that they had been opened without consecration by relics.

Asia Minor had been transferred into the interior of the Empire. Constantine made an energetic effort to draw the people into his work. He called assemblies in the large cities, where his projects were announced, and only after this preparation did he summon the Council.

The Council handed iconodules over to the State for punishment, but it was some years before any blood was shed. In 764-5 the direct attack began, with an assembly of the people at Byzantium (and no doubt at other large towns). Relics as well as ikons were removed from churches, broken, daubed, scraped; religious statues and iconodule books were also destroyed. In place of the religious pictures were set paintings of trees, beasts, birds, hunts, races. Death, confiscation or exile could be inflicted for the crime of possessing ikons.

In 765 an iconodule conspiracy involving many high dignitaries and nobles (including three Theme Generals) was discovered and crushed. The patriarch was exiled, and an iconoclast put in his place, whom the Orthodox abused as an ignorant Slav who couldn't pronounce Greek. In 766 the deposed patriarch was brought back, humiliated in St. Sophia, and made a mock in the Circus.

Now only the monks kept on the fight. They were not culturally on a high level—the main iconodule propagandist Theodore had to admit that many carried ikon-worship to extremes; and the Council that restored ikons had to take measures against the corruption and greed of abbots—but they struggled hard against liquidation.

In 765 Constantine had begun his final drive by arresting Stephen the Young, a famous ascetic whom he tried hard to win over, and by staging a show of monks in the Circus. The attack went on till 770. Its aim was to destroy monasticism altogether. 'Monks wear the Cloak of Darkness,' said Constantine. The *Acts* try to give an effect of general torture and mutilation; but the evidence, when sifted, is thin. Thus, George the Monk, writing later, cited the contemporary Nikephoros as saying 'still today the persecution's survivors bear its marks', but we have the original text, and George is shown as interpolating this statement.[1]

Strenuous efforts, however, were made to break up monasteries and to degrade the monk's status in every way. Constantine sent trusted generals to the Thracian, Anatolic and Boukellarian Themes where iconoclasm was strong among the people. Lachandrakon in the Thracian Theme, aided by an ex-abbot, was the most vigorous: he collected all

[1] Those who suffered seem those who bravely bearded the emperor—Peter Kalybitos, Andrew of Krisis. Stephen of Auxentios, their leader, had links with the nobility in Byzantium; he tried to draw in the Pope and the eastern patriarchs; Constantine left him intriguing for years, hoping to win him over.

the monks he could get hold of, in the plain of Ephesos, and told them,
'Those who want to obey the emperor and me will take a white robe
and pick a woman on the spot; those who refuse will be blinded and
shipped off to Cypros.'

There is no indication of any large-scale popular support for the monks.
Stephen, their leader, told them that they were environed with enemies.
'We are become the laughing stock of the whole people.' When Constantine cried to the assembly in the Circus, 'The cursed race of monks
won't give me any peace', the people shouted back, 'But there's no sign
of the breed left in the city!' The soldiers detested the black robe. When
George, who was acting as an *agent provocateur* in Stephen's case, appeared
in the Circus in a black robe, they shouted, tore the robe off, trampled
it, shouted for Stephen's death, rushed to the monastery where he was
lodged, pulled it down, and dragged him to the edge of the sea. When a
soldier from Armenia asked a prayer from the abbot, they denounced
him as an idolater. Later they burst into the jail, hurled Stephen into the
street, and, aided by workers who left their jobs, they finished him off
with a lump of wood.

Constantine tried to make monks and nuns ridiculous by parading
them in pairs in the Circus. He made the patriarch take the marriage-
wreath, eat meat, and listen to singing girls. (Later tales said the monks
were mated off with the nuns.) The defections were large, as the Orthodox
admit, even among Stephen's stalwarts. Monasteries and their lands were
taken over by the State or sold by public auction; some were made
hostels or inns as well as barracks; for a later Council mentions dances
going on in them instead of genuflections, satanic songs instead of canticles. Blachernai was secularised as a zoological garden, with aviary and
many sorts of trees.

THE RESULT. How successful was the persecution? On the one hand, the
confiscations and the building-up of a secular morale, linked as they were
with the revival of the free village-commune through Slav settlements
and the peasants' seizure of the land, provided the basis for a great reconstruction of Byzantine society and ensured that Byzantium as world-
centre would be able to persist powerfully through the next four
centuries, spreading its multiple influences in all directions. But on the
other hand, the contradiction of attacking one type of large estate while
fostering others meant that there was no ultimate stability in the Iconoclast
State and that in time monastic property would come back.

Nikephoros and the chroniclers speak as if all the monks of the Empire
were harried abroad or driven into caves in the wilderness. But we find

the monk Plato visiting Byzantium amid the persecution and living there with other monks. Stephen is described as shut up in a monastery, the Philippikon; his sister went into a convent at Byzantium; and later a disciple got some fragments of his body and took them to the monastery at Dion, which Theophanes says was razed but which in fact carried on. No doubt Zonaras put the facts when he wrote:

> The persecution was such that hardly a monk stayed in the City and dared to show himself in public, but many remained in hiding. And outside the City others carried on with the monastic life. Those who signed could live untouched.

In 775 Constantine died. That he had engaged the loyalty of the broad masses to an unusual degree is shown by many facts. Thus in 772 he went to protect the Berzetes, Slavs settled in Thessaly, against the attack of a Bulgarian boyar. That these Slavs stayed faithful to his iconoclast memory is proved by their attempt in 799 to get his sons from Athens and set them up against the Orthodox empress Irene. Sixteen years after his death, when Irene called her iconodule Council the soldiers came through the streets, shouting, 'Hands off the Decrees of our Dear Emperor!' and broke the Council up.

In his third discourse Bishop Nikephoros sets out to refute the admirers of Constantine, some forty years after his death. He admits that they glorify the long and happy career of his reign, and can counter only by saying that you can't judge kings by their earthly felicity. What matters is the titles they gain beside God (from the Orthodox reaction). 'Why glorify the length and brilliance of his reign?' he repeats.

And in 813, when Byzantium under restored Orthodoxy had met a series of disasters, the dissidents (Monophysites, Manicheans, Paulicians) said that the troubles were a judgment for leaving the righteous path of Iconoclasm. A rumour got round that Constantine was coming out of his tomb to drive the Bulgarians off. The people rushed to the Holy Apostles and beat on the doors. Suddenly the doors swung open. The people rushed in to the Tomb and cried, 'Wake up, Caesar, and save the City from destruction!' They saw him rise in full armour on his battle horse and ride out, leading his people once more to victory.

This was the Constantine whom the Paulicians called Conqueror and Prophet.

25

THE ICONOCLASTS: SECOND PHASE

THE ARMY AGAINST IKONS. Irene, who restored Orthodoxy, achieved power by having her son blinded in the room where she had borne him; he had outraged a section of religious opinion by marrying three times. We have noticed how her first attempt to restore Orthodoxy failed through the soldiers breaking things up; she waited a year and then held a packed Council at Nikaia, away from the army. This Council, the seventh, was the last great General Council. Irene was called a New Helena, and all confiscated monasteries were returned to the Church; but the iconoclast aftermath showed up in various reform measures, such as the prohibition of convents of both men and women. One effect of Iconoclasm had been to strengthen a reform-party, now led by Theodore of Stoudios, which wanted to end or at least curtail the State's power over the Church—to assert the principle that the Church was independent, under its own canon-law.

The second Iconoclast wave began under Leo V, after the confusion, anarchy and defeats under Irene and her successors had made it clear that the State would break down unless a strong rule was re-established. The fact that Leo, seeking to build up afresh an efficient army, felt impelled back to Iconoclasm, shows how vigorous still the tradition of Constantine V must have been among the rank-and-file. For Leo was no theologian or enthusiast like Constantine. He wanted a strong State and a successful reign. He christened his son Constantine and told his followers:

> You see how all emperors who accepted images and worshipped them died in exile or in battle. Only those who have not adored images died a natural death while still bearing the imperial rank. They were all placed in imperial sepulchres with high honours and buried in the shrine of the Apostles. I want to follow their example and destroy images so that after my long life and my son's our rule may continue till the fourth or fifth generation.

His main assistant was John the Grammarian, whose interest in science earned him the reputation of dabbling in the black art. John, said to be the son of a demoniac hermit, seems to have been an Armenian named Hylilas (Devil-forerunner, or Dish-conjurer). He had an iconoclast committee which included two senators, two ex-monks, a Pamphylian bishop: the Orthodox said one of the ex-monks had his nose cut off for adultery and the bishop was so wicked as to crack jokes with young monks. This committee met in one of the palace-rooms, and when they had drawn up their programme, Leo called the patriarch in. Ikons, he said mildly, hurt his army's susceptibilities, they ought to be hung higher up. The patriarch objected. Leo said there were no ikons mentioned in the Scriptures. The patriarch replied that he stood on the Spirit's inspiration in post-apostolic days.

So soldiers attacked the Christ on the Bronze Doors with mud and stones. Leo said the image must be taken down to be saved from insults. The bishops and abbots refused. In the new year a conference was held and Theodore of Stoudios denied the State's right to interfere. An edict then forbade the Orthodox party to meet in private houses. The patriarch fell ill, with a crowd (mostly soldiers) yelling outside his window; he was deposed and a lay iconoclast nominated in his place. Urbane dinner-parties were given in the patriarchal palace, and a council held in St. Sophia in April 815 remarked, 'We decree that the manufacture of ikons —we refrain from calling them idols, as there are degrees in evil—is neither worshipful nor serviceable.'

The dogmatic issue burst out again, centring round the Incarnation. Theodore circulated a formula of repudiation, so that all the Orthodox would say the same thing in a clear way. Rebellious monks were exiled into jails of lice, heat, cold; were bound and beaten. So it was said later; but on the whole there was not much violence, though in the end the chief resisters were exiled. We hear of a hermit on Lesbos who lived on pillar-top; he wouldn't shift, so the people kindled fires at the pillar's foot, till he came down and went off in exile to a small island. Theodore, exiled to Smyrna, continued trying to organise the recalcitrant monks and draw the People in.

At Byzantium iconoclasts put dung on ikons and there were scuffles with monks. The iconodules, now better prepared for persecution, went on resisting, though many monks came over to Leo. And though the Orthodox called Leo a Creeping Snake who brought Winter and Thick Fog, some admitted his secular merits. The patriarch whom he deposed, Nikephoros, said after his death that the State of the Romans had lost a great though impious ruler.

The proof of the general success of Leo's policy is proved by the fact that his murderer Michael, though slackening persecution, did not reverse his policy. (The only rigour used was against Methodios, who came from Rome with papal documents on behalf of ikons. That was a political act of interference, and he was shut up on an island.) Michael in the rational vein of the iconoclasts tried to get a conference with the Pope for a quiet discussion of the matter, but the Pope showed no interest. Michael then tried to win over the western rulers. He wrote to Louis the Debonair:

> Lights were set in front of ikons and incense burned, and they were held in the same honour as the lifegiving Christ. They were prayed to, and their aid besought. Some folk even used to cover them with cloths and make them baptismal sponsors for their children. Some priests scraped the paint from pictures and mixed it with the bread and wine they gave to communicants. Others placed the Lord's Body in the hands of images, from which the communicants received it.

He assured Louis that he venerated relics, and asked Louis to take the subject up with the Pope. Louis mustered the intermediate position of the Frankish Church (images permissible as decorations or memorials) and notified the Pope, who took no notice.

Michael's halting of persecution was grudging admitted by the Orthodox.

> The Fire has gone out, but it still smokes. . . . Like a crawling snake's, the Tail of Heresy is not yet scotched but still wriggles . . . winter is past, the real Spring is not yet here.

THEOPHILOS. His son, Theophilos, educated by John the Grammarian (whom he made patriarch), was a convinced iconoclast, but the fervour had gone. For him iconoclasm was simply a rational creed suited for a strong and brilliant court. A man of peace, he did not feel any kinship with the iconoclast rank-and-file of the army. However, he had a passion for just administration, was open to approach by the humblest citizen during his weekly ride to Blachernai, and had the great Count of the Opisikon beaten for taking a soldier's horse and his own brother-in-law whipped in the streets for spoiling the light in a widow's house by infractions of the building regulations. He looked in at the markets to test the wares, especially food, and to watch the prices; he allowed marriages between Christians and Persians or Moslems; he revived the palace University.

Popular tradition acclaimed him. In the twelfth-century satire *Timarion* we find him a judge of the Otherworld. Minos and Aiakos were perfectly just and tolerant of all creeds, the author says, but as the Galileans have won over Europe and much of Asia, it was only fair to appoint a third judge with them to represent Christianity, and so Theophilos was chosen. The two pagans on the tribunal were richly dressed, but Theophilos wore dark and poor clothes (as in his own life).

In 832 he held an iconoclast Council at Blachernai and resumed persecution, at least in and around Byzantium. We have an interesting picture of an interview with two iconodule monks, Theophanes, later bishop of Mikaia, and Theodore, from Palestine. (Theophilos was annoyed with the three eastern patriarchates, which had supported images.) The monks were led into the Chrysotriklinion:

'Where were you born?'
We replied, 'In the land of Moab.'
'Why did you come here?'
We made no reply, and he gave orders for our faces to be beaten. After many hard buffets, we grew giddy and fell down; and if I hadn't grabbed hold of a bystander's tunic, I'd have fallen on the emperor's stool. Grasping the tunic, I stood unmoved till he said, 'That's enough.' He repeated his questions. When we still made no reply, he spoke very angrily to the prefect, 'Take them and engrave these verses on their faces. Then hand them over to the Saracens to take back home.'
A man, Christodoulos, stood nearby with the iambic verses he'd composed. The emperor bade him read them out, adding, 'No matter if they're not much good.' He said that since he knew how we, experts in all that concerns poetry, would ridicule them.
The man who read them remarked, 'Sire, these fellows don't deserve any better verses.'

They were flogged, but still refused to communicate with iconoclasts, and so had the verses tattooed on their brows, gaining the name of the Marked Men. With benches for beds, they were jailed in Bithynia. The lines that Theophanes as a hymn-writer despised ran thus:

> *The Town where once the Word of God*
> *in sacred streets pure-footed trod,*
> *that town all hearts desire to see;*
> *these Vessels of Depravity,*
> *these evil clods of superstition*
> *working their practice of perdition,*
> *were driven from, to haunt instead*
> *our City where they seek to spread*
> *their wicked ways, and rightly stand*
> *condemned at last to take this brand*
> *black on their shamed and scoundrel faces*
> *now chased back to their native places.*

There were tales of maimed artists who produced miraculous paintings: Lazaros, a famous religious painter, was said to have been branded on the palms with red-hot irons, but he went on working.

BLASPHEMIES AND APOCALYPSES. Michael III, son of Theophilos, had his mother Theodora as regent, and she promptly deposed John the patriarch and revived images. Michael is a shadowy figure, for we have only
8*

the propaganda-picture of him given in the reign of Basil his murderer, who vindicated his action by having Michael depicted as a scurrilous and lecherous drunkard mad on horse-racing. A miniature shows him chasing a woman as she comes from her bath. We are told that in his thirst for drink he melted down the gold mechanisms of Theophilos; recklessly confiscating church-land, he ordered executions one day and forgot them the next, and so on.

What seems to have some foundation in fact is the picture of him as a sort of irreverent satanist, who carried the secularism of the later iconoclasts to the point of mocking at all ritual. His friend Theophilos the Pig, we are told, acted the part of patriarch, eleven others with Michael acted the parts of the twelve bishops, consecrated and deposed one another; with citherns sounding under their gowns, intoned the liturgy and profaned the eucharist with mustard and vinegar for flesh and blood. A miniature shows them in a church-porch with musical mummers outside. Once Michael dressed his Pig Patriarch in full pontificals in the patriarchal chair, and had his mother sent in; while she knelt at the supposed patriarch's feet, the Pig stood up, turned round, and broke wind in her face.

Bardas his uncle did much to help secular learning and Photios the Patriarch brought about the first definite break with Rome, mainly through the clash of papal and orthodox claims in the Balkans, for control of the Bulgarians. For a moment indeed there was a sort of alliance between Michael and Louis II in the West which might have wrecked the Papacy (Louis was half-heartedly supporting the anti-papal reform-movement of the archbishops of Koln and Trier); but the murder of Michael restored amity between pope and emperor—though the national feeling against Rome was already strong enough to compel Basil after a while to restore Photios.

What is clear is that Michael's reign is one of confused transition. While the Orthodox tradition depicts him as a blasphemous fool and villain, he appears as a dauntless hero in the popular epic-lay of *Armouris*. And there is evidence from apocalyptic writings that certain mass hopes of renewal attached themselves to him. As these writings testify to the excited state of the popular mind at this turning-point, they are worth consideration. Thus, in *The Revelation of Methodios of Patara*, known to Byzantine and Slavo-Russian literature, to Syrian and Armenian, we find world-history set out in a vision. We hear of the last Emperor Liberator, who in the final struggle wakes as though from drunken sleep and in time delivers up his empire to God in Jerusalem. The Ishmaelites (Arabs) will cause terrible devastation, and then suddenly will rise this emperor 'as a man from sleep, who has drunk wine, whom men regarded as dead and worthless'. After his victories over the Arabs, 'wonderful fertility will spread over the earth and all men will live in peace. The Greeks will rebuild cities, their priests will be freed from violence.' But then a disaster will fall: 'The gates of the North will open and loose the forces of the peoples who have been shut within.' These peoples are described in the usual terms for steppe-nomads (shocking appearance, cannibalism, drinking blood like water). The reference must be to the Russian attack on Byzantium during Michael's reign.

> But after seven years, when they have captured Oppe (Joppa), God will send one of his *Archistrategoi* and smite them in a moment. Then the Greek emperor will come to Jerusalem, and ten and a half years later Antichrist will be born.

In the interpolated Slavonic version the emperor is named Michael (and this name must have been in the Greek original). After thirty-three years

> the Lord will order Michael to hide himself in a sea-island, Michael will board a ship and God will waft him to a sea-island, and he'll stay there till the fixed day. And God will open the western mountains which Alexander of Macedon shut up . . .

There may be a reference here to the palace of Mamas where Michael was murdered (and which an Arab chronicler of the early tenth century described as an island where Michael went for recreation). But the basic image is that of the dead saviour-king going off to the islands of the blest —Achilles wafted to his western isle or Arthur to his Avalon, Tammuz floating in his deathboat or Scyld across the sunset waters. We may compare also the Monophysite tale of Maurice sent off in the burning ship.

Corroborations of the large part played by Michael in the popular mind are given by *Daniel's Vision* (part of the apocryphal composition put into the Slavonic version of the cited *Revelation*): we have this in several Greek versions as well as in Slavonic. The latter version mentions Tsar Michael.

Whether or not Michael deserved it, we see then that the masses, aware of his reign as turning-point, were affected by tales of his murder and consequently saw him as an emblem of the free elements that were finally stamped out by the accession of Basil his murderer. They saw him as an emblem of themselves, a pledge of the day of renewal and of reversal.

THE GROWING SPLIT. In fact the vital elements of Iconoclasm had largely gone with the death of Constantine V. Under Michael I (811–13) who carried on Irene's reactionary policy, a vicious attempt was made to put down the Paulicians and the Athingans (an allied sect, the *Don't-touch-me's*) by persecutions and massacres; and from this time on the split between the Paulicians and the State continued, every now and then intensifying. Even under Theophilos it went on, and the Paulicians made the decision of breaking with the Empire altogether. They tried to build up a society of their own, based on republican towns, in the debatable lands of the eastern borders, with Melitene as the new centre.

26

THE PAULICIANS

THE BORDERLANDS. Not only in Syria and Egypt did the Empire find discontented masses and embryonic national movements. In 636 its army was defeated by the Persians through the Armenian detachments having no interest in the fighting; and in 667 an Armenian rebel invited the Arabs in.

The Armenians looked to Gregory the Illuminator as founder of their Church. He had taught that baptism should be given to initiates at the age of thirty (the age of Christ when baptised) and that communion should be taken after the love-feast or communal meal. Monophysitism became the ruling creed, and dissidence therefore tended to dualistic formulations.

In the borderlands all sorts of creeds, varieties of Manicheism or Paulicianism, of Massilian anarchism or new saviour-cults, were to be found thriving. No doubt many of the Clubmen, the guerrillas who fought the Arabs, were Paulicians; and as an instance of the saviours we have Theophobos (Godfearer) who had much influence in the East and who was apparently looked on as a god-incarnation of the sort continually claimed in the Moslem-Persian area (Babak or al-Muslim are examples). Theophilos on his deathbed had him put to death.

The Moslem defences towards Syria and Armenia were made of a line of forts and standing-camps. The key-point was the Cilician Gates, some seventy-six miles long, reaching from the central plateaus south of Tyaɪ to the foothills of the Tauric mountains. At the northern end of the pass stood a lofty peak with the fort of Loulon, and here the western and northern roads met; the ground then rose through steep narrow glens to the top of the pass. East, high up, stood the Fortress of the Slavs, and then narrowing from a little plateau, the rocky defile, the Cilician Gates proper, high-walled, only a few feet wide and about a hundred feet long.

The Moslems now held the eastern end; but Loulon kept changing hands. If the Empire held it, the soldiers could send fire-signals on to Mt. Auxentios, whence the pharos of the palace at Byzantium could pick them up. Leo the Mathematician had worked out a code, a set of signals

related to the twelve hours of the day according to two clocks (one at
Loulon, one at the palace), which kept the same time. It was thus possible
to tell at what moment a message had been sent and to decode it.

ARMENIA. By the ninth century the separation-out of the Paulicians as a
mass-sect irreconcilably opposed to the Empire had been completed. They
might at moments look to the Arabs for aid, but never to Byzantium.

We can distinguish their area fairly well. The Constantine named as
founder of the creed was born in Mananali, an Armenian canton near
Ezerum not far from Samosata; he went to Kibossa, near Koloneia on
the Halys. Constantine V found Paulicians in the Armenian province of
Melitene, whom he transported to Thrace; under Nikephoros they were
thick in Phrygia and Lykaonia; under Leo V, in Neo-Kaisareia in
Cappadokia, where an inquisition was started against them. A large con-
gregation existed at Mopsuestia, some five hours east of Adana, and at
Tephrike on the River Chalta (which, flowing east, joined the northern
Euphrates).

The creed had a strong attraction for groups with surviving tribal
elements as in many parts of Armenia:

> The population was broken up into great independent clans, separated from
> each other by huge mountains, and led by feudal chieftains, a bishop in those
> days presided, not over a diocese, but over a clan.
>
> Inside a clan, therefore, a peculiar ecclesiastical use or faith could propagate
> itself unmolested for generations, and did so; for the religious unity of the
> clans must have been as weak and precarious as was their political unity.

So, in Armenia, the Paulician position was nationalist, and differed from
that of the peasants and artisans on the imperial borderlands. The Arab
attack on Armenia brought out a strong baffled need for a national
leadership capable of rallying the clans: but most of the clan-nobles preferred to play for safety. In south-east Armenia, however, especially
among the Bagratuni, the forces of resistance dominated. The clans
seceded from the ruling Church which had failed to beget a vital unifying trend from its centre at Valarshapat, and set up a rival church based
on Taron (where stood the mother-church of Armenia, St. Gregory's
shrine at Ashtishat). Not that they thought of themselves as seceders;
rather they were reviving the true tradition: 'We are the people who have
not swerved in faith', and 'We are of the tribe of Aram (true Armenians)
and agree with them in faith', and 'We are the Sons of the Illuminator.'

THE REBEL CREED. The Paulician creed was strongly dualistic, seeing the
world cut sharply into good and evil, and rejecting all compromise. From

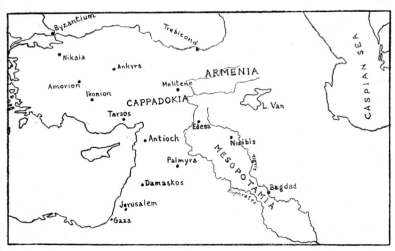

the seventh century on its exponents had steadily developed their organisation till they could hold their own between Moslem raids and Byzantine subjections. They did not accept the dogma of the Incarnation,
took the docetic view that Christ's body only 'appeared', interpreted the
Virgin as the Heavenly Jerusalem, and detested the cult-title of *Theotokos*. They looked on the *Old Testament* as the work of cheats, and disliked Peter's Epistles: Peter was the denier of Christ, the established
Church. Their canon consisted of the four Gospels, Paul's Epistles, the
Acts of the Apostles, the Epistles of John, Jude, James, to which they later
added some Epistles of Sergios, their ninth-century leader.

Strongly anti-sacramental, they interpreted Baptism, etc., on rational-
ising symbolic lines, *i.e.* the Bread and Wine were Christ's teaching.
They were ready to claim that they accepted various dogmas of the ruling
powers—merely giving the terms a different meaning. Thus, a Paulician
named Genesios (Timothy to his own brethren) was called to Byzantium
under Leo III: he swore without demur to all dogmas brought forward,
was given a certificate of orthodoxy, and was sent back safe to Armenia—
but he had in fact meant quite different things than his examiners. The
Paulicians rejected the whole organisation of the Church, particularly
detesting presbyters (priests, literally elders) who represented the Jewish
elders that denied Christ. Their leaders claimed no apostolic descent save
through the spirit from Paul. They called themselves Christians (as distinct from the congregations of the Church, whom they considered anti-
christian); they hated monks, men in a devil-devised garb. Manichee
elements appear in their dualism of body and spirit, their denial of the

Incarnation, their rejection of the Old Testament and of sacramentalism, their love of St. Paul, their ostentatious use of the name Christians, the term Paraklete for their leaders. But they differed in not being ascetics; indeed they were vigorous livers, combative and ready to take to the sword in their own defence, to found normal communities of married men and women engaged in necessary labour.

Markionite (Gnostic) elements were also present. Armenia in the fifth century had many Markionites who for some time had been leaving the towns where they were persecuted and going up into remoter regions, especially the mountain-valleys. They held to a dualism of a good God and an evil Creator, rejected the Incarnation, and had a cult of St. Paul. Markion indeed was much closer to the Paulicians in his attitude to Paul than were the Manichees. Like the Paulicians, he held Luke's Gospel the best, as the one into which the least distortions had been introduced by the compromising Church; and the Epistle of Paul to the Laodikeans, a Markonite forgery, was used by the Paulicians. But the Markonites were ascetic and not anti-sacramental.

Other sects contributed traits: for example, the Massilians, whom we have met on the dissident verges of monasticism. Their name came from a Syriac word to pray: their Greek equivalent is *Euchitai*. They denied a real presence in the eucharist, but outwardly conformed; condemned the Church and interpreted the New Testament in their own way. They held that each man was born with a demon which only ceaseless praying could expel. (I *Thes.* v, 17). They prayed themselves into delirium, jumping and dancing as they trampled the demon under: hence their names, Enthusiasts or Dancers. They refused to work, lived in poverty on charity, and often wore monks' clothes. Women could be teachers among them (as among the Manichees, Markonites, Montanists). The Edessa district seems a main spawning area, from which in the fourth century they moved into Syria and Asia Minor, specialising in missionary work among the monks. In Armenia they were still heard of into the tenth century.

Paulicianism is best seen as a fusion of these various trends adapted to the needs of a struggling peasantry, which needed an idiom to justify its hatred of the Devil and the State, its quest for a new way. The name is Armenian for Followers of Poor Little Paul (not Poor Little Followers of Paul), probably a mock term taken up in pride. With the break in magnate power in Asia Minor they came rapidly to the fore, leaders in the effort to relate the free village-commune to apostolic democracy. John the Philosopher, *Catholikos* of Armenia in 719, says they turned to the Arabs for protection, were joined by dissenting groups like the *Ikonomachoi* (Image-fighters, driven from Albania in the East Caucasus), left their lairs and came into the populous parts to preach.[1] From their centre at Djrkay they flowed over the land like a suffocating flood.

The first great organiser of whom we know was Constantine, an Armenian from a village on the Upper Euphrates, who founded many communities in Armenia, in the mid-seventh century.[2] He seems the man who threw out the cosmic-fancies of Manicheism and concentrated on modes of symbolic interpretation that kept the Biblical letter, but read everywhere the tale of a deep dualistic conflict. Admiring St. Paul, he took the name of Paul's companion Sylvanos and organised churches with names from Paul's Epistles.

Persecutions began. An official Symeon ran Sylvanos down and did him to death; then, affected by the Paulician's heroism, he was converted and took up Sylvanos' organising work. He himself was a Paul, converted to the sect he persecuted; and he took the name of Titos. Propaganda was organised from Helenopolis, till an argument on a text (*Col.* I, 16), angered one of the sect so much that he informed on his fellows to a bishop, who notified the authorities and arranged the arrests. Titos was burned alive; but the Paulicians were undeterred.

GROWING STRENGTH. On the borderlands a great leader Sergios, early in the ninth century brought about a closely knit organisation of fighting communities. They built and fortified towns near Melitene on the western borders of Armenia, with Tephrike as the capital where the military chiefs lived, and with Argaos and Amara also as important centres. They raided as far west as Nikaia and Nikomedia, and sacked a part of Ephesos. They aspired to win the whole of Asia Minor.

Sergios took the name of St. Paul's friend Tychikos. Moving all over Asia Minor, he founded three more church-centres with Pauline names, to make up the full Pauline seven—Corinth being left as the name of the mother-church (founded by Paul himself). Then under Michael I and Theodora the massacres began afresh, burnings, crucifixion, drownings.

1 Moses of Kalankatuk (or his continuator), early eleventh century, says that in the first half of the seventh century a party in Albania rejected images, baptism, salt-blessing (animal sacrifice) and church-marriage—the true priesthood having been lost on earth.

2 There was a traditional association with Paul of Samosata, which has been argued against on the grounds that Paul was not dualistic like the Paulicians, and the Paulicians did not carry on his Adoptionist attitude to Christ (*i.e.* Christ as a man 'adopted' by God as worthy, and therefore setting a standard to which men could rise). I, however, think the link was there. Both Paul and Paulicians wanted to keep close to the initiation-process of apostolic days (in which magic is at a minimum and the idea of revolutionary brotherhood at a maximum). But the theological arguments of the fifth to sixth centuries had meant a concentration on the Incarnation, which the Paulicians rejected because they interpreted such positions as leading to a dogma binding men to the world as it was.

Many Paulicians fled to the Moslem area and aided the Arabs in their attacks on the Empire; they were probably among the Melitene Emir's troops that invaded in 844 and defeated the Empire. Sergios, among the refugees, was murdered in Melitene.

There was no more outstanding teacher. The elect went round with their preaching and prophesying, called Fellow-travellers. Thirty years after Sergios' death saw a mounting wave of military power among the Paulicians. Under Theophilos (or earlier) Karbeas, who held an imperial office in the Anatolic Theme, led some 5,000 men out of the Empire, beyond Cappadokia, and put himself under the Melitene Emir.

In 859 Michael III and Bardas took the offensive, against Samosata. They rebuilt the fortifications of Ankyra to provide a base for the expedition. A truce was agreed on. But in the spring of 860 Michael marched off for the attack, and the Paulicians and Moslems suffered reverses. Then the Emir Umar invaded the Armeniac Theme and took the port of Amisos (Samsun), but at Posion the Byzantines had a great victory and Umar was killed (3rd September, 863).

THE LEADER. In Sergios we meet a man whose accents we can catch. There is a proud note of courage in his words, a faith in Christianity, not as a builded Church, but as a Church of men deciding their own way of life and cleaving to righteousness in defiance of the State.

> Let no one deceive you in any way; but having these promises from God, be of good cheer. For we, persuaded in our hearts, have written to you that I am the Porter and the Good Shepherd and the Leader of the Body of Christ and the Light of the House of God, and I am with you always, even to the end of the world. For even if I am away from you in the body, yet I am with you in spirit. For the rest, fare you well. Perfect yourselves, and the God of Peace be with you.

The main element in the Paulician creed was the effort to return to apostolic bases and to resist all later elaborations of ritual and theology. As followers of Paul, they opposed the Peter of the State-Church and kept to the simple system of an initiatory process leading to an equalitarian brotherhood.

> Knowing beforehand the tried quality of your faith, we remind you how that as the Church in previous times received Shepherds and Teachers, so also you have received a shining lamp and a beaming star and a guide to salvation, according to the scriptures: that if your eye be single, your whole body shall be full of light. . . .
> I have run from east to west and from north to south, preaching the gospel of Christ, till my knees were weary.

Sergios keeps preaching the need of true unity. 'He who whores sins only

in his private body. We are the Body of Christ.' And he remonstrates
with Leo, a Montanist:

> But do you beware of yourself. Cease now to rend asunder the true faith. For
> what charge can you bring against us? Have I despoiled anyone, or been over-
> weening? You cannot say it. But if you do, your witness is not true. Yet be it
> not mine to hate you, but only to exhort, as you have received apostles and
> prophets, four in number, so receive our shepherds and teachers, lest you
> become the prey of wild beasts.

Sergios taught, according to Photios, that he and others of the elect were
no longer mere listeners, *akroatai*, but were themselves the holy spirit.
Probably he did, for such an idiom is in accord with the dissident heresy
which did not look on Christ or the Spirit as remote abstractions but as
forms of living into which the initiate could enter.

THE STATE STRIKES. When Basil I reached the throne and the full tide of
reaction set in, no time was lost in smashing the Paulicians. The new
dynasty took as its first task the total destruction of the rebel strongholds.
Basil sent an ambassador, Peter the Sicilian, to sound out the ground and
no doubt to do some spying. The leader Hand-of-Gold (Chrysocheir)
demanded, Peter reported, the whole of Asia Minor—though that may
have only been the way an imperial official interpreted a demand that the
peasants be left to determine their own lives.

Basil attacked the small republican cities (which had *isopoliteia*—equal
rights among themselves). The first campaign, in 871, was a setback.
But next year, taking advantage of internal troubles among the Moslems,
he sent a strong army under his son-in-law, who captured Tephrike,
destroyed the Paulician confederacy, and sent the leader's head to Basil,
who held a Triumph in 872.

The surviving Paulicians took refuge in Melitene, a stronghold in the
loop of the Euphrates which had long been a trouble for Byzantium.
Basil made efforts for several years to get hold of it, but failed, though in
the process he gained many smaller Arab forts and burned a large number
of Paulician villages.

The attempt of the Paulicians to build a society of their own in Asia
Minor had been broken down. Their creed had been optimistic, seeing
the world divided, but resisting Manichean pessimism; their defeat meant
the end of resilience and hope among the peasants of the Empire. The
struggle went on, but henceforth pessimistic elements grew stronger.
The Paulician failure meant the final triumph of the feudal State and the
eradication of the free village-commune which had asserted itself in the
seventh century, modifying the State and begetting unrealised possibilities of anti-feudal development.

27

BOGOMILS

THE CONQUEST OF BULGARIA. The conversion of the Bulgarians to the Orthodox creed helped to strengthen the autocracy of the tsar. But vigorous rulers like Krum or Symeon attempted to build up a central-ised State on the Byzantine model too fast, overstrained resources and broke down, as did the similar effort of Charlemagne in the West. As the autocracy weakened, the nobles grabbed more land and oppressed the peasantry with increased burdens; and the peasantry retorted with disloyalty and heresy.

Under Samuel the Bulgarian State regained its energy, but was crushed after long and bloody wars by Basil II. Bulgaria came directly into the imperial area. The patriarchate set up by Symeon was abolished, but the Church for a while had nominal autonomy under the Archbishop of Ochrida. Then, after 1037, all pretence was set aside; Greek became the official and liturgical language; and the Church set out to hellenise the Bulgarians. After 1041 all officials in the Themes were Greeks. The Empire had its hands full, fighting off Birmans, Pechenegs, Turks, and the function it allotted to Bulgaria was the provision of men and taxes. The peasants, however, could not have paid the taxes if they wanted to; and administrative rigour increased. Michael IV imposed payment in money instead of kind, which further depressed the peasants' lot. A revolt broke out in 1041 and was put down. The peasants had to meet not only land and poll-taxes, but regular and extraordinary dues such as labour-services, provision for army-needs, and so on. Basil had set up a commission to reorganise Bulgaria with the least possible break in its system; but military control by Greek governors could not but tend to oppression and extortion.

Byzantine tax-methods were used, and all peasants with a pair of yoke-beasts were liable. The eleventh century had seen the final breakdown of tribal bases and the rise of the big landowner; by the later part of the century *pronoia* was established, land-tenures were linked with military duties, and the peasants attached to the land as *paroikoi*. Conditions went on getting worse, and after 1041 revolts burst out every now and then. This is the basis on which the great Bulgarian heresies arose. Let us look in a little more detail at the process.

THE PEASANTS RESIST. The eastern heresies could no doubt have seeped through into the Balkans by trade and other channels; but the movement was speeded up by the imperial policy of transporting blocks of population, partly to shift disaffected peoples to areas where they would be less dangerous, partly to get good fighting groups in strategic positions. The idea was as old as Diocletian; Heraklios and Justinian II had tried it under the shock of Arab attack; Constantine V moved Syrian Monophysites and Armenians westward, so did Leo IV; John I carried colonies of Paulicians to the Balkans, round Philippopolis; Basil II brought Armenians into Thrace to guard the area (they rebelled and went over to the Bulgarians). Theophanes noted how these transportations spread Paulicianism westward.

The conflict of Latins and Greeks for control of the Church increased the bewilderment and alienation of the masses from a State-Church of any kind. To some extent both nobles and peasants disliked the Church: the nobles because it helped the centralised bureaucracy, the peasants because it helped oppression. But the mass-element soon split off into its heretical forms after the first pagan revolts; the Paulician missionaries pointed to the two great competing churches, who abused one another viciously, and gained support in saying they were both ambitious liars.

Tsar Boris, writing to the Pope, had expressed his worry at finding so many kinds of Christians. As early as 870 the Paulicians of Tephrike had planned missions to Bulgaria, so that even then there must have been contacts; Bulgarian sources mention missionaries with Eastern names like Dubotin and Shubil (from Cappadokia). And we must remember how busy were Armenian merchants in the ninth century, taking Transsylvanian salt to Moravia or Byzantine goods to Central Europe; they were well-established in Thessalonika. Armenian communities existed in Thrace from the tenth to the fourteenth centuries, and there were Jewish colonies in many Balkan towns—not to mention even Moslem contact of some kind: Boris asked the Pope about Arabic books that his people had. (Pagan survivals were also strong in the ninth century. Vladimir reversed Boris' Christianising policy, and Boris had to leave his monastery to start things all over again.)

At first Slavonic was taken as the written as well as spoken language of Bulgaria. The Preslav School turned out many Slavonic literary works, both originals and translations, mainly for the educated clergy. Popular levels were untouched till the fourteenth century. But, despite the rooting of a Slavonic Church at Ochrida, the pressure of Greek influences intensified and the gap between the Church and the masses rapidly widened.

The Greeks, who had championed against the Papacy the right of a people to a liturgy in their own language, found themselves driven for political reasons to the intolerant papal position. But the monk Khrabr spoke up in defence of Slavonic letters and denounced the idea of three sacred languages (Hebrew, Greek, Latin) as a heresy.

The Bulgarian State and Church had been rent by a dilemma. They needed the Byzantine forms to build centralised controls; but in crushing the national bases they sapped their own bases of resistance to the Empire. The Bulgarian patriarchate had had its synods and hierarchy of officials on the imperial model; the clergy had appeared as a new order in the State, with legal powers based on Byzantine canon-law, claiming a regular income. And there soon grew up another gap, that between the higher clergy and the parish-priest who was generally close to the peasant-level. The Preslav court imitated Byzantium, and aspired to gain its titles from the emperor.

Semi-tribal institutions merged with the new State-hierarchies. The old noble-title of boyar came to define the new magnates who held land on a system of military services due to the emperor's person. Byzantine influences approximated this system to the matured feudal form of *pronoia*. The lords wanted increased services to sustain their growing ambitions for power and luxury, while the peasants were driven down by wars, exactions, burdens of all sorts, famines, plagues, locusts. Revolts began in 928 and 930.

The growth of monasticism helped often to stimulate heresy. For instance, round Thessalonika and along the mountains to the north-east —an area called the Second Holy Mountain or Little Byzantium—heresies thrived. The most famous ascetic was John of Rila, who lived in an oak, then in an cave. At sanctified spots monasteries were built by pilgrims and disciples. Tsars and lords founded other houses, in which Byzantine influence was strong and the rules, *typika*, were taken from Byzantine houses, generally the Stoudites.

Monasteries were thus both centres of Byzantine influence and of heretical diffusion. Many were insecure foundations, dependent on patrons who died, and after 934 subject to devastations. Hence the large number of wandering monks who spread extreme views. The priest Kosmas in his sermon against the heretics in the late tenth century attacked both the Bogomils and the extreme Monastics, and linked them. Monks often said, he tells us, that a man with wife or property could not be saved; and some persons out of piety left their children to starve. Massilian world-rejection was strong among the dissident monks.

When the Bulgarian State collapsed, and Byzantine oppression was added to the other forces making for a wretched peasantry, the heresies gained a tremendous impetus.

A NEW MASS-HERESY. In mid-tenth century the Paulicians and Massilians mingled their teachings, and the result was the Slav heresy *Bogomilism*. The patriarch Theophylakt in a letter to Tsar Peter, about that time, called it Manicheanism mixed with Paulicianism. It taught a dualism of light and darkness, and saw the creation of matter as evil and the Old Testament as evil's expression; its Christology was docetic (Christ was never incarnated in a body); it denied the Real Presence and took the sacraments as symbols. The Virgin was merely the Heavenly Jerusalem. Unlike Paulicianism, it rejected marriage and called all copulation the devil's work.

From Kosmas we learn that the creed arose from a *pop*, priest, named Bogomil, *Godbeloved*, in Peter's reign. Unaware that he was repeating the complaints of the pagan magistrate faced with the early Christians, Kosmas stresses the equivocating double-meaning that the heretics gave to words—*i.e.* they seemed to agree with orthodox statements, but gave the terms quite a different meaning. He stresses too their obstinacy: 'A man who tries to instruct a heretic will not only fail to teach him but will also pervert one weaker of mind.'

They call all nature evil, he says, and use the fable of the Prodigal Son, saying that Christ is the elder son, the devil the younger. 'And they call the latter Mammon and assert that he is creator and author of earthly things.' Generally, however, we know that they held the devil to be God's elder son; only after his fall did seniority pass to Christ. The devil was ultimately dependent on God, as the Fallen Angel and Unjust Steward (*Luke* xvi).

Dualism was thus mitigated. The Paulicians had had two absolute principles, *archai*; but though the Bogomils attributed the universe to the devil, they avoided the idea of two gods or basic principles. They condemned marriage, meat and wine (the Eastern monastic rule forbade meat). One of their myths said that the Vine, planted by the devil, was the tree of good and evil. (The Tsar Krum in his Code had forbidden business-fraud, legal injustices, drunkenness, and ordered the uprooting of all vines.)

There was probably soon a division of Believers and Perfect such as we find among the Byzantine Bogomils in the eleventh to twelfth centuries. They rejected baptism and the eucharist, and hated all material objects believed to convey grace. Kosmas says they were worse than demons who at least feared the cross. 'They cut down the crosses and make their tools of them'—a statement which shows their peasant or artisan basis.[1] They considered churches the abode of devils, ikons idols, gospel-miracles allegories; they rejected the cult of saints and respected the memory of the iconoclast emperors. They detested the church-hierarchy, making no distinction of lay and clerical—though they may have had dominant characters: there were apostles in eleventh to thirteenth century Byzantine Bogomilism. The prayers used in churches they held to be mere messes of words, *mnogoglagolanya*, except the Lord's Prayer which they said at regular intervals with prostrations, four times a day, four times a night. They confessed to one another, and women had the same status as men. They disliked the word Church and called themselves Christians to mark themselves off from the Church which they identified with Mammon.

As labour like marriage bound a man to existing society, they rejected it. 'Take no thought . . .' Kosmas points out what he thinks the contradiction that they denounced the priests as parasitic idlers. 'They teach the people not to obey their masters, they revile the wealthy, hate the tsar, ridicule the elders, condemn the boyars, regard those who serve the tsar as vile in God's sight, and forbid every serf to work for his lord.' He thus defines the social consequences of their creed: the charge of civil disobedience was likewise made against the Byzantine heretic Constantine Chrysomales in the twelfth century. But the Bogomils had no political programme.

The idea of the Two Sons of God and the exclusive use of the Lord's Prayer seem original. In the creed Slavic folk-elements mingled with Old and New Testament stories; and Manichee, Paulician, Massilian attitudes were given a new focus. What was common to all the groups was the desire to return to apostolic brotherhood and to defy the existing world as hopelessly given over to evil; but except where a pure Manicheism ruled, the dark sense of a terrific unending struggle against overpowering evil was modified by a belief that somehow, some day, the dualism would end and righteousness would triumph, in a total overthrow of Church and State.

The Massilians had no cosmic dualism, but held that a demon lived in the heart and the spirit, which must be expelled. They had a separate existence in Bulgaria till the twelfth century, then merged with the Bogomils. The Paulicians too survived apart in some areas, even after the Turks,

1 In the East the Paulicians destroyed crosses: in parts of Armenia the term *cross-stealer* was a synonym for outlaw and brigand into modern times (*e.g.* the novel *The Cross-Stealer* by Raffi of Tiflis). Paul of Taran says the heretics deny the need of cross or church. Gregory Magister says they claim an inner sense with outward conformity, and reply, 'We are Christians.'

though they were mostly converted to Catholicism in the sixteenth to seventeenth centuries. Some groups around Philippopolis, however, held to their creed of resistance and still called themselves Paulicians in the twentieth century.

CENTRES AND DIFFUSIONS. Bogomilism was the main creed of dissidence from the State among the Balkan peasantry; and the way in which the central areas of mass-heresy moved from Asia into the Balkans shows both the crushing of the free peasantry in Asia and the shrinking of the Empire back on its Balkan bases. The fusion of broken tribal forms and emotions with the heretical idiom derived from Asia was what gave the new energy and passion to peasant defiance. When Basil II incorporated the Bulgarian State in the Empire, a fresh stimulus was given to Bogomilism, which became the idiom of national resistance among the peasantry and craftsmen. The wild high lakes and valleys of Macedonia were well-suited for such a movement; but the Bogomils there were cut off from the Paulicians of Thrace. Such contacts as there were came through Armenian traders and colonists. Two routes ran from Thessalonika inland: across to the Adriatic or up the Vardar to Belgrade. In this hinterland had come the big monastic growth of the tenth century and the most rooted Slavonic elements in the Church.

Here in Macedonia, and further east in the region between Ochrida and the Rhodope Mountains, was the cradle of Bogomilism; the area where it most vigorously flourished. One line of evidence is provided by place-names which have *babun* in them, a synonym for Bogomil, which is also related to word for Old Woman, *baba*—e.g. Babua Mountains in Central Macedonia. This link of Bogomil and Earthmother is an example of the folk-bases that became entangled with the creed. The Bogomils were also called *Kudugeri* in Macedonia and *Torbeshi*, from *torba*, a bag: they carried on their shoulders a bag with the gospels in it, which they used as a scrip for alms.

An exact equivalent appears in the name *Phoundagiagetai*, poor wanderers with scrips in Bithynia and the Opsikian Theme in Asia, heretics who held that God made seven heavens, but the devil made the eighth, our world. The devil made Adam, but two things remain of God, the sun and soul—the soul being stolen by the devil from heaven. For three hundred years the devil tried to get Adam alive, but the soul went on slipping out. Then the devil had an idea, he held his hand over Adam's anus and vomited the unclean animals he had been eating over the soul (to bog it in to the flesh), and so Adam came to life with filth-enclosed soul. The devil also made paradise for man's downfall, as in the Bogomil

Book of St. John. We hear of these scripmen drawing lots as to which area they would evangelise; they had a cult of St. Paul, shed no blood, and spent much time among monks.

Contacts between such groups in Asia and the Balkans, or further west, could be kept up along the pilgrim-routes to Jerusalem.

For the organisation of the heretical churches in the Balkans, indeed, we must look westward, where inquisitions were more active and where more material is available on the methods of heretical missionaries. Through the eleventh and twelfth centuries, trade, pilgrimages, crusades brought East and West close together, and the mass-heresies moved into Dalmatia, Italy, France. Bogomil missionaries were at work in Italy at least by 1030; and thence the creed spread into France, through Aquitaine, over the whole area south of the Loire. Early in the twelfth century it penetrated north, into Champagne, Picardy, Flanders, and at the same time, with minor variations of outlook, into Hungary, Bohemia, Germany. This rapid and thorough diffusion must be linked on the one hand with trade-movements and on the other with the growth of industry (especially textile) in the areas affected. The main carriers were cloth-merchants, who smuggled the heretical books abroad—works like the *Book of St. John* that the Bogomil Dyed Nazarios took to the Patarenes (later twelfth century).

The Patarenes were the main Italian group, as the Cathars were the main group in South France. Cathars (*Katharoi*) was a Greek word meaning the Pure, openly stating the place of the creed's origin. Indeed the Cathars were often called Bulgars (*bulgari, bolgari, bogri, bugres*): hence the French and English words, *bougre* and *buggar*, as terms of abuse, since ascetics were easily suspected of perversions. It is odd that the commonest abuse-term in English perpetuates the name of the Byzantine mass-heresies.

Place-names and family-names in North Italy from the eleventh century also show the Bulgarian trail: *bulgaro, bulgari, bulgarello, bulgarini*. Cathars at the stake in Cologne in 1146 declared that their creed had stayed hidden from the days of the martyrs in Greece and such lands; and in the mid-twelfth century Marcus, chief of the Patarenes, belonged to the *Ecclesia Bulgariae* (Bogomil, mitigated dualism), as opposed to the *Ecclesia Dugunthiae* (Paulician, absolute or at least sharpened dualism). An examination of the ideas of Patarenes and Cathars reveals the whole complex of ideas we have discussed in the Paulicians and Bogomils.

In 1167 the head of the heretics of Byzantium, 'bishop' Niketas, went to Lombardy to convert Marcus to complete dualism, and later presided over a Cathar Council near Toulouse; he mentioned a Church generally taken as situated at Melnik, in the Struma Valley of East Macedonia. He was followed by a missionary, Petrakos, from overseas (Greece or Bulgaria), who advocated the milder creed. Other Churches were cited by the Dominican inquisitor Reinerius (*c.* 1250): he took the Bulgarian and Dugunthian Churches as the original centres of all the heresies, but named also the Sclavonian Church (presumably in Bosnia). Dugunthia seems certainly Dragobita, area of the Slav tribe Dragovichi, which lies in both Macedonia and Thrace; Reinerius' Bulgarian Church is best taken to mean the Macedonian Church, his Dugunthian the Thracian, one Bogomil, the other Paulician. When in the eleventh century the Normans of Bohemond, invading from Taranto, met in South Macedonia a town of heretics (which they burned with all its inhabitants), it was probably Paulicians that they murdered.[1]

Dissident groups long looked to the East, to the orthodox as well as the heretical Churches. Thus we find that the ninth of Wiklif's twenty-four conclusions condemned by the Synod of Blackfriars in 1382 advocated the reconstitution of the Church 'after the manner of the Greeks', and the first act of the Hussites after being excommunicated in 1420 was to send a deputation to Byzantium to ask for admission to the Orthodox Church. But the deeper tradition of revolt would have nothing to do with any established priesthood.

Both Patarenes and Cathars then derived their idiom and much of their organisation directly from the East; and there was organisational continuity between the early Montanist and Massilian creeds of the East, Paulicianism and Bogomilism, Catharism and Anabaptism of the West. In each case the mass-heresy arose as part of a complex historical

---

[1] The Cathars, Poor Men of Lyons, etc., by their propaganda prepared the way for the later reform-movements of Wiklif and Hus, and led straight into Anabaptism, etc. For long the East sent out its heretical influences as the Papacy could not get in with its Inquisition. 'In Eastern Europe the Inquisition never succeeded in obtaining much of a foothold. The main stronghold of Catharism was in lands east of the Adriatic . . . A practically abortive attempt was made to deal with the heretics in 1202; but in the 'twenties, the Mendicants in their untiring zeal, using Hungary as their base and with the armed support of Calomar, Duke of Croatia and Dalmatia, waged successful war against the Bosnian Cathari until the retirement of the Crusaders in 1239. . . . Catharism remained powerful not only in Bosnia, but Dalmatia, Bulgaria and Roumania. In 1298 an attempt made by Boniface VIII to establish an inquisition in the lands south of Hungary from the Danube to Macedonia, came to nothing. But in 1320 an inquisitor named Fabiano, with the assistance of the king of Hungary, made some progress . . . and a further effort was made in 1336 by Dominicans with the co-operation of the Hungarian king. Though in 1378 Urban V congratulated Louis of Hungary . . . four years later that monarch himself complains that practically all his subjects are Cathars, good Catholics being very sparse in numbers.' (Turberville.)

movement expropriating the peasantry and developing the centralised State on a basis of large magnate-estates. The heresy expressed the resistance of the peasant and the town-artisan.

In Bulgaria the Bogomils (despite backward-looking ideas of Bulgarian greatness in the past) had entirely broken with the State and its Church: each big wave of heresy represented a worsening of the peasants' lot. In Bosnia, however, the Bogomil role was different; for here the social divisions were less acute and the nobility upheld the heretical creed against both Orthodox and papal encroachments on their status, till their extermination by the Turks broke down both the Bosnian Bogomil Church and the emerging Bosnian nationhood. In South France, in the Cathar area, there developed something of a pact between the provincial secularly minded nobility and the peasantry-plus-townsfolk against the Papacy with a determined threat to Church-property. So the Papacy organised a fiendishly bloody crusade that smashed the whole of this fine Provençal civilisation that had done so much to raise the cultural level of western medieval society. Provençal society thus represented a transitional form between iconoclast Byzantium and the States where the Reformation of the sixteenth century triumphed.

THE EAST AGAIN. Though the main stream of resistance had passed to the West, heresies did not die out in the East. Thus in 1078 a Greek Paulician, married to a Pecheneg, started propaganda round Sredets (Sofia) and Nish. He was joined by another group under Dobrimir of Mesembria, and by nomads. Together they sacked Sredets and Nish, killed the bishop of Sredets, and were defeated by imperial troops. Two years later the leaders were released with gifts and high positions.

In 1081, Paulicians of Philippopolis were enlisted in the imperial army against the Normans, but deserted and refused to fight again. The emperor feared to make a frontal attack, but got some of the leaders to Byzantium, where they were arrested. Those who agreed to be baptised were let go. In 1084 a baptised Paulician in the imperial service allied himself with the nomad Pechenegs and brought about an invasion of Thrace. For two years he defied the Empire.

Paulicianism remained a fighting creed; but Bogomilism, to the extent that it mitigated the dualist idea, was less pugnacious. The heresies persisted in the Balkans, and even penetrated into Byzantium itself; but after the eleventh century the significant developments occurred in Italy and South France.

In Bogomilism we see the final cleavage between the Byzantine State and the peasant-masses.[1] The State had lost its sources of renewal and weakened to the point where the rapacious Crusaders and merchants of the West could dismember it.

[1] Along the trade-waterways they penetrated Serbia; in the later twelfth century the leader had his tongue cut out; his followers were executed or exiled, their property confiscated and badly burnt. Bogomil elements fuse with indigenous elements in Russian medieval apocrypha, and play their part in dissident movements with dualist or ascetic anti-sacramental aspects, Strignolniks, Judaisers, etc. (In the twelfth century an eclectic sort of Bogmolism was taken up by some of the higher clergy, etc., at Byzantium itself: here the revolutionary element has been dissipated.)

28

THE ZEALOTS

ZEALOT REPUBLIC. The Nikaian emperors had built up on their frontiers a kind of popular militia, *akritai*, who held lands as military fiefs. Michael VIII, to repay the *akritai* for supporting the Doukas family against the Palaiologoi who usurped the throne, deprived them of all State-aid and gave to the Treasury most of the revenue from their lands. They revolted in 1262, and the Empire lost its one sturdy line of defence against the Turks. But there does not seem to have been any religious rallying-cry in the revolt.

Though Byzantine society was able to go on maintaining itself and even to develop valuably certain aspects of its cultural heritage, there were no signs of any basis for significant advance. With a broken-down peasantry, with uncontrolled noble landlords, with a ramshackle State and with ports dominated by Italians—the centre of gravity was falling away, while in the west areas like France, England, Flanders, North Italy were rapidly developing new productive modes and State-forms.

There is one episode, however, that needs attention—the rising of the Zealots in the fourteenth century. In that rising we see expressed the element of vitality still remaining among the people, the weakness of Byzantine forms at this phase compared with those growing up in the great Italian towns, and the way in which Byzantium was tethered to ancient forms even when it had led the way in the break-through from those forms.

Fourteenth-century Byzantium had three classes: the nobles and big landlords; the middle-class, *hoi mesoi*, of traders, more important craftsmen, exponents of the liberal professions and small city-landlords; and the poor, the small producers, the *paroikoi*, small craftsmen, sailors. The poor were very poor, and the rich were few but very rich: the aristocratic families who controlled the State, some big merchants, the higher clergy, and the monks. Demetrios Kydones says that at Thessalonika (which still had about 40,000 inhabitants), some lords were able to entertain the whole city-garrison. Monasteries were swollen with property, shops, farms, gardens. The middle-class was weak: it included small producers who would have been classed as poormen in the tenth century. The poor were the mass of the population. There were a few free farmers, but most were *paroikoi*, tied to the soil under a lord. Landless men were of the same status as *paroikoi*.

The peasants' lot went on worsening, and monastic properties were enormously increasing. At Thessalonika now trade and craft were the sole means of livelihood of the people; raids from without and struggles within made it impossible to pasture cattle on the land around the city. In 1322 the State could not get in any taxes at all from the ravaged country-side. Large numbers of farms had been burned down, tools destroyed, crops requisitioned. Nikolas Kabasilas tells us how the tax-collectors hunted down a poorman, took him by the throat or the beard, and dragged him with blows to jail. The lords they dared not touch.

In 1342 revolts began in the cities, Adrianople, Heraklea, Thessalonika. A civil war was going on, John Kantakouzenos in revolt against John V; and the people had had as much anarchy as they could stand. Kanta-kouzenos had asked the nobles of Adrianople for aid, and they blithely responded; the people intervened at a public meeting, and the lords ordered a whipping for them. The poormen rose, flung the nobles in jail, and took their property; they administered the city.

Other cities heard and did the same. The poormen arrested the nobles and sent them off to Byzantium. The nobles were astounded at such be-haviour—'an unheard-of madness and misfortune sent by God to try the faithful'. Kantakouzenos in his memoirs describes the movement as born from a wish of the poormen to plunder the lords.

At Thessalonika, where there were many guilds of traders and crafts-men, sailors and armourers, the people were as much against the nobles and Kantakouzenos as at Adrianople; but here there was definite political control by the Zealots. Of Zealot aims we have only the vilifying account of their enemies, but it is clear that they had a strong social feeling and defended the rights of the poormen. Gregoras for instance tells us that they were demagogues aiming merely at mob-rule, plunder, doing whatever they pleased; but in fact they had a clear programme which wanted the freedom and independence of their city; they recognised the nobles as the worst enemies of the people and fought them. They con-fiscated the property of the lords and the monastics for the benefit of the poormen of the city and the country-side, and set up a popular militia.

It seems certain that in this programme they were drawing on the experience of the Italian cities. In particular they knew of the revolution at Genoa in 1339, when a party of merchants, using the mass-discontent over heavy taxes, had overthrown the patrician oligarchy. They knew how trade and industry were expanding in Genoa and other Italian republics, where the people had brought down the old obstructive aristocracy and limited the rights of the clergy; and they hoped to carry out the same programme in their own city. But the Zealot movement itself was entirely Byzantine and can be traced back to the twelfth century, a movement of resistance to the State among the peasants and lesser clergy.

The governor of the city was intriguing with local lords on behalf of Kantakouzenos. The Zealots therefore called the people out and led an attack on the rich and powerful without distinction. The nobles fled or hid in churches; their houses were sacked. The Zealots took power as the representatives of the central government. 'Poor men, hitherto unknown, were advanced to the highest rank', wrote Kantakouzenos, whose cause seemed in a bad way. Many of the nobles decided to make peace with the Zealots and got back to Thessalonika. But Kantakouzenos escaped defeat by drawing in Serbs and Turks to his aid. With the Serbs occupying most of Macedonia, Kantakouzenos in 1343 came up to capture Thessalonika. But to his surprise he found that the resistance of the poor was vigorous; the Zealots detected and punished the nobles who conspired to deliver up the city. Kantakouzenos got aid from a Turkish emir, whose troops cruelly devastated the country-side and carried off men and women to be sold as slaves.

The people in the besieged city suffered badly. The Turks ravaged the whole neighbourhood; peasants with their cattle, refugees in the city, were in a bad way—their cattle died from lack of fodder, and the rotting corpses provoked diseases. Under the Zealot lead the citizen militia fought back all attacks, but all Thrace and Macedonia were being wrecked and depopulated by Kantakouzenos' allies, Serbs and Turks.

In 1345 the nobles made an attempt to overthrow the democratic regime. The city was formally under the control of two officials, one representing the central government, the other chief of the Zealots; but the former, John Apokaukos, rankled under the democracy and wanted to break the too-sturdy allies of his own party. The emperor could not like a democratic city-system any more than his feudal rival. Apokaukos conspired with the remnants of the local nobility and had the Zealot chief murdered, while other Zealots were thrown into jail, deported to other towns, or expelled.

Then Apokaukos came out into the open. He called a meeting of the richer citizens and garrison-officers, and got them to agree to handing the city over to Kantakouzenos. But the guild of sailors came out against the decision, and freed the jailed Zealots, who organised resistance to the betrayal. The garrison came over to the Zealots. A hundred lords

including Apokaukos were killed in the Acropolis; and the people
hunted out other nobles all over the city.

For two more years Thessalonika held out. Then the central government reached an accord with Kantakouzenos and the civil war ended. The
Zealots refused to recognise the accord and threw off their allegiance to
Byzantium, and for two years their city was a republic, though the old
system of two archontes was kept with the protosebast representing
Byzantium. All power, however, was in the hands of the Zealots; and
when Byzantium sent an archbishop to the city, he was refused admission.
The property of the rich and the revenue from Church-property were
taken over and used to support the militia, reconstruct the half-demolished
fortifications, help the poor. In support of their action the Zealots declared that the good of the people was the supreme law and that laws can
be changed when they do not correspond to existing conditions and if
the people's good demands it.

But with the triumph of Kantakouzenos the Zealots were environed
with enemies. The nobles and the monks were ranged implacably against
them; and the monks worked hard within Thessalonika to sap their
power. The protosebast, the government's representative, managed to
get the Zealot chief (who was also head of the sailors' guild) exiled for
reasons that we do not know; the guild's house and the chief's were
sacked.

The Zealots, seeing that the nobles were regaining power, declared for
putting the city under the Kral of Serbia, Stephen Dushan. Both John V
and Kantakouzenos came to Thessalonika, and the latter at the assembly
of the people defended himself and blackened the Zealots as robbers and
agents of the Serbs. The leading Zealots were jailed and sent to Byzantium. The republic was defeated.

FAILURE. After that there was no hope of survival for Byzantium. The considered attempts of the Zealots to save the Empire by creating within it
cities of the new type that could have imitated the industrial advances
of the West was broken down by the decadent feudalism of the State and
its insubordinate nobles. And we must note that while the Zealots were
certainly imitating Genoa they were using ancient city-forms, seeking to
infuse them with a new spirit and turn them to new purposes which would
once more have set Byzantium in the forefront of the world-situation.

There were still surviving in Adrianople and Thessalonika, in the fourteenth century, both the *boule*, the council of the ancient Greek *polis*, and
the assembly of the people. The assembly had long lost its political purpose. (The last flicker had been the assemblies called by Constantine V,

9

when he told the people about his plans for extirpating monasticism
the people were merely expected to listen and acclaim, but the fact that
the emperor tried in this way to draw them into his work showed a certain living relationship.) But now the Zealots injected life back into the
ancient form and temporarily made it work inside a medieval world.

The effort could not be sustained. Only at this advanced stage of imperial decomposition could it have been made; and because of the advanced stage of decomposition it could not be stably developed. Thus
Byzantium perished under its inner contradictions; but in the long
struggle which those contradictions had evoked, from the fourth century
on, the Empire had brought forth the medieval world and laid the bases
of modern Europe.[1]

[1] The moments when the Zealots were strong were when the peasants were
gathered in Thessalonika. The city-artisans and small-traders by themselves lacked
the stamina to hold out. Compare the way in which the great Nika Revolt of the
sixth century occurred when Byzantium was thronged with peasants who had lost
their land. (There were also connections between the Zealots and the rationalistic
anti-Hesychasts in the Church; and certainly a link with the ecclesiastical Zealots of
the twelfth and thirteenth centuries, a secret organisation, anti-hierarchical and based
on the people.

From the eleventh century on we meet vague stirrings, efforts of popular
assertion (within the feudal framework). Of the tumults bringing Michael down,
Psellos says, 'The populace was already in control and furiously agitated at the idea
it was going to seize power.' The late twelfth century saw the growth of a weak
idea of Election as a Right of the People. Emperors called assemblies (1197, 1347)
of senate, clergy, merchants and artisans. Note too Michael VIII's effort to win
support by freeing public debtors and aiding the needy.

Note further how the imperial oath changed: from pledging fidelity to the State
personified in the Emperor it became from the eleventh century an expression of
feudal reciprocity (N. Svoronos, *VIe Congres*, 1950). The *mesoi* and *burgenses* (traders,
mostly Italian, who had intermarried and become citizens), the new bourgeois,
failed to assert themselves; the *mesoi* did not join the Zealots and had to be attacked
like the nobles. (The Guilds were largely in decay from the thirteenth century,
though under the Lascarids weak attempts at a regulated economy were made.)

By the thirteenth century there were still independent peasant owners (and at least
a few free village-communities), but they were rapidly lessening and hardly distin-
guishable from *paroikoi* in taxes and obligations. The thirteenth century saw a revival
of the institution of the enrolled soldier with a piece of land, which soon again broke
down. (There were also *douleutai*, poor freemen, who worked for landlords and whose
services often became attached to the estate.)—Charanis, *Byzantinoslavica*, xii, 1951.

V

Art, Drama, Music, Literature

29

THE ORIGINS OF BYZANTINE CULTURE

THE MASS-FORCES BREAK THROUGH. Many elements went to make up Byzantine art; and the formative process was not something once done and then done with. Although there are certain persisting characteristics, Byzantine art, in the millennium complex of its development and expansion, went through a large number of phases, continually drawing in new influences and in turn radiating them, east, west, north. Into its origins went elements from all over the Empire, transformed in their movement and impact with one another, drawn powerfully into the central focus, breaking that focus, re-creating it. Roman art, itself a synthesis over a long period of Italic elements with Greek and more eastern elements, lent its imperial patterns, its allegories, its impressive sense of character; Hellenistic art in the form taken in the countless Alexandrian workshops flowed in with its graceful rhythm and fresh impressionist nuances of colour and atmospherics; Syriac art brought its harsh dramatic impact and Mesopotamian art its hieratic contours. The large spiritual eyes of the Egyptian portraits met the intense brooding eyes of the Mesopotamians; the provincial simplifications of Palmyra met the symbolic crudities from the catacombs of Christian death. Linear patterns light-cut in stone merged with abstract sculptural patterns based on contrasts of light and shade. Allegory and realistic narrative, pagan motives and apocalyptic passion.

All these varying forms and forces came from the people of this world in its convulsions of violent change; they had all their meaning, their possibilities, their confusions and disintegrations—continually eddying round the effort to define a new way of life, a new kind of State and a new kind of rejection of the State.

The catacombs developed their symbolism, partly out of paganism, as when the Seasons defined Resurrection from Death (Winter), and Christ became Orpheus, or Hermes the Good Shepherd; cycles of themes were drawn from liturgy and angels devised from imperial victories, while Eastern centres like Antioch constructed systems half-narrative, half-symbolic. Christ developed from a beardless idyllic youth into an Apollo, drew elements from Olympian Zeus or bearded philosopher.

Take the last pagan art-revival, under Gallienus, with its convergence of styles, its feeling for romantic rhythms, its renewed effort to make allegory concrete, its sarcophagi with the theme of the Philosophic Sage —a nostalgia for tranquillity and courage of thought: the forms, despite their Hellenistic bases, set into monumental fixities and serene frontalities. Thus the sarcophagus in the Lateran shows the Philosopher and his Disciples in a way that foreshadows a Byzantine Christ with his Apostles, a Byzantine type of priest-portrait (the individual bishop represented as the 'eternal priesthood').

The old set forms and symmetries were breaking down. Plotinos the neoplatonist knew it:

> We have to recognise that beauty is that which irradiates symmetry rather than symmetry itself, and it is this which truly calls out love. Why else is there more of the glory of beauty upon the living, and only faint traces of it upon the dead, even though the face still retains its fullness and symmetry? Why are the most living portraits the most beautiful, even though others seem to be more symmetrical?

Life, breaking the old symmetries, and yet irradiating a new richness of vital balances, life is the clue and the seal of beauty.

Apocalyptic visions uttering the deepest pang and hope of the people; parallel scenes from Old and New Testament to express the conviction of a culminating purpose in history; classical forms intruding to strengthen the trend towards depicting history; evangelists pushing Virgil out from the frontispiece of the codex. . . .

Three-dimensional naturalism gives way in part to the pattern of figures set in a single plane. Pictures are less often centralised on a point of action shared by the figures represented; for such centralisation excludes the spectator. Now the main figure, Christ or Moses, Emperor or Saint, controls the rest of the composition and stares straight at the spectator, drawing him in. This frontality encourages monumental conceptions, but is counterbalanced by the trends making for narrative exposition.

In Dura-Europos (a frontier-town of the middle Euphrates) of the mid-third century we see the pressures from Mesopotamia that break into the new imperial art, paintings in water-colour fixed by adhesive gum, where chiaroscuro conflicts or harmonises with efforts to build form by a simple moving contour. The donor is painted as in later western medieval art. A subtle dreamy life burns through the flattening forms. The Synagogue shows a grandiose effort to express Messianic hopes in a linked series of interrelated motives. Here—as in the Roman West, on Trajan's column and in Mithraic grottos, or as in the Indian East, on Buddhist cave-walls—efforts are being made to devise a scheme for continuous narrative in art.[1]

Or look at Ravenna of the fifth century, where Sidonius heard Syrian psalm-singers, and consider the Mausoleum of Galla Placidia, built in the form of a Latin cross with a square tower closed by a conical dome, with cupola-mosaics showing blue sky and gold stars round a great golden cross. The cosmic imagery of a new art, a new world, has swung over from the East and impacted on Romano-Hellenistic forms, which are plunged into a new dimension, the vaulted sapphire of their background. The fusion is insecure, the forms resist the strong impact, the fire of colour that wants to consume the classical shapes with its new harmonies, its new demands.

We see the same clash in the apse of San Apollinare, Hellenistic forms and eastern centralising principles. A dynamic force is shaping and reforming the Graeco-Roman systems, insisting on a new relationship to nature and to men. The vivid attempts that we find at Dura to translate into picture and architecture this new relationship, to concentrate in the forms a total concept of history, of human destiny, of man's place in the universe, is here struggling with the full imperial inheritance. The new idea comes out clear in the procession of female martyrs (left of the entering worshipper) which leads to the apse, with the procession of males on the right. Each line of movement carries the eye towards the apse, the images of Mary and Christ throned among the angels. The eye moves along the less accented part to the more accented, coming to rest on Christ in the completed curve of space, the infinite sky, the womb of life.

THE NEW ORGANISING CENTRE. The Martyrs lead us to that completion, that centre of the new organising energies; and the fact is not accidental. We have already seen the importance of the martyr-cult as the mass-expression

---

[1] We can now trace something of the Graeco-Roman impact on Sassanid culture; link Antioch with Buddhist art, Hadrianic sarcophagi with the Gandhara art of North India; Dionysiac themes from Severan sarcophagi with early Sung paintings in China. The Mesopotamian art we may call a simplification (partly through a return to popular bases) of Graeco-Persian secular art, taken over by Parthian artists (as, further east, by Baktrians) and re-created in terms of the ancient style: there is frontality, arrested movement, stress on linear aspects. This secular art in turn links on with Sassanid art; and there, in its revival, bursts out afresh as a world-influence from Far East to West Europe.

And we must recall how long Graeco-Roman influences had been penetrating this area. A mosaic floor of the Roman type was found at Zeugma in Mesopotamia; a rough form of Roman architecture was used by the Parthians; a king of Armenia about 200 A.D. built a palace from which we have a sculptured fragment, in a broken-down Hellenistic style, etc.

of the demand for a new life, a rebirth. This cult displaced the imperial cult and the Greek hero-cult; it took over the forms of the Heröon. Architecturally as well as ritually, it absorbed and developed the ideas and structures of the pagan cult. Originally the rectangular or semi-circular tomb-slab, *mensa martyris*, the martyr's table, was simply used for communion-meals, with cups for the dishes allotted to the dead man and holes for the libations to be poured in. Mostly the *mensa* lay open to the sky, though enclosed with walls, and a sort of grotto or apse was designed as a funerary *cubiculum*. Later there was added a hall for the faithful to meet in for ritual acts; the open area was replaced by a covered basilica.

But the original idea of a new centre, round which the whole universe revolved, did not die away; it controlled the additions and enclosures. And here we touch the great new formative principle which Byzantine art brings into being. Architecturally it appears in the transformation of the basilica, the Graeco-Roman hall used for all sorts of public business, law, council-meetings, etc. The State-form is deeply and radically changed. This change takes many shapes, a cupola on squinches, a vaulted basilica, vaulting without arches, centralised plans of all sorts, cupola'd basilica, trefoil churches, cross-plans. And the new forms flow from the East, breaking up and reconstructing the forms previously accepted by the State. Diocletian's palace at Spalato showed the impact; Ravenna had taken in Antiochene forms by the mid-fifth century; Thessalonika, Anatolian forms. The grand completion of the new trends appeared in Justinian's St. Sophia.

The organising force throughout is that liberated by the *Martyrion*, architecture directly expressing the new mass-force, the demand for a kind of unity which the State could not supply. The key-forms here are the dome which expresses the rondure of the sky, the circle of the faithful, the womb of rebirth—a symbol at once cosmic, social, organic. The apse, which repeats the rondure on the vertical plane, linking man and heaven (the new life); and the ground-plan expressing the earth of the relics. And the problem set is how these forms are to be given stability, coherently interrelated and imposed on the basilican structure of the State.

Two *martyrion*-types evolve, that of the local martyr-hero, the people's familiar witness against the State, and that of Christ himself, derived from the local *martyrion* and applied to the holy places of Palestine. Those places are conceived as the supreme witnesses of the new dispensation.

The church as a place of assembly of the faithful need be only a rectangular hall with a timberwork cover. But such form, directly carrying over the basilican idea, cannot satisfy the mass-forces seething in Syria, Mesopotamia, Persia, Anatolia, which look to the *martyrion*, open to the sky or given a vault or dome. Already under Constantine the impact is clear and sharp: in the Octagon of Antioch, which succeeds a Heröon of the Sacred Palace; the Holy Apostles at Byzantium, which constitutes a collective heroön of the new religion; the great Palestinian foundations of the Holy Sepulchre, Golgotha, the Nativity, which merge the central plan with the basilican; and the Roman monuments, especially St. Peter, which shows the basilica transformed to *martyrion*, with the sacred corpse under the apse and at the altar's foot.

In the fourth century relics came into the churches, and soon a relic under the altar was a necessity. Otherwise the church was felt to lack the sanctifying witness against evil. *Regnum Caesaris regnum Diaboli.*

THE WORKING-OUT. Problems set by the new development are the placing of the dome on buildings which are not round, and the union of arch and column. At Galla Placidia's mausoleum, the dome rests on the four corners of the cross-form; at San Vitale the circle is enclosed in a square with a recess at each angle. Byzantium solved the union of dome and rectangle. And already at Diocletian's Salona, in the palace-peristyle, the arch leaps bodily from the column-capital. Already the whole future of Gothic is implied. 'The germ of Pisa and Durham and Westminster has been called into life.'

Structures proliferate from this vital conflict of opposites, the rectangular basilica and the circular *martyrion*. Pagan prototypes of all sorts are drawn in, transformed—the square plan, the lengthened rectangle with or without upper storey, the apse opening on an area, the triconchal shape, the room in breadth before an apse (which, completed with basilican naves, will represent a transept), round and polygonal plans, cross-form plans—the free cross, the inscribed cross, the cross in a tetraconchal plan, and so on.

Elements from this tremendous activity of new constructional forms infiltrate westwards, especially into Italy; but the lack of deep-rooted martyr-cults in the West means that generally the vital development, the conflict and fusion of basilica and *martyrion*, does not go on there. Instead there is a direct expansion of basilican forms—with a large atrium and porch, narthex, interior with three or four timber-covered naves. Sometimes galleries are contrived above the aisles, the last bays of the main nave form the choir for readers and singers, surrounded with a sculptured balustrade. The altar in the apse guards the relics, and before it in tiers the clergy take their place, dominated by the bishop's chair. Round or octagonal buildings are used for the tombs of saints or for baptismal rites; but there is no vital and continuing conflict and fusion of

9*

forms. The martyr intrudes into the basilican church without transforming its structure; he merely makes it expand to take him in.

In the East the increasing mixture of the rites and forms of Church and *Martyrion* can be clearly made out. At first the *martyrion* is often dependent on a church, set nearby or against it; but it also moves inside and compels the church to accept its plan and dispositions. The original *martyrion* was usually in a suburban cemetery; the city-church proper, however, now draws it in and imitates it. The cupola'd basilica represents the effort 'to assure to the aspect of cultural edifices a likeness to the *martyria* made fashionable by the fervour of the masses'.

In the West the *martyrion*-crypt is a construction inserted into the larger church, keeping its independence and having no effect on the general structure. In the East the dome and new centralisations flourish; relics are given a monumental setting without relation to the altar, and private burials are kept out. In the West there is slow attraction of burials in general to the altar.

The fragmentation of relics began in the fourth century, both East and West. But the East with its incomparably larger supply of holy corpses started the process, and soon all distinction of a whole or a fragmentary relic or of an authentic *martyrion* and an imitation is lost. The western practice of inhumation *ad sanctos*, of allowing burials to creep closer to the altar and its miraculous contents, to the apse, ends by modifying the apse with radiating chancels, deambulatories, and so on. The variation between eastern and western church-forms is strongly accentuated.

The martyr-cult had its effect on pictorial representations too. It provided once more an organising centre, where elements from pagan and imperial cults could be absorbed into the new systems—imagery of apotheosis and victory, epiphany and theophany. The martyr's portrait often stood in a niche, especially the apsidal one.

The Palestinian forms played an important part here. 'Not only the models of a series of essential images of Christian iconography, but also the religious bases of this imagery must be found in Palestine, and as a function of its historical relics.' This influence appears particularly in the image-types of Christ's theophany, in nativity-scenes, in scenes of the miracles and the passion.

THE NEW SYNTHESIS. Dura-Europos shows us the need to use coloured pictorial representations on the temple-walls of pagan, Jewish and Christian cults alike. The pagan concentration is on Apotheosis, the god (Zeus) in his chariot with Victories (more like Iranian Angels than Greek *Nikai*) hovering over with crowns; and on the correct religious submissions (sacrifices), with myth-scenes secondary. The Jewish concentration is on the Messianic interpretation of history and group-life. The Christian concentration is on Death and Rebirth—characteristically, only the Baptistery has paintings: the place of rebirth-by-initiation. Scenes of the Miracles and of the Resurrection lead to the back-wall with its rendering of a milleniary Earth, the idyllic Good Shepherd set over the scene of the fall in paradise.[1]

All these elements were brought together in Byzantine art; and paint was replaced by mosaic, which was well-suited to express and unite monumental design and realistic character, to give the definitions of hieratic power a richness of colour, a plasticity and weight, which paint could not achieve. The imagery became a part of the whole architectural conception; the building ceased to be a mere setting for rites or actions; it consciously embodied those rites and actions, as though the forms of stone burst into life and confirmed the deep meaning of men's progress through space and time, through history, to a goal of secure freedom and uncontaminated union.

The strong forms of a new attitude to life appear. The classical basis is there, but changed, stirred from its decadence into a tingling new life by the Syrian buffet. There are crudities, polychromatic vulgarities mixed with the many-splendoured thing; but the key-aspect is the new root-depth, the mass-force actively at play for the first time in history on such a scale. This is not the clear definitive forms of the Greek *polis*, nor the heavy mass-element slumbering inside the great statuary of Pharaonic Egypt. The slumbering element has broken out, awake; and the fullness of life, the freedom at which it desperately and confidently clutches, goes in the last resort beyond Athenian dreams; for it can be realised only by the ending of all slavery, the creation of the fraternal Earth of the Good Shepherd.

---

1 The Baptistery, the place where the initiate entered the new life, had close affinities with the *Martyrion*, the place of historical witness to the new life's reality. It tended therefore to be circular or polygonal.

MOSAIC. The building material, save in Syria and Armenia, was brick; and up to the tenth century the outsides were poor. Inside, the richness was as elaborate as possible: polychromatic pillars, marble capitals with open-work carving, walls slabbed with marble enclosed in fine sculptured borders, carpet hangings. Above the marble the walls were set with great arches, with curves of dome and apse, vaults of collaterals and tribunes, glowing mosaics; and on altar or iconostasis was a glaze of goldwork, enamelled silver, rich embroideries, under huge drifts of light.

The mosaic was the new, the typical mode of decoration. Rich in materials, with strong tonality of blue and gold, it replaced the quick interplay of lights, the atmospheric subtleties, of Hellenistic painting; in its symmetrical dignity worked the new centralising force that compelled the spectator into the heart of the imagery. Iran had brought its peacocks and griffins, Armenia its beast-patterns, Syria had brought its dramatic force which centralised a group by twisting them all with the same shock of realisation, the revelatory or annunciatory act of the new life—as distinct from the classical interrelating of a group on its point of shared interest, with a suaver rhythm that drew in rather than burst out. Hellenistic naturalism was present and resisted; but the figures were turning fullface and hard bold lines enclosed them—though on the floors birds and trees of the Alexandrian type persisted. Decorative regularities increased.

At San Vitale in Ravenna we see the new organising principle at work. In the choir the persons or events which announce and glorify the sacrifice of the Lamb are grouped round the altar; Christ in the apse is solemnly enthroned between two archangels or saints; on the lateral walls Justinian and Theodora in heavy rich court-attire look on—not the martyrs.

Sculpture, to some extent distrusted as pagan, was still made, but was secondary.[1] The vast polychromatic spaces did not foster three-dimen-

[1] The stonework most in key of the new art was that which covers a space with fine broideries (like lace or goldsmithery), digging and cutting for colour-effects suiting the general architectural design. The fifth century saw drilled work (Theodosian or acanthos capital with leaf standing out pale against deep drilled background); the sixth century saw pierced work, the design emerging as a kind of lacework seemingly detached from its background (e.g. the basket-capitals in St. Sophia).

sional forms. An Aramaic-Iranian sense of pattern geometrised the drap-
ery; features grew emphatic; a harsh symbolism struggled with naturalistic detail. Small ivory and metal work kept a wide range of invention
ranging from Alexandrian picturesque to Syrian realism, sometimes
merging opposed characteristics as in the elegant and vigorous Antioch
silver work.

The mixture and opposition of these elements showed up strongly in
the illustrated manuscripts: the picturesque genre mingled with the more
severe historical themes or the monumental gravity of ritual emotion;
allegorical figures, author-portraits, decorative richness of detail, type-
fixations, combined, separated, fought, combined. Here, as in all modes
of expression, the eastern elements tended to dominate. They were what
brought the transformative force into play.

ACTIVE IMPLICATION. Frescoes languished; but easel-paintings throve,
with a technique born from the portraits on Hellenistic mummy-cases
in Egypt. The wood was covered with a plaster layer, then with cloth,
then again with plaster: and then painted on. Poems on art carried on the
classical motif of naturalistic deception; but revealed at the same time a
sense of the transformative forces, the meaning of the new light-burst.
Paul the Silentiary writes:

> (i) *Art and not Nature gave this Bacchant gladness,*
> *for with the stone it fused the burst of madness.*

> (ii) *He's caught her eyes, just caught them—but O her hair!*
> *O the supreme lustre of her skin is gone!*
> *Paint first the dazzle-sheen of the gold sun,*
> *then Theodora's flesh will glisten there.*

And Agathias expressed the new active relation of the artist to his
material:

> *I once was a harlot in Byzantium,*
> *open to any man who chanced to come,*
> *as versatile as a bedded girl may be:*
> *here Thomas in his love has painted me.*
> *To show his soul's desire, he used his art;*
> *for, even as melts the wax, so melts his heart.*

This refers to encaustic paintings, which used hot wax. In Theokritos'
Second Idyll the girl melts the image of the lover in a magic rite, to melt
the lover; here the magic has entered into the artist, who melts into the
image he creates: a new union of artist and subject.

And as if to express this conscious entry of the artist into the theme he defines, Eulalios, the great creator of the mosaics of the Holy Apostles at Byzantium, depicted himself in his scene of the holy women at the tomb 'in his usual dress and looking exactly as he appeared when he was at work on these paintings', as a Byzantine source tells us.

SAINT SOPHIA. The destruction caused by the Nika Revolt gave Justinian a chance to rebuild portions of Byzantium, and a special effort was put into the cathedral. The ruins were cleared, near houses bought and pulled down, ten thousand workers toiled for four years under Anthemios of Tralles and his assistant Isidore of Miletos. Anthemios is a fine example of the rich cultural life of the East in the sixth century. An expert mathematician, he applied his theoretical knowledge to problems of building. One of his brothers was famed as a professor of literature, and was invited to teach at Byzantium. Two other brothers were doctors, one staying at Tralles, the other going to Rome.

The problem that Anthemios set himself with St. Sophia was to combine the basilica and the dome, the square and the cross—*i.e.* to complete the solution of the problems raised by the impact of *martyrion* on basilica.[1] He devised a Greek-cross plan (some 250 feet by 225) with a dome set over the quadrilateral space between the arms, some 180 feet high—the dome rising yet another 100 feet. At each angle of the square rose a massive pier; and the four piers held the arches and pendentives on which the rimmed dome was placed. Stability was gained by half-domes (each divided into three semidomes) east and west, with inner buttresses north and south. Light tiles of spongy earth made at Lemnos were used for the dome; and the cemented bricks of the main walls, more or less square, took in much of the tensile strain.

To employ external buttresses in the Gothic way was alien to the classical and organic line of approach, which demanded that a design be structurally adequate in itself, providing its own system of inner balances to meet the strains that its nature generated. One way of handling the dome was to use a square of polygonal bases taking the dome's thrust equally all round (*e.g.* SS. Sergios and Bacchos); but it was felt that a method which merged cross and circle was more satisfactory, more expressive of the full conflict and unity of Byzantine society. The round

[1] He may have seen the domed Serapeum of Hadrian's villa and got the idea from there of a dome as a surface made up of a rhythmic sequence of flat and concave sections unsupported by pendentives—rising flush from the drum. But the main dynamic is the martyrion form. Octagonal and rotunda structures were now common. Anatolian brick pendentives (by which a dome could be set on four square walls, themselves poised on the four central piers) made possible the fusion of basilica with rotunda or octagon moving in time into the Greek-cross form.

of the universe, cut by the four points of the compass, was the womb of
the Virgin with the crucified god within it.

Inside, the longitudinal constructions passed fluidly into the great
centralising dome which pulled everything radially up into itself and swam
aloft like a winged crown. The pillar is no longer a basic structural unit;
its purposive is decorative. Those below, set in curves, draw up the eye to
their gilt capitals; those above, lifting galleries, run into the bright upper
walls of porphyry-plaques. The four triangular pendentives, each with its
mosaic of winged cherubim move out to uphold the dome's cornice where
Christ Pantokrator looms up to judge the world. Beneath him stands the
ambo, used for rites such as a Coronation or for important proclamations.

Over it all, high in curved mosaic, brooded the Mother with Child,
blue and white and gold, on a red throne with green footstall; and at
dome-summit was Christ on the starry heavens. The roof, covered with
pure gold, mixed its lights with the endless hues of the marbles, green
white, serpentine, crocus-gold, red and white, white-misted rose,
porphyry: a blending of fires of stone, night-lighted with gold.

The great effect was one of space and light. This aerial depth was partly
gained by the half-domes, the forty windows. We know that the people
of the time responded to the new spatial quality of the construction; and
the comments of Prokopios in prose and Paul in verse are valuable as
themselves expressions of the new bases in culture.

> So the church has become an extraordinarily beautiful sight, shattering to
> those who see it, but quite incredible to those who only hear about it. It rises
> to a heavenly height, and as if surging up from other buildings it stands aloft
> and looks down over the rest of the City, beautifying it because it's a part
> of the whole scene, but also glorying in its own loveliness because, though a
> part of the city it dominates, it yet rises so high above that the rest is viewed
> from it as from a watch-tower.
> The proportions have been so carefully worked out that it may be truly
> described as specially long and also unusually broad. And it exults in a beauty
> beyond words. For it proudly displays its mass and harmonious proportions
> without excess or deficiency. It is both more imposing than the buildings with
> which we are familiar, and much nobler than those merely vast; and is par-
> ticularly lavish in light, in the reflections of sun on marble.
> Indeed you might say the interior is not illuminated from outside by the
> sun, but the glow is born from within, such an abundance of light steeps the
> shrine . . .
> It seems somehow to float in air on no solid base; it seems poised on high
> to the peril of those within. Yet in fact it is braced with exceptional strength
> and stability.

He says the dome 'less reposes on the masonry than is hung by a golden
chain from the highest heaven'—a Neoplatonist metaphor that correctly

defines the intended impression. He also says the massing colours give the walls the effect of concentrating all the essences of blossoming growth:

> You could imagine you'd come on a meadow with flowers in fullest bloom. You couldn't but marvel at the purple, the green tint, the stones of glowing crimson, and those with the flash of white, and again those which Nature like a painter varies with the richest of colour-contrasts.

When on Christmas Eve 537 Justinian entered the new church, he bade Paul the Silentiary celebrate the occasion; a few days later Paul recited in the palace the proem of his long and excellent verse-description. He saw even more fully than Propokios the cathedral as a world-image, a burst of all the energies of life in liberated colour, a renewal:

> *Spring-green of Karystos and Phrygian many colours*
> *where flowers of red and white glisten boldly,*
> *porphyry powdered with a mess of stars,*
> *crocus opening with a light of gold,*
> *milk poured out on the flesh of black below*
> *blue cornflowers growing in drifts of fallen snow . . .*

A world of joy, despite the judgment in the Pantokrator's face above— or rather because of that face, because the face still holds the sharp judgment of the people on the State of injustice and division. This light yields the secret of harmony, and not the cavernous gloom and redeeming light-burst of Gothic, not the plain light-influx and limpidity of the classical. A luminous mist gushes from the small windows set along the dome's cornice and in the walls. No shadows, only a depth. An infinite wealth of elusive reflections ending in sheer light.

For evening service a central chandelier hung by chains over the ambo; and there were many rows of lamps, silver boats and bowls, chains with discs of silver, crosses pierced to hold oil-glasses with floating wicks. The iconostasis glittered across the apse, a hanging cross glowed above, Christ in the dome lighted by unseen lamps on the cornice-top covered the white sky of the spirit. The dome shone far out at sea.

Paul saw the gleaming as a Round Dance of Lights, an image which finely relates the *martyrion*-circle to the round-dance which goes back ultimately to the fertility-rite of the tribal group. (Diogenes, bishop of Amisos, described a church as a *chorostasia* in his line 'Rest by the dancing-circuit of the blest.')

The conception was dramatic, with emphasis on the participation of all concerned, in the liturgic experience. Here, in the Byzantine world, are

> churches doing the work of theatre-halls, divided into two sections, one reserved for the immaterial, spiritual, symbolic, and spectacle, and the other surrounding the first in the form of two-storeyed galleries for the audience.

10.   CRUCIFIXION

Mosaic, at Daphni near Athens, eleventh century

Hence the symmetry of plan and the close link between the different compartments of the interior, the partitions of which are pierced by a multitude of large openings. (Brunov.)

HOLY WISDOM. Why was the supreme church of the new society dedicated to *Sophia*, who became as central for the Orthodox world as Peter for the Catholic? She was no Saint, no person at all. She was *Wisdom*, a Gnostic and Judaic concept. Underneath, she was simply the Great Mother of Asia and Syria interpreted through a screen of Greek philosophy and Judaeo-Babylonian symbolism.

The Jews had a large body of Wisdom literature in the years after Alexander the Great, when Greek thought seeped thoroughly into Palestine and Syria. The supreme god of the Jews, Yahweh, who had once had a wife, is now supplied with a female complement who would not threaten his oneness, Wisdom. An early stage appears in *Proverbs*: 'Wisdom has builded her house, she has hewn out her seven pillars . . .' and 'Wisdom cries without, she utters her voice in the streets.' Wisdom declares, 'I was set up from everlasting, from the beginning, or ever the earth was. Before the mountains were settled, before the hills, was I brought forth.'

Iranian and Babylonian personifications lie behind this idea, which the inflow of Greek thought helped to strengthen. In *Ecclesiasticus* (the Wisdom of Jesus, son of Sirach) Wisdom grows yet more important:

Forth from the mouth of the Highest and like a mist I covered the earth. I had my dwelling in the high place and my throne was upon a pillar of cloud. I traversed the heavens alone and penetrated the depths of the underworld.

Some Jewish thinkers held that she belonged to the Jews, being the agent that led and held them together. Wisdom approximates to a Messiah. In Baruch:

No man knows her ways, neither considers her paths. But he that knows all things knows her . . . and has given her unto Jacob his servant, and to Israel his beloved. Afterwards she was seen upon earth and dwelt among men.

As the emanation of Yahweh, she is also a kind of creative agent. In *Ecclesiasticus*, she says 'I caused the Light that fails not.' She here merges with the Word, *Logos*, that was becoming an important idea in the Greek-Judaic philosophies of Alexandria; and the Word too was personified. In *The Wisdom of Solomon* (an apocryphal book perhaps of the last century B.C.), Wisdom and Word are both persons with similar functions:

She (Wisdom) is the breath of the power of God, and a pure influence that flows from the glory of the Almighty; therefore can no defiled thing come unto her. . . . O God of our Father and Lord of Mercy, who have made all

things by your Word . . . Your Almighty Word leaped down from heaven
out of your royal throne, as a fierce man of war in the midst of the land that
was destroyed.

A thinker like Philo tries to distinguish the functions. He held Sophia
to be God's Daughter and Mother of All Things, and the Word to be her
Son transcendentally one with the Father. God begot the Word on Sophia,
but she was still a pure Virgin. The Word mediates between God and Man.

In the Gnostic groups of pre-Christian or early Christian days, Sophia
was a central figure. At their meetings they sang hymns in her praise on
the line of these words from *Ecclesiasticus*:

> In me is all grace of life and truth. . . . Come unto me all you that are desirous
> of me and fill yourselves with my fruits. For the remembrance of me is sweeter
> than honey and my inheritance than the honeycomb. They that eat me shall
> have the more hunger, and they that drink me shall thirst the more. Whoso
> hearkens to me shall not come to confusion.

The passage in *Matthew* beginning, 'Come unto me, all you that labour
. . .', is thus certainly a fragment from a Wisdom hymn. Wherever
Christianity tended to dissolve history and the belief in a definite world-
end into subjective symbolism and christological ideas, it tended towards
the Gnostic bases, and the ideas of *Logos* and Sophia came forward.
Athanasios could say for Sophia, 'The Lord created me in his works because my image is in them and to this extent I have manifested myself in the
creation.' Or declare, 'Wisdom is the first created essence of the creature,
because the love of God is shed abroad in our hearts by the Holy Spirit.'

In Gnostic creeds she appears as the primary hypostasis of God in creating the manifold world; she is the Great Bosom or Womb, the Guardian
Angel. Thus the Ophite sect believed in a Primal Man whose Son is the
Second Man. A Female Spirit conceives Christ as the Third; he goes up
with her, but a light-ray falls on the Waters. The ray is Sophia; her mating
with the Waters gets in her the Demiurge, Ialdaboath, who in turn begets
six Powers and (from matter's dregs) the Serpent, and calls himself
the Supreme. But Man, made by the Powers, turns to the Primal Man;
and Ialdabaoth makes Eve to ruin him. So Sophia sends the Serpent to
help Adam and Eve, to draw them into eating the fruit of the Tree of
Knowledge against Ialdaboath's command. Ialdabaoth exiles the pair
from paradise to earth; and after a long war between mankind (aided by
Sophia) and the Demiurge—a war told in the Old Testament—the Spirit
sends Christ down to enter the Virgin as Jesus. He is killed by the Jews
at Ialdaboath's instigation: or rather Jesus alone is, for Christ has gone
out of him. Afterwards Christ raises the body of Jesus, who stays on earth
eighteen months initiating the elect disciples.

To enter the Church Sophia had to shed her myth and become merely a symbol of the organic unifying factor in the universe; but the fact of dedication of churches to her shows how strong was the persisting sense of her as a person.

To grasp the nature of Byzantine art it is necessary to grasp the nature of Sophia, who provided the central organic concept from which the new art derived. The martyr, we have seen, gave the tremendous new dynamic of revolt, the concept of a centre of living and organisation opposed to the existing State, the shrine that expressed the demand for rebirth in a cosmic image, the four-square world with the sky-dome over it. But in fact the world did not and could not actualise the unity for which the martyr died; therefore a further element was required to reconcile the new dynamic forms of revolt with the State which they had modified. The intuition of a new potential unity was fused with the intuition of the unity of process in the universe, and an abstraction of unity was made from this fusion; this abstraction was then applied to the existing world to sanctify division and to construct a hierarchical system in which the cruel power-structure of the State was identified with an harmonious series of interlinked levels outside man, the angelic powers.

Thus Sophia, the Great Bosom, takes into herself the martyr-death and transforms it into the cosmic image of the domed church, where all is reconciled, all is changed into something other than it is—where power becomes mercy and class-division the necessary difference of notes in a graded scale of song. Sophia is the Virgin Mary in the world of ideas; she mediates between the One and the Manifold, and gives warmth and concreteness to the theology of the Son one with the Father; she relieves the terrible weight of abstraction, division, that issues in the lacerating self-alienation of the historical process under consideration: alienation of man from his fellows, from himself, from nature.

She reconciles discord, and thus aids the oppressor; she makes it possible for men to go on living and serve the necessary State, and thus aids the total formative process by which man keeps his difficult foothold in a world of violent alienations and continues moving forward.

She stands at the core of Byzantine art, continually drawing in the forms of revolt thrown up by the mass-movement, the mass-heresies, and transforming them to the service of the Orthodox Church and the imperial State. The full theoretical formulation of the position that she stabilises is to be read in *The Heavenly Hierarchies* composed by some Neoplatonist or Origenist Christian and attributed to Dionysios the Areopagite to give it an apostolic label and help its acceptance. Essentially heretical, it became the basic expression of Orthodoxy in its struggle against the separatist

heresies in which the revolt-sense gathered round abstractions of the One
Nature or the Two Natures. I shall deal with it further when I come to
the struggle inside Byzantine music.

THE NEW LIFE-CENTRE. The central church of Byzantine culture was therefore fitly dedicated to Holy Wisdom; and Justinian, in building the new
church, gave definitive form to Byzantine Sophia. The vast mass of new
forces liberated by Christianity, in both its orthodox and its heretical
aspects, the vast mass of new forms and colorations which the large-scale
intrusion of the common people into imperial culture had loosed, were
here stabilised and reconcentrated for imperial purposes. But in the process imperial culture had been profoundly changed. In this sense Sophia
stands for the new mass-forces which provide the elements of integration
surpassing anything in classical constructions.

With St. Sophia and all that it meant, a great new culture was matured
and stabilised.[1] And if we consider what has here happened to the basilica
(which remains the basic form for the West) we realise the gap that has
now appeared between West and East. The long arcades and colonnades
of the basilica go; the wooden roof of the naos dromikos yields to brick-
vaults, barrel or domical. The dome-centre on the square plan does away
with aisles drawn out longways; now the aisles are turned round the
central area. The need of dome-supports has brought the Greek-cross
into the ground-plan. The dome rests on four arches which it prolongs
as barrel vaults to the side-walls, to gain abutment for itself and its
pendentives. The four spaces left between the cross-arms are taken up by
square bays covered by small domes at lower levels: the four arms with
dome above form the Greek-cross. The outside is square, with short
prolongations east and west, and with a narthex or antechurch at the
west end.

In the West, however, the lack of a mass-basis for the Church means
that the main architectural form is only a remnant of the form that had
been the emblem of Roman State-power.

1 In May 558 the dome cracked: Anthemios was dead, so Isidore carried out the
restoration. He left the half-domes, but widened the arches north and south that took
the lateral thrust, making the equilateral symmetry more complete and raising the
dome more than 20 feet. Sophia has since passed through many quakes and fires:
even the fire of 1755, when the dome-lead melted and poured through the gutters.

Justinian did much more building, *i.e.* rebuilt the burned Holy Apostles, the Senate, Baths, porticoes and the parts of the palace that were burned down, generally
improved the palace-complex, built a summer-palace at Hieron (south-east of Chalkedon) and raised a township there with a fine church, markets, porticoes, with a
large mole to protect shipping and so on. But I am not making catalogues, and can
only touch on key-aspects.

31

EXPANSIONS AND INTERRELATIONS

SCYTHIC ART. The two preceding chapters have stressed throughout the rich tangle of influences from all over the Near East which converge on Byzantium; but there are further influxes and outmovements. This involved give-and-take, with Byzantium as the centre of the eddy, continues throughout the centuries. In art as in most cultural matters, the Empire fecundates west and east alike; and a thorough study of its influence would have to include a full analysis of Georgian and Armenian cultures as well as Syrian and Islamic, Russian and Scythian as well as Italian and Gallic, Anglo-Saxon as well as Germanic in general. Here I can only give examples and indications of the cultural role of Byzantium between the fifth and the fifteenth centuries.

Recent excavations of the Great Palace have found mosaics of the earlier fifth century, which are not linked with the Antiochene mosaics of the same period, where Iranian influences are strong. Late Hellenistic motives predominate—idyllic and bucolic scenes, bacchic routs, hunts, children playing (sometimes with animals). But among the monsters we meet the fantastic zodia of old Ionian art, and the fights are ferocious. Both these aspects appear in the Scythic art of the steppes from the fifth century B.C. to the fifth to ninth centuries A.D. when Gothic, Avar and Bulgarian art incorporate them. The types are Pontic creations, made for sale or barter among the folk of the Black Sea coastlands. They carry on ancient Ionian elements, which through them intermingle in the goldsmith work of the imperial epoch in Gaul.

The new-found mosaics prove that the best mosaic-artists of Byzantium, who would be used in important work in the palace, had a stock of barbarian subjects which they expertly handled. It seems likely then that the art-centre which supplied the Pontic market now was Byzantium itself. And while on the one hand the pavements show forms that Byzantium threw off into the Scythic area, with profound effect there, they also on the other hand show forms of Hellenistic finesse which supplied models from time to time later on when a classical revival arose in the capital.

The basic elements of Germanic art were derived from the forms which Iranian-Greek influence moulded on the steppes among the Sarmatians who dominated there till the Goths and Huns came. Place-names in Gaul show the widespread Sarmatian colonisation there (*Sermaise, Saumaise, Semizelles*). *Cloisonné* jewellery—with the metal hidden under clotted gems, garnet in chief, genuine or artificial, or with gems set in metal mounts—was spread by the Goths and other Germans all over the West in the fifth century: it was an offshoot of the Iranian art taken up by the Scyths and then the Sarmatians.

German art as it developed in the West was thus mainly the result of two streams of influence from the East—Greek-Iranian on the steppes and Greek-Syrian coming up from the Mediterranean. In the fifth century in Gaul we see from Sidonius how much luxury remained on the great estates, however the towns might be declining. Complicated devices like water-organs were still in use; and Iranian textiles were in high demand 'Let the fabric from a far land display the heights of Ktesiphon and Niphates' (in Armenia).

IN THE WEST. We meet stray efforts to introduce the *martyrion* form into Gaul; but without much effect. At Aix-la-Chapelle was an octagonal church; and at St. Denis the saint's tomb was in tower-form on the edge of the Roman road. In the fourth century a lady reared a mausoleum, and St. Geneviève had a Church built. In Merovingian times a dome set on columns was imposed and a railing fixed around the tomb and altar.

But in Provençe till early twelfth century the typical church was like a Roman temple with a single nave, windowless walls, fluted columns crowned with acanthus, pediments, entablatures of classical proportions —a sort of place like the church of St. Sermin at Toulouse that made Venantius Fortunatus cry in the seventh century:

> *What no man Roman-lineaged came to rear*
> *the man barbarian-born has managed here !*

Only in Italy, in Rome and Ravenna did the Byzantine forces find a soil rich enough to absorb their impact. Rome, though continuing to cling to certain imperial and early Christian traditions of its own, was much affected by the Justinianic revival, as the mosaics and frescoes of several churches and oratories show.

But if only a few places could take in anything from the main imperial stream, humbler lines of influence such as that sent abroad through Sarmatian and Gothic channels better suited the broken-down areas. Not all sites in Asia could afford rich mosaics. For instance we find self-taught Cappodocian monks piously painting the walls of their rock-chapels at Latmos near Miletos; and the effects of this kind of work spread west

and can be seen in the decorations of a series of small churches in South
Italy and even France.

And even if the impoverished West could not build grandly, it could
take in many examples of the minor arts from Byzantium. Magnates and
bishops wanted the fine textiles, ivory-carvings, goldwork of the Empire;
and such works, scattered over the West, provided standards of skill to
which local workers were continually trying to rise as soon as there was
any settled kind of life encouraging the finer crafts.[1]

ROMANESQUE. The architecture and art which in the West accompanied
early Byzantine art is generally given the misnomer of Romanesque:

> The Byzantine genius at this time, say 500 to 800, so dominated the
> expression of the arts in Italy and the West that it would be well to call
> the style Byzanto-Romanesque or even Byzantesque. (Lethaby.)

Three strains mingled, the Christian-Roman, the barbarian, and the
Byzantine (which from the sixth century exerted ever greater effect). The
ingredients of this sub-Byzantine style, with its rendering of imperial
forms in heavy ways, can be found in Romano-Hellenistic art. Thus on
ivory tablets of the Werden Casket (c. 400) and in a panel in the doors
of Santa Sabina, Rome (c. 500), we find pictured a church with two
round towers, a symbol of Jerusalem, which anticipates a Romanesque
church of some seven centuries later. Diocletian's palace at Spalato anticipated many features of Romanesque building, arches rising direct from
columns or entablature bent over to suggest a deeply moulded arch,
windows with arched heads, roll-moulding carved round a door, a long
wall-arcade on a small scale and the like. The lobed arch appeared in Syria
and Persia, already more or less like the Gothic type, and was handed on
by Moslems to South France, where it begot in time the Gothic cusped
arch. Romanesque methods of subordinating and intersetting parts into
larger parts can be found in early Byzantium or Syria, an excellent
example is in the church at Sergiopolis built by Justinian, where the
pillars between the piers have little arches fixed into the main arch. And
so on.

Under the Visigoths in France and Spain schools of builders tackled
the problem of the vaulted church. Under Charlemagne and the Lombards the forms were expanded. At Aachen Charles built his palace-chapel

---

1 Mani the prophet was a skilled painter and enjoined painting as part of his ritual.
Through the destruction of Manichean books, it is hard to evaluate the effects of their
art, though there is reason to believe that Manichean art underlay much later Persian
work. When in the ninth century book-illumination came into favour at Bagdad,
Manichean influence may well have played a part.

with a sixteen-sided wall round a high central octagon, and had the inner domical vault covered with mosaics (no doubt using artists from the Byzantine schools of Rome or Ravenna); bronze-work is imitated from the palace of Byzantium, *e.g.* a fountain in the form of a pine-cone. Other elements were Roman—some actually so: antique capitals were brought from Italy.[1]

1 At Germigny-les Près (Loiret) the church is decorated with early ninth-century mosaics of stray Byzantine influence; and so on.

32

THE ICONOCLASTS

THE NEW HUMANISM. The banning of religious art by the Iconoclasts meant a break with the monumental and abstract tendencies, and also a loss of Syrian dramatic intensity. As the orthodox destroyed Iconoclast art as well as literature, we have to interpret the results of the Iconoclast period by the descriptions of the work they favoured, by direct expressions of their aesthetic traceable in book-miniatures, and by the profound change that comes over religious art when Orthodoxy triumphs afresh. The last-named means is the most important; for the change in question can be attributed only to the fact that the religious painters after the two periods of thorough break in their art had to pick up from the point to which the Iconoclasts had carried things.

The hieratic is thrown overboard. Hellenistic and classical forms are revived, genre pictures of hunt and hippodrome, idylls of landscape with birds and flowers, portraits, historical themes. Constantine replaced the statues of Christ with statues of himself, and a fresco of the Sixth Church Council with pictures of his favourite charioteer; and encouraged historical themes likely to help morale. Nature-themes were used in church-decoration where the walls were plastered over or covered with subjects defying adoration. We have ivories of myth-scenes; and we know that humour and satire were used.

Usually the strong development of humour and caricature under the Iconoclasts is attributed to the iconodule monks, often rough peasants who brought popular elements into culture; and certainly such monks played an important part in the development. But the Iconoclasts also had their satirists; and George Asbestos, friend of Photios, did bitter drawings of the ultra-orthodox that were burned at the Eighth Council. The new mixture of elegance, fantasy, realism can be seen in the Khlidov psalter, with drawings such as that of the proud who 'set their mouth against the heavens and their tongue walketh through the earth': two bearded men with long tongues on the ground, their upper lips beaked to the sky, which is a bowl surmounted with a Cross. Fantasy runs riot in works like the Physiologos with its sirens, centaurs, nymphs.

Under Theophilos there is mixture of Hellenistic forms with new decorative impulses flowing in from the East—this time, from the art of the Bagdad caliphate (itself a synthesis of Greek, Mesopotamian, Persian elements).

ASPIRING FORMS. In architecture the ground-plan of the equal-armed cross inscribed in a square (with central dome and four lesser domes at the corners) has now finally eliminated all traces of the basilica; and this type settles down as the characteristic Byzantine expression, extending over Greece and Asia Minor, Bulgaria and Serbia, Roumania and Russia. The high vaulted transepts terminating in curved or triangular façades clarify the lines of construction and give the outside of the building as well as the inside a chance to assert itself. And the general stress of height sends the central dome soaring, raised on a high polygonal drum. For the more solid cubical mass of the Justinianic period we find an upward movement of forms, a series of lessening vaults in ascension to the main dome; for the weighty piers, slender columns; for the straight lines which could lose their majesty in monotony, a fluidity of relieving curves in a triple apse at the eastern end or in hemicycles at the ends of the narthex.

These forms, which were carried on by the Macedonians, were developed under the Iconoclasts, who completed the movement away from the Justinianic solutions into the lighter and yet more compact form which was capable of a rich diversity of adaptions in its expansion within and without the Empire. But they steadily showed the failure of the mass-element in Byzantine culture. From the ninth to the twelfth centuries the five-naved cruciform church with dome, which was typical of the capital's architecture, went on growing more dwarfed in its proportions, less functional in its structure.[1] The possibilities of aspiring form which the new forms had revealed were to be given a powerful working-out in Gothic—not that Gothic architecture was in any sense directly related to Byzantine medieval churches: the relationship was very much complex, both forms being in the last resort differentiations within a single stream of influences reaching back to the fourth century. The comparison, is however, useful, indeed necessary, if we are to understand the values, positive and negative, in Byzantine medieval architecture. We see a new start, which, however, fails to fill out with the rich organic forces born from the people.

St. Sophia is an impressive meeting-place which permits the masses to take part in the processions and grandiose rites. The churches of the Byzantine medieval

[1] The origins seem to lie in a squared nucleus made by four pillars upholding the dome—derived from a fusion of the Zoroastrian fire-temple and the early Christian type based in the free cross.

period are on the contrary reserved to a chosen élite. In the whole country-side domed churches with three naves are built on a simplified plan in the form of an inscribed cross. The capital alone constructs cruciform churches, domed with five naves, conceived from the angle of uniting spectators and adapted for processions. Their purpose in short, restricted to a small number of the faithful, remains alien to the people. Hence the unreal character of the architectural forms and the dwarfed proportions. (Brunov.)

In the same way the Byzantine medieval town, Byzantium or Thessalonika or Trebizond, thrives and develops ahead of western towns, but fails to develop the deep inner energies that lead into the commune.

A secular building which shows an effort to popularise scientific interests was the Anemodoulion, the Windslave, raised by the astromoner Heliodoros under Leo. Above a complicated mechanism this had a statue of a naked woman, visible from afar, which turned with the winds.[1]

STRUGGLE AND DEEPENING REALISATIONS. A tale about the mosaic of a beardless Christ seated on the arc of heaven in the Hosios David, Thessalonika, gives us some insight into the tussle under the Iconoclasts:

> The daughter of an emperor in pagan days, Maximian, was a secret convert and got permission to build a palace. She turned the Bath into a Church and got an artist to paint a Virgin. As it was nearly done, it was found next morning changed to a Christ. The princess made the artist leave it, and she worshipped it. Then, found out, she was put to death, and the church burned down. Later, when the Christians won, the monastery of Zehariah was built on the spot. The image was still there, hidden. Under Leo (813–20) an Egyptian monk, Senouphis, witnessed a miraculous baring of the image mid thunder and lightning. The bricks and oxhide fell off, showing it. He died from the shock and the church's name was changed to the vocable Christ the Saviour.

This tale, told by a monk Ignatios in an MS. of the early fourteenth century, is based on the fact that in the fifth century a church was built there on the foundations of a Roman bath, and was burned down in the seventh. The hiding of the mosaic is a theme from Iconoclast days; and indeed the tale of the princess equates the Iconoclasts with the pagan persecutors. The motive of the Beardless Christ, unusual in Byzantine-Syriac art, begot the tale of the Christ-Virgin. Probably an Egyptian monk-painter had left Arab-invaded Alexandria in the seventh century and introduced this Egyptian Christ-type.

[1] Secular architecture, rich under the Iconoclasts, uses the same forms (dome, trefoil, narthex, etc.). Digenis' four-storeyed house has three cupolas and a cross-form reception hall. After the seventh century pierced capitals largely give way to embroidery-sculpture (designs applied to the flat stone in ribbons and interlacing bands, around geometric figures or panels of animals and rosettes).

The tale serves to show the process that led from veneration of relics to that of images. The picture, miraculous, demands worship (and the antecedents of such worship are put into pre-Constantine days); the executed princess and the blasted monk give it the aura of martyrdom and theophany.

And poems show us the intensification of the artist's sense of unity with his material, the significance of the colour-burst. The first poem is by Constantine of Rhodes:

(i) *Virgin, to catch your face aright*
Stars more than Colours would we need :
to paint with lights the Gate of Light.
But man may cry, the stars won't heed,
and so the artist paints or draws
by nature's means and painting's laws.

(ii) *I, also Peter, who have not been granted*
sight of the Lord's lifegiving Tomb,
carved it here on this disk, where, bending
low, I see Christ's body clear.

Thus the struggle generates a deepened artistic consciousness on which the whole future expansion of Byzantine art was based.

INFLUENCES ON THE WEST. Now the West is rising towards the level where Byzantine art can have a coherent effect on it, setting off developments that leave a definite trail. Though the *repoussé* method is still used in jewellery, there is a steady turn to enamel—in altar-cloths or embroidery, chalice or book-binding. *Cloisonné* techniques are fully in vogue by the ninth century, driving out *champlevé*. Smaller objects, enamel or ivory or manuscript, were the means of diffusion rather than the solid monuments in which mosaic was imbedded. Their precious forms provided prestige-objects for gifts by the emperor to barbarian or semi-barbarians, where they gave models to the local craftsmen. Such objects were the *pala d'oro* at Venice, the enamelled reliquary at Limburg, the enamelled gold triptych at the abbey of Stabelot (Belgium), and the richly designed clothes at churches all over France and Germany.

Syrian and Egyptian styles were already strong in Merovingian Gaul, through the textiles and other imported objects. As standards rose under Charles, the direct Byzantine influence grew, *i.e.* in the Palace Group of manuscript-illuminators. These artists, of primary importance for art-developments in the West, were certainly Byzantines; one of them even appends a Greek signature. In the second quarter of the ninth century the miniaturists of Rheims handed the methods on to the ivory-carvers called the Lithard Group, who exploited Hellenistic suavities. The Adad Group, working at both manuscripts and ivories, used heavy outlines and lacked modelling by light and shade; their affinities are with the Italic art of the time in which Byzantine and early Christian influences mixed. But as they developed, they gained more spatial depth and grace of form, holding to their linear basis while absorbing Hellenistic elements. Byzantine influences thus in a complex pattern fed, speeded up, transformed local movements.

Venice was now emerging as an important trading-centre, practically a Byzantine colony, which for centuries was a basic diffuser of Byzantine objects and ideas.

Another line of diffusion westward was that of monks and ikon-painters who fled to Italy as well as Cappadocia or the Caucasus. 'Thousands of monks founded numerous cave-habitations and hermitages' in Italy and Asia, 'which were painted by Greek artists' (Jerphanion). Some small panels of early date at Kiev show aspects of this style.

ARCHITECTURE IN THE WEST. Romanesque was developing, partly through Byzantine and Saracenic impacts, partly through its own inner momentum as town-life was strengthened. In South-east France efforts were made for complete vaulting of churches, by a series of domes or by continuous barrel vaults—both eastern forms, though the barrel vault may have come to the Franks from the Visigoths. Dome-vaulting spread north, so that (about 1030) the aisles of the abbey church of Bernay are covered with domes—perhaps derived from the dome of the earlier little church of St. George near to Tours. However, in the north-west the groined vault triumphed over dome. And ribbed vaulting was devised by Romanesque architects, with the placing of towers tried out in numerous ways and the stone spire evolved.

The groined vault (which shows an arch in both directions and enables the windows in the side walls to rise nearly as high as the vault itself) was the determining factor that swung the Romanesque church away from sub-Byzantine to Gothic. It enabled the installation of rich stained windows and eliminated the dome and its central plan.

More south, however, the dome held out. In the Auvergne, chapels cluster round the choir which is surmounted by a dome. Florence and Pisa have domes over their baptistries. That of Florence has buttressing walls supporting an outer pyramid of masonry cased over with marble slabs, with the lantern on the apex protecting the open eye of the dome— here is the form that resulted in the lanterns of Renascence domes.

Pisa's conical dome is more directly Byzantine, and extremely close to Wren's dome on St. Paul's.[1]

NEW ENERGIES. The long-maligned Iconoclast period was that in which the decisive break from, and transformation of, the ancient bases were made. Historians have praised the reactionary Macedonian period that exploited the Iconoclast gains, and failed to see where the creative sources lay—in the people, in the broad masses who supported the Iconoclast movement in its vigorous phases. Now it is being recognised that the late seventh and early eighth century was

> a period of intense creative activity in the Empire, when new plastic conceptions were appearing in one technique after another, and the forms were being worked out which were to be exploited to the full after the close of the iconoclast controversy. (Pierce and Tyler.)

[1] The Holy Cross at Quimperlé is a central-plan church, perhaps the last of its kind in Western Europe. (St. Gall's church had towers circular in plan like the earlier towers at Ravenna; the early church of St. Riquier in northern France had round towers. The leaning tower of Pisa is a late example). The Norman round-tower of the donjon-keep is a derivation.

33

THE MACEDONIANS

EXPANSION AND WEAKENING. The Macedonian reaction carried on the Iconoclast bases, seeking to stabilise them as the new Orthodoxy and weakening them more and more into an aristocratic expression on the lines stated in the last chapter. Basil I's New Church, provided the key-model of the Greek-cross ground-plan. After the sixth century churches had shrunk, less concerned with the masses; domes were seldom more than 20 feet in diameter. Height and grace were thus more easily attainable; the dome could be run up on a central tower and thus becomes an important feature of the external appearance of the church; and the external appearance gained a new attention. The flat façades are now brightened with polychrome decorations, ceramic insets, courses of brick alternating with stone, cornices vandyked, dentilled or even more delicately worked into patterns.

We no longer meet the titanic anchorage in light of St. Sophia. On the positive side was a new release of a classical sense of proportions, which, married to the aspiring aims and the pleasures in picturesque elegance, brought about a series of harmonious conquests of spatial relations. The eastern elements were by no means banished; but they now lacked the driving-force, the strenuous tensions that had needed large-scale systems of balance and counter-balance to keep them in control. (For instance, Armenian influence was strong: when St. Sophia was damaged by a quake in 989, the architect who built the cathedral of Ani did the restoration. And in Russia and among the South Slavs direct Byzantine influences met and merged with influences from Armenia and the Caucasus in general.) But the positive aspects of the new development were offset by the increasing failure of the mass-element, which meant that the new forms lacked the concrete basis for renewal, for inner conflict and development—except, for instance, in Italy or Russia when they found a fuller relation to the life of the people. In the Byzantine area proper the elegance tended to become sterile, the technical controls to be exploited for their own sake.

The interior is as variously splendid as ever. Capitals with a delicate broidery of stylised leafage, beast or vegetal forms drawn from Arab

textiles, scrolls of vines, glistening stone-slabs, and the smouldering
mosaics on their gold grounds in the curve of vault, dome, apse.

The splendour of a great Byzantine church can best be realised today
in San Marco at Venice, which was built in the eleventh century by
Byzantine architects and craftsmen brought direct from the imperial
capital. As its model was the Holy Apostles of Byzantium, it does not
show the typical later ground-plan, that of the New Church; but it has
the five domes, the polychromatic marbles inside and outside, the finely
carved screens and tall nave-pillars, reredos of enamel and rich mosaics,
the gold and purple, which summon up the basic effect of the Byzantine
church at its height.

Though our surviving monuments of architecture are mainly churches,
we must not forget, however, that the secular buildings of Byzantium and
the other great cities embodied the same elements, sometimes (as in the
Great Palace) in much more extended and varied magnificence.[1]

PROGRAMMES. In art the main effect of the Iconoclast period was to compel the religious artists to incorporate the new humanism in their work,
to seek a classical balance and to develop rhythms based on the human
body, to deepen the human content of Christ, Mary, the Saints in their
expression, and to achieve something of spatial depth.

In the ninth to tenth centuries church decorations were mainly made
up of single figures, symbols and allegories, treated with the new realism
as if the stricken Church was putting all its strength into mastering the
Iconoclast humanity before it launched out again into larger and more
comprehensive themes. The single mosaics, arranged according to set
rules, appear almost wholly in the vaulted parts or in niches, contrasting
with the quieter tones of the marble-lined walls. There is an artistic unity
gained by a consistent scale of sizes, using optical devices to eliminate
distortions of perspective and differentiated keys of modelling to combat
the lighting-conditions.

The Hellenistic elements, more fully let loose in book-illustration,
acted in breaking up rigid frontality, creating the demand for a richer

[1] I cannot in my space deal with the complex criss-crossing of influences, the local
styles of varying stability, etc. Here is one point. The motive of the Cross with
Leaves, common in Byzantine art from the ninth century, was strongly developed
in Armenia, and flowered crosses were favourites of the Nestorians, carried both to
China (c. 981) and to St. Thomas Mount near Madras. 'It probably travelled
westwards from Mesopotamia along with the numerous other eastern elements',
penetrating Byzantine art in the eighth century, 'especially in the decorations of
textiles, pottery and sculpture'. In Italy direct eastern influences were slight in the
ninth century. 'The popularity of the motive there was probably due to the eastern
tastes so much to the fore in the art of the Lombards and other invaders from the
North.' (Talbot Rice.)

and less tightened-up programme, and adding scenic representations—first in a festival cycle in the vaulted part of the naos and then in a narrative series expanding over the flat walls. From the eleventh century onward the increasing poverty of the Byzantine world leads to more use of fresco painting, which in whole or part drives out mosaic and breaks down the system of balances based on marble and mosaic. Paint tends to cover the whole interior in network of pictures and upset the tenth to eleventh centuries system of optical effects.[1]

Complicated programmes have grown up, which tend to be looser and richer in the painted churches. Generally we may say that, just as once historical sequences drove out symbolist systems, now dogmatic and liturgic symbolism control history. Each group of scenes or saints has a special place and significance in the church. Christ with the archangels takes the highest point of dome or vault. In the sanctuary, round the altar of sacrifice, the earthly church is represented by Mary (who stands for the Incarnation) throned in the apse between two archangels. The naves, opposite, leading up to these conclusions, hold the saints in hierarchy, and above them the great festivals (represented by seven to twelve gospel-episodes). On the western wall breaks the Last Judgment. Miracles and lesser moments of the Passion fill the remoter parts. Scenes from the Virgin's life form in the narthex the transition between world outside and the liturgic drama within.

This type of programme, varying and expanding, spread with Byzantine influences into Russia, over the Balkans, into Sicily and South Italy (where the problem of fitting it to longitudinal churches produced further variations). The hieratic controls reached their climax in the tenth to eleventh centuries, then their concept of the festival ikon was gradually displaced by a revival of narrative. Modelling by light and shade with an effect of spatial depth and atmospheric movement was basic till the eleventh century. The climax may be found in the lovely meditative grace of the mosaics at Daphni (near Athens) where the figures are almost wholly frontal, juxtaposed in dignified and quiet attitudes, organically conceived —linked by the inner significance of the scene and the expression of face and body (unaided by the curving niche or vault which in earlier Byzantine art gave the effect of figures turning to one another). The gesture of hands, the subtle variation of the classical *contraposto* with the functional differentiation of the legs, provide the basis of the gently flowing rhythms, the indrawn but precisely defined drama of relationships.

---

[1] Probably poverty is not the decisive factor, but is merely one aspect of a total change, in which fresco is more suited to the effects desired (*i.e.* increased mobility, interrelation of forms and environment, sympathy).

10

But here we find also the thinning-down of the elements of spatial depth and the substitution of linear elements, which for the moment are defined with rhythmic curves, but which elsewhere move more strongly towards clear relief and geometrised detail. The trend to hardness, attenuation, rigidity is linked with monkish attitudes; the figures of saints grow thin and elongated; the organic element, so strong in draperies of Daphni, gives way to flat patterns. Faces become set and grave, looking out on a totally rejected world.

MONKISH CONTROLS. We can grasp this monkish element if we consider the changes of the image of Christ. In the first centuries, before establishment, he is a dreaming idyllic youth set in the Golden Age; he takes on characteristics of sungod, pagan philosopher, emperor and becomes Pantokrator, stern and righteous. At none of these phases did anyone dare to think of showing him suffering or of taking his clothes off. The oldest known representation of the Crucifixion is sixth century; in it he wears a long tunic, and no stress is laid on pain. The long tunic persists till the ninth century. Gradually men accepted the representation of some hint of suffering; the rule that his corpse was taboo as an art-subject was never transgressed. In a ninth-century miniature he holds his body straight with life in his head. But by the end of the tenth century the pressure of realism has replaced his long kolobion by a piece of linen hanging from belt to knees; his head falls on his chest; and sometimes even the convulsion of death is shown. By the mid-eleventh century, as in the mosaic of St. Luke in Phokis, the artist dares to show a meagre corpse and anguished face.[1]

OUT MOVEMENT. From the tenth to eleventh centuries on, as the areas round the Empire on the west and north rise economically and culturally, and Byzantine influence has ever stronger and fuller repercussions, the complexity of development defies compression into a few generalised paragraphs. In the following chapter I shall then merely select a few main points, and glance at the relations between Byzantium and Anglo-Saxon art, Romanesque and Gothic, Monte Cassino and Rome, Russian Art, and the Italian Renascence. In every case I believe it can be shown that Byzantine influence was fundamental, however necessary to the total result were the local elements with which the Byzantine flow coalesced. (We must recall that the local elements themselves were often developments out of Byzantine influences at an earlier phase.) The full pattern is highly complex; but we can disentangle certain basic lines without doing the complexity injustice.

[1] An expression of the power of the Virgin's cult appears at Kahre Djami (late eleventh century) where Christ becomes a kind of Mother dandling the Virgin (or rather her soul) in the form of a swaddled Babe.

34

BRITAIN AND FRANCE

LINKS WITH BRITAIN. Britain, cut off by water and by the Frankish turmoil in Gaul, may well seem an unlikely area for Byzantine influence to penetrate into; and yet a close examination shows that even during the period when Anglo-Saxon tribalism was being broken down and consolidated into kingdoms with none of the direct survivals of imperial days met in Gaul, Byzantine influence was present.

In Justinian's reign a Merovingian embassy to Byzantium had had Angles in it, and from them Prokopios may have gained such information as he had of the extreme West. The *Life of John the Almsgiver* tells that in the early seventh century the Alexandrian patriarch financed ships which carried wheat to Britain during a dearth and brought back tin and silver. This account, which shows the trade with Cornwall still carried on by the Atlantic route, was slighted as a mere literary reminiscence—though the account derives from contemporary writers. But that attitude has been upset by the discovery at Sutton Hoo in East Anglia of an Anglo-Saxon tomb in which amid several pieces of silverwork, obviously eastern, was found a dish with four control-marks of Anastasios I. The tomb's date is probably mid-seventh century. And it is noteworthy that a similar silver-piece, with five marks of Anastasios, has been found near Poltava in the Ukraine, in a burial of somewhat the same date.

It seems more than likely then that trade, however sporadic, never ceased along the Atlantic route. Spanish sources show Greek ships sailing up the Guadiana to Merida; and there was a Greek colony at Cordova on the Guadalquivir. Both these rivers flow into the Atlantic. And the letters of Pope Gregory I mention big ships able to cross the ocean.

There is no doubt of Greek influences from the mid-seventh century when the Papacy sent two teachers to reorganise the English Church and crush the tribal-monastic Celtic Church which with its devoted evangel was threatening the papal hold. The two teachers were both from the Greek-Byzantine area—Theodore from Tarsos and Hadrian from Africa. Hadrian didn't want to leave Italy and Theodore had to be given special courses before despatch to ensure that he would carry the pure papal positions to Britain. Why were they chosen? Presumably because the Latin ecclesiastics lacked the knowledge and initiative for the job; but possibly also because the Papacy recognised that Greeks had already had contacts with Britain (with the Celtic sections if not with the Anglo-Saxon). In any event the episode shows the moral and cultural bankruptcy of the Papacy in these centuries.

On the way the Majordomo of Neustria arrested the priests for some days, 'as he suspected them of being charged with a mission from the Emperor to the Kings of England'. So he at least felt political relations between Byzantium and Britain to be possible and even dangerous.

After these two teachers the Greek current was strong. The Greek language was known in Britain as nowhere else west and north of Ravenna, Ireland was outdone as a centre of Greek studies. The Greek benediction gesture got into the English rite as art shows about 800; and Kent churches show Byzantine influence.[1] 'The decisions of Roman Law and the secrets of jurisprudence' were studied at Canterbury, and soon we meet the introduction of the Cheirographa and other material deriving from the Greek-Byzantine legal tradition. Ine of Wessex invited two Greek scholars from Athens.

In the eighth century the *mancus*, the Islamic coin without an image, was the standard for Anglo-Saxon payments in gold. All over Europe the numismatic influence of Islam was felt, but in Britain alone did the mancus become the sole money for gold transactions—and stay so for centuries. Mercia made bad imitations of the gold dinar of the caliph al-Mansur (with OFFA REX on the reverse of a faulty bit of Arabic); and Offa offered to pay tribute to St. Peter in *mancusi*. In 955 Eadred of Wessex still ordered 2,000 *mancusi* to be struck.

There can be no doubt, then, of a peculiar connection of Britain with Mediterranean trade all through the difficult centuries. Aelfric of Eynsham in the early eleventh century tells of Anglo-Saxon merchants who crossed the seas for all sorts of luxury-goods, gems, gold, purples, silk,

---

[1] Round towers and central plans are fairly common. In the seventh century St. Wilfrid built a church as a round tower with four arms at Hexham; at Athelney Alfred built one as X with rounded ends (quatrefoil); the abbey church of Abingdon (675) was rounded at both eastern and western ends, and so was the original Cathedral of Canterbury. Abingdon had a round tower (and the Irish round towers belong to the same tradition). Many Saxon churches have apses—that of Wing is seven-sided (*i.e.* eastern); St. Frideswide, Oxford, had three parallel apses. There are also towers which are the main body of the church plus a small chancel on the east.

The circular tradition persisted after 1066, *e.g.* the chapter house at Worcester, the chapels at Woodstock and Ludlow Castle. This tradition seems to underlie the typical English chapter house—something without parallel elsewhere. Round churches were later brought into the West by the Templars from the East; but England has non-Templar round churches, *e.g.* that at Cambridge and at St. John's, Clerkenwell.

wine, ivory, aurichalc, glass, varicoloured clothes, etc. In Frankish times there are coin-linkages with Lombardic Italy, and political connections as well. A Lombard king fled in 662 to England, later regaining his throne, and the wife of a Wessex king later died at the Lombard capital.[1] Pilgrims and merchants had long been traversing Europe. Winfrid (Boniface) cheated the customs at Tyre by bringing balm from Jerusalem in his staff; and Charlemagne accused pilgrims in Offa's days of using their religious clothes to escape customs dues. Canute lumped pilgrims and traders together in asking Conrad II of Germany and King Rodolph of Arles to exempt 'traders as well as others travelling for the sake of prayers'. The Lombard customs-officers had trouble with the sturdy Anglo-Saxons, who fought rather than open their packs; and the Lombard *Honorantia Civitatis Papie* (Pavia) in the first half of the tenth century lays down that Anglo-Saxons must pay a forfeiture sum in place of the usual 10 per cent. Only Anglo-Saxons, apart from the Venetians and other Byzantine-Italians, are cited by name. The English commercial expansion is also witnessed by the crowds of English whores that Boniface found in the Lombardic towns.

SAXON ART. It is not surprising, then, to find that in later Saxon art Byzantine influence is strong. Some Saxon carvings show Byzantine proto-types directly behind them; others have been produced by rougher craftsmen, with whom the model is more removed. But the influence is pervasive.

Thus a slab at York of the Virgin and Child is a variant of the type called *Hodegetria* or Way-Shower, in which Mary holds the child in her left arm while pointing to him with her right: he extends his hands in blessing. The York example is close in form to the famous *Our Lady of Vladimir* (painted at Byzantium in the eleventh century). A plaque in the east wall of the west tower at Deerhurst shows another Byzantine type, in which the Virgin holds a medallion with a Child in it; and suggests an original in lead. This plaque was probably painted; a crucifixion slab at Romsey used the Byzantine incrustation method, in which a thick coloured paste (or inlay of coloured stone) was set. A crucifixion slab at St. Dunstan's, Stepney, is local work, iconographically close to the mosaics at Daphni, though the technique behind it is that of an

---

[1] The links between the Anglo-Saxons and Kievan Russia are interesting. Edwin and Edward, sons of Edmund Ironside, expelled by Canute, took refuge in Kiev. Note also that Anne, wife of Henry I of France and regent for her son Philip I, was a daughter of Yaroslav Mudry. Yaroslav's granddaughter Evpraxia-Adelheid married the German Henry IV; another daughter of Yaroslav, Elizabeth, married Harald Hardrada, who had visited the Kiev court.

ivory carving. The angels at Bradford on Avon and Deerhurst are Byzantine.

Enamel techniques were borrowed from Byzantium; possibly Byzantine craftsmen worked in England, using their native techniques on local motives—*i.e.* the Alfred Jewel in the Ashmolean is Byzantine in method, but the style is local. Byzantine styles appear in embroidery, *i.e.* the stole of St. Cuthbert at Durham, probably tenth century. Even the braided and knotted motive which we think of as specifically Anglo-Saxon in carving and illumination was widespread in the eighth to ninth centuries and was probably Coptic in origin—at least it was well-known in Egypt.

THE NORMANS. The twelfth century saw the Norman Conquest, and large sections of the English nobility fled to Byzantium, where they dominated in the Varangian guard.[1] Byzantine influences continued strong, partly through France or the German court, partly through direct contacts with the Normans in Sicily, who were using Byzantine artists and craftsmen on a lavish scale. Englishmen held offices in Sicily; scholars like Adelard of Bath and John of Salisbury made several visits, while others like Peter of Blois lived some time in Sicily before they went to England. And there were embassies going to and fro.

Byzantine influences, thus flowing in, were strong in mid-twelfth century and increased in the later part of the century. The lively rhythm of the linear forms now dominant in Byzantine art, with narrative basis, made it easily assimilable. The Winchester Psalter (about 1160) shows a rather agitated northern style but the two full-page miniatures before the text are direct Byzantine copies, and compositional and iconographical elements from Byzantium are generally present. The copyist was Anglo-Norman: he shows the Virgin between two angels holding *vexilla* (standards) instead of the orthodox *trisagia*.

[1] That there were contacts before 1066 is suggested by an odd tale in William of Malmesbury, that Edward the Confessor dreamed he saw the seven Sleepers of Ephesos turn from right to left side, for seventy-four years. He sent to the emperor to inquire. The *Saga of Edward* says he prophesied they'd stay on the left for eighty-four years and that all that time the world would be upset by apocalyptic terrors. The saga adds that the emperor received the English envoys well, sent to Ephesos, and verified that the Sleepers were on their left sides. He also sent Edward relics of the Sleepers. Probably recruiting had gone on in England as in Scandinavia for the Guard before 1066: that was why the thoughts of the young nobles turned that way in disaster. An English exile built a church of St. Nicholas and St. Augustine in Byzantium.

The first mention of English by name occurs in a 1088 bull to the monastery on Patmos, which is excused from quartering troops, Greek or foreign ' . . . Varangians, *Inglinoi*'. In Byzantine service the English had a chance to fight once more the Normans. We find them demanding to be put in the front and lead the fight. Anna Comnena tells of them getting too far ahead with their axes 'in their haste to engage in battle with the equally ferocious Normans'.

Gradually the Byzantine element increases and transforms English illumination. In the late twelfth century the wall painting of St. Paul and the Viper in St. Anselm's Chapel in Canterbury Cathedral is close to a painting in the Palatina of Sicily. The Winchester Bible, the most important English MSS. of the later twelfth century, shows the culmination of Sicilian-Byzantine influence in attitudes, draperies, even expression and facial types, and general feeling. At least two masters of it must have studied in Monreale.[1] Our Norman churches were fully painted over inside; the remains show that definite programmes were carried out.

After 1200 the direct influence slackens, though the effects of the previous impregnation are still to be seen. Now a vigorous impact from France shows itself—as a while later it shows itself in the German area.

THE RISE OF GOTHIC. But now let us turn from England back to France, where a fuller tide of Byzantine forces has irrupted—fuller because the richer town-development makes possible a more stable art-expansion.

The decisive impact comes in the later eleventh century. Steadily flat linear styles give way to modelling in light and shade. We see the process in the miniatures of the abbeys of Cluny and Citeaux in Burgundy, and then in the frescoes of churches where the artists followed the lead of the miniaturists. Often the motives are still schematised or regularised, strained or exaggerated, but the origin in Byzantine works is not in doubt. 'It is, in fact, a new type of human being which Byzantine art has helped to create in occidental painting.' And Romanesque sculpture as much as painting is thus affected.

Finally in such work as the Christ of Chartres Cathedral the integrative forces, realising organic form in its fullness and impregnating form with human significance, come to a head.

> Thus, about the middle of the twelfth century two revolutionary ideas—that of the articulated body and that of the animated figure—are carried by the crest of the Byzantine tidal wave to northern France, where a great creative genius makes them the cornerstone of a new style, the Gothic. (Koehler.)

But without cavilling at that tribute to the great sculptor of Chartres, we must recognise that Gothic is the creation of the whole new impulse stirring in the towns of France, an impulse which learns how to express itself through the Byzantine impact. The Christ of Chartres has the deep

---

[1] The Psalter was made under the auspices of a bishop of Winchester who was in Rome 1151–2 and who gave works of art to the cathedral. Note also that Peter Blois was chancellor to the Canterbury Archbishop in 1173. But English artists could in many ways now get to Sicily itself. One point of interest is the propagation of the cult of St. Thomas (à Becket), probably from Monreale Abbey, with representation of the Saint at Rome, Anagni, Spoleto.

human penetration, the artistic richness of concretion, that we find in the Byzantine work of the early tenth century, which emerged from Iconoclast humanism mastered by the ikon-painters, the masters of mosaic.

Here for the first time Byzantine art-forces meet in the West with a local force capable of taking in all that they can give and of proceeding to develop stably on its own. Gothic is both a wave of Byzantine art and a transformation of that art to new needs, a reorientation with enduring results. Gothic is Byzantine art subdued to the needs and aspirations of the young western town, the new commune.[1]

[1] The greenish-yellow Byzantine glaze is found in East England on late Saxon pots (? tenth century).—T. C. Lethbridge, *Proc. Cambridge Antiq. Soc.*, 43, pub. 1950.

Note for Chapter 35. The rebirth of Byzantine art in the twelfth century is a complex result of the central tradition and the new popular forces springing up in all directions as new national systems begin to cohere. Thus Russian art of this century is influenced, not directly from Byzantium, but via the Balkan centres, Mount Athos, the Christian East. The new Slav States are specially important. Thus, 'having introduced folk-elements into art, the Serbians succeeded in redeveloping from top to bottom the rigorous forms of Byzantine art.'—V. E. Lazarev, *History of Byzantine Painting* (Moscow, 1947–8). Lazarev takes monuments that go back to the twelfth century (paintings at Nerezi and Vladimir Suzdalski, miniatures of Dzřuč at Tbilisi and of Vatopedi) and shows there the essentials of thirteenth-century traits— optical unity, landscape complexity, figure subtlety, lightness of draperies, relief modelling—elements which co-exist with the older aspects of form, then replace them.

Similar changes occur in iconography, which is penetrated with dramatic motives and genre-themes born independently on Byzantine soil—'the logical result of the rebirth of art in the twelfth century'. The thirteenth century renews the Hellenistic traditions of Nikaia (in part as a result of the national revival looking back to the Greek past). Lazarev considers similar elements in the West to be borrowings from the Byzantine area. (V. Mole of Cracow thinks this goes too far, *Byzantinoslavica*, xii. It does, if it ignores the part played by local traditions and crafts in the West; but if it is meant to concentrate on the key-sources of creativity in the historical process, which ultimately determine the Western developments at this phase, it is correct.)

35

FINAL EXPANSIONS

FRESH OUTMOVEMENTS. The twelfth century saw a great expansion of Byzantine art-influences in Italy, Germany, Russia—and also in Georgia and Armenia. Then late in the twelfth century (that is, just before the disaster of 1204) a new human note appears in Byzantine frescoes, a note of pathos and tragic sympathy (as in the church of Nerez, near Skopie, Serbia). This note gathers round the Descent from the Cross. In the thirteenth century it shows itself added to a deepening of realism and characterisation—in work done in Serbia and Bulgaria, and at the same time a renewed interest in landscape, architectural backgrounds, life's picturesque and casual variety evoked in the midst of a set pattern. Henceforth, on to the fall in 1453 and beyond, the artists develop this vein of realism, ringing all the changes between pathos and terror, meditation and tumult, with varying rhythms and scales of colour. The movement shows its aspect of refined humanism in the frescoes of Mistra; and begets the usual conflict of Byzantine art in the clash of tense dramatic patterns and patterns of brooding gravity, in the clash of methods for drawing in the spectator —carrying a rhythm to the point of breaking strain, so that one almost reaches out to touch and control the pictorial movement at its hidden cyclonic centre; or evoking a mood of grave concentration, so that one is entranced by the form into its inturned centre of self-sufficient being. Manuel Panselinos of Thessalonika and Theophanes of Crete were the two great representatives of these trends in the final phase.

There had long been artist's books giving the basic types and models; and towards the end the compilation of Manuals was adopted.

RUSSIA. In Kievan Russia, grand architecture had received a basic impulse from Byzantium, though the forms were quickly absorbed and re-defined.[1] By applying a tradition of wooden structures to ideas born from stone or brick the Russians diversified the church with a central plan. The first Sophia in Novgorod was a church of oak with thirteen domes; that in

---

[1] Brunov points to the typical five-naved church of Kievan Russia as showing local roots that went back beyond the building of Kiev's St. Sophia.

Kiev was one of stone with the same number of domes. The Desyatinny at Kiev was of stone, with twenty-three domes.

Many influences had long met and married on the steppes. Syrian and Anatolian forms did not impact only through Byzantium; they came up also via the Caucasus. The church of Yuriev Polskiej (earlier thirteenth-century) has a richly carved exterior; its sources lie ultimately in the tenth-century buildings on an island in Lake Van, Armenia—and Iranian motives lie further behind.

The same diverse trails meet in Russian art. Greek ikon-painters came with the priests and monks. We know of Twelve who became monks of Pechersky monastery. Kiev spread ikon-styles in the eleventh to twelfth centuries throughout Rus, to Kholm of Galich, Rostov, Suzdal, Vladimir. Local materials affected the styles, the saints took on Russian features; even the costumes of a Rus prince and his family set the artist new problems. New colour-schemes and rhythms appeared.

Motives from Caucasian paintings of a Syrian type, Iranian or Sarmatian elements of organic design merged with the direct Byzantine influences of ikon and mosaic. In the latter, however, lay the new basic organising factor, round which other elements gathered. The magnificent mosaic of the Virgin in Kiev cathedral is pure Byzantine. But regional styles of much variety soon developed. Thus in the Golden-Haired Angel of early Novgorod:

> Though the composition follows that of the angel in the Kiev mosaics, the monumental manner of mid-Byzantine art which we see there has been completely left, and the Golden-Haired Angel is characterised by greater tenderness and lightness. There is also something in the rhythmical renderings of the hair which was quite individual; its swaying movement seems to have fascinated the artist, and, in addition to the colouring, this rhythm constitutes one of the features most characteristic of Russian art as a whole. (Talbot Rice.)

Russian art was now launched on its full course, but from time to time Byzantine influences nourished it afresh. In all the fourteenth century the Greek Theophanes brought Byzantine advanced techniques once more into the Russian scene, but was quickly absorbed, learning how to modify his forms in Russian terms and to give a strengthened stimulus to Russian art, both through his own work and through that of his pupils such as Andrew Rublev.

THE BALKANS. We have already noted the vital rooting of Byzantine frescoes in the Serbian area. In Dalmatia basilican forms were strong in architecture, and though Byzantine forms can be found, the Romanesque of the country looks to that of Pisa and Lucca, while the Hungarians, borrowing from France and Germany, introduced elements from those countries. But further inland in Serbia, though we sometimes meet a clash of Dalmatian and Byzantine styles (at Dečani), the latter dominates, and domed churches with an elegant interrelation of parts vary the later Byzantine forms without departing from their essential bases.

The paintings embodied all the rich and dramatic energies of the final phases of Byzantine art. And in the Bosnian area, where Bogomilism was taken up by the nobles and developed into a fighting national creed quite unlike its Bulgarian form, there was created a strange Bogomil art, owing nothing to Byzantine art or to Gothic, though in a heavy way using ideas from the Roman past, *i.e.* the sarcophagus shape as a (solid) monument. The forms here are drawn direct from the peasantry, though sometimes they treat a knightly motive, and the popular round-dance, the *kolo*, is used to express paradisiac union and happiness.

SOUTH ITALY. Throughout the centuries Byzantium had a powerful influence on Italian art-expressions, though the area of main impact varied —from Rome and Ravenna to Pavia and Venia, from Naples and Amalfi to Genoa and Palermo. In the ninth century Byzantine ivories were much imitated in South Italy; and indeed at this time the dispersion of monks by Iconoclast persecution had given a general stimulus to artwork in South Italy and Rome. The famous Benedictine monastery of Monte Cassino had come under something like a Byzantine protectorate late in the ninth century; and was friendly to Greek forms. St. Nilos (about 980) was welcomed as though he were St. Benedict himself risen from the dead and asked to officiate in Greek at the service where he used the hymns in honour of St. Benedict composed by himself. And shortly after when there were some internal quarrels, three of the monks went off east—to Sinai, Athos, Jerusalem—one of them returning to become abbot. German power was restored over the monastery in 1022, but during the schismatic troubles of the mid-eleventh century Monte Cassino tried to exert a moderating influence.

The monastery's golden age was under Abbot Desiderius, who attempted to reconcile the Pope and the Normans, and who, though politically anti-Byzantine, was on good terms with Byzantium itself. He rebuilt the abbey and its church; and gave an order to Byzantium for a set of bronze doors similar to those made for Amalfi Cathedral. Though the old basilican form was kept for the church, the decoration was wholly Byzantine. The artists who had been imported from Byzantium for the work were kept on to teach their techniques to the monks, 'in all the arts, using silver, bronze, iron, glass, ivory, wood, alabaster and stone' (wrote Leo of Ostia).

The emperor Romanos IV was enthusiastic and helped whenever Desiderius's agents came to the capital for works of art.

The training given to the monastery's monks was of much importance for Italian art. Thus, Desiderius built Sant' Angelo in Formis, near Capua, soon after 1072. The basilican structure was repeated, but the paintings were done by the Byzantine artists and their monk-pupils. Stimulated, the monks began illuminations, drawing on Byzantine forms and remembering now that they had a gospel-book given by the German Henry II some fifty years earlier (of the Ratisbon school): adding local or popular touches of their own to complete their style. The new Monte Cassino school no doubt did the paintings in St. Clemente at Rome, and prepared the way for an Italian school developing stably on the absorbed Byzantine tradition.

The response to the Monte Cassino work is of interest. Leo of Ostia declared that for five hundred years *magistra latinitas* had given up the practice of the many arts now acquired by the young monks, but at last things were to be changed. Alphanus in a poem repeated the claim. The exaggerated statement of the five hundred years was meant to link the work of Desiderius with that of Benedict himself; but it would not have been made by both writers unless there was a general sense of decadence in arts and crafts. Alphanus, who had visited Byzantium, was connected with the medical school of Salerno which he helped to found, and as a publicist wrote poems inciting the Lombards against Byzantium; he wanted a world-empire ruled by the Pope. He was probably the best poet of eleventh-century Italy. In the developments of Monte Cassino there was felt a definite challenge to Byzantine cultural supremacy, weak as the challenge actually was.

The movement started by Desiderius flagged; regional styles clogged it, but it left a stimulus towards more living articulation of the human figure, a number of compositional recipes, and a linear technique of white and gold highlights—all Byzantine elements. Wall-paintings in Italy of earlier twelfth century were broken-down provincial in style—those in the Basilian cave-chapels of the South being the nearest to a co-ordinated Byzantine style.[1] At Rome elements from the early Christian tradition revived to link with the elements from Monte Cassino.

The next decisive step came in the twelfth century when the Normans in Sicily called in Byzantine artists, architects and workers, with others from South Italy or Sicily itself, to build and decorate such magnificent edifices at Cefalu, Martorana, Palatina, Monreale. Here the developments

---

[1] Local styles have a compound of elements, from Ottonian efflorescence, Roman traditions and Byzantine influence.

already carried out in South Italy were re-fused with metropolitan Byzantine art, and some new problems posed and solved. I can only touch on a few points.

Narrative continuity is worked out to suit long walls. While merely decorative in the Palatina, in Monreale it helps to explain and underline the situation, to control the tempo, and to link two pictures. Thus, it may bring pictures together, to express a short interval of time, or may break them sharply apart. In the section where Cain kills Abel, both the attack and the fall have their main lines repeated and stressed by the two mountains in the back. In Rebecca's journey the skyline has a rolling movement, which contrasts with the tranquil edge in the preceding scene of the well.

The problem of compositional unity is being tackled from a number of angles, of which landscape or architectural setting is only one; and a keen struggle between linear design and luminous plasticity is being waged. The work of Monreale is only one aspect of a great sweep of Byzantine influence that reaches from Britain to Georgia. On the edge of the disaster of 1204 that expansion seems made by a strenuous effort fighting for internal renewal and for a deepened human and artistic grasp which will control the vast series of tensions that have been set up over the last couple of centuries.

FINAL CONTRIBUTIONS. Out of this twelfth-century expansion came the violent break of 1204; and then, as the Byzantine national forces gathered against the Latins and regained the capital, a fresh expansion appeared, stabilising the elements that were still tugging in different directions in the twelfth century.

> Italy, in closest contact with Eastern Europe, proves to be particularly susceptible to Byzantine influence, and in the second half of the thirteenth century, new achievements in Byzantine art are embraced by Italian artists with such eagerness that we are justified in speaking of another tidal wave of Byzantine influence, which this time affects only Italy
>
> And once more an evolutionary process takes place similar to that from which Gothic had sprung in the middle of the twefth century. As the process threatens to submerge what is left of an independent Italian art, the foundations of a new national style are created by Cavallini, Duccio and Giotto.
>
> Essential elements of this art, the new sense of monumentality, of actuality, and of rhythm, seem to be of Byzantine origin. Resulting in a revival of fundamental classic principles in art as well as thought, this last impact of Byzantine influence on the West set free forces which eventually were to disintegrate and to destroy the structure of the medieval world. (Koehler.)

Except that that statement seems to ignore the effects of this final wave on the Balkans and Russia, and that art was not the sole factor in releasing the forces which broke up the medieval world, the claim made for Byzantine art must stand.

We are a far cry from the textbooks that still write about the rigid and dogmatic slumber of Byzantine art from which Giotto and Duccio awoke to freedom. But the realisation of the nature and function of Byzantine art is still recent—even though it has already gone further than the realisation of the nature and function of any other aspects of Byzantine society.

> When fifty years ago mosaics dating from the beginning of the fourteenth century were discovered in the mosque of Kahrieh Djami at Constantinople they revealed an art so different from that of the Byzantine monuments which were then known that they gave rise to much perplexity. They were at first taken for Italian work; it was proposed to credit them to some pupil of Giotto who was about this time designing the frescoes of the chapel of the Arena at Padua in much the same style. (Diehl.)

But further discoveries knocked the bottom out of that theory. It was proved that the Kahrieh mosaics were only one example of a great series of works scattered over Byzantine territory and the Balkans—to be seen in Mistra in the Morea or such Roumanian churches as that at Curtea de Argès, in Novgorod or even Venice.

It is true that in its last years Byzantine art was not without certain influences from Italian art, but that fact does not in any way lessen the claim that Byzantine art underlay the Italian Renascence as much as it underlay French Gothic. Giotto and Duccio are still provincial artists of the Byzantine world, though they transform the heritage they take over. They transform it in terms of the needs and aspirations of the new Italian towns with their thriving trade and industry.

But one cannot pass from this brief account of the movements of Byzantine art and the debt of Russia and the West alike to them without mentioning the final gift of that art. As Theophanes went to Russia in the fourteenth century and used his skill to express with deepened sublety the essences of Russian art, so Dominico Theotocopuli, known as el Greco, came via Venice to achieve an art which seems profoundly Spanish till one realises that it is Byzantine of the latest phase—an art which is in fact equally Spanish and Byzantine, and which translates into terms of the Spanish sixteenth century the tremendous thrust of dramatic urgency which goes back to the Syrian heretics and Monophysites.

36

THEATRE FESTIVAL AND MASS

CIRCUS VERSUS DRAMA. We now turn to a form of music-drama, which was perhaps more integral in the culture even than art, and which provides us with the transition from art to literature. Byzantium, true, never created a great written drama; but its whole culture was essentially dramatic. We have seen how the new impulse of artistic forms burst from the *martyrion* and its ritual: that is, from a complex of historical struggle and ritual drama. And this element of ritual drama goes right to the heart of the culture. It expressed itself in the liturgy, which continually proliferates with dramatic forms and forces, though, because of its close relation with the whole cultural life, the liturgy did not split off a fully secular drama as in the West. Against that fact, however, we must set the further fact that the satirical mime never ceased to be a potent form of expression in Byzantine life, though we sadly lack all texts; and there were many attempts at secular forms of dramatic expression, which failed to build a stable tradition precisely because of the great pull of the central liturgic drama and the secure place of·the lively mime which covered everyday material.

The failure of the earlier Roman Empire to develop drama is often set down to the effects of the circus, where, amid buffooneries, the terrible things enacted (beast-fights, crucifixions, men thrown to beasts, etc.) exhausted the capacity of response to tragic patterns. There is a truth in that; but the bloody cruelty of the circus, into which the masses were drawn, must be linked with the breakdown of political freedom. It was in the long run the masses, seeking to find an effective retort of brotherhood to the State, who ended the cruelties through Christianity. Tertullian says:

> You have seen lately yourselves Attis mutilated, that famous god of Pessinos, and another man playing Hercules burnt alive. We have laughed also in the cruel noon intermission at Mercury testing the dead with a red iron. We have seen again Jove's brother, armed with a hammer, carry off the corpses of gladiators.

And Martial tells of an Orpheus, who charmed wild creatures, only to be eaten alive by a bear; of the play of Laureolus, a famous brigand, whose crucifixion was actually carried out; of a man on a cross torn by a bear.

This criminal beats the crimes of ancient tales,
for here the myth becomes true suffering.

That is, the ritual patterns, from which tragedy and comedy had been born, were expressed in a horribly debased form, actualised as an unspeakable cruelty, instead of releasing poetically their image of human suffering and triumph. Christianity, which gave the ritual pattern of the dying-reborn god anew its social significance (a significance related precisely to the hell of a society which enjoyed the sights of the circus and justified slavery), Christianity was thus the anti-circus force, through which men could rediscover the unpolluted sources of their creativity.

The Church was inevitably hostile to the mimes and actors who were linked with the circus and with pagan festival in general; and this hostility was not lessened by the fact that the mimes for long mocked Christian rites on their stage.

MIMES. John Lydos says that his Byzantium carried on the seven main forms of Roman theatric entertainment; but certainly it was the mimes, concerned with dance or satire, which took deep roots. The art-mime was based on a poem, which was danced-out to music; at its best it achieved subtlety and richness. The popular mime varied from simple buffoonery to social satire of a sophisticated kind:

> Mimes are those actors who imitate the misfortunes of others; theatre signifies only dissimulation and counterfeiting, and theatre-people are so called as people dissimulating and counterfeiting slaves one moment, then lords, generals, heads of State next. (Zonaras.)

These scenic plays were given publicly and at banquets or weddings.[1] Chorikios, a rhetor of Gaza, wrote an energetic defence of the mimes of

---

[1] Justinian forbade bishops and monks to attend shows, and (with reference to festival maskings) forbade anyone, and especially actors and whores, to dress as monks and nuns. He calmly legislates about a theatre called The Whores, where official shows were given by the consul at the New Year. Anastasios abolished a male homosexual theatre. We hear of women bathing in water on the stage, probably in connection with a Maiuma or other debased ritual.

Under Theophilos (or Valens), two circus-mimes haul a little boat before the kathisma: one tries to make the other swallow it, and when he says he can't, remarks that the Praepositos can swallow a widow's boat in full rig. The emperor inquires, finds the Praepositos has taken a widow's boat and has him burned on the spot (an improbable detail, but showing how people felt the importance of the mime's social protest).

The 591 synod forbade students of civil law to adopt Hellenic costumes, act on the stage or go into scenic competitions during their courses.

the Dionysiac cult, stressing that there were many genres, and that buffoon-turns were meant to get laughs between the races, to diminish the bad temper of losers and the exaltation of winners. Serious actors played ancient comedies and modern satirical pieces, which were valuable for making 'the lords much more prudent, while preventing them from injustice'.

The historian Menandros tells us that he trained in the palaistra, and sacrificed his lawyer's career to the thrill of circus and dance-mime; he discarded the jurist's robe and wrote a tragedy *The Death of a Persian Mage* (who was crucified for turning Christian). This was a *tragodia* for singing and dancing.

The *tragodia* in its dance-form was the ancestor of ballet. Experienced dancers could accompany any poem. Xenophon of Smyrna danced the Bacchai of Euripides. Libanios defends the dance-mime as going past sculpture as an art, and calls it the school of beauty and recreation. But he was a pagan. The Church was inexorable against pantomime-dancer, buffoon, mime alike. By the time of Theodosios the mime had fallen in status as low as he could go. Anastasios the Monophysite eased things a bit, but under Justin the full degradation reasserted itself.

FESTIVALS. Byzantium inherited the great pagan festivals of the Roman Empire. Olympic Games were held at several eastern cities, especially Antioch, with competitions for poetry and music, and with nightly shows as well as athletics. Women competed with men in song and music; the poetry contests were called *akroaseis* or *ekphraseis*, auditions or expressions, and seem to have survived in declamatory forms without competitions after Justin abolished the Games. The *ekphraseis* thus merged with the *enkomia*, celebratory verse.

The main festivals were the Kalends, a five-day New Year holiday; the three-yearly Orgies of Maioumas (combined in Byzantium with the Feast of Roses) the autumnal Brumalia, vintage-festivals. Points of interest were the continuance of saturnalian equality in the Kalends, with street-maskings by everyone and street-shows by the wreathed mimes; the linking of the Hippodrome of May, which took over elements from the Orgies, with the City's birthday-rites (preceded by the Hippodrome of the Vegetables, when greens and cakes were heaped in the arena, with rose-woven crosses and wagon-loads of fish).

In the tenth century we meet a masked dinner at court on the eve of Epiphany. Here the factions danced a war-dance of Goths with shields and staffs, a travestied pyrrhic dance, using a strange lingo thought to be Gothic but which was broken-down Latin. The Goths danced, the singers executed the Musical Alphabet (a set of verses, where the first began with A, the second with B, and so on), the Goths danced again and went off by different exits. At the circus dances generally came after the last race; but on Mayday, when there were seven races, there were dances after each race, amid the acclamations of the factions. At the vintage-festivals people tried to stand on blown-up wineskins and played the fool: Balsamon exhorts men to recite *Kyrie eleison* instead of 'thinking yourself obliged to make satanic faces to get a forced laugh'. At towns like Gaza the sophists took a leading part at festivals like those of the Roses, when they held nightly verse-contests; and Joshua the Stylite gives us a glimpse of what these holidays were like in a Syrian city such as Edessa.

> Countless torches, lighted up all along the road from the doors of the Theatre (Timarion) to the Gates, added a mystical solemnity to this festival. Yet more torches, like the first lot, were set from one end of the city to the other, on the higher levels, the porticoes, anything that made a projection, even in the river and along its banks. It was in the Theatre they all assembled, for seven days, dressed in simple shifts and tiaras, then, with torches and censers, they spent the nights singing and shouting.

Craft-groups sometimes took special parts. Thus in the Hippodrome of Butchers, the Butchers' Guild danced and sang in two groups:

> *Here's Spring the Beautiful back with its store,*
> *bringing us health wealth and laughter once more,*
> *deeds come from God to the Kings of the Romans*
> *and godgiven victory over all foemen.*

And today in Macedonian festivals much the same dance-songs are heard:

> *Where's Alexander of Macedon, where?*
> *He ruled the whole world everywhere.*
> *With deeds come down from God it was he*
> *who brought our land such a Victory.*

The Church did its best to anathematise all festivals save its own; but willynilly it tolerated and preserved popular forms, as the clergy were entangled in the great State-festivals, and in time the faction-groups were drawn into Church-festivals. Concerted movements and choir-singing were highly expert. There were *akta* or acclamations for the ends of races, for winners, for emperor and patriarch; and before long there were *akta* inside the churches and at the Church Councils. At the Vintage Festival (at least by the tenth century), the patriarch with his bishops went among the vines to bless the grapes in baskets on a marble table; first he offered a grape to the emperor, then the emperor offered grapes to the lords, while singers intoned an *apelatikon*, a hymn of praise.

WRITTEN DRAMA AND THE MASS. Literary plays continued to be written, but without any living link with the stage. Ezechiel, a Jew, wrote a play on *Exodus*, using classical idiom and iambics. But more significant of the new trend, though not a drama, was *The Banquet of the Ten Virgins* by Methodios, which shows the tendency to develop new dramatic approaches inside sermon or homily. This dissertation of the late third century, made up of eleven homilies, concluded with a dialogued poem, and has as its setting an idyllic garden oriented to the East, with a central spring. The same writer, bishop of Patara in Lycia, composed a poem on Free Will in dialogue. But such work as that of Methodios was only a straw showing the direction of the wind. The wind itself must be sought in the developing forms of Mass and Office. Here, as in other matters, the Church took over pagan forms which it merged with its Judaic inherit-ance. *Kyrie Eleison* (Lord deliver us), the cry which opens and closes Christian litanies, was taken directly from a hymn to Helios Mithras; and into one *kyrie* was incorporated part of a pagan hymn to Nemesis. In Epidauran inscriptions we find hymns in the form of a Breviary of the six daily hours of prayer; the temple had also daily liturgical rites, with morn-ing and evening hymns, burning of incense, lighting of lamps. Julian laid down pagan services, and prescribed prayer three times a day, especially at morning and evening. Pagan Calendars recorded the phases of the Sun's life, derived from Osirian and other sources, before Christian Calendars recorded phases of Christ's life through the year in a returning cycle. And the Synagogue, by 100 A.D. had accepted three daily services as binding—at morning, afternoon and evening, while its cycles of Lessons strongly affected the Christian Calendar.

The Mass was built up of two main elements, the Temple or Synagogue service on Sunday morning, and the *agape* or common meal held in private houses to commemorate the Last Supper. In early Byzantine days it was often but not daily performed; and soon lines of cleavage between East and West grew up. The West added elements from the feast of the day's saint; the East carried on the early tradition of concentrating on the sacramental theme without variations. And the East retained the Jewish form of congregational services: the psalm chanted by the Reader was accompanied by the congregation with responses after each verse. The element of communal participation remained stronger here.

Formulas increased, till Mass was a corporative act of celebrant, clergy, congregation. Hymns grew in number; but the dramatic nature of the rite stopped the indefinite accretion of songs of praise. Hymns tended to gather round the services of Morning and Evening, drawn from Syrian sources.

In 528 a decree made the three main offices, Matins, Lauds, Vespers obligatory on clergy attached to a church. The psalter was not restricted to the choir; the laity could perform it. The decree aimed at strengthening the oldest elements of Christian worship, the daily communal prayers at dawn and dusk, which had a Jewish origin in apostolic days. John of the Golden Mouth wanted midnight offices compulsory on both lay and clergy, but this was felt to be overmuch. From early days there had been four elements (psalms, reading of scripture, prayers, songs) all derived from Judaism; to these were added sermons and homilies, and, as the Church Calendar grew, a huge number of saints' festivals as well as other celebratory festivals.

Besides keeping saints' festivals separate from the Mass, the East was unlike the West in the greater mark left by the martyr-cults. Two festivals were not held inside a church at all. These were the crucially important ones of the Passion and the Ascension. They were held outside church and town, at the cemetery, at the place of the martyrs. John of the Golden Mouth underlines the point. Why, he asks, is this the tradition handed on from the Fathers? Why go outside the church for these essential rites? He pondered long, then decided the reason must be the wish to honour the Martyrs while celebrating the Passion and the Ascension.

Thus, by celebrating the Crucifixion at the spot where the Martyr had died his bloody death of defiance to the State, the eastern Church vitally linked the gospel-pattern, the generalised pattern, with the local tradition, the particular point of history which had most meaning for the local group. And there, in the open, it was easier for popular elements to flow in on the central ritual-drama. How much at home the people felt at the *martyrion* is shown by the complaints of Augustine that the Carthaginians, on St. Cyprian's day, danced and rollicked at the *martyrium* instead of praying; and by Jerome's advice to virgins at vigils 'not to budge a finger's span from mother's elbow'.

37

MUSIC

THE NEW MUSIC. If we may credit a poem by Leontios, something of the classical styles of music lingered into the sixth century. He wrote of a musician Plato

> *When Orpheus died, some Muse yet plucked the quill.*
> *But, Plato gone, the lyre in silence stands.*
> *For a small echo of ancient music still*
> *haunted his heart and hands.*

But to all intents and purposes the classical forms had long been dead. In their place new forms, entirely eastern, had arrived. Syria was the main home of the new music. An unbroken tradition 'existed from the days of the Synagogue to the Byzantine melodies of the mid-seventh century, according to which the reading of scripture was followed by the recitation or chanting of a poetical homily'.

The oldest versions of both Byzantine and Gregorian melodies go back to a common source, the churches of Antioch and Jerusalem—with the Synagogue behind them. Both Western Plainsong and Byzantine liturgical music represent new elements among the Greek or Latin-speaking peoples of the Empire. The new music is characterised by a recurrence of certain formulae, not by a basis in any particular mode, and many formulas in both Byzantine and Ambrosian (pre-Gregorian) chant are identical or closely related, going back to the Syrio-Palestinian area.

This church-music is wholly vocal, homophonic. At first readers and precentors converted from the Synagogue were used; and thus antiphonal singing and solo psalms were made possible. The soloist sang a whole psalm, the people replied with a phrase after each verse, as in the Synagogue. The liturgical music-books were of two kinds, for Lessons or for Mass and Offices. The Lessons were given in a chant, *ekphonesis*, half between recitation and song used for solemn feasts.[1]

[1] See Paul, *Ephesians* v. 19, for the three types of music: psalms, hymns, spiritual songs—found alike in Jewish and Byzantine liturgy. All Byzantine chant may be classified as psalmody (psalms, canticles), hymns (verses, stanzas, hymns, litanies, processionals), spiritual songs (songs of praise, wordless allelujas). We have no Byzantine secular music.

The early Church was hostile to music, linking it with carnality and pagan festival. The Fathers tried to evade the texts about the Jews playing, singing, dancing, by saying that the Jews, contaminated by Egypt, were permitted to do these things rather than something worse, though God didn't enjoy them. But singing could scarcely be shut out. The early Christians met for 'exhortations, corrections and censures in God's name', Tertullian tells us. Then:

> After washing hands and lighting lights, each rose in turn and sang in God's honour a canticle which he set forth according to his ways, from Scripture or from his own spirit.

That is, he improvised or drew on the psalms. Till the mid-fourth century the people prayed unanimously in church; but soon after this, as the grip of the hierarchical State-Church tightened, a violent attack was launched on the freedom and individual inspiration which the apostolic age considered the test of true conversion.

> Let no one sing in the church but the canonical psalmists for the psalms, who go up to the ambo and sing according to the book. (Laodikeia.)
> No one must read in the church psalms on private authority, or uncanonical books.
> In gatherings for divine service, psalms must not be sung one after the other but a lesson must be interpolated after each psalm.

An official book of 150 psalms is laid down.[1]

THE CRISIS IN MUSIC. But what was this new music that the Church had reluctantly to take under its control and which it sought to stereotype? To realise how the mass-forces had broken through the old forms, long sterile and restricted, we must consider both what the crisis in music was, and the groups from whom the driving force came in the development of the new forms.

The crisis from which the new music arose was a general crisis which

---

[1] The *Odes of Solomon* (first century) are written in ecstatic diction. The hymns in the apocryphal *Acts* are so Syrian as to seem direct translations. Syrian too is the *Homily on the Passion* by Meleto (bishop of Sardis, mid-second century) in oratorical prose with all the characteristics of Semitic poetry, and rhyme to stress parallel or antithetical points. A hymn attributed to Clement shows the effort to stick to classical models, though in the anapaests of the orientalising poets of Hellenistic days, and the exalted hurry begets strings of epithets and antithetical balances (cf. the hymns of Synesios). A recently found hymn shows us what was happening in music: the anapaest breaks down into rhythmical prose for the doxological formula, the music is structurally florid, using formulas linked by varying short phrases in the manner of recitation. D. Nilo Borgia has restored the poetic form of eucharistic prayers and invocations and shown it to be a kind of popular poetry, which represents the transition between classical forms and Byzantine rhythmical systems.

touched poetry as much as music. When the old Greek quantitative forms of metre broke down before popular intrusions—that is, failed to supply an effective basis for the new mass-forces of expression—the forms of old Greek music also proved inadequate. They could not be applied directly to the new texts of exalted prose or accentual verse. The main mass-thrust was in psalmodic forms based on cantillation or *ekphonesis* (elevated recitation of one kind or another). In Byzantine music the *enechemata*, the cue words and closing formulae of psalm-tones, were the main matters; the psalmodic method dominated to the end. But the Byzantines were not merely taking over the Judaic method. What they took over was the modification by the Syrians, who had been strongly affected both by Greek and Semitic forms. This modification consisted of a merging of the broken-down Hellenistic elements with elements making for psalmodic or accentual forms from the Jews. The Syrians devised isosyllabic metres and stanzas—a transitional form between the strict quantitative forms of the ancient Greeks and the strict accentual metres of later Europe.

In psalmody the unit is the whole sentence; and the parallelism of scriptural phrases begets the dichotomic structure of the music. A melodic structure emerges definitely only at the significant points, start and end and pause; the rest is recited without melody. Both psalmody and *lectio solemnis*, the cantillation of Scripture, derive from Jewish forms (which in turn synthesise a large number of eastern influences). The problem is to grasp how the psalmodic and allied forms developed into later western music (from the eleventh century on) with a secure relation between text and tone, word and note, in a rhythmically unified piece.

The liturgical function of psalmody was to keep the congregation active in the service. All the church-fathers praise its power to weld the mass into a single organism, a single body of praise. And psalms long kept a mass-emotion denied to hymns. Didymos says, 'The man of practical life prefers psalmody, the man of theoretical life prefers hymns.' And John of the Golden Mouth says the High Powers (angels) prefer hymns; the common folk should sing psalms all day—on travels, in the workshop, at home—'and no artificial accompaniment or musical study is necessary'. The ascetic or monastic trends also stressed the psalm as unlearned and penitential, opening the way to salvation for the poorest, roughest, most sinful. (Similarly among the Jews, throughout the Talmudic period, up to about 680, psalmody remained simple, drawing in the whole congregation for song or at least responses.)

THE SYRIAN HYMN. But the hymn held the clue to the next phase of development, the creation of precise form—the regaining of the precision

of ancient Greek music on an incomparably higher level of clarity and
expansive possibilities. And the first basis of the new discipline came in
the Syrian transformation of mingled Hellenistic and Judaic element in
stanzaic hymns. Here each stanza was syllabically the same as the others.
How definitely it was the new Syrian forms which conquered the whole
European world can be seen from the words for stanza. The Syriac for
stanza or for a unit of two verses was *beitha*, house (*bayith*, Hebrew: we
do not know which was first used). Translations of this term are the Byzantine *oikos*, which also means house, and the Italian *stanza*, which means
chamber. Further, the Byzantine *kukulion*, used for a prefatory or inter-
calay stanza in a metre different from that of the hymn proper, comes
from the Aramean *kulklion*, enclave or cell-compartment (to be found in
Talmudic literature). On the other hand the give-and-take of Byzantium
and Syria is shown by the drawing-in of the Greek *prosomoion* as *pismon* by
Syrian and Hebrew poetry, meaning in medieval times a refrain-hymn;
and the classic Hebrew word for poetic hymn, *piyyut*, is from the Greek
poietes, poet. The hymn-terminology of Byzantium, scrutinised, shows
a basically Syrian element.

THE CREATIVE HERETICS. The men who gave the basic new start to music
through the development of the hymn-form were the heretics, especially
the great gnostics, Basilides, Valentinos, Bardasanes, who had no in-
hibitions about expressing themselves or encouraging their flock to do so,
who stressed a give-and-take between leader and group, soloist and congregation, and who were ready to take up popular forms and use them
to spread their doctrines. They propagandised energetically with their
songs, and wanted the impact as strong and dramatic as possible; they
wanted to draw the audience into musical participation.

The orthodox Syrian Ephraem admits that the gnostic Bardasanes
certainly knew classical Greek poetry, and worked by modifying the
older patterns. His biographer Sozomen tells us that his son Harmonios

> was well instructed in Greek literature and the first to subject his native lang-
> uage to metres and musical laws; he adapted it to choirs of singers, the way
> the Syrians now commonly chant, using indeed not the words of Harmonios
> but his tunes.

Bardasanes, we may suppose, made the first steps, and his son completed
them. (The son's name suggests a paternal passion for music.) The Greek
models were probably anacreontic verse; for these rhythms were much
used for popular processions, and women seem to have sung them at
mystery-cults in strophic responses. There is little doubt that the heretics
adapted pagan mystery-forms, and the orthodox were forced to readapt.

Here, as throughout Christian origins, we meet mystery-cult and Judaism merging to provide the new dynamic.

Ephraem complained that 'the evil one has planted vociferous thorns and concealed spikes among melodies', and set out to use the new forms against the heretics. At times he stresses this motive even in his hymns themselves:

> *I chanced on tares, my brothers . . .*
> *I chanced on a book of Bardasan,*
> *and for an hour it troubled me . . .*
> *Tainted into my ears it ran*
> *and made of them a passage free*
> *for words compact of blasphemy.*
> *I hastened then to clean them out*
> *with the pure words proclaimed past doubt*
> *in scriptural verity.*

Using the heretical method, he divided melodies into strophes sung alternately and followed by a refrain.

> Ephraem rose up against the games and dances of the young folk, and he gathered the Daughters of the Covenant and taught them songs, both refrain songs (?) and alternating song .... and each time the Daughters of the Covenant gathered in the churches on the festivals and Sundays . . . and he like a father, teaching them various kinds of song and the change (? modulation) of songs, until the whole city gathered about him and the crowd of his opponents disbanded. (Yaqub of Serug.)

The last sentence shows how directly he was fighting heretics with his methods; and his seven-syllabled metres look back to anacreontics and reveal how he was matching himself against the gnostics.

ANTIPHONAL MUSIC. Antiphony was an ancient form in the Syrio-Mesopotamian area. We find it in the ancient epic of *Gilgamesh*; and Antioch and Edessa were centres from which it spread in the Churches of the heretics or the orthodox. (It is well to remember that Christianity had five basic centres of early consolidation and diffusion, Jerusalem, Antioch, Edessa, Alexandria and Rome; and Antioch had such a strong Jewish section that the Jews gained full citizenship as early as 301 B.C.) We can detect moments of increased use of antiphonal and responsorial forms in the Antiochene area. Thus Sokrates tells how Ignatios of Antioch, polemising against the Arians, saw angels in alternative (antiphonal) hymnody praising the Trinity. Then under Leontios of Antioch (344–57) two Syrians arranged the clergy and lay in antiphonal choirs for night services. Later Niketas Choniates says, 'And as Theodore of Mopsuestia writes, they translated into Greek that psalmodic species we call antiphones.' And

Basil of Kaisareia in a letter to the clergy defending antiphony declared that it was established in the monasteries of Egypt, Libya, Palestine, Arabia, Syria.[1]

OTHER HERETICAL PRESSURES. The Markionite gnostics also were famous for their hymns: 'The heretics have replaced St. Peter by Markion as prince of the apostles, and instead of psalms they write their own hymns.' They had a female choir. And Paul of Samosata composed for women.

The bad repute of hymns in the eyes of the conservative Papacy is shown by the fact that when they were common in Ireland and Gaul, they were still not approved of at Rome. The year 1000 had gone before the Roman Office-books mentioned them.

Another heretical thrust, which must have left strong marks, was that of Arianism. Unfortunately, as the evidence was destroyed by the orthodox, we can only hazard guesses at what happened. Areios composed a *Thaleia*, which seems a mixture of discussions and songs (according to Athanasios), to which the orthodox replied with an *Anti-Thaleia*. Athanasios declared that Areios emulated the 'scurrilous jests of Sotades', a mime-writer, and Philostorgos added that he made up songs for sailors, mill-workers, tramps and the like. John of the Golden Mouth described the period of Arian supremacy:

> Psalmody is silenced, blasphemous tongues babble from the sacred thrones. Add to this, dancing and screaming. Our holy mysteries are blasphemed.

It is obvious that there was an inflow of popular forms and forces, and that Areios tried to meet the common people on their own ground; but we cannot gain from the generalised abuse any notion of how hymns and liturgy were effected in detail. When, however, we recall that Arianism was dominant under Constantius II and Valens, we cannot but think that its period of triumph must have left an impress on ritual and hymn-composition. In any event the abuse of its music by the orthodox

---

[1] Antiphonal singing in the Jewish manner in octaves, seems the early custom. Up to the fifth century patristic accounts show no appreciable difference from the account by Philo and Eusebios of the Therapeutai, the Jewish pre-monastic groups of withdrawal.

Refrains were used by the Therapeutai (as also the early Hebrews, *i.e. Exodus* xv). The gnostics used free refrains; refrains appear in the apocryphal *Acts of John* and some papyri of the first four centuries. Both east and west these forms grew into larger and independent forms, the Antiphon gaining the widest propagations. The antiphon as a specific form grew from a psalm-preamble into a melismatic piece of its own: with non-metrical text in Roman music, with metrical texts in the east, *i.e. troparia* (Syrian, '*enyana*, answer) which gain independent form after originating as free interpolations between verses of psalm or canticle.

brings out the hurlyburly of popular forces which broke in through the heresies and determined the music which orthodoxy had to devise.

THE NEW FORM IS STABILISED. The *Life of St. Auxentios* in fact shows us the orthodox in the very act of fighting back. Auxentios came from Syria for military service at Byzantium; he joined a pious group and became a hermit on a hill near Chalkedon. Pilgrims frequented his cell, and he taught them songs. He himself sang the first hemistich of a line; they answered it with the second. The tunes were plain, easily picked up and remembered, tunes of a psalm or a paraphrase, so that the pilgrims could spread them far and wide.

The new form built up as the primary stabilisation of the liberated mass-forces was the *troparion*, which by the fifth century evolved out of free interpolated refrains into strophic structure. It intruded into the liturgy, which at this period was made up of psalms, the nine odes (canticles), and some ancient formulas. The liturgy gained a new life.

This was the first stage, representing a clean break from ancient Greek music and yet gathering together certain elements from that music in the fusions achieved by men like Bardasanes and Ephraem. The crystallisation of form was still unstable; the new musical energies appeared at the turning-points of psalmodic chant (beginning, middle, end) in typical melisms —short melodic formulas that preceded and underlay the growth of modal systems.

The necessary integrations of more extended and interrelated forms depended on the closer linking of text and melody. The composers of ornate chant seldom bothered much about the metrical structure of their texts; but things were different when clearly recognisable metrical forms and numbered stresses entered the liturgic field. Then the psalmodic style was no longer adequate, and gradually a closer linking of text and tone begot a clarified structure.

Certain melisms played a key-part in this whole development. The melismatic style in the Church was connected with the jubilant rendering of the Allelujah, which enabled the most unlearned worshipper to play his part in the service. (How popular this melismatic chant was in early Christian-Judaic circles can be seen from the *Odes of Solomon*.) Even when anti-Jewish feeling was at its height, no one dreamed of discarding the Allelujah, which Jewish tradition and Christian exegesis agreed in considering a song of man and angels, and which in fact went back to such magical incantations as the pre-Islamic Arabic trill *ililil*. Tertullian says it was added as an exclamation after all psalms in prayers; Cassian tells of the Egyptian monks using it; another writer speaks of the

Antiochene monks singing it with such strength after each verse that they seemed a single organism. Mid-fourth century seems the date when it was removed from the scriptural text and made a general mode of jubilation, a kind of controlled musical rendering of the possessed bab- bling so highly esteemed in apostolic days.

But fine and subtle as were the Byzantine elaborations on the melis- matic Syrian bases, they never succeeded, now or later, in fully breaking away and rising to a decisively new level of integration. The achievement of that new level, which involved the creation of a true musical notation, was in due time the work of the West. It is of interest to note the difference in the very use of the term *hymn* in West and East. The Byzantines used it often for almost any sort of sacred song, from a *troparion* to the trisagion chant, from the doxology to a psalm; but in the West from the late fourth century it comes to mean a new poem. It emerges as almost always metrical, with tactic accents and recognisable periods, and is a distinct sort of strophic music.

Even the allelujahs of Byzantium are closer to the Jewish than those of the West. The Gregorian *jubili* contain many elements not of eastern provenance, elements probably linked with the rise of the sequence and the prose, in which a new sort of musical form asserts itself. But this development, which entails the intrusion of new regional forces (Irish, Gallic, Germanic) into the stiff papal tradition, comes only later in the eighth and ninth centuries; and the Roman bases on which they build, or which they transform, were eastern, derived from the same Greek- Syrian elements as Byzantine music.[1]

[1] There was a common basis in Hebrew, Armenian, Hindu, Greek and Roman systems of accentuation; the Nestorians and Rabbinic Academy at Nisibis probably had much to do with the expansions. In the West some time in the ninth century there was used the horizontal staff to define an exact musical pitch. Outside the Byzantine area in the West notations were long lost; Isidore of Seville writes that unless tunes are preserved by memory they die, as they cannot be written. (The Syrians seem to have lost notation about 900: Bar Hebraios.)

38

LITURGIC DRAMA

DRAMATIC HOMILY. From Syria came yet another basic element of music-drama. Byzantine homilies contain a strong dramatic element, and what La Piana has called the Dramatic Homilies may be divided into three types: (1) a large group with dialogues, often quite long, which paraphrase short dialogues in the canonical texts (*i.e.* the scene between Simeon and Mary at the presentation of the child Jesus, or that of the Angel and Zachariah on John the Baptist's conception). These dialogues are often made of long *enkomia* concluding with litanies of *chairetismoi* (hails); but they are a vital part of the homily, a rhetorical mode of vivifying biblical history. (2) Homilies with dialogues or monologues that are new creations even if linked (as is almost always the case) with texts. They are not limited to one scene, but give a whole episode in various scenes; and the sermon proper is only a frame for the dramatic exposition. The style is a rich poetic prose thick with antitheses and anacruses. (3) Homilies with fully dramatised episodes of the life of Jesus and Mary with a number of scenes accompanied and followed by oratorical bursts. Here the drama has a strong rhythmical structure, with rhymes and assonances— a style close to, but not identical with, that of the hymn-writers.

In the third group the scenes were composed before they were embedded in the homilies; and the general movement revealed is from a less dramatised form to one more fully dramatised, which seems well worked out by the later fifth century. This homily-drama developed its own systems, which are exemplified by the *Enkomion* attributed to Proklos of Byzantium where rhymes and assonances are common, and where the dramatic elements make up a complete play: a rhythmic hymn to virginity, an acrostic dialogue between Gabriel and Mary, a monologue of Mary expressing her doubts, a long reply by the Angel, the acceptance by Mary, the Voice of God explaining, a Council of Demons who plan God's defeat. But, though distinct, the drama remained linked with the sermon.

We can safely assume that it was rendered in church by various voices with the aid of the choir in sung parts. We cannot prove that it was acted—not of course as realistic scenic plays, but as symbolic plays using gesture and movement—though the probability is very strong. La Piana noted that the homilies with the fullest dramatic elements were entitled *enkomia*; and in Byzantine liturgy *enkomia* are cited only in connection with Christ, Mary, John the Baptist—personages round whom the homily-drama gathered. There is further evidence that as early as the fifth or sixth century the *enkomia* were not merely hymns but complex liturgical performances such as that of the Tomb on Holy Friday.

Indeed it seems likely that Maurice was the emperor who gave definitive form to the *enkomia* as drama. Theophanes says:

> In the same year (580) Maurice gave orders that a Supplication be celebrated in the Church of the Blachernai in honour of the Holy Mother of God and that the enkomia of Our Blessed Lady be recited, and he called this celebration a *Panegyris*.

The *enkomion*-drama then appears as part of the *Panegyris* which was reserved for great liturgical commemorations and extraordinary occasions.

The iconoclast persecution, however, stopped such performances and when orthodoxy returned the tradition had been lost. Monks compiling homilies used the *enkomia*, embodying them in their composition in varying stages of completeness.

There seem to have been two cycles, each a trilogy: the Annunciation, Navity, Flight to Egypt, and the Baptism of Jesus, Passion, Hell-harrowing.

NATIVITY HYMNS. The origin of the homily-drama lay in Syria. The homilies and canticles of Ephraem are in the form of dialogues and monologues. Thus, a comparison of Ephraem's sermon on the Annunciation shows many resemblances with the Byzantine dialogues. Further, we know that Ephraem's works were familiar in Greek translations even in his own lifetime. The Byzantine homily-drama was thus a derivation of the Syriac *sogitha* or homily-canticle.

If we look at the twelve Nativity hymns of Sophronios, patriarch of Jerusalem from 634–8, we find an extended use of the *sogitha* themes. The characters are Joseph, Mary and Narrator. The first hymn opens with the Narrator's appeal to Bethlehem to prepare the manger; and the tale is carried a step further with each troparion. In the third, Joseph wants to know what all the trouble is: 'Hidden from me and all in a hurry you've brought forth. Shame instead of honour, grieving instead of joy. Blame instead of praise you've brought upon me.' And so on. The tenth describes the fury of Herod and the slaughter of the Innocents.

Another popular form which impinged on the homily-drama was that of the mime. Joseph is made out as a jealous husband.

When Mary sees Gabriel she thinks him to be a young man with evil intentions and warns him: 'The old man is jealous, and if he finds you here he will cut your head off and will make trouble for me.' The language of the mime is frankly used in the scene between Joseph and Mary when he finds that she is with child: 'My white hair is dishonoured; how can I appear before my friends; how can I stand their mockery and the laughter of the people in the town?' Mary is calm and even teases him. When Joseph in a rage tells her to depart and to go to her lover because she is now unworthy to share his bread and his roof, Mary answers: 'Willingly I would go if I knew where he lives, because he was so handsome.' But when Joseph, losing all patience, announces that he is going to the priests, Mary is frightened and invokes the help of God. The profane and irreverent tradition of the mime thus finds its way into the dramatisation of sacred history. (Wellesz.)

LITURGIC DRAMA IN THE WEST. What, then, was the relation of the western liturgic drama to the Syriac-Byzantine forms? There seems little doubt that Western developments were direct offshoots of the latter, partly through translations or adaptations of Byzantine dramatic homilies, and partly through the introduction of the homily-drama into areas where the Empire ruled, especially Italy. The resemblances, also, of the later western liturgic drama to Byzantine forms is too great to be explained by a common borrowing from apocryphal books, and so on.

The Procession of the Prophets, a very important scene in the West, certainly comes from Byzantium. The Procession which appears in Latin as part of a sermon attributed to Augustine is derived from eastern sources, of which the earliest form seems the sermon in praise of Mary attributed to Hesychios of Jerusalem.[1]

The difference between East and West may be summarised thus. In the East the deep roots of religious culture meant that in the liturgy a central form of mass-expression was evolved, which had a centripetal and unifying energy. Therefore the liturgic drama did not break away from the Church; rather it drew new elements into itself. In the West, however,

[1] 'The Byzantine Nativity cycle were dramatic in the same sense as the Italian oratorio at the beginning of the seventeenth century. . . . The same Syriac patterns, we may assume, influenced hymn-writers in Western Europe, where from the sixth century onwards the Syrians had colonies in Italy, France and Spain. It is an established fact that Syrian iconography influenced French art from the fifth to the twelfth centuries. The representation of the Nativity and the Adoration of the Magi in western sculpture, ivory and miniatures can be traced back to Syro-Hellenistic formulas. The mystery play of the Magi which appears for the first time in an eleventh century MS. of St. Martial of Limoges may be derived from the same Syrian source which inspired Sophronios. The great achievement of the West consisted in carrying the semi-dramatic form of the East on to the stage of the mystery play.' (Wellesz.) Yes, but here the Syrian influences are more likely via Byzantium, and the eastern forms became more than semi-dramatic: what they did not become was *theatre*.

the liturgy developed an inner dynamic of drama much later, as the town-forces began decisively to rise; and the secular bases of the new culture were strong enough to draw the dramatic forms away from the liturgy—step by step away from the church and into the processional streets of guild-life. But this later development and its whole surrounding nexus of cultural forces had beneath and behind it the rich movements of Byzantine society. Those movements had carried Europe, to the point where the new liberations were possible and where the resolution of the ancient world's contradictions, stabilised by Byzantium, could be lifted to an altogether new level in the struggle to break beyond feudalism.

MUSICAL EXPANSION. The new thrust, derived from the *sogitha* and strength-ened by the dramatic trend, begot a new musical form, the *kontakion*, which appeared full-grown in Byzantium, attributed to the poet Romanos. It was made up of 13 to 30 or even more stanzas all structurally alike; each stanza, 3 to 13 lines, is based on the model, *heirmos*, which can be taken from a previous *kontakion* or specially composed. A *troparion*, melodically unrelated, stands as prelude, joined by a refrain and the mode to the *kontakion* proper, which a soloist sings—the refrain is repeated between each stanza by the choir. The stanzas are linked alphabetically, or by an acrostic on the author's name or the song's title; and the title itself mentions date, festival, mode of melody. All stanzas have the same number of syllables, with stress-accents in the same places as in the *heirmos*. The poet thus has to be a highly skilled musician; and the *kontakion*, flourishing mid-fifth to seventh centuries, shows the maturing of Byzan-tine musical form.

The form came from Syrian church-songs, *memra madasha* and *sogitha memra*. At Byzantium it was used to give a poetic description of the festival's object. Romanos, its greatest exponent, was the orthodox poet of the Justinianic age; he uses the Syrian forms with strength and grace to give new life to orthodox expression. He attacks opponents, Nestorios or the ancient Greeks. Till the twelfth century his *kontakion* on the Nativity was given yearly at Christmas at the imperial palace by a double choir, from St. Sophia and the Apostles.

Musically, the *kontakion*, though developing on the *troparion*, fails to break through into definitive new structures. Allied to the Hebrew *keroba*, it shows a system of limited improvisation, based on the prevalence of standing or wandering melisms. That is, it is struggling towards the fuller integration which the medieval music of the West achieved and which in turn leads on to modern European music; but it is still basically melismatic.

ACCLAMATIONS. A subsidiary form was that of the *Akta* or acclamations which developed out of the organised cheers when the emperor entered the Circus. Nero liked the cheers so much that he tried to organise a middle-class order of augustals to do the job. In Byzantium the improvised chants by which the factions addressed the emperor were *akta*; and the term embraced both praise and protest.

They were given for the imperial family and high dignitaries of Church and State; and appeared in a church when the emperor or a high ecclesiastic visited it. Gradually they grew more complicated. Under Justinian there were already 112 readers in St. Sophia as compared with 25 psaltai for hymns; and the readers must have chanted the *akta* as well as the epistles. (Originally there had been only two readers.) The *akta* added to the pomp, regulated the order of ceremonies, processional, games.

Many of the phrases were taken from pagan athletics. 'You win.' Already the crowd shouted to Commodus, 'You win, you'll win for ever.' This phrase 'for ever' (*ap' aionos*) got into the liturgy as in *secula seculorum*. Further, election phrases from republican days—'the right man for the job', *dignus* or *axios*—were carried into *akta* and applied to emperor or bishop. The cry of *axios* ratified the bishop's election; opponents shouted *anaxios*. And this cry, *axios*, is still used in the Orthodox Church.[1]

THE PANEGYRIS. There are two matters which need a little further attention, the *Panegyris* and the concept of church-music as angelic.

The *Panegyris* was in the far Hellenic past the term for the assembly of a whole people, a tribal or city group, at a common sanctuary. Thus the Karneia, Delia, Pamboiotia, Panionia, were tribal *panegyreis*; the Ephesia, a *panegyris* of a city and its territory. The same term was used for inter-tribal, inter-city festivals like the Olympic or Isthmian Games as well as the Amphyctionic Meetings (of neighbours) which had much political importance as a unifying factor in the troubled life of ancient Greece. The *panegyris* was thus an expression of kinship by rites at a common sanctuary, a large-scale market, a place of political decisions drawing in

---

[1] Tertullian rebuked the Christian who shouted *eis ap' aionos* to a mere mortal in the circus. In the *akta* we once more meet the element of apotheosis we found shared by winning athlete and emperor—as well as by Christ and Martyr. (Sacred fraternities used *akta*: the Arval Brethren hailed Caracalla, 'With you safe we stand secure and saved.') For the election slogan see the walls of Pompeii—the formula *dignus rei publicae* became so familiar that it was put up as DRP. *Axios* was used for athletes too. It played a key-part in the idea of Imperial Virtue, taking over the Stoic idea that the Right Man gets Supreme Power: the emperor rules as *axios* or *dignus*. Pliny explains that the emperor who is *dignus* achieves godhead, consecration, at death—*dignus* thus links with apotheosis.

neighbouring States, a centre for athletics and art. To the inter-tribal *panegyris* came the rhapsodes reciting the Homeric epics. Festive speeches were given there, *logoi panegyrikoi*. Sophists took the chance to give orations; important political speeches were made, as when Lysias at Olympia preached national unity.

The panegyric speeches were of two kinds, the *epainos* with direct praise for virtue or merit and the *enkomion* which discoursed or sang of high deeds. The *panegyris* of Maurice, which embodied the homily-drama and pagan strains derived from such declamatory sophists as those of Gaza, thus had behind it a rich and complex tradition. The fair-gathering of inter-tribal concord at which the Homeric poems had been put forth was now the gathering of the faithful to witness the representation of the new life which could be actualised by nothing less than human unity.

The *panegyris* still carries on in Greek villages. The night before is a vigil, during which many folk stay in the church all night—the older ones on mattresses in a corner, the younger singing. There is a procession and service next day, a feast for all charged to the church (*i.e.* to the community itself), and the lay of the saint or martyr is sung amid round-dances. A strange return to the origins of drama and epic after the great cycle that runs from Homer and Aischylos into Byzantium.[1]

ANGELIC ECHO. At Byzantium the hymn was thought to be an Echo of Heavenly Beauty and Harmony. The writer hoped to follow a model established before all time, to write down the very music sung by the Angels on the theme he treated. Thus Romanos says of the Three Children in the Furnace that they turn the Furnace into a church by the song which merges them with the Angels and 'imitates the whole hymnody of the immortals'. He begins another hymn with the confident cry, 'Let the Choir of Angels stand amazed at this wonder and let us mortals raise our voices in a hymn.' Germanos in a hymn praises Romanos for 'composing the Angelic Hymnody'. The Trisagion was thought an angelic song heard by a boy drawn up for a while to heaven under Theodosios II. 'We who mystically represent the Cherubim', sang the singers in a rite of 874. The hymn was a mystery-act felt to turn the singers into angels and the ritual-area into a heaven. Auxentios in the early fifth century had sung: 'The hosts of heaven have hymns for offering, and we the men of earth, we the doxology sing.' These attitudes were derived from Judaism (Romanos was a Syrian Jew). Rabbinic sources are rich in tales and visions in which the heavenly host is stirred to sing by the example of the

1 The Orite, with its Greek name, is also current among the Slavonic peoples of the Balkans.

Jewish community praising their Lord in the *Qedusha* and *Exodus* xv; the Hallel psalms were taken to stimulate or imitate the angels. The Greek Fathers were familiar with the *midrashic* literature of Palestine, which was also brought directly into the Church by converts.

But the Syrian and Judaic attitudes were reinforced by Neoplatonism; the Orthodox creed absorbed and applied the Neoplatonist concept of godhead as a fountaining centre of being and haven of return. From the centre welled a ceaseless series of emanations which perpetually re-created the universe, setting up a hierarchical series of levels and at the same time organically uniting them. In true Neoplatonist thought the universe was eternal; Porphyry felt the idea of a creation in time to be irreligious. But this aspect was slurred over by Orthodoxy, which classed deviations into a too-precise Neoplatonism as Origenistic heresy, but which itself evaded all the sharp disputes and contradictions that had come up in the fourth to sixth centuries about Son and Father, or the Two Natures, by an essentially Neoplatonist position. Thus alone it could justify a self-divided world and find unifying concepts which glossed over the contradictions with a mystical glorification of hierarchy. Intuitions of cosmic or biological unity (of a chain-of-being, of monistic process) were applied to social stratification and projected in the mystical imagery of angelic hierarchies. Thus the State and the State-Church were justified; but the thesis of reconciliation, while involving the lie and cheat at which the heresies passionately protested, also made it possible for men to live, to develop their life-process under the State and the State-Church. It therefore provided an element of concretion at the heart of the alienating abstraction, which made possible the advancement of art and science.

The work which theoretically reconciled Christianity and Neoplatonism was *The Heavenly Hierarchies* of the pseudo-Dionysios, which may therefore be called the work embodying the theory of art and music-drama for Byzantium.[1]

[1] The Areopagitic writings seem composed to counteract Julian the Apostate's solar monotheism (which was still active towards the middle of the fifth century and must have had deeper roots than is generally allowed) (Ivanka, *VIᵉ Congrès*, 1950). Noutzoubidze, Georgian scholar, argues that the author was Peter, bishop of Gaza (see *Viz. Vrem.*, ii, 1949, 733).

Evagrios of Pontos, master of Cassian, did much to hand on Origen's work and fuse Christian and pagan asceticism (A. Sillem, *Downside Review*, 1951). The liturgies of Egypt and the West, it may be noted, have common forms not in the Syrian liturgies: the West seems to have borrowed in the period 340–381 (Palachkovsky, *VIᵉ Congrès*).

39

BREAK AND RENEWAL

BECOMING GOD. I should like to give here a brief account of St. Maximos; for though his career has no direct connection with music or homily-drama, his life and thought have a strong bearing on the inner struggle in the angelic hierarchical concept which had such integrative importance in Byzantine culture.

Born at Byzantium about 580 of wealthy parents, he was well educated. Heraklios made him Chief Secretary, but in 630 he resigned and entered a monastery across the waters at Chrysopolis. A rigorous ascetic, he became abbot, composed hymns, and fiercely opposed Monothelitism as a compromise with the world. He opposed it at the Council of Alexandria in 633, he swayed Africa against the emperor, and in 649 he went to Rome where he worked Pope Martin into condemning at the first Lateran Council the other imperial efforts to compromise, the *Ekthesis* and the *Type*. Constans II in rage had both the Pope and Maximos arrested and brought to Byzantium. Maximos was examined, exiled to Thrace, badly treated, brought back again, scourged, jailed, curtailed of right hand and tongue, and again exiled, this time to the Caucasus where he died.

His 'orthodoxy' was thus based in a resistance to the world and the State. He sets out what is the logical outcome of the pseudo-Dionysian position, that the ultimate aim of the worshipper is to *become* God. This position unites both the Neoplatonist desire for ecstatic communion with pure being and the early-Christian belief that full initiation made the devotee a christ. The lack of a mass-basis in the West meant that the elements of the initiatory process were more easily abstracted there and used as sacraments controlled by the priestly order; and such claims as those of Maximos or Evagrios to *entheosis* could only seem the wildest of heresies. But in the East the idea of becoming God could be embodied in positions that forced their way to the centre of orthodoxy. Knowledge and being were held to be one; to know God was to be God. As a man rises from *apatheia* to *gnosis*, from a passive acceptance to unifying insight and knowledge, he gained a *soma pneumatikon*, a spiritual body, and at last became God.

'In the Monad there are neither rulers nor ruled', says Evagrios, 'but all are gods.' And Maximos declares that 'there is one Energy of God and of the Saints'. Commenting on the pseudo-Dionysios he says, 'We are made gods and sons and body and limbs and part of God.'

Here, at the climax of hierarchical abstraction and of notions of reconciling unity, the attitudes of apostolic democracy intrude with a renewed force; and this intrusion reveals the element of concretion which, at the end of the last chapter, I noted as obstinately persisting at the core of the Church's reconciliation position—the element that lies at the heart of the great art which Byzantium produced. The organic concept inside the Heavenly Hierarchies thus burns up the thesis of social division which it set out to sanctify; intuitions of evolution and of the concrete universal break-through. And it is no accident that Maximos, in whom this line of thought comes to a head, is found to be in his own life an uncompromising opponent of the State. For him the monastic way of rejecting a polluted world was the only pledge of true human unity. Thus, in his *Liber Asceticus*, a dialogue between an Old and a Young Man, he ends with the call:

> And so, Brothers, let us turn from the World and its Rulers. Let us renounce the flesh and the things of the flesh. Let us strive heavenward, where is our City. Let us follow the divine Apostle's example. Let us comprehend the Lord of Life. Let us drink the living waters. Let us join the heavenly choirs . . .

FROM DRAMATISATION TO AFFIRMATION. The last phase of the Byzantine hymn began near the end of the seventh century in a new form, the *kanon*, in the Morning Office. A rich form made up of nine odes, each ode composed of five to nine *troparia*. Later only three *troparia* of each ode are used in the service, as a number of monostrophic stanzas are added.

The *kontakion* was basically a poetic homily; the *kanon* odes were modelled on the nine scriptural canticles and hymns of praise. Used at first for Lent, then for the time between Easter and Pentecost, then for all festival days—though the Second Ode, mourning, was restricted to Lent. The normal *kanon* thus consisted of eight odes. Whatever the theme, the commemoration of a martyr or a feast's celebration, the poet had to refer in each ode to his scriptural model.

The *kanon's* rise was aided by the canon of 692 which ordered daily preaching, especially on Sundays, from all higher clergy. The *kontakion*, sung after the gospel-reading in the morning, made way for the sermon, and as hymns were needed, the *kanones* were taken over from the Lenten period. But, more deeply, the epoch of national struggle, which had opened first with the Persian Wars and continued with the Arab wars,

needed to express the pang of its devotion. The homiletic and dramatic
kontakion waned in appeal before the *kanon*, the hymn of praise that
uttered an exaltation of resolve and a world-end mood. Exposition by
argument and homiletic dramatisation gave way before the simple expression of dogmatic ideas by repetition and variation. The surrender to
the Lord's will was matched with a devoted resistance to the national
foes: both surrender and resistance being aided by solemn rite and ikon-
splendours. Not that the dramatic element died wholly out; but it was
increasingly subordinated to the lyrical outburst, the declaration of personal participation in the ritual, the purpose, of the Church. This outburst
at first had the vitality born from the iconoclast struggle; but after the
triumph of orthodoxy the affirmation grew more and more stereotyped.
Music grew more autonomous, concerned with the elaboration of its
effects. At first *kanones* seem to have shared *heirmoi* with *kontakia*, but
soon they showed a greater efflorescence.

Andrew, born at Damaskos about 660, later bishop of Crete, is said
to have devised the form. He owed much to Romanos, often working
over his words; and though touched with Monothelitism, he was sainted
and his *kanones* were taken over. The first *kanon* school worked in the
laura of St. Sabas near the Dead Sea, mid-eighth century; its masters
were Greek, Syrian, Armenian, Coptic monks—among them John of
Damaskos and his foster-brother Kosmas. These poets were iconodules,
who found a deepened sense of participation in the initiation-pattern of
their creed through persecution. In John's *kanon* for Easter day we read:

> Yesterday Christ I was buried together with you
> with you arising I arise
> yesterday I was crucified together with you
> together with you O Saviour glorify me
> yet in your kingdom

—which can be compared with the poem on (or by) the sculptor Peter
cited above to exemplify the new passion emerging from the inconoclast
conflict. The second important school of *kanon*-writers came in the ninth
century during the second wave of Iconoclasm, led by the sturdy
Theodore of Stoudios. The Stoudite monks gave the *kanon* odes a closer
homogeneity; and though the diction was less ornate than that of
Romanos' hymns, he was still the main model.[1]

[1] *Troparia* of various kinds were also written all along, short hymns for the multifarious festivals, sung between the stanzas of the *kontakion* (or later, the *kanon's* odes)
and at start or finish of longer forms. They range from one to three-line stanzas of
poetic prose to lyric poems. Most important was the *stichera*, which (as main difference from the *hirmoi* of *kontakia* or *kanones*) combined a number of melodic formulas by simple transitional passages. Sung at times after a psalm-verse, the *stichera*

By the eleventh century there was such a huge accumulation of hymns sanctified by long use that the Church decided to cry a halt. That there were no lack of poets is proved by the fact that the Basilian monastery founded at Grottaferrata near Rome kept on producing new hymns into the twelfth century. But the Church had lost power of inner growth; it could beget no new form to give a new impulse to liturgic development, and so it tried to end the mere multiplication of existing forms. The last melode of the Byzantine Church seems John Mauropous of the mid-eleventh century.

Musical growth went on. Structures grew more complex and the text was embellished with extended coloratura through the thirteenth and fourteenth centuries by the *meliourgoi*, songmakers (called, if they taught, *maistores*). The fixation of liturgy prevented any leap into new forms, any true development; and the elaborations were sterile.[1]

A PLEA FOR SOCIALLY BASED MUSIC. Musical theory, as we see from twelfth-century arguments, never considered contemporary practice. Rather, it was a confused and lost branch of mathematical speculation. But, born from the humanist positions of the iconoclast period, claims appear for an enlarged sphere of reference for music. Psellos (friend of John Mauropos) complains of the confinement of serious music to the church. He rationalises and inverts the Neoplatonist argument. The earlier thinkers had wanted music to break through the visible world and reveal the sphere of pure angelic potences; Psellos argues that music as the revelation of universal rhythm ought to knot all the events of life, especially all the socially important moments. He wants daily life woven into the musical pattern.

> We finally discover the movements of created beings follow a rhythmical, their voices an harmonic, order, and that the dances composed from both are well constructed . . . and then we observe that the power emanating from music is extended to everything.

He deals with the relation of music to astronomy, and decides that there exist 'connections between the order in our chants, rhythms or dances, and divine music'. The ancient Greeks had various kinds of music, song and dance for all the events of life such as bridal procession or marriage-feast. But 'the kind of music that occupies our minds today is only a faint echo' of what has been.

grew in length and were used at Morning and Evening Offices (compare with Antiphons of Latins). Methodios of Sicily, a *kanon*-writer, said to have been mutilated by the iconoclasts, liked a twelve-syllabled iambic line, as did John Damaskos.

[1] I shall return to the question of musical form in Chapter 52, after the analysis of alchemy has given us further insight into Byzantine world-concepts.

He could not complain directly of church-music or belittle court-music approved by the emperor; and such secular music as existed in streets or show does not come within his intellectualist focus. So he can only complain nostalgically that once music had been fully linked with life, without knowing what positive suggestions to make. However, the advent of such a view shows the powerful secularisation already going on under the religious surface of Byzantine ideas and images. Here, as in so many other ways, Psellos is speaking as a man of the humanist renascence that had already dawned in Byzantium but was not to reach the West for some centuries.

THE ORGAN. We have one interesting example of Byzantine proficency in musical methods giving an important lead to the West. The organ was common at Byzantium, taken over from earlier Rome; it was played in the circus processions, and during banquets and receptions. The earlier type was probably hydraulic, a powerful mechanism: there had been one at Rome that sounded all over the Campus Martius. A relief of the fourth century shows the emperor in the circus, waiting with garlands for the winners, under his throne are two rows of spectators, then a row of girl-dancers, and on each side a small organ like a big panpipe. This kind was worked by wind, as we see from the organists and assistants who work blast-bags with their feet. Julian the Apostate wrote an epigram

> *I see a new kind of reeds. Have they had their birth*
> *maybe out of some strange and brazen earth?*
> *The winds may blow, and yet they do not shake,*
> *but from a cave of bulls-hide breezes break*
> *and (by the roots) pass through the hollow reeds*
> *begetting notes which a grave fellow speeds*
> *with nimble fingers in concerted play:*
> *and the music is pressed through the pipes and blown away.*

This type was portable. In the ninth century a Moslem prisoner saw one played at a reception as the guests sat down—the imperial gold organ; and when it stopped, twenty cymbalists came in and clashed all through the meal.

At times the emperor had two of his gold organs at an entertainment. The factions had each a silver one. Organs gave an harmonious background for ceremonies, generally playing as the singers ended the long-life *akta*; but also playing with singers at times. At a noble's wedding the factions went with their silver organs to the bride's house and played them; she emerged mid acclamations and mounted her horse, while tambourines and cymbals rang. There were no harmonies, but some concords may have been used. Players played with both hands and in octaves, while other instruments brought in a sort of heterophony. Organs were never used for church-services.

Some were sent as gifts to Pepin and Charles in Frankish Gaul, with Byzantine technicians to teach their use. Frankish craftsmen imitated them, and organs were used to help the teachers of plain-chant. As all this work was done by monks, the organ crept into church and spread from church to church, growing bigger till we reach such masterpieces as the great organ of Winchester Cathedral, 980 A.D. Thus the limited technical resources of the West, which kept highly skilled jobs in monkish hands, had the effect of making the organ a church-instrument—though at Rome, where the Byzantine tradition held, even today the Sistine Chapel permits no organ.[1]

FESTIVAL-FORCES. With the failure of political life in the factions, the *akta* were organised as court-ritual—greeting-chants or long-life-wishes. For the Carnival Races a week before sexagesima Sunday the Blues and Greens sang an antiphonal *Springsong* in the Circus:

> So Spring the sweet thing
> sends out anew
> to the Emperor of the Romans
> health and happiness too,
> life and wellbeing strength
> that from God flows
> and Victory godgiven
> over his foes.

A domestik of the Scholai captained each faction, precentor and chief of the performers. There were also two court-choirs and *psaltai* under holy orders.

The emperor was received by the two factions, each with domestik in front, with his head bowed, his hands crossed over the breast (an attitude from the court-ritual of Persia). The singers gave the first *akta*, faction-members making responses. The domestik made the sign of the cross thrice at the emperor. Then the second part of the aktologia began, the domestik again moved head and crossed arms, and so on.

Another Persian-Bagdad element appears in having choirs in curtained niches to sing hymns in the emperor's honour while he received ambassadors in the octagonal chamber. When the emperor entered church, court-choirs and *psaltai* sang together, with responses from the people.

---

1 Sidonius had praised Theoderic for not using the organ even on secular occasions; later Thomas Aquinas opposed the organ as a 'Judaising' force.

11*

On Christmas Eve, the players stood behind the clergy, cut from the people by standard-bearers; and there was an imperial band of trumpets, horns, cymbals, pipers. The emperor mounted the dais and curtains closed on him and his suite; they opened and he stood alone, in a new dress. The song ended, but the music went on till he waved a handkerchief. The *psaltai* sang the festival verses and then, 'Now Christ is born who crowned you King!' Then other verses; the players played; emperor and empress were praised by name; the *psaltai* sang the long-life wishes; the curtains closed; the musicians continued alone, while the standard-bearers prepared to go.

The choirs celebrated all sorts of events, promotion of officials or seasonal feasts. In mid-September the Vintage Feast was held in an open space in the summer-palace's vineyard. After the blessing and presentation of grapes, the factions sang a hymn that began:

> From the field of knowledge
> of the master of wisdom
> we're gathering the flowers outspread
> we of the sacred order of honourable patricians
> having offered up a host of songs
> will crown the head
> and offer a fragrant house of thought,
> for we've shared in his grace with all delight.
> So, king of the universe, as we've besought,
> grant the world a lengthy period
> of festivals of the imperial might
> of the emperor anointed and crowned of God.

At this period, the tenth century, the long-life wishes are kept for imperial *akta*; but by the end of the Empire the ecclesiastics get them too.

MYSTERY-PLAYS. After the breaking-down of the encomiastic shows in church, the *panegyreis* of Maurice, during the iconoclast period, did the dramatic energies of the liturgy once more take precise form? Manuscripts of mystery-plays prove that they did; what remains controversial is the date at which the mystery-play proper emerged in Byzantium. Thus, in a thirteenth-century manuscript we find a play with the actions for each speech carefully described; it opens with the resurrection of Lazarus, moves to the entrance into Jerusalem, the supper at Simon's house, the washing of the feet, the betrayal, Peter's denial, Jesus before Herod, crucifixion and resurrection, the doubting of Thomas. But whether the play itself is thirteenth-century or of earlier date is not settled. On linguistic grounds it has been dated eleventh to twelfth century, and seems a conflation of three pre-existing plays (one on Lazarus, a Passion play based on the Gospels, a Passion play mainly based on the Apocryphals); these three plays were presumably of a much earlier date than the thirteenth century. There is also a link (in the speech of Joseph to Pilate) with the dramatic homilies.

This play seems to have no connection with liturgy or sermon; and was possibly acted outside the church. If so, it perhaps reveals a western influence (at least in its conflated form), and cannot be taken as typical of Byzantine development—though further knowledge may modify that conclusion.

For at least as far as the Church is concerned, we have evidence that the method of liturgic symbolism, dramatically stressed but not moving beyond the sacramental limits, persisted until the fifteenth century. In 1422 a French traveller, Betrandon de la Brocquière, counsellor of Philip the Good, was at St. Sophia:

> One day I saw the patriarch perform a service in their manner, at which were present the emperor, his wife (a very lovely lady, daughter of the emperor of Trebizond) and his brother the despot of the Morea. I waited all day to see their way of doing it—they were putting on a mystery of the Three Children whom Nebuchadnezzar had set in the Furnace. And I was all day without drink or food until vespers.

Bishop Simeon of Thessalonika gives us some account of the method. He is polemising against the Latin Church, and wants to prove his own Church's mysteries to be good and canonical, those of the West profane and bad. He objected to the way the Latins let doves into the church to depict the Holy Ghost, use ox's blood to show Christ's wounds, employ profane settings for gospel-events and lay actors for holy persons. He cites the mystery of the Children in the Furnace as the sole case where his Church used lay actors, as the priests couldn't imitate children; and he mentions that the secular naturalism of the West was kept out, the furnace was represented by wax-candle flames and incense-clouds, the angelic messenger by the image of an angel.

We may generalise, then, by saying that though the Byzantine Church in its later centuries developed many dramatic stresses inside liturgy and festival-services, it did not see liturgic drama transformed into a secular theatre using religious themes. Such developments in that direction as may have occurred could not become centrally significant.

LITERARY AND POPULAR DRAMA. The literary drama continued weakly in Byzantium. We meet poems like that by Ignatios on Adam which take dramatic form and may have been performed or at least publicly read. We hear of a play, *Death of Christ* by Stephen the Sabbaite, written some time during the Iconoclast period. And there is the large-scale *Christos Paschon*, uncertain of date, which seeks to merge Euripidean method and liturgic drama. It was probably read in public, and shows an interesting technique, no doubt developed unintentionally, of a represented scene emerging directly out of narrative—a cinematic sort of transition. The same technique appears in some little secular pieces of later centuries.

But though there is interest in these experiments, they could not create a genuine theatre. From first to last the main streams consisted of developments in the liturgic forms, inside the Church, and others in the popular stage of farce and satire. If we only had texts of the popular theatre our views on Byzantine culture might well gain a surprising enlargement; but unfortunately we know only that it kept on vitally mocking and laughing at the world. Glimpses of the folk-elements which underlay it come tantalisingly out in church-canons and the like. Thus Balsamon in the twelfth century, commenting on the canons of 692, says:

> We see on certain festivals even clergy guising as diverse personages. Sometimes with sword in hand they enter the church, dressed up in soldiers' clothes; sometimes they come dressed as monks, and sometimes as beasts on four feet; and when I asked what authority there was for these practices, I was simply informed that it was the result of ancient custom.

He mentions the clergy (that is, the simple priests who came straight out of peasant or artisan-levels) 'clicking their fingers like drivers, painting their faces, doing female things, and committing other improprieties, to raise a laugh in the lookers-on'. And there were guisings carried on by the guilds. Thus at the festival of Notaries, the grave fellows charged with the education of young men went mumming and masquing all over the city. The guild processions can be guessed at from the sort of thing that continued at Constantinople long after the Turks took over; for in such matters there was direct continuity. But as Vogt says, 'We must resign ourselves to saying that of the Byzantine Stage we know only one thing certainly: that it existed, and that it existed under the form of a *Revue* and *Variety* Theatre, farce-comedy and political satire.'

That this theatre had an effect on the Italian Renascence Theatre is more than likely. Thus there was at Byzantium a festival called the *Bombinaria* or *Bomaria*, the Festival of the Castanettes (or Rattles)—instruments exploited by the comedy-actors. From Justinian's time derivations of the word were used to express activities that mocked at Church and State. The name itself was later given to pieces of the popular Venetian theatre played during wedding banquets. In view of the close cultural relations between Venice and Byzantium the direct borrowing cannot be denied; and further research may yet show how the Byzantine mime, carrying on the forms of ancient mockery and humour, provides the missing link between the ancient theatre and the *Commedia dell'Arte*.[1]

[1] That homily-drama, etc., influenced Byzantine art seems sure, but little work has been done on this difficult subject. It is possible that the patriarch Theophylakt (mid-tenth century) brought about an increased dramatic element in the liturgy—which would explain the hatred of him in the conservative tradition. Kedrenos says he 'introduced the custom, followed even now, that the most splendid and solemn festivities, God and the memory of the saints are insulted by musical frills, laughters, and crazy shrieks which accompany the singing of sacred hymns . . . (presumably at home). Furthermore he gathered a company of infamous fellows and put at their head one Euthymios whom he appointed Domestik of the Church; thus he had performed Satanic dances, bawdy songs, melodies picked up in the streets and whore-houses.'

'In the Far East this mime tradition' of Byzantium 'still flourishes in the character of Karagoz, the Turkish Punch, and may be traced perhaps in certain features of Indian, Japanese and especially Chinese dramatic shows and entertainments. This Eastern mime was introduced to the West during the Renascence period. Not only might *mimi*, after the fall of Byzantium, have come over to Italy, but we have such direct links between East and West as supplied by Caterina Cornero, ex-queen of Cyprus, in whose court were entertainers from the Orient. If this hypothesis be accepted, it is found that a clear explanation is provided for the sudden popularity of the *commedia dell' arte*' in the sixteenth century (Allardyce Nicoll, *The Development of the Theatre*). But mimes may well have visited Venice and South Italy long before the fall of Byzantium.

The *Christos Paschon* may well be by Gregory Nazianzen: it has some 1,500 lines adapted from Euripides, and such centos were popular in the fourth-century (A. Tuilier, *VIᵉ Congrès*).

40

LIGHT-BURST, SAINT-ANGEL AND DANIELS

IMAGERY OF ORDEAL AND LIGHT-BURST. Before I pass on to Literature, I should like to indicate something of the unity of process in Byzantine culture by some remarks based on the mystery-play of the Three Children. Simeon explained that the furnace-effect was gained in the church by a mass of wax-candles and billowing clouds of incense-smoke. We meet here then a dramatic use of the light-burst which we found architecturally expressed in St. Sophia and which there signified the transformation of earth to heaven, to a place of beauty where Christian fellowship was realised. This concept of light-transformation has a profound effect on art, and we noted poems in which a deepening awareness of the effect appears. The complex of ideas is linked in turn with the fire-leap, the sun-fire of apotheosis which is central in both the imperial cult and the hero-worship of the winning charioteer. And in a form which merges imperial and martyr cults it underlay the Monophysite legend of Maurice in the Burning Ship.

The legends of Daniel in the Lion's Den and the Three Children in the Furnace were favourites, felt to express the trials and ordeals of martyrdom, the revelation and apotheosis which redeemed from the present hell and transformed life with the light-burst. Daniel standing between lions resumed an immemorial series of heraldic images of apotropaic power; and in this form he became an emblem of deliverance and salvation, and was painted in the catacombs. In burial liturgies and prayers for the dying he appears in the whole series of deliverance-images:

> Deliver O Lord your servant as you delivered Enoch and Elias from common death, as you delivered Noah from the deluge, Job from his torments, Isaac from his sacrifice, Moses from the hand of Pharoah, Daniel from the lions, the three children from the furnace and Susanna from false accusations.

These invocations, inherited from Jewish formulas, had a magical force; uttered at the grave, they were thought to admit the dead to the land of the just, the banquet of the saints. The Figures of the *Orans* (the soul praying) and of banquets in the catacombs are further equivalents, magically ensuring the salvation of the dead.

Daniel himself became an *Orans*, a type of the soul passing through the jaws of death, an erect figure with arms outstretched or uplifted between two lions, griffins, dragons. He was linked with the rescue of Susanna, defending her against the false charge; and a September lesson in our churches, read till Elizabeth's time, begot Shakespeare's phrase 'A Daniel come to judgment.' He was linked also with the light-burst and the furnace. Thus, his relics were thought to have been translated from Babylon to Alexandria, to the Church of Cyril and John (from which later, when the Venetians were able to challenge Byzantium, they were taken to Venice). The Copts told how a patriarch sent a monk to Babylon for the relics of the Three Children, wanting to put them in a church he had built. The monk sailed off on a cloud, but at the grave was told that they wouldn't come. They promised, however, to honour the church on its dedication day. So, that evening, all lamps were trimmed ready but not lighted, then miraculously they flared up. The furnace-flame of affliction was transformed by faith into the heaven-lights of the glowing church. But despite the failure to gain the Children Daniel had a church built for him by Alexander the Great's tomb where many miracles were worked.

THE REVELATION IN REAL LIFE. Daniel the Stylite Saint of fifth-century Byzantium was named after the prophet. He expressed a wish to have the relics of martyrs laid on his corpse, 'so that if anyone wishes to visit my resting-place to strengthen his faith, he may do reverence to the saints and from them receive the reward of his good deeds and free himself from condemnation'. Therefore, records his biographer, above his body

> lie the relics of the Three Holy Children, Ananias, Azarias, and Misael. These were brought from Babylon by the emperor Leo of pious memory during the lifetime of the holy man. . . . And at the moment of Daniel's blessed death the sovereigns increased their gifts, for they bought tens of thousands of candles and illuminated both Oratories; and beginning at the very top of the column they filled with candles all the spiral scaffolding built for the descent of the holy corpse.

Thus Daniel's death-moment becomes the light-burst of apotheosis, in which the singers of Romanos's hymn become the very angels of the miraculous transformation.

EXALT THE HUMBLE. The Coptic account of Alexander the Great's interview with the Rabbis tells of his amazement at hearing that a prophet, Daniel, had foretold his career. He was then at once converted to Judaism. In art he appears in a symmetrical pattern like Daniel—between two griffins. The reference here is to the tale (told in the French *Gestes* though of Greek-Syrian origin) of his baffled attempt to ascend to heaven by griffin-power. In this guise he appears in San Marco, Venice; the pavement of the great Church of Ovieto; and carved on the façade of Borgo San Donnino.[1]

The intention was to show the king humiliated in his attempt to scale heaven (to achieve apotheosis); on the other hand the humble saint achieves deliverance, light-transformation.

THE DYING-REBORN HERO. The complex is further illuminated by the tales of St. Menas, who in art appears between two camels and is a delivering saviour. We hear of him as an Egyptian soldier in the *numerus* of the Routi-liakoi, who in Diocletian's time went to Phrygia, took refuge in the desert, then appeared before the people in the circus to declare his faith. His head was cut off outside the town and his body burned; but his relics were shared out among the people. In one version he bids his followers put his dead body on a camel and then let the camel go; they are to bury him where the camel stops.

The Ethiopian version says that troops were brought from Phrygia to put down a revolt in the Mareotic region by Alexandria. The prefect went to get Menas' relics as a protection.

> After opening the entry of the place where the body lay, a great light dazzled him, but he hid the body from the inhabitants so that they shouldn't stop him taking it off, and had it borne away in a basket.

On the sea-voyage the troops were attacked by sea-monsters shooting fire from their bodies, with 'long high necks and heads like camels'. But the relics saved them. They landed, 'fought the rebels, invoked St. Menas and his Body, defeated the barbarians, exterminated them through his intercession'. But when they tried to take the relics home, the camel bearing them wouldn't budge; they tried all available camels, but all stood immovable. So the commander had made a wooden image of Menas in soldier's uniform with camels by him; touched the relics with it to get their magical power; and then went home with the image to Phrygia.

Another life (claiming to be by Athanasios) puts Menas under Maximin. The emperor sends the Athenian Hermogenes against the saint. This envoy dreams that Three Men in shining armour announce he'll soon meet the true king. Arriving in Egypt, he argues for three hours with Menas in the circus, but Menas wins. (Menas is called *Kallirhetor*, the Fine Orator; and his defeat of the Athenian is thus a triumph of the new culture over the old.) Next day Hermogenes has his soles cut off, his tongue and eyes removed, and the rest of him sliced up. But Christ puts the bits

[1] Found in pseudo-Kallisthenes, but perhaps interpolated fifth to sixth centuries (going back to Etana myth). (Millet.)

II. REBECCA AT THE WELL AND ST. AUGUSTINE

Mosaics, Palermo, Palatina, twelfth century

together again; and when Hermogenes in repentance orders a funeral, the live man turns up. Hermogenes sees an angel on either side of him and gives up; next day he is baptised in the circus. Maximin comes with 10,000 men, and arrests Menas and Hermogenes. The latter is horribly killed, and Menas is hung in a dungeon with stones on his feet. Angels heal both men, who beard the vaunting emperor in the circus. They are killed again, and stay dead. Menas asks to have his relics taken to Byzantium (only an unimportant provincial town in Maximin's day); the emperor put them in an iron coffin and throws them into the sea. The coffin floats twenty days till it sights Chalkedon: a cloudy column with two torch-angels. Another angel tells the bishop who gets hold of the remains and hides them.

The true cult-centre was the Mareotic area. From the Arabs we know of the large church with statues and paintings, a huge tomb with two marble camels on which a man stands, one foot on each camel. Menas was patron of desert-travellers, and was visited by pilgrims from all over Europe. Excavations in 1905 found thousands of flasks, terracotta ampullai, filled with oil from the sacred lamps or the spring-water—and decorated with the symmetrical pattern of saint and two camels. The cult was very popular in France; the saint had an oratory at Arles. A scrawl on the Mareotic shrine records:

> *Take the beneficient water of Menas*
> *and your sufferings will flee away*
> *Lord help us a man from Smyrna.*

Menas then has his light-burst, his symmetrical beasts, his three shining men; and he is a persuasive talker, a Daniel come to judgment.

THE POINT OF WORLD-CHANGE. George of Cappadocia, bishop of Alexandria, was mobbed by pagans on Julian's accession, bound on a camel and paraded through the streets, then torn to pieces and burned. And Ali, the first Imam of Islam, who starts off the line of divinely ordained successors of the Prophet and who was murdered in a mosque at Kufa, is said to have climbed wounded on a camel and been carried off into the desert. Years later, Harun al Raschid, led by a deer that he hunted, came across the bones of Ali and the camel. A shrine was built on the spot and the town of Najah rose there—an important ritual centre where the hope of world-end and total transformation was uttered.

EARTHLY ANGELS. The Orthodox outlook remained much more concrete and earthly than the Latin. The idea of earth transformed by light and grace into a heavenly place is basic in it; and the light-burst we have been considering is only an aspect of the general Neoplatonist system (given a dynamic force unknown to the Neoplatonists themselves) which we traced in the belief that liturgic song transformed the church into heaven and the singers into angels.

For the Neoplatonist element we may recall the Luminous Apparition, common in theurgy: they may be traced to the *Chaldean Oracles* where certain spells bring up 'Fire shaped like a Boy' or 'an unshaped Fire with a Voice coming from it'. Chaldeans showed Julian Fire-bright Phantasms, and Proklos claimed to have seen Light-shaped Phantasms of Hekate, for which Hippolytos gives us the dangerous recipe. We hear of an adept making the eyes of statues blaze with light; and the papyri tell of *Light-guidance*. One of Porphyry's oracles speaks of 'the pure Fire compressed into holy Forms' (*typoi*).

Monks were long thought of as angels. Up to the seventh century they were commonly addressed as *Your Angel*—a phrase then modified into *Angelic* or *Equal-to-angels*. *Your Angelic Presence* seemed the natural way of speaking to a monk, and we continually meet monkish garb described as 'the angelic habit of a monk'. Anastasios was fortified by the State, but, we are told, through the deeds of St. Theodore of Sykeon it became 'ruled and inhabited by angels' under King Christ.

Augustine in the West, combining the Manicheism and the Neoplatonism which had deeply affected him, devised the notion of the Two Cities, giving a richer and more complex meaning to the Stoic phrase. In this notion Church and State, Earth and Heaven (the historical resolution of the fundamental contradictions of the existing world), are both entwined and cut apart. But in the Orthodox view the problem was to realise unity here and now, to grasp the transformative factor in experience in the greatest fullness possible. While in the State-Church, this led to elaborate concepts of reconciliation, in the heresies begotten by the total cultural complex, of which the State-Church was only one factor, the demand for unity was opposed to all existing forms and the deepest possible dynamic of revolt set up. That was why the West had to wait for the eastern heretical stream to flow into its new towns before it could generate basic idioms of revolt. And that was why, also, the eastern cultural complex generated such a tremendous artistic energy, which, continually flowing in on the West, at last raised its levels to the point where the Renascence was possible

LIGHT-TRANSFIGURATION. A few more examples to show how central was this light-image of Byzantine power and piety. Mark the Deacon from Gaza was present at the baptism of Arkadios' son, Theodosios.

And all the city was hung with garlands and decorated with silks and tassels of gold and all sorts of other decorations: no one could utter its splendour. You saw the multitudes of citizens like the waves of the sea, various with all kinds of clothes. But it's past my power to describe that splendour's glory. I leave it those the experts in words and turn to my own true story. When the baby had been baptised and came out of the church for the palace, again you saw the goodliness of the host going ahead, and their shining clothes. They were all dressed in white, the whole host seemed covered with snow: first the patricians, and illustrious, and all the dignities, with the troops of soldiers, all carrying candles: it seemed the stars were glistening out on earth.

And close to the baby was the emperor in person with a happy gleaming face, brighter than his purple; and a noble held the baby in bright robes. And we marvelled at the sight of such glory. Then St. Porphyrios said to us, 'If earthly things which soon fade may have such glory, much more the heavenly things, which eye has not seen or ear heard, neither have they entered into the heart of man.'

Both East and West Byzantium were thought to have strange gem-fires. In the *chansons de geste* Charlemagne goes to Byzantium to see the wonder-palace of the emperor lighted by a single carbuncle. The Moslems said a statue of the Virgin in St. Sophia held a carbuncle as big as a pigeon's egg that lighted up the church at night.[1]

---

[1] Evliya has a confused account of its removal to Rome on the Prophet's birth-night (a dangerous moment for talismans), and some Spanish infidels got hold of it. (Origins go back to the pseudo-Kallisthenes on Alexander and to Lucian's account of the Syrian Goddess. Compare the underground treasure-room guarded by a talismanic statue of an archer and lighted by a single carbuncle in the tale generally linked with Virgil or Gerbert, etc.)

41

LITERATURE, A GENERAL SURVEY

DILEMMA. Byzantine Literature is not as great as Byzantine Art; it lacks the universal quality, the mass-element, except in religious terms. For, though the literacy of the later Roman Empire must have been on a fairly high level, the fusion of mass-elements and the humanist or philosophic tradition of antiquity could not go on thoroughly except in the religious sphere and its direct offshoots. Though the complete gap between learned speech or writing and the vernacular which soon showed up in the West was never present in the East, yet the written language moved steadily away from common speech; it was something learned by study of the Attic classics and written as a *tour-de-force*. Thus, in modified ways, the gap between learned levels and ordinary people occurred in the East as in the West; but because the gap was never decisive and elements from below could to some extent infiltrate, Byzantine literature kept a vital and broadly based character which was quite lacking in the West till the twelfth century.

The basic dilemma of Byzantine literature appeared in the fact that when the writer moved fully into the mass-area he became a religious polemist or expounder, and when he tried to draw on the humanist positions of the pagan past he tended to fall into the élite-attitudes of that past. Still, there were continual efforts made to find points of fusion between the new Christian culture with its mass-basis and the limited humanist and scientific definitions of antiquity; and thus Byzantine literature moved slowly, despite checks, towards the synthesis which finally issued in the Italian Renascence. There the conflict of a humanist élite with mass-elements expressed in religious terms still went on, but at a higher level. What is important to grasp, however, is that the antecedents of the western Renascence lie in the Byzantine world, where the work of transforming the ancient heritage to the point where the Renascence was possible was carried out.

THE STAGES. Byzantine literature may be roughly divided into four sections. The first is that which stretches from Constantine to Justinian, when the last defences and expositions of paganism are made, when Christianity makes its first large-scale and stable statements of position and begins working out its inner conflict in terms of dogma, when ancient methods of history-writing are carried to their conclusion and attempts to find how to apply Christian idioms to history are made, and when the inheritance of Graeco-Roman poetry is reoriented.

The second is that during which the Islamic threat is met and broken. Much of the works written during this period have been lost, *i.e.* the iconoclast literature which the orthodox destroyed. But from what we have we can see the deep rooting of Christian positions, the continued development of new attitudes to history and the transformation of classical forms in poetry. A broad basis of humanism is laid, which persists, with varying fortunes, till the last days.

The third period begins in the mid-ninth century and carries on till 1204. The humanist attitudes persist, despite their own increasing limitations, despite the triumph of orthodoxy; for the defeat of the Iconoclasts and of the Paulicians has weakened the inner life of the Church, so that its triumph is in one way its defeat. A vast work of scholarship begins, with Photios as the transitional figure between iconoclast secularism and the new synthesis of humanism and orthodoxy. At the same time the popular forces are gaining in strength, and new epic forms are being hammered out.

The fourth period comes after the expulsion of the Latins and continues till 1453. It once more takes up the work of humanist scholarship; and though lacking the energy of the preceding phases, it does invaluable work in building the positions most useful for the rising forces of the West which want to absorb the humanist elements of the Graeco-Roman past.

THE FIRST STAGE. The fourth and fifth centuries had historians of the most diverse tendencies, pagans and Christians, rhetoricians and writers in whom the vernacular roughly intrudes, upholders of the aristocratic tradition and men who already begin to write for the mass-audience of monks and simple folk. Eusebios of Kaisareia made the first grand effort to combine the reach and scope of the great Graeco-Roman historians with the new evolutionary sense derived from the Christian belief that events moved coherently and progressively towards a culminating transformation. In his *History* the first part set out the materials ; in the second (the *kanones*) he gave his synthesising treatment of Jewish and Gentile histories.

The *kanones* were translated by Jerome and thus obtained at once, even in the West, a position of undisputed authority. The Latin medieval chronicle is founded on Eusebios, whose name together with his translator's, quite overshadowed all other workers in the same field, whether earlier or later.

The sixth century saw in Prokopios, with his keen sardonic mind and study of the Greek classical historians (especially Thucydides), one who carried the method of ancient history to its culmination. Ostensibly a Christian, he is in fact the last of the Roman aristocratic historians. He seems a Syrian; and despite his passionate concern for the Empire, he is bitterly aware of its discords and contradictions:

(i) Then, at last, and hardly, to the few and destitute surviving Libyans, came a period of peace.

(ii) Anxious to unite all men in the same opinion about Christ, he indiscriminately destroyed dissidents, and that under the pretext of piety; for he did not think that the killing of men was murder unless they happened to hold his own religious views.

(iii) What has happened to the wealth of the Romans is a theme for disputation. Some men assert it has all passed over to the barbarians; others think the emperor has locked it up in a lot of treasure-chambers. When Justinian dies—supposing he is human—or when he renounces his incarnate existence, if he is a lord of demons—the survivors will ascertain the facts.

In that grim conception of Justinian as a demon he shows the new forces; the thrust of the new sense of great potences, fears and hopes, which is Christianity. A medieval conception reigns at the heart of what seems at first glance an Hellenic rationalism; and the new orientation also appears in the many picturesque elements of description, such as those cited above about Byzantium's site and St. Sophia.

The turmoil of styles continues, Agathias, lawyer and poet as well as historian, writes in a precious and cadenced style, keen for metaphors but not very original, aware of the wide clash of forces. 'All things human have been set in motion.' Theophylaktos of Simokatta is even more flowery, aphoristic, allusive. John Malalas, a Syrian of Antioch (*Malalas* is Syrian for *rhetor*), writes a history from Adam to Justinian for the common man, the monk, and sees an odd hurlyburly: Britain he thinks a town and the Myrmidons of the Trojan war he indentifies with the Bulgarians. In him we meet the manifest medieval compiler.

The popular intrusion appears too in mythical histories, *i.e.* of the Trojan Wars, or fantasy-history, such as the compilation of legends and romances about Alexander the Great; and in collections of proverbs, animal fantasies coming out of Egypt and Syria.

Also many uninspired manuals on agriculture, astrology, astronomy, antiquaries, geography—even a verse geography by John of Gaza which identifies the four cardinal points with the four arms of the cross. John Lydos, a clerk who became a shorthand writer and rose fairly high in the civil service at the age of sixty, wrote discursively on Miracles, Months and Magistracies. Kosmas, retired ship-captain, tried to build up a rectangular earth and universe to satisfy Biblical geography, but had more strictly scientific attitudes as well—*i.e.* he measured the human shadow both at Axum and at Alexandria. John Philoponos of Alexandria tried to argue rationally against pagans and provided (via the Syrian heretics) the link between the nominalism of Antisthenes and the western medieval school of Roscelin. Translations from Greek medical writers were being made into Latin, especially in North Italy.

In theology the three great Cappadocian Fathers of the fourth century, Basil and the two Gregories, stabilised the relations of orthodox creed with pagan philosophy and rhetoric. John of the Golden Mouth added a more social note, addressed to the common man, and was rather opposed to compromise with pagan disciplines. Byzantine mysticism (which we have discussed in Maximos) took first shape in Evagrios and the pseudo-Dionysios, on whose works commentaries went on being written till the thirteenth century.[1] From the ninth century *The Heavenly Hierarchies* had a strong effect on the West too. Michael II sent a copy, which, translated by Erigena, had an influence on many later thinkers such as Aquinas.

Lives of Saints increased, and in the fifth and sixth centuries a vast number were written, often genuine biographies in which the miraculous element consists of faith-healings and lively pictures of life in town and country are given.

In poetry the fourth to fifth centuries saw an important Egyptian school, to whom Claudian belonged—he wrote in Greek before he went to Italy and became the imperial poet of Rome's last years of glory. Palladas, Cyros, Julian, Nonnos, Kollouthos, Tryphiodoros, Christodoros of Koptos : these men carried on the epigram or the *eidyllion*, with new orientations. Nonnos, whose main work is a vast epic on the expedition of Dionysos to India, is the most interesting. Though his *Dionysiaka* as a whole is prolix and indeterminate (beginning with the Rape of Europa and reaching its theme only in the thirteenth book), in parts it is genuinely original and lively, developing a new kind of hexameter in which accentual rhythms are appearing and the dominant elements are lightness, speed, elegance. Its imagery moves towards effects of transformation, bringing something quite new into poetry, something that links with alchemic ideas.[2]

And if the poem *A Day* found in papyri is by Pamprepios, we have another Egyptian poet, in whom the Nonnan method is successfully

[1] It owed much to Gregory of Nyssa, whose platonising attitudes had interesting parallels with Neoplatonic mysticism.
[2] There is a strong Christian influence. The epic is a pagan aretalogy closely modelled in structure, though not in detail, on the Christian aretalogy of the Gospels.

applied to a lengthy account of landscape and labour—something of the quality which *The Vigil of Venus* and the African school had been gaining in late Latin poetry, but with more intellectual background.

AMONG THE HERETICS. But we must not forget the culture of the heretical groups. In dealing with the Church in Persia we have seen how an Aristotelian approach and a rooted interest in practical applications of science, especially of medicine, were dominant in the Nestorians. The Monophysites also were keen Aristotelians. The need for orthodox theologians to reply adequately to the heretical positions forced the Aristotelian idiom into the orthodox areas as well. Thus, under Justinian, Leontios in his polemics against the heretics drew on Aristotelian terms and arguments. The basis was laid for the Aristotelianism on which the western middle-ages were later to develop their systems of logic and foster the first stages of a thorough-going scientific outlook.

The main contribution of the heretics, however, and the main way in which their systems entered the West, was the effect they had on Arabic thought. Indeed to speak of Arabic thought is a misnomer: the thought is Arabic largely in language only. It is Greek-Syriac thought translated into Arabic, and after some centuries fused with Persian and Hindu contributions. From this development of Greek-Syriac thought within the Islamic area came the works which, translated into Latin (largely through the Jews in Spain), provided the main basis of western scholasticism and medieval science. Not that only versions from Arabic affected the West from the eleventh century on. There were also many translations direct from Greek, made in the Byzantine area of South Italy.

The great contribution of the Syrian heretics to the medieval West must, however, not be undervalued. It was fundamental.

SECOND STAGE. The sixth century saw the florid prose of Theophylaktos, who wrote a *Natural History* and eighty-five *Letters* (Moral, Rustic and Amatory) as well as a *History*; he was an Asiatic who went to Egypt with his prefect father. John of Nikiou, on the other hand, is an Egyptian historian with a straightforward popular style who depicts the tumults of mass-resistance in his Monophysite native-land. There were also alchemists, medical writers, geographers.

The seventh century was one of radical readjustments with a few strong figures like Maximos; the eighth century saw the iconoclast wave. Only writers with an orthodox outlook have been let survive. In history and theology they are often competent. Abbot Theophanes shows a mixture of learned and popular elements; in George the Monk the latter dominate.

For George the iconoclast Leo is a monster born of an Assyrian lioness and an Armenian panther (*i.e.* Islam and Paulicianism), Constantine V is a mere monkey. His work in its vernacular style had a vast influence on early Slavonic literature, especially in Russia, and also in Georgia.

The disciplines of ancient study revived, and even a certain amount of scientific work was done. Leo the Mathematician studied grammar and poetry at Byzantium, rhetoric, philosophy and arithmetic in Andros; he went round the monasteries, studying in the libraries. Advanced in geometry, astronomy, music, he returned to Byzantium. The tale went that the emperor discovered his worth through a Moslem attempt to lure him to Bagdad. He was made State-professor with the church of the Forty Martyrs for his school, was deposed when Theophilos died, but after all set in charge of the new university of the Magnaura. He it was who devised the code of telegraphic fire-signals from the frontier.

John the Grammarian was so interested in science that a lot of malignant stories were made up against him by the monks. He was said to have an underground chamber for auguries and sacrifices, where he was aided by naughty nuns. Photios too was blackguarded: he had been given a charm by a Jew for denying Christ. John the Solitary, after talking about him, had a dream in which a black man gripped his throat and declared himself Lebuphas, the familiar of Photios. 'I am the helper of wizards; the guide of robbers and adulterers, the friend of pagans and my secret servant Photios. He sent me to punish you for what you said yesterday against him, but you have defeated me by the power of the cross.'

At Byzantium the most important iconodule writer was Theodore of Stoudios, who tried to reform monasticism by giving the monks some useful work, and who wrote sermons, epigrams, acrostics, hymns. His letters and funeral orations have at times an unembarrassed tenderness and vigour; and it is a proof of the inability to evade the new humanism that this fervent monk cultivates Lucianic irony and Demosthenic amplitude as well as a prophetic force.

But the outstanding theologian was John of Damaskos, who grew up in Islam, held high office under the caliph, and later went to the laura of St. Sabas near Jerusalem. He composed many hymns, set the Service Books in order, and wrote *The Fountain of Knowledge*, the first comprehensive exposition of Christian dogma, which underlies all similar work later done in both East and West. In the thirteenth century it was used by Thomas Aquinas as the model for his *Summa Theologiae*. John sees human development as a series of phases each essential in its time and place, with Christ's revelation cleaving history but not ending it. That revelation John defines as turning men into new ways and providing a goal, not a rigid set of dogmas. More important even than the sacred texts are the ceaseless labours of men to understand, to grow along the new way. Otherwise, 'the slow destruction of that which is tradition is the same as that which the removal of the foundation-stone would signifiy: soon the whole edifice would collapse.'

He accepts the world. 'I am a man and clad in a body. I desire, I need, in the body, to know and possess what is sacred.' He wants a true simplicity. Have not the common folk, he asks, the right to demand that we speak to them in terms that they are capable of grasping? And he attacks persecution. 'All that is done by force and not by conviction is brigandage.'

Thus, out of the iconoclast attack, is born the new breadth of comprehensions on which a stable intellectual advance within the given framework is made possible. Between Monophysite Aristotelianism and John of Damaskos' systematic exposition, the whole scope of Scholasticism is already defined.

Poetry moved towards medieval levels under Heraklios, in the historical epics of George of Pisidia, and in his *Hexameron*, a poem on the Creation which transposes Heraklios' Persian Wars allegorically into myth-terms. A Russian translation of the latter poem was made as late as the fourteenth century. *Hexameron* seeks to express in iambics the world renewed by Heraklios, who thus becomes a sort of demiurge. The new forces of Jehovah-Heraklios reject the ancient world:

> As Euklid's outdone by Bees, Orpheus by Swans,
> so let the Neoplatonists be dumbed by peasants.

And a magnificent religious poem, the *Akathistos*, probably written in 626 as a thanksgiving for Byzantium's preservation, combines a soaring, breathless exaltation with dramatic exposition.[1]

NEW FORCES. We get hints of the popular elements bursting through. Thus, at news of a revolt in Sicily the emperor remarked to an official, 'We may congratulate ourselves, Magister, on this revolt'; and the magister replied, 'Sire, it is no matter for congratulation', citing:

> The beginning of wars will fall on the earth
> when the reign of the Babylonian Dragon has birth
> come with greed of gold and black roaring forth.

[1] A Latin translation, probably made about 825 at St. Denis, spread through Gaul and reached St. Gall; it is known in eleventh to thirteenth century MSS., and was widely diffused in the West, where it seems to have influenced a new genre, the *versus*. Certainly it directly inspired the *versus*, *Ave sponsa insponsata* (M. Huglo, *Le Muséon*, 1951, lxvi, 1–2).

—clearly a verse-oracle whispered during the Heraklian wars. And in the tale of Theophilos' marriage we meet the use of verse-impromptu (reminding of folk-custom). The situation was that of the Brideshow: when there was any doubt about a suitable bride, there was a custom of sending officials round in the provinces with measurements to find girls of outstanding beauty, who were brought to Byzantium, and the prince chose one of them. This brideshow was made for Theophilos, whose stepmother gave him a gold apple to present to the winner. He saw the poetess Kasia and said, 'A woman was the primal source of all mans' tribulation', and she capped his line, 'And yet from woman came the force of man's regeneration.' Daunted, he gave the apple to a silent girl, and Kasia became a nun.

When the Empire wanted to gain the fort of Saniana on the Halys, which rebels held, an envoy won over the monastery steward by using the peasant Gyberis, a known singer of songs. Gyberis approached the place and sang:

> *Hearken Steward to Guberis*
> *at his message do not frown*
> *you shall win New Kaisareia.*
> *If I get Saniana Town*
> *you shall get a Bishop's Gown.*

The steward heard, understood, and was won over to the emperor.

A semi-popular trend appears in the work of the ninth-century deacon Ignatios (later Metropolitan of Nikaia) who transcribed the Life and Fables of Aesop of Phrygia, which he edited under the name of Gabrias; he wrote quatrains and little pieces like the playlet *On Adam* (150 lines of which 54 are a prologue addressed to the audience). It has the verse, 'For nowhere is a place that's outside God'. The characters are God, Adam, Eve, Serpent.

In the ninth century, as I have mentioned, the pseudo-Dionysios began to affect the West, and with him Maximos. John the Scot, Erigena, admitted that he managed to grasp the 'obscurest' idea of the former writer only through the 'marvellous manner' of Maximos' *Commentary*. He called Maximos 'the divine philosopher, the all-wise, the most distinguished of teachers', and translated into Latin his work on Gregory the Theologian. But such an Irish scholar of Greek as John was the exception in the West, and his attitude was a token of what was to come rather than of any solid advance as yet.

THIRD STAGE. Now comes an expansion in all fields from the bases laid during the iconoclast period. The classical revival, with passing setbacks, went on growing in strength. The study of Homer had never ceased.

Kometas in the tenth century amended and repunctuated; Niketas in the eleventh saw an allegory in every line; and Psellos considered himself the restorer of Schedography, minute grammatical analysis of selected passages (a method distrusted by Anna Comnena); and when the first wife of Manuel, a German, arrived, her first request was for Tzetzes to explain the *Iliad* and *Odyssey*, so that he called her the Homer-smitten Lady.

The study of Plato was revived. Arethas and Psellos wrestled with his work; and Psellos gives an amusing picture of Romanos III's effort to be a philosophic king and penetrate Plato's thought; John Mauropos was another devotee, and Italos was drawn by Pythagoreanism into heresy.

Large-scale work of compilation, codification, encyclopedic exposition went on. Photios with his summaries of books read, Constantine VII with his antiquarian projects, Arethas with his library and commentaries. . . . There are many historians, including men who wrote about their own experiences, like John Kamniates who told of the sacking of Thessalonika by Cretan corsairs. Legal writers, writers of polemics and homiletics, agricultural and medical works, hagiographers, compilers of old-wives' tales like those on the origin of Byzantium. And many of these men have strong personalities, Psellos versatile, conceited and yet full of shrewd insights and an endless zest for life and art; Kekaumenos chatting on his war-experiences and the ethics of the feudal noble; Leo the Deacon with his simple, vivid style of history; the learned friends of Psellos, Xiphilin and Mauropos, fine scholars and enthusiasts for law, poetry, knowledge, swung between court-life and monastery; Symeon the Younger with his ecstatic rhythmical outpourings, the climax of the tradition of Maximos.

In prose, important influences are pressing in from the East. *Baarlam and Ioseph* comes in from Georgian, a Christianised version of Buddha's life, a fine religious romance with vivid apologues; and *Stephanite and Ichnelatos* (*Kalilah and Dimnah*) from India also, via Persia. The probable translator of *Baarlam* was St. Euthymios, who did many translations from Georgian. His version spread among the Latins and the Slavs (also the Rumanians, probably via a Bulgarian version).[1]

The poets were many and excellent. John Geometres, who depicts the terrible devastation and the sufferings of the peasantry under war and famine, and, though a monk, delights in the beauty of earth:

> *The soft narcissus leaps joyous from earth and bold*
> *the anemone and crocus of gracious gold,*
> *the swallow pours out its song with never a rest*
> *and chatters like a girl in its morning nest . . .*

---

[1] South Italy was a diffuser of Greek literary culture as well as art. Thus, Sabbas, a rich landed proprietor of the eleventh to twelfth centuries there, had a large Greek library.

He faithfully admires Nikephoros Phokas; 'Six years the people's government I worthily held . . .' and bravely states what he thinks of his murderer:

> *Love of vile tyranny swayed my every hour,*
> *I wet my hand in blood and raped the sceptre of power.*

John Mauropous with his love of books:

> *Living among my books like a bee among flowers*
> *nourisht on words like a grasshopper on dew.*

Constantine of Rhodes singing the beauty of St. Sophia or satirising a courtier. Kometas able to call up ancient echoes:

> *Tell me, shepherd, whose trees in a row? They are olives*
> *of Pallas, but the vine for Bromios grows.*
> *whose then is the corn? Demeter's. Which of the gods*
> *owns the flowers? Hera and One who herself is a rose.*
> *Pan, dear Pan, touch the pipe with your lips, for somewhere*
> *lurks Echo in this nook where the sunlight is closed.*

Christopher of Mityele, a humanist who turns to satire, exposing a monk Andrew who collects relics, and relic-speculating imposters. (Psellos attacked a drunken monk in verses parodying the Mass.)

Simeon Metaphrastes collected and elaborated *The Lives of the Saints*; and many new ones of value were written, such as that of Andrew the Good with its picture of Byzantium's poor, the slave-market, bakeries, wine-bars, gangs of depraved guttersnipes, greedy monks, street-huxters with fruit in jars, eunuchs with blonde ringlets, whores evading the watch, drunkards picked up, peasants rolling drunk in ox-carts. Even the street-mongrels evade the saint. 'Don't you see how big your sins are?' he muses. 'Even the dogs avoid you and won't accept you as a dog, one of themselves.' And against this misery is set the vision of paradise, the journey into the future with a spirit-guide.

Or *The Life of St. Theoktiste of Lesbos*, the lonely woman on the wasted island, which is more than halfway to a romance-form.

Satirical prose too awakes. *Philopatris, The Patriot*, satirises the clergy with considerable virulence. The author, like John Geometres, is a believer in the work of Nikephoros Phokas. *Timarion* adroitly attacks medical obscurantism.

And a new force appears fully revealed, that of the popular epic, born of the marchlands where Paulicians and Clubmen and frontier-guards were to be found, fighting and fraternising with the Moslems. The first example is the lay of *Armouris*, which records the elation felt when the Euphrates was once more crossed and the Arabs driven back under Michael III;

and the full-grown form appeared in *Digenes Akritas* of the tenth to eleventh centuries, a bold, sweeping work, in which the romance becomes epic with the theme of union between Greek and Moslem.

The Carols of St. Basil, still sung in Greek areas, have elements of popular poetry going even further back than the lays; and there had been a growth of lyric forms going on—the love-poems in a fifteenth-century manuscript, called for no special reason Rhodian, are earlier than this manuscript. When the Byzantines rose and brought down Michael V, 'The people of the city and the market-place', says Psellos, 'made up dance-groups and composed *tragoudai* on these events, making up the songs on the spot.' And Liutprand says in 958 that songs against the sons of Romanos Lekapenos (in 945) 'are sung not only in Europe but also in Asia and Africa'. And Anna Comnena tells how scurrilous pamphlets were thrown into the tent of her father the emperor; her term *phamousa* (*famosi libelli*) shows the continuous tradition of such popular outlets from the early empire.

FOURTH STAGE. History had risen again in the years before the sack in the work of Anna Comnena, and Niketas Akominatos told of the sack itself; in the later centuries the line was continued, at times as in the work of Doukas, constituting a form of memoir and apologia by an actor in the events described. George Phratzes, an eyewitness of the fall of 1453, closed the series.

In the twelfth century the romance-poems of Prodromos and Eugenianos imitated the old Greek prose-romance, but in the next century the western romance had impacted and several long poems were written under its influence. Of more interest were the satiric poems of Prodromos in the form of animal fables, his begging poems with their mocking serious appeal:

> *Deliver me from poverty, loose me from hunger's rack,*
> *drive off the scorns of the world and all my creditors' attack.*

He laments the married state and abuses two abbots who presided over a monastery in which he was monk. A prose-satire, anonymous, arranges a set of curses on the lines of the Mass.[1] Manuel Philes carries on the mock-and-serious begging form. The anon *Book of Fruits* describes a lawsuit by Grape before King Quince; the titled fruits and vegetables, who compose the characters, satirise the court.

Two valuable collections of epigrams, reaching far back into ancient

---

1 There was something of satan-worship (if not in Michael III's jokes) in the Mass of the Soanos, the Beardless (thirteenth to fourteenth centuries.)

Hellas and coming forward into Byzantine days, were made—in the eleventh century by Kephalas, and in the fourteenth by Planoudes. The work of compiling encyclopedic works had continued from the days of Photios by Tzetzes, "Suidas," Gregoras, Pachymeres and others. And humanist studies gained rather than lost in force as the doom of Byzantium grew surer. I shall glance later at the part played by men like Pilatos, Michael Chrysoloras, Plethon and other Greek scholars in the Italian Renascence. Here it is enough to note the way in which from iconoclast days the humanist tradition advanced in Byzantium—and the limitations of that advance. Because of the contradiction which I have discussed, the humanist thought in some ways had less and less roots in the popular life of the Byzantine world, while refining its techniques and perceptions. What it drew from the social situation of Byzantium was an ardent patriotism for Hellas, for the classical heritage; but it knew nothing of the mass-elements which on the one hand created the hero of the frontier, Digenes, and on the other hand built up the peasant heresies of world-rejection. Its Platonism was a retreat from the world of the masses, a looking-back to Hellas as to a pre-existence of the soul. But the elements which it was abstracting from the Byzantine situation were highly valuable for the West which was now seeking to break the bonds of scholasticism forged out of Aristoteleanism.

CONCLUSIONS. What, then, is our general judgment on Byzantine literature? There are no great works, in the sense in which the writings of Homer and Aischylos, Plato and Aristotle, Sappho and Theokritos are great—or those of Dante and Chaucer, Rabelais and Villon, Cervantes and Shakespeare. But, taken in the mass, the virtue is high indeed—nothing less than the total transformation of ancient culture into the levels from which the development of modern European culture was possible. Byzantine literature is a literature of transition, unstable, confused, torn by contradictory impulses which it cannot resolve.

And yet when that is said, what a gigantic work of creative struggle appears in the total achievement. The line of historians that stretches from Eusebios and Prokopios to Doukas and Phrantzes; the line of theologians that stretches from the three Cappodocians to John of Damaskos and Symeon, and includes the Monophysites who handed Aristotlean studies to the Islamic world; the line of encyclopedists from Photios to Pachymeres; the line of humanists from Constantine V to Plethon—there is something here that humanity cannot afford to forget. And though there is no poetry of the highest scope or intensity, yet the development between Nonnos and Constantine of Rhodes is not something which can be waved away; and poets like Romanos on one side or the author of *Digenes* on the other are of world-stature.

We have only to set this tremendous work of assimilation and transformation next to what happened in the West between Augustine and Abaelard to realise what it meant to civilisation, how indispensable it has been to European development. After 1204, however valuable were certain Byzantine aspects, the central function in European development is gone. Set a poet like Prodromos next to his western contemporary, the Archpoet, and he is seen as fairly matched; set the humanists next to men like Petrarch and Boccaccio and they are outmatched; set the best of Byzantine writers of the fourteenth to fifteenth centuries next to Dante or Chaucer, and they are dwarfed. Nevertheless, the incomparable significance of Byzantine culture between 326 and 1204 remains.

42

TRANSFORMATIONS

NONNOS. I have given a very cursory statement of the development of Byzantine literature; and to make my remarks a little more concrete, I propose now to look in slightly more detail at a few of the items mentioned. Even these can only be glanced at, but a closer scrutiny, however hurried, will serve to bring out something of the richness of the development. First I shall take the poet Nonnos and one of the early saints' lives; then Photios and Psellos; then the epic *Digenes Akritas*; then some of the later prose.

First, then, Nonnos. His work has been slighted by scholars who look in it for classical qualities; but if we ask what new elements it brings, we find it of much interest despite its failure as an epic. Its origins we must look for in popular levels rather than in classical. Thus, already in the second to third centuries we find in Christian chant in the Egyptian area a breakdown of old forms, a mingling of quantitative and accentual metres, a union of ancient Egyptian prophetic idioms with the new demands of Christianity. Here we touch the core of the transformation-theme, the desperate need to reverse all values, to realise Christ as the fire of righteousness and cleansing, the innermost heart of the pang of human change.

Now you may enter on your heritage, now is the time to give, now, richly to the Poor.
God has commanded to give nourishment to the beggars. Serve the Beggars and the Weak,
*   that you may escape from Hell.*
Jesus is he whom the Father has sent to suffer, who holds eternal life, who holds immor-
*   tality's glory.*
He has brought good tidings to the Children, saying: the Poor shall have the Kingdom,
*   the Poor shall become the inheriting Sons . . .*
Jesus is Rest for those afflicted. He is the Terror, he is the Terrible Fire for the unjust . . .
Christ is the Support of the saints, Christ is Hell for the unjust.

Add the imagery of popular charm and spell. Here is fifth-century spell against headache, one of the spells aimed at controlling change, at transforming pain to well-being:

> *The house of the mystics is burned down . . .*
> *burned down on the mountains . . .*

there were seven fountains
and seven dark-eyed maidens prayed
to the dark nymphs to quench the untiring fire
and that's how the grievous fire of the head
flees from the head and flees . . .

Nonnos draws on these sources of imagery. At times he gains a rhetorical concision, as in 'Sing today on earth, tomorrow sing on Olympus'. But his main interest, apart from the new metrical possibilities he opens out, lies in the detail where contemporary attitudes force their way in, the new uses of imagery and the fantasy-method. At times the result is merely quaint, though giving myth a new realism. Artemis, bathing, moves cautiously through the water, lifts her tunic little by little, keeps its edge on the surface of the water, holds her feet and thighs together as she washes her body. This is not the ancient mountain-ranger but a girl of Nonnos' own day. Similarly Astraios takes a horoscope of his mother Persephone; or myth becomes a homely genre as when Phaethon, longing for his father, makes a little car like the sun, with a round bunch of white flowers for the morning star and so on, till he plays 'with the burning yokestraps and the whips of stars'.

But more important is the play of fantasy throughout, in which we see a world of once-stable relations breaking up, new potences emerging. Snakes shoot themselves like arrows and twine round the legs of runners; Dionysos sends vines leaping out of earth to tangle elephants' feet. At times we thus get a new fusion of images. 'Crowds of citizens with forests of fluttering hands.' And a sense of profound change, of fusions of opposites, haunts the narrative with profuse transformation pictures:

In vain I hurl the lengthy shaft. Instead of a boar
a flame uninjured flickers in the air . . .
I see a tree and aim at it, it's off
and I see a spirit of water curve in the skypath . . .

He spotted his body into a dappleback panther
he turned his limbs to a tree and a selfgrown spire
he rose up straight from the earth shaking his leaves
whistling a counterfeit whisper to the northwind . . .

The mast was a cypress with a shade of leafy green,
ivy sprang from the mastbox running into the sky . . .
The tumbling waves of the sea broke into flowers
here grew a rose and reddened the swell of the foam
rounded upon it . . .

She threw a snake at an oak and the snake curled round
and turned into moving ivy that coiled round the trunk . . .

> *The waves of the river covered her up and Kronion*
> *turned her into a fountain her breasts became spouts*
> *of falling water the stream her body the blossoms*
> *her hair her bow the horn of the horned river*
> *bullshaped the bowstring changed to a rush the whistling*
> *arrows to singing reeds the quiver passed through*
> *to the muddy bed of the river and changed to a channel*
> *hollow pouring its sounding waves out . . .*

There is an alchemic quality which goes beyond the metamorphoses of a classical poet like Ovid. There are links too with wall-painting: in the last-cited passage we seem to see the quivering image subside to a statue or fresco. At times there is a dream-touch:

> *So the mating was like a dream . . .*
> *I have seen the slope where a woman*
> *is inexplicably mated beside the bridal rock*
> *I have seen the love-mountain of Cypris where lovers filch*
> *the maidenheads of girls and then slidder away.*

There the Venusberg looms up out of the dream. Far-fetched but charming similies, linked with the transformation-motive, humanise the elements. Tyre, joined by a strip of sea-washed earth to the mainland, is a girl,

> *a girl swimmer who gives to the sea*
> *bosom and neck and head, stretches her arms*
> *between beneath waters on either side, her body*
> *whitened with foam from the waves beside her while*
> *she keeps both feet on the firm mother-earth.*

Corpses tossed on the sea are 'tripping the dance of death' (a favourite phrase). The genre-pictures or set-pieces of races, wrestling and labour-process (*e.g.* shipbuilding), every now and then break with a strange lustre like that of the new mosaic-art:

> *About her brows a chaplet*
> *shone with selfspun gleams of unquenchable light*
> *broad green emeralds and the Indian stone*
> *a scintillation born of the beaming sea.*

A new sense of symbolism is emerging, a richer and more dynamic awareness of the nature of poetic imagery. The theological stress on the analogies of prophecy and the deep attention turned to sacramental forms in the new religion play their part, as we can note through the word *type*. Thus, Nonnos describes Artemis shooting arrows into the cloud that Hera has compressed across her shoulders for protection: 'It was the very type of a flight of cranes moving in air and circling each other wreath-wise.' The simile is becoming more than a simile, suggesting further unapprehended essences of relationship and contours of contact. *Typos* is the theological word for ritual, sacraments. Thus, Gregory of Nazianzos writes, 'You leave us for the rites of hell' (*daimonikoi typoi*). And *typikon* was the term used for the rules of a monastery. The *typoi* of Nonnos have their affinity with the holy *typoi*, compressed from fire, of Porphyry.

Nonnos, then, so far from being the vaguely pretty chatterbox of a poet that academic criticism has made of him, is the lively poet of the transition from paganism to Christianity. He seizes on the subtle transformations going on in the depths of life and expresses the new orientations that lead from Hellenistic science into Byzantine-Syriac alchemy, into the medieval world. (He belongs to the second quarter of the fifth century.)

ALEXANDER AND THE SLEEPLESS. The deep changes going on in the lives of people can be read in the saints' lives. The one I select, that of Alexander, gives us a good picture of the disturbed state of things in the Asian borderlands and of the rebellious nature of early monachism.

Born on one of the islands under the Diocese of Asia, in the later part of the fourth century, he was well-educated at Byzantium and entered the group of officials forming the obsequium of the City Prefect and Praetorian Prefect. But through reading the Scriptures, he decided to reject the world, sold his property, and went into a monastery under a Syrian archimandrite. There he came on the text, 'Take no thought for the morrow', and failed to see how it accorded with the routine running of the house. For four years he meditated on the text, then he asked the archimandrite, 'Is everything in the gospels true?' The archimandrite thought he had fallen into some demon's power, and called the other monks to pray over him. Alexander repeated, 'Is everything in the gospels true?'

'Of course. It's the words of Jesus Christ.'

'Then why don't we do as he bids us?'

He argues on the text, but failed to convince the others. So he went off into the desert and took no thought for the morrow for seven years. Then he came on the text about the slothful and useless servant (*Matthew* xxv, 26), and again had qualms. So, to prove himself, he went into a near town of flourishing paganism and set fire to the temple. The people wanted to mob him, but some power held them back. The Father of the City, Rabbula, came up and disputed all night; but Alexander convinced him by bringing fire down from heaven like Elijah. The people, now converted to admiration, wanted to make Alexander bishop, but he managed to flee into the desert again, where he lived for twenty years, beyond the Euphrates, praying by day and sleeping by night in a cask fixed in the ground.[1]

He was now far-famed, and some four hundred monks had gathered round, Syrians, Greeks, Romans, Egyptians. He divided them into four choirs for psalmody, and at first instituted Four Hours daily (tierce, sext, nones, vespers); then Seven by day and Seven by night—to realise the psalmist's call for incessant praise. Now the text which obsessed him was this call, and he wanted to actualise on earth the perpetual praise of the angels. However, he had to admit that the flesh was too weak. He fasted and prayed for three years, then had a vision. God promised that his wish would come true and the praise would go on till the end of time. So a perpetual doxology was instituted by a shift-system of choirs.

He forbade organised work as a surrender to the world; so to ease temptation, he led groups out on proselytising missions. One of his schemes was to convert the pagans of Egypt; but something went wrong. He set up an abbot over the main body of the monks, and with some followers went into 'the Persian Desert' (apparently between the Euphrates and Palmyra). For several days there was nothing to eat. Thirty of the monks went off, but Alexander prophesied that there'd be an abundance by nightfall. Sure enough, at dusk they came on a detachment of imperial soldiers under a tribune, who fed them.

The monks then went along with the soldiers, visiting the kastella of the frontier lines and carrying on with the good work—that is, singing all the while. More monks and crowds of poor people had now joined them, and Alexander asked for alms for the whole lot at each place they reached. Rich citizens of one town insulted him as a beggar (and so that town had a drought for three years). At Palmyra things were worse. The inhabitants got wind of the horde coming, and shut their gates. 'Who can feed this mob? If they get in, we'll die of famine.' So the horde went on to Antioch. The patriarch there was ready (he'd been told of the horde 'by villains and hypocrites'). The horde was driven off with cudgels, but in the night they slipped into the city and squatted in some deserted baths, where they went on singing all the while. The common people left the

---

[1] The Rabbula episode seems an insertion; or the biographer, who claims to have been a disciple and who certainly knew Alexander's later life at firsthand, has by error drawn in material from elsewhere. In the Syriac *Life* Rabbula was converted by seeing the heroic virtues of the monks in the house of Abraham the Recluse, and by the teachings of two bishops. It was he who made an attack on a temple, at Baalbec. He became bishop of Edessa and fought Nestorianism. (There were several schools at Edessa: we hear of Acts signed 'by the Schools of the Armenians, Persians, and Syrians; the Artisans; and the whole Town'. The Persian School was the most famous, the breeding-ground of Nestorianism.)

churches to listen. Alms were so plentiful that Alexander founded a hospice; he acted as arbitrator in disputes (a role that the bishops considered solely theirs) and even got some rich persons to burn debt-documents; he denounced the patriarch and the Master of Soldiers of the East for misdoings or omissions.

A monk who acted like that was sure to be arrested. Hearing that the Master had been asked to exile him to Chalkis and to chase his followers out, he escaped from the city in a beggar's garb and went wandering round. (Or perhaps he went to Chalkis and then slipped off.) By chance he came on a monastery, the Krithenion, where his system was being used. Here, apparently, he gained twenty-four brethren who went on with him to Byzantium and set up near the church of St. Menas. At once monks from the houses around came to him, some four hundred of them, and he was accused (presumably by the abbots of the depopulated houses) of heresy before the prefects (who no doubt sent his case on to the church-authorities), and condemned. His group had been put in irons; but as soon as he was free again (probably with an exile-sentence), they all gathered round him.

They left Byzantium and crossed the water to the Chalkedonian suburb of the Oak, where they took refuge in the church of Peter and Paul. To send soldiers in after them would have caused a scandal, so the *archontes* got the local bishop to incite the people against them. Alexander was hustled out and maltreated, and fled to the monastery of St. Hypatios. From there he went off towards the Black Sea and founded at Gomon the house where he soon after (about 430) died. This house was the Monastery of the Sleepless, the singers of the perpetual doxology.

The polemics of St. Nilos make clear that Alexander was accused of being a Massilian. The Massilian vow of poverty, the belief that safety lay only in ceaseless prayer, the close links with the rebellious side of monasticism, the wish to live the life of angels on earth—all these were attitudes shared by Alexander. Also the Massilians or Euchitai (according to Timotheus) 'give themselves out as great understanders of the soul, to the extent of being able to tell by their conjectures . . . the dispositions of men'. This power is attributed to Alexander in the *Life* and indeed furnishes the theme of almost all his miracles. Thus, 'Truly the saint with the intuition of the Holy Ghost understood their thoughts, and he said to the brother following him, without anyone knocking on the door, "Go and take what God has sent".' Like the Massilians, too, he assumes a wandering role in defiance of all ecclesiastical regulations.

He is the type of monastic most radically opposed to the State-Church —the type whom the Church most feared and hated. His threat to the church-revenues is fully brought out in the Antioch episode: the deacon complains that he'll lose his livelihood unless Alexander is suppressed. And yet this persecuted man, who wanted to throw off every tie binding him to the world to which the State-Church belonged, founded a monastery which became the most unbending support of Orthodoxy and the hierarchical Church in the following centuries. We could not have a better example of what it was that the Church tamed in monasticism, and the way in which it did the taming. But the defiant spirit of Alexander, his relentless earnestness, his need to live a truly apostolic life, was something that the Church could never crush. Broken in one place, it burst out in another. Alexander's spirit went on wandering and calling the poor together.

43

STABILISATIONS

PHOTIOS. In the last chapter I took two examples of the period of vast up-heaval and change; here I take two examples of the steady expansion of humanism after the iconoclasts, the work of Photios and of Psellos. Photios had a full life, with many reversals and triumphs; he came at the end of the iconoclast period, in the transition-phase of Michael III, and he led the first broadly based conflict with the Papacy. No longer was it a matter of the two sees manoeuvring for tactical advantages; the clash was frontal and definite—though not till the eleventh century did it become a final cleavage. Behind the papal position lay the revival of State-power in the West, albeit in unstable shapes; behind the Photian position lay the development of the imperial State into something like the first national State of the modern world.

But here we are concerned only with the man's scholarship, which was firmly based on a knowledge of the ancient classics and the works of Byzantine authors. He dislikes artificiality and hyper-atticisms; he praises Paul's simplicity. But he is very aware of the Greek heritage, its wealth and responsibilities. In his fight with the Papacy he compares the 'poor Latin' of the West with the rich Greek of his own land. The sense of owing a key to a universal culture gives dignity to his struggle and mean-ing to his followers' recognition of him as the patriarch of all the sees and pope of the world.

His tolerance is witnessed by the letter written by his pupil Nicholas Mystikos (later patriarch) to the son of the Moslem Emir of Crete:

> (Photios) knew well that, although difference in religion is a barrier, yet wis-dom, kindness and the other qualities which adorn and dignify human nature, attract the affection of those who love beautiful things, and despite the differ-ence of creeds, he loved your father who was adorned with these qualities.

He had a reading-club at his house, and compiled for his absent brother summaries of the books read. His interests ranged among historians from Herodotos to Prokopios, and included writers on farming, medicine, grammar, orators and rhetoricians. Thus, almost all the works of the great Hellenic orators were read, except Lykourgos, whom they couldn't get round to. They read Lucian, *The Life of Apollonios of Tyana*, a book on Persian Magic, the *Lives* of Pythagoras and Isidore, the romances of Iamboulos, Tatios, Antonios, Diogenes, Heliodoros, and Agathorchides' treatise on the Red Sea. At least half as many secular as religious works were read. But he shows no interest at all in the poets of the pagan past.

His sense of history appears in passages like the following, which deal with Theodore the Presbyter's efforts to defend the authenticity of the pseudo-Dionysios:

> How is it that these treatises describe in detail rites and customs which only became established in the Church gradually, over a long period? The great Dionysios, as is clear from Acts, was contemporary with the Apostles; it is therefore improbable (say the objectors) or rather a clumsy fiction to assert that he could have set out to describe institutions which were not fully developed till long after his death.

And in the following quotations the high level of critical judgment attained in his period can be read. While using much of the old set terminology, Photios shows a new insight into the unity of form and content, he always tries to bring out the inner point of congruence between a writer's aims and the means employed. His own liking for cool sobriety also shows through the comments:

> *Herodotos.* He is fond of old wives' tales and digressions pervaded by charming sentiments, which, however, sometimes obscure the due appreciation of history and its correct and proper character . . . .
>
> *Aischines.* He uses figures of thought and speech, not to create the effect of using artistic language, but in conformity with the needs of the subject. Hence his style appears direct and straightforward, well-adapted for public speaking and conversation . . . .
>
> *Isokrates.* His main characteristics, as can be seen at a glance, are purity and distinctness, and extreme care in the craftmanship of his speeches, which often degenerates into superfluous orderliness and over-elaboration. His infinite capacity for taking pains generates lack of taste rather than resourcefulness in argument. . . . His style is weak, and the use of evenly balanced clauses *ad nauseam*, as much as anything, shows his excessive attention to petty detail. . . .
>
> *Lucian.* His composition is so well put together that the reader does not seem to be reading prose, but a pleasant song of an unobstrusive kind seems to slide into his ears. In short, his style is charming but not in keeping with the subjects he has made up his mind to ridicule. . . .
>
> *Heliodoros.* The work is dramatic, and the style congruous to the theme, being rich with simplicity and charm. The narrative is diversified by realistic incidents, expected or unexpected, to appeal to the emotions by strange escapes from danger by clear and pure diction. If, as is only natural, there is tendency to call on figures of speech, they are easy to grasp and vividly illustrate the theme.
>
> *Dion Kassios.* His style is grandiose and elevated, reflecting the consciousness of mighty events. His diction is thick with antiquated constructions, with

12*

words suited to the importance of what he tells. His periods are full of pro-
tracted parentheses and marring inversions. The rhythms and abrupt inter-
ruptions, used with care, escape the notice of the general reader on account of
the general clarity.

Eunomios (a heretic). The composition is forced, compressed, harsh: the reader
is obliged to smack the air vehemently with his lips if he wants to bring out at
all clearly the words which the author, by too much toughening, packing and
condensing, interpolating and mutilating, has painfully put together. His
periods are at times spun inordinately out, and the whole work is pervaded
with obscurity—the aim being to persuade most readers by dint of eloquence
that he goes beyond their capacity and to cover up the weakness of his
thinking. . . .

Theophylaktos Simokatta. An Egyptian by birth. His style does not lack grace,
but through overdoing figurative expressions and allegorical ideas, it is frigid
and betrays a puerile lack of taste. More, by often interpolating untimely
moral sentiments, he gives away a fondness for flaunting superfluous display.

Kandidos of Isauria. His style is not suited for history. He drags in childish and
insipid poeticalities; his composition is rough and discordant, bolstered up into
dithyrambic bombast or falling down into carelessness and inelegance. He
tries out new constructions, which do not, as in other writers, lend extra
suavity and charm, but make the work hard to read and quite unattractive.
While here and there the style shows signs of mending, his History is obviously
a medley of the most divergent materials.

PSELLOS. If we move two centuries ahead, to Psellos, we find that the
humanist element has vigorously expanded. The grave balance of Photios
has gone, and in its place is a restless eagerness, at times superficial and
hectic, yet at its heart holding a deep hunger for knowledge, a love of the
various world of men, a readiness to follow conclusions out to the point
where they threaten the whole system of existing preconceptions. Psellos,
courtier and head of the department of philosophy at the university,
studied poetry, rhetoric, history, geography, ethics, chemistry, natural
history, agriculture, medicine. He worked at all these subjects, made
abridgements of past writings about them or sought out some new method
of his own to apply in their fields. He wrote opuscules in verse and prose,
theological treatises, *eulogia*, allegories, epigrams, satires, commentaries
and *scholia* on the ancients, works on etymology, mathematics, music,
geometry, tactics, law. Unscrupulous, insinuating, shallow in many respects, he yet shows a passion and fidelity to learning which gives him
force and breadth amid all his meanderings. Pedantic, he is also fresh and
lively, keenly nosing about for new materials, new trails of thought,
new methods.

He loves the classics, zealously rebuilds the classical forms for his own
world, and makes of them a new mode of self-expression, infusing his

temperament into his style. With his quick sensibility, his warm responses and impressionable mobility, he develops a cult of the heart. 'I am not a Scythian, I haven't a stone where my heart should be.' He calls himself a harp that trembles with all modes, not with one. Nature gave him, he says, a soul like soft wax capable of taking and holding fast the supreme beauties of the sciences and of moulding in them the dearest of the graces. He shows preciosity, oratorical virtuosity, a liking for subtleties, paradoxes, pathetic violence of effect, overdone apostrophe, careful disposition of cadence, antithesis. He himself calls his motivation *sophistomania*, the quest for originality. 'The art of disposing words enchants me.'

He had to protest his religious orthodoxy, and was no doubt sincere in doing so; for he clearly never faced up to the destructive aspect of many of his positions. To defend rationality he had to insist that it did not conflict with dogma; but his whole emphasis is on the need for free and uncompromising reason. To his friend Xiphilin when patriarch, he writes, 'The process of reasoning, my friend, is neither contrary to the Church's dogma nor alien from philosophy, but is indeed the only instrument of truth, the only means of finding what we seek.' And when the subject of knowledge transcending all intelligent demonstration comes up, he gaily says that he has never experienced it and doesn't believe that anyone else has.

On the other hand, he believes in the unity of the sciences and courageously states that in the total process whereby men advance to a higher rationality both the orthodox creed and the heresies play their part.

> All the false ideas we are now attacking have derived part of their teaching from Catholic doctrine. Since I address men with knowledge, I shall not elaborate this point save as far as I reasonably must. Thus, the famous Origen, contemporary of the (Neoplatonist) philosopher Porphyrios, was pioneer of all our theology and laid its foundations, yet on the other hand all heresies spring from him.

Though there is a strong Neoplatonist element in his thinking, and though he was often confused like the other men of his day as to what constituted science and what preconceived fancy, he yet mocked at philosophy that had no relation to the life of men and held that belief in the supernatural arose from ignorance of nature and that the only rational course was to pursue yet further the study of natural law.

I have no space here to examine his multifarious works, which, taken together, mark him out as a man of a new kind of culture, a man of the kind which was to grow ever more common in the Italian cities three or four centuries ahead, but which was in the eleventh century only known to Byzantium. Here it is enough to glance at his masterpiece, the *Chrono-graphia*. In that work he breaks entirely new ground, and presents history in the form of psychological memoirs, brilliantly composed and subtly penetrative of the human conflicts depicted. With the epic of *Digenes* it represents the most complete artistic triumph in Byzantine literature, essentially new, written with complete artistry, and giving us a completed picture of the world it analyses. True, it has the limitations of its virtues; the concentrated pictorial and psychological method means that the work deals with a restricted section of Byzantine society (the court) and makes no attempt at a broader sweep (except in the case of Basil I, whom Psellos had had no close intimacy with), no attempt to define the conditions of the varying classes outside the court. Still, by presenting so profoundly and truly the confused and decadent life of the court, Psellos gives us miniatures which define the whole tempo, condition, and nature of the Byzantine State in this phase of its decline. *Chronographia* is not to be judged as History, but as Characterisations—as an imaginative creation akin to the Novel.

A few details must suffice. Note, for instance, the startling way that he quietly introduces himself into the midst of violent events, suddenly giving us a sense of the individual caught up in the vortex of history, which has no previous parallel.

When Michael V and his uncle fall, they escape in a boat to the monastery of Stoudios. Psellos slips in, and the furious crowd irrupt at the same moment. He is with the captain of the troops sent to guard the fugitives, and admits that he had his reasons for resentment at the fallen pair—

> But when I came near the altar that Michael was gripping, and when I saw the two fugitives—the Emperor clinging to the holy table of the Word itself and the Nobilissimos standing up on the right of the altar, both of them changed in clothes and spirit, both utterly shamed—then I felt the last trace of resentment ebb from my heart . . .
> The crowd that had burst into the church gathered in a circle and stood round the two men like a pack of wild beasts wanting to devour them; and I, standing against the rail on the right of the altar, went on grieving.

The fallen men talk, and the uncle puts all the blame on Michael, ending, 'If I'd been able to hold him back in his headstrong course, all my family today would be unmutilated and I'd not be given over to fire and iron.' Psellos explains with his sly and easy irony:

> That word *mutilate*, why did he use it? I'd better explain, though it holds my story up a moment. When the Emperor exiled the Orphanotroph John, as though he had crashed down the family's pillar, he hastened to demolish the rest of his kin. All his near relations, who had mostly reached adult age and

grown full beards, who had become fathers of families and been raised to the most august dignities, he forced to undergo castration and returned them to life half-dead. For, shrinking from the infliction of open death, he preferred to act with an air of indulgence and merely kill them off by mutilation.

Finally the pair are dragged out despite the monkish clothes they have put on, and are blinded.

> The executioner set about tying them up so that they wouldn't move when their eyes were being put out. 'Here you,' the uncle said, 'if you see me flinch, nail me to the post as well.' And with that he lay down on his back on the ground without any change of colour, without one cry, without one groan escaping, almost as if he lay there dead. And then his eyes were put out there, one after the other.
>
> But as for the Emperor, who had seen his own misery represented in advance by the other's sufferings, he was the one who expressed the pang which his companion was feeling—wringing his hands, or rather, beating his hands on his face and wretchedly roaring.

The picture he gives of Zoe, her cosmetics and her superstitions, her love-affairs, is a masterly thing. Here are a few words of his direct description:

> Zoe the elder had a soul quicker in conception, but a tongue that lagged in setting her thoughts out. Theodora was the contrary; she didn't easily reveal her inner thought, but once drawn into discussion she chattered on with a capable and lively voice. And Zoe moved impatiently towards the thing she desired, and held her hand ready in all eagerness for two things. I mean Life and Death. Like the waves of the sea that raise a ship up and cast it down again into the depths. But such traits did not in the least fit Theodora, whose spirit was equal to itself, and, so to say, blunted on one edge. The one had a prodigal hand, able in a single day to exhaust a whole brimming sea full of gold-dust; the other kept a good account of any money she gave, because she lacked resources from which to draw without a second thought, and had received from nature a soul more its own mistress in this matter.
>
> And to speak without reserve—since I have set myself, not to compose a eulogy, but to state historical truth—neither woman had the energy of mind necessary for power. They did not know how to carry on administration or to reason solidly on State-affairs. Most of the time they mixed trifles of the boudoir with serious matters of empire. . . .
>
> So the two sisters differed in character. And even more so in appearance. The elder was naturally more plump than her sister, but was not big in build. She had fine large eyes under an impressive brow; her nose was aquiline, but without an exaggerated curve; she had blonde hair. And her entire body glistened with its whiteness. There was little to give her age away. Anyone who noted in detail the harmonious flow of her limbs without knowing who she was, would have sworn her a young girl; not a single wrinkle showed, her flesh was perfectly smooth, firm, rounded, unbroken by a crease. But as for Theodora, she was larger in build and thinner of figure, with a face scantily

symmetrical in relation to the rest of her body. But she was quicker than her sister in speech and movement; there was nothing hard about her; she was charming and liked to laugh, and was always on the look-out for an excuse to chat.

From this basis he builds up the terror and pathos of Zoe's murder of her husband, her infatuation with Michael, and Michael's breakdown in conscience. But all that must be read at full length to appreciate the sureness of touch, the delicacy of observation, the strength of dramatic conception. Here is a detachable passage which depicts John the Orphanotroph (a charity-office which had become important through the perquisites to be gained through wardships, etc.):

For this man I'd like my account to be more detailed. It won't, however, be slapdash or incorrect; for when I'd just grown my first bit of beard, I saw him myself, heard his talk, witnessed his behaviour. I summed him up with precision. I knew praiseworthy actions of his; I can mention others not exactly to his credit.

This is how his character was made up. He had a ready wit, and as for quickness of spirit—if ever any man had it, he had. Indeed you could read it in his eyes, which threw out piercing glances. He took hold of affairs with much care, and yet he showed also an extreme activity. He became experienced in all branches of business, but it was in finance above all that he revealed a mind of the keenest and liveliest cast.

Besides, anxious not to be the cause of anyone's coming to grief, anxious too not to be looked down on by anyone whatsoever, he did nobody any harm, though in intercourse with people he assumed an air of severity and thus filled them with misgivings. This harshness never went any further than the expression on his face; for others were so scared by his mere looks that they abstained from bad actions towards him.

Truly, also, he was bulwark and a brother for the emperor. Day and night in fact he never relaxed his watchfulness. Even when he was plunged in pleasures, as sometimes happened, when he took part in festivals, ceremonies and public feasts, he never slackened from his self-appointed task. No detail escaped him; nor did anyone dare to show secrecy; all feared him and suspected his vigilance. At any odd moment of the night he was liable to hurry out on horseback and pry thoroughly into every corner of the city, passing like a lightning-flash through all the residence-quarters. The unpredictable movements of his vigilance made everyone uncomfortable; and feeling confined and repressed, men kept to their own homes. They feared to be caught in a gathering with their fellows.

Such then were the qualities that could be praised in John. On the adverse side there was this to be said: his soul was a motley and he adapted himself to accord with every idea of those that he was with. In a single moment he seemed to have a many-faceted thought. Though at a distance he censured persons coming up towards him, he welcomed them benevolently when they were near, as if he then saw them for the first time. And if anyone gave him information useful to the Empire's safety, he avoided having to give a reward by pretending that he had known the whole thing for some time, and blamed the informer for being so slow. The man went off in confusion; but John himself at once took measures in accordance with what he had learned, and by an immediate blow cut in the root an evil perhaps only beginning to push upwards.

He wanted to pass his life in great magnificence and to control affairs in a truly imperial style; but his inbred character made this difficult. He never purged himself, so to speak, of an inveterate gluttony. That was why, once he had begun drinking, he was dominated by this weakness and at once spread himself in improprieties of all sorts. Yet even in this condition he never let State-cares fade from his mind, and in spite of everything he never softened the wild-beast look in his eye or smoothed in the least his tense brow.

I have often found myself at his side in banquets, and I wondered how such a man, overwhelmed by drunkenness and laughter, bore on his shoulders the axis of the Roman Empire. In his most abandoned moments of drunkenness he still watched closely every gesture, every comment of his fellow-drinkers, and later he called them to account, like persons taken in the very act, and questioned them as to things said and done in the course of the carousal. And so men feared him much more when drunk than when sober.

What a strange creature that man was. Long past he had assumed the monk's garb; but he had never thought, even in a dream, of living up to the decency that such a garb demands. Yet all the duties that the garb imposed on him by heavenly law he carried out. Men of a dissolute life he treated with neglect. On the other hand, men who chose to live decently, men who lived as befits a freeman in the lap of the virtues, men who graced their soul with secular science, all these too he treated as adversaries, and he sought to depreciate each one's object of devotion. Thus to all other men he behaved in a ridiculous way; but to his brother and emperor he showed a single and unvarying disposition, unwavering, holding his character fast at a point of stability.

I have called Psellos a Man of the Renascence—in the sense we use that term of the Italian Renascence. And that description is true of him in his general aspect; but in his *Chronographia* he goes beyond the Renascence. It is not till we come to the later eighteenth century, in men like Boswell or Laclos, that we find this kind of relentless fascination with the spectacle of life, the bitter wit that sees into the motivations of fear and vanity, this deliberate self-dramatisation and self-implication in the scenes depicted, and, above the fascination and the bitterness and the foolery, a hard clear sober courage—a steady judgment of the whole twisted spectacle for what it is.

The *Chronographia*, like *Digenes*, comes at the height of Byzantine development—the point where the energies loosed by the iconoclast period have reached their highest and richest expansion. The later humanists may have attained a more precise discipline than Psellos in various matters of scholarship; but they lack his creative impetus, his omnivorous appetite, his power to break through the surfaces of his world into a deep realisation of its human condition.

44

THE PEOPLE'S HERO

EPIC LAY. That there were rhapsodes of the people we have direct evidence. Arethas of Kaisareia (850–932) discusses the term *agyrtes*, fair-mountebank:

> Modern example: those cursed Paphlagonians who, having fabricated I-don't-know-what songs treating the adventures of famous heroes, go from house to house to get a penny (*obol*).

The oldest example of these songs, composed in a swinging accentual line of seven iambic beats, is the lay of *Armouris*, which is linked with Michael III's defeat of Islam. In 838 the Moslems had sacked Ankyra and hoped to crush the Empire. The poet Husein ibn al Danhak wrote:

> O we have spared Ankyra nothing at all
> and mighty Amorion we have brought to its fall.

Michael refortified Ankyra, incorporating holy stones, (*i.e.* any stones from Palestine) in the walls for magical strength. The inscription says:

> Brought down upon your knees and lately ruined
> broken by the bloody hands of Persians [i.e. Arabs]
> now rouse yourself delivered from the evils
> discard the garb of griefs that boast no beauty
> receive instead the robe of bridal splendour
> strengthened behold by stones that God has trodden
> so much God's saving power now favours you:
> and give your hand with glee to him who summons
> and gloriously he'll help you up and hold you
> you who were fallen into the abyss of perils
> he stretches mighty hands out, the Lord Michael
> the Great King who is crowned and conquering
> who here renews and makes your dwelling certain
> delightful Ankyra brilliant Queen of Cities
> Glory of the whole land of the Galatians.

In 860 the defeat of 838 was avenged and Byzantine troops once more crossed the Euphrates. In 863 the Arabs were shattered at Posion. Thus the *akta* recorded the exaltation:

> Glory to God who shatters our enemies, Glory to God who has broken the godless, Glory to God the granter of victory, Glory to God who crowned

12. DORMITION OF THE VIRGIN

Fresco, Serbia, Monastery of Sopotchani, c. 1255–65

you Lord of the Earth, hail felicity of the Romans, Lord, hail, valour of your army, Lord, hail, Lord who have brought law, hail, Lord the destroyer, God will keep you in the purple, for the honour and raising up of the Romans, along with the honourable Augusta in the purple, God will hearken to your people.

The lay of Armouris is based on the fall of Amorion in 838, when the slaughter of Forty-two Martyrs by the Arabs had been made the theme of furious polemics against the enemy, aimed at restoring national morale. In the lay, young Armouropolos, precociously heroic and strong (like a folk-hero, the quickly-growing babe of fertility-ritual), sets out to rescue his father, a general made prisoner in 838. His exploits express the demand for a *revanche*, a great effort to bring home the prisoners. He passes the Euphrates, kills hosts of Moslems, and chases the survivors to Syria. The Arab ruler frees the father and gives the hero his daughter to wed.

The lay belongs to the years when the crossing of the lost Euphrates was a miraculous hoped-for event and Cappadocia was still overrun.

> *But still the Euphrates hurtles strong, and thick with mud and billows,*
> *and O its waters running deep, its waters overflowing,*
> *but just one prick of spur, and in, the black horse plunges swimming.*
> *'Now thanks and thanks, Good Lord, a thousand thanks I send you,*
> *for you have given me my strength and you can take it from me.'*
> *Then an angelic voice comes down and speaks from highest heaven*
> *'Now plant your lance, I bid you, in the root beneath the palm-tree*
> *and take your clothes and hang them on the pommel of your saddle,*
> *and spur your horse and scramble up the other bank in safety.'*
> *With one great spurring of his horse, he's right across the river.*

But after the tremendous battle-deeds of the young hero, the theme of peace and brotherhood come forward. The Emir offers his daughter:

> *'And when a son is born to them, the lad must be instructed,*
> *if he should meet a Saracen, to show him every mercy—*
> *and should he make a prize, then let them share it out together,*
> *and let them live in peace.'*

The poem has a rough humour and a good vigour, with repetition of lines or phrases effectively used. It was perhaps the army-chant of the Anatolic Theme. We know the Theme-patriotism of the soldiers by a debate, a sort of epic dialogue, between the men of the Anatolic and those of the Charsianon at the time of the pursuit of the Paulician Chrysocheir.

DIGENES AKRITAS. Behind Armouropolos, perhaps, there lies a folk-magnification of Michael III; to decide who lies behind Digenes Akritas is not so easy. Diogenes the turmarch of the Anatolics killed while fighting in 788 may have contributed memories; but if so, he is only one of many.

Some critics argue that our earliest redaction goes back to the period between Basil I and Romanos Lekapenos—the first half of the tenth century, and is linked with the rallying to the Empire and Christianity of the powerful tribe of Beni-Habib and the Emir of Melitene, Abu-Hafs. This Emir was grandson of the famous Umar, who has left his imprint deep on the poem. 944 may then be taken as an end-date because at that date the Mandelion, the Miraculous Image of Christ, left Edessa for Byzantium, and the poem knows it at Edessa. Other critics argue that the general calm on the Euphrates frontier in the poem suggests the mid-eleventh century. We have seven versions, and also a ballad-cycle.

Digenes Akritas is at least in part the Christianised form of the *Geste of Melitene*, the songs of the martyr Umar and his chevaliers: a *Geste* which seems also to underlie the Turkish romance of *Sayyid Battal*.

Digenes' tomb is pointed out on a mound with columns near Samosata. To his tomb near Trebizond mothers took their newborn sons to save them from the evil eye; and the folk of the Pontic area hoped into modern times to see him come out of his tomb and smash the infidels—as the heretical masses had hoped to see Constantine V emerge. The Cypriots took him as the ideal of strength and courage, and when a huge statue was dug up, they thought it represented him. Two tall columns in a village were called the Clubs of Digenes.

There is one literary reference. Theodore Prodromos praises Manuel Comnenos as the New Akritas, the Bulwark of Anatolia; and goes on to talk of Akritas with his big club breaking up the rich dishes that some gluttonous abbots consume to the detriment of their starving monks.

If we look at the name, we may translate it *The Halfcaste Frontier-Guard*; for the hero was half-Greek, half-Arab. But if we look deeper into the meaning of *Digenes* we recognise in it the initiation-term *Twice-born*, used of the 'second birth' of the young man who has successfully passed the tests and ordeals. And we can call our hero the representative of the initiation-ritual, the youth who supremely defeats the dark forces of the crisis-moment and who therefore symbolises his people in their death and renewal. Such an interpretation harmonises with the many elements of fertility-ritual that surround Digenes in the ballads and the lay, and that show up in the folk-beliefs about his tomb and his Heraklean Club; and in fact in the epic he does pass through initiation-tests, those of the Clubmen.

The author, while using previous lays, has expanded and developed them. Though the work remains fundamentally akin to the songs of the soldiers and the *agyrtai*, it has been raised to a higher level. The poet knows the chronicles and Homer, the earlier romances and the Alexander saga, but he is not learned. Many of the elements that he embodies may have come through popular tradition rather than by reading. What we can say with certainty is that his work reveals an upsurge from the popular levels into the literary. His lay lacks intensity and complexity of significance, but it has breadth, movement, lyrical warmth—a limpidity and buoyancy, an intellectual clarity, which marks it off as belonging to a different dimension than that of the western *gestes* or romances.

> Although the poet lacked emotional depth, he had enough originality to give his romance a purpose—its theme good government and the guarantee of peace by a union of Christian and Arab. (Mavrogordato.)

The story is in two sections, the first and shorter about the hero's father, the Emir Monsour (also *digenes* or two-raced), the second about the son. It tells how an Emir carried off the daughter of a general of the Doukas family who had been exiled to his estates. Her five brothers catch him up and outfight him. The girl (sometimes called *Eirene*, Peace) is unharmed, and the Emir, half-Greek, enters the Byzantine world as a Christian to get her in marriage. The son Digenes is born. The Emir's mother writes to him from Edessa, and the Emir, after some disagreement with his brothers-in-law, rides off and converts her with all her household. With the fourth book we meet the youth of the hero, his fights with wild beasts and robbers, his carrying-off of Evdokia, daughter of another Doukas general. Consent to the marriage is gained, and the ceremony is richly described. Then Digenes and his bride decide to live alone; they live a wandering life on the frontier, and Digenes keeps the peace by fighting brigands. The emperor rides down to the Euphrates to thank him and Digenes gives him a lecture on good government. In May Digenes defends his girl against brigands and beasts; he is unfaithful for a moment, with a girl he rescues from a ravisher, and also, after beating the Amazon Maximo, he surrenders to her urgent solicitations. But his love for Evdokia is never shaken, and he builds a magnificent palace and garden on the Euphrates for her, where he lives, spending his time in good works and the maintenance of the peace. At last he falls ill, recalls to Evdokia their lovely life in the wilds, and dies; and she dies too, of a broken heart.

There is a swift lyric gladness glinting all over the poem, which comes out in its full gaiety every now and then, in its praises of the Maytime and of love, of gardens and courage. Chivalric and popular elements mingle in passages like the following:

> *And still I must discourse of love and tell of all its wonders,*
> *for out of longing it is born, a deep and ceaseless passion,*

and out of it a tenderness desirously arises,
it thrives and strengthens bit by bit, and causes him who feels it
such a perpetual pang of grief, a sense of loss so grievous,
that he is surely offered-up a prey to every sorrow.
A young and valiant man who loves goes scornful of all danger
against a multitude of men and never thinks of shrinking
he leaves his parents at a word, he goes without a murmur
from all the friends he's cherisht most, from all his proper kindred,
he dares the worst the sea can do, and fire is nothing fearful,
he laughs at dragons as he goes, he laughs at every lion,
such boldness has he gained from love and nothing now can check it,
he has no thought of doughty men, he has no thought of brigands,
for him the nights are as the days, and any rugged valley
as quiet plains, he never fears the lair of any peril
and never once he lets his lids go down upon his vigils.

The light-burst appears as the simple glory of the return to Eden in the wilds of peace and love:

And all the inner walls were set with precious stones of splendour,
around the windows which with gold were gorgeously enamelled
went branches of the golden vine most intricately twisting
and from their tendrils hung the grapes in luscious golden clusters
and all the columns habited with gold and thickly plated
sent sparkling such a fire of gold and burned with such a brightness
that everyone who saw the place was sure the roofs were golden
and when the sun rose in the East and sent his beams towards it
the gold sent out so fierce a flame and burst with such a lustre
that everyone who stood around must turn away bedazzled.

This Edenic palace is built on a central plan with dome; and the heart of the construction is a *martyrion*.

Folk-elements keep breaking through, as in Digenes' lament for his dead mother:

O who has cut the single root that linked me with the living
and who has quenched my only light and left me crying blinded . . .
O speak a very gentle word to me, my darling mother,
and quickly call to me, I pray, and tell who holds you captive
and I shall ransom you at once with a great heaped-up ransom . . .

A cry that suggests the great wrestle with Death that bulks importantly in the ballad-cycle.

CLUBMEN AUD PAULICIANS. The elements that go to make up the poem are highly involved; but a brief glance at some of the main ingredients will help to bring out the important nature of its definition. *Akritas* merely means frontier-guard, and Digenes is in one sense the ideal figure, the heroic emblem, of the akritic soldiers. (*Akritas* may be paired off with *marquis* or *margrave*; *armaour*, Georgian; *pehlewan*, Persian; *mazpan*, Armenian; *pasha*, Turk.) In later centuries the Akritic Guard were of great importance and held a privileged position. 'When the emperor penetrates into the deserts,' says Constantine VII, 'he leaves all his court and enters with five hundred *akritai* who form his bodyguard.' The self-reliant *akritas* had in fact elements borrowed from the Clubmen and the Paulicians; and the Paulician mark lies clear on the poem. The father of the Emir Monsour is called Chrysocherpes; he is Chrysocheir, the last great military leader of the Paulicians when Basil I crushed them. Karoës, the Emir's uncle, is Karbeas, another Paulician leader, and Ambron, his grandfather, stands for the Syrian Emir, Umar of Melitene, who was allied to the Paulicians in their anti-imperial revolt. The region of the novel is the Mesopotamian section between Samosata and Melitene, and Cappadokia—the central Paulician revolt-areas.[1]

The alliance of Arab and Greek that the poem expresses is therefore the alliance of Paulicians and Melitene Arabs. But by the time the popular lays had reached the level which our poem represents, the Paulician struggle had long receded into the past, and the theme was reformulated in terms of the national struggle for survival. In a sense the theme has thus been inverted; but the mass-elements from the earlier levels persist, giving the poem its vigour, its clarity, its spirit of brotherhood, its demand for peace between peoples. The Paulician element too shows in the ignoring of the icon-cult or mariolatry, its spare and curt theology:

> *Since it has pleased the Son of the All-highest*
> *here of his own freewill for me all beggary to suffer.*

The name Digenes goes back to Leo V, iconoclast set in power by the soldiers.[2] Various emperors are named in the texts—Basil (I or II?), Romanos Lekapenos and Nikephoros. That is, the popular mind tends

---

[1] The brigands are called *Apelatai*: after combats Digenes tames them, and 'he alone was there obeyed by all the wandering Clubmen'. It seems clear that at one state of the lay he went through initiation tests and became a Clubman himself—the traces are very strong. Our text describes the tests he underwent, which are in fact quite unnecessary for his fight against the brigands. (*Apelatikon* was a hymn vaunting the emperor's exploits against the Empire's foes.)

[2] In the songs the Garden is made simply a cosmic centre, an Eden. Mary is not mentioned in the conversion of the Emir; and she only appears in a passing reference as Christ's mother in Mansur's confession of faith. In the palace the paintings are all heroic, Samson, David and Goliath, Achilles, Kinnamos, Alexander, Moses, Joshua —nothing from the New Testament, no Saints. This is iconoclast art. The *martyrion* in the centre commemorates St. Theodore (or two Theodores in some MSS.). Is this Theodore of Edessa, round whom *revanche*-patriotism built an aura? '. . . the polemic and edifying character parallel to that which Enodios had given his *Life* of the forty-two Martyrs of Amorion, which clothes the *Life* of St. Theodore of Edessa' (Abel).

to keep the memory of the fighting emperors, who had some care for the soldiers. And we get a clue to the existence of lays about these rulers in Psellos' *Life of Basil II*. This *Life* is unlike any other part of the *Chronographia*; Psellos is dealing with an emperor before his time and draws on the tales he had heard. The text suggests that these tales were in fact heroic lays. Thus the rebel Bardas Phokas is described as a sort of folk-hero like Armouropolos or Digenes. 'A man whom he struck was a man dead; and if he shouted from afar, he scattered a whole army.' He fights his rival Skleros in single knightly combat. His bodyguard of Iberians are 'fellows who grow ten feet in height and have proudly knitted brows'. When the army reaches the Hellespont, 'you'd have said they meant to cross the sea with a leap.' Again there is a single combat, between Bardas and Basil. 'Bardas comes on like a cloud driven by furious winds, troubling the plain like waves of the sea'—a sentence that reads more like Ossian than normal historical narrative.

We find similar elements in some of the Saints' *Lives*. Thus in *The Life of St. Basil the Younger*, 'When Doukas comes to fight, cry the Arabs, it's Thunder launched against us, and the neighing of his horse burns us and hurls us down to earth.'

It is not surprising then to find a resemblance between the counsel given by Bardas Phokas to Basil II in the *Chronographia* and the counsel given by Digenes to Romanos Lekapenos (or Nikephoros):

> First lessen all costs of pomp, prevent those of the army (the great military chiefs) from swelling up with resources, rather drain them with crushing taxes till they are reduced to minding their own affairs; and take no wife into the palace, hold yourself apart and admit nobody into the heart of your resolutions.

> *The rich donation you design to fill my grateful fortune*
> *I pray that you'll provide instead to poor and stricken soldiers*
> *for the imperial costs I know are infinitely weighty.*
> *The offering worthy of a king who's conquering and famous*
> *is kindness to all stranger-folk, compassion for the hungry,*
> *a power delivering men unjustly persecuted*
> *and proferring pardon to the ones who sin in their opinions . . .*

The poem has a more tolerant and popular note; but the self-reliant tone of the vassal before the emperor is similar in each case.

OTHER TALES AND EPICS. The relation of the epic to Arab tales is very close. Digenes appears as Akrates, general of Heraklios, in the Turkish epic-romance *Sayyid Battal*—the invincible champion of the Christians. But more importantly we find in the *Arabian Nights* a version of the *Geste of*

Umar, The History of King Umar-al-Neman and his Marvellous Son. Here Digenes is annexed to Islam, but the tone is tolerant as in the Greek poem. 'All the Christians were free to remain in their error.' And in the tale of the adventures of Umar's grandson, Kanmakan, we meet another akritic hero fighting brigands and beasts, who has been exiled through unhappy love and a political usurpation. His slogan is: 'We protect the weak against the strong', and in a combat with a Bedouin he has the same great wrestling powers as Digenes, who hugs wild beasts to death.

But though elements from Arab lays may well have contributed to our poem and the ballad-cycle, the basis of the latter is Greek.

Some ingredients indeed go very far back.[1] The poet tells us that Digenes displaced other heroes, whose lays are old and non-authentic. Philopappos and Kinnamos are two of these heroes. The former was the last king of Kommagene who lost his realm in 72 A.D.; but by the time of our poem he has lost his heroic quality and is half-comic. The latter was a Parthian lord who generously gave up his claims to the throne and went into exile about 40 A.D.; his renunciatory gesture must have left a deep mark on popular song.

These two characters and their songs thus go back to the first century A.D.—a surprising example of the long life that popular lays and songs can have. The rival of Kinnamos, Artabanes III, became Goderz of the Persian *Shahnameh*, thus showing an even more vigorous life than Kinnamos himself.

Indeed to understand *Digenes Akritas* correctly we must see how it embodies immemorial elements of the Asianic peoples, and must relate it to the general flourishing of epic-lay, epic-romance, all over the Mesopotamian and Caucasian area. Scholars have almost wholly missed the close relation with the magnificent Armenian cycle of epic-lays collected in 1939 under the title of *David of Sasun*, in which popular songs have been compacted under the pressure of the national resistance to the Arabs and recited right into our own day. Here we see more fully the Paulician revolt-element, transmuted into the dream of a free and prosperous earth. By comparing *David* and *Digenes* we can better understand the folk-dynamic in the latter.

The cultural effloresence going on in both Armenia and Georgia is thus linked closely with the developments in the Byzantine area which Digenes represents. The Georgian movement, more directly literary than

---

[1] In one text the hero's father-in-law is Aaron, probably Duke Aaron, son of the last tsar of the West Bulgars, who entered imperial service and fought the Seljuks, became Duke of Emesa and then of Mesopotamia in 1057; his son Theodore was famously brave.

the Armenian because of the growth of a strong State, reached its height under Queen Tamar. The great epic-romance *The Knight in the Tiger's Skin* by Rusthveli has behind it both the Homeric epics and the popular expressions that come to a head in *Digenes* and *David*; it is more chivalric and finely wrought, but it too is permeated with the folk-element that gives *Digenes* its blithe force and dominates throughout in *David*. Similarly we must link this whole complex with the heroic forms developing in Pērsia and brought to a head by Firdausi; and with the heroic lays of early Russia, where we meet *The Deeds and Life of Digenes Akritas* (with episodes unknown in the Greek forms) and which was 'of no little importance in the development of Old Russian literature'.[1]

1 The Byzantine epic had a strong effect on the French medieval epic and provided many motives for Western literature and folklore: G. Cohen, *Epopée byzantine et epopée française* (*Mélanges H. Grégoire*, II, 1950). I have not dealt with the vast flux of motives into the prose and verse of the medieval West from all areas of the East, as this aspect has long been thoroughly treated.

45

LATER HUMANISM

SATIRES. Though it is a decline to turn from the *Chronographia* and *Digenes Akritas* to later work, I should like to exemplify something of later prose before I end these remarks on Byzantine literature. First then a glance at two satires, *Timarion's Sufferings* and *The Sojourn of Mazaris in Hades*.

Timarion is a twelfth-century work, apparently by a professor from Cappadocia. Its dialogue form imitates Lucian. Timarion tells how, in a state near death, he went into the underworld; but the main point is a satire on contemporary medical theory and practice. Two shadowy forms appear at Timarion's sickbed and argues whether he is dead or not.

> This is the man who has lost the fourth of his component elements. He cannot be permitted to live on the strength of the remaining three. A sentence by Asklepios and Hippokrates has been written out and posted up in Hades, declaring that no man can keep on living if one of his four elements is missing, even though his body is in quite good condition.

So, to prove the correctness of this theory, they carry him off down a chasm into Hades. The guards let him in after abusing him as a 'wretch who holds his own opinions about the composition of the body. No one shall ever go on living on earth without all the four elementary humours'.

In Hades class-distinction still rules. The poor dead have only torches to keep off the dark, the middle-class have coal and wood fires, the richest and most powerful dead have brilliant lamps. When the conductors pass, the common dead stand up 'like boys in the schoolmaster's presence'. Timarion meets various people, a gourmand, the emperor Romanos IV (who had suffered the great defeat by the Turks at Manzikert), a rhetorician Theodore of Smyrna. The gourmand, a Palaiolog noble, keeps shovelling down bacon and Phrygian cabbage from a bowl, while two fat mice (commonly kept as pets in Byzantine houses at this time) wait till he sleeps so that they may lick his beard. Gluttony is stressed as a social evil throughout the satire. The orator who defends Timarion explains that he looks in better condition than when alive because the sparse diet of mallows and asphodel has cured him of the gout that had made him come on a litter once when orating before the emperor. All the same he asks his client to send down from aloft, as fee, some dainties to offset the meagre broth. Another dead man says to Timarion:

> Hallo, newcomer; tell me about things up above. How many mackerel for an obol? What's the price of oil, wine, corn, etc., and, most important of all, though I almost left it out, has there been a good catch of sardines? When I was alive they were my favourite dish, I preferred them even to pike.

Romanos IV lies, a man of great stature, lamenting with gouged-out eyes and trickling poison from his mouth. And he tells of his disasters.

Timarion is tried by the three judges (among whom is Theophilos in poorman's clothes, as noted above in Chapter 25). This friendly treatment of the iconoclast ruler, and the joking comment on the use of his guardian angel as a prompter in the court, show the profane element which persists throughout Byzantine culture. In a travesty of a lawsuit Timarion is tried, with the great physicians of ancient Greece as a body of assessors to guide the judges. After long argument, with Theodore defending, Timarion is found to have particles of flesh and blood still adhering to his soul and is adjudged not-dead; the conductors lose their jobs, and Timarion returns to the earth. On his return-journey, however, he visits the abode of the philosophers. A violent argument arises between Diogenes the Cynic and John Italos (who is depicted with sharp antagonism); Psellos comes in and is treated with respect but not on terms of equality by the philosophers, though offered the highest compliments by the dialecticians. (In all this we see the echoes of the controversy of Italos and Psellos.)

Then after a glance at the torments inflicted on Tyrants (among whom is an Armenian upstart, Philaretes, of the eleventh century), Timarion reaches the pit-entry and sees the stars. At last,

> there, on the river's bank, I said farewell to my guide. Leaving him, I entered through the opening in the roof, a device invented for the escape of the hearth-smoke, and approaching my body closely, I went in through mouth and nostrils. I found it very cold, owing to the frosty winter weather and even more through its having lain there dead. That night I felt like a man with a violent chill. Next day, however, I packed up my belongings and went on my way to Byzantium.

ANOTHER HELL-DESCENT. *Mazaris* was written in the second decade of the fourteenth century, when things were much worse in the Byzantine world. The narrator is dying in the midst of a bad epidemic, ringed round by ravens. In sleep he is carried to a wide, deep valley. If readers disbelieve, he says, let them bring a charge against him in the court of Minos.

Mazaris meets Holobolos, who had been rhetorician, physician and one of the emperor's secretaries, and who fell through an affair with a nun. Holobolos is depicted as the type of ruthless scandal-mongering courtier greedy for place. (His tale includes an account of his visit with the emperor Manuel to France and England.) A politically important man, here called Padiates, has overheard Holobolos' abusive remarks, and comes from a myrtle-bush with a club. He lays Holobolos out, and a court-physician comes up to cure the fallen man. He and other dead men beg Mazaris for news. One asks about his mistress, and is told that she is now faded and her fortune is squandered. Another asks about a man who defrauded him and whom he wants to prosecute when dead. Another, whose hair and beard are dyed black with ravens' eggs, asks about his son who has gone over to Islam. Another asks if his sons are as inquisitive eavesdroppers as he was himself; and so on.

Holobolos and Mazaris go to an Elysian spot. Here the choir-master, talking of his surviving relatives, fiercely attacks the monks. They use, he says, the monastic garb to cover all vices—a charge repeated throughout the tale. After a while, having got a headache with the talk, Mazaris goes into a deep shade to rest before slipping back to life.

There the tale ends; but to it are added four more pieces. In the first, a dream-chat between Mazaris and Holobolos, the former complains that the latter's advice about going to the Morea was disastrous. After fourteen months there he has come to wonder if Tartaros or the Peloponnesos was the worse spot.[1] In the second, Mazaris writes a letter of description to Holobolos about conditions in the Peloponnesos, mentioning the fortifications built against the Turks across the Isthmus of Corinth, and attacking the local lords or *archonts* for their feudal disorder and rebellion. In the third, Holobolos writes up to a doctor, consoling him for having to live in the Peloponnesos and miss the sophisticated delights of Byzantium. In the fourth, the doctor replies that the remedy proposed, a draught of Lethe, does not seem to have worked with Holobolos himself.

Points of interest are the suggestion that a change of fortune might result from going off to Crete (then under the Venetians) or to Kephallonia (under a separate despot); the mention that people are going from Byzantium to do well under the *voivodes* of Wallachia; the Turkish names of many persons of importance at Byzantium.

Though both satires show a close knowledge of Lucian and his earlier imitators—as well as of authors ranging from Homer to Aristophanes—*Mazaris* is much less classical in diction than *Timarion*. Its elaborate

[1] The author puns on the fact that an important Hades-entry was supposed to lie in the Peloponnese—'to death (moron) from Mōra (mora) you've come.'

expressions and terms from the ancient comedy-writers are based in literary reminiscence; but there is a delight in puns and word-play which has roots in contemporary life.[1] We shall not go far astray if we find in the keen satirical eye, the ironic treatment of accepted ideas, the clear sense of social malaise, a link with the mime-theatre and the popular lampoon. The classical tradition of satire has certainly not been maintained merely by means of literary imitation. It is too much alive for that, and has contacts with popular forms of expression that show up through the literary manipulations.

The author of *Mazaris* (who attacks physicians as 'manslayers' even more vehemently than the author of *Timarion*) in his onslaught on the monks and the lords, in his picture of the incompetence and corruption of law and administration, is defending Manuel's belated efforts to strengthen the State; his dislike of the people in the Peloponnese derives from their resistance to those efforts. He contrasts the impartial justice of the equal-handed underworld with the bribery and oppression of the world above. In his patriotism he thus belongs to the humanists, who lament the breakdown of their State without being able to set against the present chaos anything but a nostalgic dream of the ancient *polis* in an idealised form.

The *Timarion* and the *Mazaris*, which carry on classical forms and transmute them, are linked in their hunger for a better world with the tumultuous popular works, drawn from or based on apocryphal sources, in which Otherworld Journeys are described. The same world was producing works like *The Apocalypse of the Virgin*, which tells luridly of Mary's descent with Michael as guide into hell. And this development in Byzantine areas looks towards Dante's *Divine Comedy* and Quevedo's *Visions* rather than towards the Christian or pagan past.

BEWILDERED HUMANIST. Michael Akominatos, at the close of the twelfth century, depicts the wretched life he led in Athens. He went there bursting with enthusiasm for the Athens of ancient Hellas; and was duly greeted by solemn games and dances on his landing at the Peiraios. But the dilapidated condition of the city shocked him—broken-down walls and

---

[1] Less classical in form than *Timarion*, *Mazaris* is more soaked in ancient writings. The author 'was evidently very familiar with the classical literature, for he quotes Homer, Hesiod, Sophocles, Euripides, Aristophanes, Demosthenes, Aristotle, and Theocritus; to which we may add the Septuagint, the New Testament, Lucian, Synesius and Gregory Nazianzen; and the passages taken from these are evidently not obtained by him at secondhand. . . . Homer and Aristophanes are the authors most often cited, especially the latter, whom he speaks of as *ho komikos*, and of all his plays the *Plutus* is the one that occurs to him most readily.' (Tozer.)

suburban houses no better than huts. The villages all round were in ruins. Michael gave a sermon in the Parthenon and tried to treat his audience as the true sons of their Hellenic ancestors. But his brilliant allusive prose baffled the people who understood only the vernacular. So he complains:

> The ancient breed, eloquent and philosophic, has perished. It has been replaced by a generation that knows no Music and is pitiable, as much intellectually as physically. The city, once illustrious and great, has become a desert where you see here and there a forge or a locksmith's.

In an address to the Praetor of Hellas and the Peloponnesos, he speaks in the city's name:

> Unhappy one, I have been the Mother of all wisdom, breeding-ground of all the virtues. In many battles, on land and sea, I conquered the Persians; but now odd attacks by brigands throw me down and all my ports are given up to pillage. I have drunk the chalice from divine hands, and I fall now with hunger, hardship, thirst. Calamities assail me from within and without. The sword of pirates and the terror of tax-collectors make me barren. Hold out your hand to me in my death-throes, breathe into me a new life, so that I may count you in the ranks of Themistokles, Miltiades and just Aristides.

And he denounces the officials as ravagers because 'they behave like barbarians to Athens, this ancient and once happy city, the enemy of tyrants, in this fatherland common to all instructed persons'.

Here we see the dilemma of the humanist. His passionate love of the free and vital past cannot find points of contact with the present; he travails with a new concept of nationhood which is half an idealised picture of the past, half an intuition of future forms of social co-ordination. And the present misery and chaos seems to mock both past and future alike. Further, his new national zeal blurs out on a sense of the international or universal bearings of his concept. There is a good element in that, the conviction that the great heritage belongs to all men; but we can grasp its element of discord and confusion better if we look forward to the western humanists of the fifteenth and sixteenth centuries and see how they serve the interests both of the merging nationhoods and of the supranational financiers, how they link with the new national cohesions and yet deny them in the service of small separatist princedoms or of papal overlordship.

This inevitable conflict in men who are trying to develop a new universal outlook and who yet cannot but serve partial forces in action is already to be read in the Byzantine humanists. The unfortunate Michael Akominatos, moaning in a ruined Athens and talking to ignorant ears in the Parthenon, typifies the situation with charming simplicity.

LOST BETWEEN TWO WORLDS. Or move ahead to the fourteenth century, when the State-power is dwindling, and the scholars, however proud of their Greek heritage, know that Byzantium is weak beside the Western States. Demetrios Kydones grew up in Thessalonika, his *patris* (as he calls it). He and his family were on the side of Kantakouzenos and suffered under the Zealots; and he ended by conversion to the Latin rites. A good classical scholar, he knew Homer, the Attic tragedians, Plato and Demosthenes well; he lectured on them as well as on the Theologians. He translated some works of Augustine and grew enthusiastic over the *Summa* of Thomas Aquinas.

> After having read some pages I was so worked up that I resolved to translate passages into Greek for my incredulous friends who could not admit that the Latins might possibly have anything good in the way of literature. At that time indeed the name of Latin merely evoked among our people the idea of sails and oars, merchants, artisans, pub-keepers. Believing that they had the monopoly of wisdom, proud of Plato and his disciple, we set the Latins in the category of barbarians, leaving to them the art of war and all low trades.

Demetrios thus represents a turning-point; he becomes a missionary of Latin culture among his fellow humanists of Byzantium and prepares the way for the increased transference of savants from Greece to Italy.

His work expresses an even deeper sense of chaos than did that of Michael Akominatos.

> (1352) The catastrophe is complete and it is hard to find anywhere in the world an image of the chaos that reigns here. The barbarians have gained control of all the outer area and are the direct cause of the city's hardships; they impose such heavy tributes that the whole of the State-revenue is not enough to meet them. The poor have to be stricken with a tax in kind. . . .
>
> (Internally) the old evil that has caused the general ruin keeps on raging (*i.e.* civil war). The strife between the emperors for that shadow of power, a struggle which perforces both of them to serve the Barbarian—that is what alone makes breathing possible. What it amounts to is that the one whom the Barbarian supports will be the master in the future, as everyone knows. Thus the emperors fatally become his slaves before their own citizens do. . . .
>
> The citizens, not those who chance along, but those who pass for the most influential in the imperial palace, keep on rebelling, brawling among themselves and disputing for the highest ranks; each puts his whole zeal in swallowing everything up, if he can, all for himself, and, if he fails, threatens to pass over to the enemy, and join him in besieging his fatherland and his friends.
>
> It's a tragedy darker than those told by Homer and the rest of the poets; and who can speak of it with simplicity? You could well compare the city in its present situation with those wretches who amid a terrifying obscurity are battered by a storm and seek from within the ship to keep it from capsising.

But he still (about 1395) talks of the Empire of the Romans, though he admits that now it is 'a head cut off from its body'. In 1369 at Rome, honoured and courted by the many who wanted to learn Greek, he cried 'It all bores me, and I think of the fate of my *patris*, our enemies who mock us.' Yet later he admits 'How can you still call this city your *patris* when you have seen it devastated and helpless?'

And still, with the concepts of Empire and Nation shattered, he clings to his humanist aims. In 1349–50 he hopes that cessation of civil war means that 'virtue will flourish, science will gain freedom of thought, and the emperor will be for his people the symbol (*paradeigma*) of all fine things'. His ideal is:

> vivacity of intelligence, love of study, facility, in learning slowness in wrath, ardour in the quest of the true—in short, the harmony that results from all these qualities.

And these aims and ideals were what he and the other humanists handed on to the Italians, quickening the elements in them which were already reaching out to the same positions. He made his last visit to Italy in 1395 with Manuel Chrysoloras, and Colucci Salutati wrote of it:

> The minds of many you kindled to the tongue of Hellas, so that now I seem to see quite a large number not tepidly studying Greek Literature. . . . O how happy will I be through your gifts, your work, if, as an attainment of felicity in this mortal life . . . at the age of sixty-five I can behold in any way those sources from which all the scholarship and doctrine Latin possesses is believed to have sprung.

When the Byzantine scholars arrived at Venice, two young Florentines hastened to be taught Greek—Roberto Rossi and Jacopi Angeli. The Byzantines had no time, and Rossi went back to Florence, but Angeli was so keen that he followed the Byzantines back to the East.

VI

External Relations and Expansions

46

THE EMPIRE AND THE WESTERN STATES

FEDERATES AND FRANKS. The Empire centred on Byzantium was the direct continuation of the Roman Empire in fact and name; but its area underwent drastic changes during the 1,100-odd years of its life. After the fifth century Gaul was never regained; after the seventh North Africa and Spain were finally lost. But the hold on South Italy continued till the eleventh century. In the East, Egypt, Palestine and Syria were lost in the seventh century, and henceforth even Asia Minor was held only with varying fortunes. In the Balkans there were moments when all seemed lost, but in the eleventh century Bulgaria was subdued. Then in the last years the Serbs were rising to a strength almost as threatening in the West as the Turks in the East.

All this while the Empire zealously and jealously asserted the titles which had been its pride under Constantine or Justinian; and the element of reality in this assertion was the fact that till 1204 Byzantium *was* the world-centre, the ultimate key to the whole European development. In this section I wish to deal with the external relations, political, economic and cultural of the Empire—though many aspects of those relations have come up already in the course of our inquiry.

In the West, in the transition to Germanic States, we must recall that the invasions were mainly not invasions at all, but admissions into the Empire of Germanic federates and subjects. When Theodoric I set up a Visigothic kingdom in the late fourth century in south-west Gaul, it was done under agreement with the emperor; legally all that happened was the transfer of part of the land to federates; Roman law, administered by Roman officials, still ruled the provincials. The pact transferring a third of the land to Visigothic settlers was only a new application of the old principle of *hospitalitas*, the quartering of soldiers.

In 476, the year usually given for the Fall of the Western Empire, what happened was that Odoacer (elected king of a host of East Germans, acting Commander-in-Chief of the imperial troops in Italy, and Patrician of the Empire) was authorised to set up in Italy a kingdom like that of Theoderic in Aquitaine. This action had the consent and co-operation of the Roman Senate, who provided Odoacer's ministers; and Symmachus the Younger, consul and prefect of Rome in 485, would have been very astounded to learn that the Empire had collapsed.

Theoderic the Ostrogoth, also Patrician of the Empire, who wanted 'to live in the Roman Way' at Byzantium, succeeded Odoacer, with a constitutional position regulated by agreement with Anastasios in 497. He was defined as *rex* (vice-royalty) with the same power of law-making (*i.e.* by edict) as the Praetorian Prefect. His army was Gothic, but the civil service was wholly Roman. The *rex* nominated one of the consuls, the emperor at Byzantium the other.

Even in North Gaul, where the breakdown of imperial administration had gone much further than in Aquitaine, Clovis the Frank kept the Roman system going as well as he could. It was the inner breaking of the system, not any barbarian attack, that diminished Roman forms. Clovis gratefully received the rank of Consul.

Even when all power to control things or to impose agreements had gone from the emperor, the federate kingdoms felt themselves, however loosely, within the Empire; for they aspired to civilisation, which for them was synonymous with the Roman name.

THE PAPACY BREAKS LOOSE. In Italy the situation was more complicated. Here many of the imperial forms persisted, though at a lower level of integration than in the East. The Senate continued to exist, a local body with a ghostly aura of larger powers; and the Papacy, setting out to grab land and wealth, found itself driven to build forms of political and economic control based on those of the Empire. Thus the survival of Rome as an important city had the effect of wrecking any possibilities of an Italian kingdom, a unified Italian nation.

In the first centuries the Pope had been only a bishop of high prestige, and power was in the hands of the imperial viceroy residing in the city. Not till the seventh to eighth centuries, when the Empire has all its energies concentrated on resisting the Islamic attack, did the Papacy find itself able to manoeuvre at all effectively as a political power. What concerned the popes was the Lombard threat to their estates; they wanted to check the Lombards and keep on extending their domains. At first they found it advantageous to balance Lombardic and Imperial power in Italy; but as the Empire weakened, they swung towards the Franks as a more useful counter-check to the Lombards who had gained the areas north and south of the papal possessions.

Hence the politics of their wooing Pepin, while seeking to break any effective amity between Gaul and Byzantium; and at last the successful use of the Franks against the Lombards. But the Franks were all too

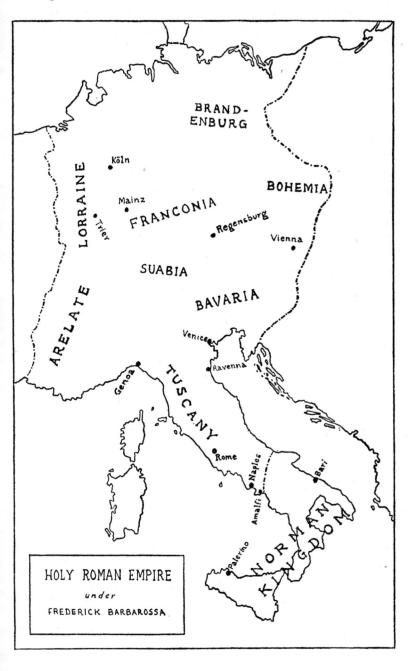

BRAND-
ENBURG

Köln

LORRAINE

Mainz

Trier

FRANCONIA

BOHEMIA

Regensburg

Vienna

SUABIA

ARELATE

BAVARIA

Venice

Genoa

Ravenna

TUSCANY

Rome

Naples

Bari

Amalfi

NORMAN

Palermo

KINGDOM

HOLY ROMAN EMPIRE
under
FREDERICK BARBAROSSA

successful. The Papacy had introduced a new danger in combatting an old one, and had to face the problem that in building an ally it had built a fresh threat to its own secular power.

Finally came the crowning in 800 of Charlemagne by the Pope at Rome, an episode which had been fantastically inflated by western historians from the ninth century onwards to the present day. It had been preluded by conspiracy and violence at Rome, a series of murders and clashes between the various groups seeking to control the Church; and it was while Charlemagne was visiting Rome to inquire into the charges against the Pope's morals that the latter crowned him. The whole episode is obscure, but connected with internal politics at Byzantium, where Irene sat weakly on the throne and was apparently contemplating a marriage-alliance with Charlemagne. Such constitutional force as the election held came from the plaudits of the 'Roman People'. The whole thing was a confused effort to make Charles a Roman Emperor (with the same title, shared or usurping, as that of the ruler at Byzantium): there was not the least intention to create an Empire of the West, which would have been inconceivable at this period. At most the idea was to bring about a situation similar to that of the fourth century when two Augusti ruled a single empire.

Charles was at a loss. He had no wish to fight the Empire to gain a title which might disturb his position as King of Lombardy. At first he ignored the thing; then, five months later, he made something of an attempt to usurp Byzantine formulas of protocol. But even so he was involved in two wars, which meant in the end territorial concessions and long negotiation before he gained recognition from the only government that could validate the title, that of Byzantium. The Empire was fighting the Bulgarians and glad enough to settle what was only a matter of prestige. Charles gained the title *basileus*.

But what, you may ask, was Charles emperor of? The answer is—nothing. . . . He himself from this time (812) dropped from his title the wondrous formula 'governing the Roman empire'—obviously part of the price paid for settlement. I need hardly emphasise the significance of this. Even those historians who have seen—and rightly—that 812, rather than 800, is the important date, have too often concluded that from 812 there really was a division of the Roman empire into east and west, and that thereafter the history of the Roman empire in the West is continuous. That is not the case. None of the Carolingians—with the possible exception, for a few months, of Louis II—nor indeed Otto I after them, ever thought to use the title 'Roman emperor', to which (as they well knew) they had no right. The Roman empire was not theirs; it was the empire ruled over by the emperors in the East. But that is not all. Charles, overjoyed by the outcome of the negotiations of 812, immediately proceeded to a step he could not earlier have lawfully taken, and in 813 he had his son Louis elected co-emperor. But even this was premature. By a curious series of accidents—it was, I think, no more—Charles died before the peace of 812 could be ratified; and it was in fact never put into force. (Barraclough.)

This matter is worth following out; for the confused falsifications about Charlemagne's 'empire' are part of the general propaganda, going back to the ninth century, which have obscured the real nature of European origins. But for the time being this propaganda was not German; it was purely papal, and was concerned to use the Franks to ensure the papal control of its vast Italian estates. The building-up of the Germanic 'empire' was, so to say, a by-product of the papal need to forge land-deeds on its own behalf.

The great papal forgery was the Donation of Constantine, which purported to tell how Constantine, suffering from leprosy, was visited by Peter and Paul in a dream and told where the bishop of Rome was hiding in a cave; the bishop showed him a painting of the apostles and he recognised his dream-visitors in the presence of his 'satraps'; after penance he was cured by the bishop and gave him supreme power over all other sees and patriarchates, plus a crown, tiara and other imperial insignia; the bishops of Rome got the right to secretaries, porters and guards on the imperial system, and the Roman clergy were empowered to ride on white horse-cloths and wear white-laced shoes like senators; Constantine further gave the bishops of Rome the city of Rome and all the provinces, districts and towns of Italy and the West as their subjects for evermore; then he removed to build a new capital in the East because it wasn't right for an earthly emperor to hold power where the head of the Christian religion had been established by the heavenly emperor. The document duly signed was set on the corpse of St. Peter.

This clumsy farrago was made the basis of papal claims and was held as the constitutional justification of the Pope's temporal powers all through the medieval period. It was made the basis for a further forgery, that of the English Pope Hadrian IV to Henry II of England to conquer Ireland, forcibly convert the Irish, and make them pay tribute to the Pope.

THE GERMAN EMPIRE. How did the western 'empire' fare? The first result was to convey something of the papal claims to the Germanic ruler. Thus, Louis the Pious, affected by the clerical idea of a 'Christian Empire', gained the aim of unifying his various dominions on the basis of a shared Christian creed. But this was too abstract a conception to work.

The Carolingian State broke down in its topheavy way. By the time of Pope John VIII the imperial title referred to a dominion diminished to the size of small Italian principality. All that had happened was that the political ambitions of the Papacy were stirred and the Popes had got hold of the title, which henceforth they clung to. From 823 down to the early sixteenth century the only emperors in the West were those who got the Crown at Rome from the Pope's hands.

But the chaos in the Frankish area meant that now both the Papacy and the 'empire' fell into the control of the Roman nobility, who set up puppet emperors from 891. In 924 the ridiculous title was suppressed. The ambitious house of Crescentius saw it as a mere nuisance impeding their aims of building Rome into a principality.

Then, forty years later, Otto I revived the title. The Frankish conflicts had begotten the idea that Charlemagne had been an emperor because he ruled over many peoples. This conception had nothing to do with the Roman Empire, but was born of the needs to build some sort of centralised control over the fissiparous dominions of the Germanic rulers. The title it envisaged was similar to the Anglo-Saxon *bretwalda*, the imperial claim of the Castilian monarchy, the 'emperors' in thirteenth century Scandinavia. But by intervening in Italy Otto I did come face to face with the Roman (Byzantine) Empire; and Otto II, to take a solid stand against Basil II, assumed the title Roman Emperor. Now the Germanic empire-of-conquest was really confronting the Roman Empire and matching itself against it. Under Otto III the Germanic policy mated with the ambitions of the aristocracy of Rome to produce a 'Roman' policy. But even so the State was not thought of as a Roman Empire. Henry II, Otto's successor, still used the term *imperium Romanum* to express only the imperial dignity, not a territory.

At last under Conrad II the term began to mean the lands collectively under the ruler's control. Now, and now only, it referred to a territorial complex and could not be bandied about (in 1024 it was offered to the French king and then the duke of Aquitaine). It signified Germany, Burgundy and Italy as linked under the Germanic ruler—no longer merely joined by a personal bond. That is, the basis of a settled large-scale German State was at last appearing. From 1040 the title King of the Romans was used to point out the emperor-elect or designated successor.

It is worth while following the history of the western title still further; for the clarification of this question is closely linked with the understanding of Byzantium's function in European origins.

The new Germanic State, loosely co-ordinated as it was, appeared in the eleventh century. Now the West was catching up with Byzantium. But the same general upward movement which had made possible the State of Conrad II had also strengthened the Papacy as an international organisation drawing tribute of various kinds from the whole West. And so there now began a sustained clash between the Papacy and the Germanic emperors, each seeking to gain the dominating position. In the long run both lost; the winners were the new national States growing up in France, England, Spain, and a result of this development was the movement of Reform that split up the Church in the sixteenth century.

But all that was veiled in the future. The three forces in the European world of the mid-eleventh century were the Germanic Empire painfully settling down into territorial stability, the Papacy with its vast landholdings and tribute-system all over the West, and the Roman Empire of the East. The institution of the Kingship of the Romans in 1040 and the schism between Rome and Byzantium in 1054 were both facets of the same situation.

In their clash the Papacy and the Germanic Empire both sought to use arguments drawn from the preceding developments and from the Roman Law which was being rapidly revived. Henry IV saw the need to link up with Peter Crassus and other legal experts of Ravenna; and a mixture of Roman Law and argument from actual historical process led to formulations like that of Hugaccio and Johannes Zemeke, 'He who is chosen by the election of the princes alone is the true emperor, even before he has been confirmed by the pope.' Frederick I now called the Empire *Sacrum* to oppose its inherent virtue to the Papacy, not to link it with papal concepts. The Holy Roman Empire was born in 1157 as an anti-papal demonstration. In reply the papal lawyers drew on Aristotelian schemata working out a doctrine of unity in opposition to that of the Two Powers which had previously dominated. 'The Empire appertains to the Apostolic See *principaliter et finaliter*', argued Innocent III. Then Frederick III wrested Innocent's weapons against the Papacy itself.

And so the struggle went on, but we need not follow it.

> The union of Germany, Italy, and Burgundy had made the Empire the preponderant territorial bloc in western and central Europe; and the national monarchies (as in the twelfth century they consolidated their position) first resisted and then challenged this German preponderance—a preponderance based not on any specific claim to imperial hegemony, but on the commanding position of the Empire in international politics; they used the conflict of empire and papacy to bring about a major shift in the balance of power, to the detriment of both. After 1197, still more after 1250, the really decisive factor is their policy, rather than the conflicting theories of popes and emperors. (Barraclough.)

What then are we to make of the nonsense which has been written about the Holy Roman Empire, of which the most outstanding example is that

13*

of Lord Bryce, who declared that this empire preserved 'the feeling of a brotherhood of mankind, a commonwealth of the whole world, whose sublime unity transcended every minor distinction', and that from Constantine's day 'the Empire was, conjointly with the Papacy, the recognised centre and head of Christendom'.

Such fantastic falsifications, whether stated with Bryce's naïve largeness of error or implied obscurely in a general focus, have in fact underlain all statements of the origins of Europe—and must continue to underlie it unless the effort is made to see Byzantium as the central fact from the fourth to the twelfth centuries. In so far as Bryce's words have any meaning they have abstracted it *from the Eastern Empire*, which did in fact maintain the concept of universality and keep the continuity of development between ancient and medieval world intact—and have then applied it to the West, where it acts as a total distortion of the truth of the historical process.

GERMANS AND BYZANTINE CULTURE. Except indirectly I have treated little of the artistic or political effects of Byzantium on the life of the Germanic Empire; but here, through the court, Byzantine art had one of its main centres of diffusion and re-development. The climax came under Otto III and Frederick Barbarossa; but I have no space to deal with the details. However, in the next chapter, where I shall look at trade-channels of diffusion some aspects of the part played by the Germanic areas in receiving and re-distributing Byzantine influences will be treated.

47

TRADE AND THE WEST

THE EARLY CENTURIES. The idea that trade between East and West at any time broke down, even during the worst of the attacks from Islam is incorrect. Trade was by far the most important single mode whereby Byzantine culture was diffused over Europe. In the sixth and seventh centuries Syrians, Jews and Egyptians were the main travelling merchants. Easterners had indeed been the missionaries of Christianity in earlier years—the confessors of the persecution at Lyons in 177 were mainly Anatolians—and now they carried Byzantine commodities and ideas.

In the sixth century there were many of them in South Gaul; Caesar, bishop of Arles, wrote hymns in Greek for his people; and in the North we hear of the Greek-speaking merchants of Orléans marching with songs to greet the king in 585. A Syrian trader (probably dealing with Britain) appears in an inscription in St. Eloi's Chapel in Eure near the Seine mouth. A Syrian bought a bishop's see in Paris, found his predecessor's *schola* incompetent and set up one of his own composed of Syrians. During the Justinianic expansion it was a big Syrian merchant Antiochos who led the imperial party at Naples.

Adamnan says that Irish monks used to visit Egypt to study monastic architecture; and pilgrims came only second to traders as carriers of tales and art-objects. A stylite (an ascetic who lived on top of a pillar) had come from the east to Yvoy. Gallic churches had the wide asylum rights of eastern churches. Egyptian Saints were highly popular. Jews were found at Clermont, Paris, Orléans, Tours, Bruges, Arles, Bordeaux; Marseilles was the centre to which they fled under persecution. They were not, however, much troubled, though the *Lex Visigothica* forbade them to proselytise and in 582 an effort was made to compel baptism—apparently at urging of the Byzantine emperor. They appear as sailors, or at least owners of ships, landowners (colons or *originarii*), doctors, but mostly as traders, specialising in spices. A Jew was agent for king Chilperic and argued with him about the Trinity. Imports included hangings, liturgical tunics, ivories, papyri. We even hear of a hermit near Nice who would only eat roots imported from Egypt. Camels were used as pack-beasts in Spain and Gaul.[1]

The return traffic was mainly slaves, though we also find textiles, amber, and perhaps madder; by the mid-sixth century and even earlier in the south the *ars barbarica* of the Germans had given way before direct Byzantine-Syriac influences. The tomb of Chilperic was made by Byzantine artists, and in textiles, manuscripts, paintings the same influence controlled the situation.

How strong the eastern influence in the Church was we can gauge by looking at the Gallican *Ordines Baptismi*, used by the Visigothic Church. Its uncouth Latin has been achieved by a word-for-word translation from Greek; and mistakes are made: *ante* is put for *anti*. Probably the same type early got into Ireland and Britain too. Its imagery betrays the merchant-class:

> Standing, dearest brothers, on the bank of this crystalline spring, bring from the land to the shore newcomers to ply the commerce of which they have need [*mercaturos sua commercia*]. Let all who embark on this voyage make their way over this New Sea, not with a Rod [*i.e.* reference to Moses and the Red Sea] but with the Cross, not with touch but with apprehension, not with staff but with sacrament. The place is small but full of grace. Happy has been the pilotage of the Holy Spirit.

IN ITALY. So strong was eastern influence in Rome in the seventh and eighth centuries that the *Liber Pontificalis* adds *natione syrus* after five popes between 685 and 731. Of the other popes in that period one is called Phrygian and two Greeks—while the Greek Zacchary held the seat 741-52. After him came the control of what has been called the 'Roman Pornocracy'. The easterners may have come from Sicily; but there were also many Greeks and Syrians settled in Rome, some of them fugitives from Islam or Iconoclasm.

As for Gaul, the contacts between Frankish and Byzantine Churches have been exemplified above for the Iconoclast period. When the eunuch Elissaros went to Aachen to prepare Rotrud as the bride of Constantine V by teaching her Greek, he found a crowd of eager pupils. One of the main problems of the Papacy in the later eighth century was to prevent a closer accord between the emperor and the Frankish king. Irene's son was betrothed to a Frankish princess—though his mother forced him to marry Mary of Paphlagonia (chosen in a brideshow). Theophanes says that Charlemagne asked for Irene's own hand—and though the relations

---

1 Though the money-circulation dwindled in the early phases of western feudalism, it never died out even at the most chaotic and backward periods. 'Money was an integral part even of primitive feudal economy.' (M. Gibbs.)

of the two courts at this moment are still obscure, they were certainly close. Michael I tried to marry his son to a daughter of Charles. The policy of the iconodules in the early ninth century seems to have been to work in with the Franks.

The Italian ports were still weak. Venice had been going through a long series of social conflicts, and was only now settling down to its role as the main link between Byzantium and large sections of the West though already, by selling Byzantine products in Ravenna, Venetians provided models in Carolingian art. The first trade-agreement with Byzantium did not come till 992. The Papacy was supplanting in the south the imperial civil service with its managers; but in some of the ports like Amalfi there were developments going on rather like those in Venice. At Amalfi the town-prefects (like the hereditary dukes who succeeded them as the port's prosperity grew) represented a local autonomy fallen into the magnates' hands; but these magnates were interested in trade-profits. Pisa had a fleet by 970; Lucca was beginning its trade in fine stuffs by about 953.

Gradually the economic level was rising; and every expansion of Italian or Frankish trade meant a penetration of Byzantine cultural influences.

WESTERN TOWNS. The tenth century brought some severe difficulties to the West—with Norman raids in the north, the Moslems thick in the Western Mediterranean. There were two Hungarian invasions, a Norman invasion of the Loire valley, and a battle between the French king and the Normans at Artois in the one year 926. The Hungarian raids went on in 933, 935, 955. Italy was devastated by Berengar in 962; and Saracen bands watched over the Alpine passes, killing travellers or holding them to ransom till 963 (or 983). Yet trade went on. Thus, we meet Greek seamen at Arles in 921.

Towns were still small, but they existed and were growing, if we define a town as a place with a permanent market. A place of some thousand inhabitants was a big city (they lay mostly north of the Seine). The great centres of the future, Florence, Siena, Pisa, Lucca, Ghent, St.-Omer were insignificant townships. The only places that show up as economically active in the eleventh century are Arras, Verdun, Rheims, and Pavia, Milan, Venice. In these towns were merchants (selling any sort of goods they could get, and transporting them): men above the peddling class, men who owned property. Thus, by the late tenth century the merchants of Milan owned the site of the market-place.

Pavia was the most important Italian city of the ninth to tenth centuries.

The Monk of St. Gall (*c.* 883) tells how the magnates of Charlemagne's army bought their luxury-stuffs at Pavia; and here (we learn in the early eleventh century) was the only place where the Venetians could sell their silks. When Liutprand was held up by the Byzantine customs who objected to the textiles he was trying to take out, he remarks how stupid it was, since anyone could buy the same materials in Italy through the Venetians or Amalfians.

Milan too was a thriving town. The merchants there were buying and selling land by the mid-tenth century, and were treated as friends and equals by the Count of Bergamo. Here also the Abbey of St. Ambrose, a vast manorial grouping, was an economic and social force that they had to consider.

In France and Germany towns were rising. Thus, at Cologne, where the old Roman enclosure had long stayed almost deserted, the traders once more took up quarters; and a small town grew up on the banks of the Rhine outside the walls. By the end of the tenth century the two towns had expanded to the point of coalescing, Dortmund by the tenth century linked the mines of the Harz Mountains and the Meuse towns of copper-workers. Verdun, centre of the slave-trade, had merchants going to Spain; Cambrai had many merchants living within its walls. (England was rather backward: even in 1377 not more than 8 per cent. of its population lived in towns.)

The areas now developing most strongly were Northern Italy, the great German rivers, Flanders. Fairs of international trading-importance were growing up after the check of the Norman attacks. In Champagne was a great meeting-place, set on the road between Britain and Byzantium; Flanders and North Italy; and there Fairs, like those described in *Timarion* for Thessalonika, were springing up.

It is, in fact clear that the end of the ninth century and the first part of the tenth saw a profound decline as a result of the invasions of the Northmen and the Hungarians. Only at Venice, which could profit by its relation with Byzantium, and in Germany soon after the middle of the century, where there was a strong government, was there the possibility of any real prosperity for the towns. Elsewhere economic life could only continue at a lower level. But we cannot speak of its disappearance for merchants continued to live in the towns, to travel, and to possess property. Many towns, after having sustained fearful injuries, arose from the ruins. New inhabitants came from the surrounding country, especially since the countryside was far from safe and the towns could at least afford some protection.

In Italy, Florence received an influx of citizens of the smaller boroughs in the neighbouring countryside. Little by little, the number of those in the towns who grew rich by trade increased, and gradually, whatever might be their origin—whether noble or peasant, from the *familia* of an abbey or bishopric—they all directed their aim towards the ideal of medieval cities: control of the government of their city. Soon it was to appear inconceivable that the rich *bourgeoisie* should not be in control of urban affairs. Even when in the later Middle Ages political disaster overtook these classes, as, for example, at Ghent in 1302, or at the end of the fifteenth century at Arras, a new patriciate rapidly re-formed in the image of that which had gone. In Germany even, where no centralised power was ever able to exert any real measure of control, and in Italy, the government of certain towns by the patriciate lasted up to the French Revolution, as at Venice; or even into the nineteenth century. (Lestocquoy.)

SAINTS' RELICS AND RISING PRODUCTIVITY. At Venice the leader of the popular party (fishers, artisans, traders, shippers) came to power in 836 and carried on a vigorous policy of trade-expansion and pirate-clearance, till he was murdered in 864. Venice was set for her rise to mercantile supremacy. And the period of her rise was marked by yet another irruption of the Martyr into our story. As the Italian ports rose, they coveted the tokens of power-prestige represented by the relics in the eastern world, and set out to gain them by buying or thieving.

There was an old tradition (no doubt fabricated after the event) that St. Mark had gone from Alexandria to preach in Aquitaine, and, driven on to the Rialto in Venice, prophesied that his bones would rest where he stepped ashore. During the reign of Doge Giustiniani (827-9) three Venetian traders had the idea of stealing what were considered the apostle's relics. They tried to bribe the guard, who was afraid. They bade him wait till the saint himself commanded. The man then felt a keen desire to remove the body, and they put it in a basket with cabbages and swine-flesh —substituting another corpse in the tomb, which was resealed. The basket was then hung from the mast. But the opening of the tomb had sent a sweet smell through Alexandria.

> Therefore the pagans (Moslems) said, 'Mark is stirring.' For they were wont to smell such fragrance every year. Nevertheless, there were many of them who misdoubted and went to the tomb and opened it, and seeing the body I have told of in St. Mark's shroud, were satisfied.

The Moslems searched the ship, but ran in dismay from swine-flesh. But on the way home the ship ran into a storm while all the sailors slept. Mark told the master-mariner they were driving in on rocks, and the master woke the others.

> And if anyone will know the truth, let him come to Venice and see the fair Church of Monsignor S. Marco, and look in front of this fair church, for there is inscribed all this story, even as I have related it, and likewise he will gain the great pardon of vii years which Monsignor the Apostle (Pope) granted to all who should go to that fair church. (Da Canale.)

At first a church was hastily put up on land bought from some nuns, while the relics lay in the ducal palace; then in the eleventh century St. Mark was built by workers from Byzantium. The theft expressed the first daring rivalry with the Byzantine world; the building of the church the confident feeling of having reached Byzantine levels.

In the eleventh century the Venetians carried out another theft of universally revered relics. In 1019 Venetian traders with a priest of Malomocco landed at a promontory called Chiledro and went into a deserted monastery. A voice cried, 'Take this holy body, carry it off.' An altar was inscribed, 'You'll find St. Tarasio's body wrapt in a cloth.' They turned and saw a cave with four lights and the corpse. The priest had an injured arm, but it was healed as he entered the cave. As he raised the weightless body, the voice again bid them carry the body off. They bore it to their ship three miles off. Monks came running after, begging for Our Father to be given back. 'Once strange folk stole one of his teeth and they couldn't sail till they gave it back to us.' But the saint wanted to go to Venice, and so the ship sailed light as a bird over the waves, and the relics were put in the church of St. Zaccaria, to Venice's greater glory.

Bari too had its great relics-theft. St. Nicholas had his tomb in Lycia, but was famous enough to have churches built to him in France as later in Russia; he was praised in familiar hymns, and pilgrims came from far to his shrine by the sea. The Moslems long ravaged the area, and in the end the local people fled to the hills. There was a fine chance for the traders of an ambitious port.

Even emperors, it was said, had failed to get the relics. So some Bari-merchants at Antioch had the idea of trying and acquired tomb-breaking tools. Hearing that the Venetians too were after the corpse, they made haste. Two pilgrims, a Greek and a Frank, reconnoitred for them. Then forty-seven men took tools and arms, and went to the shrine. A monk showed them round but refused particulars as to where the relics lay. They lied and swore that the saint had appeared in a dream to the Pope, who had sent them to follow the dream-instructions. The monk tore his hair and said he'd die first. The Bari-men held him when he tried to raise the alarm. A flask fell to the ground in the scrimmage and didn't break. A miracle. They pointed out that heaven was on their side, and Matthew, a Bari-man, drew his sword. They all started smashing things up and at last they found the manna-bathed corpse. Matthew got down into the hole and passed the bits up. The monk screamed that the saint must indeed want to go or he'd never have permitted such boldness. 'Our Prince, Our Father, why do you abandon us? . . . Now we have no defender.'

The looters decided to leave a miraculous ikon of the saint, but bore off the relics. The local people rushed to the shore, crying:

> The Lord God accords you unheard-of favour, since our Confessor Nicholas leaves us orphans and adopts you, unknown people, as his sons. . . .
> Give us back our Lord and Father, Our Defender, Our Fosterer.

They begged at least some fragments, but the Bari-men replied that they still had the tomb and the ikon, 'The illustrious town of Bari well deserves to enjoy in its turn such powerful patronage.' The people then attacked the monk who let the saint be found, but the saint came to his aid with a miracle.

At sunset the ship sailed. A lark perched on it and sang:

> Let Bari then rejoice, let her exult, the Victory of St. Nicholas is sung in Latin, in Greek, among all the people. For it is truly a Victory the Saint has won in taking Bari and Apulia under his protection, delivering them from their evils.

They arrived home on May 9th. Everyone rushed out. What was to be done with the relics? Put them in the bishop's palace or build a new church? An abbot took charge; armed men guarded the relics; when the archbishop tried to get them, sailors and populace dashed up to stop him and in the riot two were killed. A decision was taken to build a new church. Over the weekend forty-seven persons, including an Armenian girl and a Bulgarian, were cured of diseases. Villagers thronged in; pilgrimages were organised; miracles abounded. (The archbishop was a Norman priest: hence the people's fear that he'd get away with the relics.)

So runs the account by one Nikephoros based on depositions of the sailors. The Greek version laments a little over tyrannical actions, but shows bitterness only towards the Normans. Another version, in Latin, by the archdeacon of Bari smoothes down the violent aspects and draws the moral that the coming of the relics westward is proof that Catholic doctrine is better observed, and with more fervent piety in the West than in the East.

The effect was to spread Bari's name all over Europe. Pilgrims came, even from Serbia, and enriched the sanctuary. Other shrines of St. Nicholas were built (*i.e.* St. Nicholas du Pont in Lorraine). Bari became the Port of St. Nicholas, and in 1096 the Crusaders paid it special respect.

Thus the relics of the martyrs, originally the gathering-point of a deep revolutionary emotion in the local anti-imperial groups of the early Roman Empire, became emblems and focal points of the new civil life in medieval Italy.

48

TRADE IN EASTERN EUROPE

THE JEWISH MERCHANTS. Ibn Chardadbeh, Minister of Posts under the Bagdad Caliphate, compiled a *Book of Roads and Governments* (846–72). He describes the Jewish Rhodanites, the traders and carriers between East and West. They set sail from the Rhone (*Rhoddanus*) and ports of southern France, and went as far east as India, China, Japan. Byzantium and Bagdad were frequented by them in their chaffering; slaves, furs, swords, silks they took to the further east, and musk, aloes, camphor, cinnamon they brought back. They spoke Persian, Roman (Greek), Arabic, Frankish (Latin), Andalusian and Slavonic.

> Sometimes they go on that side of Romania (Byzantium) in the land of the Slavs, then to Kamlidj, the capital of the Khazars; afterwards they swim across the Georgian (Caspian) Sea, then they come to Balkh, to Maveranahar (Turkestan) in the land Tarasguz (East Turkestan) and to China.

It seems clear that Kiev was the point north of the Black Sea from which they went eastward. We find them in 904 on the border between Bohemia and Moravia; and they were well known, for Clovis, on the application of the local people, subjected them to the same tolls as under the reigns of his predecessors Louis and Carloman.

The documents divide travelling traders into three groups: natives, Slavs from Bohemia or Rugia, and the great Jewish traders. Slaves are mentioned as carried by both Jews and others; and the Slavs trade in slaves, horses, wax. The Spanish Jew Ibrahim Ibn Jakub in 965 tells of Russian and Jewish merchants at Cracow and Prague.

The rising Italian ports were determined to break the old-established systems of Jewish trade in the Mediterranean. They relentlessly cut out their Jewish competitors; and early in the tenth century Jews were prevented from using Venetian ships. So the Jews concentrated on the overland route to the East, and Jewish communities sprang up in Mainz and Augsburg (early tenth century) and then at Regensburg and Prague (mid-tenth century).

Mainz became the main setting out point for east-going trade. Arabian dirhems, seldom found below the Elbe, have been discovered there and we hear of it as rich in spices, pepper, cloves, nard, costus, galingal. From

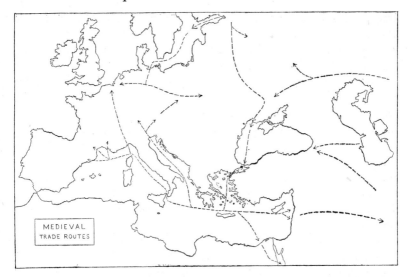

MEDIEVAL
TRADE ROUTES

the second half of the tenth century direct contacts were established with Kiev through Russian missions. The Venetians grew worried. They used the anti-Jewish policy of Romanos (932) to approach Henry of Germany and the Archbishop of Mainz with a proposal that unless the Jews accepted conversion they should be stopped from trading in metals, cloth, spices. Pope Leo VII wrote that it would be better to expel the Jews than convert them by force; but the Archbishop did nothing. The income from the Jewish traders was more attractive to him than the prospect of helping the Venetians to further wealth. Ibn Jakub mentions that Prague in 965

> is the richest city, by reason of its trade. Russians and Slavs come to it from Cracow with their wares, and Moslems, Jews and Turks come from Turkey with goods and money, and they take away slaves, lead and various furs.

KIEV. In the eleventh century the conversion of the Hungarians opened up the route of the Danube to Kiev. The road ran through Regensburg and Budapest. At Regensburg was a large rich Jewish community, and relations with Kiev were close.[1] Regensburg Jews had special privileges under the German rulers of the twelfth and thirteenth centuries.

The traders from Regensburg to Russia were *Ruzarii*; and their wares included, among the spices, gold-embroidered cloths and satins, which implied trade with Kiev and Byzantium. Kiev in the twelfth century still

[1] And as usual, trade-intercourse meant the spreading of 'heresies'. Moses Taku says of a Karaitic work, 'I was told this depraved book was brought from Babylon to Russia, and thence to Regensburg.'

traded with Byzantium and the East by caravans, *Gretchniky* (the old Russian term for travellers to Greece), which went through the steppes to the Crimean ports; from Surozh and Matarka (Tmutarakhan) eastern spices and Byzantine textiles were got.

Jews were settled in Kiev by the time of Igor and Vladimir; and the way in which cultural diffusion was aided by the Jewish groups may be exemplified from the *Sefer Hashoham* by an English Jew, Rabbi Moses Hanesiah (1170–1215) which cites a Rabbi Iza, who came from Chernigov in Russia and explained many Biblical words by a comparison with the Russian. And a rabbi of twelfth-century Kiev acted as an intermediary between the Jews of Western Europe and Bagdad Jewry. Bagdad, seat of the Exiharch and of many important soldiers of the Academy, such as Saadiah, was a vital centre of Jewish culture from the ninth to late thirteenth century.

In the eleventh century there were many Jews from Russia, speaking Slavonic, at Byzantium and Thessalonika. In earlier times they had come via the Khazars on the Volga; but after the irruption of the Polovtzy nomads, that route became dangerous. A Jewish merchant Petachiah of Regensburg has left an account of his travels to Bagdad about 1175. He went from Prague through Poland to Kiev, then six days along the Dnieper, which he crossed. He went across the area of the nomads in sixteen days, then sailed one day across the sea, landing in eastern Crimea (Khazaria). A journey of eight days brought him to the port where 'gather all those who wish to take ship for distant lands.' This was an old trade-area, once the centre of trade between the ancient Greeks and Scythians; the Khazars had held it, then the Russians, then Khazars and Polovtzy, then the Byzantines. When Petachiah arrived, it was still in Byzantine hands. He sailed across to a Turkish port (probably Trebizond) and went on via Nisibis and Mosul, to Bagdad.

THICKENING TRADE-NETWORK. These details are enough to show that apart from the direct trade of Byzantium with Kiev and Novgorod, which is well attested from the ninth century onwards, there was an increasing network of trade in Eastern Europe from the early tenth century on. This is the background against which we must read the story of the missionary work of Cyril and Methodios among the Slavs of Moravia in the second half of the ninth century, and the clash of Papal and Orthodox Churches along the line where German and Slav populations met. During this clash, Byzantium, by providing the Glagolithic and Cyrillic scripts, made a great contribution to the foundation of the Slavonic literatures.

And the pathfinding and linking work of the Jewish merchants in the East must be kept in mind when we look later at the important part played by the Spanish Jews in translating Islamic literature for the West.[1]

RUSSIAN TOWNS. Though I cannot here deal with the origins of the Russian State, it is necessary to point out the importance of the trade-relations between Byzantium and the Dnieper-area in those origins. But we must realise also that already in the seventh to eighth centuries there were many vigorous Slav towns—at Kiev, Novgorod, Yaroslav, etc.—with a flourishing artisan life. The Yaroslav area has shown fortified towns of some 10,000 sq. metres with spinning-wheels, planes, axes, pestles, crucibles, moulds, ingots, blooms, smithying tongs and pottery-implements in the graves. Norse sagas call ancient Rus *Gardarik*, the Land of Towns.

In the 9th century there was increased trade-movements from the north (Scandinavia) towards the Black Sea and Byzantium, and increased trade-movements out from Byzantium into the steppes and the Dnieper-area. These pressures speeded-up the growth of Kievan Russia into mature State-forms.[2]

[1] In the thirteenth century the Viennese closed the Danube to foreign traders and sought to get hold of the whole eastern trade. The Tartar invasion made things more difficult but did not halt trade. Plano Carpini met traders from German and Italian cities in Kiev in 1246, and Judah Crescas' map (fourteenth century) shows eastern traders came to Lemberg. Still now Kiev's importance weakened, to the advantage of Venice. Traders from Venice, Ragusa, Genoa appear in Hungary and Vienna in 1244. By the end of the thirteenth century the Jews had largely lost their position in eastern trade (partly through prohibitions aimed against them): that trade was carried on by the Hanseatic north and the Italian south. The transcontinental route across Poland and Russia faded out.

[2] We noted above that Russian art of the twelfth century was influenced via the Balkans. Kiev was in contact with Bulgaria and Macedonia and through Prague and Cracow, with the towns on the Danube and the Main, especially Ratisbon. Novgorod had links with Cologne, Lübeck, Hamburg and towns yet more southern.

Burmov (*Ist. Pregled*, viii, 1951–2) argues that Cyril and Methodios must be considered, not as Byzantine or Roman missionaries, but as apostles of the cause of the Slav peoples struggling for their own civilisation. Recent excavations in Moravia show the close relation of the six Slav tribes there with the S. and E. Slavs and with Byzantium (J. Poulik, *Jižni Morava*, 1948–50).

49

BYZANTIUM AND THE ARABS

NESTORIAN SCIENCE. I have already briefly mentioned that Arab thought was essentially Byzantine-Syriac thought, later fused with certain Persian and Indian elements, and transmitted to the West largely through Spanish Jews. Now it is time to look a little more closely into this development of Greek-Syriac thought within the Islamic world.

Both the Nestorian and Monophysite heresies were more rationalist in outlook than the creeds of Byzantium or Rome; they had a definite link with the scientific outlook of Hellenism, especially through Aristotelian theory and medical practice. Take for instance *The Cause of the Foundations of the Schools* by Marhadbsabba Arbaya, bishop of Halwen in the fourth century, who had studied under Hanana at the Nisibis school.

> By this admirable instrument (*organon*) of reasoning, the intelligence designs all the august images of certain knowledge. It creates a glorious statue after the original type. So that theory and the intelligence's reasoning may not stay inactive and useless, lacking the alphabet to construct names and to name, to instruct themselves on this essence and make manifest the power of this majesty, it has been necessary for the exercise of the faculties and as a sign of freedom, that the Creator should make this Corporeality, that he should adorn it with forces and colours, divide it into kinds and species, distinguish it by figures and operations, accord it individual properties, and set it in this vast gap between heaven and earth.

Knowledge is still looked on as the discovery of an archetype; but the whole bias of the attitude is towards an interest in the manifold forms of actuality, a belief that man can understand the world by a resolute use of reasoning.

The treatise traces the growth of Schools from Adam and Eve onwards; Plato and Aristotle are highly praised; a long account of Paul's teaching work is given, then an attack on the Alexandrian theologists for their 'bizarre fantasies. The director of this School was Philo the Jew, who as soon as he embraced this art (of Commentary) began to explain Scripture by Allegories, to the detriment of History.'

ARAB CONTRIBUTION. When the onset of Arabian tribalism, united and given its first basis of embryonic State-forms, overran Syria, Palestine,

Egypt, the conquerors had to face the problem of organising their conquests. In view of their own very low level of State-organisation, they
had no choice but to take over as much as they could of the Byzantine
forms; and this taking-over of Byzantine administration to control and
extract tribute from the townsmen and the farmers speeded up the inner
movements in Islam making for the breakdown of tribal equality and
the building-up of a State-form that controlled the Moslem warriors as
well as the subject people.

The story of the resistances put up by the tribal elements in Islam, the
forms of protest, the Messianic hopes and the continual rebellion against
the State by heretical formulations and by direct use of arms, is of the
highest interest, and throws much light on the allied but not identical
forms of resistance in the Christian world. But what concerns us here is
the ways in which Byzantium affected Islam.

To begin with, Islam itself was a product of the world we have touched
on in considering the Monophysites and Nestorians; a product of that
world impacting on the desert-tribes who were still largely free and equalitarian, defying the lure of townlife yet being continually affected by
trade and especially by the mixture of trade and holiness in the pilgrim-
centre of Mecca. To the Byzantines Islam was long only a new variation
of many-faced eastern heresy, a new fusion of Monophysite and Judaic
elements.

At its very root, Islam had integral elements taken from Palestine and
Syria. And when the Moslems came to re-organise Syria and the other
conquered areas, they simply carried on the existing forms—with certain
simplifications that often worked for the benefit of the farmer who had
lost his old lord. The Arab Empire was thus in the plainest of senses only
a section of the Byzantine world reorganised but still bearing all the marks
of its origin. Not till near the end of the seventh century did the Arabs
devise their own coinage. Their system was Byzantine; then through a
dispute which originated in the cross trade-mark on Egyptian papyrus,
they minted coins in Damaskos in 693; thus Arabic came for the first
time into the accounts, which had been till then in Greek or Persian.
The officials, however, except for a few heads, were still non-Arabs.
Under Walid, at the turn of the century, came the first attempt to displace the Christians in the administrative apparatus.

In everything except poetry and certain matters entwined with the
Qur'an, the culture was borrowed and adapted from the subject peoples.
Thus, even such a typical Moslem object as the *Minaret* (from *manarah*,
lighthouse) was devised from forms found outside Arabia: lighthouses
on Byzantine coastlands, watchtowers and churchtowers in Syria, signal-

towers and *stambhas* (tokens of deity) in Persia and India. The first architecture was directly Byzantine. In the capital Damaskos there was only
a small mosque till in 705 Walid took the church of the Baptist and reconstructed it into a triple-aisled colonnade with arcades on piers, a
transept based on the Bronze Doors at Byzantium, and a timber roof.
Over the transept was put a tall stone dome. The corners of the transept's
central aisle were linked with the dome's rotunda by semicircular arches
imitating Syrian churches. The capitals were gilded, and the walls were
encrusted with marbles or set with mosaics of cities and trees. Designers,
artists and artisans were Byzantine-trained. 1,200 workers from Byzantium were enrolled. The basic idea, followed in mosque after mosque,
was derived from the Bronze Doors and the Augusteion in Byzantium.
And when the great clock was installed in the twelfth century it was done
by a Persian.

A castle, dated in the earlier eighth century, has been found east of the
northern end of the Dead Sea: it gives us an idea how entirely Byzantine
was the court-culture of the new State. The main room has three barrel-
vaults; with apse-rooms, with baths (roofed with barrel-vault, cruciform
vault, and pendentived dome). Paintings with strong Hellenistic elements
show a haloed caliph throned under a column-held canopy, desert flying-
birds (often described by the poets), fish and a boat in the sea that laps the
throne-foot; a naked woman at cistern-edge; naked athletes; the rulers of
Byzantium, Persia, Abyssinia, Gothic Spain; horse-races, hunts of wild-
asses and antelopes, genre scenes, allegorical females. Two lunettes depict
the Creation and the Fall of Man; a pregnant woman, a man with back
turned to the viewer, and below, between them, a kicking babe; and a
woman by a dead man, with Azrael warding her off. Elsewhere the Ages
of Man in half-length figures. On the ground-squares and walls beasts
and birds abound.[1]

A NEW SYNTHESIS. In stressing the basic part played by Greek-Syriac culture in the culture of Islam I am not belittling the new element added to
the borrowed elements. The tremendous force that issued from the Arab
tribesmen did provide a new point of organising virtue, a new dynamic
unification, which Byzantium, wrangling with its heretics, could not
provide. Arab culture cannot be viewed apart from Byzantium, but it must
be seen as adding something essential to world-culture—to the synthesis

[1] Arabic architecture developed its specific forms, fusing Byzantine and Iranian
elements, and so on; drawing on local traditions (*e.g.* Visigothic in Spain); and linking with more direct Byzantine forces to help the founding of Gothic architecture,
Gothic engineering, etc.

which finally emerged in the twelfth to fifteenth centuries. Arab thought and science must be seen as a peripheral development of Byzantium in the same sense as the national States and free communes of the West. In both cases the peripheral areas were able to use elements which the central area could not fully use; they were able to break them away decisively from their roots in the ancient world and turn them to new horizons. Arab poetry had been a vital force expressing both the conflicts of disintegrating tribalism and the quest for a higher unity. It continued to thrive after Mohammed and his *Qur'an* (which used elements of tribal poetry, but within a wide focus ranging from folklore to Judaic or Christian texts); and helped to beget new forms, the philological and historical studies of tribal poetry and the *Qur'an*, and of the tribal lore closely connected with both. But it was through science and philosophy that the Arabs made their greatest contribution to world-culture—and that science and that philosophy were largely Syrian.

The great transmitters of Greek thought, in forms already attuned to a secular rather than a theological approach, were the Nestorians and Monophysites. We have traced the Nestorian movement from Antioch and Edessa into Persia, its seminary at Nisibis and its medical school at Gandisapora in Susiana. But the Monophysites in the earlier centuries toiled even more than the Nestorians at producing translations of Greek scientific work into Syriac (from which later they were sometimes translated into Arabic, though often direct translations from the Greek were made). Their school at Resaina was famed already in the time of Justinian for its translators, of whom the chief was Sergios.[1]

Monophysite scholarship seems to weaken after Islam's rise: perhaps the monotheistic element in Islam eclipsed the stress on God's Unity in the Christian heresy. (This suggestion is strengthened by the fact that when later in the thirteenth century Islamic thought has reached something of an impasse, Monophysite thought has a revival in thinkers like Gregorios bar Hebraios.) But the Nestorians, helped by the skill and high reputation of their physicians, became prominent in the Moslem world; and at Bagdad did much to spread Greek thought.

The eighth and ninth centuries saw rough but generally correct Syriac versions made of Aristotle's main works; then Arabic versions were made of these. The names of some of the translators were known even in the medieval Latin schools, *e.g.* Johannitius (Hunain ibn-Ishaq) who, by his

---

[1] Their monasteries at Kinnearin (Chalkis) sent out many versions of the introductory treatises of Aristotelian logic, concentrating on the *Categories* or *Hermeneutika*, with Porphyry's *Isagoge*, etc. These works they expounded, epitomised, used for compilations. Few students seem to have reached the *Analytics*.

own work and the work of his family, introduced to the Arabic world
many Greek writings on medicine, mathematics, astronomy. For the
next three centuries versions of Aristotle and his commentators multiplied:
in medicine Galen was most admired.

From first to last Islamic thinkers never claimed originality. Their aim
was to take over and diffuse Aristotle's ideas without alteration. But they
contributed a closer following of the texts, a barer and more realistic
exegesis, an increasing escape from religious preconceptions.

Hellenic science, beginning on a broad civic base, had narrowed in
Hellenistic days into the plaything of an élite—while at the same time
enormously developing its techniques. The mass-movement of Christianity which came to its head in Byzantium had broken down the élite-
aspects of ancient thought and made the concepts and modes of philosophic thinking the property of the common man, the artisan and slave,
even the peasant. But in Byzantium proper thought could not move from
its religious dogmas and achieve a revitalisation of Greek scientific and
humanist bases. That work, however, was carried out in its first stages by
the heretical movements. Those movements thus prepared the way for
Islam, the fulfilment of the Monophysite heresy on richer soil (that is,
among social groupings with a considerable amount of free tribal relationships still strongly alive). The intense monotheism of the creed, which
discards the sacramentalism of Judaic and Christian religions, provided
the cultural environment most fruitful for the stabilisation of the Nestorian and Monophysite contribution. (Sacramentalism tried to force its
way into Islam, in Messianic concepts of the Imamate, in the mystery-
cult of Hussein, in the cults of local saints, etc., but could not break the
central relation of Prophet and Allah.) Arab thought may thus be said to
re-secularise what Christianity had turned into dogma; but in the process
it inevitably took over the Greek ideas with something of the enriched
humanisation of the Christian phase—or rather Arab society provided the
environment in which the taking-over and re-secularisation could occur.
What Christianity had added was the insistence that the abstraction into
which Greek thought had died away should be given afresh a concrete
basis and set at the service of man. But its own terms created a new basis
of abstraction, that of dogma. Islamic monotheism, keeping Allah intact
and unincarnated, provided the atmosphere in which the dogmatic elements could be shed and the Greek ideas and methods rediscovered with
a new rational concreteness.[1]

___

[1] It is instructive to note the Arabic borrowing of various key-words; from the
Syriac the words for salvation, sign, soothsayer a priest (*kahin*), prostration, book
(*sifr*), monk, ritual prayer (*jalal*), alms, and ecclesiastic terms for godfather, water,

THE ACHIEVEMENTS. The foundations of the new synthesis were laid during the Damaskos Caliphate, in Syria itself; the development occurred after the withdrawal to Bagdad. Under Mamun (early ninth century) Greek science came into its own. At Gandisapora medicine had kept flourishing, and we know of one of its famous medical families, the Boktisho, many of whom practised in Bagdad. Indian medicine, too, came to add its skill. Harun called an Indian doctor to Bagdad, and the Barmakids had Indian medical treatises translated.[1]

Mamun, with his court library the House of Wisdom, had tried to foster these developments. He had Greek works fetched from Asia Minor; and in his reign the first important step was made to synthesise the gains. Abu Yusuf Ya'qub al-Kindi set himself to make the translated or adapted works of Aristotle and the Neoplatonists the common property of the Islamic world; he worked at natural history, meteorology, and astrology (believing the future could be foretold from shoulder-bones); and though he does not seem to have been an alchemist, he distilled perfumes. The practical bias of the new synthesis, its concern with industrial process, appears in his essay on Swords, which tells of twenty-five varieties, listed according to lands of origin; he knows swords from Yemen or Ceylon, France or Russia, and describes their qualities—*e.g.* how to tell damaged swords by gradual cooling. The first of the great Arabic encyclopedists, he stablished the new Aristotelean tradition.

Mathematics and astronomy were much studied. Euklid's works and Ptolemy's *Megale Syntaxis* (the *Almagest* of the Arabs) were translated for Mamun. Here too Hindu science was linked with Greek. *Sindhind*, an Indian work on astronomy, was translated and a summary made of it by a writer who also adapted Ptolemy's *Geographike Hyphegesis*. The same man, al-Khwarizmi wrote the first independent textbook on algebra, his name surviving transmogrified in algorithm.

Mamun also had Ptolemy's table revised on the basis of simultaneous observations in Bagdad and Damaskos, and a meridian degree calculated.

Not that we must make the mistake of thinking Islam a paradise of free

disciple, deacon, baptism, church, preacher, gong. Direct Greek loans are words for rite (*tags*), sexton, evangel, bishop, subdeacon, parish, girdle; a Greek-Syrian, priest (*khuri*), patriarch, monk's hood, heretic. Greek are the words for philosophy, music, geography; Graeco-Latin, for district, port, sailor (*nuti*). Persian are words for garden, sentry, trousers, sceptre.

1 Cultural contacts between India and Persia or Mesopotamia were many millennia old. In pre-Islamic days as Sassanid Persia was backward in music, Yezdegerd I sent his crown-prince to be educated in it at the Arab Lakmid court; the latter colonised later some 10,000 singers and dancers 'from Hindustan, all over the country'. Soviet archaeologists have found Hindu contacts rich in Khorezm (Central Asia) in this period.

enquiry. The same contraditions operated here as in the Christian State—
with the differences indicated by the analysis made above of Islamic
Monotheism. Thus, Mamun took over the theological position of the
Mutzilites who opposed predestination and held the *Qur'an* created in
time (against the efforts to make it as transcendentally mystical as the
Christian *Logos*). This position was rationalist ; but Mamun, making it
a State-dogma, handed its opponents over to the inquisition, and the
first victim was a fierce traditionalist ibn-Ranbal (who, however, later
got back into favour).

THE SIGNIFICANCE. The Islamic monotheism had to meet certain problems
which theologians tried to overcome by saying that the universe was
made up of infinite units lacking quality : God acted in every combination or change, indeed all causation was merely God's will and miracles
were as natural as nature was miraculous. To relieve the absolutism of pure
monotheistic ideas they took over the idea of Angels as the creative or
intellectual principles, and built up an hierarchical system similar to that
of Byzantine orthodoxy. Pagan Arab and Iranian ideas no doubt underlay
this development; but the organising method was largely Neoplatonist.

There is no need here to follow the movements of thought in the Caliphate of Bagdad up to al-Farabi and Avicenna, in which extended syn-
theses were attempted. But we may note how in Avicenna (980–1037)
the fusion of positions from Aristotle with those from the Neoplatonists
(who themselves often drew more on Aristotle than Plato) comes to a
head.[1] He seeks to break down the abstraction of ideas, to relate ideas to
process, to relate thought-process and natural process. The intellect (he
says) seeks to reproduce the forms of the universe and their intelligible
order; essences or forms may be looked on metaphysically, physically,
logically—in themselves, as embodied, as expressing thought-process.

Here we are only a few steps from Abaelard—and to reach even more
forward, we can recognise elements that look towards Bruno, Spinoza,
Hegel. The reorientation decisively begun by the Byzantine heretics has
been brought to a head. We may say that between John of Damaskos and
Avicenna the whole first stage of scholasticism has been worked-out and
most of the later developments anticipated. Not indeed till Nicolas of
Cusa, Copernicus and Bruno is another basic advance made. That is, the
work of western philosophy from the twelfth to fifteenth century was
rather to acclimatise Byzantine-Arab thought than to develop any new
dimensions of discovery. How little world-thought had developed be-

[1] He is followed by Ghazali, a reaction to God as the sole immanent cause; the
twelfth century sees decay and barbarisation : in 1150 the caliph ordered the burning
of a philosophical library, etc.

tween the third century A.D. and the fifteenth century can be gauged by taking a single sentence from Porphyry's *Isagoge*, the work that the Monophysites and Nestorians handed on to the Arabs. In this sentence is set down the problem that obsessed al-Farabi and Avicenna, the Nominalists and Realists of western scholasticism:

> Concerning genera or species, the question indeed whether they have substantial existence, or whether they consist in bare intellectual concepts only, or whether, if they have a substantial existence, they are corporeal or incorporeal, and whether they are separable from the sensible properties of the things (or particulars of sense) or are only in those properties and subsisting about them, I shall forbear to determine.

A sentence, also which shows how far in some ways the Neoplatonists were ahead of Plato (for whom the universal existed simply as an archetype in heaven)—or Aristotle, for that matter, since he never formulated the logical issue with this clarity. The contradictions which Porphyry stated were those which thought had to confront and resolve before it could move forward, and it took some twelve centuries before a substantial advance was made, with the dialectical concepts of Cusanus and Bruno.

This is incidentally one of the countless cultural points which demonstrate the truth of the thesis with which I began: that Feudalism was breaking through in the fourth century, and that we confront a single basic phase of history thenceforward till the seventeenth to eighteenth centuries. The problems with which men wrestled over all that phase were at root identical problems and they were posed already when the Constantinean State was formed.

DIFFUSIONS FROM SPAIN. I shall not follow out the enrichment of Islamic thought in Spain, partly through the work of Jews; but I wish to glance at the ways in which in the twelfth century the trails we have traced led into the western world. The meagre western tradition had been fed by Latin compilers like Boethius and Isidore of Seville. The first important addition came in the ninth century when Hilduin and John Erigena translated the pseudo-Dionysios. But only in the twelfth century, as the West moved to a level equalising that of the East, did the influx of Byzantine and Arab thought become large-scale and continuous.

The Crusades in some ways opened up a flow of ideas from the East; but the Crusaders themselves were mostly brutal adventurers, and the main flow was by other channels.[1] More important were the contacts

[1] There were, however, in Syria, Stephen of Pisa (*c.* 112) and Philip of Tripoli (thirteenth century). Stephen linked with the medicine of Ali-ben-Abbas; Philip with *The Secret of Secrets* (attributed popularly to Aristotle). Adelard of Bath visited Syria, early twelfth century.

between Italy and North Africa. To Africa went men like Constantine the African (who died as a monk of Monte Cassino) and Leonard of Pisa. The former translated Galen and Hippokrates and Isaac the Jew, giving a new impulse to medicine; and the latter, son of a Pisian customs-official in Africa, learned enough mathematics from the Arabs to be the leader in that field in the West for the thirteenth century. The Norman conquest of Sicily meant courts filled with Arab doctors and astrologers. King Roger commanded the composition of a great Arabic work, the *Geography* of Edrisi. In the same period Eugene the Emir translated the *Optics* of Ptolemy; and under Frederick II versions of Arabic works on zoology were made by Michael Scot and Theodore of Antioch. Frederick corresponded with rulers and scholars of Moslem areas, and his son Manfred carried on his patronage of translations from the Arabic.

But Spain was the main source of Arab works. In the twelfth century scholars from other western lands began to look to Spain—men like Plato of Tivoli, Herman of Carinthia, Rudolph of Bruges, Gerard of Cremona, Adelard of Bath. And many men inside Spain worked hard at making available the Arab texts in translation, Hugh of Santalla, Dominicus Gondisalvi, and a large number of Jewish scholars, Petrus Alphonsi, Savasorda, John of Seville, Abraham ben Ezra. Astronomy, astrology and mathematics were mainly selected. Gerard of Cremona, most voluminous of all the translators, after mastering Latin learning, was led to Toledo through desire for the *Almagest*, which he could not find in Latin; there he encountered crowds of Arabic works in every field, and, pitying the poverty of the Latins, he learned Arabic to translate them. So we are told by the account that his pupils attached to his version of Galen's *Tegni*. By the time of his death in 1187 he had translated scores of works on optics, algebra, logic, astronomy, astrology, medicine. Other industrious translators were Michael Scot, Alfred the Englishman, Hermann the German.

Usually these men worked through a converted Jew; and though the versions often had many faults their total effect was invaluable.

> From Spain came the philosophy and natural science of Aristotle and his Arabic commentators in the form which was to transform European thought in the thirteenth century. The Spanish translators made most of the current versions of Galen and Hippokrates and of the Arab physicians like Avicenna. Out of Spain came the new Euclid, the new algebra, and treatises on perspective and optics. Spain was the home of astronomical tables and astronomical observation from the days of Maslama and al-Zarkali to those of Alfonso the wise, and the meridian of Toledo was long the standard of computation for the West, while we must also note the current compends of astronomy. like al-Fargani, as well as the generally received version of Ptolemy's

Almagest. . . . The great body of Eastern astrology came through Spain, as did something of Eastern alchemy. (Haskins.)

South France also carried on the work at towns like Narbonne, Montpellier, Marseilles, Beziers, Toulouse. Here Jews played an even more important part than in Spain.

DIRECT DIFFUSIONS FROM GREECE AND SOUTH ITALY. But though the main flow was via Spain, that which came direct from Byzantine areas was not negligible. Here translation was straight from the Greek, with no Arabic intermediary. Thus Henricus Aristippus made the first Latin versions of Plato's *Meno* and *Phaidon*, and the fourth book of Aristotle's *Meteorology*. He brought many MSS. to Sicily from Byzantium, one of which was a codex of the *Almagest*, from which the first Latin version was made. Eugene the Emir, who wrote Greek verse, also did scientific translations of such works as Ptolemy's *Optics* as well as the prophecy of the Erythraean Sibyl and *Kalila and Dimna*. Many other works of Greek science were done by the Sicilian school, the *Pneumatics* of Hero of Alexandria, Proklos' *On Motion*, the *Data*, *Optics* and *Catoptics* of Euklid. And the high attention paid to medicine is shown in the foundation of the school of Salerno which played a very important part in the development of medieval science. Alphanus, the poet whom we found above at Monte Cassino (Ch. 35) belonged to the Salerno School, praised it in his verse, and was the first there to publish medical treatises. That the school at this phase had a direct dependence on Byzantium is suggested by Alphanus' *De Pulsu*, which is based, not on Galen, but on a Byzantine treatise of the seventh century. Alphanus also translated a book on *The Nature of Man* by Nemesios of Emesa, and was largely instrumental in bringing over to Monte Cassino the Moslem doctor mentioned above, Constantine of Africa.[1] Byzantine medical texts had been known in Latin versions for centuries in Italy, we must remember.

Trading towns of North Italy also played their part. Thus at a debate held in Byzantium before the emperor in 1136:

there were present not a few Latins, among them three wise men skilled in the two languages and most learned in letters, namely James, a Venetian, Burgundio, a Pisan, and thirdly, most famous among Greeks and Latins above all others for his knowledge of both literatures Moses by name, an Italian from the city of Bergamo, and he was chosen by all to be a faithful interpreter for both sides.

[1] An example of the exchange between the cultures is to be found in George of Antioch, a Syrian-Greek, who served under the Emir of Tunisia, came over in 1112 to Roger I at Palermo, rose high in his service and endowed the Mortarana church. The deed is in Greek and Arabic.

James, we know, translated Aristotle's *New Logic*; Moses was a grammarian-poet and manuscript-collector as well as translator; Burgundio translated works by Basil, John of the Golden Mouth, and John of Damaskos, which had a definite influence in Latin thought—as well as Nemesios, the Greek quotations in the *Digest*, part of the agricultural compilation the *Geoponika*, the *Aphorisms* of Hippokrates and ten works by Galen.

Other Pisans of the colony at Byzantium who translated Greek works were Hugo Eterianus and his brother Leo (Tuscus). Leo translated both the Mass of John of the Golden Mouth and the *Dreambook* of Ahmed ben Sirin. Paschal the Roman compiled a *Dreambook* at Byzantium in 1165 as well as working on occult or alchemic material.

Even remoter lands contributed something. Cerbanus, a monk in Hungary, translated a work of Maximos the Confessor; William the Physician brought codices from Byzantium to Saint-Denis at Paris; and John Sarrazin searched in the East for MSS. and translated the pseudo-Dionysios.

These details are enough to show how central a part the translations of Arabic and Byzantine works played in the revival of learning in the twelfth-century West. And to show that the number and significance of the works done directly from the Greek was fairly high. Before Henricus Aristippus the West had known of Plato only by an old version of the *Timaios*; it was through the Byzantine channels that Basil, John of the Golden Mouth, John of Damaskos, the pseudo-Dionysios, Proklos, Hero and the advanced works of Euklid were made known.

The fact that generally Byzantium and Toledo, Palermo and Bagdad were all contributing the same basic elements to western culture, brings out what I emphasised above—that Byzantine and Arabic cultures belonged fundamentally to a single complex. That important new orientations were introduced by the Arabic world does not make the statement any less true. And western thought from the twelfth to the sixteenth century is part of the same movement, though here again important new orientations are introduced.[1]

MEDICINE AND LAW. The first western university, that of Salerno, was formed in the Byzantine area of South Italy, with Byzantine influences predominant. Alphanus makes clear that the cultural movement he represented had at its core a rivalry with Byzantium. Arabic medicine did not

---

[1] I have not dealt with the diffusion of eastern ideas and themes in tale, romance, etc., as there is no dispute as to its wide prevalance. The question of Arabic influences on Provençal poetry is still unsettled in detail; but as a general fact it can hardly be denied.

enter strongly into this school, *Civitas Hippocratica*, till its highest point of development had been passed.

Direct Byzantine influence, mainly through the Justinianic Code and Digest, appears also in the next important university, that of Bologna. Legal studies had never quite died out in North Italy—at Pavia and Ravenna they persisted; and Bologna rose in the later eleventh century, with great activity during the conflict of Papacy and German Empire. At first its secular character made the Papacy suspicious but Gratian in his *Decretum*, largely compiled from faked or forged documents, showed that legal studies could be put at the service of the Church. The university, constituted at the close of the twelfth century, arose out of the earlier organisations based on student guilds.

Legal studies flourished also in the South of France. A summary of Justinian's Code written in Provençal about 1149 for the use of local judges has been found.

50

EASTERN RENASCENCE

ARMENIA. But if the twelfth century laid the basis of the later western Renascence by bringing Gothic to a fine flower and by absorbing Byzantine-Arabic science, in the East we find a similar movement—or rather a creation of literary cultures on a higher artistic level than anything yet achieved in the West, but without the strong urban element that swings the West into new levels in the following centuries.

In Armenia a script had been devised on a Greek basis; and from the fifth century a literature using this script arose. A school of translators were set up, and members were sent to Edessa, Alexandria, Athens, Antioch, Kaisareia (in Cappadocia) and Byzantium, for codices in Greek or Syriac. The Scriptures, homilies and historical works were translated including works by Ephraem and the homilies of Aphraates. Faustos of Byzantium wrote a history of the later half of the fourth century, showing the completion of the phase of assimilations. He depicts in lively way the clash of petty princes and bloodfeuds of clans, the planting of Christianity. Ananias of Shirak was another historian.

Then came a series of original work as well as more translations: history, rhetorical exercises, biographies, polemics (against Paulicians and Manichees), calendar-works, chronicles, liturgical commentaries, hymns, meditations, breviaries. Greek sources were widely drawn on; Eznik's *Refutation of the Sects* (Pagans, Mazdeans, Greek philosophers, Manichees) shows the range of contacts. Armenian works were spread abroad in turn. *The History of St. Gregory and the Conversion* by Aganthangelos is known in Greek and Arabic as well as Armenian. And the historians showed an increasing national sense. The teenth century saw a rich flowering—in the Histories of John the Katholikos and Thomas Ardzrussi, and in architecture at such places as Ani and Akhthamar.

The traffic was by no means one-way. Armenians played a highly important part in Byzantine culture—in literature, science, architecture—as well as in the political life.[1] Already with the Iconoclasts Byzantine

[1] One example: the Armenian adventurer Mleh (Melias) came to Leo VI, served against the Bulgars, was sent to Melitene (where were many Aremnians), built up a small army, and won the area east of Melitene. He took the little town of Lykandros

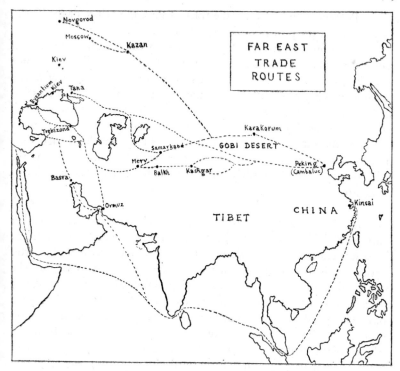

interests, economic and political, were strongly oriented towards the steppes and the Caucasus; and we find this system in full operation in the tenth century. The range of Byzantine diplomatic contacts at this phase and its wide series of vassals and semi-vassals can be seen from Constantine VII's list of foreign powers in varying degrees of close relationship with the Empire. Some sixty rulers are named. First come the Pope and the caliph of Bagdad (letters to the caliph and the emir of Egypt had specially heavy gold seals attached); and next are two Armenian princes, both called spiritual sons of the emperor. Other important potentates are the king of Iberia (Georgia), who has the imperial title of Kouropalates), the prince of Alania, the tsar of Bulgaria (to whom a note accords the title of *basileus*); then come lesser or more distant princes such as the kings of France and Germany (spiritual brothers), the rulers

(a strategic point), rebuilt the citadel; the government made it a *kleisura* with Mleh as governor. He pushed on, took Tzamandos, built a strong fort there, organised frontier-defence, called in many of his fellow-Armenians to settle the fertile area, consolidated Byzantine influence. The area was made a Theme with him as Patrician and General and the Church rushed in to arrange sees.

of the Pechenegs and Khazars, the ruler of Rus, the prince of the Turks, various emirs, the princes of Arabia and India.

The great burst of Armenian popular poetry came with the growth of national resistance to the Arabs, in the set of epic lays collected in some sixty-five versions by Soviet scholars under the name *David of Sasun*, Sasun is the City of Wrath built in the mountains, from which ceaseless war is carried down against the invaders. The folk-element is much stronger than in *Digenes Akritas*; the affinity is rather with the popular ballads of the Akritic Cycle in which Digenes is a miraculous babe, does tremendous deeds of valour, and wrestles with Death. Sasun was the wild country of the free tribes where the Paulician creed had its Armenian centre.

GEORGIA. Georgia had two main units, Kolchis and Iberia. In the earlier centuries Kolchis (Lazika), on the west, was more bound to Byzantium; Iberia was under an Iranian viceroy. The Arabs took over from the latter district and in the eighth century an emirate of Tiflis was set up. The eighth and ninth centuries saw a weakening of both Byzantine and Islamic controls, and a rise of national culture under the Bagratids, the Armenian house which had risen to dominance since 750. Finally, after an irruption of Abasgian tribes, a united Georgia was set up under Bagrat III in the early eleventh century. The new kingdom reached its height under Queen Thamar (late twelfth to early thirteenth centuries). Her reign saw also an attempt by the nobles (backed by the rising trading-class) to limit the kingship by a State Council.

Greek and Persian influences abounded in the fourth to seventh centuries. From Persian came a version of the pre-Firdausi *Book of Kings* in prose and verse; from Greek such works as the Alexander Romance and the *Physiologos*; (a citation from Homer appears in a hagiographical work. We hear of a mythological epic, which was perhaps never written down.

Then came a more fully literary culture. The terms for Poet and Poem were taken over from the Arabic; the Indian *Kalila and Dimnah* (which the Arabs had taken from Pehlevi) was taken from Arabic; and Yefimy Yver and others made many Greek translations. At the same time a national epic style in prose and verse was being created—such works as Georgi Merchul's *Grigori Khanzetli*, vivid tales of life in Georgian feudal society, with a strong feeling for nature.

Then from the late eleventh into the thirteenth century came the fusion of all these elements. There were close relations with Anatolia and Trebizond, and Georgians played important parts in the humanist revival of the Magnaura University in the eleventh century. There John Petrizi, a

Georgian philosopher, educated in Greece, was persecuted with John Italos; and in the early twelfth century universities were founded in Georgia itself, at Gelati and Ikalto, carrying on the Byzantine traditions. They were led by Petrizi, who had come home, and Arsen Ikaltoëli, an encyclopedist, also trained in Byzantium. Many of the Georgian writers of the century were trained at these universities, which they called New Athens, New Hellas. The Neoplatonists, the pseudo-Dionysios, Aristotle and other Greek thinkers were translated.

Efrem Mtzire wrote a book on Greek Mythology; and Homer, set out in abridged versions, was very popular. Rhetorical works from the Greek, the main Arabic medical encyclopedia, and the main Iranian achievements (books by Firdausi, Nizami, etc.) were absorbed in translation. The Georgian romantic epic and chivalric novel developed under this stimulus. Thriving schools of poetry arose composing lyrics, elegies, odes of high rhythmical variety, which fused Greek, Persian and Arabic elements.

This development was thoroughly humanist. In the magnificent epic of Rusthveli, which completes the movement, there is no reference to Christianity, but a rich knowledge of Arabic science and romance, and a reverence for Hellas. 'All the myriad tongues of the Athenian sages would be needed to praise their Athens fitly'. *The Knight in the Tiger's Skin* belongs to the wide complex which variously embraces *Digenes*, *David of Sasun*, Firdausi's work, sections of *The Arabian Nights* and the early Russian *byliny*. Its high chivalric tone and elaborate art links it, however, with the Iranian and Arabic forms rather than with *Digenes*.

RUSSIA. The penetration of Byzantine culture, largely through the Church, in Slav regions had as great a fertilising effect as in the Pontic or Caucasian areas. Through the struggle for a national basis, which the *Chronicle* of Nestor expresses, the Byzantine influences were absorbed and transformed. *The Song of Igor's Regiment*, an epical narrative in rich rhythmical prose describes a Novgorod raid against the nomad Polovtzy in 1185; it is a highly lyrical work with elements from folklore lifted to a bardic level of sustained power. Man's unity with nature is deeply felt, and the trees and birds help Igor in his escape. The same quality was carried on in the *byliny*, epic rhapsodies, which told of the great days of Vladimir of Kiev, of Novgorod exploits, of folk-heroes. There are many affinities with the ballad-cycles of Byzantine Greek.

Byzantine influence also appears in such works as *The Pilgrimage of the Prior Daniel* (to Jerusalem, early twelfth century), which shows how the pilgrim-routes like the trade-routes kept up a lively flow of contacts. A

large number of Apocrypha from the Byzantine areas came in, often
through Bulgaria, which merged with folklore to express the sense of
convulsion, crisis, hope of basic change and renewal: *The Pilgrimage of
the Holy Virgin to Hell* or *The Appeal of Adam to Lazarus in Hell.*[1]

But there is no need to linger over the important bases provided by
Byzantium in the Slav areas, as the matter is not in dispute. It is important,
however, to realise the way in which in the eleventh and twelfth centuries the fused Byzantine and Arabic influences spread in all directions.
The western rebirth of scientific studies and medical institutions, of legal
studies and theories of the State, was only one aspect of the process of
diffusion of Byzantine-Arabic culture. An allied development was going
on in Persia, Armenia, Georgia, Bulgaria and Russia. In each area there
were variations derived from the different economic and political levels,
the local traditions and the specific inner struggles; but it is correct to
see in the twelfth century a vast development of culture from Britain to
the Hindo Kush, from the Baltic to the Nile, in which there is a fundamental unity as well as a complex variety.

What breaks this unified movement is a nexus of new developments
in the thirteenth century. The rapid economic and political growth of the
West, with its new type of town; the irruption of the Tartars on to the
Russian sphere and the destruction of the Kievan State; the collapse of
the Bagdad caliphate before the Turkish mercenaries which it has drawn
in and which take over the Arab dominion. In the last resort it is perhaps
necessary to reduce these factors, and a large number of related and contingent matters, to the differences in the forms taken by the town in the
West, in the Byzantine area, in Russia. Not that all the towns in any one
of those areas could be reduced to a single category; but there were
certain basic factors ultimately determining the general development in
each section.

Not that the town and its forms or bases can be abstracted from the
total political situation defined by the State in each area. The new possibilities of the free commune in the West are linked with the new possibilities of the national State; and so on.

We may here leave the matter at the statement that the rich unity-and-
variety of the twelfth century is in many respects broken by the fourteenth

---

[1] In Russia the bulk of orthodox song, *Znammeny Rospey*, is syllabic like early
Byzantine; its modality corresponds to the Byzantine and eastern systems. So too
with other Slavonic church-music, especially the Macedonian and Bulgarian chant,
where we meet even the Hellenistic-Jewish *tropos spondeiakos* cited by Clement of
Alexandria.

The Phrygian mode with the augmented second is common to the music of
Byzantium, the Arabs, the Turks, the South-east Russians, and the eastern Jews.

century. A new phase arises; but this phase also has its unifying element which covers both East and West. What that unifying element was, what its inner conflict, I shall touch on in the final chapter of this book.

NESTORIAN EXPANSION. But before I leave the eastern area, I should like to mention the resolute missionary work of the Nestorians, which played a primary part in establishing distant contacts, cultural and mercantile. Nestorians reached China and India. Pehlevi inscriptions on crosses found near Madras and in Travancore testify to their presence in the seventh to eighth centuries. In 745 Thomas of Kana brought a new group from Bagdad and Nineveh, and 822 saw more reinforcements from Persia. Later we find the Malabar Christians with kings, imitating Hindu caste regulations, but still Nestorian. They had the misfortune in the sixteenth century to come under the Papal Church; the Roman Synod of Siamper tortured and burned them in 1560—though in 1812 the Inquisition of Goa was abolished by the Prince-regent of Portugal from Rio de Janeiro.

Already in 636 a mission had gone off for China. A later mission went the same way, many churches were built, several emperors patronised the faith. In the tenth century missionaries were in Tartary. In 1274 Marco Polo saw two of their churches and witnessed that they had sites all along the route from Bagdad to Pekin. Such churches stood at Halavan (Media) and Merv (Khorasan), at Herat, Tashkent, Samarqand, Baluk, Kashgar, even at Kambaluk (Pekin) and Singan fu (Hsi'en fu) in China; at Kaljana and Kranganore in India.

Finally Turkish and Mongol expansions broke their lifelines; but for centuries they linked vast areas. Nestorian monks brought Justinian the silkworm from China. They contributed elements to Tibetan lamaism and it was through the exchanges they set up that we find, for instance, a Chinaman born in Pekin come to administer communion to our Edward I in Gascony.

A CHINESE DESCRIPTION. It is of interest then to pause for a moment and look at Byzantium through the eyes of a Chinese traveller, probably of the seventh to eighth centuries—that is, during the T'ang dynasty (621–907) when exchanges with the West were at a high level.[1]

---

[1] One example of tale-exchange. Epiphanios (of Cypros, c. 315–403) tells of a valley where diamonds are got by throwing down raw sheepskins which eagles bring up with diamonds adhering. The *Liang se kung ki* tells the same story (early sixth century) of an island in the Mediterranean. T'ang pottery shows Hellenistic designs. The son of the last king of Persia fled after the Moslem conquest to the Chinese emperor T'ai Tsung. Chinese pottery of the T'ang period had been found abundantly at Samarra (some seventy miles above Bagdad), etc. But contacts of Near East, India, China were immemorially old.

Fu Lin (Byzantium) is the ancient Ta Tsin. It is situated on the Western Sea.
To the southeast it borders Persia, to the northeast is the territory of the
Western Turks. The land is very populous and there are many towns. The walls
of the capital are of dressed stone, and more than 100,000 families reside in the
city. There is a gate 200 feet high, entirely covered with bronze (the Golden
Gate). In the imperial palace there is a human figure of gold which marks the
hours by striking bells. The buildings are decorated with glass and crystal,
gold, ivory and rare woods. The roofs are made of cement, and are flat. In
the heat of summer machines worked by waterpower carry water up to the
roof, which is used to refresh the air by falling in showers in front of the
windows.

Twelve ministers assist the King in the government. When the King leaves
his palace he is attended by a man carrying a bag, into which any person is free
to drop petitions. The men wear their hair cut short and are clothed in embroidered robes which leave the right arm bare. The women wear their hair
in the form of a crown. The people of Fu Lin esteem wealth, and are fond of
wine and sweetmeats. On every seventh day no work is done.

From this country come byssos (a fine stuff), coral, asbestos, and many other
curious products. They have very skilful conjurors who can spit fire from their
mouths, pour water out of their hands, and drop pearls from their feet. Also
they have skilful physicians who can cure certain diseases by extracting worms
from the head.

This is the Byzantium of the Iconoclasts.

51

ALCHEMY

ORIGINS IN GREEK PHILOSOPHY AND EGYPTIAN CRAFTS. There have already been a few references to alchemy in our narrative; but in order to estimate the contribution of Byzantine thought to the modern world, we must look further at the matter. The ideas of change and substance which alchemy used and developed were essential for the surpassing of the Greek levels of science. Geometry was the typical Greek science; and what the Greeks could not compass was the notions of real change which appear in intuitive and embryonic form in alchemy. We distort the whole issue if we see the latter as merely a mystical system and do not realise that its origin lay in metallurgical process and that it strove to grasp the nature of material transformation.

It appears as a fusion of Egyptian metallurgy and other crafts with Gnostic and Neoplatonic philosophy (which itself derived in part at earlier phases from metallurgical symbolism and craft-spells). One of the most important alchemical writers was Zosimos of Panopolis (third to fourth centuries), a Gnostic. From Neoplatonism came the ideas of sympathetic action, action from a distance, occult and manifest qualities, star-influences, the power and significance of numbers.[1]

The idea of Gold as Lifegiving is indefinitely old, linked with craft-ritual and metal-process. The ancient Egyptians were much interested in alloys looking like gold ('so that even the goldworkers will be deceived', Leyden papyrus, first to second centuries A.D.). The coloration was felt as an act of transforming virtue; and this metal-tinting was linked with the industrial quest for fabric-dyes. Here lies the origin of many alchemical

---

[1] A fragmentary fourth century poem shows the mixture of Greek and Egyptian cosmogonic fancies in alchemic ways. Zeus creates from himself a Second or Son God, Hermes, who with gold wand ends the war of the elements. 'And they forgot their immemorial conflict. From them the Son of God builds the Sky, a sphere of seven Zones "governed by the seven Leaders of the Stars", the constellations and the Earth at Centre. He decides to make Life and then change himself into the Sun (not yet made). "Night without day flowed on alone unbroken, glistening faintly under the thin star-rays." He roams the grey skies with the third orb, the *Logos*, "seeking a temperate clime for a City's founding", and finds Egypt. This Hermes-Thoth is the gnostic Trismegistos and the Principle sought of the alchemists. He controls the elements with Golden Wand and is "clad in wonderful fourfold shape".'

methods: the dipping into mordanting baths, alloying, treatment with Royal Cement and Sulphur Water. This last reagent was a solution of sulphuretted hydrogen known as Holy Water because of its foul stink (gained by heating sulphur with lime and pouring water on). Zosimos advises care when opening up the jar; don't put your nose too near! He seems to have thought the tinted metals more yellow than gold itself and so more able to impart seed and ferment to other metals.

The three Leyden Papyri, the oldest dealing with alchemy seem to have come from a tomb. One has incantations of a fairly early Gnostic type, with lists of 37 minerals, plants, etc. (with both common and sacred names) and two metallurgical recipes. Another names substances used in the writing of magic formulas; the third has 101 recipes, of which 65 are metallurgical (mainly related to the making of gold and the alloy asemos), 11 are dyeing recipes, 15 deal with writing in letters of gold and silver; 10 are extracts from Dioskorides' *Materia Medica* on minerals used in the recipes. In a Stockholm papyrus the stress is on dyeing methods: of 152 recipes, 70 deal with dyes, 9 with metals, 73 with precious stones.[1]

Physika et Mystika by the pseudo-Demokritos (not later than third century) tells how to tint and gild metals, but shows no idea of transmutations. In the commentary by a priest of Serapis in Alexandria (probably late fourth century) practical details are blurred or ignored, and the alloying or tinting is mystically represented as producing real changes. Other followers (with names like Isis, Iamblichos, Moses, Ostanes, Eugenios) deal with colorations and the preparation of alloys by fusion.

The Neoplatonising workers took the line that experiments should begin with a nondescript metal which they felt to have no particular qualities: this they took as 'matter' in its lowest form. The problem was to impress purer qualities on it step by step till perfection was won: Gold, Light, Heaven, Regenerative Virtue. Such a base was often got by fusing the four common base metals, and was called tetrasmia.

They were here mixing the Platonic theory in the *Timaios* that matter was passive (needing to be impressed with qualities before it could produce specific metals), Aristotle's thesis of Nature as always striving towards a higher level (towards perfection), and Empedokles's theory of Four Elements, which Aristotle also set out, earth air water fire (also conceived as hot cold wet dry). And of Primordial Matter from which all came and into which all goes (so that one thing is ultimately changeable into another).

---

[1] In modern Greek the demotic word for silver is *asēmi*, with a series of derivatives parallel to those of *argyros* (silver); in origin it means bullion as opposed to coined money. Is *asemos* then an alloy, or silver proper?

The four bases were often lead, tin, copper, iron, which produced a black hue—perhaps the origin of the term Black Art. This basic fusion was whitened by heating it with some silver followed by mercury or tin. Then it was yellowed with gold and sulphur water as reagents. Finally it was turned violet, probably by certain alloys with a small amount of gold in them.

Leading writers of this school were Mary and Komarios, Hermes and Kleopatra. They used apparatus for distillation and sublimation, and were interested in the prolonged action of the vapours of arsenic, mercury, sulphur. Mary the Jewess (later identified with Miriam, Moses' sister) gained her first material by fusing lead-copper alloy with sulphur; she appears as the inventor of the main processes used by Greek alchemists, the *kerotakis*, the hot-ash bath, the dungbed, the water-bath. She is very practical, describes apparatus in detail, even the method of constructing tubes from sheet-metal. Mary's Black and the French name for the water-bath, bain-marie, preserve her memory. The kerotakis was a closed vessel in which thin copper-leaves, etc., can be exposed to the action of vapour; a continuous refluxing effect is gained by a condensing cover. With the alembic or still attributed to Kleopatra it made up the basic alchemist laboratory for many centuries.

The kerotakis and other forms of circulatory still gave the effect of a revolving space-movement, things above and things below interchanging. Kleopatra's *Making of Gold*, of which we have a single sheet, shows a still with two condensing arms and a kerotakis used for fixing metals. And the serpent Ouroboros with the words All is One. In a circle is written 'One is All and through it is All and into it goes All and if it lacks Nothing is All', and 'One is the Snake that has venom after two matings' (synthemata). The snake of unity (with its tail in its mouth) is born from the fusion-of-opposites—or rather unity gains venom (life-and-death power) after the fusion.

Mercury and sulphur were no doubt the metals most used in the kerotakis; they provided the basis for the later mercury-sulphur theory of metals—opposed opposites begetting unity, fire and water begetting gold.

COLOURS AND TRANSFORMATIONS. The alchemists were fascinated by bright red sulphides of mercury got by fusing mercury and sublimed sulphur in the kerotakis. The colour changed from black to white, to yellow, to violet. They felt that thus was gained a colour-apotheosis. Behind their ideas lay the colour-symbolism already discussed in regard to the faction-colours, which had carried the ziqqurat colours (expressing underworld, earth, heavens, sun) into astrologic meanings that attributed colours to he seven planets. In turn sound-harmonies were linked with colour-progressions. The seven vowels were aspects of the seven planets; and the same ideas gathered about the seven-stringed lyre, about scale-tones where each tone was thought to be uttered by one of the planets. Nichomachos of Gerasa developed the Pythagorean notion of a relation between the harmonies, the cosmic organisation, the system regulating musical intervals: he says that to the seven planetary tones the names of the seven vowels are given, and so on.

These fancies are worth a moment, for they give us the key to the basic unifying concepts in Byzantine culture, and enable us to see how the new architecture and art, the new drama and music, the ideas and images of the pseudo-Dionysios, are all aspects of a total process that includes the alchemic ideas and experiments. And how Byzantine culture gives a dynamic unity, on a new level, to elements from the Graeco-Roman, Egyptian, Babylonian, Syrian worlds. The clue to this dynamic element lies in the image and concept of a New Life defined in the *martyrion*. In Byzantine culture the mass-demand, which Greek and Roman cultures failed to compass, the mass-demand for a new way of life finds its first full objectification; it seethes under the esoteric forms of alchemy as much as the great heresies. Byzantine society cannot actualise the demand, but it can and does embody it in numberless significant forms. It breaks up the Graeco-Roman heritage and gives it the new possibilities that emerge in modern Europe and which are now being carried to a world-arena, the possibilities of secure freedom and universality, of a science capable of grasping and expressing the processes of change in man and nature.

Take Zosimos. Here we meet the Egg of the Four Elements, the Four Musical Elements, etc. The process of chemically colouring the Egg is dealt with. (That is, the problem of laying hold of the transformative processes of nature is raised.) He states the work of discovery as an initiation into the mystery of the Egg, the cosmic whole, which with its four elements is the embryonic stone of perfection; he related the alchemic process to the Mithraic mystery of Baptism and Death-Rebirth.

'Everything caused by nature,' he says, 'is one, not in form but in system.' *Techne* is the word used for system; it means craft or technique, the process and activity of changing nature by industrial method. The clue to unity lies in the active craft-relation to nature. By changing nature men realise the living dialectical unity within the various forms.[1]

---

[1] The social unity of the process can be guessed at from the term *stoicheion*, element, which also means letter of the alphabet. At Dura in the Zeus temple letters are given a symbolic connection with the heavenly bodies and related to the paintings. *Stoicheion*

AT BYZANTIUM. We find a fairly large alchemic activity in the Byzantine world—as far as we can judge by the manuscripts and the names of known alchemist writers. Thus we have a long alchemical work attributed to Olympiodoros the historian. Heliodoros wrote *The Mystical Way* (*Techne*) *of the Philosophers*, an iambic poem addressed to Theodosios the Great Basileus. In the sixth century a large treatise bore the signature Christianos. Under Heraklios there was Stephanos, and various writers (*i.e.* Pappos) may be set in the seventh to eighth centuries. Three poets, following something of Stephanos' declamatory style, belong to the eighth and ninth centuries, with Salmanas writing in prose. Michael Psellos dabbled in alchemy and wrote on it. But no practical advance seems made.

> Disputes as to the meanings of phrases of the ancient authors occupy much of their space. The development of elaborate analogies such as that between alchemy and music also interests them. Rhapsodical passages acclaiming the marvellous transformations brought about by the art appear, while the alchemical content remains completely static.

The initiative had passed over to the Arabs; but Byzantium still played a part as diffuser of alchemic ideas in South Italy and elsewhere. And it is clear that men like John the Grammarian and Leo the Mathematician at least kept alive something of both Hellenic and alchemic science. It is no accident that the earliest transcriptions of Byzantine alchemy are to be found in MSS. of the tenth to eleventh centuries at St. Mark's in Venice.

TRANSUBSTANTIATION. We realise the unity of the cultural trends we have discussed when we recall that the central sacrament in the established Christian Churches was concerned with the transmutation of one element into another. The Mass and the alchemical quest were different aspects of the mass-pressures operating on history, which I have noted above.

GREEKFIRE. Medicine, Geography and other scientific matters were never quite let drop by the Byzantines. Thus, in the seventh century, we find medical writers, Paul of Aigina and Theophilos, protospathar of Heraklios; and under Phokas the geographer George of Cypros was working. But there is no need to follow out such activities, which, however important in extension or codification of knowledge, open no new trails.

But an important creative development, clearly linked with alchemic experiment, was that of Greekfire. For some time fire-throwing weapons had been used, and the projectile was called Fire of Medea (naphtha), but

also meant External Soul, which at Byzantium was often thought to be lodged in a statue or work-of-art. By following this up we could relate the *stoicheia* complex to the ikon, etc.

the first large-scale use seems in repelling the Arabs in the long siege of the 670's. The perfected method was the work of Kallinikos, an architect of Heliopolis in Syria, who became a refugee from the Arabs. A liquid fire was squirted through metal tubes.

We have some recipes from a tenth-century MSS. 'Take pure sulphur, tartar, sarcocolla (Persian gum), pitch, dissolved nitre, petroleum, and *huile de gemme* (?). Boil together, saturate tow with the mixture, and set fire to it.' The flame could be put out only by urine, vinegar, sand. Another recipe comes close to gunpowder. A pound of sulphur was pounded with two of charcoal and six of nitre, put in a long narrow envelope like a cartridge which was closed at the end with wire, ignited and thrown (probably by catapult). The Byzantines knew how to purify saltpetre by treatment with potash and crystallisation. At least in one form the stuff was projected through a copper tube, and the account of its explosive propulsion implies a transformation of matter into gas and the projection of the incendiary mixture by the gas's force.

No wonder, then, that extreme secrecy was kept as to the manufacture. The Church had an anathema against anyone who betrayed the secret. The manufacture was carried on the Mangana Arsenal below the Palace, where were stored the library and maps of the general staff, and though later the Arabs managed to learn what happened in the chemical works there, Greekfire saved Byzantium at several crucial moments of attack.

> There where were stored iron-bound rams, catapults, arbalasts, stout tortoises, articulated ladders, satanic caltrops as well as cauldrons and boilers of bitumen and resin, the Arabs—disguised as simple peaceful workers or with some too-faithful friend as intermediary—certainly in the end gained some sections of the great secret.
>
> It is historically established, in any event, the Moslems made good use of it, at least from the fifth Crusade. At times they threw it in metal containers or glass bowls that broke over the enemy, covering them with fiery substance; at times the liquid fire was carried at the end of iron batons or lengths of wood —or indeed projection-machines were used, or some other method.
>
> The constant perfecting of which Greekfire was the object, gradually led to the discovery of fire-arms with tubes, rifles and cannon. It was then used in solid state, in powder form, to cast projectiles which were first of stone, then of metal.

Here, and not in China, must be sought the origin of the modern fire-arm. How far the Byzantines went in projection by explosion is still obscure; but it is certain that the chemical experiments which led to Greekfire laid the basis of gunpowder and fire-weapons in general.

SYRIANS AND ARABS. Kallinikos was a Syrian; and in Syria medical and alchemic studies were often intertwined. The Syrian medical school were transmitters of the alchemical tradition. Thus we find the medical treatise of Demokritos in ten books altogether with the works on the making of gold and silver by pseudo-Demokritos. The close relation to the Greek originals is shown by the frequent use of Greek terms and the direct taking over of signs and symbols.

From the Syrians the Arabs gained their knowledge of alchemy. Some of the works extant in Arabic are direct translations from the Greek, which as the Book of Krates which was perhaps the work of Khalid ben Yezid (died 708), a pupil of the Syrian monk Marianos and the first Moslem writer on alchemy (according to al-Nadim in the late tenth century). Avicenna and other important Islamic doctors are said to have been alchemists; but the most famous was Geber, who adds Persian elements to the Syrian traditions. His father, a druggist of Kufa, had been executed as a traitor to the Bagdad caliphate; and he himself was an ardent Shi'ite—that is, he belonged to the sect most inclining to mystery-sacraments and incarnation-beliefs. A keen experimenter, he described the preparation of nitric acid, and his laboratory at Kufa was found two centuries after his death during building operations.

It is extremely difficult to unravel the contributions of individual alchemists; but it seems certain that Geber laid a fresh stress on direct experiment. His theory was that of the Two Principles (sulphur and mercury) based on the Aristotelean thesis of Two Exhalations; and it held its ground till the Phlogiston Theory of Becher and Stahl in the eighteenth century, which provided the transition between Alchemy and Chemistry proper. Geber believed all other metals to be impure states of the Two Principles or to be not combined in the same proportions. If quite pure they fuse into perfect equilibrium, into gold; a defect in purity or proportion leads to the formation of silver, lead, tin, iron, copper. These accidents of combination can be removed by suitable treatment with elixirs.

When in the twelfth to thirteenth centuries Islamic science burst on the West, Geber's fame was vast; and many Latin treatises were fathered on him. We cannot check most of these, but in 1926 the Arabic original of a work translated as his by Gerald of Cremona was found in Cairo; and so the systematic element which seems greater in the Latin works than in his generally known Arabic works may be genuinely his. From the various versions emerge accounts of all the processes, cupellation, reduction, distillation, calcination, sublimation, used by medieval workers in the same field. They come basically from Greek-Egyptian texts; but Geber seems to have added to the idea of the kinetic quality in the two tincturing spirits or principles, which effects transformation, the idea of measurable relations, of a definite proportionate basis determining the specific mineral structure. Whether he did this, or whether he merely clarified an existent trend, this emphasis on measurable relations marks a turning-point in the foundation of modern science.

CRAFT-BASIS. That Arabic culture played a part in stabilising alchemy, and later in diffusing it westward, there can be no doubt. But there has often been an undervaluation of direct diffusions from the Byzantine area. We have noted the manuscripts at Venice; and we must never forget that wherever industrial processes involving transformations were carried on from the ancient world the alchemic tradition persisted. The high craft-skill in the Byzantine areas in works that needed chemical knowledge (jewellery, dyeing, glass-work, pottery, etc.) implied also a vital carrying-on of alchemical ideas. This fact can be proved. Thus recipe-books of the workshop such as *Compositione de Tingenda* and *Mappus Clavicula*—one known in an eighth-century manuscript at Lucca, the other in a tenth-century manuscript at Schlettstadt—include formulas found in the Leyden MSS. Similar traces of what we may call craft-alchemy appear in works like *De Artibus Romanorum* by Eraclius and *Schedula Diverserium Artium*, both eleventh to twelfth century.

And to turn back to Byzantium itself for a moment. Psellos in the eleventh century wrote his treatise on goldworking which adds nothing but shows how experiments were still carried on. But what is of greater interest is Psellos' own attitude. He speaks of descending from philosophic heights to the baser art-of-fire (that is, he feels the old Greek opposition of theory to practice) and of attempting to transform matter; and goes on to say that when he had meditated on the obligation thus imposed to bring the Hesperidean Apples to men, to turn lead into gold, he withdrew to take counsel with his reason and to investigate the causes of things. Thus, he says, after finding a rational starting-point, he might gain his end by scientific method.

He is aware, however vaguely, of the immense possibilities in the al-chemic quest, but he feels, rightly enough, that there is still a gap between the aim and the method. He wants a fuller scientific approach. It was to be many centuries before such a balanced viewpoint could have meaning in the West.[1]

---

[1] In dealing with natural phenomena like thunder and lightning, heat and cold, he tries to think rationally and bases his position in Aristotelean science as interpreted by Olympiodoros.

13. CHRIST PANTOCRATOR AND OTHERS

Mosaic, Monreale Cathedral, 1174–82

52

MUSIC AND ALCHEMY

EIGHTFOLD SYSTEMS. There is an important matter of musical development which I have left till now, as it is only after our analysis of the part played by alchemy that we can grasp its significance: this is the development of the Gregorian modes and the diatonic scale.

The concept of an eightfold modality goes far back, to the first millennium B.C. at least, and originates in the Mesopotamian area. Its origin lies in the complex of ideas we have been discussing above—ideas and images of transformation and organic relationship. One important link was with the ancient Pentacontade Calendar which originated in Sumerian and Akkadian days, and which had as unit seven weeks plus one day—a unit conceived of the seven seasons and seven winds over each of which a god was thought to rule. Over the seven gods ruled the supreme god, the Eighth. This calendar left many remnants in Christian computations (as well as Jewish); the East Syrian Nestorians still use four pentacontades: one for Lent, one after Easter, one after Pentecost, one from the first Sunday in November to Christmas. In western churches the pentacontade still appears in the period between Easter and Pentecost.

The relation of the number eight to music appears in early religious systems of the Near East, i.e. a Hittite text says that hymns to the gods are best done 'eightfold' (or in eight ways or eight hymns). Exactly what this implied is not clear, except that there is a connection with the pentacontade.

The system appears in Christian liturgy in the Monophysite work of Severos of Antioch, who composed or arranged a liturgical Oktoechos, a hymn-book for the eight Sundays of the seven weeks after Pentecost. (Paul and Jacob of Edessa also had a hand in it.) This Eightfold Song of the Monophysites was primarily a calendaric conception. But it begot the idea of a full musical correspondence to the calendaric changes of the liturgy, and by the end of the seventh century the Oktoechos was a system whereby the hymns were sung to a different mode on each of the pentacontadal Sundays.

The octave as the acoustic interval between a fundamenal tone and its first overtone (in the ratio of 1 : 2) has a concrete physical base, but does not necessitate the division of the interval into eight unequal steps. There are systems where the division is pentatonic, hexatonic, heptatonic, and the Hindu, Chinese and other eastern systems, as well as the chromatic scale, use smaller fractions. At least we can say that the eightfold division was facilitated and consolidated by various ideas and beliefs about the number 8.

Looking far back we can distinguish roughly the early moments when the basic concepts of the octave originated.

> The mathematical ratio of the octave interval (1 : 2) is an ancient Asiatic interval which preceded Pythagoras by at least 900 years. The identification of the octave interval 1 : 2 with the eighth tone of the diatonic scale seems to have taken place at the time of Pythagoras or not before. (E. Werner.)

CRAFT-BASIS. The tales connected with the latter identification are worth looking at, for they surprisingly verify the claim that mystery-myths derived from the fraternities of metal-workers underlie the alchemic fantasies and hopes. Gaudentios related the tale that Pythagoras by hearing the different tones of smiths beating on anvils realised the correlation of number and tone, cosmos and music. But Porphyrios says that he was told the secret by the daktyls, the gnome-miners, dwarf-craftsmen of the Idaian Mother. Elsewhere we are told that it was these daktyls who discovered in hammer-rhythm, in anvil-tones the clues to the nature and form of music, rhythm, melody, tone. The Idaian Mother is a form of Kybele, of the Great Mother who appears all over the early Near East, but who in this case is directly related with the Hittite Mother.

The myth then points to the origin of musical mathematics, concepts of musical form, ideas of the relations between musical rhythm and labour-process (especially metallurgical process), in the Asianic civilisation preceding the Greek.

With the collapse of Hellenistic metric and musical form, as discussed above, the problem of reorganising music on the new level required for religious group-expression led the Syrians to redefine modal bases in the same way as they redefined metrical bases. The liturgical *Oktoechos* became the modal *Oktoechos* of the new music.

NEOPLATONISTS AND HERESIES. We have seen above how Neoplatonist ideas linked musical theory and alchemy. Musical theory helped to build a sense of living organic relations, one thing (tone) passing into another in an upward or downward progression, and this progression being cut into definite stages or levels (where repetition begot something different).

It is noteworthy that the musical theorists of the early Roman Empire were mainly Syrians, Philodemos of Gadara (first century) and Aristides Quintilianos and Nikomachos of Gerasa (second century). Nikomachos takes the Pythagorean line (as also Plutarch in his ponderings on eight and the Cosmos) according to which the octave was explained as two tetrachords—manifestation of the cosmic Tetraktys of the four elements. Plotinos sets out the thesis of musical interrelations:

> The prayer is answered by the mere fact that different parts of the universe are wrought to one tone like a musical string which plucked at one end vibrates at the other as well.

And he tries to synthesise this Pythagorean view with the Orphic or Dioynsiac view (derived from the mystery-sacrament of self-identification with the dying-reborn god), saying that the tune of an incantation, 'a significant cry . . . have power over the soul, drawing it with the force of . . . tragic sounds.' Philos also uses the string-image.

The Gnostic heresies bristle with cosmic eights. In magic papyri and in the *Eighth Book of Moses* Ogdoas is the Omnipotent Name, made of the 'eight symbolic vowels'. In the *Acts of John* we meet the remarkable passage where Jesus makes the disciples dance a round-dance, holding hands (like the dance that appears in Serbian and Bosnian-Bogomil art) with himself in the middle. He ends his song

> The Eight (*Ogdoas*) sings praise with us. *Amen.*
> The Twelve (*Dodekas*) dances on high. *Amen.*
> The Whole on high has part in our dancing. *Amen.*
> He who does not dance knows not what comes to pass. *Amen.*

There are two versions in Greek and one in Latin (made by St. Augustine).

Tertullian says that the Valentinian heretics believed in a demiurge called Sabbatum 'from the hebdomodal nature of his abode' on a throne above the seven heavens; his mother Achamoth 'has the title Ogdoasa after the precedent of the primeval Ogdoas.' Here we meet a calendaric relation. Other heretics, like Kolarbasos and Markos, identified the seven or eight magic vowels with the four elements combined with the four qualities (hot cold wet dry); the seven vowels with the seven heavens (*Psalm* xix). Children used the vowels as a form of praise (vowel-combinations were substituted for Allelujah too) and the eighth vowel contained the *Logos* itself and could not be said by mortals (following *Psalm* viii, 3).[1]

Irenaios of Asia Minor makes the neo-Pythagorean link of the Ogdoas clear in his polemics against the heretic Basilides of Alexandria. He and

---

[1] The Parsees have an Ogdoas of Ormuzd and seven Amshapands on top of the realm of light.

Clement give the names of the members of the Ogdoas: *Pater, Nous, Logos, Phronesis* (Practical Wisdom), *Sophia, Dynamis* (Power), *Dikaiosyne* (Justice), *Eirene* (Peace). Irenaios also tells of the Gnostic Mother Ogdoas with names derived from corruptions of *Old Testament* terms for Yahweh. Hippolytos shows the part played by Sophia in these systems:

> outside then *Horos* or *Stauros* (Cross) is the Ogdoas as it is called . . . and is that Sophia which is outside the *Pleroma* (fullness) . . . and the animal essence is . . . of a fiery nature and is also termed the supercelestial *topos* and Hebdomas or Ancient of Days.

> Under the Ogdoas where Sophia is, but above Matter where is the Creator (demiurge), a Day has been formed and the Joint Fruit of the *Pleroma*. If the soul has been fashioned in the image of those above, *i.e.* the Ogdoas, it becomes immortal and repairs to the Ogdoas which is, says Valentinian, the Heavenly Jerusalem.

These ideas and images, which belong to the Neoplatonist and alchemic stream, show how closely linked was alchemy and musical theory with heresy. Severos the Monophysite made the liturgical *Oktoechos*, and the monks did much to carry on his work, even when they were orthodox. The Sleepless founded by Alexander were champions of the *Oktoechos* in the fifth century; and the earliest use of the term in a musical sense occurs in a story about Abbot Silvanos of Sinai in the fourth century. A monk says, 'Since the time I became a monk I have always chanted the series of the canon, the hours and the hymns of the *oktoechos*.'

THE ARABS. The Arabs, carrying on Syrian ideas, carried on this complex as well. Al-kindi shows that they knew the Byzantine *oktoechos* at least by the ninth century: and a typical statement is that by Ikhvan es-Safa of the same century:

> The musicians restrict the number of the strings of their lute to 4, no more nor less, that their work may resemble the things of sublunar nature in imitation of God's wisdom.
> The treble string is the element of fire, its tone dry, hot and violent.
> The second string is like the element of air, its tone corresponds to the dampness of air and its softness.
> The third string is like the element of water, its tone suggests waterlike moisture and coolness.
> The bass string is like the earth, dry, heavy and thick.

Bar Hebraios expresses the Arab-Syriac position:

> The inventors of the *Oktoechos* constructed it on four fundamentals, following the number of physical qualities. We cannot find a mode in pure condition without its entering into combinations with another, so it happens also

with the elements whatever is warm is also wet, as the air and the blood, or dry, as fire and the yellow bile. . . .

And he follows with a Christological application of the *Tetraktys*.

From the Arabs the ideas passed into western scholasticism, particularly through Aegidius Zamorensis.

STABILISATION OF FORM. In the same way that this complex of ideas provided the first disciplines for chemistry and medicine, it provided an organising system for the new music, which enabled the modal forms to be sorted out, given a theoretical basis, and finally developed into the scales and structures of modern European music.

> From Egypt. the new Pythagoreanism invaded Christianity, and a number of gnostic heresies resulted from that hybrid union. In Palestine, the ancient Mesopotamian calendar of seven weeks plus by one day was preserved by the Syrian and Nestorian Churches, and the conceptions of the Ogdoas and the eight modes were eagerly adjusted to the eight Sundays of the Pentacontade. It is characteristic that the ancient calendaric institutions were best preserved by the North and East Churches of Syria where ancient Aramean ideas might have been kept alive.
>
> From Syro-Palestine the Oktoechos, together with other liturgical institutions, were brought to Byzantium and to the spiritual leaders of Western Christianity. All these centres seem to have accepted the Oktoechos as a welcome systematisation of the embarrassingly abundant features of calendar, hymnody, and psalmody. Via Syria the eight modes eventually were absorbed by Arabic and Rabbinic musical theory, the latter renewing the ancient conception of the psalmists.
>
> At the same time and together with Christianised Pythagoreanism, the ideas of the magic vowels and the combined (two-fold Tetraktys: four elements and four qualities) made definite inroads on the thinking of the Near East, and later on, exerted a strong spell upon the Aramean, Arabic and Jewish thinking of the Middle Ages. (Werner.)

The fullness of the working-out varied from area to area. The Syrians seem to have implemented the theory very little in practice; the Jews made little attempt to systematise; the Byzantines developed to some extent a unity of theory and practice in regard to the *Oktoechos*. But it was at Rome, as part of the breakthrough of western music from the Syro-Byzantine bases in the ninth and tenth centuries that the substantial advance was made. For long there had been a welter of influences: *i.e.* psalmodic types that did not fit into the systematisation, such as the *tonus peregrinus*. And efforts were made at times to enlarge the number of modes to twelve, so that everything could be covered. But on the whole the great creation we know as Gregorian chant does show a definite congruence of scalar mode and melodic pattern.

Till the tenth century, however, it had not been the range of the octave that defined the mode; rather it had been the *finalis* and the relation of that to the dominant tone of the psalmody. Calendaric and astronomical correlations were floating about, as in Aurelianus Reomensis. And then with Guido of Arezzo in the eleventh century the octave plainly was conceived as the eighth tone of the scale. In his *Micrologus* he called that tone the octave. 'For there are seven different tones in music as there are seven days in the week.' (The use of the term *octava* for the eighth day of the week had been familiar since Augustine.) Now the identity of the acoustic octave with the eighth tone of the scale was solidly re-established, and the modes of the *Oktoechos* were set out in a diatonic scale.

The tremendous importance of the work of Guido (who taught in the Benedictine monastery of Pamposo) must not be undervalued; but we fail to get it into perspective unless we realise what it was putting into order—the forms produced by the creative stimulus towards a new music from the Syria of the heretics, and the tangle of intuitive concepts of transformation and organic relationship which the mass-forces had brought forward in place of broken-down Graeco-Roman science.[1]

Let us consider what the facts have revealed.

With the collapse of ancient Greek metrical systems, the systems of music also collapsed. The new rhythmical forms which expressed the mass-forces breaking in on the stereotyped élite-culture were at first uncertain, unstable. Slowly the new rhythmical systems, poetic and musical, were built up; and into their shaping went ideas born from the heart of the social process, the mass-pressures that demanded a new world. These ideas, though embracing music, had a far wider sphere of reference, and extended from the alchemic quest to the religious rituals of transubstantiation; from the new integrations of art to the struggle for Paulician brotherhood. Only thus was the discipline, which clarified and extended the new concepts of spiritual or artistic life in all spheres, effectively built up. Many centuries of effort went by before the secrets of Greek musical mathematics were rediscovered and stabilised on the new ground, the new levels. But when the discovery was made, a force of enormously greater potentiality than anything the Greeks knew had been liberated.

The shaping process was Syro-Byzantine; the stable union of scalar modes and melodic shape, the diatonic scale making possible modern music, was finalised at Rome out of the Byzantine bases.

[1] This development seems to owe nothing to the Arabs, but to be a differentiation and development of theory within the Byzantine area, which shows the rising cultural forces of the West.

53

NEW TECHNIQUES

SHIPS. To venture into the field of medieval technology is to begin a series of rather vague guesses, so little work has been done in this highly important matter. The casting of iron seems to appear much earlier in China than in the West, where it turns up in the fourteenth century; but it would be perilous to say that the last word has been said on the subject. Let us turn instead to a matter which though still obscure can be to some extent clarified, that of the modern ship.

Take the rudder. In the ancient ship the steering was by oars on either side of the stern. When did median rudder or hinged sternpost appear? What are we to make of such scattered evidence as the ruddered ship on the Belgian font (*c.* 1180), now in Winchester Cathedral, the Far-Eastern document of 1124 that described such a rudder, and the Japanese monument of about 1350 that shows one, the manuscript illuminated in 1237 by Yahya, son of Mahmud, that again shows one, the two clay-models of boats with vertical sterns (probably Saxon of the tenth century) now at Leyden?

And what is the way in which modern relations of rudder, rig, hull-design were devised? What of the fore-and-aft rig which eliminated the galley and slave-labour at the oars, and which by drastic reduction of crews made ocean voyages possible? Its earlier form was the lateen sail. A graffito of a lateen has been found on a ruined pre-Moslem church in south Palestine, but cannot be dated. Greek miniatures of the ninth century show lateen sails; in the twelfth century they appear in art-objects made at Venice, Amalfi, Benevento and other port-areas of Byzantine provenance.

The lateen sail, the first movement to fore-and-aft rig, appears then to have been devised in the Byzantine-Arabic sphere; and to have arrived in Western Europe via the Italian ports. A nexus of expanding energy, centred in Syria, seems drawing Britain and Japan alike into the adoption and perhaps development of new forms of technique. The compass certainly derives from this nexus, but where first it was adopted is uncertain. What we can certainly say is that the whole conception of magnetic forces derives from the systems of Neoplatonising alchemy.

MILLS. Look then at the mill driven by water or wind. The revolving mill seems born about the fifth century B.C.—at which date we find a large donkey-mill. Rotary hand-querns seem a little later, though this order of dating may well be the result of ignorance. However the resistance of a slave-economy to any labour-saving devices operated here too; and the Romans long clung to the use of pestle and mortar. As late as the first century A.D. the laborious method of the pestle was still used widely by bakers in grinding their corn, though we find some ass-mills at Pompeii. Meanwhile the watermill had been invented—the vertical type, certainly used round Thessalonika in the first century B.C. and still found stretching across Asia into China. This type is often used communally. The more efficient type, well developed under the Romans, had a horizontal shaft with vertical waterwheel—the shaft geared by cogwheels to a vertical spindle which turned the upper millstone. This is the type that spread all over Europe in medieval days. At Rome itself the Millers Guild resisted its introduction before the Constantinean State (that is, as long as slave-labour was plentiful). An undershot wheel (suitable for rivers of constant volume and swift current) was known by the later first century B.C.; and after the breakdown of the slave-economy the watermill rapidly developed and spread, reaching Britain by the eighth century. There were 5,624 listed in Domesday Book, in 1086.

Such mills were familiar in Byzantium, but the diffusion had occurred without Byzantine aid. The windmill, however, is a more complicated problem. The earliest form consisted of a building on a post or tripod—the whole building turning to face the wind. Later came the tower-mill, in which only the cap with the sail-beam was turned, with the turret-mill as intermediate type. As far as we know the windmill was an Iranian invention, in windy Seistan. Here the method was to use a vertical shaft and horizontal sweeps (as still in Persia). Apparently the method was noted by traders from the north, coming across Russia and the Black Sea. For the windmill seems certainly to appear in Europe in the North-west, in Normandy (about 1180) and Brittany, moving both across into Britain, and by land, southward and eastward, till it reached Italy. The change from the Persian to the western type was probably the work of people who knew the watermill of the Roman type and applied its system to the windmill, to beget the form with vertical sweeps.

From the story of the watermill then we can deduce how the breakdown of slave-economy released Graeco-Roman techniques and productive methods, which had been stifled for centuries. In the western windmill we seem to see the fruitful crossing of ideas which exchanges between East and West brought about.

With the possible exception of the potter's wheel the revolving mill is the earliest piece of machinery to replace a to-and-fro movement by a continuous rotary one. This is the principle of most modern machinery, whereby, for instance, we have the circular saw instead of the to-and-from movement of the hand-saw, and the ship's propeller instead of oars. (Curwen.) [1]

What of other circular movements in technique? What of the spinning-wheel that enabled the cloth-industry to speed up and in time led to modern textile machinery? We know nothing as yet for sure, though by 1298 enough yarn was being wheel-spun to make the guild at Speyer permit its use for the woof though not for the warp of cloth. About the same time wheel-barrows, halving the number of men needed for small loads, appeared in the West. But whether spinning-wheel or barrow were invented in Western Europe or in China is quite in doubt. The drawloom seems a Coptic invention, used for the early Byzantine silks, and not Chinese.

Church-bells with clappers may come from the West—or from China. Movable printing types may have come from Korea or may have been devised out of methods of casting used by jewellers, stamping used by bookbinders and illuminators, printing used by textile workers—methods that go back into Byzantine and Iranian spheres. The musical bow, transforming western music, may have come from Central Asia. The cross-bow may have originated in Roman days, been forgotten in China or perhaps Frankish Gaul, and then been brought to Byzantium by the Crusaders. Paper seems an application to vegetable fibre of the felting methods long used by the nomads of Central Asia with animal hair.

And what of the crank, that connected up the two basic forms of motion, reciprocal and rotary? This vitally important invention, necessary as a supplement for the wheel in any complex machine-development, seems to have been worked out by the simple folk who spread the rotary quern in the West—that is, it is a product of the breakdown of slave-economy in the areas overrun by the Germanic tribes. It is a labour-saving device that a slave-economy could not devise or adopt.

TRACTION. Two other devices which by increasing the labour-power of the horse lightened men's lot considerably and made many productive extensions possible were the horse-collar and the horse-shoe. In antiquity the yoke-method was used for harness, which begins to strangulate the beast if it pulls hard or fast; and the nailed shoe of iron seems unknown. Easily broken hooves and very low traction-power limited the use of the horse for any work, and extension of the traces for tandem harnessing was impossible.

[1] But the spindle too may be said to embody the flywheel principle.

The precise dating and place of origin of collar and iron shoes is obscure. The fact that the word for horse-collar in Teutonic and Slavonic tongues (English, *hames*) is derived from Central Asia implies that the collar itself was invented by the steppe-nomads. But however the details are finally sorted out, it is clear that these inventions could not mature under the slave-economy and were bound up with the new forms of work on the land that followed the breakdown of slavery.

Let us look then at the crucial matter of agriculture. The earliest plough was an adaptation of the digging-stick or hoe, and varying forms of this light plough continued. It was the plough of antiquity in general, used on small squarish fields. The heavy plough, with wheels, coulter, share and mould-board, seems an invention of the Germanic folk between Denmark and Bavaria. Drawn by a team of animals, it could break up heavy root-thick soil. It seems to have spread long before the Germanic invasions of the Empire. Thus, the Belgae seem to have brought it to Britain in the first century B.C., and it probably existed on both sides of the Roman-German frontier by the same period.[1]

The social effects of the heavy plough were as great as the economic; in fact the two cannot be untwined. To work such a plough, which needed oxen, the community had to pool its resources in co-operative ways. The result was the strip-field system, in which the common team ploughed in turn the strips individually owned. Here we see clan-kindred forms adapted to economic co-operation; but it is incorrect to say that the tribal element obstinately held to a backward form of production. Rather the tribal forms provided a basis of co-operative action because the resulting three-field system was the one best adapted to productive advance. It made possible spring-sowing, the tackling of rich, heavy soils, and increase of crop area with less ploughing.

There is a correlation between the new harness-method and the three-field system of the new agriculture. The first picture of the horse engaged in agricultural work seems in the Bayeux Tapestry. The horse—needing grain where the ox needs only hay—was more expensive than the ox, and needed a higher level of crop-production. By the later medieval period the horse in the open-field areas was driving out the ox, while in the two-field system of the south the ox persisted.

ENGINEERING. If we look at engineering and war-machines:

> There is, in fact, no proof that any important skills of the Graeco-Roman world were lost during the Dark Ages even in the unenlightened West, much

---

1 Pliny speaks of Italian peasants (? of Po valley) ploughing with several yokes of oxen; and the eight-ox plough team seems the system of land-division in Merovingian Gaul.

less in the flourishing Byzantine and Saracenic Orient. To be sure, the diminished wealth and power of the Germanic kings made engineering on the old Roman scale infrequent; yet the full technology of antiquity was available when required: the 276-ton monolith which crowns the tomb of Theodoric the Ostrogoth was brought to Ravenna from Istria; while more than two centuries later Charlemagne transported not only sizeable columns but even a great equestrian statue of Zeno from Ravenna across the Alps to Aachen. Incidentally, we should do well to remember that northern peoples from remote times were capable of managing great weights, as witness Stonehenge and the dolmens.

In military machines especially we might expect the barbarians to fall below the ancient standard; but at the siege of Paris in 886 we discover the Vikings, who presumably would be as untouched by Roman methods as any Western people, using elaborate and powerful artillery; while the city itself was defended with catapults. However, the Dark Ages do not seem to have improved on ancient artillery: the Roman level was not surpassed until the trebuchet, worked by counterweights, began to drive the less efficient tension and torsion engines from the field. (Lynn White.)

That claims a little too much. True, the techniques were always available —but where? In the Byzantine area. Both the examples given of heavy transport were carried out by men in the Byzantine areas of North Italy; and the Norsemen in the ninth century were in contact with the Russian cities and the Black Sea. Some twenty years before the Paris attack they had attacked, with Kievan Russians, Byzantium itself. And Greekfire was a decided advance on ancient artillery. Still, the point is correct; ancient techniques were never lost: if failing in one area, they survived in another and were available therefore for any area where the economic level rose sufficiently. And all the while the breakdown of slave-economy was creating new fundamental productive advances. The feudal epoch, generally speaking, was one of tremendous advance on the bases on antiquity; and was in no sense a retrogression.[1] But to make the statement effectively we must realise that feudal Europe includes both Byzantium and Gaul.

ORIGINS OF EUROPE. We may say in fact from the evidence presented above that Europe had three centres of origin, three areas from which originated the necessary economic and social forms and forces: Byzantium, Central Asia and the Germanic West. Each area contributed necessary elements. Byzantium preserved the ancient heritage, which included more than a literary culture; it included also the techniques of social, economic and political organisation. Byzantium transformed this inheritance in feudal terms and

[1] Even in roads, though there was breakdown, there were also gains. The Roman road was not suitable for the north, where it cracked, buckled, etc. The medieval world found a cheaper and better way of road-making with stone cubes laid in a loose bed of earth or sand.

diffused it east and west. Central Asia, linking Byzantium and China, provided various techniques such as felt and paper-making, the horse-collar, born from the contact of its free tribal life with urban civilisations. The Germanic area invented the deep plough and linked it with the three-field system.

The contributions of Central Asia and of Central Europe are in fact very hard to separate from one another. We must discard later political geography and realise that in these days something of a single region stretched from Western Europe to the Altai Mountains with its key-area on the steppes of West Siberia and Russia, and that this region devised, as well as the heavy plough that was the technological basis of the medieval manor, the stirrup that made medieval chivalry possible, and:

> trousers, and the habit of wearing furs, the easily-heated compact house as contrasted with the Mediterranean patio-house, cloisonné jewellery, felt-making, the ski, the use of soap for cleansing and of butter in place of olive oil, the making of barrels and tubs, the cultivation of rye, oats, spelt and hops, perhaps the sport of falconry and certain elements of the number system.

However much give-and-take between this area and the Graeco-Roman, the Byzantine-Iranian, and the Chinese civilisations, may have been involved in these inventions or adaptations, certainly this list gives a fair idea of the sort of contribution made by the great plains.

CLOTHES. The penetration of steppe-forms is illustrated by Byzantine dress. At Rome efforts had been made to keep out the barbarian modes. Trousers and boots were forbidden in 397 and 399; in 416 long hair and fur clothes were banned. But the pressure of change were too strong. At Byzantium the toga had been dropped in the fifth century for coats of stiff brocade. All sorts of strange costumes come in, peaked fur-trimmed hats and high turbans. Prokopios tells us of the partisan-groups, *stasiotai*, of the factions, who wore very wide sleeves drawn tight at the wrist, and who imitated Hunnic trousers and shoes. They let beards and moustaches grow, shaved their heads in front and wore their hair long behind, and went round in dangerous gangs at night. And the imperial parade-dress or *scaramangion* was copied from the Huns and apparently cognate with the Mandarin robe of China.

'We can say that almost all the nations, one after another, had their mode at Byzantium' (Kondakov). Hellenist purists like Prokopios might express scorn of such barbaric fashions. 'But these modes and novelties seduced the youth and set the law for the following generation.' Constantine VII in his account of palace-etiquette tried to obscure the radical changes that had gone on, because of the Hellenist reaction of the ninth to tenth centuries. But the account by the Kouropalate Kodinos shows that both generally and in detail barbarian modes had long dominated, 'modes, which, to ennoble them, it had long been the custom to attach to oriental models, or more precisely Persian.' The emperor and high dignitaries of the ninth century—military men, but also civil officials— preferred as outdoor costume the *scaramangion*. This riding caftan became the parade-uniform of the higher ranks of the Empire and its allies, and was made by imperial workshops as gifts to barbarians. It spread West: at the Burgundian court we meet silken *seidene scharmeyen* that derive from it; and the Italian *scaramucci* is again the *scaramangion*.

> A complete history of the diffusion of this costume would give us indeed precious indications as to the birth and evolution of the equestrian modes of Western Chivalry, which, historically, is closely linked with its Byzantine prototype. (Kondakov.)

BYZANTIUM'S ROLE. This rapid consideration of the present state of knowledge about medieval technology brings out the basic part played by Byzantium. Though the capital itself was concerned primarily with art-products, the Byzantine mercantile area passed on to the West the type of ship on which sea-commerce and ocean-voyages were to develop; and the Byzantine-Arab area created the basis of scientific theory and practice on which the West was to expand. But, apart from the direct debt to Byzantium, the drawing-in of elements from the steppe-cultures and the stimulus of new developments on the steppes was largely the work of the Empire; and in fact as soon as one attempts to generalise the process whereby later medieval Europe emerged out of the mixture of Graeco-Roman and barbarian elements, one is forced to realise the close symbiosis of the cultures in the three main areas I have mentioned; Central Asia, and the Russian steppes, the Germanic West, and the Byzantine complex.[1]

A ceremony which may be taken to symbolise something of the scope of Byzantine influences is described by the pseudo-Kodinos in the fourteenth century (though he may be drawing on earlier material). Before the Christmas Dinner in the Palace, the officials in their graded ranks chanted long-life *akta*; and after Genoese, Pisans and Venetians came the Varangians who chanted in English (*Inglinisti*) and clashed their weapons. Then another group gave *akta* in Persian, and a choir sang the Nativity

---

[1] Spaghetti seems derived from the Chinese *chow-mein;* on the other hand firearms, spectacles, and other such things were carried to China from the West. European engineers brought western siege-engines to the Great Khan, etc.

Canticle of Romanos. After that the Dinner was served. *English* may well
mean any sort of Norse noises for a Byzantine; but the apposition of
Varangian and Persian, with the canticle from the Justinianic age following, marks both the rich continuity of Byzantine culture, and its far-
flung network.[1]

[1] China certainly played a more important part in creating the techniques of the
medieval world than here suggested (see the Soviet historian Lvov), especially in
metallurgical matters and the allied sciences. But my discussion serves to show
how much work remains to be done and how inseparable are the developments in
West and East. For the eastward expansion, see J. Dauvillier, *Byzantins d'Asie centrale
et d'Extrême-Orient au moyen âge* (Actes du VIe Congrès . . . d'Études Byz, I, 1950).

54

THE ITALIAN RENASCENCE

THE OTTONIAN COURT. The German Empire, rising in the ninth century and reaching its height under Frederick II (1215-50), had steadily moved into competition with the Byzantine world; and had drawn throughout on that world for its central art-impulses as well as for such systems of organisation as it could socially absorb. That is, the movement from a domanial State to a settled system of administration, however determined and directed by local and indigenous forms and forces, looked to the East for its standards of what an imperial State should be. But though there was direct imitation in some respects, the great channel of influence was the Catholic Church.

The way in which the Roman *Curia* had grown up in the steady series of papal encroachments on imperial prerogatives and controls, and the way in which its system, extending tenaciously all over Europe after the Cluniac reforms, helped into being the State-forms that it resisted or tried to use, needs much further examination. The general fact however is clear. The Papal Church, by building up its secular system of power and property, speeded up State-forms to its own detriment and against its own will.[1]

However, the southward drive of marauding Normans and ambitious Germans brought direct contacts with both Byzantine and Arabic State-systems, with effects of suddenly heightened centralisation that could not be sustained. The Norman courts in Sicily, with their polygot secretaries, their doctors, poets and astrologers, their expert civil service and permanent archives, their lavish building in Byzantine style, were the first example. The climax of the allied Germanic movement came under Frederick II, who sought to build a complex imperial system and to encourage culture—his court becoming the cradle of Italian poetry. The

[1] Reading the *Acta* of any of the General Councils of the East, one is struck by their resemblance on the one hand to a meeting of the Roman Senate and on the other to a session of our Long Parliament (or even of the French Convention). The western medieval world had no such fine and complex procedures at its disposal, nor did it need them. But a study of the relations of feudal State-forms in East and West is badly needed, and will clarify detailed points of interaction in diplomatic, executive and other methods.

result was to wreck the German Empire, which could not sustain the clash with the Papacy.

But all the while ideas and forms were being borrowed from these experiments throughout Europe, contributing to the strength of the new national States as they emerged.

FIRST PHASES OF THE ITALIAN RENASCENCE. The great burst of Byzantine-Arabic culture on the West in the twelfth century was not followed by an equal volume of translations in the thirteenth and fourteenth centuries, though important new Greek works continued to be translated. Thus, William de Moerbeke, of Flemish origin, was sent by the Dominican authorities of Louvain to study Greek in Greece itself; and about 1273 he produced a good version of Aristotle's *Politics*.

The thirteenth century saw a considerable productive expansion in Italy, in Florentine cloth-industry, in Lucca's silk, in shipbuilding at all the trading-republics. The climax came in the later thirteenth century, then a sharp series of economic crises. Florentine production declined from 100,000 pieces of cloth in 1309-10 to 9,000 in 1382. But with the end of the fourteenth century an upward curve in production began again and went on through the fifteenth. The thirteenth century had seen con-centration of capital in trade and industry, with neglect of the land; but the crisis, caused at least in large part by this top-heavy state of things, drove capital back to the land and changed traders into landlords. With the fifteenth century the land-investment ceased to be merely concerned with the extraction of feudal rents; new land was won for cultivation, dairy-farms, canals.

This was the economic background of the revival of cultural forces which issued in the Renascence. We have already seen how Byzantine art underlay the development up to the stage of Giotto and Duccio; and though Byzantine contributions to the literary and philosophic side were naturally less plain and broadly based, yet the final phases of Byzantine humanism played a necessary part in the evolution of the Renascence.

Boccaccio and Petrarch typify the beginning of the new phase; they were hungry for Greek culture in its artistic aspects as the twelfth century had been hungry for Graeco-Arabic science and thought. One of the things bringing them together was a common interest in Greek, of which Boccaccio had gained some rudiments. Petrarch, though extremely anxious to learn Greek, never managed to read more than the capital letters of his Homer manuscript; he had to use the dry Latin version done by Leontius Pilatus, a monk of South Italy, whom Boccaccio generously set up as a teacher of Greek at Florence about 1360.

After Pilatus things languished awhile at Florence. Then came Manuel Chrysoloras as an envoy of the emperor in 1393 to Venice; he settled four years later at Florence as teacher of Greek. But, even before then, Italian scholars had been visiting Byzantium to work under him; and among them had been Guarino of Verona, whose broadcast praises of his work had been partly responsible for his Italian visit.

The efforts which the emperors of the weakened 'Empire' were now making for an accord with the Papacy and indeed with any western princes led to the conferences at Ferrara and Florence in 1438–9, at which further cultural exchanges were developed. At Ferrara, Guarino, now a leading Italian scholar and schoolmaster, acted as interpreter. (At the same time increased interest in lost or forgotten Latin writers was bringing to light many important manuscripts; the interest in Roman antiquity stimulated the interest in Rome's teacher, Hellas.)

Pupils of Chrysoloras carried on the work of translating from the Greek. Leonardo Bruni of Arezzo abandoned law through his love of Greek and translated works by Demosthenes, Aischines, Plato, Aristotle (*Ethics* and *Politics*). Scholars were eagerly collecting Greek MSS. Guarino brought more than fifty back from Byzantium in 1408; Aurispa, dealer as well as scholar, brought consignments in 1417 and 1422–3, the second of which consisted of 238 MSS.—nearly all the Greek classics. 'My whole industry, my whole cash, even my clothes I have often given for books.' Manuel II is said to have objected to his carrying religious works away from Byzantium, but did not mind how many classical texts went. Four years afterwards, Filelfo, who had been secretary of the Venetian Legation at Byzantium for some years, secured many important texts, became professor of Greek at Florence, and translated Xenophon's *Cyropaidia*. Later Cardinal Bessarion left his large library to Venice till such day as his enslaved country could redeem it.

A version of Plutarch's *Lives* was begun; Valla translated Thucydides (1452), encouraged by Pope Nicolas V, who had gained his love of Greek literature at Florence and who desired to make the Vatican a centre of Greek scholarship; Decembrio translated Appian; Traversan knew both Greek and Hebrew, and specialised in translating the Cappadokian Fathers, John of the Golden Mouth, the pseudo-Dionysios. Perotti, Bessarion's pupil (brought to Rome by William Gray, later Bishop of Ely) translated Polybios. And new Greek scholars kept arriving—Theodore of Gaza, professor of Philosophy at Rome, an elegant Latinist; Constantine Laskaris, who worked at Rome at the Messina; George of Trebizond, teacher at Rome and for long papal secretary.

But by this time the rising strength of Italian culture had given the

15

scholars and humanists for the most part a belief in their own superiority to Greek scholars. Some of the latter, who were playing their part in creating the new humanism, men like Joannes Argyropolous and Bessarion, commanded respect; but lesser figures like the fiery George of Trebizond, who was attacked voluminously by Perotti, were often trounced. Inevitably the Italian humanists felt drawn more towards Roman literature, in the language of which they still wrote and which they felt vitally related to their own political situations. And so, though the Greek enthusiasm had been a necessary phase and had brought some substantial gains, it had to be denied in the long run. 'Despite the heroic efforts of Aldus, the diffusion of Greek recedes from the beginning of the sixteenth century.'

PLATONIC THOUGHT. There was, however, one profound and enduring contribution made by the Byzantine humanists to the Renascence and to modern Europe—the study of Plato. Aristotelian method, which underlay the great twelfth century outburst, had developed scholastic philosophy, which had grown entangled at every point with the mature feudal ideology of the Papal Church; it had come to obstruct the adventures of thought which it initiated. To lift the conflict within scholasticism to a higher level, which made possible both the creation of scientific method along the lines laid down by Galileo and Newton, and the expansion of thought between Bruno and Hegel, the irruption of Platonic philosophy was now necessary. That philosophy expressed a deeper split between theory and practice, body and mind, than did Aristotle's work; but it also held in itself, only very imperfectly crystallised out, the elements of a deeper dialectic of unity than did the latter. It was precisely the element of deeper division that led on to the thought of men like Descartes and the scientific method of men like Newton, while the struggling element of dialectics, already strongly apparent in Bruno, moves on through Spinoza and Kant to Hegel and Marx.

Thus in the fifteenth century Greek thought fundamentally triumphed, and broke the spell of Aristotelian scholasticism. In 1438 at Ferrara the first shock to the old system was given. The antagonism of Plato and Aristotle was argued over between Ugo of Siena and the Greek scholars. By the time of Cosimo Medici (who died in 1464) Platonism had come to the centre of the intellectual scene. The arguments were still going on. Bessarion of Trebizond, an ardent Platonist, debated on the subject with George of Trebizond, and upheld his viewpoint victoriously in endless discussions on the same theme at the reunions at his residences, the Convent of the Apostles at Rome and the Basilian monastery of Grottaferrata.

These reunions constituted the first Roman Academy, and were frequented by Greek and Latin doctors, grammarians, philosophers, mathematicians. At Florence the visit of Gemistos Plethon in 1439, when he was over eighty years, brought about the Platonic Academy there. Plethon was steeped in Neoplatonism as well as in Plato's work, and regarded Latin scholasticism as a product of barbarism; he started off afresh the dispute on the merits of Aristotle and Plato, and wrote a treatise on the theme. A furious storm broke out, which Bessarion helped to quiet and which left Plato as victor. Plethon, absorbed in his idea of founding a mystery-fraternity of his own, went back to Mistra, where he gathered his disciples and composed a liturgy for his religion. When in 1465 Sigismundo Malatesta captured Mistra, he brought back Plethon's ashes for depositing in a sarcophagus outside the newly built church of San Francesco.

Platonist and Neoplatonist ideas soon permeated Florentine culture. Cosimo Medici set over the Academy Marsilio Ficino, a doctor, who set out to translate Plato into Latin and who later tackled Plotinos, Proklos, Porphyrios. Cosimo on his deathbed listened to Ficino reading his version of Plato's *Philebos*.

John Argyropoulos, disciple of Bessarion, carried on, to be followed by Theodore of Gaza and Demetrios Chlakondyles. Poliziano was the most famous of John's pupils. The Florentine school radiated its influence over Europe. Thus William Grocyn came from England, and so did Thomas Linacre, to study in the Academy; Grocyn became professor of Greek at Oxford, and Linacre ranks high among early humanist scholars in England.[1]

The climax of this Florentine Platonism came in the work of Pico della Mirandola, who had something of Plethon's spirit and sought in the *Qabbala* and Plato the key to a new universal comprehension. To Benivieni's *Canzone of Love according to the mind and opinion of Plato* he wrote a commentary on Platonic Love and Beauty, arguing that all science, philosophy and religion were facets of a single revelation. Ficino, Pico and Benivieni all deeply admired Savonarola; and both the culmination and the breakdown of Florentine culture appear in the premature dream of Pico and in the defeated democracy led by Savonarola. The union of Pico and Savonarola, though futile for Florence, looked forward, however, into the great struggles to follow.[2] The ideas of Plato had entered into the

[1] Other scholars were Becchi who learnt Greek from John and Platonism from Ficino; C. Landini who held the chair of Latin and Greek, and wrote a commentary on Dante; G. Manetti knew Greek.

[2] Pico brought about S.'s return to Florence and listened under a damask rose-tree in San Marco among the audience of S.'s lectures on the Apocalypse; S. wrote of him him, 'By reason of the loftiness of his intellect and the sublimity of his creed he ought to be numbered among the miracles of God and Nature.'

life-stream of Europe; and the working-out and the resolution of their contradictions were bound up with the working-out and the resolution of the conflicts inherent in the new society which was being born and which was to defeat feudalism at the crucial points of the Netherlands and England.

Thus, in its very death-pangs, Byzantium had yielded up a secret necessary to the new forces, necessary for the overthrow of medieval scholasticism and the building of the new science. The revolutionary forces, which Savonarola had sought to marshal but which were not yet strong enough, needed the anti-scholastic thought, the lines of new apprehension that led to Galileo and Bruno—to the world beyond feudalism.[1]

[1] In the process the new thought picked up the dissident lines of medieval thought (lines linked with alchemical traits we dicussed) : thus Bruno needed both Neoplatonism and Raymond Lully with his dialectic of correspondences.

Two details to suggest how even in literary matters Byzantium played an important role in Italy. The *Ritmo cassinese*, one of the earliest of Italian poetic texts, celebrates the Basilian hermits of South Italy, especially St. Nilos the Younger who came to Monte Cassino about 980 (L. Galdi, *VIᵉ Congrès*, 1950). And Dante seems to have based the moral order of the *Inferno* on a Byzantine treatise on Vice and Virtue, which was 'very probably one of the sources of our own *De Virtutibus et Passionibus*' (Trypanis, *Medium Aevum*, 19, 1950).

55

CONCLUSIONS

FEUDALISM. I do not wish to summarise the large body of material I have set forth summarily in this book; but there are a few basic points which I should like to state afresh or further discuss—the question of feudalism, the nature of the Byzantine State and its achievement, the attitudes to Byzantium among scholars, since Gibbon, and the relation of the picture here set forth to the Europe of our own day, the world-pattern of the twentieth century.

The statement that the third century A.D. was a revolutionary epoch shaking the foundations of ancient society with its basis in slave-economy, and that the fourth century saw the transformation of the Empire into a State already definitely and inevitably oriented towards feudalism, strikes at the roots of so many preconceptions that it is unlikely to command ready acceptance. It may be complained that I have given no full definition of feudalism; and so I wish here to cite some recent remarks on this point by a medievalist.

> Is not feudal society after all fundamentally determined by the relations between a landowning military aristocracy on the one hand and a vast class of peasant producers, working individual family holdings, but also organised in village or hamlet communities, on the other? I am aware that there have been many important modifications made to this simple picture [well summarised in E. E. Power's article in the *Cambridge Medieval History*, vii, (1932) entitled 'Peasant Life and Rural Conditions'] but I maintain that the picture remains fundamentally true for even economies of widely differing character, in so far as it defines the basic social relations between the two main classes of feudal Europe . . .
>
> The fact that the peasants were organised in an organic community and that they were in effective possession of their own means of subsistence is of the greatest importance. This fact contradicts, as it were, the legal claim of the landowners to the monopoly and free disposal of the arable, the meadow, the pasture, the woods, the rivers and the waste. The landowners were not, however, powerless. They were militarily an extremely powerful class, and whether the State power which they controlled was decentralised into private jurisdictions, or centralised under the direction of the most eminent of the feudal landowners, the king, they had all the means of coercion in society in their own hands.
>
> Their sustenance as a non-producing class depended on the transfer to themselves of the surplus produced by the peasant, above what the peasant needed

to keep himself and his family alive, and to ensure the reproduction of the agricultural routine year in and year out. (R. H. Hilton, *Economic History Review*, xviii (1948).)

This definition takes the essence of feudalism to be the transfer from peasant to lord of the peasant's surplus as Rent; one form of this rent is labour itself, when the peasant works (sometimes with his own equipment and seed) on the lord's demesne. There is no economic reason why the peasant should pay this labour-rent; it is coerced. Precisely because the peasant community can carry on better without the lord, a set of regulations are devised to secure the lord's claims and are ultimately guaranteed by force. Such controls and restrictions, operated in the manor court, come to be regarded as legal marks of a servile status.

How do these statements apply to fourth-or fifth- century Gaul? Fundamentally they apply as well as they do to thirteenth-century France. Fragments of the previous slave-economy were entangled with the situation; but if they were all eliminated the situation would not change in any essential. The lord existed on a basis of coerced rent; and though he may not be so militarised as the lords of the thirteenth century, landlords like Aetius were military barons as much as they were extractors of a feudal type of rent.

We must understand that no period is ever simply one thing. In the early Roman Empire we find many free workers, who work either for wages or for themselves, and slave-workers whose status approximates to forms of feudal serfdom. Still, the key-factor is slave-economy. In thirteenth-century France the towns are seething with embryonic forces and forms which will one day overthrow feudalism, and slavery is far from dead—it did not die till the French Revolution of the eighteenth century. But the carrying-on of elements from past phases and the emergence of new elements which chafe against the system is no disproof that the system exists; it is merely proof that we are dealing with a living situation. Past-traces and future potentialities are a normal and necessary part of a living organism.

Any definition of feudalism must suit both thirteenth- and eighteenth-century France. The French State in 1780, however stirring with forces of a new social and economic order, is tied still to the essentials that dominated in 1280. But what was vigorous in 1280 has become obsolescent and strained to its utmost in 1780. We must therefore beware of thinking of feudalism as limited to a single phase of history in which militarised fief-landlords coerce peasant groups into paying rents. We must be ready to recognise a series of phases in which the persistent feudal relations of lord and peasant are found to be modified variously by the stages of State-development, the stage of urban growth, the extent to which the free market is breaking through, and so on.

Once we realise these points there is no difficulty in calling feudal both the western development of centralised States out of disintegrating tribalism and the eastern development of a feudalised society within a centralised State.[1] Indeed it is the latter development which is the key to the situation, since tribal systems had often disintegrated before, and were to disintegrate later, without bringing about a feudal society and State. The ultimately determining factor behind western feudalism as behind eastern was not tribal disintegration; it was the third-century revolutionary struggle. Feudalism arose on the basis of the broken and transformed Empire, of the slave-economy of the Graeco-Roman world. That basis determined the essential lines of both western and eastern feudalism, which, as we saw, had evolved towards very similar levels by the twelfth century.

There is one other line of argument, which I have touched on lightly in the text: the basic continuity of ideological forms and attitudes between the Constantinian State and the mature medieval West, the continuity between Byzantine culture and the culture which developed in the medieval West as the economic level rose. Already at the Council of Nikaia the basis was laid which theologically persisted throughout feudalism at all phases. The Aristotelian terms of Leontios or Severos lead on to Scholasticism; Byzantine science leads into Arab science, which leads into western medieval science; John of Damaskos leads on to Thomas Aquinas. . . . The network is complicated and I have taken a large portion of this book in unravelling some of its main strands. There are many conflicts, changes of level, and so on, through the centuries; there is forward movement as well as repetition. Yet the more one penetrates into the mass of detail, the more one is struck by the fundamental unity of cultural developments from the fourth century on to the close of medieval days. The adoption of Christianity as the State-religion is not just something that happens to the ancient State; it marks a revolutionary change in society and the State, the break from a slave-economy towards a feudal basis.[2]

---

[1] Whether the peasant is tied to the land (as in the Constantinian Empire) or to the lord (as in the thirteenth to fourteenth centuries West) is unimportant: the first form is easier when the State is strong, the second when the lord has arrogated more of the State-prerogatives. The key-thing is the coerced rent.—Also feudal fees and fines, however inevitably they develop and however economically valuable to the lord, are offshoots of the primary coercion.

[2] The third to fourth centuries A.D. were the time of a general change and forward-movement on a much wider front than the Empire. In Persia it saw a political and

THE BYZANTINE WORLD-CENTRE. The first phase of a new society inevitably carries many impresses from the previous society. The Cromwellian State carried on many paternalist and other elements from the Tudor and Stuart States, which had marked the highest level and the decadence of the feudal State in England; but none the less it had broken down the feudal bases and made the first necessary liberation of social and economic forces that led to capitalist industrialism in the next century. In this sense it represents a transition from feudalism to that industrialism—but a transition that has behind it a revolutionary break in State-power. It was in this sense that I have called the Byzantine world the transitional form from ancient society. Many elements from the previous State were carried on, and slave-production was never fully eradicated, though it ceased to be the essential source of wealth. Because of the vast amount of forms and ideas that the Byzantine world salvaged from the ancient State, it was able to give the rest of Europe for many centuries the lead into new levels of social development. In this process it fed Europe with cultural and political forms, and ensured that the maximum of valuable achievement from the ancient past was carried into medieval society.

Here and there alone can be studied the key-processes of change from the ancient world based on slave-economy to the medieval world based on feudal rents.

But at a certain point, which we may roughly indicate as the eleventh to twelfth centuries, Byzantium fell back, and leadership passed elsewhere. There is nothing new in that. The ancient Greek States that led the way into a slave-economy fell back, and the leadership passed to the Hellenistic kingdoms and then to the Roman Republic. The Netherlands first broke through from feudalism in the course of their national struggle against Spain, but they soon gave way to England.

Byzantium fell back because of the very virtues which had enabled her previously to lead the way. Her centralised State inhibited the transformation of the towns, with their structure carried over from the ancient *polis*, into towns like the free communes of the West. The latter towns, while providing the economic dynamic that drove feudalism to its highest forms of development, also held the seeds of another order, the anti-feudal order of the bourgeoisie. We might say then that Byzantium fell back because it failed to develop inside itself the forces of transformation

religious revival (Zoroastrian) which had strong effects on the Christian and Arabian areas. In India it was the age of Samudragupta and Chandragupta II, the classical period of Hindu culture. In China breakdown and revival were going on, with Buddhist influences having a profound social and cultural effect. All these developments have a certain link within the international trade-nexus, in which the steppelands, Mesopotamia and Central Asia played important parts.

which were needed to advance feudal economy to its limits before they could break with feudalism and set up their own State-form.

Nevertheless, because of its long phase of leadership, during which it had taken over and transformed the culture of antiquity, it had generated a high degree of social consciousness, which enabled it to make precious and necessary contributions to the very forces of its own destruction.[1] In the long working-out of the conflict within Christianity, within orthodoxy itself and between orthodoxy and heresy, it had devised the ideology of mass-struggle that was taken over in the West by Cathar, Anabaptist, Puritan. In the long and painful effort to develop forms of cultural homogeneity against attack from outside, it moved from the traditions of the ancient imperial State to a new national concept, which, though drawing on the idiom of Hellenic city-patriotism, was oriented towards the new type of national state emerging in feudalism. Thus in the humanism which it steadily developed between the eighth and the fifteenth centuries it stabilised the old concepts of universality in terms of the new national needs; and by studying its heritage of Platonic and Neoplatonic thought it provided the element needed to crystallise out on a higher level the conflicts of the anti-feudal forces—just as at earlier phases it had provided directly or through the Arabs the ideology for the first rich stirrings of life, the conflicts in the medieval society of the twelfth century.

TERMINOLOGY. I wish then tentatively, in the light of our findings, to put forward certain suggestions for terminology in dealing with the end of the slave-holding Empire and the advent of feudalism.

The crisis of the slave-economy bursts out in the third to fourth centuries: this period is one of vast *revolutionary movements*, which fail to secure their goal (the liberation of the colons and slaves) but *which decisively shake the bases of the ancient State*.

The fourth to the seventh centuries makes up a period of *transition*, of feudalising trends. I suggest that we call this period the period of *primary feudalisations*. In the West it was marked by the merging of tribal militarism (the rise of the military noble with his clients) with Gallo-Roman landlordism and begot the Frankish kingdom, the first phase of the western feudal State. In the East it was marked by the transformation of the ancient State into a feudal State in which the old imperial bureaucracies changed and re-developed in ways facilitating the feudalising

---

[1] Materially, the Venetians and Genoese had leeched out much of the life-blood that might have provided the basis for an inner transformation; they inhibited the effective development of a Byzantine bourgeoisie.

16

trends; and begot the Iconoclast State in which a balance is attempted between a feudal nobility (with charistic tenures) and a free peasantry in village-communes—a kind of feudal State of which the West had no example. Only with the Macedonians did the Byzantine world begin to approximate towards the feudal systems growing up in the post-Charlemagne West.

The eighth century may then be defined as seeing the first stabilisation of *a definite feudal State-form*, though there are profound differences between the patterns emerging in the East and in the West. The tenth century sees the *strong extensions* of the new form; and by the twelfth century East and the West, each in its own way, representing *the mature feudal State in its first phase*, have come very close together. That is why this century issues in the decisive clash of the two halves of the feudal world in 1204. New phases of the feudal State lie ahead—*the national State* and *the absolutist monarchy* based thereon. These are the phases when the bourgeoise, not yet strong enough to challenge feudal State-power, are yet exercising a profound effect on social development.

WHY THE FALSIFICATIONS? But, it may well be asked, why has the truth of all this vast development, which conditions the whole of our culture, been obscured?

There are two aspects to the answer. On the one hand, the triumph of the anti-feudal forces led generally to a picture of the feudal era as a gap of darkness and irrationality. The breakdown of antiquity was identified with the failure of civilisation itself; and the new forms of thought were linked with ancient science and philosophy, medieval contributions being banished as barbarian. And though much work has been done to dispel the crudity of this position, yet the picture of a fall into barbarism still largely dominates people's minds.

The isolation of the historical process of Europe to the West aids this falsification; for the West does convey a picture of barbarisation for some centuries after the breakdown of the imperial State in Gaul.

But that isolation is made possible in turn by deeply ingrained propaganda, going back to the eleventh century, in which the rising forces of the West—initially the Papacy and the Italian ports, and then the German Empire—blackguarded the East. Such matters as the incredibly bloody behaviour of the westerners of the First Crusade in Antioch and Jerusalem, or the terrible treachery of those of the fourth Crusade against Byzantium, needed the compensatory depiction of the West as the source of light and high moral values.

The need of the Italian Renascence to base itself on Roman antiquity completed the tangled web of falsifications. The positions of the Byzantine humanists, which had developed out of the desire to integrate as many valuable elements as possible from their society's heritage into its present movement, were taken to justify the new social and political formations in the West at the expense of the medieval past. Hence the notion of a barbarised gap between the present and the ancient past was born; and the ancient past had to be glorified in order to build up the claims of the new State-forms, the new cultural activities. The embryonic elements of this position were indeed to be found in the later Byzantine humanists, who, as we saw, felt increasingly that the sad actuality and their patriotic aspirations were sharply cut apart; but the full split could only arrive when their positions were carried into the struggle against medieval authority which grows up in the Renascence and the Reformation.

Byzantium then blurs away from the minds of western men. The Byzantine State has fallen to the Turks, while the West survives—proof of Western superiority! Byzantine society cannot be equated with barbarised Gaul, so it is equated with the oriental despotisms that have come in its place.[1]

DU CANGE. Rather, that equation began in the eighteenth century, when the annexations of parts of India, and the increasing trade with the Levant and China, were matters of extreme importance. The birth of modern Byzantine studies, in the seventeenth century, was linked with a more respectful attitude, since those studies served to glorify the imposing growth of absolutism in Louis XIV's France. The works that may be said to found Byzantine historiography were Du Cange's *Historia Byzantina* (1680) and *Glossarium ad scriptores mediae et infimae graecitatis* (1688). Du Cange, who also edited editions of the Byzantine historians, Kinnamos and Zonaras, was a city-official of Amiens under the *Roi Soleil*, who was interested in the powerful feudal families of Byzantium, in the absolutist State-structure. Accepting without a qualm the new absolutist State of the West, he was happy to find its affinities and links with Byzantium. His great work was thus the simple though scholarly collection of materials. But the balance of attitudes he revealed could not last. As the French absolutist State rapidly began to show its limitations, its sharpening

[1] It is significant that this book of mine is the *first in any language* which comprehensively seeks to consider Byzantine influences on the West. *Byzantium* (Moss and Baynes, 1949) has chapters on Byzantium and Islam, the Byzantine inheritance in south-east Europe, in Russia and among Slavs generally, but none on Byzantium and the West. Auguste Bailly has a chapter on *Byzance et l'Occident*—starting from the year 1081(!)—and so on.

conflicts, its inability to satisfy the bourgeoisie without which it could
not function, a new concept of Byzantium appeared.

GIBBON. Now Byzantium takes uncertain shapes determined by the inner
contradictions in the ideas of the rising anti-feudal forces. Those ideas
describe the medieval world as an intrusive darkness falling between
Roman antiquity and the new States ruled by gentlemanly rationality.
And yet a glamour rises and thickens round the feudal past, the 'romantic'
past. The whole complex of confused but powerful revolt which we
group under the term Romantic Movement testifies to the strength of the
contradiction. Augustan Rome and Augustan London may alone be
'rational', yet the feudal darkness seems to hold the fire of strange potentialities which dim the gentlemanly light-of-reason.

And so, in the eighteenth century, in France and England, men began
to look again at the process whereby the Roman world broke up. Their
sense of crisis made them question the Fate of Empires. Hence writers like
Montesquieu. And in England, where a rapid mercantile expansion was
going on, largely based on the slave-trade, we find a dual theme occurring
in poetry—the opposition of feudally debased Italy (once the seat of
Roman grandeurs) and of Britain thriving in its freedom, its defeat of
feudalism; and a fear that Britain will fall like ancient Rome through
mercantile spoils, luxury and the extirpation of its free peasantry. Gibbon
therefore took up a very topical subject when he decided to define what
happened in the Decline and Fall of the Roman Empire.

As he needed to justify his world, the ruling values of that world—as
indeed he could not imagine any more rational state of things than such
a world, and as he followed the humanist tradition in identifying this
rational state with the ruling values of antiquity—so he had to define the
period following the third century as a lapse, a regression. The Empire
had to decline and fall. But the historical consciousness developed out of
the inner conflict in his society and issuing in the Romantic Movement
meant that the medieval world east and west could not just be written off
as undifferentiated loss and gloom. And so Byzantium comes back into
the picture, a powerful but unforbidding shape, an orientalised Empire
declining and falling for a whole millennium.

Gibbon feels a menace, a deep crisis shaking his world; and since he
identifies the State and the ruling values of that world with the State and
the ruling values of the Roman Empire as the point of highest slave-
development (or to be precise its phase of final decadence, the Antonine
period), he colours his picture of Byzantium with all the fears that he
feels for his own world. Byzantium is orientalised, if for no other reason,

because Britain's imperial power shows up most obviously in the East India Company, and the victim is always likely to be the avenger. Besides, he sees in the Nabob so prominent in his world the very corruptive force of oriental depravity that he fears. Byzantium is thus both the doom that falls on a corrupt imperial power and the dark force that brings it down. Gibbon's plea for enlightenment is a plea for understanding the dangers of corruption and superstition. He hopes that if the lesson is understood a system of enlightened balances may somehow hold things as they are without decay and disaster. At the same time in his creative insight he himself does not believe such lessons, and he wants deeply to understand the processes of change for a different sort of clue to safety, a fuller rationality.

This conflict in Gibbon's attitudes to Byzantium gives the depth and force to his book. Still, important as his work was in stirring a deeper sense of historical movement, he reposed in the last resort on the ruling values of his society, and accepted the thesis of decline and fall. While that thesis was accepted, Byzantium must remain an oriental degradation of the State of the Antonines.

On the other hand, if the State of the Antonines was the fine flower of rational antiquity, the need of Gibbon's own class to base its enlightened views on a society that needed the East India Company and the slave-trade was justified.[1]

Thus the liberal and the conservative elements in Gibbon jostle uneasily, struggle, and cannot resolve the struggle. But their struggle gives vitality to the book, which hands on the problems it could not solve. The formulation of the problems has been strongly advanced. Carlyle correctly states the effect made by *The Decline and Fall*—and the new start it gave to historical inquiry:

> Gibbon is a kind of bridge that connects the antique with the modern ages. And how gorgeously does it swing across the gloomy and tumultuous chasm of those barbarous centuries. . . . The perusal of his work forms an epoch in the history of one's mind. (Feb. 1823.)

FINLAY AND BURY. The Victorian age with its optimism based on a dominant position in world-trade did its best to shrug away the sense of crisis that underlay Gibbon's book. But two scholars made important contributions, Finlay and Bury. Each man deserves a word. Finlay as a youth

---

[1] Gibbon attacked 'the abominable slave-trade' in his book: 'the guilt of Europe and the weakness of Africa'. But in 1792 (during the French Revolution) he wrote to Lord Sheffield, 'In this rage against slavery, in the numerous petitions against the slave-trade, was there no leaven of new democratical principles? no wild ideas of the rights and natural equality of man? It is these I fear.'

turned from the study of Roman law to fight for Greek independence, meeting Byron at Cephalonia. An attack of fever disabled him, but he never lost his enthusiasm for the Greek struggle, and spent almost his whole life, 1825–51, in Greece. This it is that gives the new insights to his work. He sees much more of the positive factors than Gibbon, and at least theoretically grasps the need to deal with basic factors.

> The vicissitudes which the great masses of the nations of the earth have undergone in past ages have hitherto received very little attention from historians, who have adorned their pages with the records of kings, and the personal exploits of princes and great men, or attached their narratives to the fortunes of the dominant classes, without noticing the fate of the people.
>
> History, however, continually repeats the lesson that powers, numbers, and the highest civilisation of an aristocracy are, even when united, insufficient to ensure national prosperity, and establish the power of the rulers on so firm and permanent a basis as shall guarantee the dominant class from annihilation.
>
> It is that portion only of mankind, which eats bread raised from the soil by the sweat of its brow, that can form the basis of a permanent material existence.

He made some efforts to grapple with economic problems; but he sought for a middle-class in Byzantine history, as he identified civilisation with his own Victorian liberal middle-class and the curials of the early Roman Empire. What leavened Byzantium with virtue was for him 'an element that had survived from the days of municipal liberty and national independence'.

Bury may be said to combine the positions of Gibbon and Finlay. He carries on enlightment-ideas of the eighteenth century, but he stresses further positive aspects of the Byzantine world—aspects which approximate most closely to the positive aspects of imperial Britain of his own day (*i.e.* aspects taken in abstraction from the full struggle in which they appear also as dark and destructive). He pointed out that Byzantium militarily protected the weakling West for many crucial centuries, sheltering it from attacks that would have broken down its unstably emerging States; that it kept the eastern trade-routes open and fed the West economically, thus making possible the rebirth of the Western towns; that it Christianised and civilised the Slavs, and to some extent absorbed them, and so on.

These positions marked a considerable advance; but they still did not bring Byzantium integrally into relation with what went on in the West up to 1204. They left Byzantium as a sort of bulwark on the outskirt of Europe, not as a living part of it. And though Bury stressed more than any other historian the constitutional continuity between the Empire of the fourth century and the State centred on Byzantium throughout its many centuries, he did not draw any of the logica conclusions from this position. He could not enter into Byzantine history and realise its nature, its inner struggle, its concrete achievement.

THE NEW ANTI-BYZANTINES. Still, the movement of thought from Gibbon into Finlay and from Finlay into Bury represents a steady accretion of positive viewpoints, a fuller and more correct sense of what happened in the transition from the early Roman Empire to the medieval world. A similar trend of thought may be seen in French Byzantinology, with the addition of a closer interest in the manifold facets of Byzantine life. Only in Russia can we say that substantial advances went beyond the positions of Bury in Britain and Diehl in France. Partly because of the direct links of the early Russian State with Byzantium, and partly because of the general trend in Russian nineteenth-century culture towards the clarification of the basic conflicts in modern society, Byzantine studies here (linked at first to some extent with Pan-Slavism) moved towards a fuller apprehension of the part played by Byzantium in forming Europe. Russia, with her rich Byzantine heritage, was moving towards the full awareness of her own nationhood, her place in the European comity; and that inevitably involved a deepening grasp of the roots of European society in Byzantine as well as papal soil. This work, begun by the Russian contemporaries of Bury, such as Uspenskij, has been carried on, developed with new insights, lifted to a new comprehensive level by Soviet scholars, in whom for the first time the thorough understanding of the nature and role of Byzantine society is unfolded.[1]

Meanwhile, in Britain, there has grown up a trend that seeks to reverse the movement of thought running through Gibbon, Finlay, Bury. This regressive trend deserves a word; for we need to understand it if we are to understand the full significance of Byzantium's role in civilisation. The leader of what may be called the Anti-Byzantium school is A. J. Toynbee, who flatly denies Bury's exposition of the continuity of Byzantine history. He sees the Heraklian State and all that comes after as a 'successor-State' to the Roman Empire, substantially the same as the Gothic Kingdoms of Charlemagne's 'Empire'. Just one segment of a generally disintegrated situation. Since it would be hard for him to deny continuity between the State of Justinian and that of Constantine, he does not press his point for the sixth century; but declares that with

1 Vasilevskij deserves a word—Uspenskij's teacher, who is a sort of bridge between the Panslavists Byzantinologists like Destnis, Venelin, Veltman, and the generation flourishing just before 1917: Vasilev, Kondukov, Vinogradov, Ostragorskij, Uspenskij, etc.

the Iconoclasts the Empire collapses and a new State comes into existence.

> A so-called Imperial Government in Constantinople which had to look on helplessly while a Slav population supplanted a Latin and Greek population in the Balkan peninsula, and an improvised system of army-corps districts replaced the Diocletianic system in Anatolia, cannot be regarded as a real Government in any significant sense of the words.

It is hard to know whether to characterise such a statement as ignorant or perverse. True, large bodies of Slavs moved into the Balkans, and some penetrated even into Asia Minor; but Toynbee's words can have relevance only if these movements overturned the State and broke all continuity in administration and culture. No serious historian could even consider them from such an angle. The Slavs were absorbed after dislocations; the administrative system reasserted itself in the old way, the towns went on functioning, and the cultural tradition was unbroken.[1] There were no special missions needed to convert the intruders; except in some wilder parts where they kept their own tribal groupings intact, the imperial system was strong enough to sustain the shock and to Christianise the new pagans without undue strain. The effect of the Slav intrusions in fact was to *strengthen* the State; for the Slavs were the prime factor in bringing about the rebirth of the free village-commune, which restored energy to the army and vitality to culture under the Iconoclasts.

To deny that the Iconoclast State was 'a real Government' is too infantile to require refutation. To support his blank statement, Toynbee has to call the Theme-system 'an improvised system of army-corps'. This system, we have seen, took all the time between Justinian and Leo III to mature—over 150 years! And it survived stably thereafter till the end of Byzantium. An improvised system that takes so long to mature, and that survives for many strenuous centuries! If the Byzantine Theme-system was improvised and transitory, then we can scarcely talk of the British Parliamentary State as having yet come into existence at all.

But such nonsense is meant only to impress the uninformed—note the false effect of precision gained by isolating Anatolia, and the implications that the Theme-system was a simple form of militarised rule. The pre-Diocletianic State—that of the Republic and of Augustus—had combined

---

[1] Under Michael III the Slavs were in almost complete control of the Peloponnese; in 807 they had planned with African Moslems to loot Patrai, but were beaten back. Specially thick in Achaia and Elis, some tribes still kept their own customs in the thirteenth century, but by the fifteenth century were fully assimilated. But however large the settlements, the towns generally held, and the imperial system reasserted itself.

civil and military functions in its governors; and the Iconoclasts were closer to Augustus than Justinian had been in this matter. Their careful separation of fiscal matters from army-control, however, kept the Theme-government more under control of the central bureaux than had been the pre-Diocletianic provinces.

But to argue on these points is futile. Toynbee has no arguments; he has only a prejudice. Certainly there was a sharp turning-point in the reign of Leo III; but that does not make the Iconoclast a successor-State of the Justinianic State any more than the sharp break of 1649 makes eighteenth-century England a successor State of the State of Charles I.

Toynbee himself tells us why he has to deny that the Iconoclast State was a 'real Government' or Byzantium in general the true inheritor of the Graeco-Roman achievement. He identifies the Papacy with the West and the Orthodox Church with the East, Byzantium with Russia. He makes much of the fact that Church and State remained cut apart in the West while in the East the Church and State were 'one'. Certainly there is a difference here, which I have stressed in my narrative: the Papacy, by its secular ambitions and the lack of mass-bases in the origins of western Christianity, tried to control the western States was generally defeated—while Orthodoxy, the established religion of a single imperial system, was linked with the State. But the story of the eastern Church, as I have abundantly shown, is one long story of violent reactions against this collaboration, and when significant revolt against Church-authority begins in the West it is the *eastern* tradition that is being carried on.

By ignoring the rich complexity of actual history Toynbee proceeds to build up a picture of the Byzantine State as the Leviathian of all Leviathans, which by his subjective modes of logic he has no difficulty in identifying with Soviet Russia. He begins with one of his facile distortions of fact presented with the glibness that deceives the ignorant:

> The Varangians who founded the first rudiments of the Russian State by seizing command of the navigable inland waterways and thereby establishing their domination over the primitive Slav population in the hinterland, seem to have been Scandinavian barbarians who had been stirred up and set moving —eastward as well as westward by the northward march of western Christendom under Charlemagne.

The Varangians were Norsemen: there is no *seem* about it. But what march of western Christendom set them moving? They moved as raiders drawn by the loot which the urban expansion offered, and they went to Novgorod and the Dnieper, not because of any Christendom, but because there were well-off towns there for trade or plunder—not 'primitive' Slavs. They played a part in the formation of the Novgorod and

Kiev States; but not the part that Toynbee, following scholars like the American S. H. Cross, assigns them. The Slav towns had reached that phase of transition between tribal and urban forms when the old sanctions have broken down and the new ones are not effectively imposed: the result is a release of the bloodfeud from tribal safeguards without the imposition of full legal controls. At such a phase one commonly finds the group or groups calling in an external authority, which they accept in order to overcome their discord. Sometimes they select one of their own men who has a high prestige. An example of the calling-in of an outsider is the appeal by the feud-stricken people of Medina to Mohammed; an example of the appointing of a man from inside the conflicting groups is the election of a Capo by the Arengo in Venetia, in the later sixth century, to end the bloody affrays in the Pinete. The part played by the Norsemen at Novgorod was not in any sense a founding of the first rudiments of the Russian State set over a dominated 'primitive Slav population'.

But this is only a detail in his dogmatic view of the absolute opposition of East and West, Byzantium (Russia) and Papacy (Europe). 'For nearly a thousand years past the Russians . . . have been members, not of our western civilisation, but of the Byzantine—a sister society, of the same Graeco-Roman parentage as ours, but a distinct and different civilisation from our own, nevertheless.' And so 'the Russians have incurred the hostility of the West through being obstinate adherents of an alien civilisation'.

One more example of Toynbee's method in proof of this thesis:

> In the modern, as in the medieval, Byzantine world the victory has fallen to the champion of the secular power—in consistent contrast to the course of history in the West, where it was the ecclesiastical power that won the day in the trials of strength between Gregory VII and Henry IV and between Innocent and Frederick II.

The statements in the latter part of this sentence are dubious (in that they ignore the fact that the clash of Papacy and German Empire was based, not solely on a clash of priestly and secular interests, but also on a clash of the Papacy as secular power against the Germans, in which both sides used religious as well as secular arguments). By any reading of the 'trials of strength', both the Papacy and the German Empire lost, and the secular forces of the national States were liberated into rapid forward-movement.

> When Boniface VIII, alarmed by the growing power of lay governments, tried to limit their authority, he found that he was too late. The people of France and England remained loyal to their kings; there was not even a half-hearted rebellion in favour of the Pope. In France the government had such control of public opinion that it was able to seize the Church's own weapon of heresy and turn it against Boniface. (J. H. Strayer.)

Toynbee's description of the West then has only a more than dubious base for earlier periods and wipes out all history from the thirteenth century onwards. When his West has such a phantom existence, it is not surprising that his East exists only in his own subjective dogmas.

But we cannot leave the matter at a mere exposure of the lack of historical truth in Toynbee's position. We must ask what it is that drives him to these distortions of history? It is surely obvious that his arguments rationalise a blind hatred of the U.S.S.R. Indeed in his remarks to the Paris Congress of Historians in the autumn of 1950 he blandly gave away this basis. The concept Europe, he said, was defined to suit one's political convenience, to exclude the 'enemy'. At one moment it meant the union against the Turks, now it means the union against the Soviet Union. It was a pity that Russia in 1914 was drawn in as an ally against Germany. Still, she is the 'enemy', and definitions must be framed in such a way as to exclude her. Here is British Empiricism with a Vengeance—calling on moral idealism for its idiom but using the abstraction to divide men by eternal differences and alienations.

THE FULL DIALECTICS OF EUROPE'S DEVELOPMENT. That each nationality, each people, has a tradition of its own, a history of its own, goes without saying; but this tradition, this history, is not something abstractly good or abstractly bad. It is a particular phase of human development, with its own inherent conflict of good and evil, its progressions and regressions. The problem is not to deliver an abstract judgment which invokes eternal categories of fixed character; it is to realise the tradition, the culture, in its fullness, so as to facilitate the growth and stability of the valuable humanist elements. Only by falling back from this struggle and distorting history for base class-purposes can one abstractly pose one culture or tradition against another as an abstract entity.

Something happened in the West that did not happen in Byzantium, a kind of town-development (and a kind of State) which did not invade the Russian area till later than its advent and development in Italy and Flanders, France and Britain. But this is not to say that the changes going on meanwhile in Russia were worthless or irrelevant to the whole European comity. What was happening in Byzantium under the Iconoclasts was very different from what was happening at the time in Frankish Gaul; but the latter developments, though then on a lower level of social organisation than those at Byzantium, turn out in the long run to have immense importance for the total European development.

In short, there is both a difference and a unity in the developments east and west from the first century A.D. onwards. Any thorough and honest analysis must see the conflict and fusion of eastern and western elements to be a key factor henceforth in historical movement.

What separates the two areas is the stable urbanisation of the East, its higher productive level, its persistent ability to provide the basis for a centralised State, as against the slight urbanisation of the West, its breakdown, its inability for long to provide the basis for a centralised State. For reasons analysed in the text, Byzantium goes down from the thirteenth century, and in the fifteenth century the face of Europe turns westward, looking out over the Atlantic. The irruption of Turks and Tartars reinforces the breakdown in the East, as earlier the irruption of the Germans had reinforced the breakdown in the West.

The West grew up again with fresh elements vital for the advance of mankind. The East grew up in turn with fresh elements vital for the advance of mankind. From the movements in the West emerged capitalism, which carried mankind immeasurably forward beyond the levels reached by the ancient and feudal worlds; from the East emerged socialism.

But in saying this I must not be taken to commit the very sin I am protesting against. Capitalism emerged in the West, but it needed the East and its contributions as much as it needed the western bases; Socialism has emerged in Russia, but it needed the West and its contributions as much as it needed the Russian bases. Still, as long as we understand that we are speaking of changes and conflicts within the total field of Europe (in the last resort, the whole world, since the Far East, and also America, are increasingly involved), we can detach specific contributions.

We may then say in general terms that Byzantium completed the transformation of the ancient world into feudalism, and the West completed the transformation of feudalism into capitalism. The latter development involved the creation of the National State and new imperial forms; it further distorted the Christian concept of universality and brotherhood, yet gave new possibilities to its actualisation. The struggle to actualise those possibilities, to achieve a universal society in which the rich diversity of individuals and groups would be given increased freedom of growth, and in which universality and freedom would in fact become at last harmonised, appeared in the emergence of socialism—at first in religious and Utopian dreams, then in clarified theory and the union of theory and practice, then in the historical actualisation of 1917.

To work out all that is implied in these statements is not for me here. I should have to show afresh, on the new level provided by capitalism, the vital interaction of East and West, the contributions that each section of the total historical process made to the working-out. I should need to analyse nineteenth-century culture, to show the specific contributions made by Western Europe and by Russia and so on. We should find, as the tide sets in in Russia to the new level of life, a vast cultural transformation going on ever since Lomonosov, since Pushkin, in which the bases are laid for Soviet society and its lines of movement.

But here it is enough to make the broad statement; and to go on to stress afresh that we are dealing with a European process, a world process, not one of East versus West, or West versus East. We are dealing with a crisis in *human culture*, which brings to a head the problems posited when Constantine established the Church and thus set history the task of harmonising State-power with the uncompromising demand for universality, brotherhood, freedom.

If the western societies are to be true to their great part in the development of Europe, they must recognise this fact, and must set themselves the task of discovering the new universality and freedom in their own terms—that is, in terms of their own cultural tradition. Thus they will validly and vitally add their own elements of diversity to the new unity, the universal society which the development of capitalism has made possible but which cannot be achieved from within the capitalist frame of reference. They must find, as part of their own movement forward into freedom and universality, the way in which they can work harmoniously with the Soviet Union for the realisation and development of their common heritage. This is a matter in which men of good will everywhere, whatever the varying terms, Christian or Marxist, liberal or anarchist, pacifist or socialist, in which they state their positions, can validly co-operate.

Here is again a huge theme. I should fail the demands of my task if I did not sketch it here, but I must leave it at this point. My task had been to show the complex interactions, conflicts and fusions, which have made up Europe and which have involved Byzantium as well as Rome, Kiev as well as Florence, Moscow as well as London, finally Pekin as well as New York. Till 1204 Byzantium was the dominant force in Europe and (though the various areas were developing specific contributions which would later become decisive) the veins of Byzantine influence pervaded all the phases of returning urban culture. After 1204 the East did not cease to play an important part, but the dominant centres had shifted to Italy, France, Flanders, Britain. . . .

A new and fuller realisation of European unity, of human unity, comes from this research. If my book helps at all to kindle that realisation, to send others on the same quest, to vindicate a great and maligned phase of human development and to clarify the pattern of history which we must understand if we are to survive, it will have served the purpose for which it was written.

LIST OF EMPERORS

Dynasty of Constantine

1	CONSTANTINE I	*the Great* —	306–337
		(sole Emperor)	323–337
2	CONSTANTIUS		337–361
		(sole Emperor)	353–361
3	JULIAN		361–363
4	JOVIANOS		363–364
5	VALENS		364–378

Dynasty of Theodosios

6	THEODOSIOS I	*the Great*	379–395
7	ARKADIOS		395–408
8	THEODOSIOS II	*the Calligrapher*	408–450
9	MARKIANOS		450–457
10	LEO I		457–474
11	ZENO		474–491
12	ANASTASIOS I		491–518

Dynasty of Justinian

13	JUSTIN I		518–527
14	JUSTINIAN I	—	527–565
15	JUSTIN II		565–578
16	TIBERIOS II		578–582
17	MAURICE		582–602
18	PHOKAS		602–610

Dynasty of Heraklios

19	HERAKLIOS	—	610–641
20	CONSTANTINE III		641–642
21	CONSTANS II		642–668
22	CONSTANTINE IV	*(Bearded)*	668–685
23	JUSTINIAN II	*(Slitnose)*	685–695
24	LEONTIOS		695–698

25	TIBERIOS III		698–705
26	JUSTINIAN II	*(again)*	705–711
27	PHILIPPIKOS		711–713
28	ANASTASIOS II		713–716
29	THEODOSIOS III		716–717

Isaurian Dynasty

30	LEO III		716–741
31	CONSTANTINE V	*(Whose-Name-is-Dung)* Ecloga	741–775
32	LEO IV		775–780
33	CONSTANTINE VI		780–797
34	IRENE		797–802
35	NIKEPHOROS I		802–811
36	STAURIKIOS		811
37	MICHAEL I		811–813
38	LEO V	*(Armenian)*	813–820
39	MICHAEL II	*(Stammerer)*	820–829
40	THEOPHILOS		829–842
41	MICHAEL III	*(Drunkard)*	842–867

Macedonian Dynasty

42	BASIL I	Basilica	867–886
43	LEO VI	*(the Wise)*	886–912
44	ALEXANDER		912–913
45	CONSTANTINE VII	*(Porphyrogenitos)*	912–959
	(associated with Romanos I		
		Lekapenos)	919–944
46	ROMANOS II		959–963
47	NIKEPHOROS II	*Phokas* laissez faivre	963–969
48	JOHN I	*Tzimiskes*	969–976
49	BASIL II	*(Bulgar-Killer)* son of	976–1025
50	CONSTANTINE VIII	son of	1025–1028
51	ZOE daughter of		1028–1050
	(associated with husbands:)		
	Romanos III Argyros		1028–1034
	Michael IV Paphlagonian		1034–1041
	Michael V Kalaphates		
	(adopted by Zoe)		1041–1042
	Constantine IX		
	(Monomachos)		1042–1054
52	THEODORA daughter of		1054–1056
53	MICHAEL VI		1056–1057

Dynasty of the Doukases and the Comnenoi

54	ISAAC I	*Comnenos*	1057–1059
55	CONSTANTINE X	*Doukas*	1059–1067
56	ROMANOS IV	*Diogenes*	1067–1071
57	MICHAEL VII	*Doukas*	1071–1078
58	NIKEPHOROS III	*Botaniates*	1078–1081
59	ALEXIS I —	*Comnenos*	1081–1118
60	JOHN II brother to ↑	,,	1118–1143
61	MANUEL I	,,	1143–1180
62	ALEXIS II	,,	1180–1183
63	ANDRONIKOS I	,,	1183–1185

Dynasty of the Angeli

64	ISAAC II		1185–1195
65	ALEXIS III		1195–1203
66	ISAAC II	*(again)*	1203–1204
	(associated with son Alexis IV)		
67	ALEXIS V		1204

Latin Emperors of Constantinople

68	BALDWIN OF FLANDERS	1204–1205
69	HENRY OF FLANDERS	1205–1216
70	PETER OF COURTENAY	1217
71	YOLANDE	1217–1219
72	ROBERT II OF COURTENAY	1221–1228
73	BALDWIN II	1228–1261
	(associated with John of Brienne)	
	(regent)	1229–1237
	Sole Emperor	1240–1261

Greek Emperors of Nicaea

74	THEODORE I	*Laskaris*	1204–1222
75	JOHN III	*Vatatzes*	1222–1254
76	THEODORE II	*Laskaris*	1254–1258
77	JOHN IV	,,	1258–1259
78	MICHAEL VIII	*Palaiologos*	1259–1261

Dynasty of the Palaiologoi

79	MICHAEL VIII		1261–1282
80	ANDRONIKOS II		1282–1328
	(associated with son Michael IX)		1295–1320
81	ANDRONIKOS III		1328–1341
82	JOHN V		1341–1376
83	JOHN VI	*Kantakouzene*	1341–1355
84	ANDRONIKOS IV (son of John V)		1376–1379
85	JOHN V	*(again)*	1379–1391
86	JOHN VII (son of Andronikos IV)		1390
87	MANUEL II		1391–1425
88	JOHN VIII		1425–1448
89	CONSTANTINE XI	*Palaiologos*	1448–1453

It is hard to achieve consistency in the spelling of Greek names. It is pedantic to call Plato *Platon* or Circe *Kirke*: but at the same time one feels impelled to take a stand against the notion that Greek can be approached only through Latinisations. I have therefore tended to direct transliteration (with *y* for *upsilon*), except where forms were too strongly entrenched, *e.g.* Byzantium for *Byzantion*, Constantine for *Konstantinos*, etc. Though tempted, I have resisted *Kappadokian* for Cappadocian, etc. The resulting compromise is sure to annoy some, but seems to me the best under the circumstances.

ACKNOWLEDGMENTS

I have reluctantly decided not to give full references, as they would swell the Book considerably. In the following acknowledgments I therefore include only the names of works actually cited in the text and works to which I owe a particular debt. The introductory numbers are references to the chapters of this book.

1   E. Gren, *Kleinasien und der Ostbalkan in der wirtschaftlichen Entwicklung röm. K.*, 1941. Dölger, *Rom in der Gedankenwelt der Byzantiner* (*Zeitsch. f. Kirchengesch.*) lvi (1937).

2   For third century, M. Alpatov in *Voprosy Istorii* (Moscow) vii (1949) 28–39. Rostovtseff has set out something of the same thesis, but with an insecure methodology that has enabled others to disregard or misunderstand his point.
Cited: F. W. Walbank, *The Decline of the R. E. in the West*, 1946; A. Segrè, *Byzantion*, xvi, 1941, 416.

3   Cited: H. I. Bell, *J. Roman Studies*, xxxvii, 23: see also Borak, *Études de Pap.* ii, 4; Wilcken, *Arch. für Pap.*, xi, 313. Charlesworth, *J.R.S.*, xxxiii (1943).

4   Levchenko, his history of Byzantium (Leningrad) 1940, with French translation 1949; and his essay in *Vizantiskii Sbornik*, 1945, 12–95.
Cited: Vinogradoff, *The Growth of the Manor*, 1911.

5   The relation of demes and factions has been finally unravelled by Dyakonov, *Viz. Sbornik*, 1945, 144–227.
Cited: G. Thomson, *Aeschylus and Athens*.

9   Cited: M. Gibbs, *Feudal Order*, 1949; M. Bloch, *La Société féodale, les formations des liens de dépendance* (1939) 254. J. Gay, *L'Italie merid. et l'emp. byz.* (1904) 9–12; *Rev. d'hist. et de litt. rél.*, v (1908) 249; *Byzantion*, i, 215; Barthold, *Turkestan down to Mongol Invasions*: Vasiliev, *Hist. Byz. Empire*, i (1928) 290; H. Lammens, *Études . . . Modívia I* (1908) 444. Rohefs, *Hist. Grammatik des unter-italien. Gräzität* (1949).

10   Cited: Cesare Foligno, *Story of Padua* (1910) 16. For Flanders, etc., B. Philpotts, *Kindred and Clan*.

11   Cited: Aurel Stein, 'Innermost China', *Geographical Journal*, lxv, 1925.

15   Angelov, *Ist. Pregled*, iii, 1946–7, 217–30; Picheta, *Vestnik Drevnei Istorii*, iii, 1947, 95–9; P. Charanis, *Byzantinoslavica* x, 1949, i, 92–4 and *American Hist. Rev.*, lii, 1946, 74–87.

For the Farmer's Law, Ashburner, *J. Hellenic S.*, xxx and xxxii; A. Fliche and V. Martin, *Histoire de l'Église*, 1937–44 (iv–ix), vol. v, 338f.; Rostovtseff, *Stud. zur Gesch. des röm. Kolon.*, (1910) 205, 305. For *idios*, G. Vernadsky, *Byzantion*, ii, 169.

16   G. Ostrogovsky, *J.R.S.* (1947) xxxvii. Vassilievsky, *Works* (in Russian) I, iv, 256. H. Gelzer, *Byz. Kult.* 78—for the effect of Byz. coin-terms on Hebrew, S. Krauss, *Stud. zur byz. jüd. Gesch.* (1914) 109. For guilds and West: J. Lestocquoy, *Economic Hist. Rev.*, xvii (i) 1947, citing Guilland; Ganshof, *Byzantion*, iv (1928) 659; Andréades, in Baynes' *Byzantium*, 1949.

18   *Labyrs*: Cook, *Zeus*, ii, 60 (1914); Grégoire, *Byzantion*, iv, 477. Organisation: various papers by N. Baynes.

19   S. Angus, *The Religious Quests of the Graeco-Roman World* (1929) 310; *Hebel*: W. O. E. Oesterley, *The Sacred Dance* (1923); Dom Butler, *Lausiac History*, i, 235.

23   H. W. C. Davis, *Medieval Europe* (cited).

24   Vasiliev, *Byz. and the Arabs*; Grégoire, *Byzantion*, i, 250 and ii, 255; G. Ostrogorsky, *Geschichte des byz. Staates* (1940) 156.

27   A. S. Turberville, *Medieval Heresy and the Inquisition*, 1920.

28   R. Browning has discussed the Zealots with me; his sole publication on the subject is in Bulgarian. On monastic properties, M. V. Levchenko, in *Viz. Vremennik* ii (1949) 11–59—also P. Charanis in *Dumbarton Oaks Papers* iv (1948): no new efforts were made to curb the monks till the fourteenth–fifteenth centuries, and then weakly.
In general the books of Obolensky and S. Runciman; A. V. Solovjev in *Byzantinoslavica* x: I (1949) and *Bull. Acad. Belg.* (classe des lettres) xxxiv (1948) 481–534; D. Angelov in *Byzantinoslavica* x:2 (1949).

29   I owe much to Grabar's *Martyrion* (1946), though he keeps to architectural analysis and does not inquire into the wider relations.

31–3   Lethaby, *Architecture* (n.d.) 30. For the Macedonians, N. E. Brunov, *Viz. Vremennik* II (xxvi) 1949; Talbot Rice, *Byzantinoslavica* 150; also his *Byzantine Element in Late Saxon Art* (1947) for ch. 34; O. Demus, *The Mosaics of Norman Sicily* (1950); Rostovtseff, *Dura and Parthian art, Dura-Europus and its art*, etc.; Wischnitzer, *The Messianic Theme in the Paintings of the Dura Synagogue*, 1948; H. Pierce and R. Tyler in *Dumbarton Oaks Papers*, ii (1941).

34   R. S. Lopez, in *Byzantion*, xviii, 139–62. W. Koehler in *Dumbarton Oaks Papers*, i (1941); T. Whittimore, *The Mosaics of St. Sophia at Istanbul*, 1933; P. Muratoff, *La Peinture Byzantine*, 1935, etc.

37–8 My main debt is to La Piana, E. Wellesz and E. Werner. G. La Piana, *La repp. nella litt. biz. dalle origine al sec. ix con rapporti al teatro sacro d'occidente*, 1912 and his essay in *Speculum*.

E. Wellesz, *Eastern Element in Western Chant* (1947); *History of Byzantine Music and Hymnography* (1949); in *J. Theolog. Studies*, xliv (1943). 41–52 and *J. Roman S.*, 1947–8.

E. Werner, *The Conflict between Hellenism and Judaism* the *Music of the early Christian Church* and *The Origin of the Eight Modes of Music*, offprints from the Hebrew Union College Annual, xx and xxi (1947 and 1948); Vogt: *Revue des questions hist.*, Oct. 1931 (257ff).

40 G. Millet, *Syria* (1923) 85–133, *L'Ascension d'Alexandre*. He thinks the later western versions borrow motives from tales of pilgrims or crusaders.

41 H. F. Stewart (on Eusebios) in *Cambridge Medieval History* (i).

44 In general, Grégoire's various papers in *Byzantion* etc. and his *Dígenis Akritas* (1942); J. Mavrogordato in Baynes' *Byzantium* (and in correspondence). A. Abel, in *Byzantinoslavica*, x: 2 (1950) 236.
    Citation at end of chapter: Vasiliev, *H.C.E.*, i, 448; Speransky.

45 H. F. Tozer, *Byz. Satire* (*J.H.S.*, ii).

46 G. Barraclough, *The Mediaeval Empire*, 1950.

48 J. Brutzkus, *E.H.R.*, xiii (1943) Nos. 1–2, 31. J. N. L. Baker, *Medieval Trade Routes* (1938); W. Heyd, *Histoire du Commerce du Levant au Moyen Age* (123). D. S. Sassoon. *A History of the Jews in Bagdad* (1951).

49 C. H. Haskins, *The Rennaissance of the Twelfth Century* (chs. ix–x). P. K. Hitti, *History of Syria* (1951); *The Foreign Vocabulary of the Qur'an*, 1938.

50 For Fu Lin: C. P. Fitzgerald, *China, a Cultural History* (1935).

51 Greekfire: C. Lenghelis, *Byzantion*, vii, 264ff (cited); Bury, *H.R.E.* (1923).

52 E. Werner, as cited.

53 Lynn White in *Speculum*, xv (1940); E. Cecil Curwen, *Plough and Pasture* (1946); Kondakov, *Les Costumes Orientaux à la Cour Byz.* (in *Byzantion*, 1).

54 Cited on Aldus: J. H. Whitfield, *Petrarch and the Renascence* (1945) 104. In general, A. M. Woodward, in *J.H.S.*, lxiii (1943) and J. E. Sandys, *History of Classical Scholarship*, 1903.

56 Feudalism: I am aware of Ostrogorski's arguments for western influences on Byzantine feudalism; and though such influences certainly existed in the later phases, Ostrogorski's emphasis shows a failure to understand the nature of feudalism itself.
    J. H. Strayer, *Speculum* (1940) 85.

INDEX

DATE DUE